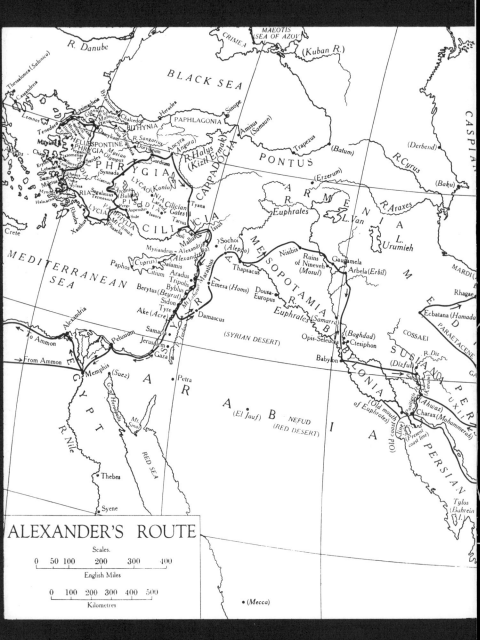

ALEXANDER'S ROUTE

Scales.

0 50 100   200   300   400

English Miles

0   100 200 300 400 500

Kilometres

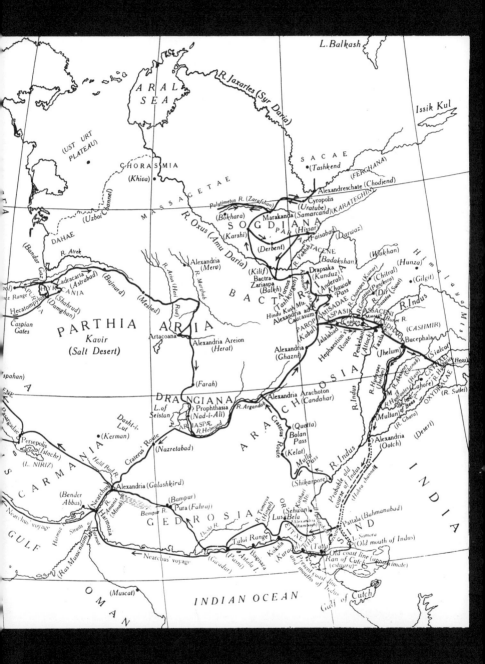

Other works by F. E. Peters

GREEK PHILOSOPHICAL TERMS: *A Historical Lexicon*
ARISTOTELES ARABUS: *The Oriental Translation History
of the Aristotelian Corpus* (Monograph)
ARISTOTLE AND THE ARABS: *The Aristotelian Tradition
in Islam*

THE
HARVEST
OF HELLENISM

A History of the Near East
from Alexander the Great
to the Triumph of Christianity

F. E. Peters

SIMON AND SCHUSTER
New York

FIRST PRINTING

SBN 671-20658-3 TRADE
SBN 671-20659-1 CLARION
LIBRARY OF CONGRESS CATALOG CARD NUMBER: 74-116509
DESIGNED BY EDITH FOWLER
MANUFACTURED IN THE UNITED STATES OF AMERICA
PRINTED BY THE MURRAY PRINTING COMPANY, FORGE VILLAGE, MASS.

The maps in this book first appeared in the Cambridge Ancient History *(Volumes VI, VII, X, XI, XII) published by Cambridge University Press. Used by permission.*

For Mary
κινεῖ δὴ ὡς ἐρωμένη

Contents

List of Maps

Preface

Eastern Hellenism, the eastern Roman Empire and eastern Christianity all have their places in the pages that follow; they were the prime historical realities of the Near East between the glories of Israel and the coming of Islam. Each is, perhaps, the preserve of a different historian—today, even as they were in the past. In antiquity a history of the Near East—the term is itself a modern (and western) designation—where philosophers, theologians, poets and politicians ran together in one narrative, would have been an unlikely project.

The Greeks themselves saw their own achievements chiefly in political terms; and politics, the study of social activity within the *polis*, or city-state, was the master science of human behavior. That is the assumption behind the famous assessment of Athens made by Pericles in the opening years of the war against Sparta, and the historian Thucydides, who reported Pericles' speech, chose the political act of war as the subject of his monumental analysis of power. The dense pages of his *History of the Peloponnesian War* ignore to the point of oblivion the cultural life of what later generations of Hellenes chose to see as their Golden Age.

Thucydides' manner of proceeding to an analysis of human affairs was adopted by most of his successors. History was the reconstruction and analysis of political events, wars, parties, coups and dynastic marriages; both biography and efforts at describing the "life style" (*bios*) of a people were left to the philosophers, as the affairs of the Church were later left to the ecclesiastical historian. The ancient separation of political, religious and cultural history, a distortion, surely, of the way the Greeks actually lived within their *poleis*, is not easily repaired. The Hellenes and the

Hellenized were relentless in their exclusion of arts, literature and philosophy from their histories, while their contemporaries who did address themselves to such cultural questions made little effort to provide a political context for the subject. Poets worked from the timeless palette of myth; and philosophers, for the most part, took scant notice of what was going on outside the doors of their academies. History and culture share separate quarters in most of the scattered reports that have reached us from the ancient world: Socrates, who looms large in the philosopher Plato, is ignored by the historian Thucydides; and Alcibiades, who finds a place in both authors and is recognizably the same man in both, seems to have different careers in the *History* and the Platonic dialogues.

The modern reporter of the Hellenic past can go down either of those paths, political or cultural history, with a certain assurance since his sources went the same way before him. Or else he can try the less certain ground of reintegration, though with the inevitable risk of writing patchwork history—a chapter on the wars of the period, the next on the literature, a third on the philosophers, then back to the wars. The skill of such a historian is not so much at integration—the compartmentalization of the ancient sources imposes severe limits on how far true integration can be carried—but at constructing transitions, smooth segues from Antigonus Gonatas to Zeno, from Ptolemy II to Callimachus or from Tiberius to Jesus, which mask the fact that Tacitus knew or cared little about Jesus and the authors of the Gospels felt roughly the same about Tiberius.

Despite the formidable dangers of putting together a pastiche, I have essayed the unitive way—not, I hope, from a lack of humility before the task or for want of common sense, but simply because no sensible reader will permit any other approach. He knows that religious movements have social contexts and that even ancient politicians could read. Alexander certainly could, and Cicero and Herod and Julian; and whom they read are of some moment in the history of ideas: Aristotle, Posidonius, Nicholas of Damascus, and Libanius. It is nonsense to report on the politicians without informing the reader on the philosophers with whom they studied and consorted, or to discuss Jesus without reference to the politics of Roman Judaea.

I have tried, then, not merely to describe Hellenism after Alexander, but to submit a reasonably complete report on what was happening in the Near East during the period from the death of

Alexander to the triumph of Christian Hellenism over the pagan version. Its completeness depends, of course, on the rather uneven flow of sources preserved from that period, and these alternately run dense and thin. One knows, for example, a considerable amount about the politics of Palestine from about B.C. 200 to A.D. 100 and almost nothing of the fortunes of the large Jewish community in Alexandria of the same period. Most of the third century B.C. is not very well known, while the fourth Christian century is more thoroughly documented than any other time in the ancient world. Hellenistic literature and the early Stoa are a shambles of fragments, and yet we have everything Plotinus wrote, and a biography besides!

Further, one knows only what the ancient writers *chose* to tell us. Their view of history had little room for economic, social or even purely physical causes: a plague of the dimensions of the medieval Black Death is mentioned almost casually in passing. Some of these deficiencies can be made up elsewhere, from archaeological findings, for example, but here too the evidence is very unevenly distributed. The climate of Egypt is kind to papyrus, whether Aristotle's *Constitution of Athens,* a tax receipt or a bill of divorce is written upon it, and so there are happy and unexpected insights which carry us beyond the literary historians. But there are few parallel finds in Syria, Mesopotamia or Anatolia, and so the economic and legal traditions of those places remain obscure and hypothetical.

Nor are biographers very helpful on questions we consider highly relevant. Anecdotes abound in the preserved biographies, and gossip of all kinds, but usually there is only silence on the youthful, formative years of their subjects. We are given occasional nuggets like the fact that Plotinus was not weaned until his eighth year, and we try to make of it what we can without any other information about his economic or social background, his parents, or indeed, where he was born. Wives and children almost never intrude in the lives of these figures from the past, except when they possess some political or dynastic significance. Ancient biography is frequently entertaining, but only occasionally enlightening.

The lights and darknesses on the pages that follow are not always the responsibility of the ancient sources; some of them are of my own making. I have tried to provide an intelligibly complete record of that time and place, but when forced to choose between intelligibility and completeness I have preferred the first. To choose thus would, of course, place any historian on the side of the angels, except that the intelligibility is his own and is tempered by his own interests and skills. So it is here; the emphases are my own, as are the somewhat more painful decisions to exclude, condense or simply hurry on. Others read the past differently, to be sure, and would speed over terrain where I have dallied or would underline what I have merely mentioned.

The writing of a history book has bound me to a certain time line and imposed certain geographical limits, but I have treated both obligations somewhat lightly. Threads of narration and analysis are picked up, on occasion, from Periclean Athens and even Homeric times, and extended, where it seemed useful, down to the sixth Christian century and beyond. For much of the period under consideration the Near East was divided between an Iranian Empire and a Roman Empire, the latter with its center in Italy and its western boundaries in Spain and Britain, and so I have not hesitated to cast refractive glances at affairs in Rome when they make what is happening in the Near East more intelligible. I have followed the careers of easterners like Plotinus when they come to Rome, and of Italians like Cicero when their work or interests carry them eastward.

It is perhaps a somewhat bumpy journey back and forth between Rome and the Hindu Kush and in the company of the familiar Hadrian and the unfamiliar Kanishka. I can plead only that the Kushan Kanishka was one of Hellenism's own as certainly as the Spanish Hadrian was, and that Alexander would have been more likely to recognize the eastern Kushan *khan* than the western Roman *imperator*. There are maps and charts to ease the passage by tying the narrative to a serial chronology and to a more exact location of places on this somewhat alien terrain; the meaning, however, is in the body of the text, and for this I must and will assume full responsibility.

I have had, of course, helpers, all innocent of whatever faults the following pages may contain. Beatrice Green, Pamela Long, Nina Natelson, and Beth Uffner labored over the typescript, and I thank them. My colleague Bluma Trell was kind enough to read much of what I wrote, as did E. P. Fitzsimmons, on whose considerable knowledge of the English language I have mercilessly, as always, drawn. I owe a considerable debt to the students of New York University on whom these lines were practiced over the last few years as a kind of rude oral epic; and particularly to one of them, Carlie Simon, who can, among her other talents, elicit a book on occasion. Dick Kluger and Diane Neustadter of Simon and Schuster have shown more than the mandatory patience and understanding; they have been kind and civilized as well. My wife has been thanked elsewhere.

)

Eastern Hellenism:
An Introduction

Our political system is called a democracy because the rule is not in the hands of a few but under the control of the majority. In private disputes everyone stands equal before the law, while in questions of public preferment it is merit rather than class membership that is esteemed. Poverty is no bar to public service; whoever has some good to perform for the polis *is recognized.*

Our private lives are conducted with the same openness as our public business; and every man is free to enjoy himself in the manner he wishes without provoking the anger of his neighbor or receiving those offensive glances which, though they do no real harm, cause grief. Private freedom is not public license; we reverence and obey the law. We obey both the authorities and the authority of the laws, especially those laws designed to protect the wronged and the unwritten laws which possess the sanction of public shame.

When our work is over we recreate our spirits in the public contests and religious festivals which fill the polis *year. There are private delights as well, pursued with moderation and good taste, whose pleasures draw away our daily cares. Because of the greatness of our* polis *the goods of the world come home to us, and we enjoy them naturally as our own.*

Our love of the beautiful is unmarred by extravagance, and our pursuit of the things of the mind has not led us into softness. We use our wealth for practical ends rather than as a subject for boasting. We do not consider a man's poverty a shameful thing;

the disgrace is in doing nothing to avoid it. We have an equal concern for our home and our polis, and even those of us who are chiefly engaged in business have a profound knowledge of politics. We alone have no respect for a man disinterested in political life. He is not minding his business; he rather is thought to be useless. We are the judges of our own actions and give careful thought to our affairs. For us discussion is no bar to action; what is harmful is to act before submitting a policy to discussion. We are unusual in that we are capable of taking risks even after we have weighed their consequences, while other men are brave as long as they are ignorant but draw back upon reflection.

Taken all in all, this polis *is the school of Hellas. Each citizen is master of his own person in all circumstances and is so with exceeding grace and versatility.*

From the funeral oration delivered by Pericles at Athens in B.C. *429 and reported by the historian Thucydides*

This is a book about a second generation, the trials of their migration, whom they met and what they said and, above all, what they did with their inheritance. The first generation was that of the Hellenes, the Greeks from Homer to Aristotle; the second generation had no name. Some of them were Greeks, but more were Macedonians, Romans, Syrians, Jews and Egyptians. They all had their own styles, born, in some cases, of long and glittering traditions. But they fell, all of them, under the spell of the Hellenes and so became a second generation, condemned or blessed to reap where their spiritual fathers had sown.

The harvest has been gathered for centuries. We are part of it and can number our own generations across a familiar landscape back to the Romans and then to the Age of Pericles. It is an attractive and generally satisfying genealogical narrative, passing in review most of the major monuments of our culture. The history of Hellenism appears to be identical with the spiritual history of the West.

It is not. We are the scions of a Latin European tradition that is only part of the harvest of Hellenism. The Hellenes' sowing fell on other ground than that of Italy, Spain, France, Germany and Britain. The people of these lands were late European arrivals to

Hellenism and already members of a third, not a second generation; what they knew of Homer and Plato and Euripides they knew first through Vergil, Cicero and Seneca. Not all of their contemporaries were reduced to the same straits, however. While Boethius was struggling to turn Aristotle into Latin for his deprived European readers of the fifth century, the original texts were still being studied in Alexandria, the intellectual center of an eastern Hellenism that was still Greek in its language and culture.

There were, then, two Hellenisms proceeding from a common source: one branch, growing from original Hellenic stock, was made up of Hellenized Latins and Latin-speaking peoples in the western provinces of the Roman Empire, while the other, the eastern branch, continued to use Greek as its medium of expression. Somewhere in what is today Yugoslavia one may trace a linguistic boundary that separated the Latin and Greek versions of Hellenism, two incredibly vital and voracious growths from a single stem with its roots in the parsimonious soil of a small corner of the eastern Mediterranean.

Obeisance has long been paid to the founding fathers of this extraordinary cultural phenomenon; the Age of Pericles is a western touchstone, and the figures of Socrates, Plato, Aristotle, Sophocles and Demosthenes are richly embalmed in our hagiography. And deservedly. Considerably less attention has been paid, however, to the almost equally brilliant achievements of the intellectuals of the succeeding generations who took the creative insights of the fifth- and fourth-century age of gold and distilled them into principles and norms which could be *taught* rather than merely transmitted.

Down to the last decades of the fourth pre-Christian century, Hellenism was a tradition embodying certain personal and institutional styles of action and certain attitudes toward those same acts. The complex of style and values is in evidence in the literature of the Greeks from Homer onward and was transmitted by the osmotic processes typical of a homogeneous society like the one in the cities of the Greek mainland and the Anatolian coast. With the conquests of Alexander, however, the political horizon of that society was extended over an immense area embracing diverse peoples and civilizations who knew little of those Periclean ideals. Almost immediately there arose the question of Hellenization. Alexander and his successors understood that if they were to survive in those new lands they must survive as

Hellenes, and so they founded their protected and protective enclaves across the Near and Middle East.

It was the savants of one of those enclaves of the Hellenic *diaspora*, the Egyptian Alexandria, who created Hellenism in the secondary sense of converting into a specific academic form what had previously been largely an unconscious and osmotic process, and who devised both the notion and the methods of *teaching* Hellenism. Hellenism as an ideal and a norm was of their making, an extraordinary feat of concept and procedure, and all subsequent converts to the gospel of Hellenism, both eastern and western, pagan and Christian, looked back upon the glories of the pre-Alexander past through their eyes.

That there was considerable distortion in the Alexandrian vision was a relatively recent discovery in the European branch of the Hellenic tradition. Indeed, Latinized Europe has required more than one renaissance to remind it whence it came. The prolonged closure of Greece within the bosom of the Ottoman Empire, for instance, meant that for long centuries Europe forgot the sight of Hellas, and its rediscovery at the beginning of the nineteenth century partook of the quality of a revelation. More revelations followed, not merely of Byron's romanticized landscape but of the very physical remains of the long-dead past.

The archaeologists of the nineteenth century almost literally stumbled over the corpse of ancient Greece and so placed the historian in a position to describe the Greek past, falteringly at first, but with growing assurance, as it really was when it still lived. No longer was it enough to receive the traditioned past, distorted in its passage through Latin hands and heavy with aesthetic and moral judgments; the nineteenth-century historian could reconstruct the Hellenic past *wie es eigentlich gewesen ist*—as it actually happened. Nor was it any longer necessary to see that past, the century of Pericles, for example, through Alexandrian or even Roman eyes. By an exercise of solidly based historical reconstruction it was possible to see Pericles whole, to admire the work of Phidias in the original instead of in Roman copies, and to meet Aristotle on his own terms rather than those of a Muslim Ibn Rushd or a Christian Thomas Aquinas.

Or so it seemed. What frequently occurred, however, was that German spectacles were substituted for Roman ones; a Hegelian reworking of Plato was little improvement over what the Stoics already had done to Platonism. There was an even more destructive result of German historicism. Both the nineteenth-century aesthete and the philologically or archaeologically oriented historian, however much they might disagree on their evaluation of Pericles, were united on at least one point: Philip's conquest of Greece marked the end of all that was meaningful in Hellenic history, the passage from the age of the giants to that of the pigmy epigones; Hellenistic art was debased, and Hellenistic political history was pointless. The vaguely pejorative and disdainful *Hellenistic* was itself a term coined to set off the style of the second generation.

Occasional scholars chose, from perversity or enlightenment, to till this cursed ground of later Greek history, the domain, largely, of eastern Hellenism. Alexander was reviled and the Macedonians were disparaged, and not even Mommsen's epoch-making work on the provinces of the Empire quite saved the somewhat more congenial Roman material from suffering a similar eclipse once the historian passed the bounds of what he considered important, the Roman Republic.

The balance has since been redressed, of course; Droysen, Krumbacher, Finlay, Bury and Rostovtzeff pursued the Greeks to their final destiny and began the reconstruction of the Alexandrian and Byzantine phases of Hellenic history. Oriental studies have come of age and provided a more informed understanding of the "mixed" Hellenism that was always taken so much for granted in its Latin version but that appeared so extraordinary when the alloy of Hellenism was not Roman Latinity but the culture of the Slavs, Armenians, Jews, Arabs or Ethiopians. And finally, and mercifully, we have survived our earlier Periclean pretensions. Either pessimism or realism now suggests that our own artistic and intellectual parent is not Athens but the neglected Alexandria; that our political kinship is rooted not in the democratic assemblies of fifth-century Athens but in Rome—perhaps, it is maliciously suggested, in third-century Rome. And Athens, once demoted to the less sensitive position of grandmother, can now be viewed somewhat more dispassionately and more truthfully than once was possible.

The historical truth about the Athens of Pericles is not in question in the following pages; what the second generations made of it is the point of departure. Nor is the validity of *their* assessment of great moment. They were formed, generation by generation, by what they thought was so, not by what we affirm is true. Except in religion, late antiquity was little troubled by the possibility that its Hellenism was degenerate. In both Latin and Greek branches, Hellenism's history was genial and serene, generally without threat of cultural competition, and not until the sixteenth century did it suffer disruptions of major and painful dimension.

Those disruptions are part of the stormy history of European Latin Hellenism, where the pressures of barbarism, science, plague, revealed religion, or corruptions of the exotic have never quite obliterated our filiation back to Homer, Socrates and Aristotle. The fate of our congener Greek Hellenism is less well known, simply because it does not debouch in us. Both branches, the Latin and the Greek, came under the political dominion of the ecumenical Roman Empire, and the European's eyes are naturally directed to the process whereby Hellenism gradually transformed that Roman state and society and eventually produced the cultures of Europe and America. But before Hellenism came into contact with the relatively callow Roman civilization, it had met and bred with the rich and ancient societies of the Near East, and it was from this union rather than from an immediate contact with fifth-century Greece that Roman—and, so, European—Hellenism was born. It was, moreover, this same contact of Hellene and Oriental that spawned related societies, the Byzantine and the Islamic, that we, as the cadet branch, so narrowly ignore.

The coming together of Greek and Easterner had been in the making for over a millennium, and scholars are only now beginning to perceive how productive were the contacts during the earliest period of an Aegean ecumenicism in the Bronze Age. It was not, however, until Alexander the Great conquered Asia that what had been isolated contacts turned into a flood tide. In the wake of Alexander's political opening of the Near East the triumphant Greeks spread their culture from the Himalayas to the cataracts of the Nile, blending with the arts, attitudes and institutions of Anatolia, Egypt, Syria and Iran. In some instances the influence was superficial and ephemeral; in others it produced the peculiar version of eastern Hellenism that had the vitality to survive for another seventeen hundred years. During this period it radically shaped Judaism, Christianity and Islam, and created an eastern Roman empire markedly different from its western cousin.

Eastern Hellenism has left its mark on all the lands once conquered by Alexander: on Buddhist art, the Zoroastrian Scriptures, the preaching of Mani, the spirituality of Christianity, the theology of Judaism, the palace architecture of Arab *shaykhs*. It produced Zeno (and through him Seneca), Apollonius of Rhodes (and through him Vergil), Posidonius (and through him Cicero), Plotinus (and through him Augustine). Its monuments are gnosticism, the university, the catechetical school, pastoral poetry, monasticism, the romance, grammar, lexicography, city planning, theology, canon law, heresy and scholasticism.

Eastern Hellenism, unlike its western counterpart, had no renaissance, because it had no dark ages. There is a straight linear progress from the death of Alexander in B.C. 323 to the fall of Constantinople in the fifteenth Christian century. The gradual separation of its Latin member during the early centuries of the Christian era was only an interlude in this progress. European Hellenism went into decline, but the eastern version, politically sustained by the Eastern Christian Roman Empire, went from strength to strength, carrying within itself the nucleus of the Greek achievement. It survived the crises of nationalist disaffection in Syria and Egypt, of irredentist nostalgia for the lost West, of mounting military pressures from the Balkans and across the Tigris, never ceasing to spin off new artistic, political and religious mutations.

It is the Hellenism of the East, then, that is the theme of this book, Greek at its base, but adapted and modified by the peoples of the Near East, planted by Alexander and harvested by succeeding generations down to the coming of Islam, and beyond.

I

A Mediterranean Oikoumene

In August of B.C. 338 the formidable national army of Philip of Macedon stood on the plain of Chaeronea at the approaches of Thebes. Drawn up opposite were the forces of Athens and Thebes, lately joined in an alliance of desperation against the man whom they had both finally come to recognize as their common enemy. Philip swept them from the plain and occupied Thebes. The three premier cities of the Hellenes—Athens, Thebes and the absent Sparta—had then to submit meekly to the Macedonian king's political rearrangement of the affairs of Greece.

The Politics of Dismay

The mutual relations of the various Greek states were shifting and uneasy even in the period before Chaeronea, and whatever the ideals and satisfactions fostered within the *polis*, they were not often transferred to the dealings of one Greek state with another or with the other powers that ringed the eastern Mediterranean. The collapse of Athens and the dispersal of her maritime allies at the beginning of the fourth century brought new alignments in Greece built, like the old, on undisguised appetites for power and self-aggrandizement. Beyond the Hellenic world lay the Persia of the Achaemenian Shahs, once again, after a disastrous peace treaty in B.C. 386, the master of the Anatolian Greeks. South across the Mediterranean was a moribund Egypt that had finally managed to free herself, during the disorders that followed the death of Darius II in B.C. 404, from more than a century of Persian occupation.

The complex military activity in the eastern Mediterranean during the fourth century was everywhere dominated by the presence of Greek mercenaries. Whatever power Persia or Egypt possessed rested firmly upon the Greek soldiery they lured into their ranks for pay, fortune or adventure. Between B.C. 385 and 383, for example, the Persians, now relieved of threats from Greece, attempted to regain Egypt. Neither side had Greek troops. The result was a stalemate and, in the eyes of some Greeks, a fiasco. Shortly thereafter, in B.C. 378, the last native Egyptians rose to the rule of Egypt in the person of the three Pharaohs of the XXX dynasty: Nectanebo I, Tachos and Nectanebo II. Once again the Shah, now Artaxerxes II Mnemon, resolved to win back the lost province, but under changed circumstances. His preparations provoked the alarmed Nectanebo I to hire the Athenian admiral Chabrias and his troopers. In the style that was to become increasingly common, Chabrias accepted the offer of employment without consulting the authorities at Athens. When the Persians complained, Chabrias was forced to withdraw, and to add balm the Shah was given the services of Athens' premier general Iphicrates, who, at the head of twelve thousand Greek mercenaries, penetrated the delta defenses of Egypt in B.C. 374. The opportunity for total success was eventually lost through Persian timidity—a satrap was in nominal charge of the expedition—and Egypt remained under the rule of her own kings for a few more years.

The Shah had gold enough to purchase mercenaries for his armies, but had considerably more difficulty in holding the loyalties of his own vassals, infected in turn by Hellenism's ideal of political autonomy and their own towering ambitions. In the eastern Aegean basin contested by Hellene and Achaemenian the cultural line that separated Greek *polis* from Asiatic city was drawn exceedingly fine. Political warfare had done nothing to halt the march of Hellenism up from the coast into the Anatolian interior. Just as the sixth century had seen the Hellenized Lydian Croesus ruling in Sardis, the fourth century had its Mausolus, the native Carian dynast whose father asserted his control over southwest Anatolia sometime after the death of Tissaphernes, the Shah's chief agent there, in B.C. 395.

Mausolus was but one of a number of western Achaemenian satraps—some of them designated, some of them hereditary, most ambitious, and all the object of suspicion at the palace at Susa—who ruled Anatolia in the Shah's name in the first half of the fourth century. In the seventies, the satrap Datames of Cappadocia had extended the Shah's realms to the Black Sea basin, and his extravagant success immediately led to plans for his deposition. But secure in Sinope, Datames could not be touched, and his assertions of independence, joined to those of Evagoras, who earlier in B.C. 389 had detached Cyprus from the empire,[1] emboldened the other satraps—Ariobarzanes in Phrygia, Orontes in Armenia, Autophradates in Lycia and Mausolus in Caria—to test their sovereign's resolve. Outright hostilities began in B.C. 366 and dragged on for some six or seven years. Datames, who had also come in on the business, was assassinated, and Ariobarzanes was betrayed to the Shah and crucified. The more agile or indispensable kept both their lives and their satrapies.

Egypt thought to profit from the disorders. To assist the rebels, Tachos fitted up an expedition under the command of no less than the King of Sparta, Agesilaus, and the familiar Athenian figure of Chabrias. This uncharacteristic display of Egyptian aggressiveness came to nothing militarily, and it cost Tachos his throne. He was deposed by the impatient Agesilaus, fled to the Shah at Susa, and Nectanebo II ruled in his stead. In B.C. 359 there was a resolute new Shah, Artaxerxes III Ochus, more determined than his predecessors to regain Egypt. But now both sides had Greek troops, and Nectanebo's Greeks threw back Artaxerxes' Greeks in B.C. 351. Persia was balked again, by a second-class power with first-class troops.

In an earlier period the Athenians too might have used the satraps' revolt to strengthen their position in the Aegean, but Mausolus had, in effect, anticipated them. His father had ruled from the inland Mylasa; Mausolus moved the capital of his kingdom down to the sea at Halicarnassus, where his own maritime ambitions were clearly displayed. He had ample encouragement in the restless state of Athens' island allies who were once again yoked in the galling "alliance" of a Maritime League. It was probably Mausolus who incited the Aegean cities to escape the

---

1. Cyprus was reduced once again in B.C. 380, but Evagoras was allowed to stay on as a ruler, nominally vassal of the Shah, but a highly visible suggestion of what was possible.

grip of Athens, and led by Chios, Cos and Rhodes, they banded together in B.C. 357 to face the inevitable Athenian reprisals. Within the year Athens struck back at the dissidents.

It was a curious war. Athens had a remarkable group of gifted commanders unequaled in her history: Chabrias, Chares, Iphicrates and Timotheus. Chabrias died early in the hostilities, but the others, frequently in command of mercenary troops raised elsewhere in Greece, operated much in the manner of satraps: jealous of each other, they pursued their own ends. The Athenians never treated their commanders gently, and the wayward behavior of Timotheus and Iphicrates during the campaigning soon brought their ruin. Once rid of his rivals, Chares turned not toward the insurgents in the islands but to the aid of the satrap of Phrygia, then in difficulty with Artaxerxes III.

How the ill-tempered Shah might react to this patent intervention on behalf of his recalcitrant satrap was only one of the issues debated at Athens in B.C. 356. Public opinion was turning against this war to maintain the crumbling Athenian Empire. Among the voices of dissent was that of Isocrates who, in his speech "On the Peace" delivered in B.C. 355, exhorted the Athenians to surrender their imperial ambitions. The counsels of Isocrates prevailed, and in the following year Athens negotiated the effective dissolution of her Maritime League: Cos, Chios, Rhodes and Byzantium were to be free and unencumbered. Their freedom did not last long. Mausolus, one of the prime movers of the revolt, entered to gather his spoils, and the democratic governments of the island *poleis* were subverted and replaced by oligarchies or, in some cases, by Carian garrisons.

Mausolus' death in B.C. 353 prematurely ended the Carian experiment in thalassocracy; his wife Artemisia followed him shortly to the grave,[2] and his successor Idrieus was not of the same stuff.

The Athenians' fears that Artaxerxes III was about to visit his vengeance upon them for Chares' interference in the Hellespont were almost certainly misplaced. The Shah's vision was myopically fastened upon the recovery of Egypt. He had failed in B.C.

---

2. The word is far too modest to describe the Carian king's final resting place that crowned the heights above Halicarnassus. It was a large and splendid burial monument, decorated for the Hellenizing king by the best Greek sculptors of the day. The tomb has disappeared, but the name survived.

351, and there were new distractions, to be sure: his troublesome satraps in Phrygia and Mysia aided, sometimes openly and sometimes clandestinely, by Athens; insurrectionist movements in Phoenicia and Cyprus; and the continued presence in Egypt of large bodies of Greek mercenaries. The Shah would have to take his chances with the latter, but meanwhile the satraps were brought under control and Athens was threatened into neutrality. Artaxerxes then proceeded to the reduction of Phoenicia by main force and, in B.C. 343, was once again ready for an attempt upon Egypt, this time with the best generals and front-line troops the Greek cities could provide for hire: Rhodians, Thebans, Argives and Ionians. The Egyptian line at Suez, also defended by Greeks, finally broke, and the Shah entered his lost province in triumph to institute a final brief and uneasy suzerainty over that land.

All of this was closely observed in Greece, and if the mercenaries in the pay of Egypt and Persia deprived the Greek *poleis* of the services of a generation of young men, they pointed another lesson as well: the obvious superiority of Greek soldiery and generalship over those of the mainland powers of Asia. The lesson was there to be learned as early as the Greco-Persian wars at the beginning of the fifth century, but it took the tumults of the succeeding hundred years, when Greek mercenaries served as the major lever of power around the eastern Mediterranean, to underscore the inescapable conclusion. Their campaigning in Anatolia and Egypt showed the Greeks the poor stuff of the native troops and their ineffectiveness in the increasingly complicated tactics of fourth-century warfare; but one event more than any other excited the imaginations of those Hellenes who had eyes to see: the Greek expedition of B.C. 399 into the heart of Babylonia and its return to the Black Sea.

At the death of Darius II in B.C. 404, his eldest son had taken the throne as Artaxerxes II Mnemon at the expense of the expectations of a younger son, Cyrus, the favorite of the Queen Mother Parysatis. Cyrus was not, however, to be cheated of the throne and late in B.C. 402 began to collect Greek troops for an insurrection. What followed was narrated by one of the participants, Xenophon, Socrates' memorialist at Athens, who kept a diary of the expedition which he later published as *The March Up-Country*.[3]

---

3. Xenophon devoted another treatise to the Achaemenians, his *Education of Cyrus*, a romanticized treatment of Cyrus the Great.

Cyrus' ten-thousand-odd Greeks under the command of the Spartan Clearchus marched unopposed through Anatolia, descended into Syria through the Cilician Gates, and headed south and east along the Euphrates until they came into contact with Artaxerxes' forces at Cunaxa, a town forty-five miles north of Babylon. The battle that followed went poorly for Cyrus' insurrectionists. His Greeks acquitted themselves well—too well, perhaps, since their headlong advance on the right wing of the battle line unexpectedly opened Cyrus' front, and Artaxerxes' cavalry poured into the gap; the rest of the line was overwhelmed and the day lost. Cyrus himself was killed in a desperate attack on his rival Artaxerxes; Clearchus and his Greek troopers stood alone and isolated deep within the Achaemenian Empire.

The Greeks slowly remounted the Tigris in a northerly direction—to return by the Euphrates, which led through the desert, was impossible without supplies—while complicated parlays with the hostile Persians took place. In one such, Clearchus and the rest of the general staff were treacherously killed. In these desperate circumstances the troops elected new generals, Xenophon among them, and resolved to strike out across the mountains of eastern Anatolia, the Armenian satrapies of Artaxerxes, in an effort to reach the Black Sea. The pursuing Persian troops soon veered off and left the Greeks to their almost certain fate, and the rest of the march was marked not so much by pitched battles as by a struggle against the elements, upland tribes, false guides and the occasional failure of their own discipline. Somehow they survived, or about half of the original force did, to reach Trapezus and eventually Pergamum.

The feat of these Greeks in Babylonia, Mesopotamia and Armenia was not so much of arms as of navigation, endurance and self-discipline, but it was read at home as something more significant, another piece of evidence of the superiority of Greek over Persian arms. So much was clear, but the real significance of the exploit was that it marked the beginning of a steady stream of mercenaries into the service of eastern rulers and the Shah's own deeper involvement in Aegean politics.

Artaxerxes II had to contend with an insurrectionist Egypt and dissident Anatolian satraps who, with Greek assistance, pursued their own ends more often than those of their nominal sovereign. He was more successful with the Greek states, on whom he imposed a harsh peace in B.C. 386; thereafter he manipulated them with considerable skill and large infusions of Persian gold. His successor Artaxerxes III Ochus did manage to win back Egypt in B.C. 343, but the price was the increased dominance of Greek troops and generals over their highly vulnerable paymasters. The Rhodian brothers Mentor and Memnon were the military mainstays of the Shah's empire during the forties and thirties of the fourth century. Mentor was the architect of Ochus' conquest of Egypt, and his commander in Asia Minor in B.C. 342–338.[4] And it was Memnon and his Greek mercenaries who had to face the first crash of Alexander's attack when he entered Asia. If Xenophon's experiences in Anatolia and Babylonia pointed to the ease with which Alexander might conquer the empires of the East, they suggested as well the chief obstacle to that conquest, Greek mercenaries under Greek generals in the service of the Shah.

The realm of the last Achaemenians, tottering on the brink of internal dissolution, was the object of considerable discussion in Greece. Its internal weaknesses were well known and its wealth the subject of varying appraisals. The two Artaxerxes bought both alliances and soldiery in the Greek cities and, on occasion, benevolent neutrality, as when Athens was persuaded or intimidated into standing aside from Egypt in B.C. 343. The Athenians never felt at ease in dealing with their traditional enemy, the Shah, but the Thebans, for whom Artaxerxes Ochus subsidized a war against Phocis in B.C. 355, showed no visible qualms. And yet the Shah allowed his allies, both the reluctant Athens and the enthusiastic Thebes, whose action—and inaction—permitted him to reconquer Egypt, to perish at the hands of another, more threatening power. Artaxerxes cared little for Philip of Macedon and actually sent troops against him when the Macedonians were campaigning in the region of the Hellespont in B.C. 340. But when Persia was called upon by her occasional friends to help against

---

4. It was during the operations there in B.C. 342 that Mentor captured and dispatched to Ochus and to crucifixion the independent ruler of the cities of Atarneus and Assos, Hermeias, who had attended the lectures of Plato and Aristotle at Athens and who invited the latter to his court. Aristotle and Xenophanes were in residence there from Plato's death in B.C. 347, when they withdrew from the Academy, until B.C. 344, when Aristotle, who had married Hermeias' niece, joined Theophrastus at Mitylene.

Philip, in B.C. 338, there was no response. After Chaeronea it was too late.

Chaeronea marked the end of the first stage in the career of the Greeks' finest institutional achievement, the *polis*. Henceforward the Greek *poleis*, deprived of the autonomy that was their prime characteristic, would serve as the generally empty counters in the game of political warfare that was played not for cities, but for the more considerable stakes of kingdoms and empires. The names were still to be conjured with—Thebes, Corinth and Sparta—but their best days were past, and their future lay in supplying the mercenaries and colonists who fought for and then settled into Alexander's conquered lands. Athens alone preserved some of her old brilliance into the new world not, as formerly, by showing forth the ideals common to all the Hellenes, but merely by virtue of continuing to preach those ideals. Athens did not lose her place as the center where the highest and finest Greek thought was taught. The new cities at Alexandria, Pergamum and Antioch might usurp her place in literature and the sciences, but until Justinian closed the Platonic school there in A.D. 529, Athens remained the city where Hellenes and the Hellenized—Greeks, Romans, Egyptians, Syrians and Arabs—resorted to study philosophy.

In its four-century life span as an autonomous organism, the *polis*, and particularly the Athenian *polis* of the fifth century, produced the complex of ideals and action that constituted what its heirs were to know as Hellenism. But there was more. Its successor, the *poleis* of the new kingdoms of Asia, provided the vehicle whereby that same Hellenism was carried to alien people on alien soil. In the larger history of Hellenism Alexandria and Antioch play as considerable a role as Athens, and even the lesser Greek cities that later dotted Anatolia and Syria displayed a vitality that not only guaranteed the survival of Hellenic ideals but was the foundation of much of the brilliance and prosperity enjoyed by the Roman Empire at the height of its eastern glory in the second and third Christian centuries.

The later *poleis* of Asia differed from their fifth-century counterparts in other than their inability to pursue a foreign policy and their tributary dependence upon Seleucid King, Egyptian Pharaoh or Roman *Imperator;* they had surrendered, as well, their claim to be the sole moral context in which a Hellene might pursue the good life. The theoreticians of the fifth-century *polis* were insistent in their joining of political institutions with moral ends. The historical *poleis* of that era had, of course, their own political goals, which find little or no place in the pages of Plato or Aristotle, but they showed as well, by their words, their actions, their public festivals and their private regrets that the moral goals urged by the theoreticians were more than a philosopher's ideal.

Though Plato and Aristotle considered the science of politics a higher form of the study of individual morality, there were some others who addressed themselves to the more pedestrian question of purely political means and ends. One such was Isocrates (d. B.C. 338) who shared the concerns of Plato and Aristotle with the moral end of the *polis*, but was enough of a pragmatist to recognize the presence of purely political activity in the dealings of one state with another. And unlike most of his contemporaries, Isocrates attempted an analysis and suggested a cure for the social ills that beset the Greeks in the fourth century.

The tightly knit fabric of the *polis* was loosening in the years after the Peloponnesian War, and the older urban areas of Greece were becoming overcrowded. The historians of the period read what was happening almost solely in political or military terms, but beneath their chronicles of wars and coups runs a deeper vein of serious economic difficulty. The birth rate in the Greek *poleis* began to climb once again after the Peloponnesian War, and this combination of more mouths to feed and the development of home industries in those areas around the Mediterranean from which Greece imported its foodstuffs and raw materials shifted the balance of trade ruinously against the *poleis*. They had to export to survive, but the markets for their manufactured exports were diminishing. Unemployment mounted, prices rose dizzily, encouraged by the large quantity of gold and silver coin dumped into the economy by the Macedonian and Persian habit of buying their allies, and war became almost endemic.

When this reoccurred in the third century the sprawling *metropoleis* of the Alexandrian age spawned an equally rootless and restless urban proletariat, but in the fourth century the more circumscribed *poleis* merely discharged their young men not, as formerly, into overseas colonies, but into the swelling ranks of the *condottieri*-like prototypes of the later professional mercenaries, highly trained soldiers ready to serve anywhere or anyone for a price.

There is little hint of this in either the *Laws* of Plato or in the *Politics* of Aristotle; the theme is sounded frequently, however, in Isocrates, who approached the *polis* with a moral perspective, but through the avenue of action rather than constitutional analysis. For Isocrates, Panhellenism was a real if fugitive ideal that demanded more than a self-congratulatory reunion every four years at the Olympic Games, where the Greeks celebrated their common Hellenism. In his "Panegyric Oration" he called for a program of political action that would unite the *poleis* not as an empire but as a confederation, and that would have as its object the opening of new frontiers on old soil, western Anatolia. Isocrates was no imperialist in the sense of the expansion of a single state, as Athens had done in the preceding century, nor again in the creation of a superstate. Salvation still lay in the *polis,* even though its fourth-century versions were marching from crisis to crisis.

The calls and convictions of the preceding decades converged on Philip. A Persian crusade in the cause of Greek unity had been preached by Isocrates in a Panhellenic oration delivered in B.C. 380, and a similar call had been sent out even earlier by others. In B.C. 346 Isocrates addressed himself directly to the Macedonian king and once again urged the policy that he had been advocating for over three decades: the *poleis* were doomed unless they were united in some common cause like a crusade against the Shah. Isocrates' horizons were more modest than those later revealed by events; he advocated no more than the liberation of the Greek cities of the Anatolian coast which the Persians had held firmly in their grip since the shameful peace of B.C. 386. The project would be simple enough, since recent history had proved that the forces of the Shah were no match for Greeks. The reconquest of Asia Minor would unify the mainland *poleis* in the pursuit of a common goal, the liberation of Anatolia, and, if successful, provide a colonial outlet for the energies of the *condottieri* who had been the instruments of violence for the last half century in the eastern Mediterranean.

This was Isocrates' message in the "Philippicus" of B.C. 346, as it had been of his "Panegyric Oration" of B.C. 380. The later tract pointed directly to Philip, and it is doubtful whether he needed much urging. The Macedonian king's Hellenic pretensions were considerable, and the liberation of the Greek cities of Asia by a Panhellenic army marching under his banner was a gesture that appealed simultaneously to his imperialist ambitions, his sense of Hellenic solidarity, and his love of adventure and gain. There were, moreover, the Shah's hostile moves in the Hellespont in B.C. 340 and the unmistakable fact that only Achaemenian gold was capable of loosing Macedon's hold on Greece.

Artaxerxes III fatally misjudged Philip. The Shah knew well enough that his direct military intervention was likely to be suicidal, but he had the financial means at his disposal to thwart Philip if he so wished, and willing instruments in Athens and Thebes. But Achaemenian pride was apparently more concerned with the empty aspirations of the reannexation of Egypt than with checking the far more dangerous Macedon. Artaxerxes' ear must have grown accustomed to talk of crusades and the seemingly unproductive threats to liberate the Greek cities of Ionia. Persia was safe behind its wall of Greek mercenaries, its Mentors and Memnons.

Artaxerxes III was murdered shortly after the battle of Chaeronea, and the presence on the throne of the Shahs, first of Arses, the untested son of the Grand Vizier Bagoas, and then, when the ephemeral Arses had been poisoned by his own father, of Bagoas' other creature, Darius III Codomannus, must have made an Asian expedition even more tempting to the triumphant Philip.

At a congress of the *poleis* expansively summoned to meet at Corinth in B.C. 337 Philip announced his intentions: he would lead a Panhellenic force across the Hellespont and free the Greeks of Asia from their political bondage to the Shah. If there was any enthusiasm for the plan it must have been subdued; but there was not, at any rate, overt resistance, and the cities represented at the assembly dutifully elected the Macedonian king commander in chief and distributed the responsibility for ships and men among the various *poleis*—all except Sparta, who held herself resolutely but impotently aloof. By the spring of the next year preparations were complete and some advanced units had already crossed over into Asia when they received the news that Philip had been assassinated at the instigation of person or persons unknown, his wife Olympias, perhaps, or even his twenty-year-old son, Alexander.

Alexander's Conquest of Asia

As the news of Philip's death spread through Greece, there sounded an almost explosive note of jubilation and release. It was decidedly premature. Philip's generals rose to his son's support, and Alexander rushed into Greece, secured Thessaly, and reasserted his position as Philip's heir both as king of Macedon and captain of the armies of the Congress of Corinth. A little later, while Alexander was putting down some unruly insurgents in the Balkan marches of his kingdom, a mistaken report reached Greece that he too had been killed. The democratic faction at Thebes unhappily took this occasion to rise up yet once again. The sudden reappearance in Greece of a very lively Alexander provided a stark and unforgettable object lesson to the *poleis;* he razed the city of Thebes and sold many of its men into slavery.[5] It was a move that in its speed and decisiveness recalled the Philip from whom the Greeks had so lately thought themselves relieved. Thenceforward Alexander had little or no trouble with his "allies." By the spring of B.C. 334 he was ready to resume his father's interrupted design for the reduction of Anatolia.

Some test of the Persians' resolve on their own ground had already been made under Philip when his general Parmenio crossed over into Aeolis and took some fortified points on the Asiatic side of the Hellespont. When Darius III came to power in B.C. 335 he dispatched against the intruders the Rhodian Greek Memnon, who with his brother, Mentor, had been war lord of the Achaemenian Empire for more than a decade. Some few of the Macedonians were dislodged by Memnon and his Greek mercenaries, but the essential bridgeheads held for Alexander's eventual arrival were securely covered by Parmenio.

Alexander came to Asia clothed in two official roles. He was king of Macedon and, as such, was the liege lord of his Macedonian barons and their troops. In an earlier day the lords of Macedon served their ruler as an elite cavalry, accompanied, doubtless, in their picturesque and dashing campaigns through the valleys of the Balkans by a ragtag body of foot soldiers. Philip, who served

---

5. The only exception to the general destruction of Thebes was the house of the poet Pindar, the first appearance of a broad streak of literary romanticism that ran through the personality of Alexander.

as a cadet at Thebes under Epaminondas, the greatest military mind in Greece, reorganized the army: he kept the elite cavalry, shaped the infantry into a new formation, the phalanx, a more elastic and yet more cohesive fighting instrument than the solidly packed and heavily armed hoplites of the Greek cities,[6] and wielded the two into a single tactical unit. There were light-armed troops as well, the hypaspists, trained and armed in the manner of the fourth century's newest offensive weapon, the skirmishing formations popularized by the mercenary armies. But the high professional sheen Philip gave to these various bodies of fighting men was not the chief grounds for their success. By the skillful management of the cadres Philip managed to professionalize his troops while preserving their feudal loyalties and their consciousness of being a national army. As Philip's successor as Macedonian liege, Alexander inherited this marvelous fighting instrument bound to him in its upper echelons by ties of personal loyalty and pervaded throughout by a sense of national and tribal cohesiveness.

Alexander's progress through the East was not, however, merely an exercise in Macedonian imperialism. Alexander, like Philip before him, was conscious of—and insistent upon—his Hellenic role in Asia. He was the captain of a Greek League coming against the descendants of those Shahs who had humiliated the Hellenes in the past. Philip's Hellenism was real enough; an admiration and active support of things Greek was a dynastic policy in Macedon at least since the time of Alexander I (*c.* B.C. 495–450), who claimed Greek ancestry, competed as a Hellene at the Olympic Games, and invited Pindar to his court in Macedon. Archelaus (B.C. 413–399) lured Euripides to his new capital at Pella, and when Philip invited Aristotle into Macedon to serve as the tutor of the thirteen-year-old Alexander, he was merely continuing his house's attempt at drawing the somewhat rude and un-Greek northern kingdom into the cultural orbit of Hellenism. Philip fought his way into Hellenic politics as well, and the two motifs of culture and politics came into triumphant conjunction

---

6. The Macedonian phalanx, which was brigaded into battalions of 1,500 men, was armed with a new lancelike weapon, the *sarissa*, a pike of somewhat less than fifteen feet in length, that at first glance might seem more appropriate in the hands of a cavalry trooper, but whose unwieldy length kept the enemy both engaged and at bay, which was the primary mission of the phalanx.

in B.C. 346, when the Macedonian king presided at the great Pan-hellenic games celebrated at Delphi.

Alexander's Hellenism was of a different sort, more personalized and urgent than his father's had been. The Phrygian shore of the Hellespont was far more Hellenized than his own homeland, but when Alexander finally crossed over there in the spring of B.C. 334 he saw himself coming as a Greek to an alien Asia, prepared to repay to the full Xerxes' earlier descent on his own spiritual homeland. And once on that sacred shore, he turned not to the east to face the forces that Darius' satraps were drawing up against him, but hastened instead to Hellenism's holiest shrine, the site of Troy, in Alexander's day the rather modest town of Ilium. He sacrificed in Athena's temple, inspected the antiquities, including the tomb of his hero and putative ancestor Achilles,[7] and exchanged his own armor for some antique pieces that he was told dated from the Trojan War.

The Shah's forces marshaled at the nearby Granicus River were no match for the Macedonians. Memnon's advice that they fall back and scorch the land was ignored by the Asiatic satraps, who distrusted the only man among them capable of facing Alexander on equal terms. A rout followed in which many of the Shah's relatives and high command were killed or captured; it is unlikely that Darius himself was even in Anatolia at the time. Alexander sent an offering of three hundred suits of full Persian battle armor to Athens for dedication at the Parthenon. The inscription was his own: from Alexander and the Greeks (except the Spartans), taken from the Persians of Asia. The Athenians probably grasped the point, but were restrained in their enthusiasm; they still did not send the fleet they had long ago promised as their part of the undertaking.

Alexander, temporarily freed of Persian attention, headed southwest and "liberated" Sardis and Ephesus. Magnesia and Tralles quickly offered their capitulation. Miletus and Halicarnassus caused some difficulty, but Alexander's siege equipment was equal to the task, and those *poleis* too eventually yielded. There

---

7. The Macedonian house claimed descent from both Heracles and Achilles. Alexander's conversion of this harmless and not uncommon genealogy into a fixation may have been due to the habit of one of his tutors—not Aristotle—of calling the Macedonian prince Achilles and himself, naturally, Phoenix.

was very little vengeance, even against those who had their doubts about the Macedonian version of political freedom. As he gathered the mainland cities into his net, Philip had replaced the democratic factions in them with oligarchic politicians sympathetic to his hegemony. In Asia, Alexander reversed the policy. And though the Hellenic cities were now "free," they paid the same taxes they had paid under the Shah. The mood, however, was quite different. Before, the cities had been tributary subjects of the Achaemenian Shah; now they were contributory members, together with the mainland *poleis*, of the League of Corinth.

Alexander appeared reasonably secure as he rounded the Lycian corner of Anatolia and turned inland for the reduction of the cities of Pamphylia, Pisidia and Phrygia. The Persian fleet, now under the command of Memnon, freely coursed the Aegean coast behind him, but succeeded neither in prying loose from his grasp the Greek cities of the Asian coast nor in raising insurrection in Greece, where the Macedonian general Antipater vigilantly saw to it that none of the cities forgot the terrible example of Thebes. Athens, for one, did not, and Antipater's only serious trouble was with Sparta, which had never been a member of the League of Corinth and now under Agis III was in diplomatic touch with Darius. The negotiations are obscure, as are Agis' motives for trying Macedonian sovereignty at this point, but in B.C. 331 Agis was on the move in the Peloponnesus in direct defiance of the League. Antipater met the Spartan forces at Megalopolis and defeated them. Agis died for his hopeless cause, but Alexander treated Sparta with mercy and restraint, and Greece remained quiet until his death.

After less than a year of campaigning, Alexander's mission, whether he is viewed as captain of the League of Corinth or king of Macedon, was completed. His circle through western Anatolia came to term in Ancyra in Phrygia in B.C. 333, and through that wide arc behind him he had freed the Greek *poleis* of Asia of their political subjection to the Achaemenian Empire. His political work was done; there remained only the strategic and psychological prize of the Shah himself. Darius was still at large, and if the death of Memnon in B.C. 333 deprived him of his best commander, his forces were still intact, lodged somewhere south of the Taurus. Alexander turned south from Ancyra, and with rapidity of movement that was his most characteristic tactic,

passed through the Cilician Gates into the vicinity of Tarsus on the plain beyond. Darius lay somewhat farther to the south.

The battle fought at Issus in the fall of B.C. 333 came about when Alexander and the Shah stumbled upon each other across their broken lines of communication. Alexander was eager for the contact; Darius less so, but when the Persians discovered that they had cut across Alexander's southward path from behind and stood between him and his camp, the opportunity could not be resisted. The two forces were evenly matched, and the fighting was straightforward and hard. The difference was in the commanders. Early on Darius cut and ran, and as the news traveled along the line the Achaemenian army became demoralized, and they broke and fled. It was a major confrontation and a major victory. Darius' field quarters fell into Alexander's hands, as well as the imperial harem, which was treated with courtesy and tact. And when Parmenio shortly afterward moved out on Alexander's eastern flank and occupied Damascus, he found there the personal treasury of Darius and his high command.

Darius had veered off to the east, toward the safer precincts of Mesopotamia and Iran, but Alexander pushed on to the south, through the Phoenician coastal cities of Byblos and Sidon, which yielded without a struggle. Here in the shipyards and sailors of Phoenicia was the source of Persian naval strength. Alexander argued, not very convincingly, that it would be dangerous to leave either Phoenicia or Egypt untaken at his rear. He may have been tempted by the promised ease of the assault, but if so, he was cruelly disappointed at Tyre, whose island garrison resisted his siege for seven months in the summer of B.C. 332.

On the eve of the fall of Tyre, Alexander received terms from the Shah: a ransom for his family so large that it appeared more like an indemnity, the hand of his daughter in marriage, and the cession of all the Achaemenian holdings west of the Euphrates, an area including not only the still unconquered parts of Anatolia but Egypt as well.[8] Alexander, speaking now in his own voice, answered that he had no need of money and that the rest of the Shah's offer, his daughter and Asia, belonged to him already. It was close to the truth; except for a show of obstinacy on the part

---

8. The latter offer was a strange portent of the future. The lands that Darius offered to cede to Alexander marked almost exactly the limits that Alexander's latter-day successors at Rome and Constantinople were able to hold against Parthian and Sasanian Iran.

of the Arab defenders of Gaza, Alexander marched almost casually into Egypt.[9]

Perhaps as early as Issus, Alexander was dropping his role as the delegated commander in chief of a Greek expeditionary force, but in Egypt the physiognomy of a new Alexander is clearly revealed in two significant events: the founding of Alexandria and his visit to the oracle of Zeus-Ammon at Siwa. The site of the future Alexandria was in the western Delta near the village of Rhacotis and opposite the offshore island of Pharos. Alexander's intent was frankly commercial, perhaps to establish a maritime rival of the recently troublesome Tyre,[10] and his intentions were marvelously fulfilled: Alexandria, as the terminus of the sea routes to the East, became in time the chief commercial emporium of the eastern Mediterranean. Alexander's Macedonian successors in Egypt were to prove commercially aggressive, and the chief instrument of their economic imperialism was the magnificently endowed port of Alexandria, supported and serviced by the factories, warehouses and banks of the city itself. But Alexander's city served far broader ends than purely commercial ones. Shortly it was to replace Memphis as the administrative capital of Egypt, a Greek city in the midst of an Egyptian sea, to which were drawn Greece's and Asia's premier scientists and scholars to share in Alexandria's other triumph, the Library and Museum that remained the intellectual focus first of Hellenism and then of Christianity down to the Muslim invasion.[11] All of this was perhaps implicit, if not intended, in Alexandria's foundation. By it the introverted and traditionalist Egypt of the later Pharaohs was opened outward into the new Hellenic *oikoumene*. Egypt never

---

9. The later Jewish tradition found it incredible that Alexander should pass Jerusalem without notice, and in Josephus' later narrative of the events of this period Alexander is fictitiously carried to Jerusalem for an encounter with the High Priest. By the time of the Talmud what had earlier been a piece of tendentious historical fiction was converted into pure fantasy.

10. If he did intend to undermine the position of Tyre, as some have suggested, he did not succeed. The overland trade routes from the East inevitably ended on the Syro-Phoenician coast, and the factories of Tyre and Sidon continued to thrive on the eastern raw materials delivered there at the end of the caravan trek. The chief check on the Phoenician emporia was the remarkable growth in the next decades of the Seleucids' capital at Antioch.

11. See Chapter V, pp. 193–94.

ceased to rest heavily upon its agricultural base, but now other vital strains of commercial activity quickened and the land that had lain dormant for centuries was reintegrated into the general Mediterranean economy.

The phenomenon was general in the lands of Alexander's conquests, the drawing of the East closer into the orbit of Hellenism; but as Alexander stood in Egypt there began to appear as well the first signs of current in the opposite direction. Alexander's new Greek city in the Delta had, according to the founder's express intention, temples not only to the Greek gods but to the Egyptian Isis as well, and at Memphis he sacrificed to the sacred bull Apis. Historical precedents counted heavily with him: Cambyses, the mad Shah who had first conquered Egypt for the Persians, had slain Apis in an earlier age, and already perhaps Alexander had begun to think of himself not so much as a Greek captain as the successor of a doomed Darius. And beyond politics stirred the mythic images of Achilles, Heracles and Dionysus. Propaganda values and the peculiar combination of personal vanity and the piety of the true believer drew Alexander toward that Libyan oasis which sheltered the famous oracle of Amon-Re, well known in the Greek world as Zeus-Ammon, and which possessed some of the towering prestige of Delphi and Dodona.

The journey to the oasis of Siwa was difficult, and what went on in the temple precinct once the eminent visitor arrived is not entirely clear. At a later date, when Alexander's apparently self-proclaimed divinity became an issue, it was said that the seeds of his delusion were planted at Siwa. Perhaps so. He was almost surely greeted by the priests there as Pharaoh, the divine offspring of Amon-Re. Another man might have been alternately amused or impressed; for Alexander the greeting could have been no more fantastic than his own growing image of himself as the scion of divine and heroic forebears. The titles of Pharaoh and Shah merely opened new dimensions in an already highly charged religious sensibility. Alexander never resisted his new roles. He grasped them firmly and used them skillfully for both political and ideological ends.

Even before Siwa, Alexander assumed the prerogatives of Pharaoh, and after he returned thence to Memphis he set about reorganizing the government of his new kingdom. As earlier in the non-*polis* territories of Anatolia, the civil administration was left in the hands of the Egyptians, originally two men but subse-

quently under the control of a single native governor; Macedonians remained unmistakably in control of the military establishment, not one but many officers with interlocking commands. Garrisons were posted at Memphis and on the eastern approaches at Pelusium.

In the spring of B.C. 331 Alexander was once again in Syria dealing with the increasingly complicated problems of government, while Parmenio secured the Euphrates crossing at Thapsacus and prepared pontoon bridges for the moment when the Macedonian armies once again took up their pursuit of Darius. Farther east the Persians were making their own preparations. The satraps brought together an army considerably larger than the one that had faced Alexander at Issus. There was a particularly heavy concentration of cavalry, with contingents from both the western satrapies in Anatolia, Armenia and Syria, and the more formidable horsemen from eastern Iran and the Central Asian marches where Alexander would later meet his fiercest opposition, Bactrians, Sogdians and Sacae. Elephants in war panoply were brought in from India,[12] and another of the Persians' terror weapons, chariots with projecting scythe blades attached to their wheels, were collected in great number.

Alexander appeared at Thapsacus in August, marching up from Tyre via Damascus, Emesa and Aleppo. The Euphrates crossing was uneventful, as was the transit across northern Mesopotamia. The Tigris was forded south of the rising mountains of Armenia, and the army began its descent of that river. Darius had drawn up his army at Gaugamela, eighteen miles southeast of Nineveh, and it was there that the two armies clashed. As at Issus, the fighting was hard and the outcome still very much in doubt, when Darius fled the field of battle. The issue was decided at that point, even though the struggle ran on for some hours more. Ominously, only the Bactrian and Iranian horse under the satrap Bessus

---

12. The tactics of elephant warfare were simple: to terrify the enemy and particularly to thwart cavalry charges by causing the horses to shy. Alexander later captured Darius' elephants at Susa, and they became a standard and sometimes successful feature of Near Eastern warfare. One man who had faced them in India and had been impressed was Alexander's general Seleucus, who, when he later became master of Iraq and Iran, bartered Alexander's Indian conquests for five hundred war elephants which were used at the battle of Ipsus in B.C. 301 (see Chapter II, pp. 80–81).

remained intact. They caught up with Darius after the rout was complete and accompanied him on his flight eastward. It was presumed that Alexander would continue his march south into the heart of the empire, toward Babylon, Susa and Persepolis.

Babylon offered no resistance. Its satrap Mazaeus, who had commanded the Persian right at Gaugamela, surrendered and was probably surprised to have Alexander reinstate him as civil governor; as in Egypt, the military affairs of the province would be under Macedonian supervision. With a sure instinct, the conqueror ordered the temple of Bel, which had been destroyed by Xerxes during his vicious suppression of an earlier revolt, to be reconstructed, and he piously consulted the Chaldean clergy on the correct worship of the Babylonian god. While this ceremonious good will was being displayed toward the Babylonians, an advance column of the army, dispatched immediately after the battle of Gaugamela, reached Susa and reported that the city— and its treasures—was secured. Alexander, his respects paid to Babylon, followed shortly after and quickly sent a large sum of money from his new reserves to Antipater for financing the war against Agis of Sparta. From Susa, Alexander forced the passes into the Achaemenian home province of Persis (Fars), where lay the great temple and palace complexes of Persepolis and Pasargadae.

The Macedonians wintered at Persepolis (B.C. 331–330), and what occurred there during those months is somewhat puzzling. Up to this point Alexander's policy had been to punish resistance and treat capitulation with mercy and compassion. There was no resistance at Persepolis, and yet Alexander ordered the destruction of the Great Palace of Xerxes. Legend later fashioned a story about the whim of a courtesan, but the only motive for the act known to the older sources was that Alexander thus avenged Xerxes' burning of the temples on the Athenian acropolis. If so, it was a passing and isolated recollection of why he, the king of Macedon, was standing, thousands of miles from home, at the center of the Achaemenian Empire. And once he performed the symbolic act of revenge on behalf of the Hellenes, Alexander sent home his League troops; thenceforward he was in Iran by his own mandate and authority.

The homebound troops, deaths and disabilities were thinning the army's ranks. Some of this loss could be easily sustained; the campaigns to date had shown that cavalry was the major fighting

arm in Asia, and all along the route the Macedonian infantry was bolstered by fresh detachments of horse troops recruited locally. Darius too was running low on his precious heavy-infantry mercenaries and so, of necessity, had come to rely more and more on his eastern cavalry. But Alexander was not content with mere military calculations. In a bold, and perhaps dangerous stroke he made arrangements over that winter for the training of young Iranians in Greek culture and manners to eventually take their place in the sacrosanct files of the phalanx.[13]

There was more of this to follow, but Darius was still at liberty, lodged, according to report, to the north of Ecbatana, the Achaemenian summer palace in Media. There were said to be troops there too, the remnant of the Greek mercenaries upon which the last Shahs so heavily relied, as well as the corps of Bessus' eastern cavalry. With the return of campaigning weather in the spring of B.C. 330 Alexander headed toward Media. While still three days short of Ecbatana he learned that Darius and his troops had withdrawn farther eastward, toward the Bactrian redoubt that Bessus thought offered the best ground for support and defense. He was possibly right, but once past the Parthian Gates that marked the passage from Media to Parthia and the eastern satrapies where his own power was more secure, Bessus decided that Darius was more of a liability than an asset and put his sovereign under arrest; Darius could be sacrificed if Alexander, then in hot pursuit, got too close. Bessus' troopers took their cue and acclaimed their former satrap, who himself had royal blood in his veins, as Shah. Darius' arrest was brief. As Alexander, who had dropped off the regular infantry and was following closely on horse, drew dangerously near, Darius was struck down and left for dead. The Macedonian advance riders found him gasping out his last, and when Alexander arrived the Shah was already dead.

There were mopping-up operations, surrenders to be accepted, and delegations to be received. As before, local governors were confirmed in office, here a Parthian for Parthia and Hyrcania, and given a Macedonian counterpart to supervise the military. Then

---

13. Alexander's understanding that more than close-order drill was necessary for success in the disciplined Hellenic fighting techniques may have been helped by the Persians' own failure in this direction, particularly the experiment of the Cardaces, Darius' ersatz hoplite force made up of native Persians, that had so signally failed at Issus.

the news arrived that Bessus had proclaimed himself Shah under the dynastic name Artaxerxes. Alexander had been cheated once more; the tiara which he craved rested on another's head. He set off after this new prey, scarcely noting the report that Antipater had met and defeated the insurrectionist Agis at Megalopolis in the Peloponnese.

As Alexander emerged from the mountains of Hyrcania he faced the flatlands that ran up to the northwest across the Oxus and the Jaxartes to the steppes of Central Asia.[14] The area, dominated by the Achaemenian satrapy of Bactria, was not all of a piece. The corridor to Central Asia was then pasturage, which on its northern side became desert between the Caspian and Aral seas. The lower reaches of the Oxus was delta land, the home of the Khwarazmian tribes and a settled culture. The upper reaches of the river, whence it descended in a broad valley from the Hindu Kush, had some agriculture, chiefly rice, and its inhabitants lived in towns, the chief of which was Bactra (later Balkh). Between the Oxus and the parallel Jaxartes there was another plain. Here too there were other towns, Maracanda (Samarkand) and Sogdiana (Bukhara), that even during this period prospered as trade emporia, since on the upper Jaxartes beyond Maracanda lay the valleys of Ferghana that connected eastern Iran with Kashgar and the western reaches of China, and beyond Bactra were other routes that passed over the Hindu Kush into India.

Alexander did not pursue Bessus up the corridor to Bactra, but turned instead southward into the mountainous province of Aria, where the governor, Satibarzanes, having earlier promised fealty and been confirmed in office, was now stirring up insurrection. It was Alexander's first taste of a different kind of political climate. Here in eastern Iran the satraps ruled like autonomous barons in their own fiefs, and if they gave the Shah less public trouble than the western satraps, it was only because they ran under a looser rein. Henceforward Alexander was embroiled in a series of local wars fought by much tougher troops than those Darius had in his lines at Gaugamela and Issus.

The resistance did not, however, begin in Aria, since Satibarzanes decided to decamp and join Bessus in Bactria. Alexander

14. Both rivers flow into the Aral Sea, but the Greeks, whose knowledge of the area was as sketchy as its Herodotean foundation, thought they debouched into the Caspian.

founded a new Alexandria (Herat) as a capital for the Arians and then pushed on into Drangiana, which had also promised and then withdrawn its support of his regime. Here too the resistance collapsed, but a far more serious check occurred. For the first time evidence of serious disaffection appeared within the army, indeed, in Alexander's own circle. Word of a planned coup came to the king's ears and with it the report that the responsible party was Philotas, commander of the elite cavalry and the son of Parmenio, Philip's former general who had almost made a botch of Gaugamela and whom Alexander had left in the rear at Ecbatana. It is unknown whether Philotas was guilty—he denied complicity—or how much substance there was to the talk of a coup, but the accused was tried, found guilty by his Macedonian peers, and executed. Parmenio had not been accused, but in cases of high treason the death penalty was not infrequently visited on the family of the guilty as well. Alexander chose this course, and Parmenio was dispatched at Ecbatana.

Deep in the mountainous country of Carmania (Kerman) and Gedrosia (Makran) Alexander decided not to return the same way he had come but to mount the Helmand river valley, cross the Hindu Kush northward from the direction of India, and descend on Bactria from its eastern end. It was now the spring of B.C. 329 and it took the better part of the next eight months to gain Kandahar, Ghazni and Kabul, accompanied by the usual labor of founding new settlements, confirming Persian satraps in their civil authority, and leaving Macedonian troops along the way to garrison the land. The army wintered in the southern foothills of the Hindu Kush and, early in the spring of B.C. 328, began the difficult passage of the range known to the Greeks as the Paropamisus. It was a fearsome ascent in blinding snows and with minimum rations, but the column finally gained the Panjshir-Khawak Pass and curled down the northern slopes to Drapsaca on the frontier of Bactria. Even here, in his home territory, Bessus did not feel sure enough to take a stand. He scorched the countryside but left the cities of his former satrapy for Alexander to occupy without a struggle while he scuttled across the Oxus.

The weary Macedonians crossed the Oxus at Kilif and were on the road to Maracanda when news was brought that Bessus had fallen victim to the same treatment he had meted out to Darius: the barons of Bactria and Sogdia had arrested Bessus and were willing to hand him over to the invader. Alexander was considerably less moved by the capture of this usurper Shah than he had been by that of the legitimate Darius. He sent his delegate Ptolemy ahead to collect Bessus, whom he later treated to the humiliation of a public flogging. Maracanda was occupied in due course and a further march brought the troops to the banks of the Jaxartes.

No one of the Greeks knew what lay beyond the Jaxartes—which they mistook for the Don—save the ominous gathering of nomads on the far banks. It is doubtful that Alexander even knew precisely where he was—the nearby valleys of Ferghana led directly to Sinkiang—but he did realize the importance of the Jaxartes crossings and constructed still another Alexandria, "the Farthest," later Khojend, to cover the approaches to Sogdia, which he doubtless intended to hold. That was to be by no means a simple undertaking. The entire province was in revolt behind him, and Spitamenes, the baron of Sogdia, now held Maracanda under siege and had cut to pieces the relieving force. Alexander rushed back from his adventures across the Jaxartes and managed to save Maracanda, though Spitamenes slipped off to his capital at Sogdiana when Alexander withdrew to winter quarters at Bactra (B.C. 329–328).

Two seasons were spent in Sogdia and Bactria before the area was at least superficially pacified. Reinforcements arrived from the west, but Spitamenes was a strong and intelligent foe who felt he could count on sanctuary among the nomads who roamed the desert interior of Sogdia toward the Aral Sea. He was mistaken. Alexander kept up a relentless pressure until the nomads finally lost heart and slew their embarrassing guest. On another foray into mountainous eastern Sogdia he captured the family of a local dynast among whom was the chieftain's daughter Roxane. Soon afterward Alexander married her in what the later historians relished as a true love match between the handsome world conqueror and the ravishing Central Asian beauty. If it was such, then it ran counter to everything else we know of Alexander, whose only apparent interest in women was bestowed on his mother Olympias and other less flamboyant but unmistakable mother figures like the dowager Queen Ada of Halicarnassus and the mother of Darius.

The marriage to Roxane was doubtless contracted for political considerations, never very far from Alexander's mind. And here in the remote eastern fastness of the Achaemenian Empire there is further evidence that politics was converging with ideology. Since the death of Darius, Alexander had increasingly taken on eastern airs; he was, after all, the successor of the Shah, and to wear native clothes and the tiara might be reasonably defensible policy in a land where the safety of his few Greeks and Macedonians hung on the thin threads of public image. But Alexander was nowhere so calculating as that. His intimates in the confining camps of the Macedonian field army grew uneasy precisely because they sensed that the Oriental Alexander was somehow more than a mask donned for the gulling of eastern Iranian warlords. The ranks were thinning in Asia as age, weariness, garrison duty and changes in tactics bore in upon them all. The army that wintered in Bactra in B.C. 328 was far different from the one with which Philip had triumphed at Chaeronea only ten years before. Iranian governors and grandees freely came and went; it was they, for example, who finally tried Bessus and sent him off to Ecbatana for execution. Troops of Bactrian and Sogdian horse, more skilled in the guerrilla warfare of Central Asia, were posted next to the elite Macedonian squadrons. Alexander seemed to thrive on the exotic mix that he himself had created and encouraged, but the sentiments of many of the others, deeply committed to the traditions of a national army and a national king, were deeply offended.

Two events brought the seething discontent into the open. Drinking was becoming increasingly heavy among the troops in the East, and Alexander, whose personal asceticism had been marked by all who met him, was himself turning more frequently and heavily to wine. In one such drinking carouse some courtiers were moved by the occasion and the wine to suggest that Alexander's achievements placed him above the traditional gods. For Cleitus, a general who went back to the days of Philip and who had saved Alexander's life at the Granicus, the outrage had gone far enough; he charged that the drunken bragging demeaned the old-time gods, and moreover, Alexander's deeds were not his alone but all the Macedonians'. It was no haphazard remark. Cleitus had been brooding about the changed atmosphere and Alexander knew it. There was an exchange and Cleitus hoarsely asked why Macedonians had to petition Iranians for an audience with their own king. Some of the other guests tried to thrust Cleitus out of the tent, but he persisted. Alexander, now near the edge of hysteria, picked up a spear and ran his general through on the spot.

What Cleitus had said to his own misfortune was probably on the minds of many of the conservative Macedonian officers. Their nerves had been worn thin by the recent defeats inflicted by Spitamenes and his guerrillas. The real issue for them was not blasphemy but the shift from Macedonian to Iranian command and, beneath that and connected with it, the execution of Philotas and Parmenio. The affair provoked by Cleitus signaled an outrage to the feudal sensibilities and military pride of the Macedonians. Something else occurred at about that same time that touched more deeply into the fiber of Hellenism. Alexander's half-romantic and half-political penchant for Oriental dress and behavior led him to introduce the prostration (*proskynesis*) into court ceremonial. For the Iranians, who normally approached the Shah in that fashion, it was no matter; for the Greeks it was at very least in poor taste in that it required them to act out the charade of Alexander's divinity. The Ionian cities had proclaimed that divinity when Alexander liberated them, just as the mainland Greeks would in B.C. 324. That, however, was a question of legislative enactment; here in the camp at Bactra, with its tension between Iranian and Hellenized Macedonian, the act of obeisance that was demanded was personal and not legislative. Political deification signified one thing at Athens and ritual prostration quite another in Bactria.

The act of *proskynesis*, later a feature of Roman Imperial ceremonial, was particularly opposed by the official historian and unofficial philosopher in Alexander's train, Aristotle's nephew Callisthenes. His account of the expedition up to this point had been uniformly flattering to its captain, but he somewhat unaccountably opposed the practice of prostration. It is perhaps worth noting that there were other philosophers with Alexander, and at least one of them, Anaxarchus of Abdera, who had begun the trip as a somewhat mordant skeptic, ended as the most convinced and urgent absolutist of them all. It was he, for example, who suggested that Alexander was superior to Heracles at the banquet that cost Cleitus his life. There was doubtless jealousy between the two scholars, and Callisthenes was not remarkable for his tact: Alexander's reputation, he claimed, would eventually depend more on his report than on the king's own deeds. The *proskynesis* issue, then, may have served as a trial of strength between the two court philosophers.

Callisthenes won on this occasion; Alexander backed off from his demands for prostration from the Greeks at his court. But shortly thereafter Callisthenes was compromised. One of the corps of pages who waited upon Alexander impetuously bungled a piece of protocol on a hunt and Alexander had him publicly flogged. The boy was stung by the humiliation and with some other malcontents hatched out a plot against Alexander's life. The king learned of it, arrested and tortured the conspirators, who then said it was all Callisthenes' doing. It was known that Callisthenes was tutoring the page in questions of philosophy and that seemed to suggest complicity. Callisthenes was tortured and hanged. But it was by no means the end of the business. The partisans of the dead Callisthenes had their revenge on the dead Alexander.

All of this occurred in the eastern satrapies during the years B.C. 329–327. If the disturbances had any effect on Alexander, it cannot be detected at this point. He had been invited by the king of Khwarazm to explore the northern reaches of the Black Sea, but in the summer of B.C. 327 Alexander turned instead to India. He had first to recross the Hindu Kush, though this time by a higher but shorter pass, then, once having regained the Kabul valley and paused a season to reestablish his rule there, he divided his army into two columns which went separate ways through the hill country and, after some hard fighting, eventually joined at the Indus River in the spring of B.C. 326. Alexander's base for the Indus country was at Taxila, a considerable city, whose king had already allied himself with the Macedonians. His motive was not too difficult to fathom. Taxila was at war with a formidable enemy, a towering Indian prince whom the Greeks knew as Porus. Porus' territories ran east from the Hydaspes (Jhelum) River, and in the summer of B.C. 326 he held the east bank in strength. By a combination of feints and assaults Alexander forced the river, brought Porus to terms—characteristically he left him ruler of the area—and kept marching and fighting toward the east.

There may have been some plan in this or, rather, a geographical assumption that in a due-easterly course India would end on the shores of Ocean, the semimythical body of water that circled the known world, whence the army could be put on ships and transported to Egypt. The troops doubtless had the same general picture as their navigators, but it was colored by other, more human considerations. They were weary of fighting, and against opposition that appeared to be getting fiercer as they proceeded. The army demanded to go home. Alexander was forced, at last, to yield.

The return journey that began in the winter of B.C. 326 was a complicated and difficult business. The troops descended the Indus, some by ship and some on foot, accompanied by a second army of dignitaries, prisoners and camp followers. There was hard fighting on the way, and in some of the engagements here one can detect a note of almost sadistic fierceness on the part of Alexander, a more than normal recklessness that eventually cost him his life. He was almost fatally wounded in his rash attempt against an Indian town of no great consequence. He partially recovered from the wound, enough to continue traveling, but Susa and Babylon were still a year away across an almost total desert. From Patala in the Indus delta the general Craterus was sent across the mountains to Kandahar with the heavy siege equipment and the women. Nearchus took the fleet and was instructed to coast the Indian Ocean and Persian Gulf to its head. Alexander would march overland with the army through Gedrosia.

Behind them the Macedonians left the Punjab command and the Indian satrapies with some flesh but with very little bone, and they did not long survive Alexander's departure. Sometime in the next decade all of northern and western India was united in its first great empire under the Mauryan Chandragupta, who, if he had not met Alexander, had certainly heard of him. Alexander may well have created his Indian successor either by destroying the network of petty princes who had ruled the region heretofore, or by kindling the nationalistic resistance of the priestly cult of the Brahmans.[15] More importantly from the point of view of Hellenism, Alexander's conquests in India, as ephemeral as they were, let loose in the Greek world a flood of information about India and the Indians that not only exercised its fascination on generations of readers but put down as well the foundations of

15. See Chapter II, p. 81.

close commercial ties between the two cultures. Both the Ptolemies and the Romans reaped handsomely of Alexander's sowing.

The return across Gedrosia was a nightmare of heat, thirst and hunger. Somehow all of them made it. Alexander, Craterus and Nearchus rendezvoused in southern Carmania as planned, and the worst was over. By the spring of B.C. 324 their combined forces were back in Susa. More than one man was surprised by what must have seemed like a return from the dead, and Alexander's first acts were to reestablish his sovereignty among his governors, some of whom were already busy recruiting private armies against the day of his end. The guilty were peremptorily punished, all except his longtime friend and financial administrator Harpalus, who took all of what he had not already embezzled from the treasury and sought refuge in Greece. All was not well in Greece. Antipater and the Queen Mother Olympias were at odds. Nor did Alexander much care for the unfortunate Antipater's habit—actually it was Philip's habit—of governing the League cities by supporting reactionary governments within them. Antipater would have to be replaced. Meanwhile, Alexander sent memoranda to the Greek cities asking that they restore their political exiles and officially acknowledge his own divinity. There was some grumbling about the exiles, but the *poleis* complied, as they knew they must.

Focusing on the problems of Greece must have been difficult for a man with more grandiose schemes in his head. The old project of a Hellenic-Iranian synthesis was not forgotten. The officers were encouraged and even bribed to take native wives and, to set a further example—he was already married to Roxane—Alexander took as his wife a daughter of Darius, a move which had the additional felicitous effect of underlining his legitimacy as lord of Asia. The mass marriages went off well enough, but another order touched a far more sensitive spot. Alexander moved to demobilize ten thousand veterans, the core of his army, back to Greece under the command of Craterus, and to replace them with Iranians in Macedonian gear and under Macedonian regimental standards. The reaction was outrage, but Alexander remained firm. When new troops finally did arrive from the west he designed a new phalanx with Macedonian longpike men in the front files and behind them the more mobile Iranian files with swords and javelins. Such a hybrid had never been seen before, but it did not disappear from history; the legionary formations of the Roman Republic closely resembled Alexander's creation.

Plans began to go forward for the next venture, or rather the whole complex of ideas which centered on Babylon as the capital of a new commercial empire that was clearly designed to compete with, if not replace, the older centers in the eastern Aegean. Great new docks were to be built at Babylon, and the Euphrates was to be cleared and dredged down to its mouth. The eastern shore of the Persian Gulf would have to be colonized and, more immediately, Arabia would have to be circumnavigated and explored. It was, somewhat oddly, a not too distant vision based on peace, not war. None of it, however, was to be. Alexander died at Babylon in the grip of some sudden and mysterious disease in June of B.C. 323, after twelve years of rule and a mere thirty-two years of life.

The New World

The son had overshadowed his father, but almost everyone who has looked at the two men has understood that the astonishing feats of Alexander are inexplicable without the techniques that Philip devised, perfected and placed in the hands of his son. At sixteen Alexander was his father's viceroy in Macedon, and at eighteen he commanded the left wing opposite the elite Theban Sacred Band at Chaeronea. He was groomed for kingship, and when the moment came, unexpectedly, in the wake of an assassination, he put firm hands upon his birthright. More at home in his Hellenism than Philip, Alexander ruled with equal ease in feudal Macedonia with its tribal and personal loyalties and among the more sophisticated republican Greeks who vacillated between the niceties of constitutional rule and the necessities of *Realpolitik*.

Philip was more suited but less likely to have achieved what Alexander did. Though it was his son who crossed into Asia and liberated the Anatolian Greeks, and who with his loyal, tightly knit and highly trained army brought the empire of the Achaemenian Shahs to an end, it is likely that Philip could have, and would have, done the same. There was, however, a point where one suspects Philip would have turned back, not in retreat but to the work of consolidation, and that that point would have been far short of the Indus—after Gaugamela, perhaps, or Ecbatana.

Alexander came to Anatolia as the liberator of the *poleis*, stayed to become the pursuer of the fugitive Darius Codomannus and then, at the moment of triumph, ran right past his dead prey, attracted to some new goal only imperfectly understood by the men who accompanied him. After Hecatompylos, Alexander was almost transfigured, ridden by strange complexes of Heracles and Dionysus. We know what he did, and in considerable and accurate detail; why he did it is not always clear from a reading of the historians, almost as romance-prone as their subject.

Alexander was well supplied with historians. His secretary Eumenes of Cardia, the future satrap of Cappadocia,[16] was charged with recording the events of the expedition in the official journal (*ephemerides*), which was later published, while others kept geographical records and even collected zoological and botanical data, all quite in the spirit of a student of Aristotle. Some of this essentially factual material filtered down into the later biographical tradition—into Plutarch's *Life of Alexander*, for example, and Arrian's *Anabasis of Alexander*—and other bits were incorporated into the learned literature of the geographers, natural historians, and mongers of the exotic.

Of more interest to Plutarch and Arrian than these quasi-official records were the works of the men whose contact with Alexander turned them to history and memoir. At least three members of the expedition, Aristobulus, Ptolemy and Callisthenes, produced their own recollections of the campaign. The first two were soldiers or technicians—Aristobulus, like Eumenes, a Greek; and Ptolemy, the future king of Egypt, a Macedonian—and their histories were, as far as can be seen, personal statements issued after Alexander's death and valuable as eyewitness accounts of what went on. The third observer, Callisthenes of Olynthus, was Aristotle's nephew and a trained historian and philosopher, a dangerously tendentious combination among the next generation of Aristotelians. His report covered only the first four years of the expedition and was grossly flattering in

---

16. An early associate of Eumenes was another historian, his townsman Hieronymus, who later served as the court historian of Antigonus Gonatas. (See Chapter II, p. 90.)

tone.[17] Callisthenes had occasion, as has been seen, to change his mind about Alexander.

The execution of Callisthenes marked a turning point in the historical tradition about Alexander. Up to that point the reports on Alexander, mostly from the king's own propaganda establishment, were highly favorable, but by putting Callisthenes to death Alexander earned the hostility of the Aristotelian school of historians. There was no one in either camp, the supporters or the detractors of Alexander, to deny the reality of the Macedonian's success. The debate was conducted in somewhat more philosophical terms, whether the achievements of Alexander were the result of luck (*tyche*) or were the product of his own virtue (*arete*), with the Aristotelians strenuously arguing for the first. The topic became a favorite assignment for declamation in the rhetorical schools, and an early exercise of Plutarch on the subject has been preserved, *On the Luck of Alexander*.

Plutarch went on to give Alexander a somewhat more formal biographical treatment in his *Life*, but the noise of the debate can still be heard there. Plutarch had a good range of sources available on Alexander, including the Peripatetic moralists who gave the work its color,[18] but he stood nonetheless with the defenders of Alexander's virtues, qualities which he could do no other but explain in terms of the conventional school morality of his own day.

The categories of historical and philosophical analysis were clearly not capacious enough to catch and hold this extraordinary man. The sheer extent of what Alexander did, miles traveled, peoples liberated or subjugated, cities founded and plans hatched, is staggering enough; the *quality* of his feats almost defies understanding. The defeat of Darius, for instance, at Issus or Gaugamela is comprehensible: a resourceful commander with a disciplined professional army meets and overcomes a larger but less well organized force under the leadership of a fearful man. The result is satisfactory, because it is almost completely predictable in terms of what was previously known about the combatants.

---

17. During the Roman Empire a romantic and legendary account of Alexander was put together from various sources, chiefly imaginative, and falsely ascribed to Callisthenes. This so-called *Alexander Romance* was diffused in a great number of vernacular translations all over Europe and the Near East during the Middle Ages.

18. See Chapter II, pp. 113–14.

But what is to explain Alexander's pursuit of a beaten and almost completely deserted Darius into eastern Iran? Or the extreme personal risks he took during the descent of the Indus on his way home, when he leaped down alone *inside* the walls of a beleaguered city? It was a foolhardy gesture, but totally of a piece with everything else he ever did.

Philip could have been Greece's Napoleon, a bold and resourceful commander of totally loyal troops, a diplomatic and military genius prepared to take calculated risks. Calculation was not in Alexander's nature, nor was he, perhaps, even a soldier. His energy, self-discipline, physical prowess and personal asceticism were not carefully considered habits harnessed in the service of some higher end; as in the case of a superb natural athlete, they were his own traits, which he displayed for as long as they pleased him but which could be replaced, on the instant, by their opposites. Energy yielded to lassitude, and self-restraint gave way to self-indulgence, not because he was moody but simply because it suited him. Challenge, and perhaps challenge alone, excited him. He lived by an almost perfect political and military instinct, which never betrayed him, because it was an instinct toward action and not fantasy; Alexander had plans but not dreams.

Hellenism was an important part of Alexander's plans for Asia. Neither Hellenes nor Hellenism were new in that part of the world. The Greeks were early and indefatigable colonizers, and not even in the Bronze Age were they confined to the peninsula that had become their homeland. War, trade and sheer adventure carried them all over the Mediterranean, east and west, and from the eighth century onward there were well-established Greek settlements lining both shores of the Black Sea and along the western coast of Anatolia. Elsewhere in the East, in Phoenicia and Egypt, there were more modest trading posts.

The Greeks traveled and traded by sea, but they must have pushed inland even at this early date, not to settle, but to sell and to see. Wherever they did go to stay the Hellenes brought their institutions, particularly the *polis* complex, and it was through these that their manner of life spread into the hinterland. The Hellenes enjoyed a more refined style of life than any but their most royal neighbors. Those neighbors, whom the Greeks somewhat contemptuously lumped together as "barbarians" (*barbaroi*), found the style endlessly attractive and took to using Greek artifacts and aping Hellenic manners.

The process of Hellenization, the assimilation of Greek culture on whatever level, began early in the Mediterranean as a natural and unpremeditated admiration, unsponsored and unencouraged. The Hellenes themselves found it amusing rather than flattering. In their eyes, to be a Greek was a tribal act, and to be a Hellene was a political one. To don a chiton or even to learn to speak Greek was not enough; one had to live the life of a *polites*, a citizen of the *polis* to vote, hold public office, attend the *polis* festivals and worship the *polis* gods.

There were those who tried. Foreign immigrants came into the classical *poleis* to live and work there. They remained, however, outside the residual tribalism that lay at the bottom of many of the city institutions. The foreigner had no affiliations and so no real entry into the *polis;* he was well treated but was kept at political arm's length as a "resident alien." Elsewhere he had to be content with lavish but empty imitations. Hellas had her royal admirers who could affect the Hellenic style in their own capitals, an expensive affectation, doubtless, but one which gave a certain panache to princes on the fringe of the Greek world.

Croesus in Lydia and Mausolus in Caria were just such image builders, perhaps, but elsewhere the roots went somewhat deeper. Both the Etruscans in Italy and the northern Macedonian neighbors of the Greeks were drawn more closely into the orbit of cultural Hellenism. The conversion of the Etruscans went generally unremarked in mainland Greece, but Macedon breathed hard upon the *poleis* from the middle of the fourth century, and the kings there did not hesitate to use their assiduously but lately acquired Hellenism as a lever for their political ambitions.

No Greek, even in the middle of the fourth century, envisioned cultural Hellenism as either a weapon or a religion to be used on the *barbaroi*. For ethnic Hellenism they did, however, have some political feeling, and Isocrates among others had tried to construct something on that tribalism. Without much success. Tribalism, a Hellenism of the blood, eventually died in the Hellenistic age, but only because there was not enough blood to sustain it. Alexander's own quarrel with the Achaemenians was a reflex of the old tribal solidarity which he and his father, though Macedonians, felt secure enough to use against the Shah. Alexander on campaign deliberately summoned images of the Greeks at Troy once again, of Thermopylae and the burning of the acropolis avenged; it was Darius I and not Darius III who was the prey.

Having once invoked a national vendetta in Anatolia, Alexander dropped it in Iran. Whatever was behind his later plans for a mixed Greco-Iranian army and the mass weddings between Macedonian officers and Iranian brides, it was neither Macedonian nor Greek. It profoundly violated the Macedonian notion of a national army, and it ran counter to almost everything Alexander had been taught by Aristotle. In his *Politics*, Aristotle was explicit on the difference between the Greeks and the *barbaroi:* the latter were naturally inferior, and a war conducted against them was a just war. Alexander never wasted a great deal of time justifying his wars; he fought whoever opposed him with stunning and sudden vigor and then accepted surrender without vengeance. He must, however, have changed his mind about the *barbaroi.*

Some have ascribed the change to idealism, a pre-Stoic presentiment about the brotherhood of men, which led him to an attempt at fusing the races. It seems unlikely. Alexander's plans for fusion did not extend much beyond the Iranians; there were no places reserved for the Egyptians, Arabs, Phrygians or Jews in his alleged republic of the races. The change seems to have had other motives, some lying close to the surface, others subject only to surmise.

Alexander was a remarkable blend of the romantic and the pragmatist. He could weep for Achilles one moment and in the next turn into the general and master tactician. In his latter roles he faced and decisively defeated the Achaemenian armies, but in the doing he too fell under the spell of the grandeur of Achaemenian history. The Shah represented the most potent and majestic state that the Greeks had known during the last two centuries of their history, and their military and political disdain of the Achaemenians was tempered by the kind of subtle awe that is reflected in Aeschylus' *Persians,* in the pages of Herodotus, and in Xenophon's *Education of Cyrus.* Alexander was susceptible to such sentiments, and at some point he was gripped by the idea that he was not merely the conqueror of the Shah, but his successor as well.

Alexander's marshals, later turned kings in those same lands of Asia, took up the same notion easily enough, but it was Alexander who had to make the initial adjustment. Ptolemy could later play a Hellenic Pharaoh, because Alexander had first chosen to play a Hellenic Shah. A republican Greek might have had trouble with the role, but it must have been considerably easier for the feudal lord of Macedon.

Alexander's choice of the role in which he would subsequently rule what he had won carried certain implications. If he did not intend to return to Macedon, as he certainly did not, then he must rule in the East. The Shahs had governed their huge empire from their home province of Persis. Alexander chose to rule the same empire, extended by the inclusion of Greece, but his practical eye told him that Babylon was a better seat of power than Susa or Persepolis.

The last months of Alexander's life were filled with the bustle of commercial plans; docks, dredging and exploration filled his mind. He had seen the East and understood some of its commercial possibilities, possibilities which the Shahs, who were anchored by their ancestral ties to upland Fars and by their traditions to the land, had only very partially exploited. Alexander passed over the Achaemenian homeland for the more commercially promising Babylon, a choice which his successors ratified by building the three capital cities of Seleucia on the Tigris, Ctesiphon and Baghdad in its near vicinity.

The commercial opportunity was all gain; there were, however, disadvantages to an eastern empire. Alexander had to rule with Greeks and Macedonians. They were the best soldiers in the world, and not even a Shah Alexander could afford to send them home and rely on the imperial Achaemenian army, a body whose elite corps were even then Greek. He needed his Macedonians to garrison the land and Greeks to run it,[19] and he apparently judged that there were not enough of either of them to do the job, nor could he count on there being enough in the future.

On both counts he was wrong in the short run and correct in the long run, as the history of his successors was to show. They could and did control the Near East by resorting not to intermarriage, but to drafts from home. Colonization served the needs of all of them, but eventually colonization failed and the Greeks

---

19. The earlier experiment of appointing or reconfirming Iranian satraps had already collapsed. Of the eighteen original appointments only three were still in office by the time of Alexander's death.

lost the lands east of the Euphrates because they did not have, as Alexander had foreseen, the Greek manpower to hold them. The garrisons dwindled and were finally swept away by nomads or native dynasts.

Alexander intended to solve the problem differently. He understood that the Greeks would have to settle in the East if he were to continue in his extraordinary role as Hellenic Shah. He encouraged the settlement of his soldiers by promoting their marriage to Iranian women and the establishment of ties in Iran. Further, he chose to solve his manpower problem not by fusing the races, as it is sometimes seen, but by deliberately converting Iranians into Greeks. His new Iranian cadets were to have instruction in Greek literature and learn to fight in the Macedonian phalanx formation. As Shah he might assume the Iranian style, but he was not so mad as to want to convert his valuable Macedonians and Greeks into Iranians.

Alexander thus encouraged Hellenization, though on what must have been a modest scale and for severely pragmatic reasons. He had had the insight that reading Homer produced good soldiers; that it might also produce citizens seems not to have entered his head. Citizens of what? A *polites* was a citizen of a *polis* and of nothing else; kingdoms and empires possessed only subjects, not citizens. Whatever deliberate Hellenization occurred, it was intended that it occur in the army and not in *poleis*.

There were *poleis*, of course. Tradition credited Alexander with being a prodigious builder of cities. He certainly did found some, including the most famous of them all, the Egyptian Alexandria, but here tradition may be suspected of projecting some of the achievements of later dynasts back onto Alexander. It is sure that Alexander set the pattern of city building that was to characterize the Near East for the next five centuries, and he did so by planting his garrisons in the kind of protective environment in which they would survive, a Greek environment. But they were, for all that, garrisons.

Alexander passed through the East on the run leaving military settlements in his wake. The foundation of a *polis*, as the Greeks understood the term, was a far more complex process than building a fort and calling it Alexandria. It meant the creation of political institutions and the physical setting in which they could function, a citizen roll, a city council, market inspectors, a gymnasium, temples, courts and a constitution. Alexander's pace generally outstripped the possibility of such foundations, and once clear of Syria, the bulk of his prospective citizens was composed of Macedonian soldiers with doubtful credentials as *politeis.*

His successors had both the leisure and the manpower to build something more substantial. The Ptolemies in Phoenicia and the Transjordan, and the Seleucids in Syria and Mesopotamia founded genuine *poleis,* where the true Hellenization of the East occurred. They had not only soldiers but artisans, merchants, architects and teachers to flesh out a *polis,* and the Seleucids in particular embarked on an ambitious project of urban Hellenization in the Near East, the same policy inherited and imitated by the Romans after them.

None of this would have been possible without Alexander. It was he who opened the possibility of a Hellenized Achaemenian Empire. It had a very brief political life. By the time of Ipsus in B.C. 301 it must have been clear to all the interested parties that there was to be not one empire but many kingdoms. With hindsight the death of the Achaemenian idea—perhaps it really died with Alexander himself—does not appear very important. What had far greater consequence was a political reality of an even briefer duration. For something less than five years Alexander effectively ruled what none had ruled before him, a domain that included *both* Greece and the Achaemenian Empire. As an idea, that lasted far longer and penetrated more deeply into the marrow of the next age than whatever Iranian aspirations Alexander may have had in putting on the Achaemenian tiara.

The conquests of Alexander shattered the homogeneity of Greek political life that had previously been pried open only by the Hellenized Macedonians. Greek race and Greek rule were no longer coextensive. Before Alexander, Hellenic tribalism, politics and culture were inseparable in the eyes of the Greeks. With the events of B.C. 334, they had necessarily to separate. New Macedonian kings, once Alexander's marshals but now rulers of the *barbaroi,* were bound to Hellenism by political necessity. For many decades Macedon continued to be their political home and its throne the object of their political ambitions. Their most important constituents, even in those barbarian climes, continued to be the Hellenes, and the Hellenistic kings were forced to play out a complex role compounded of Macedonian political piety, a well-displayed cultural Hellenism, and whatever minor crotchets the local tradition demanded. Alexander had dashed into the part headlong and played it with gusto and a kind of eccentric brilliance; within a generation, however, it demanded a far more nuanced performance.

In the post-Alexander age Hellenes and the *barbaroi* were locked in a political embrace that neither of them had willed. After Alexander's death no one of his generals was willing to surrender the "spear-won land," nor were any of the *barbaroi* strong enough to drive the Hellenes out. They lived, if not together, then in the same land, the Hellenes in their scattered *poleis*, and the natives at their fringes or in the countryside. The protective *polis* prevented the Hellenes from being absorbed into the body of the natives, but the experience of isolation, or at least diffusion, created in the conquerors a new sense of solidarity.

The Hellenes had known it before, but their Panhellenic enthusiasms, celebrated periodically at the games in honor of Olympian Zeus, were diluted by the essential political parochialism of the pre-Alexander *polis*. Now it was political parochialism that was diluted within the great new kingdoms born from Alexander's own and was replaced by a renewed sense of cultural solidarity. Hellenism, a community of values, aspirations and style, bound together the dispersed Greeks in a novel type of polity without politics.

The Greek dispersal of the years after B.C. 334 created the *oikoumene*, the "known inhabited world," not in the literal sense, to be sure, but as a kind of spiritual empire coterminous with Hellenism. The *oikoumene* was as far as the mind could reach, a Greek mind thinking Greek thoughts, elastic enough to recognize, salute and co-opt what lay outside its pale. It differed from the then forming Jewish Diaspora, which saw itself as a community in the form of a network within a larger alien body. The Hellenic *oikoumene* was at once more grandiose and more self-assured. It was the domain of a Hellenism diffused over an area from Italy to India, possessed of many states but of a single set of cultural ideals and a single language innocent of dialectical variations. In fact the *oikoumene* too was a network, but in the eyes of the Hellenes who inhabited it, the *oikoumene* appeared to be a blanket.

The *oikoumene* was the creation of Alexander, not so much by intent as by what he did. He freed Hellenism from its political limitations and so released into the new areas of his conquest an almost tangible wave of energy. Émigrés streamed forth from the old Greek centers to take up their residence in the new lands, not merely, as before, in enclaves along the littoral, but deep inland. They did not come as pioneers in the wilderness, to be sure; the overseas Greeks settled where it was prosperous to settle, at the crossroads of what were now international highways.

In the generation before Alexander, Greece's chief export to the Aegean was the restless mercenary; after him a cross section of society left the unpromising mainland for whatever lay abroad. The emigration cured, for the time at least, some of the economic and demographic woes that burdened Greece in the fourth century. Mainland population figures drifted downward, and as the manpower went off, money came in. New markets opened for Greek goods and the hoarded treasures of the East were at least partially unlocked.

Greece abused the promise of prosperity offered by the new *oikoumene*. A recovery in the third century was followed by a decline in the second. The mainland *poleis* were the least successful in their adjustment to the new political order of things and fell to almost uninterrupted fighting. The new eastern centers, at first markets for mainland manufactures, gradually became competitors. In the end Rhodes and Alexandria replaced Athens and Corinth as the commercial leaders in the *oikoumene*.

The vitality released by Alexander was not merely economic. A standardized currency and a common language created the international trade of the Hellenistic world. Kings and cities grew rich on that trade, and their peculiarly Hellenic civic consciousness induced them to turn the profits into *polis* institutions, to elaborate building programs and patronage of the arts, all on a scale never seen before. The public glories of fifth-century Athens could be rivaled in the new *oikoumene* by every other *polis* in Anatolia, Syria and Mesopotamia. Oasis cities knew a grandeur that Thebes never had known and never would know.

Thebes had been—and Athens, Corinth, and Sparta as well—a city of mixed social and economic structure but of a homogeneous culture. The culture of the new *poleis* was also unmistakably Hellenic, but with subtle undertones of the native tradition. The undertones are not always easy to catch in the literary sources; the scholars and poets of the new age, whether they came from Athens, Alexandria, Pergamum, Apamea or Gerasa, were as relentlessly Greek as their predecessors, and it is not localism but a new ecumenicism of language and vision that betrays them as citizens of a world different from the fifth-century one. It is in the decorative arts that the native tradition appears. In all the Mediterranean cultures the fine arts were enlisted in the public service of politics and religion, and these latter were, from Alexander onward, faced in two directions.

Ptolemy in Egypt was constrained to be both Hellenic king and Egyptian Pharaoh, and the religious product of this political dualism was the cult of Serapis, Greek in its language and art, Egyptian in its myth and its liturgy. The Seleucids built Hellenic temples to house the Syrian Atargatis and the Babylonian Marduk. In India the Euthydemids presented their proud numismatic portraits in the pure Greek style and read out the royal titulature on the reverse side of the coin in Indian Prakrit. The native tradition accepted the embrace from the other direction. Baal Shamin became Zeus; and Dushara Dionysus. Ashoka proclaimed his Buddhist piety in Greek. The Arab *shaykh* of Petra, the Parthian Shah of Iran, and the Jewish High Priest in Jerusalem, all officially and publicly proclaimed themselves "Philhellenes."

The *oikoumene* created by Alexander carried within itself the twin implications of universalism and localism. In the first generations of its existence it was the intellectual community, and particularly the Stoics, who exploited the ecumenical possibilities suggested by the common culture and common language of the *oikoumene*, while the kings, disappointed in their hopes of ruling a single empire in Alexander's place, were constrained to go the way of particularism. The localism never died. The Jews fought off the main thrust of Hellenism, and in the fourth and fifth centuries of the Christian era the Syrians produced a marvelous and vital subculture out of their still-living native tradition. Hellenism embraced, but it did not suffocate.

In the end, however, it was the universalism and not the particularism within the *oikoumene* that triumphed. A state, Rome, and a religion, Christianity, both originally local phenomena in the *oikoumene*, moved onto the terrain already conceptually plotted by the Stoics, and the promise of Alexander's achievement was fulfilled: one state, one culture, one God.

II

The Struggle for Power

At his premature death Alexander left neither clear-cut plans nor a designated successor. Of heirs presumptive there were many who ambitioned the role but none who could claim it. Dynastic considerations were put forward and were quickly undermined for reasons of political expediency. The only male survivor in direct connection with the royal house of Macedon was Arrhidaeus, an illegitimate and half-witted son of Philip by a Thessalian mistress. There was one additional possibility: Roxane was pregnant, and Perdiccas, who may have been Alexander's senior officer at the time of his death, suggested that the interested parties await the birth of the child; if a son, he could be proclaimed king and assigned a regent.

The Heirs of Alexander (B.C. 323–301)

This solution of the succession question, which did justice to both the dynastic principle and the political realities—the real power would remain in the hands of the generals—was unacceptable to those who, by Macedonian custom, had the right of choosing the new king. It raised once again the difficult issue of national sentiment versus Alexander's Orientalizing policy. The generals, drawn from the cavalry elite, either accepted that policy or considered it irrelevant at this point, but for the conservative and by now thoroughly unhappy foot soldiers of the phalanx the raising of the son of a barbarian woman of Bactria to the kingship of Macedon was unthinkable. The army was a national body, the nation under arms, and they asserted the privilege that was undoubtedly theirs: Arrhidaeus would be their king. Better a Macedonian half-wit than a bastardized Iranian.

Roxane did, indeed, bear a son, and for a brief time war was very close between the nationalist supporters of Arrhidaeus, now crowned Philip III, and the general staff that backed the infant Alexander IV. But war was averted and a mischievous and confusing compromise worked out. There would be two kings, Philip III and Alexander IV, and since neither was competent, they would be supervised by two of the most trusted generals, Craterus and Perdiccas, the former to oversee Philip III and with the right of veto over Perdiccas; the latter would assume executive control over what was left of the Army of Asia.[1] The plan was full of holes. It did not spell out primary responsibilities, nor did it conform to the emerging realities. Craterus, for example, was off in Greece dealing with an insurrection when the arrangements were being made, and further, he had no control over Philip III, who was in Babylon with Perdiccas. Antipater, Alexander's long-time viceroy in Greece, was not even consulted. Perdiccas had, in short, an apparently strong position almost unsupported by legitimacy. Trouble had inevitably to follow.

The first two discomforts of the new regime were in the making even before Alexander's death. The garrisons that Alexander had left behind in eastern Iran were unhappy with the prospect of indefinite service in those alien parts, and a large number of them gathered in Bactria to make their way home, by force, if necessary. The mutiny was far from being universal, however, and Perdiccas managed to stiffen his loyal governors in the east to block the path of the recalcitrants and force them back to their posts. The arms of the loyal satraps insured compliance, but by no means caused the issue to disappear.

Back in Greece something far more serious had been brewing. The example of Thebes and then of Agis III at Megalopolis had kept the Greeks under tight self-restraint in the face of Antipater's viceroyalty. But Antipater was a hard master, and the presence of Macedonian garrisons in some of the *poleis* had done nothing to lessen the tension. The uneasy calm might have held,

---

1. The Macedonian army, aptly described as a "mobile *polis*," was never completely dispersed but attached itself, in whole or in parts, to various marshals struggling for succession. It was in itself a token both of legitimacy—it could choose the king—and of political and military power.

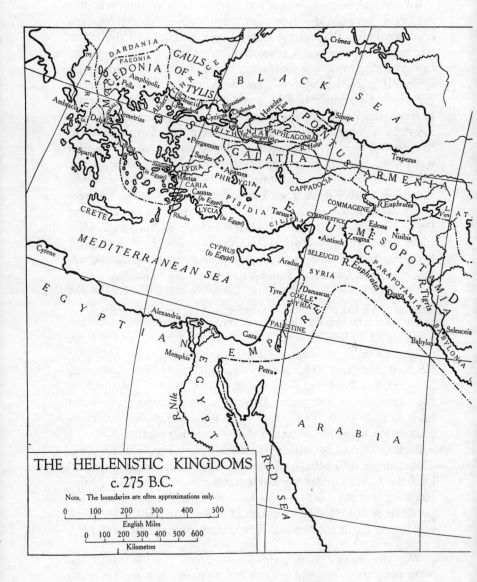

THE HELLENISTIC KINGDOMS
c. 275 B.C.

Note. The boundaries are often approximations only.

0   100   200   300   400   500
English Miles

0   100   200   300   400   500   600
Kilometres

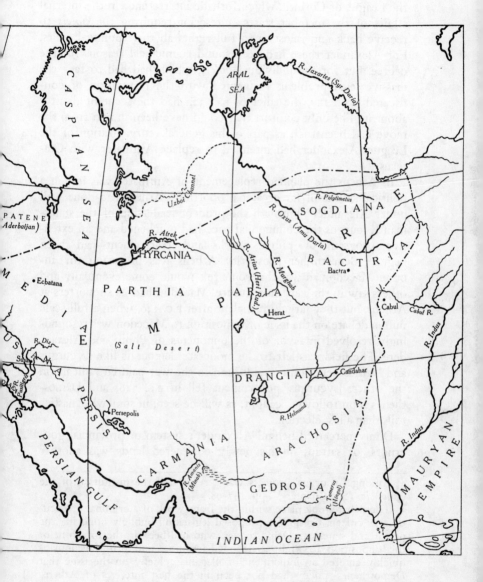

CASPIAN SEA

ARAL SEA

R. Jaxartes (Syr Daria)

Uzboi Channel

R. Polytimetus

SOGDIANA

R. Oxus (Amu Daria)

R. Atrek

HYRCANIA

R. Arius (Heri Rud.)

R. Marghab

BACTRIA

Bactra

ATPATENE
(Aderbaijan)

Ecbatana

PARTHIA

ARIA

Herat

Cabul

Cabul R.

R. Indus

MEDIA

M

(Salt Desert)

R. Diz

Susa

PER.
Pasitigris

USA

DER.

PERSIS

Persepolis

DRANGIANA

Candahar

R. Helmund

ARACHOSIA

R. Indus

MAURYAN EMPIRE

PERSIAN GULF

CARMANIA

R. Anamis
(Minab)

GEDROSIA

R. Tomerus
(Hingol)

INDIAN OCEAN

however, but for Alexander's own intervention. In B.C. 324 he had sent to the Greek states, in direct violation of the terms of the League of Corinth, which forbade interference in the internal affairs of the member states, a rescript requiring the *poleis* to receive back and reinstate to full rights all their political exiles. For Alexander there had been sound ecumenical reasons for the decree, but for the individual *poleis*, which had had to face the massive legal problems connected with the restoration of confiscated property, the edict of B.C. 324 had the scent of disaster about it. The only comfort that could have been drawn from the move had been that, as part of his general reorganization of the League, Alexander had intended to replace Antipater with Craterus.

In Athens the planned replacement of Antipater was lost in a political shuffle of far greater proportions. Athens had done well under Alexander. Through the prudent leadership of the statesman Lycurgus the commercial pace had quickened and an extensive program of public works—and rearmament—had been begun.[2] Beneath her prosperity Athens was preparing for another Macedonian war that some felt would come eventually and others saw in the very near future. Macedon had its supporters at Athens, but they largely fell silent after B.C. 330, when a full-scale public debate on the issue of opposition to Macedon was resoundingly resolved in favor of the opponents of Philip and Alexander.[3] The field was left to the moderate democrats like Lycurgus and Demosthenes on one side, and to the war-painted radicals on the other. Lycurgus' government fell in B.C. 326; and Demosthenes soon followed, caught, as will be seen, in somewhat nastier toils than a lost election.

Dimly perceived behind Alexander's system of provincial governors, or satraps, in his newly conquered lands was another

---

2. Among Lycurgus' projects was a reform of the institution of the *ephebeia*. (See Chapter V, pp. 197–98.)
3. The debate took place within the framework of a criminal prosecution. A citizen, Ctesiphon, proposed legislation publicly honoring the orator and statesman Demosthenes, who had been in the forefront of the opposition to Philip before Chaeronea. The pro-Macedonians quickly entered an indictment of illegality, chiefly on the issue that Demosthenes' policy had not been in the best interests of Athens. Demosthenes himself defended Ctesiphon against the indictment, and another eminent orator, Aeschines, defended the pro-Macedonian position. Ctesiphon was acquitted.

institution, the beginnings, perhaps, of an imperial bureaucracy, though its initial operations had to do chiefly with finances. This centralized organization Alexander had consigned to a certain Harpalus, who was directly responsible to the king. Harpalus held great power in his hands, and when Alexander disappeared over the Hindu Kush, never, as many thought, to return, that power began to be exercised more and more outrageously for the benefit of its wielder. When Alexander later reappeared in the Persian Gulf, Harpalus, who had tried Alexander's patience before, gathered up what was left of the treasury, recruited a mercenary army, and quickly made for safer ground.

That ground was Athens. The Treasurer General had been generous with Athens and so had reason to believe he would be welcome there in the spring of B.C. 324. There was some hesitation when Harpalus first arrived, but he was eventually granted political asylum. Alexander's gold soon began to flow in Athens, particularly into the radicals' pockets, since their own desire to have it out with Alexander coincided with Harpalus' own plans to save his skin when Alexander struck back, as he surely must. Demosthenes and the moderates resisted, but the ground began to slip from beneath them with Alexander's unpopular demand for the restoration of the political exiles.[4] Meanwhile, the gold of Harpalus, who had been confined to prison while the Athenians decided what to do,[5] had its effect. Perhaps the sum was thought to be larger than it actually was, but the general feeling at Athens was that it was not all in their possession and *someone* must have it. The gathering political storm centered on Demosthenes. He was tried for embezzlement, convicted and sent into exile. Whether or not he had taken anything from Harpalus is unknown.

The removal of Demosthenes, the leader of the moderate coalition, was followed suddenly by the report of Alexander's death in Babylon. The war party at Athens, now in almost complete control,[6] felt that their moment had come. Alliances were

---

4. For the Athenians that meant disgorging the entire island of Samos, which had been seized from the people living there and recolonized.
5. Harpalus shortly escaped and was subsequently murdered by one of his own supporters.
6. It was unsafe to hold any but strong anti-Macedonian views at Athens then, and as a direct result of the political climate Aristotle was forced to vacate the Lyceum and flee to Euboea, where he died the next year.

scouted wherever Antipater's garrisons left some freedom of action. Sparta as usual would make no move, but there were others willing to desert the League of Corinth for a new federation which did not include Macedonian hegemony. Troops could be gotten, and above all there was the fine Athenian navy that Lycurgus had patiently rebuilt over the years.

The forces marshaled against the new Hellenic League were too strong, however. Antipater had his own troops, supplemented by those of the satrap of Hellespontine Phrygia. Craterus, who had been dispatched by Alexander with demobilized veterans to replace Antipater, soon joined forces; and finally there was Alexander's fleet under Cleitus. The odds proved too great, and after a series of naval disasters Athens was isolated from her allies and forced to sue for peace within a year. The terms were pure Antipater: the restoration of the oligarchs to power, limitation of the franchise, and a Macedonian garrison in the port of Athens. Demosthenes, who, in a burst of national good feeling, had been recalled from exile early in the war, in B.C. 323, was once again forced to depart, this time pursued by Antipater's agents, who left him no escape but suicide.

The war, in which Perdiccas had little part, cast doubts on some of the arrangements made in Babylon. During the hostilities Craterus, though a regent, fought under the command of Antipater, something which Craterus apparently found perfectly natural, but which also tended to move him somewhat aside and bring Antipater and Perdiccas into a direct line of collision. That course could, perhaps, have been avoided by the fairly simple expedient of a political marriage between Perdiccas and Antipater's daughter, and plans for such a union were going forward when a new card was played. Antipater had had his troubles with the strong-willed Queen Mother Olympias almost from the moment Alexander departed from Macedon. Now in a final effort to undercut Antipater, Olympias offered Perdiccas an even more intriguing alliance, a marriage with her daughter and Alexander's full sister, Cleopatra. Perdiccas found the offer most attractive. Antipater was naturally enraged, and his new dark view of Perdiccas was fed by another of the satraps, Antigonus, "the One-Eyed," who had had his own falling-out with Perdiccas and had taken refuge in Macedon at the side of Antipater. The three generals, Antipater, Craterus and Antigonus, managed to convince themselves that Perdiccas' next move must obviously be the occupation of Macedon itself and they began to prepare for war. Perdiccas had more immediate problems, however. At Alexander's death the Macedonian general staff had almost immediately begun parceling out among themselves the provinces of their dead commander's empire. While Perdiccas, Craterus and Antipater debated the question of the regency, Leonnatus in Hellespontine Phrygia, Antigonus in Central Phrygia, Lysimachus in Thrace, Eumenes in Cappadocia, and Ptolemy in Egypt each took possession of his satrapy. The first two could not sustain themselves: Leonnatus died in the war against the Hellenic League, and Antigonus came under fire from Perdiccas; Eumenes and Lysimachus had trouble within their own satrapies. But in Egypt Ptolemy quietly and efficiently slipped into place. He may have begun with a tactical error, the annexation of the neighboring Greek *polis* of Cyrene in Libya, but his position was so secure that he followed this with something considerably more daring. It had been arranged in Babylon that Alexander should be buried in Macedon. A magnificent funeral cortege set out from Babylon in B.C. 322, but it was diverted by Ptolemy at Damascus and led into Egypt. The corpse of Alexander was interred in the Egyptian religious capital of Memphis while something more lavish was being prepared at Alexandria.

Ptolemy alleged that Alexander had wished to be buried at Siwa. That is possible, though at this point highly irrelevant. What was occurring was a struggle over the charismatic bones of the leader as a token of legitimacy. Perdiccas had them and lost them to another. Over the winter of B.C. 322 he had to make his decision, to move against Antipater in Macedon or Ptolemy in Egypt. By the campaigning season of B.C. 321 it was clear that Ptolemy was the target of the offensive thrust; Eumenes was persuaded by the promise of extended domains to engage Antipater in a holding action in Anatolia. Antipater quickly realized what was happening. He dispatched Antigonus with a fleet to Egypt. The main body of the Macedonian field army would be led across the Hellespont—hopefully with Lysimachus' cooperation—and then divided. Craterus would lead one army group to confront Eumenes in Cappadocia, while Antipater himself hastened with the main body to Egypt to help Ptolemy against Perdiccas.

The plan misfired in various directions. In Cappadocia Eumenes roughly handled the forces of Craterus, who lost his own life in the battle, but Perdiccas quickly found himself in serious trouble attempting to cross the Nile. A number of his troops were needlessly lost and the rest mutinied. Perdiccas' fellow officers, among them Seleucus, one of Alexander's younger officers now moving into prominence, and Peithon, chief of the far-eastern satraps, saw the fortunes of empire shifting once again and assassinated the regent. Antipater had won out over Perdiccas but lost his chance to share in Ptolemy's victory and so curb the Egyptian satrap. No matter now. Antipater was proclaimed sole regent of the two innocuous kings and generously rewarded his co-conspirators. Ptolemy was allowed to keep Cyrene in defiance of convention. Seleucus was installed in Babylon as satrap, and Peithon was given a wider jurisdiction in eastern Iran. Antigonus was made Commander in Chief of the Army of Asia with a mandate to hunt down Eumenes. Antigonus' son Demetrius, though still only a boy of fifteen, got a bride out of the business, another daughter of Antipater, Craterus' recent widow. Finally, and as a pointed restraint on the highly favored Antigonus, Antipater appointed his own son Cassander as Antigonus' second in command. His arrangements completed, Antipater gathered up his token kings, Philip III and Alexander IV, and returned to Macedon.

Antigonus set about faithfully executing his commission; he had run most of Perdiccas' supporters in Cappadocia to ground and had Eumenes bottled up in Cilicia, when Antipater succumbed to old age in B.C. 319. The old issues of succession were suddenly reopened. Antipater had providently designated another of Alexander's officers, Polyperchon, to succeed him as guardian of the kings. The troops in Macedon agreed, but it was clear to most of the other interested observers that the question of legitimacy was rapidly becoming a mask for a power struggle, to get and to hold, as Ptolemy had done with Cyrene. Here too Ptolemy showed the way by immediately attacking and annexing the satrapy of Syria-Phoenicia, acting not as the member of a large holding company directed in the name of the kings by a regent, but as the king of a sovereign state. Technically, Ptolemy and all the other satraps owed their position to the regents, Perdiccas, Antipater and Polyperchon, but all now knew that this was a pious fiction engineered to keep Alexander's empire in one piece.

Antigonus grasped the point as firmly as Ptolemy. He let Eumenes off and concentrated instead on dislodging the governors of Lydia and Phrygia and on constructing a fleet. Polyperchon, whose strongest claim to power was his legitimacy, had little room for maneuver. Antipater had planned that his son Cassander would serve as Polyperchon's second in command, with the right, one supposes, of eventual succession. But Cassander, despite the fact that of all the men in question he alone did not bear the golden talisman of service with Alexander, had not the patience to wait upon that prospect and cast in his lot with Antigonus. Polyperchon did manage to attach one man to his cause, Eumenes, who, with first-class Macedonian troops and part of Alexander's original treasury—the gold had earlier been moved from Susa to Cilicia to be more accessible to Europe—was an ally of some substance, if he could manage to stay in communication with Polyperchon.

Immediately the strategic moves began, Antigonus to destroy Polyperchon's fleet, and Eumenes to raise his own fleet in Phoenicia. Antigonus achieved his objective first. Alexander's Aegean fleet, which was under the command of Cleitus and loyal to Polyperchon, was caught unawares and destroyed in the Hellespont. Antigonus was then free to hasten south in pursuit of Eumenes. Eumenes realized that it was now pointless to attempt fitting out a fleet, and in the summer of B.C. 318 struck out instead for the east with the hopes of raising the eastern satraps, Seleucus in Babylon and Peithon in Media. They refused to be moved and summoned Antigonus to their aid. There was other support in the east, however, in the form of the satraps who were gathering their forces in a coalition against Peithon. In a few months Eumenes had a formidable army collected in Fars, made up of his own troops and those of the eastern satraps. Antigonus, now reinforced by Seleucus and Peithon, pushed on after him, nonetheless. An inconclusive engagement was fought near Isfahan in the autumn of B.C. 317. Eumenes withdrew into winter quarters, but the relentless and skilled Antigonus made a final, desperate attack, whose surprise tipped the scales in his own favor. Eumenes was captured and executed.

Polyperchon was having difficulties maintaining himself in Greece. Athens was uneasily his, but he was effectively locked out of the Peloponnesus. Once his fleet was destroyed in the Hellespont, Athens, whose lifeblood was still maritime commerce, also began to waver. Cassander came back to Greece from Antigonus in B.C. 318, and his judgment that Athens was

ripe for the plucking proved correct. The Athenians capitulated
to his terms: his garrison in the port and his man as governor.
The latter was Demetrius of Phalerum, an Athenian statesman
and scholar of the Lyceum who ruled the city in Cassander's
name for ten years. From this powerful foothold Cassander sailed
north and deposed Polyperchon from Macedon.

All was not over. In Epirus, where Polyperchon fled, were
Olympias, her daughter-in-law Roxane, and her young grandson
Alexander IV. Philip III now belonged to Cassander, and while
Olympias may have had no great commitment to Polyperchon,
she did want the throne of Alexander for her grandson. The Queen
Mother had influence in Epirus. An army was raised on her behalf, and while Cassander was off campaigning in the Peloponnesus, she invaded Macedon. No one would fight the fearsome
and revered old lady, and in the summer of B.C. 317 she was in
full control. The hapless Philip III was executed; whoever supported Cassander was shown no mercy. The spilling of Macedonian blood by Epirote troops was to no one's liking, and
Olympias' support vanished as quickly as it had sprung up. When
Cassander returned to Macedon the following year there was no
saving her. He had Olympias executed and took Alexander IV
and Roxane into close custody.

When the dust cleared the new protagonists could survey the
ground. Cassander had Greece, Macedon and the last shred of
legitimacy. Ptolemy was still carefully ensconced in Egypt and,
more recently, in the ports of Phoenicia. But Antigonus lorded it
over the rest of Asia and had, moreover, Alexander's treasury,
which in theory belonged to all of them. The theory was to
prove far different from the practice, as became clear at least to
Seleucus in Babylon when Antigonus returned there from Fars
and demanded an audit of the finances of the satrapy. Seleucus
did not stay to protest the legality of Antigonus' request, but fled
in haste to Egypt to alert Ptolemy and, through him, the others,
Cassander in Macedon and Lysimachus in Thrace, to what they
in turn might expect.

Their fear of Antigonus drew Ptolemy, Cassander and Lysimachus into coalition. They issued an obviously preposterous
proposal that would have confined Antigonus to territory in the
center of Anatolia. Antigonus' response was a double of Perdiccas' earlier strategy: to hold against Cassander and Lysimachus in
Anatolia and strike out against Ptolemy. In the spring of B.C. 315

he drove Ptolemy's troops from Syria, began to construct his own fleet, and opened a diplomatic offensive against Cassander. He cited Cassander for his crimes against Olympias, Alexander IV and Roxane, and promised complete liberty to every *polis* that would come over to him. Cassander had been hit in a vulnerable point. Like his father before him, he relied everywhere on unpopular oligarchic governments and Macedonian garrisons.

Antigonus must have judged that his propaganda was having its effect, since in B.C. 313 he left his son Demetrius to keep watch on Ptolemy from Gaza while he disembarked his troops in Greece and began taking Cassander's strongholds, even though he himself was held up by Lysimachus' stubborn defense of the Hellespont. Cassander cried for relief, which he finally received in B.C. 312. Ptolemy won a great victory over Demetrius at Gaza and, with the way open before him, sent Seleucus at the head of a flying column to seize Babylon deep at Antigonus' rear. Ptolemy himself could not hold Syria and Phoenicia for long, but the damage had been done. The disarrangement led to stalemate, then to peace. By its terms Cassander was confirmed in Macedon as regent of Alexander IV until the boy came of age in B.C. 305, Ptolemy in Egypt as before, Lysimachus in a greatly enlarged Thracian satrapy, and Antigonus in central Anatolia, Syria-Phoenicia and Mesopotamia. In theory the eastern satrapies were his as well, but he never occupied them, and Seleucus reigned guardedly but undispossessed in Babylon.

The peace of B.C. 311 has been read as an open invitation to Cassander to do away with Alexander IV like some piece of antiquated stage machinery. This is indeed what he did in the following year, and the male line of Alexander came to an end.[7] It is likely that Cassander was content with the arrangement of B.C. 311, and Antigonus too could afford to let the western Asian situation simmer, contenting himself with administering the

---

7. Save for one brief but intriguing moment of doubt. In B.C. 309 Polyperchon, who had been evading an almost uninterested Cassander, resurfaced with a newly discovered heir, a youth named Heracles, who was allegedly the son of Alexander and the Iranian princess Barsine. Polyperchon contemplated an invasion of Macedon with Heracles in his van and some financial support from Antigonus in his pocket. Cassander persuaded him, however, that he was being used by Antigonus, and Polyperchon had the suddenly useless Heracles done away with.

Greek *poleis* under his control and founding new ones. He did attempt to dislodge Seleucus from Babylon and thus open the corridors of his power toward the east. Ptolemy could not, however, allow Seleucus to fall, and his somewhat bizarre adventures in B.C. 310–308 may have had the relief of Seleucus behind them. Ptolemy took Cyprus, established naval bases in southwestern Anatolia, showed his ships in the islands, and climaxed his new Aegean imperialism by landing in Greece and convening a Congress to announce yet one more liberation of the land of the Hellenes. The result was a political fiasco, but it did serve to rouse Cassander's suspicions against his former ally. And Antigonus, perhaps as intended, turned from Seleucus in Babylon to affairs in the eastern Mediterranean.

Up to B.C. 308 these had been delegated to the care of Antigonus' brilliant and deadly son Demetrius, who snapped at Ptolemy's heels whenever and wherever possible. Now the holding stage was over, however, and Antigonus was ready to attempt what must necessarily be, for the eighty-year-old general, a final effort at empire. The blow was directed, as Cassander's had been ten years before, at Athens. In the summer of B.C. 307 Demetrius sailed into the Piraeus with a large fleet and announced that at last her days of subjugation, first to Antipater, then to Cassander and his governor, were over. It was as if the promise of the ill-fated Hellenic League of B.C. 323 had suddenly and unexpectedly been fulfilled. Cassander's governor Demetrius of Phalerum was packed off to a merciful and even illustrious exile,[8] while the new Demetrius and his absent father Antigonus were greeted like gods.[9]

Thus far Antigonus' plan was a resounding success. The loss of the prestigious Athens would cripple Cassander for a time, and meanwhile Antigonus could round fully on Ptolemy. In B.C. 306 Demetrius was sent against Ptolemy's fleet at Cyprus and won a stunning victory. Antigonus took the road to Egypt, supported, as he hoped, by the descent of Demetrius' victorious fleet on the Egyptian coast. But he had waited too long. Weather impeded the fleet, and deep in the fall of B.C. 306 Antigonus began to lose heart. Ptolemy was buying off his troops, and supplies were running low. With the example of Perdiccas vivid before him, he

---

8. Eventually to end in Egypt. See Chapter V, p. 193.
9. See Chapter XII, p. 467.

decided not to attempt a Nile crossing and withdrew instead to
Syria.

After his son's victory over Ptolemy at Cyprus, Antigonus
assumed for the first time the title of king and bestowed it on
Demetrius as well. Ptolemy too called himself king after he repulsed Antigonus from the Nile. Previously all these men, as well
as their contemporaries who had already passed from the scene,
had ruled as governors for a ghostly Alexander only partially
reincarnated in his witless half brother or infant son. Now both
these sacramental figures were gone, as was Olympias. Cassander
and Demetrius had not even fought with Alexander. Ptolemy and
Antigonus, the relics of a passing generation, must have grown
weary under the shadow of a semilegendary saint. The declara-
tions of kingship of B.C. 306–305 were a final casting-off of that
shroud: the living would rule in their own name. From B.C. 305
Ptolemy, Cassander, Lysimachus and Seleucus were all kings in
their own domains.

Antigonus' project for B.C. 305 was the capture of Ptolemy's
important commercial ally Rhodes. Like Demetrius, who conducted it, the siege of Rhodes was showy but wasteful, a spectacular demonstration of the sophisticated siege techniques,
offensive and defensive, that the Greeks had evolved within the
last century, but it cost Antigonus a year of time and expense for
nothing more glorious than a negotiated settlement. Demetrius
came away wearing the new laurels of "Besieger" (*poliorcetes*),
while the thrifty Rhodians sold his abandoned siege machinery
and from the proceeds built themselves the colossal statue of
Helios that adorned their harbor to the wonder of the ancient
world.[10]

When his Rhodian adventure was finally, if unsatisfactorily,
finished, Demetrius returned to Greece, where Cassander had
been profiting by his absence to put great pressure on Athens. In
B.C. 304 Demetrius lifted the near-siege of the city and followed
by sweeping northward through Greece up to Thermopylae,
purging the cities en route of the last remnants of Cassander's
oppressive influence. And as he had promised, Antigonus restored
a federal union of the type that Philip and Alexander had envi-

---

10. The subsequent history of the Colossus was something less than
wonderful. It was thrown down by an earthquake, and what was left
of it was sold for junk in A.D. 656.

sioned in the League of Corinth and Athens had fought for against Antipater in B.C. 323–322.

This promise of political reform had been the high-handed Cassander's vulnerable point from the beginning, and now its fulfillment, coupled with the obvious military strength of Demetrius, moved Cassander in B.C. 302 to ask for peace. Antigonus caught the echo of desperation and refused to negotiate. Cassander thus was forced to throw himself among his allies, Ptolemy, Lysimachus and Seleucus, who up to this point had shown little disposition to help. Now, however, they began to close ranks. Surprisingly it was Lysimachus, formerly satrap and now king of Thrace, who struck the heaviest blow. He crossed the Hellespont and caught Antigonus' client cities in western Anatolia completely unawares. Antigonus was in Syria at the time.[11] Hastily he summoned Demetrius to his side and proceeded across the Taurus to face Lysimachus. Now acting in concert, Ptolemy came up from Syria and Seleucus from Babylon. Ptolemy allowed himself to be frightened off in mid-march, but to his glory Seleucus pressed on to the place of final confrontation, Ipsus in Phrygia.

Seleucus had lately been fighting other enemies on other fronts. All of Alexander's eastern conquests from Babylon eastward to beyond the Indus were his by reason of the dim campaigns he fought in the east ever since Antigonus relieved the pressure on Babylon in B.C. 308. Alexander had left the Indian Porus as his governor east of the Indus, and he had been reconfirmed by Perdiccas. But the hostilities in which Perdiccas was subsequently embroiled invited power to find its own level farther east. Porus was murdered by a certain Eudamus, who with the native Taxiles ruled the area between the Indus and the Hydaspes. The prize was Porus' war elephants which had so startled the Macedonians when Alexander first arrived in those parts. Their possession doubtless strengthened Eudamus' position in the coalition formed in B.C. 317 to thwart the growing eastern ambitions of Peithon, satrap of Media. When the coalition yielded to the higher neces-

---

11. Up to this point Antigonus had ruled his holdings from Celaenae in Phrygia. When Lysimachus unexpectedly burst into Anatolia, Antigonus was at that very moment inaugurating his new capital, Antigonia, on the middle Orontes in Syria. It was destroyed by Seleucus after Ipsus.

sities of Eumenes' struggle with Antigonus, Eudamus sacrificed his life and his troops to Eumenes' losing cause. The immediate result was a dangerous political vacuum in the lands east of the Indus, and the first to profit from it was the powerful Mauryan king Chandragupta, already lord of a large empire across northern India. He began his occupation of the Indus basin sometime about B.C. 315 and remained unchallenged there until the appearance of Seleucus over the rim of the Hindu Kush sometime after B.C. 308.

The fighting in the Indus valley must have gone badly for Seleucus, since he eventually drew back into the highlands and left all that Alexander had won beyond the passes of the Hindu Kush to the Mauryan emperor. The Greeks were rolled back politically, but their influence took far longer to recede. Chandragupta probably had some of the ubiquitous Greek mercenaries in his own employ, and the lines of communication between Babylon and the Mauryan court at Patna remained open. Seleucus' ambassador there was the voluble Ionian Greek Megasthenes, whose *Indica* kept the Hellenes in the west well apprised of the marvels of India.[12] But the Greeks were never again to have a state in the Punjab, and Seleucus' sole return for the cession of those lands was a brigade of Indian war elephants.

Seleucus and his elephants joined Lysimachus on the field of Ipsus in B.C. 301, and the two forces swelled into a mighty army. Opposed was an even larger force led by the still aggressive Antigonus and his son Demetrius Poliorcetes. It was the elephants that won the day. They blocked the charging Demetrius from returning to his father's flank and the fates of war closed in around the old man. Antigonus died with a cry for his son on his lips. Demetrius saved his own life only by headlong flight from the field.

With the death of Antigonus another of Alexander's marshals was gone, and with him any hope that the empire would hold together. The survivors, now kings, divided the spoils without embarrassment or rhetorical subterfuge. The histories of the lands they ruled drew apart during the following two and a half centuries until Rome reestablished as one empire most of what Alexander had won. But the dissolution was merely political.

12. See p. 112.

Cassander in Greece, Lysimachus in Anatolia, Ptolemy in Egypt, and Seleucus in Asia were bound together by their common political origins, the increasingly valuable Greek and Macedonian mercenaries and colonists on whom their power rested, and their association in the Hellenism that was at the same time their master and their servant. The dream of one empire was lost, but the *oikoumene* remained intact.

The Contest for Greece (B.C. 301–196)

Demetrius Poliorcetes managed to escape the general disaster of Ipsus with a few troops, the most potent fleet in the Aegean, and the popularity of his father's lenient policies in the Greek *poleis*. It was a popularity tempered by Demetrius' own excesses; his profligate and tyrannous behavior during the winter of B.C. 304–303 was still remembered by the Athenians who had deified their liberator three years before, but who now had reason to regret their impetuous gratitude. Even at his lowest Demetrius could not be written off. A scattering of cities around the Aegean were still in his possession, and he was, nominally at least, the president of the Hellenic League. There was no ground to rest there, as he discovered when he returned to his bastion Corinth; he could have what he could hold. And after B.C. 301 that did not include Athens, which, freed of Demetrius, seemed once more to be drifting in the direction of Cassander.

Cassander may already have been in the grip of his last illness when the third century began. His policy was cautious and unaggressive. After Ipsus he resigned any claims on Asia[13] and seemed unwilling to contest Greece with Demetrius. Cassander died in B.C. 298, and Demetrius, ignored by the other kings, saw a new avenue of power opened to him, Macedon itself. But first there was Athens, and Demetrius profited by the party strife there in B.C. 296 to attempt taking the city by force. This time the Athenians fiercely resisted the embrace of their erstwhile divinized liberator. Demetrius was forced to starve the city into submission. He treated his illustrious captive mercifully, but left

---

13. He did manage to extract some territory in southern Anatolia from Caria round to Cilicia for his brother Pleistarchus, perhaps to threaten Ptolemy, but showed no inclination to support its existence. The kingdom of Pleistarchus soon disappeared into hungrier maws.

no doubt that this was no longer B.C. 307; a permanent garrison of occupation was established.

Shortly there came to Demetrius an unexpected but welcome invitation to intervene in Macedon. After the brief reign of Cassander's son as Philip IV, the kingdom was unfortunately divided between two surviving sons, Antipater and Alexander, who promptly fell upon each other. It was the younger, Alexander, whose claim was somewhat less secure, who issued the summons to Demetrius. The latter was at the time engaged in heavy fighting with some of the *poleis* of the Peloponnesus and so could not respond with the same speed as another who had received a similar invitation, Pyrrhus, the monarch of the federated kingdom of Epirus on the western coast of Greece. Pyrrhus was no newcomer to the sophisticated game of Aegean politics. On and off the throne of Epirus since B.C. 307, he had served and been served by both Demetrius, after Ipsus, and Ptolemy, who in B.C. 297 had finally planted him securely in his kingdom.

It was Pyrrhus who shored up Alexander and who received territories in western Macedon as his reward. Demetrius paid his call nonetheless, and when told that his services were no longer required, murdered Alexander, expelled Antipater, and in B.C. 294 had himself proclaimed king of Macedon. The noise of the event was perhaps somewhat too loud, since it attracted the attention of his rival Macedonian dynasts across the Aegean. His potential rivals had up to now been content to give Demetrius his head in Greece, a gesture not so much of benevolence as of respect for his fleet. Demetrius did indeed become deeply embroiled in Greece, which, now that the son had shed the mantle of his father Antigonus' policy of liberty, required constant surveillance. Boeotia became troublesome and found allies in Pyrrhus and the nearby League of Aetolians. Demetrius nonetheless took Thebes and garrisoned it in B.C. 291.

Perhaps Demetrius understood the impossibility of reducing the hard core of his enemies in Greece, Epirus, Aetolia and Sparta; or perhaps the fantasy of Alexander's empire exercised a more provocative magic than the more constrained dimensions of Alexander's kingdom. In any event, in the years after B.C. 290 Demetrius had unmistakable designs on Asia. Lysimachus, who had never had the courage or the opportunity to intervene in Greece before this, was obviously the target of first choice as master of Anatolia and the chief instrument of Antigonus' failure at Ipsus. Demetrius' fleet was formidable, and since the odds must have appeared better in Macedon than in Asia, the compliant Pyrrhus was persuaded to cooperate with Lysimachus in a joint invasion of Macedon in B.C. 288 to forestall Demetrius' descent on Asia. Seleucus showed no great interest in the project at this point, but Ptolemy undertook to send his growing fleet across the Aegean to harass Demetrius at Athens and Corinth.

The conquest and partition of Macedon by Lysimachus and Pyrrhus went remarkably easily. Demetrius had used up most of his credit there and barely escaped with his life. At Athens Ptolemy landed troops, and Demetrius' partisans within the city were overthrown. It seemed that this must be the end of an extravagant career; but just as he had done after Ipsus, Demetrius somehow managed to survive. As before, he still had his fleet and, with the exception of Athens, his garrisoned cities in Greece. He made a dash for Athens, which sent out a hasty call for Pyrrhus. By all appearances Athens was to be the scene of a destructive battle between Pyrrhus and Demetrius, but the city sent out a delegation of its philosophers to ask Demetrius to forbear. He had no stomach for Pyrrhus at this point and acceded to the plea. Athens was spared.

There was one more gamble to be made, and Demetrius rose from his latest adversity to a final throw of the dice, his planned invasion of Asia. He left his son Antigonus Gonatas behind to watch over what was left to him in Greece, and in B.C. 287 he landed at Miletus in Ionia. It was a bold gesture and almost worked. There were some successes—he took Sardis—but as soon as Lysimachus' army appeared in the spring of B.C. 286, Demetrius' progress turned into flight. The pressure of superior forces pressed him ever southward through Anatolia and finally over the Taurus into Cilicia, where he became the problem not of Lysimachus but of the previously unconcerned Seleucus. Seleucus, who relished the presence of Demetrius in Anatolia, had no great appetite for this confrontation on his own doorstep, but Demetrius was far too dangerous to be allowed to run free in Syria. Seleucus' new capital of Antioch was nearby, and he had a lively recollection of Demetrius' father, Antigonus, ruling not too many years before in this same area. The two armies finally closed, and Demetrius had no chance for success. He escaped, was hunted down and finally was starved into submission. Seleucus did nothing with his quixotic prize except confine him; in a short time Demetrius pronounced sentence upon himself; he drank himself to death in captivity (B.C. 283).

Things were not much altered in Greece by Demetrius' capture. His son Antigonus Gonatas hung on by the slender thread of his garrisoned cities, while Pyrrhus and Lysimachus divided Macedon. Lysimachus soon had second thoughts about that project and began to exert pressure to dislodge his political bedmate. Pyrrhus eventually yielded, and by B.C. 285 Lysimachus was in total possession of Macedon and Thessaly, Thrace, and all of western Anatolia. Gonatas was reduced to the role of an increasingly impoverished onlooker. He first lost his fleet—it defected to Ptolemy after the death of Demetrius—but managed to recoup somewhat in B.C. 281 by taking his father's former showplace, Athens.

When Gonatas assumed his father's almost empty crown in B.C. 283, his prospects must have seemed dim. Ptolemy had possession of the fleet, as well as a firm grip on the commercially important and prestigious League of the Islands that centered on Delos. Lysimachus ruled unchallenged in Macedon, Thessaly, Thrace, and Anatolia down to the Taurus. Seleucus was unshakable in Syria and was securing his succession by the association of his son Antiochus in his rule (B.C. 292). Gonatas' kingdom, then, was little more than the Greek cities, Athens and Corinth chief among them, that he held by main force. But beneath his rivals' outwardly strong positions new currents were flowing, released, in the first instance, by Ptolemy's repudiation, sometime before B.C. 287, of his wife Eurydice in favor of his mistress Berenice.

The change went smoothly enough in Egypt, and even its most dangerous consequence, Ptolemy's adoption of Berenice's son in B.C. 285 and the new heir's accession to power two years later as Ptolemy II Philadelphus, created no domestic problems. But it did send abroad into Mediterranean politics Eurydice's disinherited son, Ptolemy Ceraunus, who within a short time encompassed the ruin of the last of Alexander's Successors and eventually won for Gonatas what neither arms nor fortune seemed to promise him in B.C. 283.

Ceraunus took his failed expectations first to Seleucus and then to Lysimachus, lately of Thrace but now master of an empire. There was a familiar face in the court of Lysimachia. Both Ptolemy I and Lysimachus had profited by Antipater's largess of daughters; Ptolemy had received the now repudiated Eurydice, and Lysimachus had been given Nicaea.[14] Sometime after Ipsus, Ptolemy used the same tactic of matrimonial insurance, and once again Lysimachus was provided with a bride, Arsinoë, the daughter of Berenice. Lysimachus later returned the gesture by bestowing his own daughter Arsinoë (born not of the Egyptian Arsinoë, but of his first wife Nicaea) to the young Ptolemy II Philadelphus. It is doubtful that Lysimachus was about to break the bond of these matrimonial alliances for the sake of Ceraunus; Ptolemy II was his son-in-law, and Ptolemy's sister Arsinoë was his own wife. His own succession was clearly settled on another of Nicaea's offspring, Agathocles.

There was but one impediment to that arrangement, albeit a formidable one, the current queen, Arsinoë, who, like her mother Berenice, was intent that her own children would rule. She supported them all too successfully, and the aged Lysimachus was persuaded by his still young, ambitious and ruthless wife that Agathocles was plotting treason. In the same year that Ptolemy I passed peacefully away in Egypt, his daughter brought about the execution of Agathocles (B.C. 283). Ceraunus, who was probably no more than a bystander to these events, must have seen doors open before him.

He was forestalled by someone swifter than he. At the execution of Agathocles, who was competent and popular, unrest spread through the Greek cities of Anatolia, and Lysimachus, never the gentlest of rulers, reacted harshly. The malcontents streamed southward to Seleucus, who seized the opportunity that Arsinoë had so unexpectedly provided and marched into Anatolia. The cities were ripe for revolt. Bithynia, Sardis and Pergamum came over to him without a struggle. Finally Lysimachus came up with his army and was decisively defeated and killed at Corupedion in Lydia (B.C. 281). Arsinoë made good her escape from Ephesus, but Seleucus did come into possession of the doubtless bewildered Ceraunus.

In B.C. 281, fifty-three years after Alexander crossed into Asia, Seleucus was the last of the surviving generals of the Grand Army. Egypt could never be his; Ptolemy had planned and worked too well there. But Macedon itself was near, and forget-

---

14. Whose name he gave, in the manner of the Hellenistic rulers, to the Bithynian city previously called Antigonia. Antipater's third daughter, Phila, went first to Craterus, and then, at his death, to Demetrius Poliorcetes, to whom she bore Antigonus Gonatas.

ful of the considerable problems that still beset him in Asia, he hurried toward that prize. Ceraunus may have read Seleucus' problems more acutely. He assassinated the aged marshal as he crossed over into Europe and claimed the crown of Macedon from Lysimachus' troops as the avenger of their rightful king. They accepted him and then, in an act of considerably greater bravado, he offered his hand to his half sister and the widow of Lysimachus, Arsinoë. The lady, who was holed up in eastern Macedon, may have outreached her ambition; she too accepted.

The rapid events of B.C. 281–280 provoked different responses around the Mediterranean. Gonatas saw his own opportunity in Ceraunus' somewhat uncertain hold on the throne of Macedon. He gathered up his mercenaries, sailed north with a new fleet, but was quickly and effectively beaten by Ceraunus. Seleucus' son Antiochus could do nothing from his side, because a powerful coalition was forming along the southern and western shores of the Euxine, where Byzantium, Chalcedon and then the kingdoms of Bithynia and Pontus blocked all passage into Europe. In Egypt over that winter Ptolemy II celebrated his own inexpensive leap in prestige by a magnificent festival in honor of his divinized mother and father, capped by his own version of Panhellenic pretension, Olympic Games.

Ceraunus was undone, and Gonatas was suddenly propelled into power by a force that neither of them could have foreseen in B.C. 280. For over a century detachments of Celts had been moving, unseen by Greek eyes, from north of the Alps to the lower Danube. In B.C. 279 they fell suddenly and violently upon Ceraunus' new Macedonian kingdom and thus passed into Hellenic history under the name of "Galatians." They cut through Ceraunus' army, captured and executed the newly minted king, while another part of their horde passed southward into Greece proper, burning and looting in the open countryside. There was apparently no force to resist them. Gonatas was thoroughly demoralized after his defeat in B.C. 280 and his Greek cities were falling away.[15] Pyrrhus was occupied with his new role as savior of the western Greeks in Sicily and Italy from the imperialism of the Roman Republic, and as yet there was no move from Asia. But the Galatians were stopped, miraculously as the Greeks be-

---

15. Led, incredibly, by the long dormant Sparta under its king, Areus (see p. 88).

lieved, on the very threshold of rich and tempting Delphi. The credit was shared by Apollo and the Aetolians, who hounded them back out of Greece. The Galatians recrossed Macedon and joined fresh contingents in Thrace.

In the following years it was Anatolia that had to face the Galatian menace. But before they crossed the Hellespont the marauding Celts left one curious postscript. In B.C. 277 Gonatas, who had a precarious grip in eastern Thrace, fell upon a detachment of Galatians there and destroyed them. In the almost continuous stream of Greek warfare the event was little more than a ripple; in psychological terms, however, it was an immense victory, magnified by the Greeks' terror of the new northern barbarism. Hellenic military cruelty was by then almost institutionalized but could still provoke the cries of outraged consciences. The Galatians' tactics were a new and raw experience even for the Greeks, who were habituated to war but not to nomadic invasions. Folk memory had to go back to the Cimmerians and Dorians centuries earlier to find a parallel.

Gonatas, then, was exalted amidst the anarchy and for his feat was acclaimed king of Macedon, where his family ruled uninterruptedly for more than a century.[16] With this base his fortunes began to revive. Pyrrhus returned from Italy in the next years and demonstrated that he was capable of unseating Gonatas whenever he chose; he had, moreover, both encouragement and subsidy from Egypt, where Ptolemy II viewed Gonatas with growing alarm. But Pyrrhus allowed himself to be lured into the Peloponnesus by false prospects there and met his death in Argos, caught between the armies of Sparta and Macedon. From B.C. 272 Gonatas proceeded in a somewhat more leisurely fashion to reconstruct the mosaic of mainland *poleis* that his grandfather and father had held before him.

Though Gonatas' conquests were as yet limited to the Greek mainland, he was still the object of suspicion in Egypt, a suspicion fed by the reappearance at the side of Ptolemy of his sister Arsinoë. The widow of Lysimachus and Ceraunus had her own claim on the rule of Macedon, a claim that obviously counted

---

16. After the Romans decimated the Macedonian army at Pydna in B.C. 168, they deported Perseus, the last king of the Antigonid house, to Rome. After an unsuccessful twenty-year experiment with four Macedonian republics, the former kingdom was finally converted into a Roman province (B.C. 148).

very little with Gonatas, who, shortly after his own accession in
B.C. 277, took care to evict Arsinoë's eldest son.[17] Arsinoë was no
mere political exile in Egypt. She had persuaded Ptolemy II to
repudiate his other Arsinoë, Lysimachus' daughter, and marry
her, his own full sister. Arsinoë did not live long enough to savor
the direct confrontation between Ptolemy and Gonatas which
she doubtless provoked. For the time being, Ptolemy contented
himself with calling upon seconds in his duel with Macedon, first
Pyrrhus, then Sparta, and finally Athens, provoked in B.C. 267
into her final excursion into Aegean politics.

The Chremonidean War—so called from the Athenian statesman who proposed the resolution of war—declared by Athens
against Gonatas in B.C. 267, though founded on strong anti-
Macedonian sentiment at Athens and elsewhere, was clearly
conducted with Egyptian connivance and support: the Egyptian
fleet would undertake to supply Athens in the face of a likely
Macedonian siege. It was, after all, a sad and disorganized affair.
Spartan nerve collapsed at the death of her King Areus in B.C.
265. The new king of Epirus, likewise drawn into the war by
Egyptian money, allowed himself to be defeated by Gonatas'
thirteen-year-old son. Athens was left to bear the final Macedonian onslaught alone. It came in B.C. 263 in the form of a
blockade, which Egypt made no strong effort to break. In two
years the city was starved into subjection, and a Macedonian
garrison once again took up its post in Athens.

During those terrible years death came to the philosopher
Zeno, the founder of Stoicism, who had lived and taught at
Athens since sometime about B.C. 310. The Athenians well under-
stood their loss—they voted a public funeral—but so did
Gonatas. Most of the other Hellenistic princes supported the arts,
some sumptuously, like the Ptolemies in Egypt and the Attalids in
Pergamum, but none with greater conviction or personal com-
mitment than Antigonus Gonatas. His first contact with philos-
ophy was probably with Menedemus, an early Cynic of the
Socratic tradition,[18] who had assembled a literary circle of his

---

17. Arsinoë's other sons by Lysimachus never survived her betrothal
to Ceraunus, whose bridal gift was the murder of Arsinoë's children.
The eldest survived to lurk in the shadows of Macedon until Gonatas
prudently got rid of him.
18. See Chapter XI, pp. 413–14.

own at Eretria in Euboea.[19] Menedemus' bluff and unrelenting, if somewhat anti-intellectual, moralizing—like his model Socrates, he wrote nothing—attracted the youthful Gonatas. Later at his father Demetrius' duchy of Athens he found an even more appealing teacher, Zeno, and as a result of their lifelong friendship Gonatas became the first of a long line of philosopher kings on the Stoic model which reached down to the Roman Antonines.

In B.C. 276, when Gonatas had finally come into his father's kingdom and was celebrating his marriage with Phila, the half sister of Antiochus I, he invited Zeno to join the circle of historians and poets that he was then already collecting at his court in the Macedonian capital of Pella. Menedemus was likely there, as was that other, somewhat more commercial Cynic, Bion of Borysthenes.[20] Aratus of Soli, a transient between Pella and the Stoic circles of Athens and the author of the *Phaenomena*, a poet and scientist's appreciation of the Stoic doctrine of universal providence,[21] was commissioned to compose the official marriage ode. Other poets and writers were drawn by Gonatas' largess and intellectual promise, but some deeper loyalty to the house was behind the presence of the era's most imposing historian, Hieronymus of Cardia. Hieronymus' career, as a soldier and diplomat, not yet a historian, began with his early attachment to the cause of his fellow countryman Eumenes. After Eumenes' defeat near Isfahan in B.C. 317, Hieronymus attached himself to the cause of Antigonus and served the family for three generations, under Antigonus as a scout against the Nabataean Arabs, under Demetrius as a garrison commander in Euboea, and finally under Gonatas as confidant of the house and the official Antigonid historian of the period between the death of Alexander and the destruction of Pyrrhus.[22]

Zeno justifiably pleaded old age and could not be tempted to Pella in B.C. 276. He sent in his place his student Perseus, who was

---

19. Which included, among others, one of the rare contemporary tragedians of any merit, Lycophron (see Note 25, p. 93).

20. See Chapter XI, p. 415.

21. See Chapter V, p. 220.

22. His *History of the Successors*, which draws upon his deep involvement in the events of his time as well as upon the Macedonian archives, is lost and must be read chiefly in its adaptation by Diodorus of Sicily and by Plutarch in his *Life of Pyrrhus*. For all its Antigonid bias the work seems to have avoided the flagrant faults that marred that of Peripatetic historians like Duris of Samos (see p. 91).

appointed to serve as tutor of Gonatas' son and as the theoretician
of Antigonid kingship: what probably emerged was a Stoic
Mirror for Princes tempered by the realities of the Macedonian
political tradition. In Macedon, where the divinization of rulers
was and remained an alien custom, the rule of the king was
solidly grounded in the popular will as expressed by the nation
under arms, the Macedonian army. This notion had led to no
great stability in the past, and it must have been with sovereign
envy that the kings of Macedon watched their Ptolemaic contemporaries in Egypt cementing their position by recourse to the
divinity of the ruler.[23]

The fault was not, perhaps, with the Macedonian system as
much as with Alexander's crossing it with his own peculiar style.
It is not entirely clear whether later claimants wished to succeed
Alexander or become king of Macedon, functions that were
partially the same but in some respects totally different. Gonatas,
assisted to be sure by the course of events down to B.C. 276, cut
the knot. He and his successors disclaimed, by their lives and the
styles of their rule, any association with the charismatic kingship
of Alexander. They resisted as well the temptations of Phar-
aonism that worked so well in Egypt and even among the
Seleucids.

For the Antigonids kingship was a natural bequest given by the
people to individuals who promised to merit well of them.[24] In
Perseus' phrase it was a "noble servitude," performed for the
good of the people by the ruler, the latter, it should be added,
under the guidance of the Stoic sage (*sophos*). The Antigonids
ruled at home modestly and simply in an age of divine kings and
gods-made-manifest, and faithfully followed the path charted by
the undeified and restrained Gonatas down to the latter days of
Philip V and his son Perseus.

The survival and practice of that tradition was surely a tribute
to the character of Gonatas and the idealism of his Stoic mentors,
but owed something as well to the peculiar nature of Macedonian
kingship. Macedon began as an association of peoples under a

---

23. See Chapters IV (p. 156) and XII (pp. 467–68).
24. Their status was, of course, quite different in the *poleis* under
their control. Gonatas ruled there by garrisons and tyrants no less
than Antipater had originally done, a fact rendered perfectly clear by
the Chremonidean War. Chremonides, no less than Gonatas, was a
disciple of Zeno.

king, and the Macedonian state never lost its national tone. Its army, the people joined together under arms, had the right to elect the king, and from Philip II to Philip V and Perseus they exercised it frequently. At first the monarchy turned on the dynastic claims of Philip II's family, but with the evaporation of that hope in the deaths of Philip III and Alexander IV the ground broadened to include the inner circle of Alexander's staff, men who were not merely generals in an arduous and successful campaign but who were, by the feudal standards of Macedon, members of the national elite: Antipater and his son Cassander, Polyperchon, Antigonus and his son Demetrius, Lysimachus, the ephemeral Ceraunus, son of Ptolemy, and finally, Demetrius' son Antigonus Gonatas and his descendants.

The political life of the Macedonian monarchical state was but poorly institutionalized; the court in Pella was almost Homeric in comparison to the growing bureaucracies of Alexandria and Antioch. The old feudal nobility that in Philip's and Alexander's day still had some power and distinction melted steadily away, eroded in part by the growing Hellenization of the realm, until the latter-day Antigonids ruled as they would, save for an occasional testing of their position against the popular will. The Macedonian king possessed a court, but no real helpers in the business of government.

The collision between this form of "democratic autocracy" and the tradition of parties and politics in the *poleis* was felt from the first moment that these latter, self-governing units outside Macedon fell under the sway of Philip II. After a few false starts Philip, and then Alexander, attempted to govern them, at least in the general lines of their policy, through the instrument of the League of Corinth, a loose federation of mainland *poleis* organized on the principle of proportional representation. It governed and tempered the relations of the Greek states among themselves, and its overseas policy was, not coincidentally, exactly that of its Macedonian presidents. The League of Corinth had no power to intervene in the affairs of its member *poleis*, except in extraordinary circumstances. These latter were precisely one: the threat of what the feudal lords of Macedon and the oligarchies of Greece most feared, social revolution. Both Alexander's prescription for the League and Demetrius' revived version of it in B.C. 302 made specific provision for Macedonian intervention in any state that began to display the classic symptoms of revolution:

proposals for the cancellation of debts, the redistribution of land, or the emancipation of slaves. Though Rome had to face a number of such proletarian uprisings in the second century, they were not unknown in third-century Greece, where there was a revolutionary *coup d'état* in Cassandria in B.C. 279,[25] and the politics of the Peloponnesus were dominated during almost the entire second half of that century by the social and economic ferment in newly awakened Sparta.

The League of Corinth was born not of a shared need of the *poleis* but by the will of its Macedonian presidents. With Alexander's death it not unexpectedly lapsed, though fitfully revived by Antigonus, Demetrius, and finally in a less comprehensive but more imaginative fashion by Antigonus III Doson in B.C. 224.[26] It did not, however, represent the Greeks' only attempt at federation. The self-sufficient and self-contained *poleis* might be difficult to unite into larger political organisms—as Isocrates had well understood—but there were other grounds for confederation. From far back in their history the Hellenes of both Greece and Anatolia grouped themselves in amphictyonies, tribal unions around a central religious shrine like Delphi. Philip II had toyed with the Delphic Amphictyony on his way to Hellenic hegemony but apparently discarded it as a political instrument in favor of the League of Corinth. The importance of a religious center in supplying a rallying point for confederations of whatever order did not disappear. Antigonus experimented with various sectional leagues in the waning years of the fourth century, a League of Ionians, of Aeolians, of the Islands, and in each case

---

25. What took place in Cassander's former capital in Chalcidice is not entirely clear. What is clear is that it was a bloody time of mass confiscations whereby the newly enriched proletariat bought themselves mercenaries to maintain their position. The affair was celebrated in a lost drama, *The Men of Cassandria*, written by Menedemus' friend Lycophron of Rhegium from the aristocrats' point of view and in obvious violation of the normal prohibition against using contemporary history as a subject of tragedy.

26. This latter version ceased functioning in the crisis of B.C. 212–210, when Macedon became embroiled for the first time with Rome, and its king, Philip V, called upon Doson's Hellenic Confederacy to come to his aid. The invitation was greeted by silence, largely because of the reluctance of the Achaeans, a fact that later led Philip to ignore the fiction of the confederacy and revert to the tougher policies of Antipater, Cassander, and even Gonatas.

had the perspicacity to weave his political fabrics around larger-than-life shrines like Delos or Ilium.

In all these instances the aim of the association, no matter what the grounds of its foundation, was to persuade the members, by one means or another, to take concerted action for what was presumably their common advantage. Superficially at least these were alliances, formalized on occasion by the presence of a deliberative body to debate the courses of action; beneath the talk there was the political reality of power: Athens imposing her will on the Maritime League, Thebes on the Boeotians, Philip governing his Thessalian Federation, and Alexander dictating terms to the Congress at Corinth. There were, however, examples to be found among the Hellenes of the genuine surrender of sovereignty to a higher political body. The clearest examples come, to be sure, from the least urbanized areas of Greece, where the autonomous *polis* had not yet taken root. The various tribes of Epirus federated themselves under a common king. In Aetolia, which knew neither kings nor *poleis*, a different pattern emerged. The unity of the Aetolians was like that of the Macedonians and the Thessalians, a national one, but they possessed no king of their own and neither chose one, like the tribes of Epirus, nor succumbed to someone else's, like the Thessalians. The Aetolians were a tough, individualistic, if unsophisticated people and, as their national self-consciousness sharpened, governed themselves by a kind of tribal democracy: the adult free males under arms, assembled twice a year, constituted the sole legislative body of the nation. Decisions were made en masse and were executed by an elected president and commander in chief. A smaller representative body sat as a judiciary.

This is what the Aetolian League looked like about B.C. 275, to all appearances a throwback to a much earlier age. Indeed, Greek political history seemed to be marching backward. With the ascendancy of the northern and western states, political life regressed to the earlier form of kingship, and now in Aetolia to something earlier still. In one sense, however, the Aetolians were remarkably ahead of their times. They did not consider citizenship as a function of blood descent, that is, an Aetolian tribal pedigree, but rather as a legal fiction that could be extended by fiat. By this insight, unheralded by any of their contemporaries, the Aetolians had devised a manner of extending their polity other than by annexation or occupation, both of which were practiced by monarchical states but were considered impossible or inappropriate by the Greek democracies. The Aetolians could and did extend joint citizenship (*sympoliteia*) to any contiguous unit that wished to become "legal Aetolians," to sit with the Aetolian assembly and share in its duties and privileges. The constituent towns kept their local governments and rights; *sympoliteia* could not, however, be extended to any political unit larger than a town. Other, larger polities had to dissolve themselves down to the town units which then could be received piecemeal into the League.

This experiment in mass democracy was essentially altered by its own success. In B.C. 290 the Aetolians took possession of Delphi, a position of prestige enormously enhanced by their successful defense of the sanctuary against the Galatians in B.C. 279. Victory over the feared and hated Galatians established the Aetolians as firmly in north-central Greece as it did Gonatas in Macedon. The Aetolian League had become a major power, but the increasing number of its tribal members, real or fictive, turned its democratic assembly into a shambles, out of which emerged a very much smaller group of "delegates" who took over the effective control of League business. The League's business seems to have been chiefly plunder, and their predatory habits, marked even amidst the escalating barbarism of the third century, kept the Aetolians constantly embroiled with Macedon. It was a serious defeat at the hands of Macedon in B.C. 219 that drove the Aetolians into the arms of the Romans, an embrace that eventually suffocated them. If the Aetolians expected the Romans to share with them the spoils of their victories over Philip V, they were much mistaken. Disappointed, they turned desperately to Rome's rival, the Seleucid Antiochus III.[27] Once the Romans disposed of Antiochus, they stripped the Aetolian League of its powers and allowed it to die a quiet death.

While the Aetolians were still riding the crest, in B.C. 251, a similarly constituted body of Achaean towns in the Peloponnesus found themselves in unexpected possession of the *polis* of Sicyon, which joined their League after a daring and well-executed coup. The Achaean League had a constitutional structure almost identical with the one in Aetolia across the Gulf of Corinth. As in its model, all foreign policy was in the hands of the League and not

---

27. See Chapter VI, p. 249.

subject to the individual decisions of the member towns. And as the Aetolians were to do, the Achaeans gave over the operation of the League to a smaller representative body; the general assembly was summoned only for emergency matters, the declaration of war, for example. Membership could be extended by *sympoliteia,* and as the League grew, Dorians and Arcadians were admitted on an equal footing with the original Achaeans.

In B.C. 245 the Achaeans elected as their captain Aratus, the young man of republican sympathies who had brilliantly engineered the coup in his native Sicyon, and for the next thirty years it was his liberal, anti-Macedonian policy that guided the League's fortunes.[28] As captain he could not succeed himself in that annually elected office, and so it was not until B.C. 243 that the first stroke against Macedonian tyranny was delivered, the liberation of Corinth from the grip of Gonatas after almost a century of Macedonian occupation.[29] The capture of Corinth was a remarkable feat, but Aratus did not rest there. There were other blows against Macedon, the Aetolians, and Athens, the last almost an anomaly in the new politics of the third century. Surrounded on all sides by polities that dwarfed the old-fashioned *polis,* the Greek states were slowly reassembling themselves into blocs. Federalism was a kind of political mimesis in which the small entrepreneurs of the preceding century were merging in the face of corporate competition. The way was led, as has been seen, by those peoples whose adolescent political organisms had not yet matured into the hardened lines of a *polis.* For the Athenians, neither crippled like Thebes nor demoralized like Corinth, *sympoliteia* would have been unthinkable, and so the

---

28. Aratus, like growing numbers of his contemporaries, left behind *Memoirs* which eventually found their way into a number of Plutarch's biographies and into the history of the League's chief apologist, Polybius (*c.* B.C. 200–120), the Arcadian of Megalopolis who shared Achaean *sympoliteia.* Polybius served the League as both soldier and diplomat, and after the battle of Pydna in B.C. 168 was deported as a hostage to Rome, where he became an important apostle of Hellenism (see Chapter IX, pp. 360–61). Polybius' work is, of course, strongly pro-Achaean in tone, and he is an undisguised admirer of Aratus, but more significantly his *Ecumenical History* signals the Hellenic intelligentsia's recognition of the fact that Rome was now part of the *oikoumene* (see Chapter X).

29. Perseus, Gonatas' Stoic vizier, now promoted to a military role, died in its defense.

city was condemned by its sophistication and its tradition to go its own way, which in the third century led nowhere.

Among the Achaean League's allies was another political dinosaur, Sparta. Its once proud military tradition had received a rude check at the hands of the Thebans at Leuctra in B.C. 371, and Sparta had withdrawn into a brooding silence within the Peloponnesus. It could not be lured out to face Philip at Chaeronea, nor did it join the various Leagues that the Macedonians promoted as instruments of their hegemony. Agis III had taken the field against Antipater in B.C. 331 and the unlikely Areus may have had his own dreams of a Peloponnesian League in B.C. 280; but these were isolated incidents, provoked more by Sparta's insecurity in the Peloponnesus than by any aspirations to Panhellenic leadership. Sparta, in fact, lay crushed between the millstones of the myth of its image and the terror of its reality.

In the fourth century Sparta was still the darling of both the militarists and the political theoreticians around the Hellenic world: a well-ordered, rationalized state governed by a warrior class free to exercise itself in all the rigors of military perfection. Rural and untormented by urban proletariats, it coasted serenely on its plantation economy, and if there were occasional chilling thoughts about the rising of its slave class of helots, they were reassuringly suppressed by the tight grip that the true Spartiates kept on the land and its neighbors. New among the latter was the fortress city of Megalopolis, founded by the triumphant Thebans in B.C. 371 to serve as a sty in the bright eye of Spartan ambition. It did. Megalopolis' policy was unfailingly anti-Spartan, and its presence in the near vicinity challenged fourth- and third-century Sparta to be strong or perish.

In the Greek world strength was judged by twin criteria: internal stability and military prowess. The ordinary means of gauging these suggested that Sparta had nothing to fear. Its constitution was an authoritarian model of good order (*eunomia*) that delighted Athenian theoreticians like Plato, Aristotle and Xenophon, whose own society seemed uneasily in the grip of demagogic rabble rousers. Even Zeno, another Athenian by adoption, whose moral viewpoint was somewhat more pragmatic than the institutionalized ethics of his predecessors, found Sparta to his liking as a state in which equality and justice for all men could be guaranteed. And if the myth of Spartan military invincibility was punctured at Leuctra and elsewhere in the fourth century, it was still true that the Spartan was the most capable fighting man produced by any of the *poleis*. Spartan mercenaries were the best value money could buy, and the fourth century even witnessed the unlikely sight of a Spartan king serving as a mercenary in Egypt.

But these criteria belied the truth. Sparta was like a forcing chamber of all that was economically and socially wrong in the third century. The mounting crises of the middle of the fourth century had been averted by Alexander's conquests that opened new markets for Greek manufactures and brought monetary stability to the *oikoumene*. The restless mercenaries of the pre-Alexander generation were converted into the colonists and soldiers of the new regimes. But in the third century the pattern of decline began to repeat itself: as earlier in Italy, the Black Sea littoral and Asia, so now the new *poleis* of Syria, Palestine and Egypt outgrew their need of Greek manufactures, and once again unemployment climbed in the mainland cities, urged upward by the growing number of slave laborers that were a by-product of the frequent wars. Macedon, Achaea, Epirus and the savage Aetolians marched and countermarched across mainland Greece, and their incessant fighting all but destroyed the middle class in the *poleis*, leaving the wealthy and the poor to confront each other across the ruined landscape.

Sparta suffered most of all. Its young men had gone off to fight for pay in the armies of other states. At home the franchise was inextricably tied to the ownership of property, and the general impoverishment meant that the poor Spartiates, those born to citizenship, had to sell their land and their citizenship to survive. And as the class of property owners shrank, so too did the state that was theirs, and theirs alone, both to govern and to protect. By the middle of the third century there were no more than seven hundred fully enfranchised Spartiates, a remnant from a glorious past standing amidst the wreckage of institutions that once embodied the Spartan ideal of a communal state, but were now no more than generally ignored fossils. Sparta was still an agricultural state in the third century, but the careful safeguards against the introduction of a money exchange had broken down during the reign of Areus—the policy was Areus' but the gold bore an Egyptian mint mark—and the primitive Spartan economy was faced with the additional burden of contracted debts.

Third-century Sparta, which had no middle-class buffer to

begin with, had, then, to face the hazards of class warfare and its own obvious inability to protect itself from its external enemies. These latter were of different stripes but are simply characterized: whoever threatened Sparta's position in the Peloponnesus. In B.C. 280 this was Gonatas and his Macedonian garrisons in Megalopolis and Argos. Eight years later it was Pyrrhus of Epirus who allowed himself to be persuaded by a Spartan malcontent to undertake an invasion of the Peloponnesus and paid for his folly with his life. In B.C. 267 it was once again Gonatas, as Sparta allowed herself to be used as one of Ptolemy II's pawns in the Chremonidean War, a struggle that won Sparta nothing and cost the life of her ambitious king, Areus.

In B.C. 243, when Aratus, the master of Sicyon and Corinth, was captain of the powerful Achaean League, the anti-Spartan factions so carefully cultivated by Gonatas were still in power in Megalopolis and Argos. It was a difficult time for Sparta. The new king, Agis IV, was forced, again probably at the prodding of Egypt, to reach out and take the hand of Aratus as an ally. Both states wished to destroy Gonatas' power bases in the Peloponnesus, Aratus because they were seats of Macedonian tyranny, and Agis because they threatened Sparta. In B.C. 241, when hostilities erupted north of the Isthmus, Aratus summoned his Spartan ally to come to his side. Agis dutifully complied, broke off important business at home, and came up to Corinth only to discover that Aratus did not as yet feel secure enough to fight at his side.

Aratus' hesitation had nothing to do with the quality of Agis' troops, but rather with the state of affairs in Sparta. When Agis received the call from Aratus he was in the midst of a social and economic revolution largely of his own making, a revolution that inspired as much mistrust in the bourgeoisie of the Achaean League as it did among the wealthy landlords of Sparta. Agis' ideas may have derived from philosophical sources, but they were crossed with a healthy strain of nationalism: seven hundred Spartiates meant seven hundred hoplites to fight in the phalanx, a dangerous situation in the late third century. What the young king proposed—he was barely twenty at his coronation in B.C. 244—was the cancellation of debts and the redistribution of land into 4,500 equal lots. The first proposal would restore the franchise to the impoverished Spartiates and the second would doubtless promote to new Spartiate status a number of the unenfranchised class of the "dwellers around" (*perioikoi*).[30] This was mild revolution indeed, the extension of the upper class, but it provoked reaction among those at Sparta who profited most from the unequal distribution of wealth.

Agis' plans were only half fulfilled. He had pushed through the cancellation of debts before Aratus' inopportune call came in B.C. 241, and was prevailed upon to postpone the redistribution of land. When he returned home in the following year he discovered that the forces of reaction, led by his co-king, Leonidas, had engineered a countercoup. Rather than provoke a civil war, Agis chose exile but was shortly betrayed and murdered, and Leonidas ruled without colleague until his death in B.C. 237.

Leonidas was succeeded by his son Cleomenes III, and the Spartan revolution passed into its second phase. Leonidas had betrothed the young Cleomenes to Agis' equally young and attractive widow, Agiatis, perhaps with the hope of justifying by this interdynastic marriage his own and his son's single but unconstitutional possession of the dual throne of Sparta. If this is so, the maneuver was only partially successful. Cleomenes did recall Agis' brother Archidamus from exile to rule at his side, but when he too was murdered Cleomenes settled on the illegal appointment of his own brother as royal colleague. A more important result of the marriage, however, was Agiatis' conversion of Cleomenes to an even more radical version of the dead Agis' program of social reform.

The marriage was not the only force carrying Cleomenes in the direction of reform. As a young man he was tutored by the Stoic philosopher Sphaerus, another of Zeno's students, and a clearly distinguishable influence on the Spartan king. Gonatas may have wasted his Stoic adviser Perseus by involving him too deeply in political and eventually military affairs, but Cleomenes did not repeat his mistake. Sphaerus was put in charge of the social aspects of the "Lycurgan restoration" and served as a kind of Spartan Minister of Education down to Sellasia.

Sparta had for the Stoics the same fascination that it had for the older schools of philosophy. The ideal of a classless society of citizens was institutionalized in the Spartan constitution, and if this community of equal citizens rested upon the hapless masses

---

30. The *perioikoi* were settled in villages around the Spartan heartland. They had rights in their local governments and could serve in the Spartan army, but had no say in the general policy of the state.

of the semi- and non-enfranchised *perioikoi*, resident aliens and enserfed helots, it did not offend Greek sensibilities, which concerned themselves solely with the relationship of one citizen to another. Zeno, Perseus and Sphaerus had all written on the Spartan polity, the one state in the Greek world whose institutions were directly aimed at the equality and morality of its citizens.

By the days of Agis and Cleomenes the ideal had all but disappeared from practice. The equal lots of land enjoyed by the Spartiates had coalesced into plantations in the hands of a few wealthy landowners and the social institutions like the communal meals and a prescribed ascetic life style had fallen into abeyance. Paradoxically, the philosophical Agis had put his hand only to economic reform, but the more aggressive and activist Cleomenes intended a social restoration as well. The difference, perhaps, was Sphaerus, and the yoking of the two men, the Stoic theoretician and the Spartan nationalist, almost carried off the nearest thing the Greeks ever had to a revolution.

Between the reigns of Agis and Cleomenes the political geography of the Peloponnesus had changed. Antigonus Gonatas was gone (B.C. 239), and his successor in Macedon, Demetrius II, mistakenly tried to fight both the Leagues—a war that went badly for him—and at the same time hold at bay his aggressive new neighbors, the Dardanians of Illyria. He died in B.C. 229, and the ten years of his rule saw the end of a political system that had been in force since the days of Alexander; the last traces of Macedonian influence disappeared from the Peloponnesus. Aratus achieved his goal, and the cities there were no longer Macedonian fiefs but members of the free association of the Achaean League.[31]

The success of Aratus changed the relationship between the Achaean League and Sparta. Whoever controlled Megalopolis and Argos, whether Macedonian or Achaean, was viewed with suspicion in nearby Sparta. Hostilities between Cleomenes and the League for possession of the towns of Arcadia broke out shortly after B.C. 229 and dragged on inconclusively for more than a year, hampered on the Spartan side by the suspicion with which Cleomenes was regarded by the reactionary elements at

---

31. Athens, freed of the Macedonian presence in B.C. 229, had no inclination to trade Demetrius II for Aratus and chose instead to go the way of a feeble and meaningless independence.

home, and on the Achaeans' by Aratus' lack of enthusiasm for the war.

In the winter of B.C. 227 Cleomenes broke off the fighting in Arcadia, left the Spartan troops in quarters, and returned home with his presumably more trustworthy mercenaries to settle his problems there. He seized the chief organs of the state and proceeded to enforce the revolution for which Agis had timidly refused to spill Spartan blood.[32] Sphaerus was installed with orders to reinstitute the original "Lycurgan Constitution" in all its communist, ascetic vigor, while Cleomenes himself canceled debts, redistributed the Spartan lots of land and began the enfranchisement of the *perioikoi*. Money began to come in again from Sparta's old and self-serving ally Egypt, where Ptolemy III saw Cleomenes and Sparta as his next cudgel against Macedon. Now on the tide of rising expectations, Cleomenes rearmed and reorganized his army, a project that doubtless stood closer to his true intent than Sphaerus' bizarre attempts at resuscitating a dead Lycurgan past.

Cleomenes' new army was indeed formidable, but he had in hand another, more terrible weapon, the promise and the threat of social and economic reform that could be brandished over the attentive heads of the League cities. From B.C. 226 things began to run Sparta's way in the field, and the allies of the League tripped over each other in their haste to rally to Cleomenes' banner. Finally the Spartan king offered the battered Achaeans his terms: his own permanent captaincy of the League. There was considerable support for the offer within the League cities, but Aratus still commanded enough votes in the federal assembly to defeat the proposal.

It was a dangerous moment for the Achaean League and a personal crisis for Aratus. Cleomenes had both arms and ideology on his side, and Aratus knew that his votes against the Spartan would eventually evaporate. There seemed to be a single, unattractive alternative to capitulation, to invite Macedon into alliance. Aratus had devoted an entire career to freeing the Peloponnesus from Macedonian rule only to be forced into summoning its new king, Antigonus Doson, to help save him and the League, for the price, at the very least, of Corinth. Aratus

---

32. Cleomenes himself spilled very little of it. His coup was effected at the cost of fourteen lives.

came to the reluctant decision that, whatever may have been true in the past, Cleomenes was the present enemy.

At the death of his cousin Demetrius II in B.C. 229, Doson had come to power in Macedon as the regent for the nine-year-old Philip V. He soon took the crown for himself, stipulating the eventual restoration of Philip as the true heir. Doson served Macedon well. He restored the frontier in Illyria, resumed his position as head of the Thessalian Federation, and kept the Aetolian League in check. He seemingly had no ambitions in Greece proper, but when Aratus proffered his alliance late in B.C. 225, Doson recognized the opportunity for what it was and accepted.

In the spring of B.C. 224 Cleomenes stood at a fortified line on the Isthmus as Doson approached from the north. The line held, but Doson turned it by landing troops in the rear at Argos, where Cleomenes' revolution had failed to materialize and his supporters were disappointed and embittered, as they were almost everywhere. Cleomenes fell back upon Sparta, and Doson spent the winter in political warfare. He reconstituted the Hellenic League of Philip II, Alexander and Demetrius Poliorcetes around the nucleus of Macedon and its allies (Thebes, Epirus, Boeotia) and the Achaean League; the Aetolians and Athens clung to their neutrality and Sparta was, of course, excluded for the present.

The fighting resumed in the central Peloponnesus during the campaigning season of B.C. 223 and was marked by unusual savagery on both sides. Doson took Mantinea and handed it over to Achaean vengeance; the population was sold into slavery. As a counterstroke Cleomenes battered Megalopolis into subjection and then razed the city. It was probably the fiercest fighting that Greece had ever seen. In B.C. 222 Doson returned once again. Cleomenes, from whom Ptolemy III had withdrawn his subsidy, could no longer avoid a direct confrontation. It occurred at Sellasia, in the valley eight miles north of Sparta, in June of that year. Cleomenes' army was annihilated,[33] and Doson entered Sparta in triumph, the first general in history to have done so. He

---

33. The king himself managed, however, to escape to Egypt with Sphaerus. Both Ptolemy III and IV treated him with kindness, but Cleomenes, now deprived of his army, tried his other weapon, revolution, on his hosts. It did not succeed and Cleomenes and his retainers committed suicide in B.C. 219.

annexed the city to the Hellenic League and Cleomenes' reforms were promptly undone.[34]

Doson died in B.C. 221 and, as promised, the seventeen-year-old Philip V came into his inheritance. In a few short years he convinced his supporters in Macedon and both his allies and enemies abroad that a new force had been released in Greek politics. By B.C. 217 he had finally curtailed the troublesome Aetolians and brought Greece to the brink of national unity. What he had accomplished was done by imagination and daring, qualities that in an earlier day had opened an enfeebled Asia to Alexander the Great, but in the late third century carried Philip and his kingdom into direct collision with a mighty new neighbor, Rome.

The second century was a Roman one in Greece, provoked in the first instance by Philip's maritime ambitions. In both the Adriatic and the Aegean Philip, who had rebuilt his fleet after its neglect by Doson, indulged in that form of institutionalized piracy first popularized by the Aetolian League. In the west it brought him up against Roman trade in the Adriatic and in the east against Attalus of Pergamum and the republic of Rhodes. These maritime states soon discovered their common cause and entered into alliance.[35]

Philip was less happy in his allies. He might naturally have expected Doson's Hellenic League to rally to his side; they did not. Instead he threw in with Rome's chief enemy in the Mediterranean, Hannibal of Carthage. It was a serious miscalculation, which bore its destructive fruit after B.C. 202, when Rome had

---

34. To be revived on one final occasion. In B.C. 207 Sparta was ruled by Nabis, who, with the paradigms of Agis and Cleomenes before him, reintroduced the revolution as a means of strengthening Sparta. He went somewhat further than either of his predecessors in that he freed some of the helots—selectively, however, and not on a large scale. Sparta was indeed strengthened, but not to the point where it could challenge the new Greek power, Rome. Nabis' revolutionary and imperialist ambitions were restricted by the Romans to Sparta itself. It was not enough for Achaea, which in B.C. 189 suddenly came down upon Sparta and wiped out the last traces of the revolutionary regime.

35. Quickly joined by the Aetolian League, which had its own debt to settle with Philip V. Both the Rhodians and the Aetolians had their own misgivings about Rome, but Philip, as usual, left his enemies little recourse to the preferable.

finished, for the time, with Carthage and could intervene more directly against her Macedonian *provocateur* in the Adriatic. From B.C. 199 a Roman expeditionary force tried the Illyrian passes into Macedon and finally in B.C. 197 forced its way into Thessaly, where on the field of Cynoscephalae Roman and Macedonian arms collided in pitched battle.[36] The Romans under Titus Quinctius Flamininus won out, and if Cynoscephalae was not yet the end of Macedon, it did give the Greeks their first close look at their future rulers from across the Adriatic.

Rome's terms to Philip were generous under the circumstances: to evacuate Greece and to curb his fleet. Philip had no choice but to accede, and at a Panhellenic gathering at Corinth for the Isthmian Games of B.C. 196 Flamininus magnanimously announced Rome's gift to the Hellenes, their final liberation from the yoke of Macedon. Two years later Rome withdrew her armies; for the first time since B.C. 338 the states and leagues of the mainland had to confront the promise of freedom and the now desperate prospect of governing themselves.

Academic Athens

From the moment that Philip II triumphed at Chaeronea down to the death of Demetrius II in B.C. 229 political life at Athens withered under the shadow of Macedon. The older party divisions of oligarchs, democrats and all the varieties between yielded to the simpler polarity of pro- or anti-Macedonian sentiment. There were garrisons in the ports of Athens during much of that time, or a Macedonian governor, and these alien bodies in the *polis* organism stifled genuine political activity. The oppressive Cassander ruled the city through his governor, Demetrius of Phalerum, and the more enlightened Gonatas too had his man in Athens for six years after the Chremonidean War or until he felt

---

36. It was not the first such encounter. In B.C. 280 Pyrrhus of Epirus, whose Greek fortunes were going badly—Lysimachus had just driven him from western Macedon—allowed himself to be persuaded that he could save the Greeks of southern Italy from Roman encroachments. He landed at Tarentum with a considerable army, and at nearby Heraclea the phalanx and the legion met for the first time. The subsequent Epirote victory was indeed "Pyrrhic"; it cost him four thousand irreplaceable front-line troops.

secure enough to withdraw his troops and govern his prize by remote control. His analysis at the time was correct; there was no further trouble from Athens, which preferred apathetic neutrality to political adventure.

The progressive paralysis of political action in Athens was not accompanied by either economic or intellectual decline. The Macedonian kings, and particularly Gonatas, treated the city liberally, and it is likely that Athens was a generally more prosperous place in the post-Alexander age than it had been in the mid-fourth century. It suffered, as did most of Greece, from the third century's increased tempo of war, but except for something like the Chremonidean conflict the close and protective grip that Macedon kept upon the city shielded it from the worst of the fighting.

In an earlier day Athens' propagandists could claim that the city was the "school of Greek culture." At the turn into the third century that statement was more literally true than when it was first uttered. There were still poets and dramatists at Athens—none the equal of the earlier giants—as well as the errant street Cynics spawned by Socrates. But from the time that Plato turned from that Socratic tradition and founded his Academy in B.C. 387, the intellectual life of the city, and through it the entire *oikoumene*, was dominated by the great schools of philosophy. It was their methods and interests, particularly Aristotle's Lyceum, that provided models for the new centers of Hellenism at Alexandria, Antioch, Pergamum and eventually Rome.

Some of the men working in the Lyceum at Aristotle's death in B.C. 322 went back to the old days with Plato, Heraclides of Pontus, for one, Aristotle's fellow student in the Academy who quit Athens in B.C. 338 when Xenocrates succeeded to the directorship of the school. Theophrastus, Aristotle's successor in the Lyceum, was another graduate of the Academy. Others were Aristotle's own students: Eudemus of Rhodes, Aristoxenus of Tarentum, and Dicaearchus of Messene. Finally, there were the younger men trained by Theophrastus: Cassander's future governor, Demetrius of Phalerum, Strato of Lampsacus, Duris and Chamaeleon.

In general these scholars remained faithful to the patterns of research set out by Aristotle: detailed, analytical studies based on as wide a sampling of material as possible, whether in politics, in literature or in botany, an interest in ethical questions and character typology, already noted in connection with the lives of Alexander and later to have an important influence on biography,[37] and the pursuit of historical antecedents.

The historical approach to the arts and sciences was a particularly strong tradition in the Lyceum. Eudemus is the first scholar we know of to have written a history of the sciences; Duris holds an analogous position in the history of art, and Chamaeleon in literary biography, the latter doubtless the source of much of the totally unhistorical and useless gossip we possess on ancient authors. On an even broader scale was Dicaearchus' *Life of Hellas*—or perhaps better, *The Life Style* [bios] *of Hellas*—a general cultural history.

Aristoxenus came to music from exactly the same direction. The Hellenic world's greatest theoretician of music was a native of Tarentum in the South Italian heartland of Pythagorean speculation. It is curious that he should have chosen to study with Aristotle rather than in the more mathematically inclined Platonic Academy. He was not, at any rate, a great admirer of Plato and frequently echoed Aristotle's charge that Plato had plagiarized the Pythagoreans. But Aristoxenus was the only member of Aristotle's school with more than a passing knowledge of mathematics, and if he had succeeded Aristotle as head, as apparently he expected to do, the course of the Lyceum would probably have been far different.

Aristoxenus was an exceedingly complex scholar. He was clearly a Pythagorean moralist of the old school and equally conservative in his musical tastes. In his view—the traditional one—music was an educational instrument, and so its modes should be restricted to the old-fashioned types calculated to instill the manly virtues. Yet at the same time he was enough of an Aristotelian empiricist to blame his Pythagorean predecessors for an a priori rather than an inductive approach to musical theory. Aristoxenus' preference for the latter course produced, in the image of Aristotle's work in politics, not only the work of general theory, the *Elements of Harmonics*, but historical surveys of the ground in his *History of Harmonics*, and supplementary studies of the careers of various poets and practicing musicians.

As might be expected, Aristoxenus stood with the naturalists

---

37. See Chapter XI, pp. 422–24.

like Dicaearchus and Strato in the Lyceum's controversy over the nature of the soul (*psyche*). After an earlier flirtation with a Platonic version of the human soul, which was an immortal and divine substance separate from the body, Aristotle later attempted to approach the nature of the soul through its functions, and these results were quite different. In his work *On the Soul* the *psyche* is defined as the "in-functioning" (*entelecheia*) of an organic body, a considerably more materialistic view than the one he put forward in his early dialogues. And yet Plato has not completely vanished, even in *On the Soul*. Aristotle was prepared to admit that one part of the soul, the intelligence (*nous*), is immaterial, immortal, and somehow separable from the body.

For the naturalists of the Lyceum this vestigial legacy of supernatural Platonism must have been an embarrassment, and Aristoxenus, among others, resisted it. For him the *psyche* was, as it had been for at least one branch of the older Pythagoreans, a harmony of the elements of the body.

The debate over a theological versus a naturalistic explanation of causes ranged far wider than the soul and must have been a considerable one in the Lyceum. Eudemus of Rhodes represented the former position in metaphysics, where he stood close to Aristotle, and in ethics, where he went beyond Aristotle's more or less naturalistic ethics to more profoundly theological orientations.[38] On the other side stood Dicaearchus and Aristoxenus, the side that eventually triumphed with Strato of Lampsacus. The middle ground in the debate was held by the "second founder" of the Lyceum, Theophrastus (B.C. 382–287), the prodigious scholar who more than any other reflected his contemporary and master, Aristotle.

Theophrastus probably began, as did Aristotle, as a student of Plato in the Academy. Aristotle withdrew from the Academy at Plato's death, and in the company of another disgruntled Platonist, Xenocrates, took up residence at Assos in Asia Minor. Later the two men, Aristotle and Theophrastus, came together on Theophrastus' native Lesbos and were both at Philip's court in Macedon.

---

38. The question of Eudemus' authorship (or editorship) of the so-called *Eudemian Ethics* is still a very much open one. In this case the argument that it was written by a young Aristotle still under the influence of a Platonic theology is somewhat vitiated by the fact that Eudemus returned to something approximating those same positions.

In B.C. 335 they returned to Athens, Aristotle after an absence of twelve years; and the following years were spent in teaching and writing in Aristotle's new school, the Lyceum. In B.C. 323 Alexander died, and the subsequent anti-Macedonian demonstrations at Athens forced Aristotle to migrate once again, this time to Euboea. Theophrastus remained behind to care for the affairs of the school; and when Aristotle died in the following year, Theophrastus took up the responsibility of guiding the Lyceum through the next three and a half decades, temporarily aided, to be sure, by the rise to political power of his student Demetrius of Phalerum. In the end he was immensely successful; under his stewardship no less than two thousand students passed through the Lyceum.

Theophrastus was a determined empiricist but an even more determined disciple. Where Aristotle had erected theory, Theophrastus left it largely untouched; where details remained to be filled in or new areas explored, there he devoted himself to the close and painstaking study of data that had become the hallmark of the Lyceum. His work on botany provides the classic example.

As in the case of Aristotle's parallel work on zoology, the botanical studies of Theophrastus were of two types, the largely descriptive *History of Plants* (probably also, as in Aristotle, the result of a great deal of cooperative research)[39] and the more theoretical and philosophical *Causes of Plants*. Where before there had been only information, and certainly not on this enormous scale, Theophrastus erected the science of botany, faithful in type, procedure and accuracy to the Aristotelian model.

The same indwelling of the Aristotelian spirit, now not in the natural sciences but in ethics, is visible in the *Characters*, thirty sketches of archetypal personalities drawn with acute brevity. Aristotle had already essayed some character typing in the *Ethics*, but the sketches of Theophrastus suggest even stronger affinities with the kind of "type casting" already prevalent in rhetorical studies (including Aristotle's) and the new style in Attic comedy typified by Menander.

While the main features of the massive Aristotelian synthesis

---

39. Some of it drawn from earlier pharmacopoeias, some the fruit of Alexander's expedition with its Peripatetic "observers," but the bulk done by Theophrastus and his considerable number of students.

of the *kosmos* and its scale of substances remained intact, Theophrastus was somewhat more than a gifted apprentice detailing the master artist's design. There were places in the system where teacher and disciple disagreed, nowhere so radically as Aristotle had departed from his own teacher, but on intriguing points nonetheless.

Theophrastus had genuine difficulties with the Aristotelian logic and, more significantly, with his celestial theology. He was unconvinced by the plurality of prime movers that Aristotle seemed to think necessary, by the way the heavenly bodies were moved, and in general by Aristotle's separation of the causality of the supralunary world from that here below. Indeed, he raised questions on the basic Aristotelian notion of teleology and the universality of its application. Nature does nothing in vain, Aristotle had maintained;[40] Theophrastus could raise in contradiction a whole catalogue of obviously natural vanities, like men's breasts.

It was by no means Theophrastus' aim to drive God from the universe; he abhorred atheism, and though he recognized Aristotle's unmoved First Mover as God in the absolute sense, he extended the divine purpose, somewhat in the manner of the Stoics, to the entire order of nature. His student and successor as director of the Lyceum from B.C. 287 to his death *c.* B.C. 270, Strato of Lampsacus, had fewer qualms in that direction. His explanation of the universe did very nicely without either God or teleology. Though he held that the world operated through natural causes, Strato was no mechanistic atomist who reduced everything to quantity and contact. For him the basic principles in the universe were corporeal forces (*dynameis*), a notion with venerable pre-Socratic antecedents that was to have an illustrious career in late antiquity.[41]

According to a later tradition it was Strato who turned the school from ethics to the physical sciences. Aristotle and Theophrastus were, of course, interested in both ethics and the sciences, and there were any number of later Peripatetics, Ariston of Ceos for one,[42] who were deeply committed to ethical studies. But the statement makes a great deal more sense if it is construed to mean that the directorship of Strato marked the triumph of

40. And Theophrastus echoes him, in the *Causes of Plants* at least.
41. See Chapter XI, pp. 434–35.
42. See Chapter XI, p. 424.

the naturalistic wing among the Peripatetics over those who, like Eudemus, preferred theological explanations. It may have been the salvation of the school. It was precisely the supernaturalism of later Platonism that forced its confrontation with and eventual capitulation to Christianity, while the Aristotelian tradition, remote, technical and scholarly, survived.

Stratonic naturalism was but one side of the tradition flowing from the Lyceum.[43] The same men who did such painstaking empirical work in the natural sciences devoted an almost equal part of their energies to more popular forms of literature. As has already been observed, the history of the arts and sciences was an important part of the research program in the school. Some of this work was purely historical—chronological precisions, lists of Olympic visitors, students and teachers, etcetera—but other facets of the same program were connected rather with Aristotle's attempts at placing the Socratic focus on the moral life of man (*bios*) in a scientific context.

Aristotle marked the beginning of an empirical ethics, the collection of a great deal of material with moral coloring from which one could generalize the *bios* of both individuals and larger social groups. Theophrastus' *Characters* was one such generalization of an individual typology, and the same author's cooperative work with Aristotle on the "manners and customs of the *barbaroi*" was a descriptive beginning of what might have been designed as a more general sociology.

There need not have been a scientific excuse for these collections. Aristotle and his student were doing no more than betraying the long-standing Greek curiosity about their neighbors, a curiosity shared, incidentally, by very few of those neighbors but which was and is one of the prime characteristics of the Hellenic spirit. Herodotus had given his readers elaborate and entertaining instruction on the non-Greek cultures of the Near East. Now, with Alexander's conquest, the extent and exactness of the information feeding into the Greek sources was enormously enhanced. Some of it was merely wonderful, exotic or bizarre. Some of it, too, was ethical and religious, cut to Peripatetic specifications or to provide grist for the rapidly turning mills of religious syncretism. But it was not all fantastic; Alexandrian tastes for chronology and geography were also satisfied.

---

43. For the impact of this materialistic tradition on the Academy, see Chapter IX, pp. 354–55.

The reportage of this lore was normally done by Greek travelers and historians. The Greeks continued to travel in ever-widening arcs, and the result of such restless voyaging in the new age was a work like the *Indica* of Megasthenes, an Ionian Greek who between B.C. 302 and B.C. 291 served as the envoy of Seleucus I to the Indian king Chandragupta. Megasthenes may have been a Peripatetic scientist; the *Indica*, at any rate, is an ethnology in the Aristotelian-Theophrastan style on the physical and human milieu in India, and it served as a major source on the subcontinent for subsequent historians, geographers and naturalists.

With the Hellenization of the non-Greeks, however, native informants could address the Greek readers directly. A Greek had given the Hellenistic age its first real glimpse of India, but the *Aegyptica* of Hecataeus was a frank piece of political and philosophical propaganda that sounded a theme heard more and more frequently in Hellenistic times: *ab oriente lux,* all culture and wisdom proceeded from the East, in this case Egypt. His contemporary Manetho—both men lived under the first two Ptolemies—was, on the other hand, a native Egyptian, a priest of Heliopolis, Hellenized, to be sure, and instrumental in the Ptolemaic campaign to win the Hellenic world to the cult of Serapis.[44] In his *Aegyptica* the material, though uncritically used, was at least authentic; Manetho could read and use the native records, and so supplied a chronology of Egyptian history which provided later Christian historians with a synchronized framework for Biblical and, so, world history.

Another native "converted" to Hellenism who served as a valuable informant on the new lands and old lore was Berossus, Marduk's priest[45] at Babylon under Antiochus I (B.C. 281–261). Here the information was more than chronological or historical. Berossus was an immediate contact, through one who knew, with the astrological schools of the "Chaldeans," and so one of the moving forces in that unmistakable change in Greek religious habits associated with the spread of astrology.[46]

---

44. See Chapter XII, pp. 471–72.

45. As priests both Manetho and Berossus obviously had access to archival and traditional material closed or unknown to others—e.g., merchants and soldiers. Herodotus had himself used priests as informants in Egypt.

46. See Chapter VI, pp. 235–36, and Chapter XI, pp. 436–40.

These were technical works of interest only to specialists. The empirical approach to ethics and its newly articulated medium, the literary *bios* which approached literary and historical personages through character analysis, found a far wider audience. The Peripatetic *bioi* were directed not at the philosopher or the *grammatikos* diligently conning his texts, but at the wider Hellenistic reading public. From Chamaeleon onward, however, the genre of literary biography unfortunately loses almost all contact with historical verisimilitude. The object was plainly to construct a "personality," and to this end and for the delectation of his audience the biographer plundered the older sources, and particularly comedy, for whatever anecdotes or gossip might prove useful.

The same evolution can be traced in the Lyceum's treatment of political figures. Across the stage of Hellenistic history marched a procession of extraordinary men, fortune's darlings or rejects, whose meteoric rise and equally rapid fall provided endless grounds for speculation on the vagaries of Lady Luck (*tyche*). Demetrius of Phalerum, whose own life was a paradigm for the reversal of fortune, was early into the field with a comprehensive treatment, *On Fortune.*

Other historians of the time were grounded in a different tradition. Theopompus, for instance, of the "school" of Isocrates, had already begun integrating ethical characterization and biographical sketches into his general histories;[47] but for the scholars of the Lyceum, whose ethical and moralizing interests suffocated disinterested political analysis, history provided a broad canvas upon which to trace the moral constitution of the age's great men.

Two early Peripatetics, Hieronymus of Rhodes and Duris of Samos turned their hand to history, and, insofar as their work can be reconstructed, it betrays both the strength and weakness of Peripatetic historiography: a catholic view of history which embraced social and ethnographic investigation, accompanied by a vulgarization of tone and style.

Duris, who was Theophrastus' student at Athens and then became, sometime after B.C. 301, ruler of the island of Samos, is

---

47. As had Aristotle himself in his *Athenian Constitution.* The normal distinction between the two genres was that *historia* dealt with the deeds (*praxeis*) of men, while the *bios* concerned itself with the character (*ethos, arete*) of the individual.

an almost perfect examplification of the Peripatetic interest in history. He wrote a general history of the Greek world from Leuctra to Corupedion, a local history of Samos, some Peripatetic-style biographies (probably including one of his ancestor Alcibiades), and studies in ethnography, literary criticism and the history of art.

Art history in antiquity was a composite and complex affair. From the fifth century various Greek artists, tragedians, painters, sculptors and architects had attempted to give literary expression to the technical side of their art. Some of these manuals had to do with materials and processes, others concentrated on the theoretical—that is, the mathematical—basis of the arts. The Lyceum's research into ethical biography added a new dimension, so that next to *The Craft of the Painter* and *On Perspective in Painting* there now appeared *Lives of Painters*, *bioi* concerned with character and personality and little interested in deeds; the whole series is visible in Aristoxenus' bibliography. What the earlier scholar had done for music, Duris then did for painting and sculpture.

The final ingredient in ancient art history is another creation of the Hellenistic age, purely descriptive works on the art and architecture to be found at various sites in the Mediterranean world. The genre to which they belong is really an adjunct to geography; the *periegesis*, or "circuit," as it was called, is a description of a trip by land or sea through a certain area, with a fairly detailed inventory of the historical and artistic monuments located there.[48] The best known of the antiquarian guidebooks is the *periegesis* of Greece written by Pausanias under the later Antonines, but it had eminent Hellenistic forebears: the *Guide to Alexandria* of Callixenus of Rhodes from about B.C. 200 and the slightly later researches of one of the era's most distinguished antiquarians, Polemo of Ilium,[49] who wrote guides to the Acro-

---

48. Related in form but different in intent is the "pictures at an exhibition" exercise much favored in the rhetorical schools, particularly during the Second Sophistic. The exercises were highly imaginative and designed to illustrate the verbal powers of the student, not his ability to report what he had actually seen. A number of such have been preserved, notably the *Pictures* by one or another of the famous Philostratus family (see Chapter XV, p. 547).
49. Polemo's home town was already a kind of Hellenistic Williamsburg, but the full-scale restoration had to await the expansive and expensive Hellenic piety of Hadrian. Ilium had a special attraction for

polis, the treasure houses at Delphi, Dodona, Samothrace and, of course, his native Troad.

The vulgarization of history by the descendants of Aristotle had its roots in two increasingly coincident attitudes. The first has already been touched upon, the feeling that moral characterization was important to both the historian and the biographer. To this end biographers worked hard at creating full-bodied, interesting portraits that "lived" in the same sense that a character on the contemporary stage was alive. What resulted from their labors most frequently has been far closer to somewhat tendentious historical novels than to any recognizable history. The scurrilous and titillating were painted in broad strokes; the merely true was not enough.

The other attitude was stylistic and was related to the evolution of rhetoric. As Cicero later read the history of public speaking, the staple of the old school, of Demosthenes for instance, was a political oratory whose simple but powerful style was akin to concerned conversation. With the decline of political autonomy the existential quality of the old speechifying disappeared and was replaced by a kind of school oratory which was softer and more graceful in expression and whose object was to please rather than to move to political action. In Cicero's eyes the change was associated with Theophrastus' student Demetrius of Phalerum.

The enervation of rhetorical vigor was to lead directly to the florid and baroque style known as Asianism,[50] but it had its effects in historiography as well. The graces of Demetrius were reproduced in history by Hieronymus and Duris, and Duris for one found the Isocratean tradition in history a little too stiff for his liking, neglecting as it did both lifelike characterization (*mimesis*) and the motive of pleasure (*hedone*).

The Peripatetic biographical style quickly made inroads at Alexandria. The Library had provided a seedbed of scholarly

---

the Romans, who fancied themselves as descendants of the Trojans, even though no one was quite sure where Troy had been. Demetrius of Scepsis, an impressive Trojanophile (he wrote a five-volume commentary on the muster of the Trojan army which occupies all of sixty-three lines in *Iliad* II) of the generation after Polemo, held for the modern Bunarbashi; others were equally convinced that the original site was to be located at Hissarlik, as indeed it was.

50. See Chapter XV, pp. 539–40.

endeavor there, and the tradition of exact biographical investigation, as exemplified in the *pinakes* of Callimachus,[51] was now cross-fertilized by the more florid strains of Peripatetic biography. Callimachus' student, Hermippus of Smyrna (*c.* B.C. 200), is described in the sources as a Peripatetic. In his approach to biography he proved to be a rather decadent example of the tradition. He attached to his teacher's sparse catalogues biographies that were models of maladroit fiction[52] but became part, nonetheless, of the schoolbooks of the era.

Alexandrian scholarship eventually survived this crisis of method and attitude. It had its own recuperative resources that enabled it to resist the tendentious fancies of biography. There was particularly the Alexandrian commitment to accurate philology and the historical awareness of the when and where of events; at Alexandria chronology was taken seriously. From the middle of the fourth century various Greek states had been putting their archives in order, and Aristotle too had insisted on the compilation of accurate lists of such chronological indices as archons and Olympic victors, so that by the time Eratosthenes succeeded Apollonius of Rhodes as Chief Librarian at Alexandria (*c.* B.C. 246) enough material was at hand to make possible a systematic attempt at a more comprehensive chronology.

The *Chronographies* of Eratosthenes was the beginning of a new learned science. The Spartan king lists and the Olympic records were marshaled into a continuous structure. Greek literary history was provided with a fully articulated chronological scale against which its data could be studied and measured. The system of Eratosthenes was subsequently expanded and improved by Apollodorus of Athens, a student of Aristarchus of Samothrace, who wrote his own *Chronics* sometime about the middle of the second century. Apollodorus' scheme covered the ground from the Trojan War to B.C. 144 and included political, literary and philosophical history, traced not now against the scale of Olympiads but the succession of Athenian archons.[53]

---

51. See Chapter V, p. 194.

52. He was to all purposes the inventor of the death-bed scene, which became almost mandatory in the *bioi* of philosophers.

53. Another innovation of Apollodorus was his notion that a known date in a man's life could be presumed to have occurred at his "flourishing point," or acme (*akme*)—i.e., the fortieth, or middle, year of his life span. It was neither chance nor the salubrious climate that caused so many ancient authors to have apparently lived until eighty!

The desire for precision implicit in the work of Eratosthenes and Apollodorus enabled Alexandrian scholarship to recapture, at least to a degree, the lives of the poets and philosophers from the general reading public. The style became tighter and flatter; the material was scrutinized somewhat more critically. But the Peripatetic ethical coloring never quite disappeared. The *bioi* composed by Diogenes Laertius and Plutarch betray, each in their own way, the triumphs and failings of the later Lyceum's excursion into biography.

In the last years of its brilliance Athens harvested a great crop of men learned in philosophy and the sciences. Very few of them were native-born. Most were attracted from other Greek *poleis*—the Hellenization of the Near East had just begun; that of Italy was still in the future—trained in the academies of Athens and either stayed on there to earn their living as teachers or else migrated to the new centers of learning or patronage in Macedon or the East. The last major figure of her own that Athens gave to the new age was Menander.

Menander (B.C. 343-292) was a celebrity in an era of celebrities. He was on familiar terms with Epicurus, Theophrastus, Athens' governor Demetrius of Phalerum, and was well enough known in international circles that Ptolemy I invited him to grace his clutch of imported luminaries at Alexandria. Menander declined the invitation and continued to write and present comedies at the Athenian festivals, over a hundred in all. On only eight occasions was he awarded the first prize.

Cicero's comment on the not altogether ungraceful descent of Greek oratory between Demosthenes and Demetrius will be recalled. Speechmaking had lost its political reality and compensated with refinement. Attic comedy of the days of Aristophanes was, like the oratory of Demosthenes, a form of political communication. Even during the latter years of Aristophanes that had ceased to be true, and by the time of Menander politics was an alien ingredient in comedy. The New Comedian wrote with ease and elegance; the turns of phrase were facile and eminently quotable, but they proceeded from a *corpus* that was all but dead.

In antiquity Menander was frequently praised for his realism, and his characters do bear a strong resemblance to the types that walked the streets of Athens at the end of the fourth century. Indeed they *are* those types, detailed with the archetypal features that graced his friend Theophrastus' *Characters*. Both the *Characters* and their analogues in the comedies of Menander are faultlessly lifelike, but they are not alive.

Menander was popular with a Hellenistic readership that was cut off from political comment and solaced itself with situation comedy played by the familiar types of middle-class life in Athens, soldiers, slaves, courtesans, and ingénues. The plots are complex, if highly predictable; the action is amorous, though never erotic. New Comedy is Euripides vulgarized, without the saving grandeur of the myths or the excitement of the pathology, closer to life and yet far more remote. Style had not yet deserted the Athenian spirit, but it was increasingly a style without artistic substance.

Menander died in B.C. 292 and by that date Athens had already begun her decline from a political power to a university town. The failure of her statesmen and armies, however, masks a profound intellectual, if not artistic, vitality. Menander's comedies catch reflections of the life of a prosperous but politically inane bourgeoisie in the Athens that had to reckon with Antipater, Cassander, Antigonus, and Demetrius Poliorcetes. One can perhaps read between his lines the failing morale of political impotence, but there is no hint there of the intellectual energies that were at work in the Lyceum or of the serious moral issues being debated in the Stoa and the school of Epicurus. The moral and intellectual fiber of the new post-Alexander world was being woven at Athens during the half century after Aristotle's death. Menander was aware of it—he was a student of Theophrastus— but neither the new learning nor the new morality had any place in his art.

III

The Fearless Universe

The version of the history of philosophy fashioned by the academicians of late antiquity did scant justice to the extraordinary variety in the modes of philosophizing current in Hellenism. It threw into the background, for example, the Cynic progeny of Socrates the street philosopher by emphasizing Plato, the disciple of Socrates the dialectician.[1] The academicians identified Pythagoras as one of their own, while history continued to resuscitate Pythagoras the *Wundermann* and political reformer. The school tradition overlooked the continuing tension between popular and technical instruction, discourse by dialogue and by treatise, private and social ethics, and the variants in philosophical postures that were still possible at the time of Socrates and even beyond.

It is, of course, true that the political events of the latter half of the fourth century reduced the options open to a philosopher. The premise of an open political discussion in a free society was only precariously operative after B.C. 338, and Plato's even earlier withdrawal from the *polis* life at Athens pointed the prudent course to philosophy. Chaeronea had effects on the substance of discourse as well. Philosophers were forced, for instance, to re-think their presumption that personal ethics was subordinate to the master science of politics. The Hellenistic age brought into sharp focus the plight of the individual shorn of the customary network of political, social, economic and religious relationships that constituted him a *polites* in the fifth-century sense of the word. In fashioning a suitable goal for the good life the philosopher of that new age had to operate without the conventional starting point of the *polis*.

1. See Chapter XI, pp. 410–13.

Two widely divergent methods of procedure were open to philosophy in the last decades of the fourth century: the informal, anarchic and almost anti-intellectual way of the Cynics, and the scholastic, learned and technical way of the Peripatetics. The Stoics, for all their Cynic touches, followed the latter course. Epicurus attempted something quite bolder, to provide a viable alternative to the other, unacceptable two.

Epicurus: The Hedonist as Hero

The biography of Epicurus (B.C. 341–271) presents violent contradictions. He is portrayed as the scornful vilifier of his philosophical contemporaries and predecessors, and at the same time as a gentle philanthropist, the beloved and revered center of a circle of friends and disciples. Temperamentally he was doubtless the latter, but for the philosopher there was a crucial issue at stake, an issue to which Epicurus addressed himself with the weapons of rhetoric. And if the case against the philosophical tradition seems overstated, it is probably because the truth was somewhat otherwise than Epicurus' shouted protestations would have had it.

In the mid-fifth century Socrates had felt that his physicist predecessors were on the wrong scent and quietly dismissed them, if not from his thoughts, at least from his public considerations. By the time Epicurus set up his "school" in Athens in B.C. 307,[2] the irregular and loosely realized philosophy dismissed by Socrates had become, at the hands of Plato, Aristotle, Speusippus, Xenocrates, and Theophrastus, an organized and established tradition that could be ignored only by taking to the streets in Cynics' rags. Cynicism was not Epicurus' style. By training at least, he belonged with the academics. His father was a schoolmaster of Samos and he appears to have studied philosophy at Athens and elsewhere in the traditional manner, though with some apparently untraditional interests.

The insistence at a somewhat later date that Socrates was the founder of "modern" philosophy has had the rather unfortunate effect of closing off the "pre-Socratics" as an antediluvian stage in

---

2. The association of master and disciples was by then five years old but had been located at Colophon, Lampsacus and Mitylene.

the history of philosophy and of lumping in their number Socrates' own contemporary Democritus. The works of Plato and particularly of Aristotle do not easily lend themselves to that reading of history; it is clear enough that even Socrates' immediate successor picked up the threads of Parmenides, Empedocles and Anaxagoras that Socrates had disdained, and that Aristotle was deeply interested in the atomism of Democritus.

It is not, then, totally incomprehensible that there was still a healthy "pre-Socratic" tradition in the Greek cities in the generation after Aristotle. Through one of its representatives, Nausiphanes of Teos, Epicurus was carried more deeply into the works of Democritus. What direction the teaching of Nausiphanes took we do not know. Democritus' own work is today reduced to fragments, but what is left suggests interests more complex than the mere arrangements of atoms. Certainly the two men shared a belief in physical atomism, but how much more what appears peculiarly Epicurean was, in fact, inspired by Democritus can only be surmised.

Epicurus took some pains to insist on his own originality. He rejected in strong language the parentage not only of Nausiphanes but also of Democritus, of Leucippus, and indeed of the whole of the philosophical tradition that had come before him. The harsh words seem to betray some kind of personal pique, but there is other evidence that this disassociation from the philosophical past was somewhat more pragmatic than personal and was directed rather at the burgeoning scholasticism of philosophy. For Epicurus philosophy was the child of neither rhetoric nor dialectic but was simply a direct and common-sense approach to the problem of leading the good life.

There is a good deal of the Socratic in that attitude, but if Epicurus was a latter-day Socrates, he was a Socrates torn from the context of the *polis*. The philosophy of Epicurus was to a degree the philosophy of common sense, but it was no longer public. The two men shared the same moral earnestness, but in the case of Socrates it was exhibited on the streets of Athens; Epicurus withdrew to the company of his friends and disciples. Socrates' method was dialectical; Epicurus eschewed dialectic and preferred to express himself in clear and commonplace assertions, without resort to irony or paradox.

The disciples and successors of Epicurus preserved the memory of his charismatic leadership. The birthday of the Founder was celebrated and his portrait prominently displayed. The Epicurean "school" held to its original quality as a conventicle of disciples joined in quiet seclusion and remote from both the cosmopolitan social consciousness of the Stoa and the academic and technical interests of the Lyceum.

Epicurus did not withdraw from his immediate political environment to retreat into metaphysics or mathematics. His ethical concern was serious and deeply felt, but it was addressed to the isolated figure of the individual rather than the ills of society. If Socrates found the ideal of the good life inconceivable apart from the *polis*, Epicurus wasted little thought on the Athens of Demetrius Poliorcetes. The contemporary *polis* supplied neither an end nor a point of departure for human activity and so the disenchanted but pragmatic philosopher of the new era turned within, to an analysis of behavior, for his moral guidelines.

Epicureanism was not, for all that, a fresh start dispassionately begun. It took up and accepted the premises of the atomist tradition of Democritus, and it was shaped by its moral indignation at the present, its own and Athens'. Epicurus' mother was a religious quack, who eked out a living by hawking charms and spells, and her young son was called upon to accompany her. The acolyte of the past was to turn into the religious cynic of the future, but the adult Epicurus had the witness of his own eyes to the degeneration of religion. Demetrius' "liberation" of Athens in B.C. 307 was greeted by the inhabitants with a burst of exaggerated religious fervor that bordered on travesty; during his own days in Athens Epicurus saw Demetrius' mistress installed in the Parthenon as Aphrodite.[3]

The experiences of youth and maturity left their mark, and Epicurus dedicated himself to dismantling this dangerous façade of religious superstition, not merely by attacking it with the weapons of science, history and sarcasm, but also by attempting to construct in its place a thoroughly naturalistic view of the world and its workings, an edifice sans metaphysics and sans mysteries, but resting instead on a common-sense view of phenomenological reality. Atomism, perhaps already a somewhat old-fashioned scientific theory, supplied him with the materials for

3. See Chapter XII, p. 467.

such a construct, and Epicurus expropriated them, not because he was a traditionalist Democritean—he left no doubt of that—but because they suited his ethical purposes.

His criticism of contemporary values thrust Epicurus toward Athens' Cynics and know-nothing skeptics, but his own constructive theory anchored him equally firmly in the scholastic tradition he so vehemently denied. He was a careful reader of Aristotle[4] and had earlier studied with a Platonist. His own literary work was extensive, and even though the tiny preserved fraction of it is not in the form of school treatises,[5] it is nonetheless a collection of closely reasoned documents and by no means free of the technical jargon of the schools. There was only one style of Greek philosophical rationalism and Epicurus was caught up in it.

True to his antischolastic principles, Epicurus disparaged logic and concentrated instead on setting forth a solid epistemology upon which his physics and his ethics could rest. Put in its briefest form, it held that the clarity of our sensations is the sole criterion of truth, and that the affective states that follow upon each of them are the sole criteria of good: if the state is pleasurable, the experience is good; if it is painful, the experience is evil.

In Epicureanism all knowledge is sensation and all sensation is reduced to one form or other of physical contact. Both the premise and the conclusion here is that there is one grade of

---

4. Certainly of the *exoterica* and very probably of the school treatises, notably the *Nicomachean Ethics*, as well. On this distinction of the works of Aristotle, see Chapter IX, p. 364, note 19.
5. Chiefly three letters and a doxography entitled *Principal Opinions* preserved in Diogenes Laertius. The rest of ancient Epicureanism must be reconstructed out of the curious philosophical advertisement set up in billboard fashion in his native Lycia by Diogenes of Oenoanda and from the fragmentary remains of the first-century Epicurean Philodemus of Gadara in Syria. At the end of the second century Epicureanism was part of the flourishing philosophical scene at Rome. On the testimony of Cicero, Zeno of Sidon, Phaedrus and Philodemus all lectured there. A number of converts were made, notably Lucretius (*c*. B.C. 90–55) whose epic *On the Nature of the Universe* is the chief monument of at least the physical theory of Latin Epicureanism. The first book of Cicero's *On the Nature of the Gods* consists of a résumé of Epicurean theology and is probably derived from either Phaedrus or Philodemus.

being, matter, and so the formal distinctions elaborated by earlier philosophers between matter and spirit, body and soul, sensation and intellection are meaningless. All is mass, movement, collision and dislocation, the latter indifferently knowledge or feeling.

What appear to us to be "bodies" are in reality conglomerates of the only true bodies, the ultimate, indivisible (*atoma*) particles of matter that come together quite fortuitously in various combinations and various densities. In some instances they cling together quite tenaciously,[6] in others the individual particles do not even touch; their unity consists in a subtle integration of movement as if they were all dancing to the same tune. Man's "body" is an example of the first type of cohesion; what has been called his "soul" is nothing more than the latter—the finer and more mobile atoms within the grosser conglomerate vibrating in unison to their own peculiar rhythm.

Each conglomerate is constantly casting off images (*eidola*) of itself, and when these impinge on another body they cause a dislocation of the atomic structure of the recipient. That dislocation is in a sense the communication of information which on its cognitive level is sensation (*aisthesis*) and on its affective level is feeling (*pathos*). The cognitive dislocation differs only in degree ranging from the crude blow to the midriff, through the impressions on the sense organs whose atomic organization is such that they can "read" the information more discriminately, to the most subtle type of dislocation that leaves even the relatively refined sense organs unaffected and causes a dislocation so fine that it is detected only in the "soul."

The *aisthesis*, or sense perception, is the primary form of cognition for Epicurus, but there is another related to it. By repeated exposure to similar *eidola* we begin to form on our inner sensibility a more generalized impression, which Epicurus calls an "anticipation" (*prolepsis*) and which serves in different contexts as a kind of residual universal of predication, a standard for the identification of subsequent impressions, and a paradigm for production.

There is, then, a perfect correlation in the system between what exists, what strikes one, and the reading of that contact:

---

6. The *atoma* are not all of the same size, shape or weight, and their irregularity contributes to their adhesion, as do their "hooked" edges.

epistemological and ontological truth are identical. If I know it, it is, and it is in the way that I know it.

A difficulty arises almost immediately. What of these *atoma?* Man has no direct perception of these indivisible particles of matter that are the building blocks of the higher conglomerates. Epicurus explained that though knowledge necessarily begins with the perceptible, perception does not mark its limits. Things perceptible also function as "signs" of another class of beings, the imperceptible (*adela*) that the mind reaches by the reflective process called reasoning (*logismos*). The behavior of perceptible bodies points to the existence of things imperceptible like atoms and the void that the mind grasps by inferential reflection. Consider the parallel question of error. In reasoning the mind uncovers imperceptible information that is implicitly contained in what we "read." Error arises when opinion (*doxa*) creates information that is neither perceptible nor implicated in perception.

Truth, then, is in the senses, and the senses tell us that the universe is a world of bodies governed by the laws that pertain to bodies, that is, physics. Epicurus admitted ignorance into the universe, but not mystery; there is no "other," the heart of every mystery; there is only "this." Rocks and men, animals, gods and planets are nothing more or less than bodies, differently organized perhaps, but all subject to the same laws of a mechanistic physics.

In antiquity Epicurus was accused of being an atheist without the courage of his convictions. Perhaps so; the force of tradition and sentiment may have prevented him from doing away with the gods entirely. But he was, on the other hand, faithful to his own logic. The gods are perceived, therefore they are. They are perceived in the dreams and visions that the Greeks and all other primitive peoples understood as direct communication from the supernatural. Since the *eidola* of the gods, too subtle to affect the cruder sense organs, do drift into man's consciousness, it must follow that the reality behind the *eidola* exists; the system will allow no other conclusion. Further Epicurus will not go. To his contemporaries the scandal of his position was that he denied to the gods the function popularly associated with them since the time of Homer and crucial to philosophy since Empedocles and Anaxagoras, the governance of the universe.

The break with tradition was complete and irreversible. The gods, their existence guaranteed by the fact that men perceived their *eidola*, were banished to a pleasant but meaningless existence in the *intermundia*, the space between the worlds, where they were not exposed to the elements and so enjoyed a *de facto* if not an essential immortality. The universe meanwhile pursued its own course, subject not to the will of the inefficacious Epicurean gods but to the laws of physics.[7]

His contemporaries, and particularly the Stoics, were exercised by the obvious impiety of this position, and only somewhat less so by Epicurus' ethics. His correlation of epistemology and morality has already been noted: if the atomic dislocation that follows upon physical contact transmits information, the result is perception; if the dislocation transmits value, then the result is an affect (*pathos*). But unlike the case of the *aistheseis*, where a false perception is a contradiction in terms, there are both good and bad *pathe*, and here Epicurus is forced to desert the mechanistic simplicities of his theory of cognition to face the realities of moral choice: those *pathe* are good that are accompanied by pleasure (*hedone*); the evil are attended by pain (*ponos*).

Epicurus was not the first Greek to adopt a hedonistic ethic. There was speculation on hedonism in the intellectual circles contemporary with Socrates. Plato too had measured the possibilities in his *Philebus*, and at least one eminent Academic, Eudoxus, offered pleasure as the highest good for the simple but persuasive reason that all men as a matter of fact pursue it. Another of Plato's contemporaries, Aristippus the Cyrenaic, had a more sophisticated proof that Epicurus found attractive: pleasure is the highest good because men pursue it *instinctively*.

Epicurus borrowed Aristippus' argument from instinctive behavior, but he had read enough of the *Nicomachean Ethics* to realize that Aristippus' pleasure-of-the-moment theory was naïvely untenable. Epicurus agreed with Aristotle that the end of life was happiness and that one swallow does not make a summer. Ecstasy, though pleasant, was not happiness, but the pleasurable life was a happy one. Even though the logic of his materialism

---

7. But to a physics of a very special kind. The mechanistic quality of the Epicurean universe, though it suited Epicurus' ethical aims, was the logical outgrowth of the static, geometricized physics favored by Pythagoras, Democritus and Plato. Aristotle returned to the vitalist tradition of a physics of qualities and powers (*dynameis*), which provided a quite different model of the universe. On the subsequent career of this dynamic physics see Chapter XI, pp. 436–38.

demanded the reduction of pleasure to physical pleasure,[8] the nature of happiness made desirable the choice of long-term pleasures over more immediate ones. Aristippus' theory allowed for no such distinction, and so Epicurus offered his own analysis of the nature of pleasure.

The classical analysis of pleasure derived from medical theory and rested upon the notion of the balance of elements in an organism. Pain followed when one of the constituents of an organism lapsed into deficiency. The imbalance triggered a desire for redress, and the resulting "filling up" of the deficiency was the source of pleasure. Both Aristippus and Epicurus accepted this analysis of pleasure as the kinetic "filling up" of a deficiency. Epicurus recognized, however, that there was an additional and higher "catastatic" pleasure that followed from the equilibrium of forces or elements in an organism. Pleasure, then, was the equilibrium of painlessness of the body and of unperturbedness (*ataraxia*) of the soul.

The throwing back of pleasure to the mind broke with Aristippus' crude, momentary pleasures of the now by involving in Epicurus' calculus the memory of past pleasures and the anticipation of future ones. In this way Aristotle's requirements of happiness extended over a lifetime could be fulfilled even within a hedonistic ethic. But no one seemed to be much impressed by such subtleties of analysis; the Epicureans were relentlessly branded as hedonists of the flesh, godless men who worshiped their stomachs. Epicurus was, as a matter of fact, a genial but abstemious man, and his followers were considerably tamer than some of their contemporaries. If the egocentricity of their theory was appalling, the manner of their life was certainly not.

The egocentricity of Epicureanism was perhaps the root issue under the rhetoric and vilification. As no other philosopher had done, Epicurus made man his own measure, subject to no will other than his own, bound into a system of physical necessity, but at bottom free to pursue self-dictated goals of conduct.[9] In

---

8. Epicurus' admission that pleasure, being at root physical, can vary only in quantity appears to be another somewhat unhappy example of following premises to their conclusion, but his reduction of all physical pleasure to that of the stomach betrays the psychologist at work.

9. Epicurus recognized that the price that would have to be paid for a mechanistic universe was nothing less than the freedom of the human

Epicurus' eyes the other-directed life was symbolized by religion and its works. Religion was rooted in fear, fear of death, and to save himself from that fear man threw himself on the gods and gave vent to his anxieties in the name of religion.

Without the fear of death the temples would be deserted, and Epicurus did his best to liberate men from that fear. The afterlife was a mirage; no spiritual entity lingered on after death to suffer torments or to peer back across the grave with grief and nostalgia. The laws of nature cried out that death was simply the end. Happiness was to be achieved in life, and, despite the taunts of his opponents, Epicurus did not suggest that it was to be found in indulgence. His hedonism was as calculated and as reasoned as anything that emerged from the Stoa or the Academy.

To the controversialists, first Stoic and then Christian, Epicurus was a pig; to his disciples he was a Promethean hero. At the opening of his poetical Epicurean manifesto, *On the Nature of the Universe*, Lucretius described in awesome tones the deeds of the Founder. The world lay crushed by religion. Then came this Greek man who was the first who dared break through her embrace to course out beyond the flaming battlements of the universe and bring back to man the truth about the limits and powers of nature. Because of the intellectual bravery of Epicurus, religion was cast down and man raised to glorious victory.

Not many other Romans rallied to the cause at Lucretius' side. The essentially private character of the Epicurean sage could not compete with the Stoic preachment of One World and One God, particularly when later theoreticians devised a proper Roman climax: and One Empire. And if the Greeks were rather offhand about the role of religion in their state, the Romans knew well enough the intimate connection between their own highly institutionalized religion and the *res publica*. Epicureanism languished and eventually died in the Roman *oikoumene*.

---

will, a value he was not about to sell for a mess of atoms. To preserve this freedom, the basis of all moral responsibility, Epicurus introduced a fortuitous element at the beginning of the system. The regular primordial rain of the atoms through the void was first disturbed by an unexplained swerve (*parenklisis*) that started the atomic collisions and combinations and at the same time broke the links of physical necessity to the degree that would allow the appearance, at a later point, of human freedom from that same necessity.

The Organic Kosmos

By all appearances Stoicism came from the same Athenian environment that produced Epicurean hedonism. The immediate surroundings were the same—academic Athens was a society of modest proportions—but the paths that led the two men there were different. For all his protestations, Epicurus grew almost directly from the Athenian school tradition; the substance of his physical system derived, without any great innovations, from older atomistic sources, and even his hedonism had scholastic antecedents. What drew men to Epicurus was, however, the personal magnetism of the man and the deep coloration that his own unhappy religious experiences cast upon an otherwise pedestrian atomism. Democritus had taught essentially the same propositions without either the ethical conviction or the moral sensibility of Epicurus and produced only students; Epicurus created a generation of disciples and after them other generations who still cherished the memory of the Founder.

Zeno, the Hellenized Cypriote of Phoenician stock, came to Athens sometime about B.C. 310, a few years before Epicurus opened his school, as his father's sales representative. The young commercial traveler—he was twenty-two—was "converted" to philosophy by a chance reading of Xenophon's *Memoirs* with its moving portrait of Socrates as a moral teacher. That Socrates, far different from the earnest dialectician of most of the Platonic dialogues, was still spiritually alive in the Athens of B.C. 310, not in the Academy or in the Lyceum, but in the person of the Cynic Crates of Thebes.[10] So Zeno judged, and though he later attended lectures in the Academy and read in the traditional literature of the schools, the Socratic and Cynic note of a serious concern for the practice of virtue never deserted the school that he founded.[11]

His school came into existence about B.C. 300, a century after the death of Socrates, and even in its founding there was something Socratic: barred by his alien status from enjoying the villa-

---

10. Whom Zeno honored, as Xenophon had Socrates, in his own *Recollection of Crates*.

11. On the later academic debate on who were Zeno's teachers, see Chapter IX, p. 352.

style arrangement that served both the Academy and the Lyceum (again, it is typical that Epicurus held forth in his house, "The Garden"), Zeno was thrust out on the streets where Socrates had talked and where the Cynics still held forth. The city gave him some space in the public Painted Colonnade (*Stoa Poikile*), and there Zeno taught his severe but attractive morality.

Under its first two leaders, the founder Zeno, who led the discussion down to the time of his death in B.C. 264, and his successor, the pious and plodding ex-boxer, Cleanthes, the Stoa (as the school came to be called) was notable for the free-wheeling and often acrimonious debate that went on there; the hallowed aura of reverence that surrounded Epicurus was totally absent. And yet Zeno was personally popular and appreciated in his adopted city. At his death a grateful Athens built him a funerary monument at public expense.

When Chrysippus, another non-Greek from Soli in Cilicia, became director of the school (B.C. 232), the times had changed. The school was then dominated by easterners, some, like Diogenes, from as far away as Babylonia. And in the place of Cleanthes stood a man who brought to the Stoa the rapier skills of the greatest dialectician of his day. Chrysippus had need of such skills. During the years when he was head of the school, down to his death in B.C. 204, the Stoa had to face constant attack from a highly skeptical Academy. Out of Chrysippus' clashes with Arcesilaus and Carneades came a new Stoa, stronger in ideology and argument than it was under Zeno, and more rationalistic as well. Competition with the "schools," from which the Stoa had differed from the outset, converted Stoicism into a full-blown academic enterprise. It was by then scattered over the *oikoumene* as well, with important centers in Pergamum and Rhodes, and later at Rome.

Most of what is known of the early Stoa of Zeno, Cleanthes and Chrysippus at Athens derives from the later ecumenical phase of the school under the Roman Empire. By then the original issues had become heavily overgrown with polemic and revisions, and it is neither simple nor always convincing to reconstruct the debates at the beginning of the third century from material three or four hundred years later. The beginnings of the school must be put together from fragments painfully gleaned from the Stoa's adherents and opponents from Cicero (d. B.C. 43) to Seneca (d. A.D. 65), Plutarch (d. *c*. A.D. 125) and beyond. These later writers provide, however, little context in which to locate the fragments; that must be supplied from Zeno's immediate predecessors.

A philosopher taking up his work in Athens at the turn of the fourth century stood upon freshly cleared ground. An immense problem had been lifted from the philosophical tradition, and both Zeno and Epicurus were free to explore something that had been forbidden for almost two centuries, a physics and an ethics unaccompanied by metaphysics. Philosophers of their generation witnessed a momentous event, the death, albeit a temporary one, of the influence of Parmenides.

From his own day until that of Plato and Aristotle, Parmenides (*c.* B.C. 480) gave shape if not substance to the problems that faced the Greek thinkers. Others before him had expressed doubts about the validity of the kind of sense knowledge that lay at the foundation of most speculation about natural forces and the constitution of the universe. With Parmenides that doubt became radical and, in the face of the full stop to which he had come, he constructed a system of rationally deduced being which owed nothing to the senses and everything to the higher faculty of intellect. Parmenides thought it methodologically impossible to deal with sensible things and their effects, and so motion, change, time and the notion of corporeality itself were all but banished from his construct of reality.

Parmenides' version of "reality" was severe in its intent and its method of logical exclusion. The doubts raised by its creator caused everyone who followed gradually to abandon the earlier view of a *kosmos* pulsating with life and change. Plato's hypothesis of an immutable and transcendental reality was, to a large extent, his solution to Parmenides' problem, and the sole Socratic legacy in the Platonic metaphysic is the fact that some of those transcendental beings, the Forms (*eide*), have an ethical content.

Within the course of his own career Plato seems to have grown dissatisfied with his Parmenidean-style solution to the problem of being, and in his *Timaeus* he descended from the metaphysical heights back in the direction of our own material and philosophically unmanageable world. Even then Aristotle may have been leading the way for his teacher in the Academy, and once he had been released from his discipleship by Plato's death in B.C. 348, the younger man gave fuller reign to his own empirical and naturalistic bent. Aristotle thrust the transcendental *eide* back into material beings as immanent structures of organic fulfillment and intelligibility, and then went on to resurrect the old problems of motion, change and becoming that Parmenides had stifled. "Nature" (*physis*) once again made its respectable appearance as an internal principle of growth, and the activities of substances were explained in terms of their equally internalized "powers" (*dynameis*).

Aristotle never completely shook his Platonic and Parmenidean legacy. His thought still had room for a transcendental God who was linked in its activity with the system's only other transcendental being, the human intellect (*nous*). Aristotle defined, described and analyzed the human soul in terms of its functioning in a natural relationship with the body. To do so was to deny the Platonic soul, and yet at least part of Aristotle's version of soul, the *nous*, continued to exude, as has been seen, a Platonic aura: it was immortal, impassible, and separable from the body. There was a great deal of awkwardness about this in terms of Aristotle's naturalism, but the awkwardness did not long survive him. At about the time that Plato's successors in the Academy were unceremoniously dropping the *eide*,[12] their contemporaries in the Lyceum were busily engaged in purging the unresolved supernaturalism from Aristotle's teaching: the eighteen-year-long term of Strato of Lampsacus as scholarch of the Lyceum (B.C. 288–270) marked its successful conclusion.[13]

Zeno's universe was essentially that of Aristotle cleansed of its last traces of transcendentalism and pushed even further back toward the dynamism of the pre-Parmenidean philosophers. Despite the fact that Aristotle had relocated the Platonic *eide* within material beings, they were still *eide*, principles of structure. Aristotle's own ambivalence between the Platonic formal and structural way of looking at being and his own interest in dynamism is accurately reflected in his own shifting between the notion of a static Platonic "Form" (*eidos*) and that of a dynamic "being-in-function" (*energeia*) to describe what goes on within substances.

All vestiges of *eidos* are gone from Zeno. He saw both being and the universe of beings as an immense physical organism and so was led by the analogy with living beings to an internal prin-

---

12. See Chapter IX, p. 350.
13. See Chapter II, pp. 110–11.

ciple that had been discussed in fifth-century medical circles, the vital spirit, or *pneuma*. Here too Aristotle had gone before, and when he had allowed himself to speak with the voice of a biologist rather than that of a reformed Platonist, Aristotle had explored the possibilities of this hot, foamy liquid serving as a link between the physical organism and the spiritual soul. The *pneuma* carried the commands of the psychic faculty to the nervous system and in the act of generation transmitted soul from parent to offspring by means of the seminal fluid in which it was mixed.[14]

Zeno promoted the *pneuma* to a prominent position as the vital fluid or breath that flows throughout organic being. At first glance one seems to be back in a kind of Homeric psychology where soul appears in the form of the breath of life. Stoic *pneuma*, however, is more than a mere fiery breath of life that can be inhaled and exhaled. It is a subtle, almost spiritual substance that mixes through the grosser material of the body without ever losing its own identity.[15] Within the *pneuma* are carried, again in the manner of Aristotle, the "seedlings of reason" (*logoi spermatikoi*).

The *pneuma* served, then, as the vehicle which transmitted the principle of reason (*logos*) from parent to offspring. For Aristotle it solved the problem of the passage of the soul from one generation to the next, but for the Stoics *logos* was a principle that extended throughout the system, from the individual man to the entire cosmic organism, and in exploring its wide range of connotations they reached far behind Aristotle.

For the Greeks *logos* had a great many related meanings: intelligence, reason, discourse, speech and finally, in a usage shading off into a technical term of geometry, proportion. The term had become domesticated in philosophy through Heraclitus (*c.* B.C. 500), who used it across almost its entire range of connotation. The Heraclitean *logos* was the wisdom of philosophy, obscure in

---

14. This solution for the problem of transmitting soul from one generation to the next was not a particularly happy one insofar as it concerned the immortal and completely immaterial *nous*, which, according to *Aristotles platonizans*, came "from the outside." This latter notion, alien to the Stoa of Zeno's day, made its appearance there when Posidonius returned to a Platonic view of the soul.

15. The Stoics had, perforce, an elaborate theory of mixtures to explain, among other things, this joining of a quasi-spiritual with a material substance.

its essence and difficult to utter; it was as well the related *state* of things, an underlying equilibrium between conflicting forces that constituted the true being and the true meaning of the universe. An immutable *logos* underlay the apparently constant flux visible in the sensible world. To illustrate it, Heraclitus resorted to a staple of the pre-Socratic physicists, fire. Fire was the basic element of the universe, all-pervasive, directive and intelligent.

The Stoics, who were as little naturalists as Heraclitus was, took up the notion of *logos*-fire and joined it to the sophisticated physiology of the fourth century. Fire and *pneuma* were parts of the vital continuum that ran through the organism of the universe, in its upper regions as the pure fire of the sun and the planets, and in a progressively grosser form as the corporeal *pneuma*. Everywhere, above and below, it represents reason, *logos*, the creative and providential force that is also God.

In the Stoics' view of cosmic history there was, in the beginning,[16] fire, which in the course of time was transformed into the other elements—earth, air and water. Through all of them permeates the divine Fire-and-*Logos* which is individualized as the *logoi spermatikoi* and is carried in the pervasive *pneuma*. The *logoi* animate, shape and order the various parts until the universe (the *kosmos*, as an earlier generation of Greeks had begun calling it) is constituted in all its interrelated variety. The process continues, however, and the *Logos* absorbs and consumes all within itself until at the end of the cycle the *kosmos* is dissolved into the divine fire whence it came, and the *logoi spermatikoi* are reabsorbed into the single *Logos*.[17]

In Stoicism, as in Epicureanism, all is matter, but Zeno's temptations toward the spiritual were even more flagrant than those of Epicurus. There is, as it turns out, matter and matter, one active and creative, the other passive and inert. Epicurus was forced by the logic of his system to manipulate matter into *immaterial* postures in terms of the size, shape and motion of some of the atoms; Zeno, who was a physiologist and not an atomist, could afford to stand closer to Aristotle's distinction

---

16. There was not, of course, a literal beginning; the series was circular, not linear.
17. The cycle, which is signaled by a final conflagration, is repeated at fixed intervals measured off, according to Zeno, by the completion of a "Great Year," the period of time required for all the heavenly bodies to return to a given point of departure (see Chapter XVI, Note 33).

between *being-in-act* and *being-in-potency*, converted, to be sure, into a materialist terminology: form and matter, act and potency become, in the Stoic version, active matter and passive matter. The Stoics were neither as materialistic nor as monistic as they at first appear. They could no longer bring themselves to assert the existence of transcendental beings, but they were equally incapable of totally surrendering their belief in some kind of quasi-spiritual dimension in the universe.

The differences within the primary active element in the universe which separated one level of being from another the Stoics ascribed to a tension (*tonos*) in the *pneuma*, another notion borrowed from Heraclitus who had described the *logos* of the universe as "a tension, as in a bow or lyre." In simple organic beings this tension generates little more than a feeble circulatory movement, but as one progresses up the scale of organisms the more sophisticated forms of tension give rise to the nature (*physis*) or growth principle in plants, the soul (*psyche*) or stimulus-response mechanism in animals, and finally reason (*logos*) in men and higher organisms, for the Stoics, as for Plato, the principle of self-induced motion which is exemplified by the free assent that men give in their reasoning process.

In each case the tension in the *pneuma* and its passive surrounding matter constitute organic systems of increasing complexity. Man is one such, and like all the others he is a mixture of *pneuma* and passive matter. The *pneuma*, which is mixed with blood, circulates through an intricate internal system which centers in the directive faculty (*hegemonikon*) located in the heart[18] and terminates in the five senses and the speech and genital organs. There is input into the system through the sense organs and output through the speech organs and genitals, the former emitting external discourse (*logos*), which reflects man's internal reasoning,[19] and the latter the seedlings (*logoi spermatikoi*), whereby one animal generates soul in another.

18. There were brain partisans among the Greeks, but Greek medicine knew a great deal more about the circulatory system than about the nervous system, and so the majority opinion held for the heart as the vital center. The Platonists alone among the philosophers located it in the brain.

19. Hence the great Stoic interest and skill in grammar, logic and the linguistic sciences. The connection of internal and external *logos* in Stoicism also became an essential ingredient in Philo's "Mosaic Philosophy" (see Chapter VII, pp. 304–05).

For both Plato and Aristotle the human soul was one of the transcendentals, in whole or in part capable of escaping the body and so of enjoying immortality. Zeno had scant grounds upon which to rest human immortality. Men were different from animals, the entire Stoa conceded it, but only in degree and not, as in Plato and Aristotle, in kind. The human soul was like that in animals in that it was nothing more than a certain tension in the pneumatic system of the organism. Death was, in effect, the dissolution of that system. Zeno seemed to hesitate in drawing the conclusion, though the later Stoic Panaetius (*c.* B.C. 180–110), who had to debate acute Academic critics as Zeno did not, was later forced to it: the soul perishes with the body.

Zeno, however, allowed the human *pneuma* to survive the body for an unspecified time, in order, perhaps, that it might undergo the pleasures and pains of the traditional afterlife. Eventually it dissolved, though what could be called the universe's soul, the central Fire, survived what was analogously cosmic death, the periodic conflagration.

It is not inconceivable that Zeno's physics would have pleased a Socrates who had just turned away from Anaxagoras' physics because of its ineffective teleology and had not yet been introduced to Plato's metaphysics. In Zeno the teleology is complete, because it is enclosed within a system, that of the *kosmos* as an organism. The latter was not a new idea among the Greeks. The Pythagoreans who had first called the universe an "ordering" (*kosmos*) understood something of its complex unity, though their model was a mathematical rather than a biological one. Some of the other pre-Socratics, however, had looked upon the universe as a gigantic living creature endowed with a unity and life of its own. By Zeno's time the biology of organisms was far better known than it had been in Anaximenes', and the implications of a biological model could be elicited at great length.

If the universe is conceived of as a single living and breathing being, as even Plato had conceived of it, the conclusion is inescapable that its parts cooperate in some spectacular sense toward the good of the whole. There were patent signs in nature that this was so, the interconnection of the movement of the heavenly bodies, the seasons, and the life cycle here on earth, for example. Why it was so was also manifest. An organism is a system under the control of a central power located in a central organ. In man this was his *hegemonikon*, or reasoning faculty, located in the heart. There were similar systems in other living beings, and it was natural to assume that it was also true of the animal that was the *kosmos*. Clearly fire was the "blood" of the universe, carrying the directions of *Logos* throughout the system and emanating from a central fire in a central organ, the sun.[20]

All of this had immense implications. The Stoics' biological model of the universe suggested that the cosmic system was controlled, that the control was rational, as in man, and that there was a close connection between corporal, psychic and ethical function in both man and the universe. Not all of the implications were pursued immediately. The early Stoa was concerned with more or less traditional questions of physics, theology and ethics; it was only later, in a very different political and religious environment and after the original system was much overgrown with a revived Platonism, that some other extraordinary aspects of this highly organic universe began to reveal themselves.[21]

The Stoics' God betrays the same uneasy blend of the corporeal and the spiritual within a materialistic system that their view of man does. God, like all else, is material. He is not himself a natural organism distinct from the others, but the active, life-giving and life-guiding principle that Zeno consistently identifies with the material element of an older era, fire. The materialism is softened, however, by a parallel identification with reason and intelligence, not now in the manner of the divine Intellect of Anaxagoras and Aristotle or the Yahweh of the Jews standing outside the universe and directing what is within. The divine *Logos* of the Stoa is immanent in the *kosmos;* it simultaneously creates and directs, everywhere and in everything.

Stoicism was pantheism, though not with the total lack of definition that the term suggests. The object of Stoic piety was, indeed, the nature of things, but nature was legitimately worshiped under many different aspects. The faces of nature were the faces of the universal God, and when the poets or popular religion spoke of this or that god they were celebrating various functions, blessings or appearances of a single god. Stoicism thus provided a way of salvaging both traditional religion and the

---

20. There was some debate in the school on the question of the central organ of the universe. Cleanthes, Zeno's successor, held for the sun, and from Posidonius onward it became a standard and important part of Stoicism.

21. See Chapters IX, pp. 367–68, XI, pp. 440–42, and XII, pp. 469–70.

traditional myths. It was unbothered by anthropomorphism, because it saw under what were different manners of speaking a single and universal God.[22]

The Epicureans had banished their gods to an ineffective place beyond the universe and harm's way; the Stoics placed the divine *Logos* right at the cosmic heart of things and subjected all to its beneficent control. The world unfolds in both its internal evolution and its human history according to a divinely conceived plan. The plan is achieved, not as Yahweh achieves his, by intervention in human affairs, but by structuring all life and existence from within. The *kosmos* and all within it are in the grip of an inexorable chain of causality (*heimarmene*), but the Stoic "series of causes" differs from the similar Epicurean chain—with its embarrassing broken link—in its intelligent and divine purposefulness. Epicurean causality is perfectly naturalistic, a godless physics with neither purpose nor direction. Stoic causality was, on the other hand, utterly purposeful, and the clicking of its series of automatic causes and effects is really a hymn to the *Logos* which operates, indeed, which *is* the system.

The notion was not, perhaps, an entirely attractive one, save that the divine architect and engineer or, to use a more common Stoic figure, king, is a benefactor, and so what appears as a restrictive *heimarmene* when viewed from the angle of causality is something quite different when held up before God's benevolence. Against the Epicureans' God-deserted universe the Stoics opposed their own strongly held doctrine of divine providence (*pronoia*). God wishes well for the world, and since he is omnipotent he can bring that good about. The universe is directed by the divine plan of an omnipotent and benevolent God. That plan shines forth everywhere, in the orderly working of nature, in the beauty and majesty of natural phenomena, and in man's own possession of reason. Civilization, culture and nature all converge to point toward a providential plan for this best of all possible worlds.

Zeno's almost naïve optimism made a tempting target for the Voltaires of the skeptical Academy, and it fell to Chrysippus to answer them. In the face of an imposing catalogue of cosmic slings, arrows and outrageous fortunes, Chrysippus had to con-

---

22. On Stoic exegesis as applied to the traditional myths, see Chapter XII, pp. 451–53.

struct a theodicy that would either explain or excuse the presence of evil in the universe. Stoics were fond of using the cosmological argument in their proofs for the existence of God, but the reverse of the argument could quite as easily be turned against them when the discussion came to the question of divine providence: how can an all-good and all-powerful God who cares allow such evil things to occur in his *kosmos?*

It was not enough to retort, as a contemporary Pharisee might have done, that it was part of a divine chastisement; there were examples enough of children and the innocent being struck by natural disasters. The Stoic had other responses, that the misfortunes of a part may serve toward the good of the total organism, for example, but one such betrays the dimly perceived limits of their cosmic optimism. In the *Timaeus* Plato had pitted his creator's good intentions against the relative intractabilty of matter: he did as well as he could under the circumstances, which were, for Plato, nature's own "necessity" (*ananke*), a natural causality which in part resists the benevolence of the demiurge. The Stoic identification of God, providence and nature would seem to have removed that conflict. But Chrysippus' theodicy reveals that the Platonic *ananke* has not been entirely banished from the universe and that nature has its own refractory causality, which sometimes escapes the operations of divine providence. God does not intend physical evil, Chrysippus contends, but it follows on occasion as a kind of unwanted but necessary side effect to some of God's beneficent plans.

This may be, after all, little more than Chrysippus caught in the trap of dialectic. The main thrust of Stoic ethics was to deny the intrinsic evil of such external events in the *kosmos*. The Stoic sage struggled to rise above both grief *and* earthquakes, secure in the knowledge that the only evil was sin, a moral state in man, and the only good was virtue. The concern for theology and theodicy was inevitable in the school's movement away from its pragmatic Cynic origins into the academic tradition. The learned theological debates among Epicurean, Academic and Stoic reported in the pages of Cicero's *On the Nature of the Gods* shows the Stoic divine at his academic best, polished and well supplied with dialectical weaponry, but somehow remote from the more primitive but more engaged Zeno.

All of this was accomplished with as little resort to supernaturalism as can be found in Epicureanism, and with no trace of the transcendentals on exhibit in Plato or even Aristotle. By B.C. 300 Parmenides was intellectually dead, and his metaphysics was buried with him. For the next generation, or until a new methodological doubt began to creep into the Academy in the middle of the third century, the Greek philosophical tradition has a curiously old-fashioned look in its fascination with an immanent and vitalistic physics. The appearance is, of course, fundamentally deceptive; the Hellenistic philosophers harnessed their old-style physics to an ethical purpose in a way that no pre-Socratic could possibly have done. Zeno's world was indeed once again "filled with gods," as Thales had said at the very beginning of the Greek philosophical tradition; but these gods were now inextricably connected with a Socratic concern not shared by Thales, what was the good life for man.

The Harmonious Life

There is a disturbingly false note in the history of Epicureanism. The Founder's physics is laid out with all the assurance of a man who is resident in a universe without surprises or mystery. Epicureanism brought light to the previously opaque and misunderstood corners of the *kosmos*, but there are signs that Lucretius' "first Greek hero" was whistling in the dark all the way out and back along the battlements. The Epicurean appears to be peculiarly ill at ease in the world that he has just so masterfully and rationally explained away. The "hidden life" might seem to be an ideal preparation for a self-recollecting prophet or an apt setting for a world-despising ascetic. The Epicureans did not flee to the wilderness, to be sure, but both the direction of their ethics and the manner of their lives were toward withdrawal into a quiet, protective, and reinforcing environment or retreat. It may have been the most explicable of all worlds, but there is a whisper that it is not the best, and the lucidity of Epicurean physics apparently did nothing to reduce that fear of the machine that drove Epicurus and his disciples into the garden.

The Stoic appears far happier in his organic universe than the Epicurean in his mechanical one. He was, after all, at home in the *kosmos*, secure in the knowledge that he was part of a universal and benevolent purpose. More, within the universe the individual had a specialized and natural role in a human society.

The Epicureans' analysis of instinctive behavior led them to conclude that man's primary drive was toward the enjoyment of pleasure. Stoicism began with the same methodological premise, to lift man from his social environment, which may after all be the product of irrelevant circumstances, and to observe him perform under his own instincts. For Socrates, Plato and Aristotle, the realities of human existence were the realities of the *polis*, to the point that the *polis* itself was thought to be an appropriate level at which to attack the problem of human behavior. Plato's *Republic* was an exercise in social psychology designed to support the conclusions of individual psychology, and Aristotle too subscribed to the notion that *polis* activity was a more intelligible field of study than individual activity; politics was the master science of which ethics was a subordinate part. In Epicurus and Zeno the attitude is quite reversed. The individual was the only appropriate point of the departure, and if the Stoics did at a later point in their analysis construct a social theory, it was only because of what they had observed about the natural and unstructured behavior of men.

The results of their observations were not so very different from Epicurus'. Where Epicurus had detected the drive to pleasure, Zeno found another form of self-love which he described as "self-acceptance" (*oikeiosis*), a desperate clinging to life and the means of survival. Both men had proved to their own satisfaction that men were animals. Zeno, however, continued to observe the specimen and noted that man's desire for self-preservation gradually extended itself, first to his own offspring, as did all animals', and then to family, to tribe and finally to all of human society. It was in this final stage that man left behind the rest of the animals and created for himself, from his own natural instinct, a society of rational beings. Thus, man's proper nature revealed itself as that of a social animal (*zoön koinonikon*) endowed with reason.

All Stoic morality, individual and social, rested upon this foundation. Because Epicurus' analysis did not proceed far enough he remained anchored, in the Stoic view, within the confines of an individual and egoistic ethic, and there on the still narrower ground of an animal ethic. As a self-protective and self-gratifying animal, the Epicurean drew back from the world, while the Stoic was encouraged to explore not only the entire domain of nature to which he was organically related but also the body of human society in which he was, by his rational constitution, a charter member.

It was Zeno who first expressed the goal of Stoic morality in the formula "to live harmoniously." There may have been some ambiguity in this. If "harmoniously" is glossed as "naturally," it summons up the two meanings that the Stoics were already attaching to "nature" (*physis*)—nature as the creative principle of the entire cosmic system, and the specialized nature which is the peculiar property of man. Where Zeno stood is uncertain, but Cleanthes read "naturally" in the first sense,[23] while the more intellectualistic Chrysippus understood it in the second sense.

The Stoa ended by reading it both ways and, so, constructing a cosmic religion and an individual ethic of highly rationalistic tone. The first step along the path to the latter was to deny any moral content to actions performed in fulfillment of the earliest human instinct to survival. Life, death, pleasure, pain, riches and wealth might all be "natural" or "unnatural" for an animal organism, or an Epicurean, but they had no connection with the ground of *human* morality. Moral values, good and evil, are applicable where man is capable of functioning *qua* man, as a *logos* organism.[24]

The good life for man consists, then, in the perfections which are proper to his rational nature—wisdom, temperance, fortitude and justice—while their contraries are morally evil. Between these two classes of absolute goods and absolute evils are all those actions and states which are morally indifferent (*adiaphora*), an area which would later attract a great deal of attention, but which created difficulties from the very beginning.

Zeno made some distinctions among the morally indifferent activities of man. He regarded them as having at least some

---

23. This is the reading that shines through the cosmic pieties of his *Hymn to Zeus*, the most considerable piece of work preserved undamaged from the earliest days of the Stoa.
24. Hence the importance of determining the onset of the "age of reason" in human animals. The linking of the genital system in the pneumatic network leading to the *hegemonikon* provided the clue. For the Stoic the age of consent, and so of moral responsibility, was signaled by the onset of puberty, somewhere between the seventh and fourteenth years.

bearing on the categories of good and evil and so thought that they should be judged accordingly, in terms of their indirect contribution to living a moral life. Health, wealth and intelligence, for instance, though not strictly moral in content, can contribute to virtue and so should be classified as "desirable." It was a common-sense approach, but in proposing it Zeno was speaking with the voice of Aristotle rather than that of Crates, and the position must have outraged the still tender Cynic sensibilities of some of Zeno's followers. The opposition was led by one of them, Ariston of Chios, who broke with Zeno over the *adiaphora* and founded his own schismatic group. Ariston urged a position of absolute moral vigor: there is only one good, no matter how one chooses to subdivide it, and all else is either evil or morally indifferent; there are no distinctions within that latter class, and so the moral man should care nothing for either health or illness.

The Stoa did not follow Ariston; instead they concentrated their attention more and more on making correct choices from among the *adiaphora*. The Academics of Chrysippus' day assailed him with a barrage of moral conundrums in the form of concrete "cases of conscience" which rested upon conflicts of interest—between the self-preservation inherent in man's animal nature, for example, and some social good flowing from his rational nature. The Stoa had no choice but to answer and so was drawn away from the simplicity of Zeno's earlier insistence that virtue was absolute—so it was, in his definition—to a recognition that the actual pursuit of the moral life, as opposed to its theoretical fulfillment in the Stoic sage, reduced itself in practice to a correct choice among those acts so casually labeled "morally indifferent."

The sage (*sophos*) continued, nonetheless, to be the center and showpiece of Stoic ethics, a remote and forbidding ideal. On the Stoic scale, virtue was an absolute; it suffered, as Ariston had said, distinctions but no grades; and before its confrontation with Academic casuistry, Stoic morality was writ large in black and white. As there was no such thing as partial or relative virtue, so there was no partial sage. There was only the man who possessed virtue: superior to life because he had mastered it, self-sufficient in his virtue, and happy by definition.

Most of these characteristics, typical of the presocial stage of Stoic ethics, derive from obvious Cynic antecedents—the Cynics' oft-proclaimed superiority of the virtuous man to the politician or the king, for instance—but others came from the nature of virtue itself. Zeno had defined the end of man as a life harmonious with nature, and virtue was the internalization of that harmony, a disposition of the soul in conformity with man's rational nature. Happiness follows upon the possession of virtue and upon that alone; all else is vanity, or evil.

For the Stoic to act he must first, in the best Hellenic tradition, know; and both knowledge and virtue converge as a certain disposition in the soul. From the moment a child is born his senses are presented with a series of images. At an early stage he can only react, as an animal reacts, but as his *logos* system matures, the entire complex of rational knowledge and rational activity comes into operation. The image is converted into a concept (*ennoia*), first by reason of some quality of its own which counsels assent, and then by the voluntary assent itself. Thus the image to which assent had been given has undergone "apprehension" (*katalepsis*) and becomes part of the furniture of the rational *hegemonikon*.

Our way of knowing is neither mechanical nor, again, perfectly natural. Assent of the will, a free and undetermined action,[25] must be given before apprehension is possible. The quality and depth of the concepts can in turn be affected by outside forces—by instruction, for example; the Stoics took education seriously. There is, however, a class of concepts which are natural and spontaneous. The "common concepts" (*koinai ennoiai*), like all else in Stoic epistemology, are acquired through prior sense images; but they are gotten without a great deal of reflection and are the common possession of all mankind. In this category falls knowledge of the existence of God and of the first principles of the moral life.

Zeno's emphasis on the role of assent in knowledge is a clear departure from Epicurus' more mechanical way of knowing. There is another difference between the two men which leads back into the heart of the Stoic ethic: for Epicurus everything that happened to an organism was simply one form or another of experience (*pathos*), and the moral life reduced itself, in effect, to choosing those *pathe* which induced pleasure rather than pain; in Zeno and at the beginning of the Stoic tradition there was a

---

25. Or so it was in Zeno. Chrysippus appears later to have shifted the burden away from the free assent to the compelling quality of the image presented to the mind.

rather sharp distinction drawn between the rational, cognitive experiences, the images served up for apprehension, and another class of emotional and nonrational affects which fell upon the soul and for which Zeno reserved the name of *pathe*.

The test case on the *pathe* is Plato, and his varying reactions to them are an anticipation of the Stoa's own positions. When, at the beginning of his career, Plato held for a unified and rational soul, the affective *pathe* appear as intruders in the life of the philosopher, and though he does not use the term, the extirpation of the *pathe*, the state of *apatheia*, is a fair description of the philosopher's moral goal. Later, as his naturalistic conviction that man's soul embraces more than pure intellect grew, Plato began to relax on the subject of the emotive *pathe*, even to the point of granting one of them, pleasure, a role in the good life.

Zeno too had a naturalistic view of the soul, but his conviction that the reasonable part of that soul is the true nature of man made him as fierce as the early Plato in denying to any of the irrational *pathe* a place in moral consideration. The goal of the truly virtuous man should not be a sifting of these violent and irrational *pathe*, as in Epicurus, or their moderation and balance, as in Aristotle, but resistance to them. The ideal of the sage is *apatheia;* he does not allow himself to be affected by external and morally worthless impressions like grief or fear or pleasure, because they perturb the soul and interfere with its proper function, rational thought.

Chrysippus had trouble with this, not because he wished to vindicate the morality of the emotions, but because he could not see how it was possible for a nonrational experience to affect a rational faculty. Chrysippus held as strongly to the unitive and rational nature of the human *hegemonikon* as the early Plato did, but Platonic dualism between soul and body was denied him, and so he could not explain the emotions as resonances of an alien body. He had instead to reduce all the *pathe* to intellectual experiences, to judgments.

Stoicism, following upon the heels of Socrates and the Cynics, internalized virtue. Virtue was a disposition of the soul, and so, intentions were more important than actions. The Peripatetics had wished to argue that external goods had some bearing on man's happiness, a notion that the Stoics relentlessly resisted. A man was happy if he possessed virtue, and no purely external circumstances could avail to change that, neither poverty nor sickness nor even torture. Virtue made men happy and it made men free. It knew neither social nor economic classes; the only slave was the slave to passion.

For the Stoa the *pathe* lay at the root of sin, which is no other than a perversion of man's nature. In a larger sense it is impossible for man, or any organism, to act unnaturally. The possibility of perversion arises only from the peculiar human dualism: Man is both a natural animal and a natural *logos* organism in which the parts are subjected to the good of the whole. That good is determined by man's directive faculty, his *hegemonikon*, or reason. In all other beings from the lowest to the highest, the *kosmos* itself, the subordination of parts to the whole is predetermined by providence and regulated by the causality of *heimarmene*. Man is the exception; he alone can, if he so chooses, act unnaturally, and it is from this unique condition that the moral imperative arises: man *must* act naturally.

If man can apparently burst the chains of *heimarmene*, can he also disrupt and distort the divine plan for the world? If he can, then God is not omnipotent; if he cannot, then human freedom— and human morality—would seem to be a fiction. The dilemma was a real one, but unyielding to solution stated in those terms; neither the Stoics nor any Greek was willing to deny either horn of it. The Stoics and the Epicureans, it is true, were caught more firmly on it than others, because of their insistence on the determinism of physical causality, even though the former put that in the hands of God, and the latter put it under the rubric of physics.

The Epicureans chose to escape the dilemma through a chink in their omnipotent physics, the fortuitous swerve (*parenklisis*) in the atoms that they posited to save human freedom.[26] The Stoics preferred to work on the problem of free will from the direction of causality, and Chrysippus in particular tried to fashion a theory that would keep *heimarmene* intact and at the same time not extend its necessity to that act of assent which was the fulcrum of human knowledge and action.

There was no question, Chrysippus explained, of man's changing either the plan or the execution of divine providence; the human role was fixed, and so man's real choice reduced itself to following along or being dragged along. Viewed in the light of

---

26. See Note 9, p. 127.

providence, living harmoniously with nature might be more correctly expressed as accepting a life which was harmonious with nature. In man's case there is, however, a further twist. Since man possesses reason it must be that God's plan requires that he not only possess it but exercise it. That providential fact can be reconciled with the necessitating *heimarmene* by a more careful analysis of causality. An external cause, and *heimarmene* operates in that area, determines that an effect shall be, but the precise mode of the effect is determined not by the external cause but by the inner constitution of the effect. Thus, *heimarmene* dictates a being's role in the universe, but its manner of playing that role is in accordance with its own nature, in man's case, the free exercise of reason. The Stoics replaced the missing link in Epicurus' chain of causality with a distinction of causes.

The Stoic sage was at home in a providential world, but in another sense he had to struggle against it. He had his natural habitat in the society of men, to which his most primary instinct directed every man. That society, even though it was founded on a common possession of reason, was not a necessarily rational one in practice; it knew sin. The dual nature of man as animal and rational being created problems of individual and social conduct and made the choice of the good a difficult one. The possession of virtue was an unrelenting struggle, and it was Heracles, the energetic battler against overwhelming odds, who was the prototype of the Stoic saint.

The internalization of virtue and the constant exhortation to an indifferent attitude toward external goods would seem to be an open invitation into an insulated and passive cultivation of virtue, since the *kosmos*, though natural, did not appear to be moral. It was not moral, as the Stoic understood morality; but the microcosm of human society was moral ground, and every individual had, by reason of his own rational nature, both a membership in and obligations toward that society. "I am human," exclaimed a character in one of the Roman Terence's plays, "and nothing human is alien to me." Stoicism had a new and strong sense of a moral imperative, first to choose the absolute goods, and then to select among the *adiaphora* those actions and states that most contributed to the common good. Living harmoniously with nature imposed severe social and political obligations.

The Stoic's social obligations unfolded within a new and revolutionary view of society. For Aristotle man was still a *"polis* animal" (*zoön politikon*), but in Zeno he became a "social animal" (*zoön koinonikon*), a resident in a new society, which knew no Aristotelian distinction between Greek and barbarian, free man and slave. The Cynics had already glimpsed this ideal, though only in a half-realized form. Diogenes of Sinope identified himself as a "citizen of the *kosmos*," but only because he wished to point up the superiority of the Cynic's "natural" virtue to the conventional morality expressed in the law (*nomos*) of the *polis*. The point was doubtless an ethical one, but the expression *kosmopolites* as used by Diogenes owed more to rhetoric than to philosophical theory.

In Stoicism not only is the organic structure of the *kosmos* fully realized, it is transcended by another, human community with its own constitution resting upon the *kosmos* organism. The Cynic "citizen of the *kosmos*" led a secular existence in a world that knew little of God or providence; Zeno's society was a genuine City of God. Men and God shared the fellowship of reason (*logos*) and membership in the community that was founded upon reason.

The Stoics' City of God did not end their commitment to the City of Man. Cynic and Epicurean individualism, though very much in the spirit of the times, was foreign to the Stoa. Their view of human society and the course of contemporary history no longer permitted them, however, to see the state solely in terms of the classical *polis*. In their eyes the state was no longer limited by the narrow confines of cultural and ethnic homogeneity that characterized the *polis;* it was now "a group of men living in the same place under the rule of law [*nomos*]."

Law was the foundation stone of Stoic political and social ethics. The question of convention (*nomos*) versus nature (*physis*) had been endlessly debated in an earlier generation, but for the Stoics the two were synonymous. *Nomos* was, in the first instance, God's will immanent and operative in the universe; it represented the conversion of his providence into a moral imperative. As Cicero later put it, "law is the supreme *logos*, immanent in nature, which commands what ought to be done and forbids the contrary." He is speaking, of course, of the divine and immutable law of nature, but there is, in a sense, no other.

Human laws drawn up by men for the governance of their states are—or, rather, should be—an echo of the law of nature. The Stoics did not deny that this was frequently not the case;

there were immoral laws, and the Stoic man of virtue had an obligation to change them so that the laws of states might conform more closely to the immanent natural law. In the later Roman Republic, with its own highly developed tradition of law, Stoic legal theory worked its effects through juridical channels; but in Zeno's generation the notion of a sovereign law was subservient to that of the sovereign lawgiver, the Hellenistic king, and Stoic influences were to be found not in the law courts but rather at the side of those kings, Perseus with Antigonus Gonatas at Pella in B.C. 276, and later Sphaerus with Cleomenes at Sparta in B.C. 235.

In his utopian *Republic*, written while he was still a student of Crates but now lost, Zeno had apparently foreseen a state in which men would live together in the harmony that Cicero later described as *humanitas*, without laws, institutions or formal religion. Alexander's *oikoumene* had opened the tantalizing possibility that one day the theoretician's dream might become a reality; but in Zeno's own day it was still the tiny polity of Sparta that stood closest to the ideal of a classless, communist utopia of virtue. The individual's obligation to become involved in the murderous political life of the Greek *poleis* was not greatly stressed or much heeded by most Stoics, and with Chrysippus the school apparently lost interest in its own political theories as it became progressively more academic, dialectical and individualistic.

In Rome the Stoa discovered itself and eventually found in the Roman Empire what even Alexander had only fitfully offered, an ecumenical state ruled by a single king under a single law. And in Stoicism the Romans, for their part, found a philosophy that fitted their needs and their aspirations. Strenuous, activist, practical Stoicism, with its own stern sense of duty and often simplistic attitude toward the moral life, suited the Romans, as it later suited the Christians. Egocentric Epicureanism the Romans found little to their liking, and the revived metaphysics of Plato and Aristotle aroused interest only among the Hellenized professionals. And only the Stoics' political theory was large enough to understand and explain what the Romans' arms had, in fact, won.

We know about the mutual attraction between Stoic theory and Roman power simply because our records are better for that period, Cicero during the Republic and a number of Stoic authors during the Empire; in the personalized Imperial histories of Tacitus and Suetonius we can observe Stoics at the court of the Emperors. But before this rich historiographical stretch begins, one must first traverse the literary wreckage of Hellenistic Stoicism. Polybius, the chief source for the events after B.C. 221 was concerned with the philosophical consequences of political action, but had no interest in the history of philosophy. One suspects, dimly and uncertainly, the activity of individual Stoics at the courts of Hellenistic kings, but there are few details. The preserved philosophical information has to do with the school and its debates with other schools, not the source of the ideology of the Seleucids or the Ptolemies.

That there was an ideology is unmistakable, whether derived from the Macedonian model of kingship, or the *polis* ideal which the new monarchs carried with them from Greece, or the ancient precedents of the lands over which they ruled. For the Ptolemies in particular, surrounded as they were by a dense population caught up in a severely regimented economy, and living in the shadow of the millennial tradition of Egypt, ideological innovation was a precarious business anywhere outside the confines of Hellenized Alexandria. The Ptolemies might call themselves "Benefactors," in the approved nomenclature of Stoic kingship, but Stoic notions of brotherhood, equality and harmony were never given a serious hearing in Egypt. There, as in the early days of Roman rule in the East,[27] political Stoicism would have been tantamount to revolution.

---

27. See Chapter VIII, Note 5.

IV

The Ptolemies of Egypt

When the Romans withdrew their armies from an enfeebled Greece in B.C. 194 a successor of Antigonus Gonatas still ruled in Macedon as the claimant of Alexander's throne. That throne had once been savagely and single-mindedly contested by Alexander's generals as the key to his inheritance. The Successors were Hellenes who were more impressed by the legitimacy of being King of Macedon than by the more romantic prospects held out by the title of Lord of Asia. Seleucus' impetuous bolt for Macedon in B.C. 280 is witness enough to the power of the magnet. They were all drawn by the attraction of the Macedonian kingship and the source of the manpower upon which every Hellenistic kingdom rested. They all coveted Macedon—all save Ptolemy Soter, who from the first wisely contented himself with strengthening his position in his "spear-won" land of Egypt. The first Ptolemy appears generally immune to the Macedonian fevers that gripped his fellow generals, and his cautious behavior allowed his son and heir, Ptolemy II Philadelphus, freedom to follow the call of a new imperialism that was heard around the eastern Mediterranean in the second quarter of the third century.

An Egyptian Empire (B.C. 322–217)

The Ptolemaic position in Egypt was paradoxical. The land was rich and, unlike many of the rival kingdoms and states, potentially self-supporting. Earlier Pharaohs had ruled there in isolation, trading across the Aegean on occasion from the free port of Naucratis in the Delta, where Greek businessmen conducted, in

MEDITERRANEAN SEA

Arsinoe-Teucheira
Ptolemaïs
Apollonia
Berenice-   Cyrene
Euhesperides   Barce
CYRENAICA

Paraetonium

LIBYA

Canopus
Alexandria
Naucratis
Saïs
Bubastis
Memphis
Tanis
FAYÛM
Philoteris
Theadelphia
Arsinoe (Crocodilopolis)
Oxyrhynchus
Hermupolis
Lycopolis
Ptolemaïs
Tentyra
Latopolis   Thebes
Arsinoe
Apollinopolis
Elephantine Kom-Ombo
Philae   Syene
             1st cataract

Philometoris?
Cleopatra?

COELE-
Damascus
Tyre   SYRIA
Ptolemaïs (Ake)
          Gadara
          SYRIAN
Rhinocolura
Raphia   DESERT
Gaza   Philadelphia (Rabbath-Ammon)
PALESTINE
Pelusium
Heliopolis Petra
Pithom-Heroopolis
Arsinoe-Cleopatris
Berenice?   Aelana
Heracleopolis
Philadelphia
Crocodilopolis
Philotera?
NABATAEANS
Arsinoe?   Teima   ARABIA
Myos Hormos
LIHYANITES
         Dedan
Coptos
Ampelone
Berenice
             Iathrippa
             R. Euphrates
             Seleucia

2nd cataract

AETHIOPIA

Meroe

Ptolemaïs Epitheras

Berenice the Golden

TROGODYTE COAST

RED SEA

MINÆANS
Karna
Mariaba
SABÆANS
KATABANI
Arsinoe?
Berenice Epidires

HELLENISTIC EGYPT

Scales.

0   50 100   200   300   400   500

English Miles

0 50 100 200 300 400 500 600 700 800

Kilometres

Greek bottoms, whatever international commerce was necessary. After Alexander, however, an isolationist Egypt was no longer viable. Greek states then ringed the entire Aegean and extended as far east as India. They were bound to each other as surely by their commercial needs as by their common culture. Under an ineffective ruler Egypt might be a weak link in the *oikoumene*, but it could hardly choose to disappear from the newly vitalized trade routes that ran around and through it.

Ptolemy Soter's own position there was anomalous. He was neither a native Pharaoh nor the governor of a foreign power of occupation. He was a Macedonian sovereign of an Egyptian state who had promoted himself with conspicuous ease from satrap to king. As such he had to survive in the company of other aggressive and energetic Macedonian kings. And like them he was supported by the company he kept, his Macedonian and Greek mercenaries, traders and colonists. The home states had, of course, the largest supply of these, and whoever ruled Macedon was in the soundest position. Anatolia too had its *poleis* of long standing, and both there and farther south, in Seleucid Syria and Palestine, Hellenization was taking hold to the extent that the home-grown product would eventually serve both the military and commercial needs of the regime.

In Egypt, however, Ptolemy, his court, his soldiers and his factors lived on the Hellenized island of Alexandria floating in the midst of a boundless Egyptian sea, drawing sustenance but no nourishment from the environment. His domain was the richest of the lands given to Alexander's marshals, but its richness was natural, a granary rather than a treasure house. Egypt's rulers had to work for their increase on the new international exchange.

Ptolemy's problem of rule was twofold. He had to govern his Egyptian subjects in some intelligible way, likely as the sensible successor to the Pharaohs. This role could be augmented but not easily changed, and the ways of the Pharaohs, tested and refined over the millennia, had almost necessarily to be the ways of the Ptolemies. At the same time, the founder of the dynasty could not afford to disappear behind the traditional and, to the Hellenes, exotic ways of the land. To his immediate and indispensable circle of Greeks he had to play the Hellene, at home in Alexandria and abroad before his larger Mediterranean audience.

Ptolemy's domestic policy was exceedingly shrewd. He kept his Hellenic house in order and even made a modest attempt at enlarging it by founding the Greek colony of Ptolemais in Upper Egypt. His show place was, of course, Alexandria, where in B.C. 294 he commissioned the Peripatetic scholar—and lately political exile—Demetrius of Phalerum to organize the Museum, where Ptolemy Soter and his successors could patronize in their lavish fashion the cream of the Hellenic intelligentsia drawn from all over the Mediterranean.

For his tradition-minded Greek subjects and as an emblem of legitimacy to be waved before his rivals abroad, a cult of Alexander with its own endowed priesthood was instituted over the dead hero's earlier kidnaped corpse. To the Egyptians Ptolemy was, of course, Pharaoh, though not perhaps with the same ritual insistence as some of his descendants. His mindfulness of his Egyptian image, his local Hellenic pretensions and his overseas ambitions were all on display in the cult he organized in honor of Serapis, a hybrid deity with a calculated hybrid liturgy.[1]

Abroad, Ptolemy was cautious and showed no great lust for the crowns of the other Successors, but he did not hide in the Delta. The nearby *polis* of Cyrene early tempted him to annexation, and in the years B.C. 310–308 he was in every corner of the Aegean, chiefly at the expense of Demetrius Poliorcetes. His activity won him Cyprus, ports in Caria and Lycia, and some of the islands.[2] The end, however, was bathos. Ptolemy landed at Corinth and proclaimed the liberation of Greece. No one seemed to be interested on that occasion, but his brief contact with Greek soil did prompt one Panhellenic gesture: an announcement, in his own name, of the Isthmian Games.

In their anticipation the victors over Antigonus at Ipsus apparently divided the spoils before that battle in B.C. 301, and Ptolemy Soter's share may have been Antigonus' holdings in Phoenicia and Syria. It was a rich reward for expected services, but the services were never rendered; Ptolemy's troops were frightened off before they even reached the Taurus. It was Seleucus who played the major role at Ipsus, and the eventual settlement gave all of Syria to him. By then, however, Ptolemy was in full possession of the prize territory; his armies never reached Anatolia, but they had come up from Egypt as far as the river Eleutherus south of

---

1. See Chapter XII, p. 468.
2. On one of them, Cos, the future Ptolemy II was born in B.C. 309. His mother Berenice was then only the mistress of Ptolemy I.

Aradus and there were no signs of a voluntary withdrawal after Ipsus. Seleucus made no countermove at the time. He contented himself with occupying northern Syria where he unmistakably signaled his Mediterranean ambitions by moving his capital from the distant Mesopotamian Babylon to the new city of Antioch near the mouth of the Orontes.

Antigonus' son, Demetrius, as has been seen, was far from dead after Ipsus. He still possessed the most powerful fleet in the Aegean and ports to harbor and provision them: the Cyclades; Cyprus once again after his signal victory over Ptolemy there in B.C. 296; and the great commercial cities of western Anatolia and Phoenicia, where Ptolemy held only the hinterland. Demetrius too allowed himself to be seduced by the throne of Macedon, and though he was successful there, he paid for his prize out of his Aegean holdings: Lysimachus, Seleucus and Ptolemy all gathered up his overseas cities. Lysimachus came down to the coast in Anatolia and took over the *poleis* there, while Seleucus moved up to the foot of the Taurus and annexed eastern Cilicia. Ptolemy's share was Cyprus and the former "Kingdom of Pleistarchus" along the southern coast of Anatolia.

The fall of Demetrius in B.C. 285 shook more wealth from the tree, chiefly into the hands of Egypt, the only other power with naval aspirations in the eastern Mediterranean. Ptolemy came into the possession of Demetrius' fleet, its ports in the Cyclades, and the great arsenals of Tyre and Sidon. And though Ptolemy's position was strong, a certain equity had developed between the surviving dynasts of a passing age. Lysimachus, Seleucus and Ptolemy all appeared to be secure in their holdings.

In B.C. 285 Ptolemy Soter was the master of a sprawling thalassocracy based in Egypt and extending over the entire eastern Mediterranean basin. From his Hellenic metropolis of Alexandria his ships straddled the sea lanes across the Aegean, to Cyprus and Phoenicia. Alexandria was developing as the head of overland traffic running down from Upper Egypt and the Red Sea. Ptolemaic Tyre was the terminus of another overland route leading in from Babylon, though it faced increasing competition from Seleucid Antioch. Trade from the east also continued overland through Anatolia to the Ionian *poleis* Miletus and Ephesus, and here too Ptolemy was in contention as a rival of Lysimachus.

It was Ptolemy himself who introduced a fatal disequilibrium into Aegean politics. Sometime before B.C. 287 he repudiated his wife Eurydice and married his mistress Berenice. For the succession he passed over Eurydice's son Ptolemy Ceraunus and instead associated Berenice's son to his own rule as Ptolemy II in B.C. 285. Two years later Ptolemy I was dead, and the people, already accustomed to his son's rule at his side, accepted the sole rule of Ptolemy II without difficulty or contest. But elsewhere abroad others of the Successors paid a fatal price. Ptolemy II's sister Arsinoë brought Lysimachus to Corupedion and his death, and the disappointed Ptolemy Ceraunus encompassed the ruin of Seleucus.

Ptolemy II shared some of his father's cautious political habits, though in B.C. 280 the obvious strength of his position tempted him to more aggressive action. He was the undisputed master of the seas, while his potential rivals, Ceraunus, Gonatas and the newly crowned Antiochus I in Syria, had their own pressing contentions. His first move must surely have been a signal of what was to follow. Sometime about B.C. 280 the new ruler of Egypt made public—and international—declaration of the divinization of his dead mother and father as "savior gods" (theoi soteres). The practice was widely imitated throughout the Hellenistic monarchies—except the Macedonian—and later among the Romans, where the act of canonization was simultaneously a gesture of filial piety and a cementing of the dynasty's claim to rule. The first Ptolemy had insured himself with the cults of Alexander and Serapis; his son, who had no immediate connection with Alexander, needed something more suggestively dynastic.

It was not the intention of the new Pharaoh to bask solely in the illumination given off by his divinized but dead father. Taking advantage of Antiochus' distractions in Macedon in B.C. 280, Ptolemy pinched off two of the Seleucids' important commercial centers, Damascus in Syria, whence the eastern overland trade could be diverted from Antioch, and the important Aegean terminus Miletus, once the possession of Lysimachus but now the presumed inheritance of the Seleucids. The Egyptian action had one healthy consequence: it forced Antiochus to give up his hopes of winning Macedon and to come to terms with Gonatas.

By treaty Gonatas and Antiochus divided their spheres of influence at the Hellespont, but a more realistic and divisive buffer separated them. The Galatians, who had already killed Ptolemy Ceraunus in B.C. 279 and were to be Gonatas' stepping-stone to the kingship of Macedon, roamed the Thracian shore in uncontrollable bands. They had already thrown Greece into turmoil and now stood on the edge of Asia ready to be drawn into Anatolia by the forces that were gathering there against Antiochus.

When Seleucus defeated Lysimachus at Corupedion in Lydia in B.C. 281 he was the presumptive heir of the Thracian satrap's enlarged domains in Anatolia. His son Antiochus soon discovered the error of his presumption. Not even Lysimachus' foes were his allies, much less his subjects. It is doubtful whether Lysimachus ever had much effective control of north-central Anatolia. From Chalcedon on the Bosporus, to Trapezus in the east, on the coastal plains of the Black Sea and in the highlands behind them, native dynasts ruled without consent or recognition from either Lysimachus or Antiochus. One of them, Zipoetes of Bithynia, the westernmost of the kingdoms, the most Hellenized, and the most important, since it sat directly astride the lines of trade and communication that crossed the Bosporus, fought both Lysimachus and Seleucus with equal enthusiasm. Farther east, Mithridates of Pontus also kept Seleucus at bay. The monarchies resisted incorporation into the Seleucid Empire, and so did the independent *poleis* of the littoral, Byzantium, Chalcedon and Heraclea, which united themselves in the defensive alliance of the Northern League.

The Anatolian resistance to Seleucus and Antiochus had an initial ally in Gonatas, but the Galatian invasion convinced both Antiochus and Gonatas that their mutual interest should make them allies, not antagonists. It was the treaty of B.C. 279 between the two men that eventually brought Antiochus' half sister to her nuptials at Gonatas' court in Pella in B.C. 276, and enabled Antiochus to turn southward and take measures against the growing aggression of Ptolemy II. Or so it seemed. Freed of Gonatas on his northern flank, Antiochus had still to reckon with the northern kingdoms of Anatolia.

Zipoetes of Bithynia died about this time, and his successor Nicomedes compensated for the loss of his alliance with Gonatas by recruiting new helpers against the Seleucids, the Galatians in Thrace. Celtic bands were ferried across the Bosporus, armed by Nicomedes and Mithridates of Pontus, and passed forward into the territories of Antiochus. Hordes of them roamed the countryside in western Anatolia creating panic among the *poleis*. Only at Pergamum was there some semblance of resistance; its semiautonomous governor Philetaerus managed somehow to turn the marauders away. Farther south, Antiochus showed remarkable energy under the circumstances. By shuttling back and forth across the Taurus he succeeded in B.C. 276–275 at least in blunting the edges of his two most pointed threats. He wrested Damascus back from Ptolemy, and in Anatolia in B.C. 275 his war elephants inflicted a painful defeat on the Galatians.

After this check the Galatians did not withdraw, as they had done in Greece a few years earlier, but were settled by Nicomedes round about Pessinus and Ancyra in central Anatolia as a buffer between the northern kingdoms and whatever ambitions Antiochus might have in their regard. They played their role well for another century. The Seleucids were indeed screened from Bithynia, Pontus, the Bosporus and the Black Sea, but Anatolia got in the bargain a dangerous and only fitfully tamed body of warriors ready to serve where summoned or paid. But they had made Antiochus' reputation in Anatolia, as they had Gonatas' in Macedon and the Aetolians' in Greece. For his victory of B.C. 275 the Seleucid king was hailed as Savior (*Soter*) by the Ionian *poleis*, and he wore his title—as yet without its later divine accouterments—with as much right as the recently canonized Ptolemy I Soter in Egypt.

Ptolemy II had lost Damascus in his earlier exchange with Antiochus and was perhaps in difficulty in Miletus. He stood to lose considerably more in the next encounter, since Antiochus' hands were at least temporarily freed of the Galatians in Anatolia and the Seleucid king had in addition procured himself important allies. He could now work in concert with Gonatas and, more to the present point, he had persuaded Magus, Ptolemy's half brother, who was viceroy in Cyrenaica, to repudiate Egyptian sovereignty. Magus married Antiochus' daughter Apama in the bargain and prepared, in B.C. 274, to invade Egypt, while Antiochus undertook a coordinated assault on Coele-Syria.[3]

---

3. The "Syria" of antiquity was a broadly used term and covered all the territories from the Taurus mountains to Gaza, and from the Mediterranean sometimes as far as the Tigris. The ancient geographers normally made a further distinction between northern and southern Syria. The first was known as Syria Seleucis and embraced the rectangle of land from the Taurus to the river Eleutherus and eastward to the Euphrates. This was the heartland of Seleucid power, and south of the Eleutherus lay Ptolemaic Syria, commonly known as

Ptolemy was not without his own support, chiefly his remarkable sister Arsinoë who had earlier fled to Egypt from Ceraunus. In B.C. 275 Ptolemy repudiated his wife and raised Arsinoë to the throne beside him. The marriage between brother and sister, which lasted only five years, until Arsinoë's death in B.C. 270, violated the deepest Hellenic taboos against incest, even though there was more than adequate precedent in Egyptian Pharaonic custom. Pragmatically, however, it worked, both as a political act for Egypt and as a personal one for Ptolemy, who found in the marriage a wife and a queen as well as a formidable piece of political and dynastic insurance. Under their dual reign Egypt reached its Hellenistic pinnacle.

It is the verdict of historians that it was Arsinoë's energy and ambition that converted Ptolemy's difficulties of B.C. 276 into the glories of B.C. 272. Magus' invasion was checked and the Egyptian fleet continued to rule the Aegean. Antiochus' invasion of Coele-Syria was blocked, and though the Seleucids held on to Damascus, the entire Phoenician coast remained firmly in Egyptian hands. Ptolemy was even more successful in Anatolia, where by B.C. 272 Egypt held all the cities from Miletus south round the coast as far as eastern Cilicia. On land and on the sea Ptolemy II had no rivals.

At home Ptolemy and his queen were sung by the poets and scholars whom he and his father had collected at Alexandria. Their position was now so strong that Ptolemy could attempt a completely unprecedented move, the declaration, sometime before B.C. 271, of his own and his sister's divinity. The incentive may have come from Arsinoë herself, and its success may be judged by the fact that it quickly became a standard policy of the Hellenistic kings to proclaim their own divinity under a variety of cult names that set forth their claims and their image to their subjects—"Savior" (*Soter*), "Benefactor" (*Euergetes*), "Victorious" (*Nikator*)—as the occasion seemed to warrant.

Ptolemy's activities were not limited by the sweep of his fleet. The growing success of his commercial enterprises put the diplomatic weapon of gold in his hands. He spent lavishly in Greece, chiefly to raise opposition to Gonatas. Pyrrhus was in Ptolemy's pay after his return to Greece from southern Italy, and

---

Koile ("Hollow") Syria. This latter could be further divided in various ways (Philistia, Phoenicia, Judaea, etc.), but as used in the pages that follow, Coele-Syria means southern Syria and Palestine.

after the king of Epirus' misadventures and death in the Peloponnesus in B.C. 272, Ptolemy found new bludgeons against Gonatas in Sparta and Athens. Areus of Sparta was Ptolemy's creature, and the Chremonidean War was largely of his making.

Egyptian gold failed to bring Gonatas down in Greece, but Ptolemy had more success in Anatolia, where he connived with Eumenes, the new governor of Pergamum—Philetaerus had died in B.C. 263—to throw off the very nominal suzerainty of Antiochus.[4] It was more than merely substituting the portrait of Philetaerus for that of Seleucus on the Pergamene coinage. Eumenes' ambitions were geographical as well as numismatic, and with the help of Ptolemy's subsidies he began to detach Pergamum's neighboring cities from the grip of Antiochus. When Antiochus came up to protect his interests Ptolemy swung into action in person and took the rich city of Ephesus as his own. Antiochus had then to deal with this more threatening enemy, and as a result Eumenes held what he had, the nucleus of a new kingdom of Pergamum that dominated the northwest corner of Anatolia and which he and his successors husbanded into an Asian power.

Ptolemy's undoing in Anatolia came about through a shadowy figure known only as "Ptolemy the Son," very probably the son of Arsinoë and Lysimachus who had been chased from Macedon first by Ceraunus and then by Gonatas.[5] If this is indeed who he was, he seems to have been earmarked for the succession in Egypt at the expense of the children of Ptolemy's first marriage and to have been entrusted with the rule of the Crown Colony of Ephesus, doubtless at the urging of Arsinoë.

Ptolemy the Son may have felt the ground slipping from beneath his feet, since he risked his chances for a legitimate succession to his stepfather by supporting an insurrection at Ephesus in B.C. 260. Miletus and its Ptolemaic governor went over to him. Antiochus I Soter had died in B.C. 261 and had been succeeded by his son as Antiochus II Theos, and the new Seleucid ruler was promptly on the scene in Ionia in B.C. 260. Gonatas too was by

---

4. About the same time the territory of Cappadocia likewise deserted the Seleucids and constituted itself an independent kingdom.

5. The anti-Gonatas policy pursued so relentlessly by Ptolemy II probably rested there, on whatever familial loyalty he may have felt to the claim of Ceraunus and, more likely, on Arsinoë's disappointed hopes of having her son rule in Macedon.

then free of the encumbrances of the Chremonidean War and eager to revenge himself on Ptolemy. Rhodes was another maritime ally, and in B.C. 259 it was a Rhodian adventurer who took Ephesus—Ptolemy the Son was killed by his own troops—and in the following year Miletus fell to Antiochus II. At about the same time, Gonatas' fleet won a huge and unexpected naval victory over Ptolemy II off the island of Cos.

The peace that was finally concluded between Ptolemy and Antiochus II in B.C. 255 left the former Egyptian Empire considerably diminished from her days of glory a mere fifteen years before. Ptolemy had to surrender the Cyclades and Delos, Samothrace,[6] his Ionian cities and the provinces of Cilicia and Pamphylia. Antiochus annexed the Phoenician coast southward from Aradus to Sidon and appropriated to himself the title of God (*Theos*).

Ptolemy was not overawed by the newly fashioned thalassocracy of Gonatas and kept up the pressure on his rival in Greece until his death in B.C. 246. He interfered in Greece as the opportunity presented itself, but his best contrived stroke was an alliance with Antiochus II Theos, sealed, in the usual fashion, by a dynastic marriage. In return for the renunciation of his claims on Phoenicia, Ptolemy offered his daughter Berenice[7] and a staggering dowry to Antiochus. Antiochus accepted, repudiated his wife Laodice, and in B.C. 252 married Berenice, who soon bore him a son.

All seemed to be going according to plan, except that Laodice, who had children of her own by Antiochus, refused to follow the example of her more docile predecessors and go into quiet exile. She continued to hold forth at Ephesus, while Ptolemy's daughter Berenice played the Seleucid queen at Antioch. Where Antiochus stood is unclear, and perhaps unimportant, since at Antiochus' death in B.C. 246 Laodice imperturbably claimed that it was her son, Seleucus, who was the designated heir. Berenice's own son by Antiochus II was still no more than a child, but the strength of her position obviously rested on her Egyptian connections.

---

6. Where, on the island that had once sheltered Arsinoë in her flight from Ceraunus, Gonatas erected the *Winged Victory* to commemorate his naval victory over Ptolemy.

7. Berenice, like Ptolemy's son and successor, Ptolemy III, was the offspring of his first wife. Ptolemy II and his sister Arsinoë had no children.

Ptolemy II died at the beginning of B.C. 246, and so it was his son and Berenice's brother Ptolemy III who responded to her call for assistance. The Seleucid territories began to polarize between the rival queens—Anatolia for Laodice and Seleucus; Syria and the east for Berenice. Ptolemy's first act was to move his fleet into position off Cilicia and seal off the Taurus. It was a sound move but apparently rendered pointless when some of the palace guard at Antioch rose up and murdered Berenice and her son. The issue did not, however, disappear in this flurry of violence, because somehow the murder of the queen and the child was kept quiet. In the spring of B.C. 246 Ptolemy III came in person to Antioch, as if in response to a summons from the legitimate heir. He was received with acclamation, marched through Syria eastward to Seleucia on the Tigris to receive the fealty of the eastern satraps, and liberally sprinkled the Seleucid domains with Egyptian garrisons before returning home. It was an altogether incredible performance, and Ptolemy himself can hardly have thought that it would hold up.

It did not. Laodice's son Seleucus II was scouting an army in Anatolia,[8] and the death of the pretender was eventually revealed. Seleucus came over the Taurus and had no trouble in regaining the paternal estates in northern Syria. But Phoenicia would not and did not yield to him and he never reestablished Seleucid control over the eastern satrapies beyond Babylon. An attempt at confronting Ptolemy on the sea also came to nothing when a storm destroyed the Seleucid fleet. In the end the only real reversal that Ptolemy III suffered was a naval defeat by Gonatas off the island of Andros in B.C. 245. Gonatas could not, however, follow up his success, because of the pressures from the increasingly aggressive Achaean League, whose captain Aratus took from him his base at Corinth in B.C. 243. Corinth was the anchor of Gonatas' "empire," and its loss announced the presence in Greece of a far more dangerous foe than the distant Ptolemy.

The war on his sister Berenice's behalf may have been a fiasco, but the events of B.C. 245–241 otherwise played into Ptolemy's hands. There was no one to hinder him in the Aegean once Gonatas and Seleucus II had perforce to withdraw, and so he was able to reassemble almost all the pieces of his father's domain.

---

8. He raised allies from the suspicious northerners by parceling out a nubile sister each to Mithridates of Pontus and Ariarathes of Cappadocia.

And in the balance Egypt gained twenty years of peace. Ptolemy III ruled in security, while the Antigonids, Sparta and the Leagues fought for the control of Greece, and while Seleucus struggled to maintain himself in Asia.

The war for Laodice was a disaster for her son. To raise an army against Ptolemy III in B.C. 245, Seleucus II had had to barter away all but autonomous control of Anatolia to his younger brother Antiochus Hierax. Once freed of Ptolemy, Seleucus tried to regain what he had given away, but only succeeded in making his own position even more insecure. For support Hierax turned where others had turned before him, to the Galatian tribes of central Anatolia. They did as they were bid by Hierax and inflicted a crippling defeat on Seleucus near Ancyra (B.C. 238). But Hierax was in no position to restrain them from further action. His rampaging Celts pinned Hierax in Sardis while they once again overran the *poleis* of western Anatolia.

Seleucus II was powerless in Anatolia, as now was Hierax. Resistance to the Galatians fell to others, to the armies of the newly hatched kingdom of Pergamum. Eumenes' cousin and heir now ruled there as Attalus I (B.C. 241–197), and in B.C. 230 he faced down the Galatians in the upper Caicus valley. He won the gratitude of the other Hellenes of Asia, who understood how close they stood to disaster, and once secure in the knowledge that no one would now rise up to the defense of the discredited Hierax, Attalus drove the Seleucid pretender from Asia. Hierax was still capable of mischief, however. He raised some troops in Armenia, but rather than face Attalus, he turned once again against his brother. Hierax stirred up trouble in Antioch and did some campaigning on his own in Mesopotamia. Seleucus was left with little choice but to break off his pressing projects farther east and return to the challenge of his brother. It was a decision that cost his house its possession of Iran.[9]

Hierax was eventually dispatched, but Seleucus II died in the same year as his brother (B.C. 226), and the three years of the reign of Seleucus III saw little improvement in the affairs of the dynasty. His generals had some initial success against the now dangerous Attalus, but at Seleucus III's death in B.C. 223 they began to make their own plans for the future in despite of Seleucus' younger brother and heir, Antiochus III. They had

---

9. See Chapter VI, p. 243.

gravely miscalculated. The young Antiochus dealt first with his insurrectionist governor in Babylon in B.C. 220, left Attalus temporarily to do his work in Anatolia, and turned instead to what he judged to be the root of his troubles, Egypt; it is almost certain that both Attalus and Hierax had been drawing subsidies from Ptolemy III.

Antiochus III wasted little time in displaying his energy. Ptolemy III died in B.C. 221, and no sooner was Ptolemy IV Philopator installed in Alexandria than Antiochus began probing the Ptolemaic defenses in Syria. Nothing came of this campaign, except that it served notice that Antiochus would not rest content with the *status quo* in Syria. Once he had put down the revolt in Babylon he could deal with the Egyptians more vigorously. He recaptured Seleucia Pieria, the port of Antioch, in B.C. 219 and drove down the coast of Phoenicia.

Antiochus, it is clear, could have taken Egypt in B.C. 219–218. Twenty years of peace had taken its toll on the Egyptian army. But if Ptolemy IV had few or no troops in those days, he did possess a minister of considerable talent. The reins of state were firmly in the grasp of his vizier Sosibius, whose diplomacy and determination in those difficult years saved Egypt. Antiochus was given to believe that a large Egyptian army awaited him at Pelusium on the frontiers of Egypt, and while he spent two years in an almost leisurely dismantling of the Ptolemaic strongpoints in Phoenicia and Palestine, Sosibius brought that shadow army from rumor to reality by the unprecedented move of recruiting native Egyptians to take up arms. By the summer of B.C. 217 Sosibius had put in the field a phalanx manned by twenty thousand Egyptians. Under the personal leadership of Ptolemy IV and his sister and future bride Arsinoë, they took up their stand at Raphia near Gaza. The scenario called for a rout of the Egyptians, but the native troops held against Antiochus' charge and Egypt was safe.

Raphia was an opportunity wasted for Antiochus. His armies withdrew through Syria, and in the subsequent peace the Seleucids kept the port of Seleucia Pieria as their own, but lost what they had so briefly held in Coele-Syria. The portrait of the two kings of Egypt and Asia sketched in B.C. 217, Ptolemy IV triumphant and Antiochus III in dispirited retreat, was seriously flawed, however. Trouble awaited Ptolemy at home and, in a sense, Egypt never recovered from the victory at Raphia. Sosibius' policies of taxation and recruitment, necessary in the face of the dangers of B.C. 219–218, bore painful fruits in the following years. Antiochus, on the other hand, was far from quelled. No more than two years after Raphia he was campaigning in Asia Minor, settling down the insurrection that had been brewing there since the days of Seleucus II. And if he made no serious inroads against the power of Pergamum, he was firmly established north of the Taurus and the Aegean was once again within the Seleucid grasp.

The Pharaonic Corporation

Ptolemy I Soter found Egypt a sound if sluggish giant. The land was rich, and there was a kind of primitive efficiency in the manner in which it was controlled. At the head of the state was the divine Pharaoh. He ruled Egypt as his own property, a personal monopoly governed in his name by an army of bureaucrats and a second army of priests, both of which rested on the broad base of the peasantry, who tilled the soil and paid the taxes and rents. It was the way Egypt had been ruled for centuries, a method sanctioned by both immemorial tradition and unmistakable success.

No one had ever succeeded in radically altering the system. Ptolemy I and his successors merely grafted a new class between the body and the head. The Ptolemies ruled as somewhat newfangled Pharaohs, but to do their bidding they had a new class of Hellenes—Greeks and Macedonians—to govern the state, fight its battles, enhance its commercial life, and add that intellectual panache for which Egypt became famous during the Hellenistic age.

The early Ptolemies were somewhat more and somewhat less than Pharaohs. Their survival rested on their claim to Hellenic kingship, and so the face they turned to the Mediterranean was a Hellenic one: successors of Alexander, patrons of the arts and, on the Stoic model that gained currency in the post-Alexander world, benefactors of mankind. The first four Ptolemies were fastidious in their Hellenic imagery. They were crowned according to Greek formulae and kept the personal cult, first of the dead Pharaoh and then, with Ptolemy II, of the living ruler, on public and splendid display in Alexandria and such international show places as Delos. Their laureates, Callimachus and Theocritus, sang their praises in ecumenical Greek.

The Ptolemies' Hellenism was well advised. The twin sources of Egypt's new power were its Macedonian army and its Greek entrepreneurs. It was the former that had shielded Egypt from the rival ambitions of Perdiccas and Antigonus and then garrisoned the Ptolemaic cities in Anatolia, Phoenicia and the islands. Constructed around the central core of heavy Macedonian infantry, twenty to twenty-five thousand men in the phalanx formation, the total field strength of the army was probably about double that size when fleshed out with mercenaries like the Galatians or with native Egyptian auxiliaries. In support were the inevitable elephants which the Ptolemies procured at great expense from east Africa.

The Macedonian phalanx was the heart of the army, and in Egypt as elsewhere the Macedonian fighting man was a valuable commodity. He could be—and was—replaced by Greek troops that were recruited from the mainland at a good price; but, until Raphia, natives were considered unsuited for phalanx service. To pay off their troops the Ptolemies gave both money and land in exchange for services. The troopers were given "lots" (*kleroi*) of land, and since the lot holders and their descendants were liable to further service, the Ptolemies constructed for themselves a kind of local militia and, at the same time, the cadres of a military reserve.

The reward of stability was empire, and as time passed, the offensive front line of the Ptolemies passed from their army to their fleet. Out of the wreckage of Demetrius Poliorcetes' ruined ambitions Ptolemy Soter constructed an Aegean thalassocracy that was still intact almost half a century later. From B.C. 285 to B.C. 241 Egypt was the paramount naval power in the eastern Mediterranean. She controlled the trade depots and arsenals in Ionia and Phoenicia, the timber lands in southern Anatolia, and the way stations in the Cyclades and throughout the Aegean. Cyrene was her colony, and she traded extensively with Sicily and Carthage in the west.

In fifth-century Athens the fleet had been the rallying point of lower-class democrats, but by the Hellenistic period a curious reversal had taken place. The light and highly maneuverable ships powered by citizen rowers of the earlier day had given way to the gigantic dreadnoughts cherished by the Hellenistic rulers. Like their elephant counterparts on land, they counted on shock and ram tactics. These showy if ineffective warships were born as much from the lack of trained and skilled rowers as from the penchant for monumental overstatement that characterized the style of Hellenistic kingship. Aboard their ships the Ptolemies had whatever manpower they could afford, local rowers and native Egyptian marines on the royal fleet and, on the private craft supplied by the rich citizens of Alexandria, mercenary Greek crews.

Shielded behind their army and their impressive but inefficient navy, Ptolemy Soter and Philadelphus could lord it as Hellenes in the Mediterranean, while at home they practiced a blend of the old and the new in the management of their estate. The basis of Egyptian prosperity in international trade was her grain exports. The Egyptian political presence in the ports of the Aegean certainly enhanced this trade, but it did not eliminate the need for middlemen. That role was played for Egypt, and for the other grain-producing areas like southern Russia, Cyrene and Sicily, by the bankers and shipowners of Rhodes. The grain supplies upon which the eastern *poleis*, and eventually Rome, depended for their existence passed through Rhodes, on Rhodian ships, and floated on Rhodian capital. Not until Rome possessed herself of the *oikoumene* and so could import her grain directly from Egypt did Rhodes' position falter.

The Ptolemies actively scouted markets for their grain. We know that Philadelphus was in touch with Rome as early as B.C. 273, possibly for commercial reasons, and thereafter there were frequent initiatives tendered by Egypt to this burgeoning new market in the west. The Ptolemies were likewise careful to cultivate the Rhodian brokers who did their business. Frequent gifts of grain are recorded, and when the earthquake that destroyed the Colossus struck Rhodes in B.C. 227, Egypt was among her many commercial clients who hastened to the island's assistance; from as far away as Sicily in the west and Pontus in the east help came to the port that served them all as sales and purchase agent. Nor was grain the only tie between Egypt and Rhodes. Even the caravan routes which terminated in Phoenician ports under Ptolemaic control moved their goods first to Rhodes, thence to be transshipped to Alexandria and the rest of the Mediterranean.

Egypt's new posture on the international markets was the creation of the early Ptolemies. The state was reorganized from within, and doors were opened to new suppliers and new markets without. Egypt's had always been a controlled economy, wherein not only the means of production but the land itself was held, in one form or another, in the Pharaoh's name. The Ptolemies did nothing to change the system at its root—Greek notions of private property and laissez-faire economy remained alien concepts along the Nile—but they did improve the organization and operation of the Pharaonic system. Greek managers and control mechanisms were installed. The land, upon which Egypt's wealth ultimately rested, was more carefully registered. Its possession continued as before, land held directly by the king or land granted in lease by the king, and though the Ptolemies did not tamper with the theory, their leases did reflect the new circumstances of their rule.

Land was leased, as has been seen, to their soldiers in the form of inalienable lots (*kleroi*). Some tracts were newly attached to their few experiments with the *polis* to serve as a kind of hinterland on the Greek model. Finally, in an attempt to stimulate more enlightened and aggressive cultivation, large tracts were granted as "gift estates" (*doreai*) to members of the new Greek civil-servant class. From all these carefully supervised holdings came the Ptolemies' wealth in the form of rents and taxes. Down through the system were ranged Greek bureaucrats, from the chief manager (*dioiketes*) in Alexandria to the supervisors and comptrollers in the provinces. The registries were checked, and both the planting and harvesting of grain were carefully watched. The wheat itself was stored in local royal granaries and eventually shipped to Alexandria.

The productive capacity of the land rose from the more efficient supervision imposed by the Ptolemies, but the export economy that guaranteed their place in the commercial *oikoumene* demanded greater and greater surpluses. The Ptolemies met this need by putting more land under cultivation. The irrigation system was improved, and new, modern agricultural tools were placed in the hands of the cultivators.[10] A different form of wheat grain was introduced to compete on the international market.

The Ptolemies' decision to introduce a new wheat strain that conformed more closely to the consumption patterns of the Greek market was not the only example of the adaptation of traditional ways to the demands and tastes of the Greek-oriented *oikoumene*. A self-contained Egypt on a subsistence economy drank beer, for example, and dressed itself in linen; Egypt of the Pharaohs raised olives for eating. But now there were nearly one million Hellenes or Hellenized in Egypt. Under the Ptolemies they drank wine, dressed in wool, and converted olives into oil for hundreds of purposes. The Egyptian economy had not only to cater to the tastes of this new ruling class, it had also to sell its goods around the Mediterranean to other Hellenes of similar tastes. The culture of the vine and the olive tree took enormous strides forward. Sheep raising was begun, and entire sectors of the industrial economy were converted to supplying the demands of Hellenic taste in pottery, utensils, jewelry and costume.

Over all of these industries the Ptolemies exercised an exclusive monopoly which regulated operations down to the smallest details. And in accordance with a long-standing Pharaonic tradition, both transportation and manpower could be commandeered. In the statist practice of Egyptian rule, both were resources of the ruler, who was the state, and were to be used at his discretion. Frequently this would be done under contract, but in emergencies there stood readily at hand the *corvée* (*angareia*) or the unabashed requisitioning of matériel. For the ordinary and oppressed Egyptian the only recourse was service or flight (*anachoresis*) into another district or into the desert wastes beyond the reach of the commissars and the tax collectors.

One of the most important of the Ptolemaic enterprises was that in papyrus. The growth in both chancelleries and schools during the Hellenistic age stimulated an increased appetite for writing materials. The parchment of Pergamum would one day challenge Egypt's grip on the papyrus trade, but under the first

---

10. The iron age in weaponry had come to Egypt centuries earlier, but the Ptolemies, incredibly, were the first rulers to introduce agricultural instruments made of the rare iron into the life of Egypt.

Ptolemies, and particularly Philadelphus, the Mediterranean world inscribed its records and its literature on papyrus, and this came from Egypt. It is not clear whether the Ptolemies originally exercised a total monopoly on its manufacture, but their opening of Egypt to international trade finds no more striking illustration than the plunge in the price of papyrus rolls after B.C. 300. The price began to climb again some twenty years later, perhaps by reason of Philadelphus' monopolistic capture of the trade and its consequent manipulation.[11] Egypt must have remained, however, her own best customer for papyrus. The highly centralized bureaucracy there kept records on every person and every acre in the land, and at one point the Library at Alexandria possessed 700,000 papyrus rolls in its collection.

As impressive as was the early Ptolemies' internal organization of their inheritance, their casting of their lines abroad was an even more remarkable feat, particularly when viewed against the closed and introverted patterns of life and rule that characterized the most recent periods of Egyptian history. The very first Ptolemy, Soter, set the land on the path of economic imperialism from which it never departed until its own internal problems made Alexandria yield its place to Rome.

The commercial prosperity of Egypt rested upon two bases, its own agricultural wealth, which made it one of the Mediterranean's chief exporters, and its ability to control the trade routes that ran into the Mediterranean from the south and east. Some trade items Egypt reserved for her own use—horses, copper and timber from her dependencies in Cyrenaica, Cyprus and Cilicia, gold to stabilize her coinage imported from Ethiopia, and the indispensable elephants hunted in east Africa—but the rest was shipped, either in raw form or as manufactured items, from Alexandria and Rhodes to the urban markets of the Aegean and the west.

Their Mediterranean fleet and the course of events after Ipsus gave the Ptolemies a hold on many of the termini of the overland routes from the east, notably at Ephesus, the end of the trans-Anatolian routes, and at Tyre and Sidon; but as long as the

---

11. That monopoly within Egypt could lead to a manipulation of the international commodity market was made clear in Alexander's lifetime when Cleomenes, his agent in Egypt, withheld Egyptian wheat from the Aegean markets and provoked or contributed to a famine that had particularly severe results in Athens.

Seleucids held Babylon or Damascus the flow of goods was regulated by foreign and hostile hands. Egypt had other ways to the east, however, and under Philadelphus she began to exploit them in conjunction with her unshakable monopoly on the routes to Africa. Trade with Africa could come down the Nile through various hands until it reached the Egyptian frontier, but under Philadelphus explorers from Egypt moved up the river to the sources of that trade. Greek voyagers sailed beyond Meroë as far as Ethiopia. Meroë itself began to be Hellenized under their influence, and as the kingdom there extended its domain southward over Ethiopia, raw materials flowed in increasing quantities from the south to the warehouses and wharves of Alexandria.

Though the Nile route to the south had its attractions, Ptolemy II showed far greater interest in the maritime routes that led down through the Red Sea to the Somali coast of Africa and the great trading emporia across the Bab el Mandeb in Arabia. Soter had begun the exploration of the Red Sea, but Philadelphus exploited that area more thoroughly. From Arsinoë (Suez) and Myos Hormos in the north to the Bab el Mandeb in the south, Philadelphus and Euergetes founded coastal stations along the western shore of the Red Sea to serve as eastern ports of entry to their kingdom. At first Philadelphus opened the old Pharaonic canal between Suez and the Nile, but this appears to have fallen into disuse and silted up, replaced within a short time by the port of Berenice, which was connected to Coptos on the Nile by a well-patrolled and well-maintained caravan route.

Egypt was not the only Red Sea power in the third century. At the southern tip of Arabia were the Arab Sabaeans of the Yemen, the resident masters of the proverbially rich "Araby the Blest" (*Arabia Eudaimon*), who effectively controlled the trade coming overseas from India. The Ptolemies' lust for elephants eventually brought the Somali and Ethiopian side of the straits under their control,[12] but during this period, at least, nothing broke the Sabaean lock on the Red Sea; the Egyptians were contained within and the Indian trade lay beyond. Nor did the Sabaeans necessarily hand on the Indian goods for shipment to Alexandria. In the third century before Christ there was already a thriving overland caravan route up the western coast of Arabia, through the Hejaz to Petra, the capital of the Nabataean Arabs

12. Adulis, the chief port of Ethiopia, began as a Ptolemaic settlement.

and the distribution point to Egypt via Gaza and to the north via Damascus.[13]

Philadelphus made at least one direct attempt at cutting out the Nabataeans in B.C. 278–277, when an expedition was sent to northern Arabia. It seems to have done little good; the commercial power of Petra grew undisturbed. Philadelphus probably paid his price and took his stuffs, in this case spices and gold from Arabia, and ivory, pearls, spices, dyes, cotton and silk from India. There was apparently enough value in the trade that all three middle-men—Sabaeans, Nabataeans and Egyptians—could grow rich upon it. And yet it must have been only a fraction of what it was later to become when the Roman market and its insatiable craving for luxuries began to open. By then, however, none of the third-century reapers was strong enough for the harvest.

This rich international trade was controlled, as all else in Egypt, from Alexandria, where the factories, warehouses, port facilities, banks and most importantly the royal exchequer were located. There may have been private capital involved, and certainly privately owned ships for transshipment across the Mediterranean, but all else was in the hands of the Ptolemies. They owned the facilities, regulated the tariffs, pocketed the considerable taxes on trade, and above all controlled the currency. Alexander had introduced a standard coinage based on Attic weights into the *oikoumene*. Soter at first followed suit, but ended by minting his own silver coins on the standard used in the Phoenician cities. It was doubtless a recognition of Egypt's new role in the caravan trade that had in the past centered in Phoenicia and whose clients were accustomed to that standard. But at the same time it was an act of isolation, curiously different from Soter's other Panhellenic gestures. This departure from the Attic standard was but another example of Egypt's Janus posture under their new rulers. The coinage itself was schizophrenic. The natives had no experience with gold or silver coinage, and so business in Egypt was conducted through bronze coins, while the international trade used gold and silver, a distinction observed nowhere else in the Hellenistic world.

---

13. When the Ptolemies took control of Palestine the latter route shifted somewhat to the Ptolemaic cities of Philadelphia (Amman), Gerasa (Jerash), and Ptolemais (Acre). With the loss of Palestine to the Seleucids of Antiochus III, the cut across Galilee was abandoned for the Damascus-Antioch route to the sea.

Aegean entrepreneur or Asian caravan master? International silver or local bronze? King of Alexandria or Pharaoh of the countryside (*chora*)? Hellene or Egyptian? Before Raphia the choice was very much in the balance for Egypt's masters. Egypt was a land of nearly seven and a half million inhabitants during Ptolemaic times, of whom seven million were Egyptian natives resident in the *chora*. Alexandria may have numbered about 300,000 inhabitants under the Ptolemies—it was later to grow to a million in Roman Imperial times—of whom perhaps no more than half were Greeks or Macedonians. The figures are tentative in the extreme, but the impression is doubtless correct: amidst the natives a tiny minority of Greeks lived self-contained in their Hellenic enclaves like Alexandria and Naucratis or else strung out in thin lines through the administrative network that covered Egypt. The Ptolemies had to rule both Greeks and Egyptians, and a very mixed body of Mediterranean immigrants in the bargain.

Alexandria was a Hellenic city with a mixed population that under the Ptolemies grew into the greatest urban complex in the entire *oikoumene*. It is not difficult to understand why. All the intellectual, social and commercial energies of Egypt focused there, without distraction or diversion to other centers. In the colonial territories, in Cyrenaica, Palestine and Syria, the Ptolemies possessed other cities which they themselves had founded or whose growth they encouraged; but in Egypt, Alexandria was supreme and all but unique. And yet its position there was anomalous. Alexandria was the residence of the Egyptian ruler and his court, and yet it was, in a sense, outside Egypt, an artificial organ that was, according to the official nomenclature, "by Egypt" (*pros Aigypton*), but certainly not of it. It was among the largest Greek cities in the world, but it lacked the signal criterion of *polis* status, self-government. The Greek residents of Alexandria had their own local laws, but rule in any real sense of that word issued to them from within the royal precincts that dominated the city. The analogies with Washington, D.C., are almost exact.

The city founded by Alexander and adorned by his successors in Egypt has not notably yielded to archaeology. The little we know of it we know chiefly from literary description. It was a new foundation and, so, a planned city on a rectangular grid, and bisected, at right angles, by two main streets. Walls covered the

land approaches on the east and the west, and on the other two
sides the city fronted on water—on the north the natural harbor
created by the offshore island of Pharos,[14] and on the south the
waters of Lake Mareotis which connected with the Nile.

Within the city the palace complex of the Ptolemies dominated
the urban landscape. Within it were the palaces proper, the
offices of the sprawling bureaucracy that ran the Pharaonic
corporation, the Museum and the Library, the magnificent
Mausoleum of Alexander, parks, temples, promenades and the
Royal Zoo. Alone outside the precinct the temple of Serapis, the
Serapeum, and its auxiliary library, could rival what was within.

It was an altogether splendid place, a city of the *oikoumene*
rather than of the land that gave it sustenance, and it held within
its walls the most polyglot urban population in the world. Homogeneous populations were never very common in the East, and
Alexander's opening of that world to further immigration merely
encouraged what was already the normal state. His one city in
Egypt was Greek in style, designed as the home territory for the
Greek masters of the land. It became, however, a commercial
city and the seat of an empire, and so there came to it not only
Greeks and Macedonians to use its Hellenic institutional facilities
and amenities, but the entire range of ethnic and social classes in
pursuit of money, dreams or preferment, or drawn on by the
simpler but equally persuasive manacle of slavery. Egyptians
moved self-interestedly into the orbit of Hellenism then, and
Indians and Africans arrived in the wake of trade. The bulk of
the foreign immigrants must have come, however, from the
Ptolemies' nearest colonial possession, Syria-Palestine. Ptolemaic
armies ranged over that territory at frequent intervals, and they
dragged or led back with them mercenaries, traders, prisoners
and slaves. One ancient account has Ptolemy I Soter bringing
back 100,000 Jewish captives. The number is too high, but Soter
fought four campaigns in Palestine, and it is likely that the considerable colony of Jews in Egypt, most of them located in Alexandria, began with the first Ptolemy.

In Alexandria and elsewhere the Jews frequently constituted a

---

14. Alexander had himself linked Pharos to the mainland with an
artificial mole and thus created two harbors. The western of these was
relatively open, but the eastern, where the royal fleet was berthed, was
heavily fortified and dominated by the gigantic lighthouse constructed
on the eastern end of Pharos island.

corporation, or *politeuma*, a form of association originally applied to new urban centers of mixed population which did not qualify as fully constituted *poleis*,[15] but later came to be used of homogeneous communities *within* larger urban complexes. They may originally have been collections of alien mercenaries, but the term *politeuma* soon broadened beyond its original military associations. Egypt had within it *politeumata* of Cretans, Phrygians, Boeotians, Lycians and Cilicians, and, at Alexandria, a *politeuma* of Jews who lived together[16] and were allowed, like other similarly constituted bodies, a considerable degree of self-government under its "ethnarch."

The Jews at Alexandria were apparently not full citizens of the polity, probably because of their inability to participate in the religious life of the state. At this point it was a matter of no importance, since even the legal "citizens" of the city, the Greeks who were not part of the royal complex, had no real rights but stood under the control of the Ptolemies' city prefect.

Even here, in the city where the Greek tradition was the strongest, it was transparently clear that Egypt belonged to the Ptolemies. Self-government was an alien notion in Egypt, and the Jews probably possessed as much of it as anyone did. For its surrender the Greek in Egypt received the perquisites of a ruling, though ruled, class. The institutions and public monuments of Alexandria were those of a Greek city. Temples, baths, theaters and gymnasia were lavishly supplied for the most refined of Hellenic tastes. State-supported education provided the means for either creating a new generation of Hellenes or saving the current one. The Museum belonged to the Ptolemies and in a sense to the *oikoumene*, but even the *chora* was not lacking in schools and teachers to spread the rudiments of Greek culture and style.

No effort was made to keep the natives, the "folk" (*laos*), from slipping into the lists. If Hellenism was a discriminatory criterion in Egypt, Greek blood never was, and as the sources of immigration from Greece began to dry up, the rulers of Egypt had to decide between broadening their Hellenization program or facing the eventual orientalization of their realms. They inevi-

---

15. And thus was similar in intent to the military colony (*katoikia*) that had a degree of self-determination but not the full range of urban privileges associated with the *polis*.

16. Though not of necessity; Jewish synagogues were located in all quarters of the city.

tably chose the former, and the ruling class of Ptolemaic Egypt, though sorely pressed by the economic and social dissatisfaction of the *laos,* never surrendered their distinctive Hellenism. Erosion there was and, after B.C. 200, a marked increase of Helleno-Egyptian syncretism in the once pure culture of the upper classes. The roots, however, held until the Romans occupied the land and reversed the policies of the later Ptolemies. Like Soter, Philadelphus and Euergetes I, Rome saw in Hellenism the key to Egyptian prosperity.

The Later Ptolemies (B.C. 214–131)

The victory at Raphia in B.C. 217, it turned out, had been dearly bought. Antiochus III had been held at bay, and for the rest of his reign Ptolemy IV Philopator had nothing to fear from the otherwise distracted Seleucid. But the price exacted by the vizier Sosibius, calculated in terms of cash and as a lien on the future, sealed Egypt's doom. An independent Egypt dragged on its existence for nearly two centuries after Raphia. During most of that time, however, it was sheltered by the power of the Romans, who would eventually annex it. Freed of foreign tampering by Rome's nervous benevolence, Egypt was free to orchestrate her own downfall with the twin discords of financial disintegration and dynastic quarreling.

The cost of Raphia, both in raising the army before the battle and in rewarding it afterward, had to be exacted in taxes dealt upon the land by Sosibius in the name of Ptolemy. There had been hard times before, and doubtless Egypt could have survived this new squeeze had it not been compounded by far more ominous stirrings within the populace. In their reversal of the traditional practice, Philopator and Sosibius were driven by military necessity to grant to the *laos* a share in the operation of the state. The military parity of Greek and Egyptian signaled by Raphia had subsequently to be redeemed by political and economic parity, and the exchange of these expectations for higher rents and the introduction of a poll tax raised native discontent to the level of insurrection. Raphia was a national, not a Ptolemaic, victory, and the nation was cheated of its rewards.

Both Philopator (B.C. 221–204) and his youthful successor Ptolemy V Epiphanes (B.C. 203–181) were faced with serious revolts that served merely to increase the financial drain on the already laboring state and, more seriously, distracted Egypt from its other source of income, its holdings in the Aegean. After Raphia the foundations upon which Soter, Philadelphus and Euergetes I had constructed their empire were allowed to rot. Nationalism, its rise and the efforts made to counter it, ruined Egypt's earlier internationalism, and with it disappeared the economic prosperity that had made the land a Mediterranean power for more than a century.

Events both at home and abroad conspired against Egypt. Men and money had to be thrown into the fight against the rebels, who nonetheless gained control of important areas of Upper Egypt. A Nubian secessionist dynasty ruled around Thebes for nearly twenty years at the beginning of the second century, probably with the encouragement of Egypt's former vassals farther south. The Ptolemies' supply of gold may have been choked off by the trouble, and at the very least the Central African trade was seriously dislocated. At the same time, Egypt's two great markets in the western Mediterranean were locked in the Punic War.

Times were not good in Egypt, and when Philopator died in B.C. 204 the kingdom passed into the uncertain hands of a boy heir, Ptolemy V Epiphanes. The dead king's two ministers, Sosibius and Agathocles, and his sister and widow, Arsinoë, grappled for control of the power, while Philip watched from Macedon and Antiochus III from Syria. The struggle led to Arsinoë's murder in B.C. 203, the disappearance of Sosibius, and the lynching of Agathocles by a bloodthirsty Alexandrian mob. Ptolemy was crowned in B.C. 203 to the accompaniment of native revolts and bloody deeds in the countryside. More threateningly, Egypt's two rivals in the Aegean took advantage of the uncertain circumstances to conclude an unholy alliance against Egypt. In B.C. 202 Antiochus III and Philip V of Macedon agreed, it was said, to partition the empire of the enfeebled Ptolemies. For Philip, sobered but unscathed from his first brush with his Roman neighbors in Illyria, the pact was of little practical consequence. He ignored the ports that were to fall to him and embarked instead on the course of ill-disguised Aegean piracy that drove the terrified Rhodians and Pergamenes into the arms of Rome and carried Philip himself to his fatal collision with the Roman legions at Cynoscephalae (B.C. 197).

Antiochus, who had little taste for Rome, now or later, concentrated on the matter at hand. In B.C. 201 a Seleucid army invaded Syria and once again, as in B.C. 219, swept as far as the last Palestinian outpost at Gaza. There was a temporary setback—Epiphanes had found an able general in Scopas, a recruit from the military organization of the Aetolian League—and the Seleucid forces were driven back into Palestine. This time, however, the inevitable could not be postponed. The rival armies clashed in B.C. 200 at Panium near the Jordan's source, and the issue of who was to possess Coele-Syria, contested since the settlement after Ipsus a century earlier, was finally decided in favor of the Seleucids. Except for the ephemeral events of B.C. 147–145, no Ptolemy ever ruled there after Panium, and in the following years Antiochus swept into his net the last traces of the Ptolemaic empire strung along the southern coast of Anatolia. Overseas all that was left to Egypt was Cyprus, and at home the dependency of Cyrene.

Ptolemy V came to terms with Antiochus in B.C. 195, ceded Coele-Syria and whatever else he had to give, and received in return the dubious gift of Antiochus' daughter who ruled Egypt at Epiphanes' side as Cleopatra I, the first of a number of eminent ladies to bear that name in Egypt. Epiphanes lost his father's empire, but in effect he bought himself time to face the problems that his father had created. The path of survival was now clearly marked for the Ptolemies, an accommodation with the *laos*, at the expense, inevitably, of the Greeks, upon whom the kingdom had so long depended.

Egypt was now almost severed from the *oikoumene* in any commercial or political sense, and the Greeks who ruled the land would have to live with the Egyptians who inhabited it. Concessions were made: a new class of Egyptian veterans were granted lots of land (*kleroi*) as the Greeks had been; the temple estates were enlarged and their privileges extended. The Ptolemies themselves attempted to construct a new image of their rule. The custom may have begun with Philopator, but by the time of Epiphanes it was assuredly the order of the day that the Ptolemy, once the proud heir of a Macedonian kingship, was crowned with full *Egyptian* protocol by the priesthood at Memphis.[17] Even the

---

17. Both the concessions to the native elements and the new monarchical style are in evidence in the most famous of all Egyptian inscriptions, the Rosetta stone, a priestly decree of B.C. 196 in honor of Ptolemy V Epiphanes. The decree, transcribed in Greek as well as

calendar, important for the regulation of the religious life of the land, was converted from the Macedonian to the Egyptian style.

The success of the new policy was limited; revolts and insurrections continued to wrack Egypt, and Epiphanes was forced to harden his concessions with more active operations against the dissidents. Thebes was finally recaptured in B.C. 187, and the insurgents in the Delta were put down some five years later. Successful repression may have given birth to some feeble hope, but Ptolemy V did not live long enough to savor it. He was poisoned in B.C. 181, aged twenty-eight, and left as his legacy to Egypt three small children and his widowed Syrian queen, Cleopatra. For the eight years of Cleopatra's regency on behalf of the young Ptolemy VI Philometor Egypt remained quiet, but at her passing, the government was taken over by the ministers, who judged the time ripe for the recovery of Coele-Syria.

The temptation was obvious, even though the results might be dangerous. The Seleucids had by then been badly chastised by the Romans in both Greece and Anatolia, and by the treaty of Apamea they had had to surrender not only Anatolia but their fleet and war elephants. The new king in Syria, Antiochus IV, was an erratic and untried quantity. Under other circumstances Egypt could likely count on Rome's help against Antiochus, but by B.C. 170, when the hostilities began, Rome had already embarked upon her final confrontation with Macedon.

Antiochus did not wait for the invasion. He swept across the Egyptian frontier and by B.C. 169 he held Ptolemy VI captive and was in possession of Memphis, where he had himself proclaimed Pharaoh. But Memphis was not Alexandria. The Egyptians at the Greek capital recognized Philometor's younger brother Euergetes II as king and prepared to defend the city. Antiochus, who had other plans in the East, possessed no appetite for a prolonged siege and withdrew, leaving the erstwhile Ptolemy VI to deal with his younger brother, the now Ptolemy VII. We do not know how Antiochus read the situation between the brothers and their respective factions, but it could not have turned out as he expected. No sooner had the Seleucids left Egypt—they held on to the frontier post at Pelusium—than the brothers were reconciled and Egypt, which had witnessed the joint reign of father

---

hieroglyphic and demotic Egyptian, was unearthed by Napoleon's troops in 1799 and led within two decades to the first decipherment of hieroglyphics.

and son and of brother and sister, now had the experience of two brother kings enjoying simultaneous rule.

Antiochus had no choice but to return. By B.C. 168, however, the Mediterranean political picture had been significantly altered. The Romans had inflicted their final defeat on the Macedonian army of Perseus at Pydna and so were free, if not eager, to deal with the Seleucid ambitions in Egypt. Nothing in the treaty of Apamea forbade the Seleucids' expansion at the expense of the Ptolemies, but Roman interests would be served neither by the growth of Antiochus nor by the disappearance of Egypt, already an important source of Roman provision. The Senate made its decision, and while the Seleucids were reoccupying Egypt and Cyprus it sent its envoy, Popilius Laenas, with a demand to Antiochus that he immediately evacuate the land. Laenas found Antiochus at the Alexandrian suburb of Eleusis, and though the ultimatum was delivered under insupportable circumstances—at Antiochus' request for time to consider, Laenas traced a circle around the Seleucid king and demanded an answer before he stepped out of it—Antiochus swallowed the affront to his pride and abandoned Egypt.

Whether Egypt was now behind a Roman shield or caught in a Roman net was not immediately apparent; what was clear was that the Seleucids could entertain no pretensions there. Ptolemy VI Philometor never quite forgave or forgot Antiochus, but henceforward Egyptian policy, internal and external, was conducted with one eye on the Roman Senate. First there was the question of the double kingship. Of late the populace of Alexandria had been taking a more energetic role in the making and unmaking of their rulers, and now there began a shuffling back and forth between Rome and Alexandria of first one brother and then the other, each pleading his case to his dual constituency, the Roman Senate and the Alexandrians. The latter were finally persuaded that the Roman solution was better. *Roma locuta est; causa finita est:* Philometor would rule in Egypt and Cyprus (B.C. 168–145), while the younger Euergetes II could have the Egyptian dependency of Cyrenaica as his domain.

Philometor was not exempt from the internal difficulties of his predecessors. There were more insurrections and more of the same royal reaction: bloody reprisals mixed with political concessions. But the old reflexes never quite disappeared. In B.C. 147 Philometor was provoked by an abortive Seleucid coup against

Cyprus to intervene once again in Syria. The dust swirled around various Seleucid pretenders there and for a brief moment Philometor regained possession of the lost territories of Coele-Syria.[18] The adventure cost him his life. In B.C. 145 he died in battle near Antioch, and Egypt quickly forfeited the unexpected restoration of her empire.

At Philometor's death there was a brief move in the direction of the king's minor sons,[19] but Euergetes II quickly made his appearance from Cyrenaica, married Philometor's widow and their common sister, Cleopatra II, and settled into the kingship (B.C. 145–116). Euergetes then made the rather extraordinary move of marrying and associating in his rule Cleopatra III, the daughter of Ptolemy VI and his current wife, Cleopatra II. This curious *ménage à trois* bred almost immediate trouble. There were more revolts at home, and the polarization of the people, the Alexandrians who supported Cleopatra II, and the priests and the *laos* who stood behind Euergetes II, led in B.C. 131 to the king's flight to Cyprus. It took Euergetes five years to plot and fight his way back to Egypt and Alexandria, and only after the growing pressures had forced Cleopatra II to decamp to Syria. Euergetes, who detested his sister as heartily as she disliked him, found that he could not rule in Alexandria without her, and since the lady preferred a throne to exile, even if the price were association with Euergetes and her equally objectionable daughter, Cleopatra II returned to Egypt in B.C. 124, and the troika somehow ran on for another eight years.

Like his predecessors, Euergetes II took measures to stem the now endemic civil war. The situation in Egypt had, perhaps, gone too far to be saved by the likes of the enfeebled Ptolemies. The strongly centralized state of the early members of the dynasty was disappearing, undermined by the growth of increasingly privileged underlings and rapacious bureaucrats. Euergetes II could not afford to curb privilege—the state now rested upon it—but he could spread it somewhat more widely in the direction of the one power group that stood as the partisans of the non-Hellenized *laos* against the Greeks of the Alexandrian establish-

18. See Chapter VIII, pp. 271–72.
19. Sometimes a dynastic number is assigned to the ephemeral Ptolemy Neos Philopator, Philometor's son, and sometimes not. He has been omitted here and Euergetes II has been reckoned the seventh Ptolemy.

ment, the native priesthoods. The temple corporations were given wider powers and grants in the hope that they might shield the *laos* from the Ptolemies' own mechanisms of rule.

Euergetes II favored *laos* institutions at the expense of the Greeks of Alexandria. Natives rather than the Hellenized received gift estates and the new Egyptian soldier class—new since Raphia—continued to be rewarded with their lots. Nor were the "Greeks" themselves what they had been in an earlier day. The racial distinction which had earlier underlain cultural differences was blurred by intermarriage and the increased association of Greeks and native Egyptians on all levels. From the third century onward the "Greeks" were merely the Hellenized, a route that in the second century was giving evidence of being a two-way street. Even those who had gone through the acculturation process were showing increasing signs of a residual Egyptianization. The Greek language was becoming barbarized, Egyptian customs like embalming and brother-sister marriages appeared among the Hellenized, and native gods dislodged the traditional Hellenic deities.

More immediately, the Alexandrians, the standard bearers of Hellenism and the disappointed supporters of Cleopatra II, made representation to Rome against their king. The Romans sent out Scipio Aemilianus, son of the victor of Pydna, Aemilius Paulus, and himself the hero of the recent sack of Carthage. A tough soldier might have understood Euergetes' policy. But Scipio Aemilianus was something more, a cultured "Hellenizer" in his own right and the center of a brilliant intellectual circle at Rome, where he served as patron of both the historian Polybius and the philosopher Panaetius.[20] This time the Roman triumphed over the Hellene, and though he treated Euergetes to a considerable degree of personal and public disdain, Scipio recommended to the Senate that they let their Egyptian client be.

Euergetes II died in B.C. 116 after he had willed the Ptolemaic appanage of Cyrene to his illegitimate son Apion as an independent kingdom.[21] His heirs in Egypt itself were his young sons who had to struggle with their mother, Cleopatra III, for their inheritance. Egyptian history had by then degenerated into *opera buffa* played out by a mixed cast of mothers and sons against a

---

20. See Chapter IX, p. 360.
21. At Apion's death in B.C. 96 he in turn bequeathed Cyrenaica to the Romans, who incorporated it as a province in B.C. 74.

strident chorus of Alexandrians, the whole under the frequently disinterested direction of the Roman Senate. The only noteworthy event of those decades was the passing, in B.C. 80, of Ptolemy X, the last legitimate male descendent of the Ptolemaic line, at the hands of an Alexandrian mob.

The Alexandrians' choice for a successor was an illegitimate son of Ptolemy VIII who was crowned as Ptolemy XI Theos Philopator Philadelphus Neos Dionysus and nicknamed "the Flute Player" (Auletes). His situation was desperate. Rome ignored him and his pleas for confirmation over the years, and at the point when his gold finally recommended him to Rome's benevolent attention (B.C. 59), the Alexandrians turned on their king and drove him out. It was three more years before Auletes could find and then bribe a Roman commander to restore him to his throne; Aulus Gabinius, the governor of Syria, agreed, for a price.[22] In B.C. 51 the long but troubled reign of Auletes was over, and Egypt came into the hands of his still immature offspring, the transient Ptolemy XII and the future consort of both Caesar and Antony, Cleopatra VII.

The single greatest achievement of Ptolemy I, son of Lagos, and his successors was their drawing of a moribund Egypt back into the *oikoumene*. Life does not easily change along the Nile, and for the greater part of the land the new international status of their nation must have been no more than a vague report which they could praise or blame in good years or bad. For others, however, the effects of the coming of Hellenism and a new regime were more sensible. There was a different managerial style in the government ministries, and a new language took its prestigious place among the native Egyptian dialects. Egypt turned to building once again, and along the length of the Nile the Ptolemies raised their temples to the traditional gods in the accepted Pharaonic manner.

In the Delta and along the Nile the Ptolemies might be taken as a new, enlightened and vigorous Egyptian dynasty; in Alexandria, however, there is no mistaking who they were—Hellenized kings who had come to Egypt in the name of Alexander and who ruled in his city and his manner. Alexandria was immense by *polis* standards of the fifth century and possessed an economic and intellectual vitality undiminished for over a thousand years,

---

22. See Chapter VIII, p. 336.

until the Muslims founded their rival capital of Cairo. The city set the new styles in poetry, scholarship and the sciences for the entire *oikoumene;* it taught the Romans their Hellenism, the Christians and Jews their theology, and the Arabs their philosophy. As Athens had once boasted of being "the school of Hellas," the capital city of the Ptolemies was the university of the entire Mediterranean world in the Hellenistic age newly born in the fourth century before Christ.

V

The New Intelligentsia

To even the most untutored eye it is obvious that the art historian's distinction between "Hellenic" and "Hellenistic" reflects a real and acute change in the vision informing the plastic arts of the Greek world. The Periclean age was characterized by a strong sense of proportion, balance and restraint; and the same awareness of "the fitting" (*to prepon*) that inhibited the rehearsal of scenes of carnage upon the public stage guided as well the fifth century's almost faultless instinct for line and mass and for the sublime and easy grace subsequently judged "classical."

The world of the compact, homogeneous *polis* that produced this art was riven in the days of Philip and Alexander. Fifth-century *polis* art was admired and imitated, but never again produced with the same unselfconscious facility as in the days of its masters. The new sprawling monarchies of the Successors brought forth something quite different. Mannerism succeeded Classicism. The brooding and twisted sculpture that appears from the fourth century onward betrays the anxieties of a new world and a new breed of artists. As surely as the idealism of classical Platonism succumbed in these same latter days to almost fatal bouts of skepticism or sought refuge in mathematics, the artists and littérateurs of Alexandria and the other centers of the new Hellenism deserted, or were deserted by, the idealized visions of an earlier day. Men were portrayed as they were in everyday life or were caught in the thousand crises of soul and body devised by the newly liberated imagination of the artist. Those who found neither joy nor inspiration in naturalism took their solace in the academically revived past or the equally unreal delights of Arcadia.

The disjointed passage to the Hellenistic style must surely be read in terms of the collapse of the *polis.* Classical Greek art and letters were, in an almost unparalleled fashion, the products of the complex of political, social, religious and economic relationships expressed in the untranslatable term *"polis."* Within it the man who will later identify himself as an artist was still the *polites,* and whatever he did—whether cutting, shaping or dressing the stone that would be transformed into the Parthenon—his work was a political one. Indeed, we are hard put to ferret out the fifth-century term that corresponds to our "art" and "artist"; every search for "artist" turns up "artisan" (*technites*). All art was public and was subsumed into the larger concerns of the *polis,* just as ethics was regarded as a subdivision of the master science of politics.

Perhaps the only currently recognizable artistic figure in the pre-Alexandrian landscape was the bard. By the days of Plato the ambivalence between the religiously inspired and possessed bard (*aoidos*) and the craftsmanlike "maker" (*poietes*) had not yet been resolved in favor of the latter. In the *Phaedrus* it was still possible for Plato to compare the eccentric and individualistic "singer" with the madman, the lover or the prophet, as an awkward but useful inhabitant of the all-enveloping *polis.*

The Hellenistic age knew nothing of this. With the unraveling of the carefully contrived web of the *polis,* the premises of both life and art were undercut. The *polites* found himself invested, willy-nilly, with the unfamiliar, uncomfortable, and sef-contradictory role of the "private citizen" (*idiotes*). The kingdoms of the Successors were enormous political institutions ruled by a remote sovereign of immense, almost divine, stature and governed by a new class of professional civil servants. In the Athens of the fifth century it would have been unthinkable to speak of "the government" as an entity separate from the people governed; in Alexandria, Antioch or Pergamum it was as natural as it had been in Achaemenian Iran or Pharaonic Egypt.

Just as the fifth-century *polites* had become, by the third century, either a private citizen or a civil servant, the earlier *polis* artisan eventually came into the employ of "the government" or pursued some private vision. In the army, in politics and in art it was the age of the professional. From this separation of functions, formerly bound together in the *polis,* emerged the familiar figure of the professional artist and, divested of its political teleology, the doctrine of art for art's sake.

The new Hellenistic artist, freed of public judgment and beholden only to his patrons or his colleagues, was easily betrayed into bombast, pedantry or sentimentality. His wider audience had changed as well. In Periclean Athens there had been both socioeconomic classes and political parties that reflected a broad spectrum of interests; and it is possible to see displayed in the literature of that era the not too delicate tones of partisan appeals. But there must have been, at the same time, a remarkable homogeneity of culture constructed on a Homeric base and guaranteed by the obviously public nature of art, literary, pictorial and plastic. And if the public—and well-attended—performances of the dramatists are used as a gauge, there was an equally remarkable level of taste and cultural literacy.

After Alexander the symptoms of cultural heterogeneity begin to appear, not so much, perhaps, by reason of the deculturation of some, as the only partially successful acculturation of others. The events of B.C. 334 signaled the beginnings of the ingestion of large numbers of non-Greeks within the Hellenic body politic. Previously Hellenism had traveled beyond its own political frontiers and "converted" diverse peoples like the Lydians, Macedonians and Romans. Now, with the conquests of one of those Macedonian converts to Hellenism, Greeks and *barbaroi* were yoked together in common political systems. What had once been sporadic and random now had to be faced on the level of policy, the acculturation of the previously despised *barbaroi*.

In places, the Hellenization process worked marvelously well; the macro-Hellenization of Antioch and the micro-Hellenization of a place like Dura-Europos are eloquent enough testimony to its success, as are the eminent Hellenized *barbaroi* who will appear on the pages that follow. But its undeniable and inevitable side effect was the creation of perceptibly divergent "highbrow" and "lowbrow" cultures. The *nouveau*-Hellene, like his later brothers, frequently settled for surface effects ranging from the adoption of a Greek name and nakedness in the gymnasium to a smattering of Greek sufficient to read tax regulations or bills of lading. The very methods of "conversion," with their educational short cuts through the glib terrain of digests, anthologies and handbooks, contributed to the same end.

The Hellenistic artist had, then, a variety of audiences to which he could direct his work. The general citizen body of Antioch or Alexandria had tastes that were at once more vulgar and more sophisticated than those of their predecessors of the fifth century. The general culture was somewhat debased, surely, but there were compensations. The immediate horizon of the earlier Athens was the ports of the Delian League, beyond which lay the shadowy perspectives of Herodotus. For the new *kosmopolites* of the third century, Central Asia, East Africa and India crowded in upon the now-familiar Armenia, Babylon and Arabia. There was a fresh appetite for the exotic, but it was frequently accompanied by a somewhat wider understanding of the world and its workings. The parochialism implicit in the *polis* yielded to broader perspectives, novel ideas, other ways of doing things.

The new reading public in Anatolia, Syria, Palestine, Mesopotamia and Egypt were not the immediate products of Alexander's conquests. They had quite literally to be created before they could be served. Both sides were eager for the encounter: for the rulers Hellenism meant prosperity; for the non-Greek ruled, entry to the seats of power and affluence.

The Instruments of Hellenism

The heritage of Hellenism has been overwhelmingly literary and artistic. Time has not been kind to the physical monuments of the Greeks, and thus it has been the word, and precisely the written word, that has been the vehicle of choice and chance whereby the values and ideals of their civilization have been transmitted to succeeding generations of Romans, Slavs, Arabs, English and Germans. The Greeks themselves, however, saw the matter somewhat differently.

It is true that there was always a close association between the word and the deed in the Hellenic consciousness; the history of *logos,* whether sung, chanted, recited or written, is venerable. What is surprising to the latter-day partisans of the literary side of this combination is the degree of intensity and care with which the Greeks cultivated the physical side of their lives, a facet of their existence that archaeology and literature can only suggest. Attic tragedy is an almost perfect paradigm: we possess the words, but the music and dance have been lost forever.

Part of this loss is due to the sheer inability to preserve activity except as frozen in stone or sublimated in words. It is also the result of a deliberate attempt on the part of the Greeks themselves to convert a culture compounded of a variety of elements into one that was strikingly and predominantly literary. The change was finally achieved in the Hellenistic and Roman phases of Hellenism, but it had been in the making for some centuries before.

A central fact in this conversion of values was the rise of democratic Athens to a position of importance and influence in the Hellenic world. The earliest Greek culture had been unrepentently aristocratic, and the values that appear in the Homeric epic are those reflecting the function and aspirations of the upper classes. The Homeric heroes were aristocrats of the blood, bred to a code of conduct derived from their function as the warrior class in the society. Physical bravery, skill, speed, strength and cunning were all central to the code and were rewarded by the tokens of honor, whether they were exercised in war or in those surrogate military activities designed to keep the warrior at fine edge during peacetime: the panoply of war games in which aristocrats have always delighted and which remained, until quite recently, alien and unthinkable to people whose role in the society was to work rather than fight.

Training up to this standard began with breeding; a man of common birth might hurl the javelin forever without becoming an aristocrat. But given the proper blood lines, excellence (*arete*) was achieved by doing, training not at random or in private but in a kind of apprentice system. The young squire joined himself to a perfect knight to imitate, listen and learn. Achilles was formed by the wise Chiron and Phoenix.

Despite the progressive weakening of the aristocratic dominance of society, the pattern of apprenticeship kept its hold on Greek education not only in form but in substance; even the more liberal and open new *poleis* of the eighth century and later relentlessly pursued the aristocratic ideal of physical excellence. Education was essentially physical education or, to put it in a way more accurately designed to banish the image of altruistic Swedish gymnasts, education for sports.

If the sweaty pursuit of excellence at track, field, wrestling, boxing and the obviously aristocratic hippic contests had any competition, it came from the desirable training in *mousike*, the arts of the Muses: singing, dancing and the playing of musical instruments. Literary studies ran an inconsiderable third.

It was to be many centuries before the physical exercises at the heart of Greek culture were dislodged from their place of honor—gymnasia and palaestra were features of every Hellenistic and Roman town that prided itself on its culture and amenities—but they were tied to the aristocratic premises of a long-dead society, and the arrival of the new-style democratic *polis* numbered their days.

Education in the old manner was carried out within the family, by parents or individual tutors, but the extension of the full *polis* life to larger and larger numbers of the population made such arrangements obviously uneconomical. Out of this need came the school, the attempt at training—at first chiefly physical training—in larger groups; the tutor had yielded to the teacher.

The growth of the *polis* as the paramount political institution also accelerated the progress from physical to literary culture. The physical skills of the warrior-athlete, still admired and nurtured in the more conservative and aristocratic world of the Dorian states, were replaced in the open political society of Athens by the skills of discourse. *Arete*, "excellence," took on, in the changed political circumstances, a distinct verbal tone. The itinerant professors of the fifth century, the Sophists, undertook to teach the new *arete*.

The Sophists' extraordinary achievement was that they had in a sense duplicated the feats of earlier Greek thinkers in converting phenomenological data into intellectually negotiable concepts, not, as in the case of the *physikoi*, the raw material of a changing physical world, but the more intriguing stuff of man's moral activity as reflected in literature and life. Both ethics as a branch of philosophy and literary studies as a branch of science had their beginnings here; Socrates and Aristotle alike had distinctly Sophistic antecedents.

There was a great deal of contemporary wonder at the Sophists' techniques and, as far as it can be reconstructed, their methodology does betray a pioneering quality; paradigms, exercises, manuals were all in use, probably for the first time. But the teaching of the Sophists, for all its revolutionary ingredients, appears to have been highly unorganized. It was not until first Plato and then Aristotle founded their schools in the next century that the new pedagogical weapons found an organized and structured housing within which to operate with maximum efficiency.

We are not very well informed on the operations of either the Platonic Academy or the Aristotelian Lyceum. While it is true that they strike a modern observer as somewhat closer to a religious and social confraternity than to a highly organized university, it is also likely that they were juridically recognized institutions with "permanent" staff and students, and that they included both research and formal teaching based on a curriculum, a combination of interests and pursuits that are particularly visible in the Lyceum, where the preserved Aristotelian treatises betray both the formal nature of classroom instruction and the cooperatively organized research projects.

Nowhere here was it a question of inculcating Hellenism. Though future events were to show how well such institutions "traveled," the Academy and the Lyceum both give the appearance of being *polis* institutions tailored to the higher intellectual aspirations of the homogeneous population typical of a fourth-century city-state. There may have been aliens enrolled there, but it is certain that they learned their Hellenic rudiments somewhere other than at the feet of Aristotle.

Political boundaries mean little in the process of acculturation; institutions count for a great deal. The Romans normally relied on institutions that operated within their own political boundaries: the *barbaroi* of whatever variety were drawn *within* and then institutionalized in numbers sufficiently small to ensure the integrity of the institution—in the Roman case, the army. But there are other institutions which cross borders with relative ease and serve the same ends. At times merchants have been entrusted with modest cultural wares which they have transported across frontiers. Far more effective, however, have been religious institutions. The Roman state could draw the Germans into bastions like Cologne, seed them into the Roman army, and turn them out, a quarter century later, as passable Romans. The Christian Church, on the other hand, could cross the Rhine and Christianize—and Romanize—the Germans on their own soil, as they later did in the East with the Ethiopians and the Slavs and—very nearly—with the Mongols.

The Greeks of the Hellenistic period used neither army[1] nor church to Hellenize the *barbaroi*. They relied on a political institution, the *polis*. Alexander occupied Egypt as an already established political entity and by some judicious surgery placed a new head on its already well-articulated body. His Asiatic conquests, however, were on a terrain without well-defined and genuine political frontiers and here, as in the later American conquest of its West, he contented himself with planting a series of outposts held by a Greek garrison. His successors there managed to group these under a tenuously administered central government.

Some of these posts may have begun their life as fairly close approximations of the older Greek *poleis*, but by far the majority, particularly in the Anatolian and Asian hinterland, began as military colonies (*katoikiai*) pure and simple. In Anatolia and Western Asia many of the military colonies eventually passed into the more sophisticated *polis* state, but farther east their life span must have been exceedingly short, since there was little or no emigration from Macedon or Greece to support them. By B.C. 250 there were Greeks but no *poleis* east of the Tigris.[2] The scores of "cities" bearing the name of Alexander are a mirage.

Hellenism did put down solid roots in the new *poleis* of the Mediterranean littoral, like Alexandria and Antioch, and in the more venerable urban centers of the immediate hinterland, like Oxyrhynchus, Damascus, Emesa, Baalbek and Philadelphia, where Greeks settled in sufficiently large numbers to preserve their identity. None of these *poleis* enjoyed the absolute political autonomy that their illustrious models in Greece once had, but they did possess, outside Egypt at least, some degree of self-government effected through the normal instruments for such: elected officials, a municipal council, perhaps even a popular assembly.

In almost every case the population of these latter-day *poleis* was highly mixed, and it was here, in these centers, that the

---

1. Alexander did some experimenting with the army as an instrument of acculturation in Iran, but his successors preferred to take their Macedonian phalanxes neat. It was only when sorely pressed at Raphia in B.C. 217 that the Ptolemies allowed native Egyptians into the ranks.
2. Seleucia-on-the-Eulaeus, the former Susa, possibly excepted. There can scarcely have been enough Greeks in the Bactrian kingdoms, now further cut off by the Parthians, to constitute anything resembling a genuine *polis*. But we can only surmise.

native population was assimilated to the Hellenism of their masters, superficially by aping the manners of the ruling class, but more truly and effectively in the educational institutions that were an inevitable component of each settlement. Within the controlled environment of the Hellenistic *polis* the process had some chance of success; outside it could do nothing, as in Egypt, where there were not enough centers to make any but the slightest impact on the mass of the Egyptians who inhabited the "countryside" (*chora*).[3] It is ironic, then, that it should have been at Alexandria that the instruments of Hellenization, so little used in Egypt itself, were forged.

The Museum and Library at Alexandria, not the most spectacular but surely the most permanent monuments of the first two Ptolemies in Egypt, were direct lineal descendants of the Aristotelian Lyceum. There is some evidence that both those institutions were designed for Ptolemy Soter by Demetrius of Phalerum, whose tenure as Cassander's governor for Athens ended in B.C. 307 and who came to Alexandria in B.C. 297 at Ptolemy's invitation. Earlier, during his stewardship at Athens, Demetrius had made the necessary arrangements for regularizing the foundation of the Lyceum as a private school under the directorship (B.C. 322–288) of Aristotle's student and successor Theophrastus. Demetrius, who had studied with Theophrastus and whose own philosophical achievements and interests were considerable, helped the new scholarch around the alien-property Laws.

The Academy and Lyceum were both private institutions; the Museum was created, subsidized and controlled by the Ptolemies. Its grounds and buildings were part of the Royal Quarter, and the scholars who lived and worked there as part of a formal cult association dedicated to the Muses were supported by royal subvention and had at their disposal the immense resources of the Library. Here too the Aristotelian antecedents are clear. But again, what Aristotle had done on a private scale (with financial help from Alexander, to be sure),[4] the Ptolemies converted into a

---

3. Both Greek gymnasia and, later, British cricket fields were in short supply in Upper Egypt; there are, be it noted, mosques there, and the inhabitants speak neither Egyptian, Greek nor English, but Arabic.

4. It was the rediscovery of Aristotle's library in the first century B.C. that led to the new edition of the Aristotelian *corpus* by Andronicus of Rhodes and the consequent revival of the fortunes of a moribund Aristotelianism (see Chapter IX, pp. 364–65).

public institution that provided the model for similar royal libraries in most of the urban centers of the Hellenistic East.

The volatile political climate of Alexandria was not always conducive to tranquil scholarship,[5] but during the Museum's heyday, for about a century and a half from its foundation, the Ptolemies attracted there the finest scholars of the Hellenic tradition. Athens continued to exercise its special authority in philosophy, but in philology and the mathematical sciences Alexandria reigned without serious challenge.

The director of this remarkable literary and scientific establishment was nominally the chief priest of the Muses' Association, but the effective lead was given by the chief librarian, who doubled as tutor to the Ptolemaic crown prince. The likely list of men who held this post illustrates well enough the encyclopedic interests of the post-Alexander intellectual establishment: Zenodotus, the editor of Homer, and an epic poet; Callimachus,[6] author of hymns, epic vignettes and epigrams, and the architect of the great catalogues (*pinakes*) of the Library; Apollonius of Rhodes, fashioner of the model Hellenistic epic, the *Argonautica;* Eratosthenes, who won academic laurels by being the second-best-informed scholar in every discipline; Aristophanes of Byzantium, grammarian, lexicographer, and editor, who prepared the second edition of Callimachus' *pinakes;* another Apollonius, about whom little is known; and finally, Aristarchus of Samothrace, editor of Homer and the lyric poets, and commentator on the entire range of Greek literature.

The obvious and almost obsessive interest in Homer was another Aristotelian legacy. Here, as in the case of the Attic dramatists and the lyric poets, the focus was primarily textual. The chosen rule of the Alexandrian *grammatikos* was to present

---

5. Demetrius of Phalerum himself fell from favor under Ptolemy II Philadelphus, and the Library and its annex in the Serapeum were frequently threatened by the fire, deliberate or accidental, that inevitably accompanied Alexandria's troubles, first with the Roman occupation forces before Actium and later at the hands of rampaging mobs bent on finding solutions to theological and ethnic problems in the streets.

6. There is some doubt that Callimachus, for all his reputation, ever actually held the post of chief librarian, a possible source of the difficulty between him and his student Apollonius of Rhodes, who certainly did hold it.

the text, word by word, line by line, book by book,[7] to produce that Holy Grail of scholasticism, the annotated edition of the master, rendered as authentic as the diligent comparison of manuscript readings could make it, and clarified by the not inconsiderable philological resources at the scholar's disposal. He was, as Cicero later described him, a *poetarum explanator*.

The Alexandrian scholars of this early period were literary critics only in a very limited sense. They did not hesitate to introduce the criterion of "the fitting" (*to prepon*), a peculiarly Greek combination of the moral and the aesthetic, in passing judgment on the *authenticity* of one or another Homeric passage, but they eschewed any more philosophical consideration of the text. Allegorical exegesis there was in quantity during the period; it came, however, from other sources—the Stoics, who at Pergamum and elsewhere felt no inhibitions against exploring philosophical levels of meaning in the classical literary texts.

Nor were the Alexandrians much interested in the literary disciplines for their own sake. Their lexicographical and grammatical studies were pragmatic and textually oriented. Here too it was the Stoics, proceeding from a far broader philosophical base, who were the first to pursue the language disciplines as sciences in their own right instead of mere *ancillae textus*. The earliest Stoic attempt at a systematic grammar of verbalized discourse— as distinct from their prior studies in logic as a "grammar" of internalized *logos*—was probably that of Diogenes of Seleucia (*c.* B.C. 155),[8] followed by the Alexandrian response in the *Techne Grammatike* of Dionysius Thrax (*c.* B.C. 170–90), the student of Aristarchus of Samothrace.[9]

The Alexandrians, like their predecessors in the Academy and Lyceum, were concerned with problems of classification and organization, as well as with the text itself. Callimachus' bibliographies have already been mentioned, and Eratosthenes worked out a complex chronological schema into which the biographical material could be fitted. Zenodotus, the first of their number, probably began the practice of drawing up lists of "acceptable" authors, thereby initiating the process of critical winnowing that

---

7. Free-standing treatments of larger aspects of the work in question were a later development.

8. See Chapter IX, p. 373.

9. For the wider effects of this grammatical breakthrough, see Chapter XV, pp. 544–45.

was to continue down through the Middle Ages and reduce the remnants of Greek literature to the slim traces that remain today. Chance did not preserve Sophocles, Demosthenes and Pindar; their survival was the result of a deliberate choice by the literary mandarins in the Museum, whose own work, in turn, was excluded from the canon by the even more refined tastes of the classical revival that occurred at the beginning of the Roman Empire. Ironically, the same age of Romans that fed upon and was formed by Hellenistic literary styles rejected their own masters as "unclassical" and so perpetrated the utter ruin that is today Hellenistic literature.

The Museum was a training ground for specialists, almost totally innocent of what were later called "humane" or "liberal" studies. But the work done there, both in its method and in its substance, eventually found its way into the burgeoning new institutions of secondary education, where it set the formal, academic tone of most of the middle ground of instruction and much of its higher reaches as well. The long reign of the scholastic method was inaugurated in Alexandria.

Periclean Greece had what passed as primary schools, modest institutions where the rudiments of reading, writing and arithmetic were taught to children between their seventh and fourteenth years. From then until his compulsory military training at age eighteen the young Athenian was formerly at loose ends. After Alexander, formal schooling was extended upward from the primary level and downward from the advanced training offered by the Academy and the Lyceum. Eventually the Athenians' attitude toward the years of military training (*ephebeia*) changed as well.

In Hellenistic times the literary and scientific formation of the well-to-do occurred during the years of secondary education. The "curriculum authors" canonized at Alexandria were studied by adaptations of the methods worked out at the Museum. Recitation and declamation there surely were, but the main effort was expended on an explication of the text. Special vocabularies of the dead epic or already dying Attic dialects were prepared, glossaries consulted, plots digested, characters identified. Grammar was studied in the formal mode of Dionysius Thrax, and simple literary compositions were assigned. Most of the activity in these secondary schools shows unmistakable signs of Alexandrian influence, but when it came to moral formation the educators turned rather to the Stoics. Theirs were the exegetical methods used to extract an appropriate moral lesson from the literary classic under consideration. Homer became not only the philologists' paradise but the perennial moral paradigm for all Hellenes. The allegorical interpretation that had been developed by the Stoic philosophers enabled the nimble and imaginative secondary-school teacher to elicit from Homer or the dramatists any and all moral lessons necessary for the edification of his charges.

Secondary education was designated as *enkyklios paideia,* or "general education," a sequence of studies that the philosophers considered the ideal preparation for their own discipline. In its canonic form the *enkyklios paideia* appeared sometime in the first century, though its essential point, the combination of literary and scientific studies, went back to the issues debated by Plato and Isocrates in the fourth century. It embraced seven disciplines: the later Carolingian literary *trivium* of grammar, rhetoric and dialectic, and the scientific—or better, mathematical—*quadrivium* of arithmetic, geometry, astronomy and music.

Upon graduation the Athenian gentleman of eighteen might pass into the *ephebeia,* the two years of compulsory military training that came into prominence at Athens after B.C. 338. The two years, later reduced to one, whatever its original intent, eventually evolved into something far broader and more ambitious than military drill and tactics; the *ephebeia* became, ironically, at a time when citizenship meant relatively little, a kind of physical and moral preparation for citizenship. The purely military side of the training gradually declined—the Hellenistic kingdoms had little use for citizen-soldiers—and the later ephebes apparently spent most of their time at sports, rounded off (or interrupted by) an occasional talk on literature or philosophy by one of the itinerant lecturers of the day, a gentleman's finishing school unmarred by a curriculum, but with a fine equestrian team and a splendid opportunity for contacts with other young aristocrats of Athens.[10]

At Athens or in the other older *poleis* of Greece the *ephebeia* might follow naturally upon the secondary school, but elsewhere in the Hellenistic world, where the school structure was considerably less formal, the *ephebeia* was apparently pushed pro-

10. At a later date, about B.C. 119, foreigners were admitted.

gressively forward into adolescence, where it served, in its own peculiar fashion, the function of both the secondary school and, for the non-Greeks, the all-important entryway to Hellenization. The process of acculturation was achieved as much in the gymnasia of the *ephebeia* as in the classroom. It was in the halls of the former that the Egyptian, Syrian or Jew acquired the dress, manners, style and connections that marked him as part of the ruling class and distinguished him from the non-Hellenized *barbaroi*.

Beyond the *ephebeia*, essentially a civic institution, lay the world of higher private education—for the more serious and professionally inclined, a career at the Museum or matriculation at one of the four major philosophical schools at Athens, or perhaps the medical school at Pergamum; for the amateur, enrollment with one of the sophists-at-large for advanced instruction in philosophy or rhetoric, the two Hellenistic claimants to the title of supreme science. The popular version of philosophy hawked from one end of the Mediterranean to the other attracted some attention, particularly in the diatribe form adopted by the street Cynics, but it was far surpassed by rhetoric, which developed into a passion and left its profound mark on the popular culture of both Greek and Latin Hellenism down to the Middle Ages.

To serve this now formally articulated literary culture the anonymous masters of the Hellenistic age produced the academic tools necessary for the work: grammars, lexicons, textbooks, digests, concordances, biographies, histories of schools, and lists of eminent scholars, poets, inventors, famous men with the same name, marvels of the world,[11] prodigies, omens, miracles of nature and syntax.[12] And the new reading and listening public, attuned alike to the cultured, the pedantic and the exotic, absorbed it all.

Little or none of this diffusion of Hellenic literary culture from Alexandria over the Near East would have been possible without the prior existence of a cultural lingua franca that could serve as its medium. Since the days of the Persian Wars the Attic dialect of Athens was evolving into just such, encouraged equally by the Athenians' growing cultural dominance in Greece and

---

11. Some of the wonders of the animal world, live and stuffed, were on display at Alexandria.

12. For the use of some of these academic accessories in the study of philosophy, see Chapter IX, pp. 372–73.

their more aggressive foreign policy in the Aegean.[13] By B.C. 400
their manner of expression had visibly diverged from the fifth-
century literary language. It was some form of this Imperial
Attic that had replaced the native tongue in Macedon by the days
of Philip and was carried by his son's victorious armies to Asia.

Imperial Attic provided the basis for the Hellenistic age's
common speech (*koine dialektos*), the *koine*, a syntactically and
morphologically simplified version of the language of Thucydides and Plato but a nonetheless natural and flexible idiom capable
of further evolution. The *koine* was used as both the spoken and
the written tongue without notable dialectical differences
throughout the Hellenistic kingdoms and the eastern Roman
Empire from the death of Alexander to about the time of Justinian. The older Greek dialects, the symbols of *polis* parochialism, gradually disappeared;[14] in their stead the *koine* served as a
single ecumenical vehicle for the whole range of Greek literary
production, technical and popular, from Polybius to the New
Testament.

Alexandrian Poetry

Menander is not the archetypal Hellenistic poet. He was, after all,
the epigone of a still-living tradition, and the empty activity on
the Athenian stage was still suffused by the stylistic echo of
something better. All the motifs of the new age were present in
Menander's comedies, but so too were the Attic stylistic reflexes
that could still redeem the banal. With the death of that tradition,
however, the elegance of poetry became more studied and, where
the inspiration failed, more labored. The Hellenistic artist
worked at his considerable passion. In the end poetry deserted
drama; the latter-day stage was occupied by revivals, pantomime
and Handel-like oratorios.

The new age was nothing if not productive. All tastes, from
the highest to the lowest, were served a hearty if not exciting
fare. The Athenian theatergoer was treated to an almost endless
succession of Menandrean-formula comedies, which have since

13. And whose political alliance with the Ionian maritime *poleis*
explains the noticeable Ionic tinge to the later *koine*.
14. Their final doom was hastened by the vogue during the Empire
for an artificial "pure" Attic (see Chapter XV, p. 542).

mercifully disappeared. The Attic New Comedy never fared well at Alexandria or elsewhere, however. The Alexandrian public took their places at the far ends of the literary spectrum; their tastes ran at one extreme to the naturalistic mime, and at the other to the "high" poetry of the professors, on whom the reputation of Hellenistic poetry ultimately rests.

The mime represents antiquity's most adventuresome probe into realism. Other forms flirted with realism; the satire, romance, Old and New Comedy show realistic brush strokes, but the broad canvas was romantic, utopian or fantastic. The mime came at realism head on. Our preserved instances had fairly lofty literary ambitions and, so, are not exactly examples of the genre in its most direct form; they are doubtless somewhat more artistically contrived, for instance, than the mimes that were being acted on the contemporary stage. But even in what we have, in Theocritus and Herodas, both literary men and in no sense primitives, one sees illustrated with only a minimum of typing and schematization a segment of life but little revealed in the ordinary Greek view of literature.

The Greeks preserved a strict separation between the tragic-epic and the comic approach in literature. The former dealt only with "serious" subject matter, with the result that whatever did not fall into the category of the serious, the noble and the grand was incapable of any treatment but the comic. The lower social and economic classes and humble occupations obviously did not qualify as subject for either epic or tragedy and so became the exclusive preserve of the comedian. It was precisely argued against Euripides, for example, that he was attempting to introduce just such mean characters, disguised in the ennobling raiment of mythology to be sure, into the center of tragic action.

The literary mime was no exception to this disjunction. The figures were sketched sympathetically, but there was a broadness of characterization and good-natured parody that belongs unmistakably to the comic tradition. The buffoon is never very far away.

For all the vaunted realism of Menander, the mimes of Herodas were considerably closer to "life" as realism understands that word. Menander's characters have their plastic analogues in comic masks; Herodas' in the old women, cripples and battered slaves that Hellenistic art delighted to portray, "warts and all." This is not photographic realism, of course; there was an artist at work. The mimes were composed in a literary iambic meter in a literary dialect in the distinctly literary and urbanized milieu of the island of Cos. The poems are vignettes of everyday life, almost impressionistic glimpses of the seamier side of the great urban centers of eastern Hellenism. As a poet, Herodas is of no great stature, but he does expose part of the hidden reality that had no place in the works of the great academic literati.

It appears unlikely that Herodas was in any way a member of the literary establishment assembled at Alexandria by Philadelphus or Euergetes. Even at Cos, which had its own brilliance under the early Ptolemies, Herodas may have had his difficulties with the critics.[15] Another practitioner in the literary mime had, however, a more successful time there. The career of Theocritus unfolded during the first half of the third century at the court of Hiero of Syracuse in his native Sicily, in the poetical circles at Cos, and at Alexandria, where he enjoyed both the patronage of Ptolemy II Philadelphus and the instruction and encouragement of the leading poet of the day, Callimachus.

Theocritus was, as a matter of simple fact, a better poet than Herodas, far broader in his range and greater in his depth. Herodas' gift was for honest reportage; Theocritus' for art. Where their work runs somewhat parallel, in Herodas' mime on the two women of Cos (IV) and Theocritus' on the women at the feast of Adonis (XV), the superiority of the latter's insight into human nature and his skill in its portrayal is immediately clear. Theocritus sang in many forms—pastorals, erotic lyrics, mimes, hymns, encomia, miniature epics and epigrams—and had a different voice, and often a different dialect, for each.

Theocritus was not very different from his Alexandrian contemporaries, perhaps merely better. His encomia for Ptolemy and Hiero praise, as they should, without being fulsome. His mythical excursions on Hylas, Helen, Heracles and the Dioscuri are learned in the manner of the times, but Theocritus knew how to distinguish learning from pedantry. The urban mimes do not sacrifice art to realism. Theocritus' reputation does not, however, rest on being merely better than a Callimachus, an Apollonius or a Herodas; in one important respect he was also different: he was the first to exploit the genre of pastoral poetry.

---

15. Mime VIII casts them as goats, a perhaps not too subtle comment on the current madness for shepherds and their flocks.

The connection of shepherds with poetry and literary reflections on that and other aspects of their life were not lacking in earlier Greek literature. Rural types, frequently in song or at the pipes, can be found from Homer to Aristophanes. Daphnis, the semilegendary shepherd beloved by a nymph and then blinded by her, had already appeared in a poem by Stesichorus about B.C. 600. But this was folk tale converted into myth. Theocritus applied to the rural life with its already stereotyped preoccupation with love and song the realistic techniques of the mime. Here now languished more or less real shepherds in a more or less real Sicilian landscape. More or less, because these are shepherds who never herd and are, in addition, beneficiaries of some quite unshepherdlike mezzotints.

It would be left to another, Roman age to convert these shepherds into sentimentalized and romanticized Rousseauvean prototypes, but the city dweller Theocritus was already blurring the edges of realism with notions drawn from other sources. From the time of Socrates the Cynics had been preaching and actively demonstrating a disdain for the values of the *polis* urbanism, even the relatively circumscribed version of the fifth and fourth century. By their conduct they seemed to be leading men back to a simpler, more natural behavior. "Nature" was very much in the air in the post-Alexander world, not yet in the sense of rural primitivism, but as the Stoics understood it, the cosmic rhythm that provided a paradigm for man's activity. Plato had urged harmonic behavior as an ethical ideal, but had expressed it in mathematical notation. The Stoics read natural harmony in physical terms and contrived an ethics of material naturalism. The call of the wild was implicit in a philosophy grounded in an analysis of instinctive behavior.

Theocritus' approach to the pastoral was literary, not philosophical; his Sicilian shepherds were singers and poets without any suggestion that the melodies that issued from their untutored lips masked Stoic harmonies. But they are equally clearly idealized types unencumbered by real herds or interests beyond their erotic fancies. Their song flows forth in faultless hexameters. They are better lovers and poets than shepherds.[16]

Theocritus stood at the boundary of a real and romanticized

---

16. In at least one Idyll, VII, they are real poets. The shepherds here lightly mask members of the Coan poetical circle.

landscape, and it was the latter perspective that caught the fancy of later artists and readers. Romanticized myth and sentimentalized shepherds went hand in hand into the second century, finally to be enshrined in later Greek romances like *Daphnis and Chloë* or, in a form much more akin to Theocritus' own, in the *Eclogues* of Vergil, where the shepherds, transported from Sicily to Arcadia,[17] already smell more of Watteau than of sheep. The world of Vergil's Tityrus, "stretched out in the dense shade of the beech tree," is compounded of a tempered Theocritean realism, myth, historical allegory and utopian escapism, a combination that the inheritors of Hellenism found endlessly attractive.[18]

It is unreported what Callimachus thought of his contemporary Theocritus' bucolic innovations. Presumably he would have approved, since he had his own fondness for the cottager. What is more, Theocritus stood firmly on his side in the contemporary controversy on the epic. It is not entirely clear what the argument was about, since the relevant poetry of one of the major protagonists, Callimachus, has been reduced to shreds. What remains of the issue are a series of programmatic utterances, from which one can, it is true, construct an Alexandrian poetic. Traditionally Callimachus' remarks were directed against his student Apollonius of Rhodes, but Apollonius' only crime may have been that he was appointed chief librarian at Alexandria, instead of his mentor.

Callimachus' (*c.* B.C. 310–240) program for poetry dealt chiefly with the revival of the epic in full swing during Hellenistic times. At an earlier date tragedy had expropriated the mythical and heroic material of the epic for its own dramatic and ethical purposes; tragedy was no longer popular in the third century, however, and the narrative verse forms, the hexameter and its derivative, the elegiac couplet reclaimed the rich mythical legacy

---

17. For the Romans Sicily was far too familiar to provide an idyllic landscape. Vergil may have come upon the notion of Arcadia, a remote province in the central Peloponnese, in Polybius, who had once lived there and reported in his history that it was an altogether tuneful place, filled with singing rustics, if little else.

18. Particularly when blended with nuances derived from the shepherds of Bethlehem and Christ, "the good shepherd." The latter image, which began its career as a Pharisaic metaphor, derived its iconography from Hellenic sources, chiefly Orpheus as "master of the beasts."

of the past. By now, however, the older myths were scarcely recognizable. Euripides had romanticized them and undermined the once grandiose figures with the tools of psychological realism; scholars had collected and studied the immense body of variants lying outside the standard accounts. Myth was reduced to history and, in the knowing manner of the new scholarship, invoked to explain local cults and practices.

Callimachus attempted to set down some guidelines for the use of this rich and complex material. The ideal poem should not attempt to reduplicate the feats of the older epic in rearing long poems over the Homeric base; the age of the cyclic poets was past. "A big poem is a big nuisance," Callimachus is reported to have said. Poets are not paid by the yard, and so they should concentrate on the quality of their art (*techne*). Vulgarity of tone was to be avoided, as were overblown effects; the masses would have to look elsewhere for their entertainments.

Such standards are not entirely unexpected from a man who, fresh from Cyrene, rose from the position of suburban Alexandrian schoolmaster to be the most commanding scholarly and literary figure in the Museum and who spent most of his life in the establishment compound at Alexandria working on bibliographies. What does come as a surprise is the graceful sense of humor that Callimachus can bring on occasion to the execution of such a limiting poetic. Even in the hymns, the best-preserved part of his work, when he is engaged in the deadly serious work of fashioning an encomium to the recently (B.C. 285) enthroned Ptolemy Philadelphus in the form of a *Hymn to Zeus,* there are not altogether serious references to the debates of the Higher Critics of mythology. On another, somewhat less sensitive subject, the *Bath of Pallas,* the wit of the poet is on full display.

The thinly veiled political allusions in the *Hymns* betray Callimachus in his guise as court poet and propagandist. There was political propaganda in Aeschylus and Aristophanes, doubtless; but they spoke with the voice of an interested individual *polites,* not as a government spokesman. Callimachus, supported and sustained by the Ptolemies, was in turn giving voice to their policies: the exaltation of the ruling house and the propagation of Hellenism in a changing Egypt. There is no suggestion that the poet was not personally convinced of those policies, any more than later Vergil or Horace disagreed with the Augustan propaganda that they disseminated. The price for the comforts of the Museum, if not onerous, is, however, unmistakable.

The *Hymns* are not, for all their interest, the critical works in Callimachus' career; the controversy on the epic was fought elsewhere. It may have begun with Callimachus' criticism of Antimachus of Colophon, an "Alexandrian" before his time, who died early in the fourth century. Plato had been an admirer of his work, but Callimachus, it would seem, was not. He found the older poet's reworking of the Theban cycle overextended and tedious. Callimachus' own early work, the *Aitia*, or *Causes*, illustrated his own more modern point of view; it is—or was; there is little left—a mosaic of impressionistic pieces on mythological themes held together by the flimsiest of unities. An elegant and flashy piece of work, Callimachus' critics retorted, but it did not prove that he could carry an extended theme. Callimachus responded with the *Hecale,* a miniature epic, or epyllion, of about a thousand lines dealing with a somewhat homely part of the Theseus legend.

It may have been at this point that Callimachus' student Apollonius of Rhodes (*c.* B.C. 295–215) entered the lists. Formally speaking, his *Argonautica,* a four-book treatment of the quest for the Golden Fleece, was an epic in the old fashion, an extended (though nowhere as long as either the *Iliad* or the *Odyssey*) treatment of a heroic theme. Substantially it was utterly Alexandrian in its romanticism, its Euripidean psychology, its sheer picturesqueness. But that was not the issue at stake, and the *Argonautica* was probably a direct reproach to the position of Callimachus. At some point in the debate, perhaps about B.C. 260, Apollonius succeeded Zenodotus as chief librarian and the relationship between student and teacher degenerated to the point that Callimachus took pen directly against Apollonius in his satirical *Ibis.* Theocritus may have joined in too; some have seen his *Hylas* (XIII) as a well-aimed corrective to Apollonius' treatment of the same theme. Callimachus had the last word, however: Apollonius was eventually forced to leave his native Alexandria and take up residence in Rhodes.

The entire debate has an unreal quality, an obscure academic battle which must be reconstructed out of the wreckage of Hellenistic poetry. Was an evaluation of Homer the focus of the contest or the personal jealousies of inbred scholar-poets scrambling for preferment? At this remove from the evidence it is impossible to say, but in the end nothing was settled. Antagoras of Rhodes and Rhianus of Crete among others wrote extended epics, and Vergil gracefully transferred the Apollonian tradition into Latin in his *Aeneid*. Callimachus' poetical theory was sustained by Euphorion, the librarian of Antiochus the Great (B.C. 223–187) at Antioch, and profoundly affected Latin Hellenism through the *Metamorphoses* of Ovid.

All these men, the original combatants and their Greek and Latin seconds, have profound similarities, which the debates on the dimensions of the epics should not obscure. They may have differed in degree, but they were one, for example, in their emphasis on the erotic elements in their mythical narratives. Eros reigned supreme in Alexandrian poetry. When in the first century before Christ the Greek elegist Parthenius wanted to encourage the Roman poet Cornelius Gallus[19] to take up the genre in Latin, he could do nothing more appropriate than prepare for him a prose résumé of erotic material.

By all the evidence Gallus (B.C. 70–26) took Parthenius' suggestion, but it is not entirely clear whether he used the material, as the Alexandrians surely had, to describe in elegiac verse the erotic adventures of the figures of mythology, or whether his elegies reflected subjective experience of his own. Later Roman masters of the subjective erotic elegy like Propertius seemed to think the latter, but they claimed as well that they had drawn their own inspiration from the Alexandrians, particularly Philetas, Callimachus, and Euphorion.

The Roman elegists knew their Alexandrian forebears directly or by anthology, but we, who are reduced to scanning fragments, know little of what to make of this piece of reported literary history. Did the poets of Samos, Cos and Alexandria write subjective love poetry? The answer lies somewhere back at the beginning of the Hellenistic period.

The unacknowledged father of the Alexandrian mode was the poet who has already been mentioned in connection with the controversy on the epic, Antimachus of Colophon, to us little more than a name. Almost all the characteristics of the later age appear to have been present in his work: a penchant for the epic,

---

19. On his political career see Chapter X, p. 388.

a learned and even obscure diction, and the use of the elegy for narrative, in Antimachus' case to commemorate the death of his wife Lyde. It is not at all certain what was in the *Lyde*, but if, as seems likely, it was a series of vignettes drawn from mythology and paralleling the death of his beloved, then Antimachus must also be credited with another Alexandrian motif, the elegy used to commemorate erotic scenes.

There is no evidence that Antimachus used the elegy to transcribe his own feelings, except possibly by way of preface to the collection. Nor is there any way to elicit a similar subjective approach from the work of the pioneer elegist Philetas under Ptolemy I, or from the elegies or elegiac collections of his students and successors at Cos and Alexandria under Philadelphus: Hermesianax, Phanocles, Alexander Aetolus.[20] There is not much to choose between them. They were for the most part scholar poets whose favorite vehicle was a collective theme—for example, women beloved by poets—upon which they could string their considerable learning in mythology and their equally impressive technical mastery of the elegiac form.

Not much is left of their work; what remains has been preserved in anthologies, like that of Meleager.[21] Passion runs through their lines; they are poets of love, but someone else's. It may have been the tone, the style, and the erotic *loci communes* that they and Callimachus transmitted to the Romans. The almost painful personal note appears, on the face of the scant evidence, to have been Tibullus', Propertius', and Ovid's own.

The shifting tides of Greek sensibility eventually tired of the Alexandrians. The Attic purists of the second Christian century condemned them to oblivion. Like all virtuosi they went out of style. They can be read very surely, however, through the lines of their Roman imitators, and their stamp on Latin literature was an enduring one. Ovid was their creature, and through him the entire body of Latin Hellenism. The Alexandrians' antiquarian interests in a sense fashioned the instruments of their own de-

---

20. During Zenodotus' directorship of the Library Alexander was in charge of the tragedy collection. Comedy was the responsibility of Lycophron, the author of a curious piece of Alexandrian pedantic fantasy, the *Alexandra*, a long and almost totally opaque prophecy put in the mouth of Cassandra.

21. See Chapter XI, p. 416. The Romans may have read them in the same source.

struction, since their careful preservation of the past, their canons, *pinakes* and learned editions enabled later generations to recreate that past and consequently hold the Hellenistic poets in the contempt reserved for "middle ages."

The Mathematical Sciences

Some of the "moderns" of the Hellenistic age, notably Menander, Callimachus and Apollonius, found their way into the literary *trivium* of secondary-school education, a terrain otherwise dominated by the "classical" authors of pre-Alexander Greece. But the scholars of Alexandria reigned supreme in the scientific *quadrivium* that made up the other half of the *enkyklios paideia*. "Scientific" is clearly too broad a word to apply to the *quadrivium;* its components, arithmetic, geometry, music and astronomy, were all branches of ancient mathematics, a prejudice toward the suprasensible that betrays Platonic and even earlier Pythagorean influences on the curriculum. Among the physical sciences some, most notably chemistry, were still considered a mere craft (*techne*), while others, like physics and biology, formed part of the all-embracing discipline of philosophy.

The Ptolemies obviously supported literary studies, but may have had a greater personal interest in the sciences. Demetrius of Phalerum was not the only eminent Peripatetic summoned to Alexandria during the formative period of the Museum; Strato of Lampsacus also received the call under Ptolemy I, and some of his influence at court can be seen in Philadelphus' (for whom Strato served as tutor) interest in the sciences. It is likely too that Strato, one of the first men in antiquity to write on the subject of mechanics, fathered the cluster of theoretical and practical engineers that later blossomed at Alexandria: Archimedes, Ctesibius, Philo and Hero.

Neither Strato nor many others in the Lyceum except Aristoxenus were much interested in mathematics for its own sake. Aristotle's approach to phenomena was a relatively physical one, and his qualitative view of the *kosmos* passed uninhibited to his immediate disciples. But not, however, to Alexandria where the influences of Demetrius and Strato appear to have been on the whole more programmatic than substantial. In science the Alexandrian masters returned instead to the mathematical interests of the Platonic Academy. The affiliation is particularly clear in the very first of them, Euclid.

Euclid (*c.* B.C. 330–275) may have received his mathematical formation at Athens, but it was at Alexandria under Ptolemy I that the creative period of his writing and teaching took place. Its exemplary fruit was the *Elements,* a work whose vogue as a textbook has doubtless overinflated its author's reputation as a mathematician. Most else of what Euclid wrote has disappeared, but the *Elements* at least was a stocktaking, laying out in marvelously systematic and lucid form[22] the progress of Greek mathematics and geometry since the Pythagoreans. And that most of this history unfolded in circles connected with the Platonic Academy is perfectly clear from the text itself. Pythagorean geometry (Books I, II, IV, VI) and arithmetic (Books VII, VIII, IX) from the Founder to Archytas of Tarentum[23] had made considerable progress, but seem to have foundered, at least temporarily, on the discovery of the incommensurability of certain magnitudes, most notoriously the diagonal of a square with its sides.

We do not know how the early Pythagoreans proved the irrationality (non-*logos*) of $\sqrt{2}$, but the existence of such a quantity without a corresponding number (which were, by definition, integers) caused a contemporary scandal in that it cast doubts on one of the basic premises of Pythagorean science, that of the proportionality (*logos, ratio*) thought to exist between quantity and number. The crisis eventually passed, and by the generation of Plato mathematicians with whom he worked, Theodore of Cyrene and Theaeteus,[24] were busy at work proving the irrationality of the other surds up to $\sqrt{17}$, and otherwise domesticating these once fearsome beasts (Book X of the *Elements*).

---

22. Not even the form is Euclid's. It already appeared, in a fairly sophisticated garb, in the slightly earlier Autolycus of Pitane. The notion of reductive (*apagoge*) proof, a major feature of Euclidean geometry, may go back as far as Hippocrates of Chios, a mathematician of the mid-fifth century.

23. Plato met Archytas during his first trip to Sicily in B.C. 388, and Pythagorean mathematics was still alive when Plato returned there in B.C. 361.

24. Both of whom figure in the Platonic dialogue named after the latter.

The theoretical basis for the rehabilitation of the irrationals was provided by another mathematician, Eudoxus of Cnidus (*c.* B.C. 408–355), who was at Athens twice, first about B.C. 385 as a student at Plato's newly opened Academy, and again some twenty years later as a renowned mathematician in his own right. Eudoxus followed the lead into geometry provided by two somewhat earlier men. The celebrated atomist Democritus had attempted to work out the volumes of cones and pyramids by reducing them to a series of stratified cylinders and prisms, and the mathematician Hippocrates of Chios restored confidence in the theory of proportionality with his investigation of the area of a circle in terms of its radius, isolating in the process a new "number," *pi*. From this base Eudoxus worked out his own general theory of proportions (Books V and VI of the *Elements*).

In Euclid's description of proportions (V, VI) and the irrational numbers (X) the keystone in the structure is Eudoxus' method of exhaustion, that is, to approach a quantity inexpressible by one of the integers through its upper and lower limits.[25] Exhaustion may have been implicit in Democritus and Hippocrates, but to Eudoxus belongs the credit of fashioning it into a rigorous procedure whereby the mathematician may proceed to give a mathematical demonstration of Hippocrates' theorem of area $= \pi r^2$ (Book XII).

The crown upon the work is Book XIII, wherein Euclid demonstrates the exclusive existence of the five regular convex solids (pyramid, cube, octahedron, dodecahedron, icosahedron) that were first built by the Pythagoreans, then later geometrically constructed by Theaetetus, and finally given an exalted position as the building blocks of the sensible world in Plato's *Timaeus*.

The *Elements* was the vehicle whereby the tremendous mathematical progress of the previous two hundred years was transmitted into Hellenistic and Byzantine times. The work was frequently elaborated by commentators, by the later Alexandrian mathematicians Apollonius of Perga, Hero and Pappus, and then, somewhat more ominously, by the Neoplatonist philosophers. The Alexandrian commentators, working in a more antiseptic scientific tradition, generally restricted themselves to the mathe-

---

25. This in turn rests upon an earlier Pythagorean procedure; the application (*parabole*) of one area to another and the measurement of its consequent excess (*hyperbole*) or deficiency (*elleipsis*).

matical side of Euclid, but this was, in the light of the earlier history of the discipline, somewhat of a distortion.

The mathematical *quadrivium* was originally intended as a preparation for the study of philosophy, and in the Pythagorean and Platonic scheme of things numbers and geometrical figures were invested with deeper moral and metaphysical implications. The revival of religious Neopythagoreanism at the end of the Roman Republic and its fusion with the newly vitalized Platonism assured the return of mathematics to its former haunts. Euclid might hold the first place in geometry, but the prime exponent of mathematics for late antiquity was the Neopythagorean Nicomachus of Gerasa in the Transjordan (*c.* A.D. 150) in whose *Introduction to Arithmetic* a number theory—or better, a metaphysics of number—divorced from geometry was presented to the would-be philosopher in both the Greek and Latin[26] traditions of Platonism.

Most of the later luminaries of Neoplatonism were formed on Nicomachus' *Introduction* or on the roughly contemporary *On the Mathematics Useful for a Study of Plato* by Theon of Smyrna. Proclus, the last, fifth-century high priest of the cult, wrote commentaries on both Euclid and Nicomachus.[27] He was little interested in mathematics as such, but a mathematicized version of Platonism was very much to his taste (as it had been, in a somewhat more secular form, to Plato's immediate successors), and the mathematical commentaries in question provided an excellent opportunity to set down the foundations of the physical and metaphysical structures to follow, entitled, not coincidentally, the *Elements of Physics* and the *Elements of Theology*.

All of this was remote from Archimedes (B.C. 287–212), the product of a purer mathematical tradition, who studied and worked at Alexandria and then at the court of Hiero II, where he perished in the Roman siege of Syracuse. His interests were far wider than Euclid's. In geometry he pushed the Eudoxean

---

26. The *Introduction* was adapted or translated into Latin by Apuleius and Boethius.

27. See Chapter XVIII, pp. 679–81. Proclus, whose commentary on Euclid is a treasure-house of information on the history of Greek mathematics, is said to have thought that he possessed the reincarnated soul of Nicomachus. That is somewhat more likely than that it was the soul of Euclid.

method of exhaustion to new limits of both fineness and application. The areas and volumes of various curvilinear figures like the circle and the sphere were assayed, first by mechanical demonstrations,[28] and then more rigorously by the method of exhaustion. By this latter he reached a closer reading for the value of *pi*.[29] The study of mechanics was pushed forward from where it stood under Aristotle and Strato by Archimedes' construction of a sounder theoretical base by the application of mathematics to his work on equilibrium. He was the absolute pioneer in hydrostatics, and his *Sand Reckoner* expanded the extremely restrictive Greek mathematical notation by coming to grips with very large numbers.

Latin Hellenism had only an indifferent knowledge of Archimedes the mathematician; his reputation, mediated by Plutarch's biography of Marcellus, was rather that of an engineer of heroic dimensions who provided Hiero's Syracusans with a series of astonishing military machines until he was slain, unawares and absorbed in a geometrical problem, by a brutish Roman legionary. The same is true of his brilliant successor, Apollonius of Perga, who was active in Alexandria and Pergamum about B.C. 200. Both men were far too advanced in their mathematics to be folded into the Latin handbook tradition, and so it was not until the thirteenth century that Latin scholars had available, courtesy of new translations made from the Arabic versions, at least some of the work of Archimedes and Apollonius. The heirs of eastern Hellenism, the Arabs, who interested themselves in all parts of the mathematical *quadrivium*, had at their disposal, on the other hand, an immense range of translations from the Greek. Every major Greek mathematician from Plato to Diophantus was presented in translation, many from the ninth century.

Apollonius' genius lay in pursuing the fecund notion of application, excess and deficiency into the problems of conic sections. His strenuous and difficult effort marked the end of the extraordinary Greek tradition in plane and solid geometry. Where further advances were made in mathematics they were either

---

28. By the application (*parabole*), for instance, of the known area of a rectilinear figure to that of a curvilinear one. The elements of the former may then be weighed.

29. Since the Greeks did not have a decimal notation the Archimedean value was expressed in terms of fractions: 3-1/7 is greater than *pi*; 3-10/71 is less.

connected with the still vital interest in astronomy[30] or in the form of a significant breakthrough into another area.

The single most serious limitation on Greek mathematics was not, as might be thought, its cumbersome system of notation which used letters to designate numbers, each letter possessing only one value, whatever its position, but rather the Greeks' persistent connection of number and quantity. As Aristotle himself perceived, the Pythagoreans had hopelessly confused the geometrical point and the arithmetical unit, and, despite Aristotle's admonitions, the Greek mathematicians never quite freed themselves of the habit of counting on their fingers. This manner of viewing things converted, for instance, fractions into proportions between segments of lines and raised the whole question of "irrational" numbers. Here was the precise point at which geometry beckoned. Tempted to choose between numbers and lines, the Greeks remained on the path that had led them this far, geometry.

Apollonius had pushed pure geometrical analysis to the limits that its concomitant number system would allow, and his successors contented themselves with investigating various forms of curves, but always with the same analytical tools. Not until nearly five hundred years had passed was the geometrical premise itself put aside, and the possibility of an algebraic solution of mathematical problems revealed itself anew. The Babylonians had possessed what appears to have been a very sophisticated algebra built upon their sexagesimal system of positional notation. Whether this had somehow survived or Diophantus of Alexandria (c. A.D. 270) discovered it anew cannot now be determined. He was, at any rate, the first Greek to substitute for the prose recipes of geometry a symbolic notation that included shorthand signs for operations and for an unknown number, whether in the first, second or third "power."[31]

---

30. Which led, via the use of chords, from plane to spherical triangles in the direction of trigonometry. A rudimentary form of this branch of mathematics was probably employed by Hipparchus and is clearly visible in Menelaus (c. A.D. 100) and Ptolemy (see Chapter XI, pp. 436–40).

31. Two "squared" reveals the normal Greek geometrical approach: a line of two segments was constructed into a square; "two to the second power" shows Diophantus at work; DY, his symbol for an unknown of the second power, is an abbreviation of *dynamis*, "power."

At least partially freed from geometrical analysis, Diophantus could manipulate even quadratic equations (always reduced by Diophantus to one unknown) and perform the basic algebraic operations of reduction and cancellation.[32] It was, for all that, a wasted effort. Diophantus' work, eventually rediscovered by both eastern and western Hellenism, was borne under in his own day by the rising tide of Neopythagoreanism, astrology and the "new physics," which had little use for, and even less interest in, pure mathematics.

The question has frequently been raised as to why this considerable learning in mathematics was not converted into technology. The answer is, quite simply, that it was, though not uniformly nor as a matter of policy. At all times and all places the conversion of what is known into what is done is regulated by a complex of factors, political, religious and economic, and in this the Hellenistic period was no different from the thirteenth, eighteenth and twentieth centuries. In certain areas—architectural engineering, military technology, city planning and road construction—the later Greeks and their Roman successors made remarkable progress, a progress that is almost predictable in terms of publicly supported building projects, new professional armies, urbanism, and larger political units with communications problems. The application of theoretical science to what the ancients conceived of as the "life sciences" was no less remarkable.

If, however, the question is directed more specifically to the problem of work, it then strikes at the heart of the peculiar nature of applied science in the ancient world. A whole series of remarkable engineers worked at Alexandria; Archimedes, Ctesibius, Philo, Hero; and yet it was only the first and greatest of these, Archimedes, who gave much thought, albeit reluctantly, to converting to practical, chiefly military, ends what remained for the others mechanical toys. Little or no attention was paid by even the most skillful masters of what was called "organics" to the problems of power and work.

Perhaps "problems" is the wrong word. Since the domestication of animals the peoples of the Mediterranean had employed

---

32. It is the first of these two terms, in Arabic al-jabr and al-muqabalah, that gave its name to the discipline through the Latin translations of al-Khwarizmi, the ninth-century Muslim mathematician, whose own algebra seems to be independent of Diophantus'.

two chief sources of power: men and animals.[33] Other "prime movers"—water, wind and heat—were of course available to the Hellenistic East. Horizontal water wheels were known to the Greeks in the first century B.C. and soon enough a Roman engineer placed the wheels in the more efficient vertical position where they could be adapted to either an undershot or overshot water source. But their use did not become common until the fourth Christian century. Again, Hero constructed various complicated gadgets moved by wind and steam. Nothing came of them, however, and the far simpler contrivance of the windmill was unknown in the East until Islamic times.

Clearly there was no real problem urging the development of these new power sources. For everything, from grinding their grain to building their basilicas, aqueducts and roads, the Greeks and Romans had a plentiful supply of animals and men, free and slave. Capital was never reinvested in equipment but only toward the purchase of more slaves or more land. It was only when the sources of manpower were beginning to dry up in the third and fourth Christian centuries that any urgency toward mechanization was felt. By then both Christianity and Stoicism were making serious inroads against slavery. The Empire was at the same time in the grip of a serious social and economic crisis provoked by a disastrous progression of wars and plagues attended by a decline in population and sheer mismanagement.

Equally important in this complex of causes were some basic Hellenic attitudes toward science and work. The philosophers, some of whom made broad use of the notion of function (*ergon*) in their speculations, never considered work (likewise *ergon*) as one of the functions of man. Both the notion of school (*schole*) and the "liberal" (*eleutherios*) style associated with the life of the mind were closely identified with leisure. The schools might debate the superiority of the active (*bios praktikos*) to the contemplative life (*bios theoretikos*), but nowhere in the discussion figures the productive or "making" life (*bios poietikos*). Scattered through Aristotle's *Politics* are frequent disparaging references to the "life of the mechanic" (*bios banausios*) devoted

---

33. The latter were not always used very intelligently. Down to the tenth century A.D. ox harnesses were used on draft horses and donkeys. The throat and girth harness gradually slips upward and chokes these latter animals as the draft pressure increases. Their limited efficiency was further impaired by the absence of suitable traction shoes.

to making things for use, an occupation which automatically bars one from the enjoyment of full citizenship and the pursuit of virtue itself.

Certainly there were those in the *polis* who valued such work and took pride in its skillful accomplishment; Greek craftsmanship allows no other conclusion. Even some scientists, notably Plato's contemporaries Archytas and Eudoxus, used mechanical contrivances both as "elegant illustrations of geometrical theorems"[34] and as proofs of propositions that could not be handled analytically. The latter use of "machines," forced on the Greek by the faults in his notation and theory, had, of course nothing to do with technology, and when Plato objected to it on the grounds that it undermined the purity of geometry, his remarks proceeded not from an aristocratic prejudice against work, but from a need of defending the peculiar position of the "mathematicals" in his philosophical system.

A combination of this fastidious mathematical Platonism[35] and Aristotle's objections to the *banausiai technai* affected most of the Hellenistic scientific establishment. One of the reasons that the Romans were better engineers than the Greeks was probably that they were far weaker in theory and, so, relatively untouched by the Greek theoretician's instinctive embarrassment at debasing the theoretical for the benefit of the merely useful.

The Hellenistic advances in geometry, underscored by the almost full stop at Apollonius of Perg, are useful in illuminating other dark corners in Greek science. The scholars at Alexandria, Athens and Pergamum showed remarkable strength in the mathematical and classificatory sciences where the procedure was deductive, analytical or organizational. Progress was quickly blocked, however, wherever resolution depended upon chemical analysis, of which the Greeks had only the most rudimentary "craft knowledge," or where the data of direct and unaided

---

34. In this category fall all the working models of the heavens that Greek astronomers continued to build to illustrate their constructs.

35. The Platonic attitude, sometimes quite explicitly identified, colors, for example, Plutarch's account of Archimedes in his *Life of Marcellus*. Archimedes' own *Method* reveals, however, that he knew the difference between mechanical, constructive and experimental approaches to geometry and physics and the kinds of proofs achieved through rigorous mathematical analysis. While the latter was the eventual goal of the scientist, Archimedes in no wise despised the former.

observation did not suffice either to form or resolve hypotheses. At the end of antiquity, for instance, scientists in medicine and astronomy were confronted with a range of hypotheses on the nature of digestion and the movement of the heavenly bodies. Given the state of the art, no further observational data could be expected; the eye had reached its natural limits. The scientist was forced, then, to choose between hypotheses on other grounds.

The astronomical case is particularly instructive, since it reveals some of the fundamental strengths and crippling premises of ancient science. Neither the Greeks nor any of their contemporaries had that close control of environment which makes possible the laboratory with its infinitely repetitive experiments. Nature, however, provided approximations of such in its apparently eternal preservation of species, and particularly in the regular and never-ending procession of the heavenly bodies across the skies.[36] Observers in Greece and throughout the Near East charted those movements and in Hellenistic times even began to exchange data. And in the tradition of Greek science the astronomer attempted to construct a model of the movement of the heavenly bodies that would, in his phrase, "save the phenomena."

There were a number of such hypotheses to explain how the heavenly bodies moved as they apparently did; the deeper teleology of *why* they moved in that fashion, a question of little interest to the astronomer working with geometrical methods, was supplied by the physicist-theologians. The two schools could not, of course, ignore each other. Eudoxus was guided by Plato, and Aristotle by Callipus, and as the belief in the divinity of those heavenly bodies took an ever firmer grip on public consciousness the two types, the astronomer and the theologian, tended to run together in men like Hipparchus and Ptolemy.

The starting point of all the models of celestial movements was the basic Pythagorean tenet that the universe was a finite, circumscribed and circular system. The size of the system was gradually extended by trigonometric methods, but the Pythagorean premise was never quite rejected. What went on *within* the system was the subject of considerable debate in Pythagorean

---

36. Aristotle had made the natural connection between the two phenomena: the eternal movement of the sun in its orbit guaranteed the eternity of the species.

circles in the fifth century—was a stationary earth or sun the center around which the other planets revolved, or was the earth the rotating center of a fixed system?

Plato, whose interest in geometry was intense, gave some thought to the problem of the celestial model, and it was probably he who set the terms of its solution: which uniform and ordered movements must be assumed to account for the apparent movement of the planets? The answer was supplied by Eudoxus, who provided an ingenious and elaborate geometrical analysis of the motion of the planets. The planets moved in homocentric circles around the stationary earth, but to "save" the increasingly complicated observational data each revolving planet and the circle of the fixed stars had to be resolved into a number of concentric spheres, twenty-seven in all, before the desired geometrical pattern could be achieved.

Eudoxus' model was unmistakably a geometrical one, but Aristotle, who appropriated it with the refinements of Callipus, an astronomer working with Aristotle in Athens about B.C. 330,[37] had little use for such *entia rationis* as geometrical figures and converted it into a physical system of stars and planets. In that altered state it was canonized at the heart of the *Metaphysics*, and whatever conviction the theory of homocentric spheres carried with it into later times was due to that glorified setting.

Eudoxus' geometric scheme could be and was refined, but the earlier Pythagorean musing on the heliocentric hypothesis was never absolutely hushed. It was revived in the Academy during Aristotle's stay there by Heraclides of Pontus and by the later astronomer of Alexandria, Aristarchus of Samos (*c.* B.C. 280) one of Strato's students. In Heraclides' compromise version, Venus and Mercury revolved about the sun while the sun, in turn, and the other planets revolved about the earth. The earth, moreover, rotated daily on its own axis.

Aristarchus rejected the compromise: the earth rotated daily, but it also revolved around the sun. There might be geometrical and physical objections to this hypothesis, the parallax of the fixed stars, for example, but it raised even graver doubts in another area, theology. We know that religious misgivings were

---

37. On geometrical grounds Callipus added seven spheres to Eudoxus' twenty-seven; Aristotle's own physical considerations—he had to account for the *transmission* of movement from the outer rim inward—raised the number to fifty-five concentric spheres.

expressed by the Stoic Cleanthes, but he was unlikely to have been alone, since the heliocentric hypothesis disturbed an essentially religious view of the universe. The stationary earth was, in a sense, at the bottom of the universe; ranged above and beyond the moon were the heavenly bodies, whose divinity was eloquently testified to by the common consent of mankind and, if scientific evidence was required, by their regular and eternal motion. In that supralunar world, motion and causality were different from what occurred on our disordered earth.

These attitudes rise from every page of the *Timaeus* of Plato, who had demanded a celestial hypothesis in terms of "orderly and regular motion." They are equally obvious in the *Metaphysics*, where they provide the basis of Aristotle's distinction of types of substances. To exalt the earth to the position of a divine planet and to relegate the sun, increasingly the focal point of celestial activity for the Stoics, to the "bottom" of the universe were equally unthinkable.

A solution, then, had not only to save the "appearances"; it had to save the theological premises as well. Motion in the heavens had clearly to be circular, for example, since this type of motion was the most honorable and fitting (*prepon*) to the divine and living substances that progressed stately across the skies. The "appearances" (*phainomena*) that showed not only variable velocities but even retrogression had thus to be resolved into circular orbits; the Hellenistic astronomer, who knew well enough about ellipses, never explored that rather irregular possibility.

The final Greek hypothesis, adequate to the demands of geometry and theology alike, evolved between the time of Apollonius of Perg (B.C. 280) and Hipparchus (B.C. 130), and received its final statement in the *Mathematical Collection* of Claudius Ptolemy (A.D. 150).[38] As stated there, each of the circular orbits around the earth was reduced to smaller circles, or epicycles, which had as their progressive centers points along the larger circular orbit of the planet. The elegant system of Ptolemy, compounded of the best the Greeks could achieve by unaided observation and geometrical analysis, served as the model of the heavens for the pious and the learned alike down to the time of Copernicus.

---

38. See Chapter X, pp. 406–7.

The *Mathematical Collection* was, however, a learned work and few in the Hellenized reading public could follow its complicated mathematics. Popular interests in the heavens was unlikely to have been mathematical;[39] what the public knew about the skies was couched in far more pictorial terms, derived, by and large, from the poet laureate of popular science, Aratus.

Aratus (*c.* B.C. 310–245), born in Soli in Cilicia and educated in the best scientific and philosophical circles at Athens, was court poet to both Antigonus Gonatas at Pella and Antiochus I in Syria. His extravagant reputation in antiquity rested solidly on the *Phaenomena*, a verse reworking, in the style of Hesiod, of a similarly titled work by Eudoxus, a description of the visible heavens with a kind of appendix on weather signs derived from Theophrastus. In Aratus, however, the description is integrated with various star and planet myths, and the whole is overcast with a noticeable Stoic piety. The poem, which was widely read in Hellenistic circles and later at Rome in Cicero's Latin translation, further solemnized the wedding between the heavens and religion that had been in the making for at least a century and that would eventually overwhelm the serious study of astronomy.

The *Phaenomena* was a work of scientific vulgarization, and, if the number of citations and commentaries is used as a criterion, an immense success among Hellenized readers. Aratus' popular science, combined with piety and myth and unencumbered by the sophistication of contemporary mathematics, is a perfect example of what the literate Hellene—Greek, Egyptian, Syrian or Roman—fed upon. Research in higher mathematics, philosophy and rhetoric was the business of scholars in places like the Museum or the Lyceum, and most of our preserved treatises come from just such academic circles. But the results eventually passed outward to the middle schools and into the hands of interested readers in the form of textbooks and works of popularization like Aratus'.

Not many of the latter class of writings survive, and with their disappearance judgments about the popular culture of the time are rendered extremely perilous. The learned read Ptolemy; the

---

39. Except for the mathematics necessary for casting horoscopes. As the illiterate might go to the professional scribe to write his letters, so the astrologically inclined of Alexandria or Rome had recourse to the *mathematici Chaldaei*, the store-front sages who for a fee worked out the computations. See Chapter XI, pp. 438–39.

literate, Aratus. The difference between the two groups was by no means immense, but taken together they constituted a small fraction of the population of the *oikoumene*.

Whatever literacy did exist centered in the urban *poleis*, where the motives and means of Hellenization came together. Literacy was tied to prosperity, and prosperity to Hellenization. At the time when new *poleis* were being founded across Asia, the first connection, between literacy and prosperity, may not have been perfectly understood, since the new literary culture was still in its infancy. Great city founders like the Seleucids were concerned not with spreading literacy but with creating a class of municipal managers responsible for local trade, commerce and administration.

Only a *polis* would produce such men, just as only a Hellenized environment could produce the soldiers who conquered and occupied the Near East. And even though the Seleucids and others who pursued a policy of Hellenic urbanization in the East may have intended primarily economic and political ends, their chosen instrument, the *polis*, was from its inception a social organism with values as well as methods. Those who shared its life became more than managers and soldiers; they were drawn into the Hellenic culture of the *oikoumene*, spoke its common dialect, read its literature in Antioch no less than in Athens, and absorbed its evolving ideals.

VI

The Seleucid Empire

The battle of Ipsus finally promoted Seleucus, former junior officer under Alexander and then satrap of Babylon, to the position of a king of the *oikoumene* by giving him access to the Mediterranean along the Syrian coast. Twenty years later his victory over Lysimachus at Corupedion crowned his achievement by putting the old Hellenic centers in western Anatolia into his hand. Ipsus guaranteed his survival as a Greek rather than an Oriental king, but Corupedion may have exposed him and his successors to Aegean temptations that brought about his house's ruin. Seleucus forfeited his own life en route to the throne of Macedon, and Antiochus III allowed himself to be drawn once again to Greece and into the overwhelming arms of the Romans. The treaty of Apamea that followed withdrew the promise of Corupedion by thrusting the Seleucids back south of the Taurus, beyond the reach of the vital Greek manpower without which no Hellenistic kingdom of the East could hope to survive. When other upstart powers and disloyal or uncontrollable vassals amputated the Iranian and Mesopotamian provinces at their rear, the last Seleucids suffocated to death in their pocket in northern Syria. Antioch, like the disembodied Constantinople of the later Byzantine Empire, survived as a head without a body, until the Romans saw fit to deliver their almost casual *coup de grâce*.

The Greeks in the East

The great land mass running from the Phoenician coast of the Mediterranean eastward across the Syrian steppe, the Mesopotamian river systems, and the Iranian plateau up to the watersheds of the Hindu Kush was the testing ground of Hellenism in the East. In Anatolia Hellenism had come early to the western littoral and was proceeding slowly inland even before Alexander's conquest; Alexander and his successors there merely hastened a process that had begun some five centuries earlier. In Egypt Hellenism came with Alexander,[1] but it was in effect quarantined in the highly protected atmosphere of Alexandria. The result was a glorious hothouse bloom which sent its remarkable fragrance throughout the *oikoumene* but put down no roots into the native soil.

Hellenism in the Seleucid heartland was a very different matter. Here too it came with Alexander; but then it was broadcast over the land from one end to the other in the form of Greek cities and Macedonian military colonies, first by Alexander himself and then by his Seleucid epigones. Alexander may have had the rather novel idea of a mixture of races, Greek and Iranian, that was to be, however, Hellenic in its culture. No such ideal transfigured the Seleucids. Their aim was simply to hold the land and make it prosper, and Hellenic urbanization converged on both those goals. They dotted their immense empire with these urban centers, some large and some small, here dense and there isolated, but all exposed, as was not the case in Egypt, to destruction or survival, political, military and cultural.

The outcome depended on the strength of the institutions, which the Greeks had every reason to think were more than adequate—Sicily, Macedon, and the Black Sea littoral had already tested them—and more directly and more dangerously on the sheer number of Hellenes that could be attracted to these new lands.

To colonize this huge territory that extended from the Mediterranean to India the Seleucids had primarily to draw upon the Greek and Macedonian homeland and the *poleis* of Ionia. There were from the beginning soldiers or mustered-out veterans in the area, like the garrisons that Alexander left behind in the course of his conquest or Antigonus' Athenians whom Seleucus transferred from Antigonia to his new city of Antioch. The bulk had to be

---

1. There were, of course, Greeks in Egypt before Alexander, wandering tourists like Herodotus and mercenaries like Agesilaus and Chabrias, but the great bulk of them was limited to the commercial enclave of Naucratis.

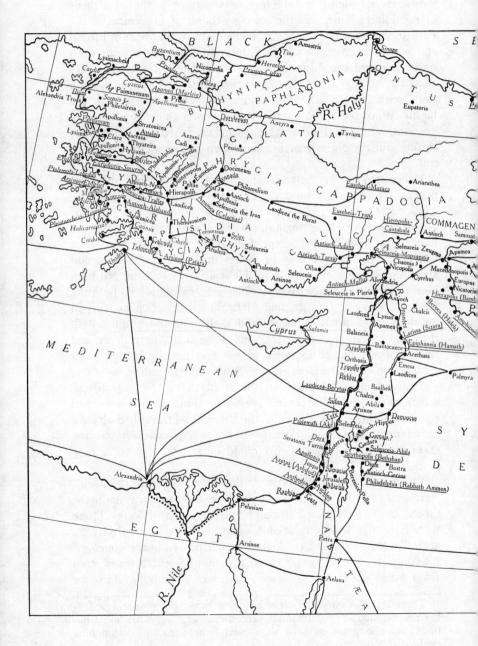

A

Phasis

arnacia (Cerasus)

CASPIAN SEA

R. Cyrus

Antioch-Edessa (Orrhoë)

themus

Antioch Nisibis

Charrae (Harran)

(Carchemish)

ce

Ichnae

Nicephorium

M E S O P O T A M I A

Demetrias ?

Singara

Alexandria (Arbela)

Europus (Rhagae)

A

Apamea

(Thapsacus)

R. Euphrates

Libba

Seleuceia

Doura-Europus

Epiphaneia (Ecbatana)

M E D I A

Apollonia

Chala

Doura ?

Artemita

Apamea ?

Heraclea ?

Akkad

Neapolis

Ctesiphon

Seleuceia (Opis)

Sinnar

Gabae ?

Babylon

Cutha

Seleuceia (Susa)

Borsippa

Apamea ?

S U S I A N A

Alexandria ?

Nippur

Seleuceia

Orchoi (Uruk)

C H A L D Æ A

Laodicea

Apamea ?

R. Euphrates

Alexandria-Antioch

Methone ?

Seleuceia

Arethusa

Larissa

Antioch

HELLENISTIC ASIA

drawn from home—soldiers willing to serve for pay and the promise of land, merchants in pursuit of profit, or simply economic and political refugees from an unpromising and overcrowded Greece. What the total was it is almost impossible to say—we do not even know the exact number of the settlements—but the sensible conclusion can be no other than that the Greeks were a small minority of the total population of the empire.

Ringed about them were the native peoples ruled by the Seleucids by right of conquest: Lydians, Phrygians, Carians, Galatians and the other tribes of Anatolia; the Syrians, Arabs and Jews of Coele-Syria; Babylonians and Iranians; nomad Sacae, Sogdians, Bactrians and Indians on the eastern frontier—all yoked together by the political overlordship of the Seleucids, who offered, in varying degrees in different places and different times, economic prosperity, physical security, and a control tempered with toleration.

What came out of the association was to a perceptible degree an open-ended society in that the ruling class, the Hellenes, permitted, if they did not encourage, additions to their ranks by the process of cultural assimilation. From the moment Alexander came to Asia, down to the Arab invasion, Hellenism provided the single operative criterion of caste in the East. A free man of whatever origins might choose to submit himself to the acculturation process in the *polis* institutions like the gymnasium and *ephebeia*. The Greeks, it would appear, did not much resort to exogamy in the East, but their cultural liaisons were splendidly promiscuous and the acculturated easterner, no matter what his tribal or ethnic origins, had no trouble in the *oikoumene* if he bore the talisman of a Greek *paideia*. There is no appreciable difference between the Greek-born Polybius and Plutarch and their eastern contemporaries Posidonius of Apamea and Lucian of Samosata. The Stoa was filled with easterners in the second and third generation of its existence, and it excited the attention of no one except the modern scholar.

The Seleucid view of political citizenship was somewhat narrower. We do not know precisely how Hellenization worked in this context, but in the gross forms of political life citizenship, membership in the *demos* of a constituted *polis* was not granted *en bloc* to the considerable body of natives who might inhabit it. As in Egypt, the native inhabitants of the *polis* were grouped in a *politeuma* with a degree of self-regulation but under the general jurisdiction of a municipal or royal official.

This is the view from within the protective confines of the *polis*, where Greek and native lived together in a highly Hellenized environment. Outside its walls, however, was the *chora*, the countryside of the peasant serfs, the nomads, the temple states and tribal societies that also rested under the hand of Seleucus I and his descendants. The Seleucids inherited from their Achaemenian predecessors a complicated system of political and economic tenure, to which they added their own peculiar Greek conceptions. First and foremost they ruled an empire; the Seleucid monarch held sway over various vassal lords, who acknowledged in varying degrees his sovereignty and paid him tribute. Such were the kings in Media Atropatene and Armenia, for example, or in central Anatolia. These native dynasts ruled national or tribal states with their own dynastic traditions and could not be easily removed by their Seleucid overlord. Their relations with the central authority, loose as they were, were probably regulated by treaty. An even looser relationship was maintained with the "nations" (*ethne*), nomadic and seminomadic tribes that wandered across Iran and the Syrian steppe. They were in theory tributaries of the Seleucid king, but it is doubtful whether there was much control of them or whether there was much tribute paid into the Imperial coffers from such sources.

In theory the satrap, or provincial governor, was somewhat different. He was part of the central administrative system and was appointed and removed by the king, to whom he was immediately responsible; the moneys that came from him were calculated as tax, not tribute. In reality, however, some of the satraps, particularly those in the East, must have operated little differently from the native dynasts. Indeed, they may have been more dangerous, since they had under their control, or that of their military counterpart, the *strategos*, that part of the Seleucid army that was drawn from the various military colonies (*katoikiai*) scattered over the empire. The Achaemenians, who earlier had set the pattern of a loose rein over their governors, had trouble with their satraps, and the Seleucids were not exempt from the same difficulty.

The *katoikiai* were governed by the satrap or other district chief through his local supervisor (*epistates*). There were other political units within the satrapies that were, on the other hand, autonomous, the Greek cities (*poleis*) and the temple states. Here too there were Achaemenian precedents in western Anatolia, where the *poleis* of Ionia were part of the empire of Darius and Xerxes. Like the temple states, the *poleis* were, by definition, self-governing units which were at best only partially assimilable into the organization of the province or the empire. The Achaemenians had difficulty with their fiercely independent *poleis* and not infrequently resorted to coups and tyrannies to ensure that a pro-Persian faction governed with them. When Alexander marched through Anatolia he declared the liberation of these same *poleis*—for which they made him a god—and, in contrast to his vicars in Greece, returned liberal and democratic governments to power. More, he founded new *poleis* as the preferred unit of political and social life within his empire.

Every successor to Alexander in Anatolia followed the same policy of Hellenic urbanization, a policy that promised economic prosperity and military security, but held out as well the ideal of political autonomy. The Seleucids followed the same path for as long as they were in Anatolia, but extended *polis* urbanization into areas where there was little or no precedent. Babylonia had been urbanized by the Assyrians, but certainly not on the Greek model, and Syria and Iran were still generally operating on the level of a village economy when the Seleucids arrived there.

Under the Seleucids and the Ptolemies a pattern of *poleis* was established from the Taurus southward to Gaza on the borders of Sinai. In an easterly direction the Seleucids connected their Syrian show place and capital of Antioch to their chief eastern mart and *polis* at Seleucia on the Tigris by another dense band of cities across northern Syria and Mesopotamia. There were other cities in Media and, after Alexander's own example, a cluster of settlements at the head of the commercially important Persian Gulf. Lines of *poleis* stretched farther east to Central Asia and India.

In some instances the Seleucid colonizers merely took older settlements and raised them to *polis* standards by settling Greeks within them and organizing city life around Hellenic ideals and institutions. Babylon eventually received this treatment, as did the Achaemenian Susa. In other instances the foundations were new, as in Seleucia on the Tigris and what was to become the capital of the entire empire, Antioch on the Orontes.

Before Ipsus, Seleucus had ruled his eastern satrapy from a new Greek city of his own divising on the Tigris and named, as the other Successors were doing in their capitals, after himself. His rival and former overlord, Antigonus "the One-Eyed," was following an identical policy in Syria, where he collected the Greeks and Macedonians under his sway into the city of Antigonia on the Orontes. Once Seleucus fell heir to Syria he promptly shifted the center of his empire westward. His first foundation after Ipsus was another Seleucia, this one at the mouth of the Orontes; and from its dedication in B.C. 300, Seleucia Pieria, as it was called, served as the western center and official capital of the realm all during its founder's lifetime. A month later, farther up the Orontes, though five miles short of the site of Antigonia, Seleucus founded a second city, Antioch, originally intended to control the overland trade routes that passed nearby, but later, with the accession of Antiochus I, to become the capital of the Seleucids. Seleucia Pieria, an otherwise admirable site, was highly exposed to attack from the sea, and the Seleucids had, as yet, no navy.

Antioch was laid out carefully on a gridiron plan, as were most of the other Seleucid cities, with the public buildings centered around an *agora* and the whole enclosed by a rectilinear wall. The population of the original settlement was purposefully controlled at the figure of 5,300 adult males,[2] a number that yields a tentative total of 25,000 Greek inhabitants exclusive of slaves.[3] Within the walls the population was Greek and Macedonian, including the Athenian settlers whom Antigonus had originally planted at Antigonia and whom Seleucus transported to Antioch, and a number of Jews, mercenaries mustered out of Seleucus' army. Outside the walls and excluded from the citizen population, the *demos*, were the local Syrians, drawn in increasing numbers to these glittering new Greek cities.

---

2. A figure not coincidentally close to the number 5,040 set down by Plato in his *Laws* as the optimum number of householders in an ideal *polis*.

3. During Roman times the population of Antioch had grown to about 500,000, and in its heyday Seleucia on the Tigris was even larger.

Antioch was one of a cluster of four major *poleis* that Seleucus founded in northern Syria: Seleucia Pieria and Laodicea on the coast, Antioch and Apamea inland, the last serving as the Seleucid war camp and arsenal. Round about these to the south and the east there were eventually others: Beroea (Aleppo) astride the north-south trade route, Europos, formerly Dura, on the Euphrates crossing, and in northern Mesopotamia the fortress cities of Edessa and Nisibis. This zone of northern Syria and Mesopotamia the Seleucids converted into another Macedon with a dense network of *poleis* bearing reminiscent Macedonian place names or the dynastic titles of their royal founders.

The essence of the *polis* was that it was self-contained and self-ruled. This was its status in Greece and Ionia, and Seleucus and his successors had little difficulty in converting the decentralized government of the Achaemenians, who had once ruled these same lands, into their own version of municipal *laissez faire*, a system that the Romans found and imitated in the East until well into the third Christian century.

The Seleucid *polis* could be distinguished not so much by its visible Hellenism as by the presence of certain institutions of government: a body of enfranchised citizenry (*demos*), a consultative or legislative body (*boule*), and local magistrates (*archontes*). This urban complex, planned, walled and adorned according to the wealth of the inhabitants and the munificence of the king, was supported by its own surrounding territory of "city land."

These self-contained *poleis* floated like cells within the larger units of the central administration, the descending scale of satrapies, eparchies and hyparchies borrowed from Achaemenian practice. The satrap and his military opposite number in the province, the *strategos*—the Seleucids kept Alexander's distinction of the civil and military powers in the provinces—generally supervised only those affairs of the province that did not fall within the purview of the *poleis:* peace and order among the unconquered or semiconquered elements of the population, the collection of rents and tithes on the king's land, and the upkeep of the postal and road system.

The foundation of a *polis* was, then, no simple matter; it meant that a new or existing urban center of some considerable size had to be brought to a level of organization and institutional sophistication where it could not merely govern itself but govern itself in the Greek manner through an apparatus of demes, tribes, city councils, elections and elected officers. It is likely, then, that many of the Seleucid settlements designated at one time or another as a *polis* began their careers as somewhat more humble military colonies (*katoikiai*), garrison encampments set down near native towns. The two could coalesce in time, the soldiers put down roots and families, and from the common growth of the town and the camp emerged in time a *polis* which then contained within itself the original native population organized in the form of a *politeuma*.

That the military settlers should put down roots was the obvious intent of the government. The *katoikia* had land attached to it, just as the *polis* did, and the tillage was distributed to the soldiers in the form of lots (*kleroi*), which carried with them (whoever the owner—the original soldier, his son, or another party to whom the lot had been sold) the obligation of continued military service.

The Seleucids' treatment of their *poleis* was never uniform. A *katoikia* could be governed by a royal overseer appointed from Antioch or Seleucia, but the *polis* was in theory ruled under its own laws by its own elected officials drawn from the local citizen body. What then was their relationship with the king? Some he had himself founded and others, the older settlements in Anatolia, he had won by conquest. Neither group of cities, then, was free to go its own way. Unless specifically exempted, the *poleis* had to pay a tax into the royal exchequer. Nor did the king hesitate to put one of his garrisons into a *polis*, an infringement of *polis* autonomy that was already provoking considerable unrest under the Antigonids in Greece, or even to appoint an *epistates* to run the city—or perhaps merely to oversee the "aliens" of the *politeumata*—as Cassander did with Demetrius of Phalerum at Athens. There was no question of the city's maintaining its own army or conducting its own foreign policy.

The same attitude can be detected in the Seleucids' relations with the large temple states that had for so long existed all through the Near East. They allowed them to rule themselves within the premises of their own constitution and to continue to function as quasi-autonomous social and economic units. But the temples too belonged to the king in the larger sense that the *poleis* did. They too paid taxes, and the Seleucids did not scruple to tamper with their land tenure.

The king had outright and direct ownership of all other territories, that is, all the land not joined to a *polis*, *katoikia* or temple state, or given in grant to another. The peasants who worked it, like those who worked the temple and gift states, were tied to the land in the condition of serfdom and they paid their taxes directly and individually to the king.[4] It is here in the "king's land," that the Seleucids' commitment to urbanization can be seen most clearly. Great tracts of the royal domain were detached to form the hinterland of the *poleis*, new and old. The effects of the transfer were twofold. As occupants of *polis* land the peasants ceased to be serfs and became free settlers of the *polis*, inhabitants of the villages outside the urban center, or at liberty to take up residence as members of a *politeuma* within it. Second, the money from rents, leases and taxes was fed into the *polis* exchequer instead of to the king. The central administration recouped some of it in the form of a tax on the *polis* itself, but the Seleucids were in effect encouraging the investment of capital in *polis* institutions rather than in the monarchy.

To rule this immense hybrid of political and ethnic units the Seleucid monarch had few institutions and powers. The army and the fleet were, of course, his, and the determination of foreign policy. He had at hand the loosely knit fabric of a court and the central administration of civilian governors, financial comptrollers and military commanders. He held the lines of internal communication, the road and postal systems, and he regulated trade by his twin powers of taxation and the minting of currency. Finally there was the image: the savior (*soter*) and benefactor (*euergetes*) of the people; by descent a god (*theos*) and by action a god-made-manifest (*epiphanes*).

His victories in the field and his generous patronage at home kept the image before his subjects. The Seleucids, like all other Hellenistic monarchs with the exception of the Macedonian Antigonids, were worshiped as gods. The claim to divine affiliation back to the Olympians began with Alexander, and just as the Ptolemies claimed descent from Heracles and Dionysus, so Seleucus was reputed to have been the son of Apollo, and the dynasty as a whole was placed under the special protection of both Zeus

---

4. Unlike their Egyptian counterparts, the Seleucid serfs paid an annual percentage of their produce and not a fixed amount. A bad year did not threaten to wipe them out.

and Apollo. Zeus was the tutelary deity of Antioch, while Apollo was given sumptuous quarters at Daphne, a suburb of Antioch made sacred as the site of the god's pursuit of a nymph of the same name. The sacred enclosure there had a large temple containing a monumental statue of Apollo,[5] a sacred grove, and an oracle of the god,[6] the whole simultaneously glorifying Apollo, the Seleucids who sponsored such magnificence, and the city of Antioch to which pilgrims were drawn from throughout the *oikoumene*.

The descent from Apollo was doubtless officially propagated, but the instruments for its propagation were the various Greek *poleis*, which by their altars, statues, priesthoods and feasts advanced the cause of the living sovereign and, indeed, his ancestors in the ruling family. As in the case of Alexander, these were municipal cults spontaneously offered to the sovereign and not the products of some imagined Oriental perversion. Each *polis* offered divine honors to the king in its own fashion, linked, in one form or another, with the cult of the two tutelary Olympians, Zeus and Apollo.

The variegated and localized honors paid to the Seleucids stand in obvious contrast with the divine kingship in Egypt. The Ptolemies were the object of an official *state* cult that was, as all else in Egypt, highly centralized and skillfully manipulated. It was probably an imitation of the Egyptian model that Antiochus III finally attempted the first empirewide cultus in the Seleucid realms. In each satrapy he appointed archpriests and archpriestesses to supervise the divine honors to be paid to himself and his wife. The search for some unifying principle was natural enough under the circumstances, but the lands ruled by the Seleucids were not and could not be another Egypt. Antiochus was defeated by geography and the diversity of cultural and ethnic strains over which he had to preside.

The Seleucids' wistful longing for a unified empire did not

---

5. The work of the same sculptor who had earlier established his credentials for the grandiose by doing the sculpture for the tomb of Mausolus at Halicarnassus.
6. The oracle continued to function down to A.D. 350, when Constantine's nephew Gallus moved the bones of a martyred Christian bishop into the vicinity and so silenced the voice of Apollo. By the time the Emperor Julian arrived at Daphne some ten years later the entire complex was deserted and ruined (see Chapter XIX, pp. 710–11).

tempt them to the repression of the cultic variety which surrounded them. They rebuilt and richly endowed the older Greek temples in western Anatolia, particularly Apollo's venerable oracular site at Didyma. Nor were the Oriental gods neglected. Babylonia in particular was the recipient of a great deal of Seleucid patronage. The temple of Marduk in Babylon, that of Anu in Orchoi, earlier known as Uruk, and of Nabu in Borsippa were all reconstructed and readorned under Seleucid auspices.

This liberal and tolerant policy in Babylonia paid dividends. The Seleucids put down roots there and were accorded the same kind of legitimacy as successors of the Babylonian divinely inspired kings that prompted Alexander to choose Babylon as the center of his embryonic empire. At first the Seleucids seemed to be of two minds about Babylonia. After the settlement of B.C. 321 Seleucus began his career as satrap there, and the entire Seleucid Empire marked as the beginning of its official chronology Seleucus' entry into the city of Babylon after the battle of Gaza in B.C. 312. And yet he deserted Babylon and founded the new city of Seleucia on the Tigris to serve as his first capital. Seleucia was, moreover, a Greek *polis*, free of the Oriental associations of the old Babylonian culture. Indeed, Seleucus and Antiochus I seemed bent on reducing Babylon to a ruin when they transported a large number of its inhabitants to their new *polis*. Other *poleis* ringed the old city; Susa was converted to another Seleucia, and there were even attempts at Hellenizing Uruk and Babylon themselves.[7]

And yet Babylonia held a special position. Seleucia on the Tigris was a second capital of the empire upon which all the eastern satrapies depended, and from the beginning it was entrusted to the crown prince, who took up his residence there. Though Seleucia succeeded Babylon as the trade and administrative center of the entire East, the older centers, Babylon, Uruk and Borsippa, were not allowed to disappear. They became instead the centers of a new Babylonian renaissance, encouraged and subsidized by the Seleucids, partly Hellenized, but essentially devoted to the preservation and cultivation of the still-living past. Akkadian was still in use there, though it was rapidly being

---

7. The former, Hellenized as Orchoi, never became a full-fledged *polis*, but Babylon under Antiochus IV Epiphanes' building program received the full Greek treatment, including a theater and a gymnasium.

replaced, outside of learned and priestly circles, by Aramaic and Greek.

The priestly class in Babylonia was severely reduced in number from its days of glory and, likely, Hellenized in its upper reaches. Beneath them the scribes, likewise far fewer than before, continued their work of study and transcription. The entire temple corporation kept up the old rituals and worked over the traditional Babylonian law that was still operating in that region. The libraries were carefully kept up, and much of what is known today of the ancient Babylonian tradition in literature, law, religion and science depends on the careful work done in the temple archives during the Seleucid era when that same tradition was already more than a thousand years old.

This lively intellectual activity, which contrasts so sharply with the diminished native tradition in the Egypt of the Ptolemies, did not leave the Greeks untouched. Hellenized citizens of the Seleucid domains could pass into the *oikoumene*, as Posidonius did from Apamea and Meleager from Gadara, and there were a number of such from the farther East, the geographer Isidore of Charax and Diogenes of Seleucia on the Tigris, the Stoic who succeeded another Seleucid product, Zeno of Tarsus, as head of the school and who participated in the famous embassy to Rome in B.C. 155.[8] Neither man came trailing clouds of Babylonian lore, but there were others who remembered whence they came. One such was Berossus, the priest of Marduk in Babylon who reported, like Manetho in Egypt and Josephus in Palestine, the traditions of his native culture to the Hellenes of the *oikoumene*. His introduction to Babylonian civilization, a work entitled *Babylonica*, was dedicated to Antiochus I and likely composed while Berossus was teaching on the island of Cos about B.C. 270.[9]

Berossus' sophisticated chronological calculations attracted some attention among the historians and naturalists, and doubtless

---

8. See Chapter IX, pp. 357–58.

9. The *Babylonica*, which is only very partially preserved, began with the mythical tale of Oannes and ended with the death of Alexander the Great. The book was in vogue during Roman Republican times; both Posidonius and Alexander Polyhistor (see Chapter X, pp. 399–401) used it, and from them it passed into wider circles: Seneca, Pliny, Plutarch, and the Christians Clement of Alexandria and Eusebius of Caesarea.

they noted as well other material that the author considered germane to his purpose—to introduce the Greek reader to Babylonian astrology. Berossus had access, of course, to the Babylonian archives, and there is some evidence that back in Babylon and Uruk the accumulated astronomical—and astrological—lore of centuries was passing into Greek, some of it for the first time. Even as pure science the material was accurate and the calculations advanced—very complete tables on the phases and eclipses of the moon, for example—and its passage to the Greeks had a perceptible influence on Hellenic mathematical astronomy. As already noted, the astronomer Hipparchus of Nicaea (*c.* B.C. 161–126) had the Babylonian periodic tables available to him in one form or another. Hipparchus himself was not innocent of the other side of Berossus' legacy, the Babylonian astrological beliefs that gave the "Chaldeans" the reputation among the Hellenes of being the foremost practitioners of that science. The reputation was, as a matter of fact, somewhat ill deserved, since antiquity's classical version of an astrological system was formulated in Egypt. It is clear, nonetheless, that the Greeks' and the Egyptians' first taste of that exotic discipline came from the learned centers in Babylonia. Babylonian astral influences are in evidence in the later years of Plato and have been detected, somewhat less surely, behind Zeno of Citium's universe that is consumed by a periodic conflagration and under the domination of fate (*heimarmene*). By the time of the directorship of Chrysippus in the middle of the third century the Stoa knew well enough about Babylonian astrology, either through the circulation of Berossus' work or through the immediate presence in Chrysippus' circle of students of the Babylonian Diogenes.

Later historians of the sciences had no very clear idea of the details of this transmission at the point of its origin. They had some names, one of which, the Greek "Kidenas," has happily turned up in its native form of "Kidinnu" in a second-century cuneiform text. Another "Chaldean," Sudines, who was also interested in lunar tables, illuminated the court of Attalus of Pergamum as a diviner. Earlier, there had even been a Chaldean in the Academy. We, who possess the fragmentary remains of the Babylonian libraries, are not much better informed than the ancients. In some few cases the actual translation of the astronomical texts into Greek can be traced, but in general the movement of Babylonian learning to the Hellenes is only apparent at its origins and terminus; the passage itself is concealed.

This is the transmission of knowledge from one culture to another; there is very little evidence of a synthesis of those two cultures. In Egypt just some such synthesis was coming about, because the later Ptolemies could not avoid it, but in Babylonia the gulf between Hellenism and its older environment never appreciably lessened. Of composite Greek-Babylonian names there are a few, very few, and not much else besides. By B.C. 125 a sacked and burning Babylon was in the hands of the Parthians and the opportunity had passed.

In Syria too, where the Greek settlements were far denser than they were in Babylonia, the Seleucids tolerated and even encouraged local cults. At Heliopolis, Palmyra and Gerasa there were temples of local gods and goddesses—Hadad, Baal Shamin, or Atargatis—frequently concealed under Greek names or cult epithets. Seleucus I had himself set the tone in making initial sacrifices to Zeus Casius and Zeus Ceraunius, two local versions of sky gods, before founding Antioch. His wife Stratonice personally supervised the reconstruction of the temple of the Syrian goddess Atargatis at Hierapolis-Bambyce.

Their attitude toward the temple states in their realms—most of the great ones in Anatolia lay outside the Seleucid domains—was somewhat more ambivalent, since here crossed religious and economic considerations. Religious practices were rarely interfered with—Antiochus IV Epiphanes' treatment of Jerusalem is a rather extraordinary exception—but the early Seleucids, like the early Ptolemies, did not hesitate to curb the economic and political power of the temple corporations by joining them to nearby *poleis*.

The Seleucids could afford to be tolerant on questions of religion; it was, after all, good business, and economic prosperity is what kept them alive. Under their rule the land thrived and trade prospered. They had, however, to fight for their success. The century of warfare that raged between the Ptolemies and the Seleucids for the possession of Coele-Syria was a struggle for ports and trade routes rather than the genteel dynastic sparring it is sometimes made to appear. Both the east-west and north-south overland trade routes funneled through that region, and the Seleucids who, for most of the period down to B.C. 200, were

restricted to the narrow Mediterranean frontage between Seleucia Pieria and Laodicea, had carefully to guide the eastern
overland trade to Antioch. Nearby Damascus to the south was
generally in Ptolemaic hands, and even the routes that passed
onward into Anatolia ended at termini like Miletus and Ephesus
that were only fitfully under Seleucid control.

Trade came westward to Antioch through the *poleis* and forts
of northern Syria and Mesopotamia after having mounted the
Euphrates and the Tigris from the chief eastern emporium at
Seleucia on the Tigris.[10] Administratively all the eastern satrapies
depended on Seleucia, and commercially all the routes westward
from India converged there, overland from Bactra or by sea to
the head of the Persian Gulf.[11]

The most frequented route to India was the great caravan road
that passed to the north of the Iranian plateau through Ecbatana
(Hamadan), Ragae (Rayy), Hecatompylos, Merv, Bactra
(Balkh), and then crossed the Hindu Kush and descended to
Taxila. Many of these posts from Seleucia out to the frontier
beyond Bactra were *poleis* staffed by the Greeks for the transparent purpose of protecting a major trade artery.

The thinly stretched lines of trade and communication that
bound together the scattered outposts in the eastern satrapies
created military, political and cultural problems far more acute
than any that arose in the deliberately dense areas of colonization
in Anatolia, Syria and Mesopotamia. Invasion and secession came
to the Seleucids' eastern domains less than a century after Seleucus I first possessed himself of Babylonia. An occasional raid
thereafter might bring a temporary restoration, as in the case of
Antiochus III, but the Seleucids could not hold Iran. Their
regime had some success in the Semitic Fertile Crescent. Media,
however, they clung to by main force and even that did not avail
farther east. When the Romans banished them from Anatolia the
Seleucids lost contact with their sources of Greek manpower;
and their eastern garrisons, unsupported by new drafts from the
west, dwindled, then vanished into the Iranian population. And
where there were few or none from the beginning, as in Persis

---

10. The more direct route westward across the Syrian steppe via the
oasis of Palmyra came into heavy use somewhat later.
11. The Persian Gulf also was the Seleucids' connection with the spice
trade from southern Arabia as the Red Sea was for the Ptolemies.

(Fars), the Iranian tradition went on unbroken and undisturbed.

Hellenism, on the other hand, made inroads in Iran, as it did throughout the East, and it was strong enough to survive even the political collapse of the Seleucids. Their successors in Iran, the Parthians, are the evidence—a native Iranian dynasty for whom it was still politically profitable to flaunt its Philhellenism.[12] From even the most remote centers of Iran, Greek inscriptions dating from Parthian times have been unearthed. And even farther east of Iran, at the very rim of Alexander's conquests, there survived the kingdoms of Bactria and India that preserved their specifically Greek quality until late in the first century.

Hellenism in Iran stirred no countercurrents westward as it had done in Babylonia and Egypt. The religious resurgence of Babylonia may have inhibited that possibility, just as Seleucid support of the Babylonian cultural tradition may have prevented their being more effective in Iran. There was, however, richer soil in the former western satrapies of the old Achaemenian Empire. Iranian influence was strong in Anatolia long before either Alexander or the Seleucids arrived there. The Iranian goddess Anahita, for example, was firmly domesticated in some of the great temple states there. It was from this ground that Iranian religion later bloomed in the *oikoumene* after the Seleucids had come and gone.[13]

On balance the Hellenization of the Near East under the Seleucids was a remarkable success. Their empire passed after a considerably briefer tenure than those that preceded or followed them there. While they were in possession, however, they changed the face of the land. Under the two Hellenizing powers, the Seleucids and the Ptolemies, Syria, Mesopotamia and Babylonia entered periods of great prosperity that continued, with minor gains and lapses, down to the Mongol invasions of the thirteenth century. Syria was one of the garden spots of the Roman Empire, celebrated for that blend of urban sophistication and agricultural richness that few other provinces could equal. In a larger perspective Rome's success in the East was of Seleucid manufacture. The Romans came with new capital and fresh armies to lands where the Seleucids pioneered the methods and

12. See Chapter VIII, p. 343.
13. See Chapter XII, pp. 475–76.

techniques. The Romans built upon the same foundations and pursued the same policies as their predecessors and reaped even richer rewards of wealth and prosperity.

Another harvest of Seleucid planting came to Rome. The *poleis* of the Near East, founded or Hellenized by the Seleucids, turned out a steady stream of poets, philosophers and historians, who not only maintained the Hellenic traditions when Greece faltered but passed as well into the service of the new ecumenical Roman Empire.[14] The Greek of the Gospels came from Seleucid and Ptolemaic sources, and the Hellenization of the Christian Church occurred not in Greece nor in Rome but at the hands of Hellenized scholars in the Near East. Christianity's two great schools were at Alexandria and Antioch.[15]

And the tradition ran on. Syrian Christians preserved their Hellenism into the eighth and ninth centuries in a vital enough state to transmit it to the new Arab masters of the Near East. This tenacious Hellenism owes little more than its mere possibility to Alexander. The conversion of the possibility into a reality fell chiefly to his successors, who had first to found and then to man the cities, garrisons and schools. How well they did can be attested to by the fact that, in the eleventh century, Plato and Aristotle were still being read in Baghdad, not far from the long-deserted ruins of Seleucia on the Tigris.

Antiochus the Great (B.C. 223–187)

The successors of Seleucus I were unsuccessful in holding together the immense empire that the founder of the dynasty acquired by his skill and energy. Antiochus II had to surrender his sovereignty over Pergamum, and Seleucus II, whose rule began in the confused circumstances of rival queens putting forward rival heirs,[16] lost important parts of the Seleucid holdings in northern Syria to Ptolemy III Euergetes. Seleucia Pieria, for example, the lifeline of Antioch to the sea, was under Ptolemaic control from B.C. 246 onward. And there were disquieting reports from the eastern satrapies of rampaging tribes and assertive princes.

---

14. See Chapter X, pp. 399–408.
15. See Chapter XVII, pp. 621–27.
16. See Chapter IV, pp. 161–63.

Seleucus II (B.C. 247–226) came to the throne as a disputed monarch but did manage to save his threatened kingdom from complete emasculation at the hands of the Ptolemies and from perishing in a civil war provoked by his brother Hierax. He was succeeded by his elder son Seleucus III (B.C. 226–223) whose first task at hand was to restore order, Seleucid order, to western Anatolia, which since the days of Hierax's revolt was regulated at the pleasure of the kings of Pergamum. His first attempt, directed by his uncle Andromachus, was a total failure. The Seleucid army was defeated by the Pergamenes, and Andromachus was captured by Attalus I, who promptly shipped him to Ptolemy in Egypt like a captured chess piece for a future Syrian war. The second attempt was fatal. En route Seleucus III was assassinated by his own men. The murderers put forward no pretender, and so their resentment must be presumed to have been personal rather than dynastic.

The dynasty itself seemed to be in good hands. A younger brother of Seleucus III was just approaching majority, and for the moment things were under the capable direction of Andromachus' son Achaeus, who had led the demoralized troops of Seleucus III back to Syria. The new young king was crowned as Antiochus III and immediately confirmed Achaeus as his deputy to continue the efforts against Attalus. The king's own attention was diverted eastward, where, almost immediately after his accession, two of the eastern satraps, the brothers Molon in Babylonia and Alexander in Persis, declared their independence and assumed the title of king. They likewise prevailed upon the vassal king of Media Atropatene to repudiate Seleucid sovereignty. It was not merely the youth of Antiochus III and the unsettled circumstances in Syria that prompted the move; within the preceding three decades local governors had asserted their independence as kings in Pergamum, Cappadocia and Bactria, while another, Tiridates, was carving himself a domain in Parthia and Hyrcania.

The first army raised against the eastern rebels fared poorly. Antiochus was forced to raise new levies and lead them in person against Molon and Alexander. He drove a wedge between the rebellious satraps and their allies in Atropatene, and as soon as he turned south toward Babylon the dispirited troops of Molon began deserting. By B.C. 219 it was all over; the revolt had been put down and Molon and Alexander confessed defeat by taking their own lives. The new Seleucid king had been blooded in the East.

Once returned to Syria, Antiochus was faced with a difficult choice. Achaeus, whose initial campaigns in Anatolia were marked with unexpected success, had lately been exhibiting dangerous symptoms of independence. It may have been that Achaeus' captive father was now being played by Ptolemy III to save his ally Attalus. Achaeus, who had Attalus in his grasp at one point, broke off the siege of Pergamum and turned instead toward Antioch. Like Molon in Babylonia, he proclaimed himself king. His troops, however, would have none of it, and Achaeus was stranded in Anatolia, caught midway between a recouped Attalus and the returned Antiochus III.

Antiochus' choice was to leave the impotent Achaeus to face down Attalus and to concentrate on the Egyptian director rather than the Anatolian actors, a choice that was doubtless aided by the presence of a new ruler in Egypt, Ptolemy IV Philopator. That decision led directly to Raphia and defeat in B.C. 217.[17] Antiochus was baffled by Ptolemy's vizier Sosibius and the new native contingents in the army of Egypt; all the Seleucid had to show for his campaigning in Coele-Syria between B.C. 219 and B.C. 217 was the recovery of his link to the sea, Seleucia Pieria, which the Ptolemies had held for thirty years.

Antiochus was not dismayed. He returned to Antioch and marched directly against the rebel Achaeus. Attalus was now willing to connive at the pretender's destruction, and with the cooperation of the Pergamenes, Antiochus backed Achaeus onto the acropolis at Sardis. The siege was prolonged, but in B.C. 214 the position was betrayed to Antiochus, and the unfortunate Achaeus was mutilated, beheaded, and crucified in the skin of an ass.

By B.C. 213 Antiochus had ended the civil wars in his domains, held Sosibius at bay, and regained some of the earlier Seleucid leverage in western Anatolia. In B.C. 212 Antiochus once again turned eastward. Armenia, a vassal kingdom that had defected when Hierax was stirring up insurrection in those parts, quickly came to terms, and for the restoration of tribute to the Seleucids the king of Armenia received Antiochus' sister in betrothal. From there the king took up the more formidable task begun but never

---

17. See Chapter IV, pp. 164–65.

completed by his father, the restoration of Seleucid control over Alexander's original kingdom in the East.

The Iranians had been quiet since Alexander deposed the last feeble Achaemenian ruler; whatever revolts subsequently occurred in Iran were more likely the work of dissident and ambitious Greek governors than the result of any native stirrings. Some areas there, like Media Atropatene (Azerbaijan) and Persis (Fars), the Seleucids never colonized and so never really controlled, and they had to content themselves with occasional tribute. But there was no real power in the East to threaten what they did, in fact, possess.

Such a power made its appearance sometime about B.C. 250, though it could scarcely have seemed so at the time. The Seleucids numbered among their subjects a great number of tribes (*ethne*) whose nomad habits made them all but invisible to their supposed overlords in Antioch. Nomads drifted down from the steppe between the Caspian and the Aral Sea, and one confederation, the Parni, came into the line of sight of the Greek settlements in Bactria. It was a critical time in Bactria; Diodotus, the Greek satrap there, had just ended what must have been a prolonged period of *de facto* autonomy by proclaiming his *de jure* independence from the Seleucid Empire.

The two events of the middle of the third century cannot be related, but the independence of Bactria and its repelling of the oncoming Parni must have occurred at about the same time. The Parni were driven westward into the neighboring satrapy of Parthava, where another satrap had lately severed his ties with Antioch. He was not so fortunate with the nomads, who, first under Arsaces and then under his brother Tiridates, completely overran the province. Tiridates proclaimed himself king. Substantially, these developments all took place during the troubled reign of Seleucus II, who had to contend with the Ptolemaic annexation of northern Syria and the rebellion raised by his brother Hierax in Anatolia. In B.C. 230 Seleucus II was at last free to turn his attention to the Parthian problem. At first he may have had the support of the now independent kingdom of Bactria; but with or without that support Seleucus II had Tiridates and his cavalry hot in flight back into the steppe, when reports of new activity on the part of Hierax forced the king to break off and return to Syria. It was a glittering opportunity unhappily lost.

Antiochus III armed himself for the assault on Parthia at

Ecbatana, a western post on the great caravan route astride which the Parthians now sat in their new capital of Hecatompylos. For his financing, Antiochus plucked at a near and tempting source, the treasury of the goddess Anahita's temple. We do not know whether the spoliation marked an official change in Seleucid policy toward the temples or was a random act dictated by an immediate need. It was to have a number of unfortunate sequels.

Fortified with the Anahita bullion, Antiochus took the road east in B.C. 210. The campaign that followed, though hard fought on both sides, went well for Antiochus. Hecatompylos fell and Tiridates' successor, Artabanus I, withdrew farther east into Hyrcania. The more heavily armed Seleucids had hard going over the Elburz range, but once on the plains of Hyrcania, they overtook and defeated Artabanus. There was, of course, no question of removing the Parthians; Antiochus had to content himself with a pledge of fealty and the promise of tribute.

Beyond Parthia lay Bactria, the richest and apparently the firmest of Alexander's conquests east of Babylon. The satrapy was at once a frontier, a trade corridor, and a granary. Across the Oxus lay the middle ground of agricultural Sogdia, and beyond that, over the Jaxartes, the Iranian nomads of the steppe, fenced off from the plantations of Transoxania and Bactria by the Macedonian garrisons that Alexander had left behind there. Across the Hindu Kush from the southeast came the caravans from India. Bactria, then, by reason of its agricultural produce, its pastureland—the best cavalry horses in the empire came from Bactria—and the flourishing transit trade was a rich and prosperous place, though no longer directly to the advantage of the Seleucids; Bactria, now an independent kingdom, was ruled by the ambitious Euthydemus, who had seized power from the son and successor of Diodotus.

Antiochus III planned to restore Bactria as well as Parthia to his rule, but his success there was at best indifferent. He came to grips with Euthydemus a number of times, but the capital at Bactria would not yield. A stalemate developed, and in B.C. 206 Antiochus had to settle. Euthydemus was confirmed as a vassal king and handed over war elephants and supplies as his pledge to Antiochus.

The settlement was hastened by Euthydemus' resort to an argument calculated to impress any ruler of Iran: continued warfare between the two Hellenic kings could serve no other end but to open Sogdia and Bactria to the Sacae nomads of the steppe. The Sacae had been there for centuries, Iranian nomads roaming the Kirgiz and Mongolian steppes from the borders of China to southern Russia.[18] They were continually probing the borders of Iran, and both Xerxes and Darius had earlier conducted campaigns against them. Alexander too had experience of the dangers that lay across the Jaxartes. The settled and flourishing Iranian communities in Bactria, Sogdia, and Khwarazm were a constant temptation to the horsemen of the steppe, and Euthydemus probably had little difficulty in enlisting Antiochus' Hellenic sentiments against the exterior barbarians. Euthydemus may have intended no more than to throw a good fright into the Seleucid king, but he spoke with a strange prescience. Not long after he used the Sacae threat on Antiochus, events in western China brought about an almost exact fulfillment of what Euthydemus feared.[19]

Antiochus passed on like a curious tourist to the lands once visited by Alexander but now little more than a memory to be renewed by the literary reminiscences of earlier Seleucid ambassadors to the East. South of the Hindu Kush he went little farther than Kabul, though the way to India was open. There was no Porus now, and the massive Mauryan Empire lay in scattered pieces. Antiochus was scarcely in a position to put the pieces together again. He collected some tribute and some elephants in a perfunctory fashion, then passed via Arachosia and Seistan back to his eastern capital at Seleucia on the Tigris (B.C. 205). There were some further campaigns along the eastern shores of Arabia to keep the Arab merchants there honest—they were the middlemen for the Seleucid spice trade to the Hadramaut—and by B.C. 204 the great eastern *anabasis* was over.

Antiochus III spent eight years in all in the east. During his absence he suffered no losses by invasion or insurrection in his western domains, an impressive tribute to the thoroughness of his work during the first years of his rule. What his contemporaries admired was, however, his flamboyant repetition—or a reasonable facsimile thereof—of Alexander's eastern adventures. The Iran-

---

18. It was from this latter region that one branch of the Sacae, the tribes known to the Greeks as the Scythians, had earlier penetrated into Anatolia and Thrace, where they eventually settled down as neighbors of the Greeks.

19. See Chapter VII, p. 276.

ians saluted him, as they saluted their Achaemenian lords of the past, as *Shahan shah*, and the Greeks called him Antiochus "the Great King."

What he had accomplished had no lasting significance for the Seleucids, since within five years of his return Antiochus was cut off from the only means he had for holding the east on a more permanent basis; his loss of Anatolia cut him off from the sources of Greek manpower to colonize these eastern *poleis* and *katoikiai*. What he did do was to buy time for Media and Babylonia against the Parthians. By showing the Hellenic flag in Bactria Antiochus may have bought time for the Euthydemids as well.

When Antiochus returned from the east in B.C. 203 he found that another contemporary of his had grown to aggressive manhood. Philip V of Macedon had made his name by inflicting a painful defeat on the unpopular Aetolian League (B.C. 217), and his later brush with Roman power in Illyria had done little to curb his ambitions. He continued to be active in the affairs of Greece and more recently was intruding himself into Aegean politics. Rhodes and Pergamum were immediately put on guard, wary of Philip, but not yet willing to use the ultimate Roman weapon, whose power they themselves feared.

Antiochus and Philip might have clashed over this aggressive Aegean policy; some of the western Anatolian ports were, after all, Seleucid either by claim or by possession, but Antiochus had a more pressing intent, Egypt. Sosibius too knew that Antiochus was attempting to avenge Raphia, and negotiations were already under way to enlist Philip as the guarantor of Egyptian sovereignty while Sosibius built up his defenses. While the diplomatic maneuvering was proceeding at a heightened pace during the winter of B.C. 203, the news leaked from Egypt that Ptolemy IV was dead—when it had happened, no one was sure—that his queen, Arsinoë, had been murdered, and that the child heir, Ptolemy V Epiphanes, was in the hands of his viziers.

Now it was Antiochus' turn. He opened direct negotiations with Philip in which he offered to share a dismembered Ptolemaic overseas empire. He would buy off Philip with the promise of the Egyptian-held ports in the Aegean and so free himself from possible interference in Syria or Egypt. Faced with the choice of being Egypt's protector or its jackal, Philip chose the latter, though not, indeed, with enthusiasm, since when he once again took up arms in the Aegean in B.C. 202–201 he did not show any great interest in the Ptolemaic cities which the treaty with Antiochus had given him.

Antiochus, however, proceeded directly to the spoils and in two years had driven the Ptolemies out of Coele-Syria and Palestine. The last Ptolemaic stand in B.C. 200 at Panium by the sources of the Jordan was unsuccessful. Antiochus did not invade Egypt but attacked instead the last Ptolemaic footholds in southern Anatolia. By B.C. 195 Ptolemy V Epiphanes had little choice but to sue for peace.[20]

After Panium and before moving his army to Cilicia, Antiochus devoted some months to mopping-up operations in Coele-Syria. There were still pockets of resistance in the cities, including, as it turned out, in Jerusalem in the temple state of Judaea.[21] Here a Ptolemaic faction continued to cling to the inner city even after the surrender of their Greek mercenary general, Scopas, on the battlefield. Antiochus eventually dislodged them, perhaps as late as B.C. 198, with the help of his own Jewish supporters within the city.

The coming of the Seleucids to Judaea is like the lifting of a veil. Palestine under the Ptolemies was a silent land, and the later Jewish sources, such as the books of *Maccabees*, were so intent in their focus on the Jewish Hasmonaean dynasty that all of what happened before B.C. 167 was left almost unnoticed. The events of B.C. 198 are the beginning of quite another kind of revelation. From a rather peaceful Ptolemaic backwater, Jerusalem was about to be thrust center stage in Coele-Syria. Already in B.C. 198 there were hands helping to move it into the camp of the Seleucids, including, it would seem, the ruler of Jerusalem himself, the Judaean High Priest, Simon the Just.

Antiochus handsomely rewarded his partisans in Jerusalem. By an official rescript to his governor in Syria he remitted and abolished several taxes to his new possession and affirmed the right of the Jews to "live according to their ancestral laws." The latter was surely something more than a proclamation of religious toleration—the Seleucids and, indeed, all the Hellenes, tolerated

---

20. See Chapter IV, p. 178.
21. The territory of Judaea embraced the narrow enclave of land between Modin and Bethel north of Jerusalem to Beth Zur on the south. The eastern boundaries were the Jordan and the Dead Sea, and the western, the divide between the Judaean highlands and the coastal plain of Philistia.

every and all forms of religion—as much as the recognition of Judaea's continuing legal status as a temple state, free to govern itself as before according to the prescriptions of the Mosaic Law under its own High Priest and Council of Elders. It was a simple, uncomplicated act, quite in the Seleucid tradition, and from it Antiochus turned to the larger affairs of the *oikoumene*.

Philip did badly in the treaty of B.C. 202, or rather, in his own peculiar enactment of its terms. His reckless behavior in the Aegean provoked Rhodes and Pergamum to summon Rome to their side. Philip chose to ignore the Senate's ultimatum in B.C. 200 and the issue was settled three years later at the battle of Cynoscephalae. At least the issue of Philip was. In Rome's eyes it was replaced by the issue of Antiochus the Great.

Antiochus thought to profit by Philip's inability to possess what the treaty of B.C. 202 had so magnanimously given him. While Philip and the Romans talked armistice and peace, Antiochus sailed the Anatolian coast accepting the surrender of the Ptolemaic cities there. About the time that Flamininus was making his theatrical proclamation of the freedom of Greece at the Isthmian Games of B.C. 196, Antiochus had crossed over the Hellespont and was taking possession of Lysimachia in Thrace.

Antiochus was involved in a risky business and he knew it. He had to amputate the Ptolemaic port cities without rousing Rhodes or Pergamum as Philip had, and he had at the same time to convince Rome that he was merely repossessing what was rightfully his. Antiochus had ambassadors at Rome reassuring the Senate and he would have managed to carry off the entire business but for two recalcitrants—the cities of Smyrna in Ionia and Lampsacus in Aeolia refused to submit and chose to carry their case against Antiochus to Rome.

The Senate and Antiochus closed several times on the diplomatic front. The Romans wanted the Seleucids out of Europe— that is, Thrace—while Antiochus refused to admit the Roman right of arbitration in the cases of Smyrna and Lampsacus. Antiochus received and rejected the Roman terms at Lysimachia in Thrace in B.C. 196, and once again legates were sent to him at Ephesus three years later. The terms were the same at Ephesus, but a new ingredient had been added to Rome's doubts about Seleucid intentions: since B.C. 195 an illustrious and, to the Romans, familiar faee was to be seen at Antiochus' court, the defeated Carthaginian general, Hannibal. Once again Antiochus declined.

Events were leading to a confrontation, and its staging ground was already prepared. The Aetolians, who had been Rome's allies against Philip, were unhappy with their share of the settlement after Cynoscephalae and were urging Antiochus to direct intervention in Greece. Hannibal was pressing for a stroke at Italy itself, but Antiochus chose Greece as politically safer ground. He would arrive there as the Hellenes' liberator from Rome, as Flamininus had done against Philip V. The plan *was* politically sound but its military execution proved, in the sequel, indefensible. The Aetolians seized the port of Demetrias on the Gulf of Pagasae as planned, but Antiochus landed there in B.C. 192 with no more than ten thousand troops. The Aetolians were of little subsequent help to Antiochus, and when the Romans came down from Thessaly in force the following year they were armed with an alliance with Philip V, from whom Antiochus had also expected some support against his former enemies. Antiochus' meager force was pinned at Thermopylae and the king himself barely escaped alive to Ephesus.

The war was far from over. A Roman fleet pursued and there was hard fighting in the Aegean, while Antiochus prepared his field army for the Roman invasion of Asia.[22] The legions came in B.C. 190, led by the redoubtable Scipio Africanus, Hannibal's conqueror at Zama in B.C. 202. Antiochus had a far larger army but lost his nerve; he offered to the Romans the concessions they had demanded in B.C. 196: the evacuation of Thrace and the autonomy of Smyrna and Lampsacus. Now, however, they were unacceptable. The Romans demanded a total Seleucid withdrawal from Anatolia and an indemnification for the entire cost of the war to date.[23] Antiochus could scarcely do worse by fighting. At

---

22. Rhodes and Pergamum, whose king Eumenes II was behind the provocation of Smyrna and Lampsacus, were now openly on the side of Rome and their navies took part in the fighting. On the Seleucid side, Hannibal now assumed the role of admiral in charge of a Phoenician detachment. He did poorly.

23. There were other terms, including the surrender of Hannibal. Antiochus allowed him to escape, however, and Rome's chief enemy eventually took service with Prusias, king of Bithynia. Here too the Romans exerted pressure on Hannibal's new host and rather than submit to extradition the Carthaginian commander committed suicide in B.C. 183 or 182.

Magnesia on the plain at the foot of Mount Sipylus, Antiochus took his stand on ground of his own choosing. The battle was fiercely fought but quickly decided, and not entirely by Roman arms; the decisive blow was struck by Rome's most faithful ally in the East, Eumenes II of Pergamum, and the disaster was compounded by the Seleucids' most prized weapons. In the final stages of the battle it was a stampede of the Seleucids' war elephants that broke the phalanx.

Antiochus did not retire to fight another day; he surrendered almost immediately to the Roman terms. According to the provisions of the treaty concluded at Apamea in Phrygia in B.C. 188, Seleucid political power disappeared from north of the Taurus, the armed forces were pared down, and Antiochus and all his successors were saddled with a staggering indemnity. It may have been the latter that led to Antiochus' death. He was murdered a year after Apamea struggling over a temple of Bel in Elam; the struggle was doubtless for the temple's treasury.

Antiochus IV Epiphanes (B.C. 175–163)

After Apamea the Seleucids were in pressing but not impossible circumstances. The Roman indemnity was large, but Syria was a prosperous land and would survive. Far more critical was the dynasty's exclusion from the sources of manpower, military and colonial, in Anatolia and Greece. Even at Magnesia, Antiochus' muster was chiefly non-Greek, and now there was no hope that the situation would ever greatly improve. A political reaction might also be expected among the Seleucids' various vassals, never very tightly controlled, even by an Antiochus III; it is likely that the increased independence of Euthydemus in Bactria was a direct result of his reading of the implications of the battle of Magnesia.

What the Seleucid Empire needed in B.C. 187 was prudent, unaggressive management, and this is exactly what it received during the reign of Antiochus' son Seleucus IV (B.C. 187–175). There were no adventures, no gains and no losses. His only victory was the modest diplomatic one of marrying his daughter to the new king of Macedon, Perseus (B.C. 179–168), as a possible hedge against another Roman descent into Greece. Seleucus' mind must have been chiefly on the financial crisis provoked by the Roman indemnity, and so it was probably with a great deal of interest that he heard from his Syrian governor that a Jewish official had come to him with the suggestion that there were funds to be had in the large deposits at the temple in Jerusalem.

This was an extraordinary piece of business coming from a temple official, but it had a plausible ring. The current High Priest, Onias III, stood at opposite political poles from his father, Simon the Just, and possessed known Ptolemaic sympathies. The official suggested that the money was in danger of being appropriated to subvert the Seleucid position in Palestine. Seleucus sent his chief minister Heliodorus to investigate. It is not known exactly what happened in Jerusalem, but after talking to Onias and breaking into the treasury, Heliodorus returned to Antioch without the gold. The incident created no great stir at the time, and Heliodorus was better remembered as the assassin of Seleucus IV, whose life he took, for reasons unknown, in B.C. 175.

The throne should properly have passed to Seleucus' eldest son Demetrius, but it was grasped instead by Seleucus' brother, Antiochus IV. The instigator of this move may have been Eumenes II of Pergamum, Rome's great and good friend in Asia. Antiochus may indeed have been the candidate of Rome herself. He was one of an entire generation of eminent Roman hostages,[24] having gone there in B.C. 188 in pledge for his father Antiochus III as part of the treaty provisions of Apamea. It is unknown how long he had remained—he was replaced by Seleucus IV's son Demetrius, who was currently in Rome—but he was a known political Romanophile. He was something more. After his release at Rome, Antiochus took up residence in Athens, where he held public office, and whatever may have been his fascination with Roman political institutions, he hewed hard to the Hellenism that had always been the center of Seleucid policy.

Antiquity knew little of what to make of Antiochus IV. He was vilified by the Jews, but the historians of the *oikoumene* were somewhat more ambivalent. He had a theatrical and erratic temperament, and yet he was a serious and determined man, interested in Stoicism and a later convert to Epicureanism.[25] The

---

24. The historian Polybius, to cite but one other (see Chapter X, p. 400), was one of a thousand Achaeans taken there after the battle of Pydna.
25. The Seleucids' ties with contemporary intellectuals were nowhere so strong as the Ptolemies'. There was a library at Antioch and one

Epicurean school was remote from all forms of religious fanaticism, while the Jews read him out as a religiously motivated monster. What appeared ominous to the Jews alternately dazzled and puzzled the citizens of Antioch. During his early days there as a ruler he delighted, for example, to play the Roman candidate for office, moving about the city as if he were a republican canvassing votes in a popular election. This was the same ruler who inscribed his coins with the legend *Theos Epiphanes* ("The God Made Manifest") and whose coin portraits of Zeus bear a curious resemblance to the king himself.

Antiochus IV was neither madman, playboy nor savior of Hellenism. He was an energetic and dedicated ruler who worked to save his kingdom under the ominous double threat of Rome and Parthia. We can see the hand of Antiochus at work in the modernization of the Seleucid army along Roman lines and in the traditional urbanization program. He founded few if any new *poleis*—the manpower was no longer available—but he did raise many older cities of predominantly non-Hellenic character to the level of *poleis*. Antiochus IV seems to have reinforced his father's innovation, under the rubric of Zeus Olympius, of an empirewide ruler cult which was intended to complement, not replace, the other local cults.

When Antiochus IV came to Antioch in B.C. 175 to assume the diadem, he found awaiting him there a client from Jerusalem, the High Priest Onias III, who had become alarmed at the accusations being made against him by his rivals in the temple and had come to Antioch to explain himself to his overlord. His position was complex but comprehensible. Politically Onias stood with the pro-Ptolemaic party in Judaea. We have no idea of the dimensions of that faction in Jerusalem, but whoever they were they must have stood on very shaky ground after Antiochus III annexed the temple state to the Seleucid Empire in B.C. 200. Ranged against him were not only those who were politically aligned toward the

---

rather eminent poet, Euphorion (see Chapter V, p. 206), is known to have been librarian there under Antiochus III. Antiochus' philosophical leanings, like those of most of the Hellenistic kings, are likely to have been in the direction of Stoicism, since this philosophical school provided an intellectual justification for their kingship. Antiochus IV's conversion to Epicureanism, as well as that of his successor Demetrius I, was effected by a certain Philonides, a Syrian of Laodicea, who studied in Athens but later opened an Epicurean school in Antioch.

Seleucids—Onias' father, the High Priest Simon, had been one such—but another faction of considerable strength, the Hellenizers.

Hellenism was not something new in Judaea. The territory of the temple state was surrounded by *poleis* planted earlier by Perdiccas, Antigonus and their Ptolemaic successors in Palestine. The land was filled with Greek bureaucrats and soldiers, and though there is not a great deal of direct evidence—Ptolemaic Syria was a quiet and unreported land—it must be presumed that the residents of Jerusalem and Judaea were enmeshed in the political, economic and social implications of the Hellenic settlements round about them. And without complaint.

We do have some evidence on how one Jewish family was caught up in that complex. The Ptolemies distributed military land holdings (*kleroi*) east of the Jordan to stiffen the defenses there, and the head of one such settlement was a Jewish officer named Tobiah. Tobiah was himself connected by marriage with temple circles in Jerusalem, but it was during the lifetime of his son that the family moved directly into the affairs of the temple state.

By the time of Ptolemy III Euergetes (B.C. 246–221) there must have been men of substance in Jerusalem who saw that their own political future might be better served by the Seleucids than by the waning Ptolemies, and it was probably some such pro-Seleucid sentiment that prompted the High Priest Onias II to withhold Judaea's tribute from Egypt. The situation became threatening but was saved by the intervention of Joseph, Tobiah's son, who was invested with full civil powers, appeared before Euergetes, and patched things up between Judaea and its sovereign in Alexandria. Joseph himself came out of the affair in handsome fashion; he was designated the Ptolemaic tax collector for all of southern Syria and Phoenicia.

Joseph and the other sons of Tobiah grew rich upon the arrangement, but the Tobiads' immense leap up the ladder of preferment moved other changes as well. Joseph was linked to Ptolemaic officialdom at a high level and simultaneously became an important member of the Jerusalem establishment. The position of the High Priest had been compromised by the sharing out of his financial powers with another, in effect with a layman whose responsibilities lay not only in Judaea, as the High Priest's did, but in the *poleis* of Phoenicia and the Transjordan and, ultimately, in Alexandria. By Onias' act and Joseph's counteract Judaea was drawn more closely into the *oikoumene*.

At the coming of the Seleucids in B.C. 200 both the High Priest, now Simon the Just, and the sons of Tobiah effortlessly changed their political allegiance to the new regime. Not entirely, however. Onias III adopted, as we have seen, a pro-Ptolemaic stance sometime about B.C. 180, and one of Joseph's now rich sons, the youngest, Hyrcanus, allied himself with the High Priest. The rest of the brothers and their supporters were by then a wealthy cabal, stanchly pro-Seleucid in their politics and increasingly Hellenized in their cultural orientation. It was their reaction to the position of Onias III and Hyrcanus, who had large sums on deposit in the temple, that prompted some of the Tobiads' partisans to approach Seleucus IV and invite his expropriation of part of the temple funds.

While Onias III stood before the newly crowned Antiochus IV in Antioch, the Tobiads took advantage of his absence from Judaea to install in his place his brother Joshua, better known under the Hellenized form of his name, Jason. Joshua-Jason followed Onias to Antioch to make his own case before Antiochus. Jason was clearly an illegitimate usurper of what was a hereditary office, but in this case money spoke louder than legitimacy; Jason bought himself the High Priesthood. He did not rest there. He purchased for another large sum the conferral of a highly esteemed and valuable privilege—the city of Jerusalem was permitted to constitute itself into a *polis*.

The action could be considered a coup. Prosperity in the East was inevitably Hellenic urban prosperity, and now that Antiochus had been prevailed upon to grant the *polis* status to the city, Jerusalem would share more fully in that affluence, as a colleague and rival of Philadelphia and Gerasa. For Antiochus it was a welcome and typical step; he would later do the same for another eastern temple city, Babylon, and with good results. The conversion of Jerusalem into its new character of Antioch in Judaea must have begun immediately. A list of citizens who would constitute the *demos* had to be drawn up, and since the selection was in the hands of Jason, it is easy to imagine that the *demos* rolls, those who would immediately share in the expected windfall, embraced the entire ruling aristocracy, the political, religious and commercial elite of the city, probably about three thousand male citizens in all, including, to be sure, the large

Tobiad establishment. The former Council of Elders was converted into a municipal senate (*boule*) in line with Greek procedure. Finally, there appeared the two essential instruments of a Hellenic *paideia*, a gymnasium and the institution of the *ephebeia* to serve as the gateway of Hellenization for the next generation. All went well. Antiochus IV came up to Jerusalem in B.C. 172 to inspect what had been done and confirmed Antioch in Judaea as his newest Hellenic *polis*.

Trouble of another sort was brewing in Judaea. During Jason's tenure as High Priest (B.C. 175–172) the Tobiads became disenchanted with him. He could not have usurped his brother's place without their support, but it was now withdrawn, almost certainly on political grounds. The family's willingness to go down the road of political Hellenism, evident since the days of Tobiah himself, had necessarily to be stronger than that of the High Priest with his traditional background and dual constituency of the Hellenized *demos* of the new Antioch and the conservative and economically deprived middle and lower classes.

One member of the Tobiad faction, Menelaus, made his way to Antioch and bought from Antiochus IV what Jason had bought before him, the High Priesthood. But Jason was not Onias; he stayed and fought, supported by partisans in the city and the countryside. He was finally chased out, and sometime later Menelaus completed his work by contriving the murder of the exiled Onias III at Antioch.[26]

If Jason resisted Antiochus' financial demands on occasion, Menelaus showed himself far more compliant. To pay off his debt to the Seleucid king Menelaus was even willing to put his hands on the temple plate. Now the resistance grew fierce. The deposition of Jason had drawn into the conflict the body of the Jews, mostly urban proletariat and agriculturists living in villages around Jerusalem, who up to that point had been unconcerned with the power struggle between two families. Fighting broke out in the new Antioch and Menelaus' brother had to call out the Hellenic militia to protect the fragile *polis*.[27] He lost his life in

---

26. When Onias felt himself in danger he claimed asylum in the safest place, the temple of Apollo in Daphne.

27. There was likely an imperial Syrian garrison stationed in the city as well. The Seleucids' admiration for the *polis* system did not prevent their stationing garrisons and imperial overseers (*epistates*) in these theoretically independent cities.

the street fighting but order was restored and Menelaus still clung tenaciously to his power and position, supported by Seleucid authority.

Suddenly an entirely new issue exploded. Ptolemy V had died in B.C. 181 and for eight years after his death, Cleopatra, the sister of Antiochus IV who had been bestowed upon Ptolemy as balm for the rapacious peace treaty of B.C. 195, ruled as regent for her minor son. Now she was dead and Egypt was back in the hands of the viziers, who were openly plotting to regain their lost provinces in Coele-Syria. Antiochus struck first, however, and in B.C. 169 had taken Memphis and captured the young Ptolemy Philometor.[28]

Antiochus may have thought that the business in Egypt was well in hand—toward the end of B.C. 169 he sent troops eastward to Bactria—but on his way back from Egypt he looked in at Antioch in Judaea. The earlier trouble seems to have died down, but in the flush of victory Antiochus followed the unfortunate precedent of his father at Ecbatana and Elam and despoiled the temple treasury. He may have had some local Jewish encouragement in this, but it was a serious miscalculation. Antiochus was summoned back to Egypt in the following year to suffer his public humiliation at the hands of Popilius Laenas. During the campaign the full force of Jewish discontent was unleashed in Jerusalem.

Jason had been hiding out in the Transjordan, and in B.C. 168 he returned to the city, not merely to turn out the usurper Menelaus but to engineer a Ptolemaic coup against the distracted Antiochus. Menelaus was in fact captured and imprisoned, but then Jason was in turn expelled by the people who had once been his supporters but who now outstripped their former High Priest in their revolutionary zeal. The *polis*, the creature of Jason as much as it was of Menelaus, was overturned. This time Antiochus returned from Egypt not merely greedy but in a towering rage at the insurrection. The rebels were massacred by direct assault and Menelaus was liberated. Savage reprisals against the dissidents followed; the *polis* of Antioch was restored.

Antiochus probably read what had occurred during his absence in Egypt in B.C. 168 as a political insurrection, and to a degree, it was; Jason had raised the city in the former Egyptian province in

---

28. See Chapter IV, pp. 179–80.

the name of Ptolemy, and there were known Ptolemaic sympathizers in Judaean politics going back to the time of Onias III and Hyrcanus the Tobiad. What he did not understand was that the trouble went far deeper. Antiochus' raising of older eastern cities to the rank of *poleis* must have everywhere encouraged the kind of class warfare that broke out in Judaea. A city that began as a *polis* had within it Greeks of all classes and ranks of society; in the eastern cities without an appreciable Greek population, on the other hand, a *demos* had to be constructed out of those who had become Hellenized, inevitably the aristocratic upper classes, the higher priesthoods, as in Babylon and Jerusalem, and the commercial entrepreneurs. The non-Hellenized inhabitants of these cities found themselves converted into a *laos*, disenfranchised strangers in their own land. Conversion to a *polis* institutionalized differences in society that had previously been present but blurred by an ethnic or cultural solidarity. Menelaus, the radical Hellenizer, and Jason, the moderate Hellenizer, both belonged to that institutionalized aristocracy in Judaea and neither was acceptable to the disgruntled *laos* in B.C. 168.

Antiochus departed from Jerusalem after the savage repression and in B.C. 167 sponsored his lavish display of imperial pageantry at Daphne, his retort, it seemed to Polybius, to the games ostentatiously celebrated by the Romans to celebrate their victory over Perseus of Macedon at Pydna. The mood was quite different in Judaea. No sooner had Antiochus quit the city in B.C. 168 than the sedition flared up again. This time it fell to Antiochus' governor Apollonius to put out the fire. The city had to be stormed once again. This time, however, there was no talk of the restoration of the *polis*. The Judaeans had forfeited that privilege, but instead of degrading the city back to the rank of temple state, Apollonius devised an economically more painful alternative. Jerusalem was converted from a *polis* to a *katoikia*, that is, became a garrison city in which the land of the Judaeans was confiscated and redistributed to a colony of transplanted Syrian soldiers to hold as their *kleroi*. Two groups, the Syrian lotholders and the now terrified Judaean Hellenizers, lived within the heavily armed and walled inner city of Jerusalem.

The economic consequences of this were extremely serious; the confiscation and redistribution of land must have dispossessed most if not all of the Judaeans. And for the first time in the entire controversy a distinct, if unintended, religious note was sounded.

The Syrian soldiery naturally brought with them their gods and their cults. Whatever their names, these were clearly Syrian gods—Baal Shamin among others—whom the soldiers could identify, in the manner of the times, as easily with the Zeus Olympius of the Greeks as the Yahweh of the Jews. In sum, the action was a purely military and security action, punitive rather than reformatory, which had nothing to do with Hellenization. Menelaus presumably continued to conduct the temple rites and serve as High Priest for the Jewish Hellenizers within the *katoikia*.

The accounts in the various books of *Maccabees* are highly condensed for the events before B.C. 167, and we must surmise that the economic losses to the Jews and the direct and immediate affront to their religious sensibilities by the worship of Syrian gods within the temple precinct increased the tempo of the revolt. What is much clearer is that Antiochus had become aware of the new religious dimension that had been added to the conflict. When he made his retort in the escalating struggle in the winter of B.C. 167 his edict was directed unmistakably at Palestinian Judaism and not merely, as before, at the temple state of Judaea. Both custom and cult were affected: the Sabbath observance and circumcision were prohibited; the temple was rededicated to Zeus Olympius and pagan sacrifices replaced Jewish ones;[29] all the inhabitants had to celebrate the King's birthday and join in the public processions in honor of Dionysus. In short, the Mosaic Law was abrogated, something that had not been done previously.[30]

Antiochus' action of B.C. 167 united all except the minority of Hellenizers in Judaea against him. They were, it is true, the men of substance and power in the state, but the others, those dispossessed of their lands, the lower clergy and the scribes, and the

29. That Antiochus' understanding of what constituted a Jew was somewhat wider than merely an inhabitant of Judaea appears clearly enough from what happened in Samaria; under the terms of the edict, the Samaritan temple on Mount Gerezim was rededicated to Zeus Xenius. Later Jerusalem sources, which delighted in slandering their northern neighbors, altered the story to make the Samaritans *petition* Antiochus for the desecration of their temple.

30. Antiochus III had recognized the juridical right of the Jews of the temple state of Judaea "to live according to their ancestral laws," that is, the Mosaic Law, and even the constitution of the *polis* of Antioch in B.C. 175 did not abrogate that right, but merely placed in the hands of the *demos* of Antioch the choice of their own constitutional forms.

religious pietists all joined hands in a full-scale rebellion. From B.C. 166 onward Palestine was seething with revolt. Antiochus was aware of what was happening, but Jerusalem was firmly held, and though he sent fresh troops into Palestine in B.C. 166, he felt secure enough to turn to what he considered a far more serious threat, the Parthians.

Antiochus' campaigns in the East began in B.C. 165 as auspiciously as his father's great *anabasis* had. The troublesome Armenia was once again reduced to tributary status. There is no sign that the recent events in Jerusalem dissuaded Antiochus from his confidence in the *polis* system; two other eastern cities were raised to *polis* rank, Ecbatana in Media and the venerable Babylon. The undiscouraged Antiochus may even have put his hand to some new temple treasuries. All to no end. While preparing for a new assault against Parthia in Media during the spring of B.C. 163, the Seleucid king fell ill and died, his sins, according to the exultant authors of *Maccabees*, scarlet upon him.

The sin of Antiochus IV Epiphanes was that he was politically ill-advised on the problem of Judaea. When a later Seleucid, Antiochus VII Sidetes, had Judaea temporarily in hand, some of his counselors advised him to solve the problem of the Palestinian Jews by dispersing them. Sidetes refused their advice and attempted, as Epiphanes had done, to find a political solution. Antiochus IV had grievances in Judaea, attempted treason among others, and this in a state where he had tried a particularly imaginative political experiment: the granting of the rights and privileges of a *polis* without, at the same time, imposing a totally Greek form of political association (*politeia*).

By the rescript of B.C. 175 it was apparently left to the Jews to choose their own form of *politeia*, and even though those currently in power, Lysias and the Tobiads, were Hellenized, they had no intention of repudiating the Mosaic Law. There were conflicts, of course; Greek *polis* institutions and a Mosaic Law constitution were not natural bedfellows. Some compromise could probably have been worked out, as it had been in Egypt, but the details of it were not Antiochus' concern. What was his concern, however, was civil disorder, which he read, perhaps correctly, in the context of his troubles with Egypt, as treason.

Antiochus IV reacted like the political animal he was; in B.C. 168–167 he suspended the Mosaic *politeia* and cashiered Jerusalem back to a *katoikia*. His action encouraged a whole spectrum of discontent, some of it latent, some of it already out in the open, ranging from the economically dispossessed to the outraged pietists who saw Jews toiling manfully but nakedly in Jerusalem's Hellenic gymnasium.[31] Religious scandal, cultural shock, xenophobia, family ambitions and the tax rate were all weapons in the Maccabean arsenal and they used them to bring the Seleucids down.

---

31. The naked athleticism created some additional transparent problems for the would-be Hellenized Jew, and the conservatives were even further scandalized when they observed that some of their socially climbing brethren had resorted to some primitive form of plastic surgery to conceal from their fellow gymnasts the fact that they had been circumcised.

VII

Hellenes and Jews

The arrival of the Seleucids in Coele-Syria set in motion events of enormous consequence for the Jews. The Seleucid policy of Hellenization raised issues that eventually tore apart the Jewish community of Judaea and profoundly affected the other colonies of Jews scattered around the *oikoumene*. And yet few people in the *oikoumene* had any awareness of what was happening in Palestine or what it meant, until Josephus' later *Jewish Antiquities* introduced the Hellenized reader of the Roman Empire to the traditions of this people who could be seen in every corner of the Mediterranean.

In their public role as farmers, merchants and soldiers, the Jews were familiar figures around the *oikoumene*, little different from the other easterners who had migrated from their homeland into the *poleis*. The Jews were like their neighbors in all save their intransigent monotheism and their claim to an extraordinary document that provided an ideal and a norm for human behavior. Other peoples possessed both myth and law describing their own past and regulating the conduct of society; the Jewish Torah was both of these, and more. It described the historical unfolding of God's providential plan for his own people and provided a code of conduct that had become, in recent times, the sole and authoritative basis of Jewish life.

Hellenism made no issue of history; one might think about the past as one wished. And though it knew nothing of providential destiny cast in national terms, it could afford to ignore or to patronize such claims. Jew and Hellene clashed, rather, on the issue of conduct. The *polis*, that exemplification of the Hellenic ideal, was essentially a field of action. Some Jews were either unwilling or unable to share in that *polis* life, because of their attachment to a different and competing ideal, the Mosaic Law. Their refusal, which had no real parallel in the *oikoumene*, was noted but never really understood. As Pericles had pointed out in his funeral oration, Hellenism could allow almost any eccentricity in private behavior; what was unspoken in that speech, however, was that the *polis* found it difficult to accept a large-scale and public refusal to share in its life and rites.

By the time that Josephus made his report to the *oikoumene* late in the first Christian century, the struggle between the two competing ideals, that of the Hellenic *polis* and that of the Mosaic *politeia*, had already reached its denouement.[1] National aspirations, social injustice, an inequitable tax policy, insensitive governors, and party politics had all sharpened and deepened the tension between the conflicting ideologies during the two and a half centuries before Josephus. Earlier, before either the Seleucids or the Romans came to Coele-Syria, the people of the former kingdoms of Judah and Israel were introduced to Hellenism in a somewhat gentler fashion, it would appear, by the Ptolemies. Not a great deal is known about the Ptolemaic occupation of Palestine, but there are three more or less contemporary documents that reveal the changes in the Jews' attitudes toward their new masters during the first century of Seleucid sovereignty over the land.[2]

The Wisdom of Jesus bar Sirach was written in Hebrew in Palestine about B.C. 180 and translated into Greek by the author's grandson some seventy years later in Alexandria. Bar Sirach knew, then, the Seleucid occupation, but not the crisis of B.C. 167 and the following years. He was a pious teacher in a still-provincial Palestine—the prototype of the later Hasidim, Pharisees and rabbis, less self-conscious, perhaps, than the last and less politically involved than the first two.

The social conditions later invoked by the Maccabees are all present but as yet unkindled in Bar Sirach: the distance between the powerful rich and the oppressed poor; there are echoes of

---

1. Josephus was himself involved in the final playing-out of the drama as a moderate Pharisee willing to accommodate with the Roman state (see Chapter X, pp. 404–5).

2. The work known as *Ecclesiastes* ("The Preacher") may also be from Judaea on the eve of the Seleucid occupation, but both its date and its exact area of origin are still highly uncertain.

unrest and trouble in the towns. Present too are the first signs of a stirring in the land, the new prosperity of Hellenism and the rewards and dangers of a money economy. The author's reactions are measured and his moral teachings reveal a gentle and humane piety. Bar Sirach was aware, it would seem, of the implications of the Hellenic intellectualistic ethic on his brand of traditional Judaism, but remained serene and undisturbed in the face of what must have still seemed a remote, if interesting, challenge.

The book of *Daniel* was completed less than twenty years later, but it belongs to another world and another theological dimension. The book is a composite, but in the later chapters the edicts of Antiochus IV are in force, but not yet, apparently, the counterinsurgency of the Maccabees. Bar Sirach's humanistic optimism has totally disappeared under the savage course of events, and the author of *Daniel* views those events and their significance within the almost cosmic flow of Jewish history. Humanism is incapable of providing a meaning for what has occurred, and in *Daniel* it is replaced by a theology of history where both the punishment leveled against the Jews and the relief from that oppression can come only from the hand of God moving in history. *Daniel* takes refuge in the apocalyptic revelation of God's justice; only in the light of the past and the future is the present endurable.

In the pages of *Maccabees* the apocalypse has been achieved, though by somewhat more pedestrian means than those foreseen in *Daniel*'s vision. In I and II *Maccabees*, prophecy has been replaced by the realistic satisfactions of triumph. The first of the two is the more sober account, composed during the reign of John Hycranus (B.C. 134–105) by someone with access to the archives and imbued with the official Hasmonaean point of view. The author works well within the traditional historiography of the books of *Kings:* the wicked and ungodly (Antiochus) versus the righteous observers of the Law (the Maccabees). It is an intelligent but highly tendentious account.

I *Maccabees* was composed in Hebrew, but the original of II *Maccabees* was in Greek, a work for the Diaspora readership by an otherwise unknown Hellenized Jew named Jason of Cyrene, who appears to have been a contemporary of Judah Maccabaeus. The preserved version is an epitome done some forty years later. Jason's volumes—there were five books in the original—though highly condensed in our version, are a more colorful and emotional piece of work that betrays many of the highly rhetorical effects of Hellenistic historiography.[3] It has, moreover, a marked theological cast absent from I *Maccabees*. The work abounds with omens and prodigies and God's Euripidean hand is everywhere apparent.

In both works, whatever their virtues or vices, the lesson is the same: the Law has been avenged on the godlessness of the Hellenes. The Maccabees as the pious upholders of that Law celebrated an inevitable triumph over the Gentiles. In both texts the Hellenizing Jews are ranged with the impious Seleucids, while the Hasidim play only a minor part in the events. Of politics, social discontent and economic oppression there is only the faintest wisp of breath between the lines. The reality, as will be seen, was far more complex.

Seleucid Successor States in the East

Before Antiochus began his march against the Parthians he placed both the government of his western satrapies and the care of his young son, Antiochus V, in the hands of the regent Lysias, and it was upon him that the responsibility of insuring compliance with the Judaean decrees fell. The *katoikia* of Jerusalem was firmly in hand; Syrian troops were in the citadel, the land around the city was distributed to military colonists from abroad, and the Hellenizers under Menelaus were in charge of the temple establishment. Lysias' charge was to enforce similar measures in the rest of Judaea. Copies of the Torah had to be collected and burned, and the obstinate resistance to Hellenization ended.

There was opposition, of course, the same opposition visible beneath the anonymous fighting around Menelaus and Jason at an earlier date. But Antiochus' stringent measures of B.C. 167 brought new opponents into the lists. Who they were is almost lost under the later Maccabaean claim to the lion's share of the victory, but one group that antedated the Maccabees is the faction known as the Hasidim. If, as seems likely, the Hasidim were connected with scribal circles in contemporary Judaism, then the institution of the *polis* under Jason rendered them increasingly

---

3. See Chapter II, pp. 113-15.

superfluous and the decrees of Antiochus converted them into a party of political opposition. It was the scribal class that had the single greatest institutional investment in the Law of Moses, whose guardians and interpreters they were. Under Jason and Menelaus the cultus in the temple of Jerusalem went on as before, firmly in the hands of priests. What had changed with the coming of the *polis* was the former total reliance on the Mosaic Law—and its authoritative interpretation—to provide a basis for social and individual conduct. Hellenization may have had its syncretizing effects on the cultic side of Judaism, but they must have been minor compared to its undermining of the legal prescriptions of the Mosaic *politeia*.

The Hasidim went into active opposition to Hellenized Jew and Seleucid alike, though we cannot trace their exact role in the events preceding B.C. 166. They come to the fore only after that date, when the resistance in Judaea took a new turn. At Modin, north of Jerusalem, one of the agents of Lysias was assassinated as he attempted to enforce the new cult regulations. His assassin was identified as Mattathiah of the family of Hasmon in the lower clergy. It was a minor incident, but it brought into the struggle the military and psychological masterminds of all the subsequent resistance, the sons of Mattathiah, known collectively as the Maccabees,[4] who after their father's death fled into hiding in the countryside, where they began to organize a full-scale guerrilla war.

The guiding spirit of the revolt was Judah Maccabaeus who from B.C. 166 onward conducted war on all fronts, against the Seleucid armies sent by Lysias into Palestine, against the Hellenized but non-Jewish Syrian colonists, whom Antigonus' policy intended to plant in Judaea, and finally, against the Hellenized Jews at Jerusalem and in the villages of Judaea.

The official historians of the house of Hasmon, writing when it was the ruling house, read the struggles of the years after B.C. 166 in theological terms, as a resistance movement against the godlessness of the Seleucids. In reality it was far more, a bitter civil war across the breach between the upper and lower classes of Jews that the Seleucids' policy of Hellenization served to enforce and illumine. The Jewish Hellenizers were the class of substance and

---

4. The etymology of "Maccabaeus" is uncertain; it may mean "hammer."

power in Judaea, supported from Antioch and sharing in the fruits of Seleucid prosperity. The Hasmonaean tradition converted them into traitors against the God of Israel, because the Hasmonaeans chose a certain version of Judaism as their initial issue. For the Hasidim the Mosaic Law may, indeed, have been the chief issue, but as the sequel was to show, the Hasmonaeans operated on the more complex ground of *Realpolitik*. They did not scruple, for example, to abrogate the principle of the Sabbath rest in the name of the resistance, something the Hasidim had never done. And they were also aware that, whatever their quarrel with the local Jewish establishment, there were other things at stake beyond the borders of Judaea.

Since about B.C. 300 the Jews had been moving from their earlier enforced confinement in Judaea not only to the possession of their other former haunts in Palestine, but into the wider world of the *oikoumene:* Egypt had a considerable Jewish population early in the post-Alexander period, and there was a sizable Jewish colony in Antioch as well. The Maccabees had no plans for either metropolis, but in Palestine itself the presence of colonies of Jewish emigrants in places like Joppa and Jabneh gave the Maccabees a claim against those cities and at the same time raised irredentist fears among the inhabitants. Their fears were, as it turned out, justified.

The Seleucid armies fared poorly against the effective Maccabean guerrillas, and in B.C. 164 Lysias was forced to come in person to the troublesome province. He had some initial success, but by that time Antiochus IV was deeply committed in Armenia and so Lysias thought it wiser to negotiate a compromise settlement than to pursue the business to its end. The compromise was worked out with the Hellenizers at Jerusalem and by it Lysias thought to undercut the Maccabean and Hasidic opposition. He promised to petition the abrogation of Antiochus' cult restrictions against the Jews—Lysias could scarcely do so on his own authority—and meanwhile permission was granted to those Jews who wished to return to Jerusalem to take up residence in the city. It was clearly an attempt on the part of Lysias and the Hellenizers to wean some of the war-weary moderates away from the Maccabee brothers. Judah recognized it as such and reacted swiftly with a countermove of his own. Later in B.C. 164 he seized Jerusalem, all except its Syrian-held citadel, and swept away the entire program of Antiochus. On December 25 of B.C. 164 the temple was purified and rededicated to Yahweh.[5]

The Maccabees, now in possession of the holy city, embarked on an ambitious program of reform. The Mosaic Law was re-established as the law of the land and the Hasidim could once again function as its authoritative interpreters. What was done with the temple priesthoods is more difficult to say, but since the Hellenized upper clergy was now under a state of siege with the Syrian garrison on the citadel, it seems likely that Judah made new appointments to these positions. As for the High Priesthood itself, nothing seems to have been done; the Hasidim would certainly never have tolerated Judah in that post. The Council of Elders, the former *boule* of the *polis* of Antioch in Palestine, was doubtless also reformed to make room for the middle-class and provincial supporters of the Maccabees.

Judah and the Maccabee faction were now in control of the seat of power in Judaea, and the fighting took on a new savagery on both sides. The Syrian communities outside his immediate reach—which was growing longer—took reprisals against the Jews who dwelled in them, while Judah for his part struck across the land murdering non-Jews and putting the temples of the Greek and Syrian gods to the torch. Idumaea to the south and Ammonitis across the Jordan were visited with Maccabean raids and in some cases the entire male population was slaughtered. What had begun as an insurrection had become a veritable jihad.

For two years Antioch did nothing, and then finally at the beginning of B.C. 162, after the death of Antiochus IV in Elam, Lysias was forced to act. His own future was in doubt, but the position of the Syrian garrison in the Jerusalem citadel was becoming critical and the Hellenizers there appealed to Lysias for direct intervention. A large army was mustered, and once again Lysias led them into the field in Judaea. And once again there

---

5. Why this particular date was chosen to mark the "dedication of the temple" (*Hanukkah ha-bayyith*) is not immediately apparent. A common suggestion has been that it marked a Hellenic festival day that the Maccabean one was intended to supplant. If so, it was likely to have been one connected with the winter solstice, like the feasts commemorating the "birth of the Sun" under the Romans (see Chapter XI, p. 443). The theory is reinforced by the fact that Hellenized Jews later referred to the Maccabean festival as the "Feast of the Lights."

were initial successes canceled in the end by Lysias' inability to conclude the war. On this occasion the interruption was the return from the East of Antiochus' legate Philip, who claimed that he had been designated by the dying king to replace Lysias as regent of Antiochus V.

Lysias was forced to another compromise with the Jews. He issued a decree in the name of the young Antiochus V restoring the affairs of Jerusalem to the *status quo ante* of Antiochus III: permission to the Jews to "live according to their ancestral laws." It was no more than the juridical recognition on the part of the sovereign of Judaea of what Judah Maccabaeus had already achieved by force in B.C. 164. The Seleucids yielded on the question of the Jerusalem *polis*, and the Maccabees on their side had to accept the Jewish Hellenizers, who very likely continued to live in the citadel compound.

They did not have to accept Menelaus. Some token had to be yielded up, and the obvious candidate was the Hellenizing High Priest who for years had been the bone of contention in Judaea. Lysias brushed him crudely aside, had him tried and executed. The regent did not, however, surrender his control over the office. For Menelaus' place he made a shrewd choice, Alcimus, both an Oniad and a Hellenist.

The Maccabees were unwilling to accept Alcimus, and Lysias had no time to install him by force. He had to return to northern Syria to deal with the claims of the counterregent Philip, which he did in short order. It was not the end of Lysias' troubles. In addition to Antiochus V there was another quite legitimate heir to the throne in Rome, Demetrius, the eldest son of Seleucus IV whom the Senate had taken as a hostage in place of Antiochus IV. With the support of the historian Polybius, himself a hostage in Rome, and of some Roman friends—officially Rome was interested in Syria, but not quite sure of what practical course to follow—Demetrius escaped from Rome without the Senate's leave. He landed in Syria late in B.C. 162 and almost immediately the support for Lysias and Antiochus V drained away. The young king was murdered by his army after a reign of less than two years.

The early days of the new Seleucid monarch, Demetrius I (B.C. 162–150), did not appear to hold much promise. His vassals Ariarathes of Cappadocia and Artaxias of Armenia were in scarcely disguised revolt against Seleucid sovereignty; the High Priest-designate Alcimus was still not seated in rebellious Judaea; and in the East, Timarchus, the satrap of Babylon, had openly proclaimed his independence. All the actors in these political dramas, incumbents and insurgents, now played their roles with their eyes fixed offstage; Rome, without holding an inch of territory in Asia, was a paramount power there. She had thrust Antiochus III from Anatolia in B.C. 188 and saved Egypt from Antiochus IV twenty years later. Kings and would-be kings fought for her recognition, and in B.C. 160 Rome was visited by a number of eastern embassies. Both Demetrius I and Timarchus had their representatives there, followed by another from the Maccabees. The Roman Republic was generous with recognitions but chary with help. The Senate held off from Demetrius for a while, but both Timarchus and Judah Maccabaeus received the Roman stamp of approval.

It was of little real help to either. Toward the end of B.C. 161 Demetrius dispatched strong forces to Judaea while he himself marched against Timarchus in Babylon. The revolt quickly collapsed and Demetrius I was acclaimed in Seleucia on the Tigris with the old Seleucid appellation of Savior (*Soter*). When he returned westward the Romans too generously acknowledged that he was indeed the legitimate ruler of the Seleucid Empire. The Judaean problem appeared equally easy of solution. Demetrius' general Bacchides managed to install Alcimus while Demetrius was still in the East and so brought about a major reconciliation between the Hellenizers and the Hasidim. The latter broke off from the Maccabees and declared their religious grievances satisfied by the restoration of the Mosaic Law in the land and an Oniad as High Priest in Jerusalem.[6]

The rift between the Hasidim and the Maccabees is not unexpected. Not only had the Maccabees gained the alleged purpose of their revolt, judicial recognition of the Mosaic Law in

---

6. Connected with the withdrawal of the Hasidic objections to Alcimus may have been the fact that the true hereditary heir to the High Priesthood, Onias IV, had fled to Egypt at about this time. Two events are connected with his name there: his intervention in Alexandria at the head of a body of Jewish troops on behalf of Philometor's widow Cleopatra (see Chapter IV, p. 181), and his earlier petition to construct a Jewish temple at Leontopolis, a town near Memphis. The site and purpose of this latter are puzzling. Nothing points to its supplanting the temple in Jerusalem, where Egyptians continued to resort for pious purposes.

Judaea, they had, on occasion, acted in a religiously unprecedented fashion. Mattathiah had himself announced the abrogation of a Mosaic Law, the Sabbath rest, on his own initiative and without any basis in Scripture. Judah had followed the Hellenic practice of adding one of his own declared festival days to those prescribed by the Law. Hanukkah, the annual commemoration of the rededication of the temple in B.C. 164, was a man-made innovation with no justification in the Bible.[7] The political aspirations of the Maccabees were beginning to come into relief and relations between what was rapidly becoming the ruling house of Judaea and their former spiritual supporters continued to degenerate.

Demetrius I's negotiated settlement, based on the earlier one of Lysias, did not disperse the Maccabean movement. Judah Maccabaeus still roamed the countryside with his guerrilla bands and savagely mauled a Syrian army sent against him in March of B.C. 160. Another appeared a month later and finally ran Judah to ground. His brothers Simon and Jonathan made good their escape to the wilderness.

In B.C. 160 the party of rebellion was still intact, though its goals were now unabashedly political. Jonathan assumed the place of the dead Judah at its head and continued his evasive maneuvers. In B.C. 159 Alcimus died and the embarrassment of both the Hellenized Jews and the Seleucids is revealed in the fact that they could find no suitable successor. Demetrius and his generals were perhaps beginning to realize the impossibility in which they had involved themselves. The guerrillas could not be totally eradicated, even by a major display of force, and the Hellenizers were not strong enough to protect themselves without direct and constant Seleucid intervention. Each of the preceding compromises had merely strengthened the Maccabees' hand, yet the Seleucids had little choice but to go down the same road again. An arrangement was agreed upon whereby Jonathan and his brothers would be granted amnesty with the proviso that they did not tamper with the situation in Jerusalem. Jonathan used the respite to good

---

7. Nor would it ever have. The Hasidic party of Judaism long survived the Maccabees and later had their revenge on their former allies. The rabbinical descendants of the Hasidim rejected the various books of *Maccabees* from the canon of Sacred Scripture (see Chapter XIV, p. 536). Some Scriptural purists like the Qaraites (see Chapter XIV, Note 26) did not even celebrate Hanukkah.

purpose; the Hellenizing Jews were attacked wherever they could be found, except in Jerusalem.

Demetrius may have been anxious to reach a solution, since his problems were deepening elsewhere. He had clashed with Attalus II of Pergamum over who would rule in neighboring Cappadocia. Then, foolishly, Demetrius created another enemy for himself by sponsoring an unsuccessful coup on Ptolemaic Cyprus. At home, too, his support was growing thin, and more and more frequently Demetrius, who owed his reign to popular support in Syria, enclosed himself in his fortified castle near Antioch and held himself remote from his disenchanted subjects.

Once Attalus and Ptolemy Philometor were working in collusion—with the encouragement of Rome, one may be sure—trouble had swiftly to follow for Demetrius. It appeared in the form of a protégé of Attalus named Balas, whom the Pergamene king put ashore at Ptolemais (Acre) in B.C. 153, supported by Pergamene and Ptolemaic troops and armed with a claim to be the son of Antiochus IV Epiphanes and the prior recognition of Rome. Demetrius had few places to turn, but the obvious fact that Coele-Syria was likely to be the critical area of contestation with a Ptolemaic candidate for the throne of Syria drove him into the arms of Jonathan Maccabaeus. In B.C. 153 concessions were made to Jonathan, and the Seleucid garrisons were withdrawn from Judaea. To no avail, since Balas dangled a far more tempting piece of bait before Jonathan—the High Priesthood.

In October of B.C. 152 Jonathan assumed his priestly robes for the first time and placed Judaea and its surrounding areas firmly in the camp of Balas. With the way now free, Ptolemy Philometor's armies crossed the frontier and marched northward in support of Balas. Cut off from all support, Demetrius eluded his enemies for somewhat over a year until he was finally trapped and killed in battle (B.C. 150).

It appeared that a bright day was dawning both for Jonathan the Hasmonaean and for Philometor. When Balas celebrated his triumph and his nuptials with Cleopatra Thea, the daughter of Philometor, at Ptolemais in B.C. 150, both the Egyptian king and the Jewish High Priest were there in person, the latter now openly acknowledged as the Seleucid man in Judaea. Balas' reign (B.C. 150–145) was not, however, very successful. He seemed uninterested in the affairs of state and preferred the Egyptian milieu of Ptolemais to Seleucid Antioch. The government was in the hands of the ministers, and some measure of the local in-security may be gained from the fact that for a few brief years (B.C. 149–147) Antioch and Seleucia Pieria entered into some sort of mutual-defense league. The central administrative power was clearly disintegrating under the pressures of civil war.

In B.C. 147 the dissatisfaction with Balas came to a head with the appearance in Syria of Demetrius II, the son of Demetrius Soter. Balas had little chance for survival, but Jonathan held for him in Judaea and closed with the pro-Demetrius governor of Coele-Syria in a series of engagements. Jonathan's armies took and held Joppa, Ashdod and Ascalon on the coastal plain of Philistia, and the High Priest was rewarded with new civil honors by the fading Balas. Whatever chance Balas may have had vanished at the appearance of Philometor in Coele-Syria with a Ptolemaic army bent on recouping this lost province of the Egyptian Empire. Philometor's intentions regarding Balas were not at first clear, but once in possession of Coele-Syria, he declared for the adolescent Demetrius II and offered him what he had earlier given to Balas, the hand of Cleopatra Thea.

For one brief moment in Antioch in B.C. 145 Philometor was himself tendered the throne of the Seleucids,[8] a notion that he resisted. Instead he prevailed upon the Antiochians to accept Demetrius II. Balas, who had fled to Cilicia, promptly returned to the contest and was defeated by the combined armies of Philometor and Demetrius II. Philometor died shortly afterward of wounds received in the battle. His death marked the end of the last brief Egyptian occupation of Syria and the initiation of a turbulent new chapter in Egyptian history.[9]

There is only silence about Jonathan's role in the events of B.C. 145, but he seems to have painlessly transferred his allegiance to Demetrius II. The High Priest of Judaea had now grown from his former rebel status near to being the chief Seleucid official in southern Syria. And he learned to be a faithful subject. Demetrius II had come to Syria on the arms of Cretan mercenaries, who, once the fighting was over, devoted themselves to thrashing about Antioch. Demetrius soon had riots on his hands on their account and he summoned his vassal Jonathan the Hasmonaean,

---

8. To which he had some claim by blood. His mother was Cleopatra I, daughter of Antiochus III, who had given her to Ptolemy V Epiphanes as part of the peace treaty of B.C. 195.

9. See Chapter IV, pp. 181–83.

who came to Antioch with three thousand Jewish troops. Jonathan's men quashed the trouble in short order, but at a very steep price in blood and ill will. The Jewish community at Antioch had doubtless to live with the latter when Jonathan returned home.

The civil war in Syria dragged on. A new infant pretender was put forward with the unimpressive credentials of being the son of Balas (B.C. 143). The real pretender was, of course, his regent, a military leader named Diodotus, whose real issue was the behavior of Demetrius' Cretan and Jewish mercenaries, an issue that in no way inhibited him from concluding an alliance with the commander of those Jewish mercenaries, Jonathan the Hasmonaean. There was doubtless a price, and doubtless well worth it for Diodotus, who now disposed of the infant and assumed rule for himself under the name of Tryphon. Tryphon had Jonathan and his troops in his van all through the fighting of B.C. 143–142, and Hasmonaean armies that had once done most of their campaigning between Jerusalem and Beth Zur now fought from Gaza to Damascus.

The useful alliance came to an end late in B.C. 142, when Tryphon decided that Jonathan was either too dangerous or too ambitious an ally in arms and had the High Priest taken and executed. His successor was his elder brother Simon, who had held a high civil position under Tryphon. Simon had now perforce to return to the camp of Demetrius II, but there were handsome rewards far surpassing what had been granted before. Earlier Demetrius had been pressed by Jonathan to remove the two final signs of Seleucid dominion over Judaea, the payment of tribute and the continuing presence of a Seleucid garrison in the Jerusalem citadel. Demetrius had temporized with Jonathan, but now he was in no position to resist Simon's demands. In B.C. 142 Judaea was freed of both. The Hasmonaeans now ruled a free and sovereign state.

The gesture was not sufficient for Simon. His legal status vis à vis the Seleucids had been clarified, but his legitimacy among the Jews was still suspect. In the eyes of some he was not an Oniad and so had no claim on the hereditary office of High Priest. This was rectified in B.C. 140. At a convention of the Great Assembly of Judaea—probably Judah's democratized version of the earlier aristocratic Council of Elders—there was placed in Simon's hands the chief spiritual, military and civil power of the new state. Not even David and Solomon, with their far broader empire, had held that kind of authority; only the medieval papacy provides analogies.

The contest for Syria between Demetrius II and Tryphon was broken off by news from the East. From about B.C. 171 the reviving Parthians were under the rule of Mithridates I. At first the new Shah's energies were contained by the aggressive eastern policy of both Antiochus IV Epiphanes and his general Eucratides, but with the death of Epiphanes in B.C. 163 and the subsequent civil disorders in the western satrapies of the Seleucids, the Parthians were given a free hand to resume their activities in Iran. Eucratides in Bactria probably bore the first Parthian assaults and lost some of his westernmost territories to the invaders. After that it was the turn of Media, which Mithridates occupied sometime about B.C. 155. The threat of Mithridates against Media immediately to the north of his own satrapy adds another dimension to the revolt of Timarchus in Babylonia and Demetrius Soter's prompt response at the outset of his reign. It seems doubtful whether Timarchus could have held Babylonia against Parthia in any event.

In the long run the legitimate Seleucids proved as impotent as Timarchus would have been. Elam followed Media into the growing Parthian Empire, and by B.C. 141 Mithridates was in possession of Babylonia, including the Seleucids' eastern capital of Seleucia on the Tigris. Either because he despaired of holding Syria against Tryphon, or because he judged it pointless to try to hold Syria without Babylonia, Demetrius II broke off the struggle in Syria in B.C. 140 to lead an army into the eastern satrapies. The sequel is not entirely clear. Demetrius seems to have retaken Babylon, perhaps with the help of the Bactrian Greeks on Mithridates' eastern flank. But as he pursued Mithridates farther into the Iranian highlands the Seleucid king was betrayed and captured. With his valuable captive in tow, Mithridates soon regained Babylonia.

The capture of Demetrius II was the signal for the appearance of the last great Seleucid, Demetrius II's brother, Antiochus VII Sidetes (B.C. 139–129). Tryphon he disposed of with remarkable ease. The usurper had no real support and it was only the general dislike of Demetrius II that kept him in power. Antiochus VII was a legitimate Seleucid and immediately strengthened his claim by marrying his brother's wife, the now familiar Cleopatra Thea.

With Tryphon once out of the way, Sidetes turned to restoring his badly shaken empire.

His first target was Judaea, where there was an immediate attempt to bring Simon to heel after the heady events of B.C. 142–140. Sidetes' terms were moderate: the Hasmonaeans were to evacuate those towns outside Judaea—the seaport of Joppa chief among them—which they had taken during the civil wars; they must also restore a Seleucid garrison to the citadel in Jerusalem. Simon refused, and in B.C. 138 Antiochus' army descended into Coele-Syria but, like so many earlier expeditions, found itself unequal to the Hasmonaean guerrillas. Sidetes did nothing further for the moment, until the assassination of Simon in B.C. 135 reopened the possibility of intervention.

On this occasion Sidetes came in person and in force. Out of the scramble for the High Priesthood Simon's son John Hyrcanus had emerged successful, but in the field he was now no match for Sidetes. Jerusalem fell and Hyrcanus had no alternative but to accept the terms. Sidetes did not insist on turning back the clock. He did force the Hasmonaeans back into the borders of Judaea and imposed a heavy indemnity, but talk of a Seleucid garrison of occupation in Jerusalem was dropped, and there was no attempt otherwise to curb the status of the Hasmonaeans as the rulers of a sovereign state.

Judaea was sovereign but still allied to the Seleucids. When Sidetes felt strong enough to dream that recurrent Seleucid dream, the restoration of the eastern satrapies, his considerable field army included detachments of Jewish troops under the command of Hyrcanus. Like Demetrius II before him, Sidetes began well. In B.C. 130 he once again held both Babylonia and Media against the new Parthian king Phraates II, but it was a brief triumph. In the spring of B.C. 129 the Seleucid camp was surprised by the Parthians, and Sidetes perished in its vain defense.

Phraates was less successful on other fronts. Early in B.C. 129 he had released Demetrius II back to Syria, to divert, one suspects, attention and support away from his brother in the East. As it turned out, Demetrius arrived just in time to succeed the dead Sidetes (B.C. 129–125). Then, after ten years of rule, Phraates II was engulfed in the great storm of nomads gathering over Greeks and Parthians alike in Bactria and along the eastern frontier in Iran.

The end of the Hellenic kingdom of Bactria was prepared by a series of unconnected events in Parthia and China. The Chinese sources reveal that the Mongol steppe was in turmoil in the second century before Christ. In western China the stirrings of a new nomad confederation called the Hsiung-nu[10] dislocated the weaker tribes of the steppe, and about B.C. 160 one of them, the Yüeh-chih began an enforced trek westward. Whatever the ethnic coloration of the Hsiung-nu, the Yüeh-chih were, at least in their leadership cadres, Iranian.

The passage of the Yüeh-chih horde westward was attended by further pressures along the route, pressures that thrust them onward until finally, at the western edge of the steppe, the Sacae began experiencing the presence of the Yüeh-chih confederation behind them. Sometime about B.C. 130, the Sacae burst through the frontiers and streamed into Bactria, where they disrupted the Greek kingdom that was clinging to life there. The Sacae then passed farther south to Herat and Seistan, where two Parthian kings died resisting them, Phraates II (c. B.C. 138–128) and Arta-banus II (c. B.C. 128–123), and eventually came to rest in north-west India. When, some ten years later, the Yüeh-chih followed on the heels of the Sacae into Bactria, the political fabric of eastern Iran, which had been more or less stable since the time of Alexander, began to disintegrate. North, south and east of the Hindu Kush, Greeks and Parthians had to fight against extinc-tion, first against the Sacae and then against the Yüeh-chih.

Neither was successful. The network of Greek kingdoms that stretched from Bactria to India disappeared, the last one about B.C. 100, and in their place in Iran and India sprang up various mixed Saca-Parthian principalities, and finally a sprawling empire constructed and dominated by the Kushans, the ruling tribe of the Yüeh-chih confederation. But before their end the Greeks of the East who were the farthest outpost of Hellenism created a marvelous if minor culture under the kings of the Euthydemid line.

When he was freed of the presence of Antiochus III in B.C. 204, Euthydemus ruled the lands of Sogdia and Bactria that Diod-otus had raised from a satrapy to a kingdom.[11] The frontier

---

10. The temptation to identify the Hsiung-nu with the Huns of the later western sources is strong, but attempts at bridging the six cen-turies that separate the two peoples have not been entirely persuasive.
11. See Chapter VI, p. 243.

remained secure and the rich and Hellenized land behind it prospered on agriculture and trade to the point that Euthydemus felt
strong enough to essay some modest expansion at the expense of
the Parthians of Merv. At his death sometime about B.C. 189
Euthydemus was succeeded by his son Demetrius, a far more
aggressive empire builder. By B.C. 184 Demetrius was on the
march south, had crossed the Hindu Kush, and occupied without
difficulty the Seleucid satrapies of Aria, Arachosia and Seistan in
what is now Afghanistan, and in the following year descended
into the Indus valley to batten on the remains of the disintegrating Mauryan Empire.

Demetrius was not, of course, the first Greek to go that route.
Alexander too had gone down to the Indus and for about ten
years at the end of the fourth century the area was under Greek
political control. Seleucus I had, however, lost or bartered away
the Indian satrapies of Alexander on the eve of the battle of
Ipsus,[12] and thenceforward the passes of the Hindu Kush marked
the political frontier between the Seleucid satrapies and the
provinces of Chandragupta's Mauryan Empire.

Contacts continued between the two empires. Seleucus I sent
his ambassador Megasthenes to the Mauryan court at Pataliputra
(Patna), and sometime about B.C. 250 Ptolemy Philadelphus'
legate was also there. There were doubtless commercial visits in
the other direction as well, but with the accession of Chandragupta's grandson in B.C. 269 the West began to feel a different
kind of presence. When Ashoka (B.C. 269–232) came to
the throne he ruled an empire that extended from Afghanistan to
the Ganges delta and southward deep into the Deccan plateau,
the entire subcontinent except the southern tip and parts of the
eastern coast. He began his career by extending his father's and
grandfather's conquests down that eastern coast, but sometime
early in his reign, perhaps about B.C. 261, he was converted to
Buddhism and spent the rest of his life practicing a kind of sturdy
pacificism. Religiously Ashoka tolerated all sects, but at the same
time he converted Buddhism into an aggressive missionary faith.
A Buddhist ecumenical council was held under his auspices at
Pataliputra, where the teachings of the Buddha were codified and
the obligation to proselytize was announced. All over his empire
Ashoka erected lapidary proclamations of his goals and ideals,

---

12. See Chapter II, pp. 80–81.

including, in the manner of the Achaemenian Shahs, claims of victories far afield.[13]

Ashoka claimed conquests for his new faith in the kingdoms of Antiochus II, Ptolemy Philadelphus, Antigonus Gonatas, and even Megas of Cyrene and Alexander of Epirus. There may have been some substance to the boast; evidence has been found to suggest that there were indeed Buddhists in Egypt at the time, though not perhaps with any great effect. The recipients seemed to know nothing of the Buddhist missions, and the Hellenes of the West continued to prefer Megasthenes' reports to Ashoka's Pauline Buddhists.

The westernmost part of his empire, the old satrapy of Arachosia (Kandahar) included communities of mixed Hellenic-Iranian stock, and Ashoka posted his edicts there in Greek and in the former Achaemenian lingua franca, Aramaic. As one passes farther east the preserved Ashokan edicts, though still in Aramaic, betray the more visible stamp of one dialect or another of Prakrit, the Sanskrit-descended language of northwest India.[14]

Ashoka's huge empire survived his death by no more than half a century. His sons quarreled, and the throne finally fell into the hands of a Brahman usurper. Shortly thereafter, in B.C. 183, the first Greek army since that of Seleucus I came over the Hindu Kush led by the Greco-Bactrian king Demetrius, and there began a century and a half of Greek rule in the former domains of the Mauryan emperors. It was, in effect, an interregnum, a brilliant pause between the dissolution of the Indian Mauryas and the arrival of the Iranian nomads.

Demetrius settled in at Taxila and sent his general Menander to probe eastward. The probe turned into a conquest, and by B.C. 175 the Greek invaders were in possession of most of the Maurya holdings in the north of India, including the imperial capital at Pataliputra. It did not suit Demetrius to rule his new holdings

---

13. The royal style in edicts was not the Achaemenians' sole bequest to the Mauryan Empire. The architecture of the imperial palace at Pataliputra appears to have had distinct Achaemenian antecedents.

14. Aramaic must by then have been in its final stages of currency in the farther East since even the bilingual coins of the later Bactrian Greek rulers were inscribed in Greek and Prakrit. There was, however, a legacy. From the Aramaic script developed the Kharoshthi alphabet, the script in which some of Ashoka's Prakrit edicts were written. The Bactrian Greeks likewise addressed their subjects through Kharoshthi.

from that far east, nor, indeed, did he contemplate returning to Bactria. He chose an Indian rather than a Bactrian base for his empire, and in the complicated system of subkings in use in the East since the time of Euthydemus it is probable that the chief seat of power was at Taxila (Rawalpindi), while other members of the family took up royal residence at Bactra, Alexandria-Kapispa (Begram, north of Kabul), and perhaps even at Pataliputra.

The line considered itself pure Seleucid; Euthydemus had married a daughter of the sister of Seleucus II. But even under its earliest Greek kings the Iranian element in Bactria was strikingly mixed with the Hellenic in religion, art, architecture and language, and with the accession of Demetrius the ambitions of the line toward syncretism become obvious. The coins of the Euthydemids are for the most part of the purest Greek type and on the Attic standard of weights.[15] Many of them bore, on their reverse side, however, legends in Prakrit written in Kharoshthi script. Indians were admitted into the *demos* rolls of at least one of Demetrius' cities in India, and the evidence points to at least the possibility that one of his successors had been converted to Buddhism. The Euthydemids, who ruled on both sides of the Hindu Kush, obviously became more fully domesticated on its eastern side, and not improbably by reason of just such a policy of Greco-Indian fusion. That union of Greeks and Iranians that Alexander had anticipated Demetrius and his successors came closer to achieving between Greeks and Indians than any other Hellenistic dynasty. The Bactrian Greeks ruled not in artificial Greek enclaves like Alexandria and Antioch but in the full-blown Indian cities of Taxila and Sagila.

Antiochus IV was not impressed by the Bactrian dynasty's claims of Seleucid legitimacy. In B.C. 169 he sent his cousin Eucratides against his house's former vassals, whom even Antiochus III had failed to tame. Eucratides' work may have been made

---

15. They were minted from gold imported, from the time of Euthydemus, from China. At this point Chinese imports into Bactria had still to pass through the hands of middlemen. The Chinese came in person to Bactria for the first time in B.C. 128, when the Han diplomat Chang Ch'ien reported back to the Emperor Wu Ti on the state of affairs in Bactria. About ten years later the first through caravans began arriving from China, to be greeted not by Greeks but by the new Kushan masters of Bactria.

easier by atomization within the Bactrian Empire; he had, at any rate, a notable success, and by B.C. 167 had destroyed Demetrius. In Iran the results were not happy. The coalition over which Demetrius had presided was disjointed and the immediate beneficiary was not Epiphanes' viceroy but Mithridates I of Parthia. Antiochus IV perished in B.C. 163 at the beginning of his own campaign against Parthia, and once Mithridates was relieved of the threat of a western invasion, he could turn his attention to the rich satrapies of Sogdiana and Bactria. Eucratides was cut down by the Parthians in B.C. 159, and his son and successor Heliocles, the last known Greek king of Bactria, though capable of some response to the Seleucid Demetrius II's attempt to curb Parthia in B.C. 141, was finally carried under by the oncoming hordes of the Sacae and Yüeh-chih.

The Greeks in India survived somewhat longer. In his first great advance Eucratides marched as far as India and destroyed Demetrius' brother Apollodotus before Menander came up and checked the attack sometime after B.C. 165. Eucratides had then to return to Bactria to face the mounting pressures of a Parthian invasion at his rear, and Menander was left as the reigning sovereign—legitimized to a degree by a marriage to a princess of the Euthydemid house—over the Indian half of Demetrius' Bactro-Indian empire. Like most of the other Bactrian kings, his chief monument is in his coins, still magnificent examples of Greek workmanship, and in the curious *Milindapanha* (*Questions of Milanda*), a quasi-Platonic dialogue written in a Prakrit dialect and describing a conversation between a Greco-Bactrian ruler (Milinda/Menander) and the Buddhist sage Nagasena. In India the tradition arose that Menander himself became a Buddhist.

The date of Menander's death is not certain, but his Indian empire could not have long survived him. The Sacae, pursued by Yüeh-chih and Parthian alike, were already on the road to India, and by the middle of the first pre-Christian century all political traces of the Greeks—or the Yavanas (Ionians), as the Indians called them—were obliterated. Their scattered principalities became the property of various Saca-Parthian dynasties and were eventually swallowed up into a state whose limits were almost exactly those of Demetrius', the Kushan Empire.[16]

In the West the second reign of Demetrius II (B.C. 129–125)

16. See Chapter XV, pp. 561–62.

was an unhappy one and a fitting prelude to the utter decline of Seleucid energies that followed. Demetrius was assassinated in B.C. 125 and was followed on and off the throne by a succession of meager and impotent relatives. Either Rome or Parthia could have had Syria for the taking, but Rome, though by now possessed of territory in Anatolia,[17] was as yet disinclined to move south of the Taurus, and the Parthians were totally and dangerously engaged in holding the eastern nomads at bay. Not much of the Seleucid Empire was left to be possessed, a tiny corner of northern Syria, and even that temporarily disappeared in B.C. 83 when Tigranes, king of Armenia, had a fleeting glimpse of a Mediterranean empire. The Romans forced Tigranes to disgorge his precious slice of Syria, but everywhere else the Seleucids' former vassals expanded into the political vacuum: the Nabataean Arabs east of the Jordan, Commagene on the middle Euphrates, and, most impressively, the Hasmonaeans in Coele-Syria. Only the equally enfeebled Ptolemies failed to profit from the Seleucids' distress.

Hellenic Kings and the Mosaic Politeia

The success of the descendants of Mattathiah of the house of Hasmon is impressive, even seen through the adulatory haze of the various books of *Maccabees*. The later Seleucids faced almost constant rebellions in their wide-flung empire, and most were doubtless caused by the growing independence of a local ruler measured against the progressively weakened central administration. The Seleucids, who ruled loosely from the beginning, could, in their distress, devote neither attention nor resources to their decentralized provinces and so had to face either ambitious Greek governors or firmly entrenched native dynasties. In most cases, however, the arrival of the Syrian field army and the judicious showing of the flag of Seleucid legitimacy served to restore order, if only temporarily.

The Maccabees and the revolt they championed had a far different quality to them. The family itself constituted no established native dynasty, nor did they merely legitimize, in the manner of a Timarchus in Babylonia or a Diodotus in Bactria,

---

17. See Chapter VIII, pp. 315-16.

power that they already in fact possessed. The Hasmonaeans began from ground-zero but tapped two major sources of national self-consciousness not much in evidence elsewhere in the Seleucid dominions: they joined natural leadership to the twin issues of socioeconomic repression and religious persecution. Elsewhere the taxes were too high, local officials rapacious, and mercenary garrisons an affront; in Judaea the Maccabees perceived that these were institutionalized vices and so attacked the institution, the Hellenized *polis* system.

Since the *polis* and its institutions were the focus of attack, the Seleucids were not given the choice of correcting or alleviating the inequities of their rule in Judaea but had of necessity to withdraw the system itself. No compromise caused the central issue to disappear as long as the Maccabees clung tenaciously to it. They saw the question of a *politeia* the way a Hellene saw it, as the indissoluble union of politics, economics, morality and religion. The Jewish Hellenizers on their side and the Hasidim on theirs were each willing to separate Caesar and God, but the Caesaropapists, Epiphanes on his side and the Maccabees on the other, obstinately refused to do so. After Epiphanes the Seleucids understood that they were too weak to enforce their own quite traditional Caesar-God combination on their Jewish subjects; Seleucid armies did not terrify the early Maccabees. They had popular support, which never deserted them; and their guerrilla tactics used that support to advantage. The Jewish mercenary of the post-Alexander world was an excellent soldier and widely used by the powers of the *oikoumene*. On his own ground he was almost invincible, except by an overwhelming force, something the Seleucids could rarely muster.

There were, of course, other Caesaropapists in the *oikoumene* who could muster such forces, and when Hasmonaean ideas were thrown against Rome, not, to be sure, by the Hasmonaeans themselves, who had long since learned the wisdom of keeping Yahweh and their Hellenism out of each other's way, it resulted in a disastrous bloodbath. In these early days, however, both the Hellenizers and the Hasidim understood compromise as the Hasmonaeans did not. Such blind tenacity harvested national glory for a century of Hasmonaean rule.

Antiochus VII Sidetes (B.C. 139–129) was the last Seleucid successfully to curb Hasmonaean ambitions in Coele-Syria. Even while he lived it was becoming clearer what those ambitions were and how the Hasmonaeans intended to fulfill them. The triumph over the Hellenizing Jews confined for so many years in the citadel of Jerusalem was not enough; Simon the High Priest carried the war abroad, beyond the narrow boundaries of the former temple state into areas that were once the possession of the kings of Israel. There were still Jews in those lands, in Galilee, Samaria, Transjordan and Philistia—how many cannot be said—but since the days of the Greek colonization in the wake of Alexander they lived in an atmosphere dominated by Hellenism and the Hellenized Syrians who ruled the cities. There is no evidence that the Jews found that atmosphere oppressive, indeed many grew prosperous feeding upon it, until the Hasmonaeans chose to make Hellenism the issue of their struggle against the Seleucids. Except in Samaria, which was in some lesser and obscure sense a Jewish temple state adjacent to Judaea, Antiochus IV made no hostile or oppressive moves against Judaism outside Judaea; it was the *politeia* of Jerusalem that concerned him.

Nowhere else but in Jerusalem was there a question of a Jewish versus a Hellenic *politeia,* but in many places the citizens expanded the issue on their own account, encouraged, for good or for ill, by the Hasmonaeans' willingness to intervene in force outside the borders of Judaea. After the Maccabean revolt the Jewish population of Coele-Syria was nowhere safe from the Syrian majority, and the Hellenized Syrians were nowhere safe from the possibility of a sudden and bloody Hasmonaean raid.

Under Seleucid pressure, the Maccabees' early activity was held to the level of guerrilla warfare. As that pressure relaxed, or even, in the civil wars under Balas onward, turned to encouragement, the Maccabean guerrillas evolved into something more substantial. By the time of Simon they were organized as a paid professional force in the manner of a Hellenistic army, and by the first century the transformation was so complete that the nucleus of Alexander Jannaeus' forces was a corps of Greek mercenaries from Cilicia.

Success brought other changes as well. In the sophisticated company of Hellenistic states Judaea could not be run from a cave in the Transjordan as the resistance under Judah had been. When, seven years after the death of Alcimus, Simon accepted the vacant High Priesthood from the hands of Balas, he accepted as well the institutionalization of the charismatic qualities of his house. There were many in Judaea who felt that revolutionary charisma was no qualification for a hereditary Mosaic priesthood and their discontent was enhanced by the growing recognition that in reaching for the High Priesthood Simon had also firmly grasped what the Seleucids had been thrusting upon him and his predecessors for years, a Hellenic kingship.

The black and white tones in which the authors of *Maccabees* paint the struggle between the godless Hellenes and the righteous Maccabean partisans of the Mosaic Law make the conversion from guerrilla leader to Hellenistic king an abrupt and incredible *volte face*. Beneath the propaganda, however, there is another, softer reality. The Maccabees' opposition to the Jewish Hellenizers of Jerusalem and Judaea was political, as was their oppression of the Hellenized non-Jews of the cities of Palestine. Just as Antiochus Epiphanes made no move against the Jews of the *oikoumene*, so the Maccabees gave no evidence of taking a rigorous stand against their Hellenized brethren of the Diaspora —one of whom, Jason of Cyrene, was the author of the original of II *Maccabees*—or of scrupling to deal politically with other powers, notably Rome, every whit as devoted to the worship of false gods as were the Seleucids. Even in questions of cult the line was not firmly drawn; when Judah Maccabaeus restored the temple it was in the Hellenic style of decor, and his proclamation of the feast of Hanukkah had Hellenic, not Biblical, precedents.

Simon's activities between B.C. 142 and B.C. 140 were more overt. He was, in fact and by ratification of the people, the ruler of the Jewish territories of Coele-Syria. Behind him stood the monarchical tradition of David and Solomon, a misty historical paradigm that might be useful for some local propaganda or to establish irredentist claims over larger territories. More nearly at hand, however, were two other traditions of somewhat greater consequence. For nearly four centuries the Jews of Palestine and Babylonia had been adjusting to life under a Mosaic *politeia* without magistrates. The High Priest was a mere creature of the Torah, responsible for the discharge of certain cultic functions and little else. Since the arrival of the Greeks in the Near East he had been making a modest political comeback, because the Hellenic rulers chose to deal with the Jews and other denizens of temple states through their priestly corporation. The Jews confined within the *politeuma* system had to be represented to their sovereigns by someone, and whether he was the High Priest, as in Judaea, or an ethnarch, as in Ptolemaic Egypt, made little juridical difference. It is unlikely that this arrangement caused the Jews themselves to change their views on the true function of the High Priest, a cultic official of some prestige, but bound, as were they all, to the service of the Mosaic *politeia*.

At Simon's other hand was the current notion of Hellenistic kingship, by then deeply compounded of Macedonian, Stoic and Oriental elements. The Hellenistic king was an absolutist. His was the land, the people, and the panoply of state, and his absolutism was mitigated only by the presence of Greek-style autonomous *poleis* in his dominions. His legitimacy flowed from his Macedonian origins and was validated by his role in the state as the savior from external perils, victorious leader in war and benefactor of the people. Around him shone the haze of a divinized king.

To rule as a feudal David in second-century Syria was a patent impossibility. To attempt to govern as a Mosaic High Priest must have appeared equally unfeasible to Simon. He chose the only course open to him: in B.C. 140 he was crowned in the manner— not yet in the name—of a Hellenistic king and took the reins of government firmly in his hands. Quickly the apparatus of state appeared around him, a bureaucracy and a foreign service replete with Hellenized names, a professional army, a calendar based on his regnal year, and, somewhat later, the unmistakable sign of independent rule—coinage issued in the Hasmonaean name and soon to bear Greek inscriptions. Members of the family were entombed in splendidly royal mausoleums at Modin.

For some in Judaea the behavior, public and private, of Simon must have been a painful wrench from the sacred traditions of Judaism. Formal opposition to the Hasmonaeans does not appear until the reign of Simon's son, John Hyrcanus, but there is reason to think that the stirrings were already present. Archaeology has revealed a strange community of apocalyptic Jews living at Qumran on the shores of the Dead Sea at the beginnings of the Christian era. They had traditions about their own origins, but they are woven in an opaque manner through their private and sectarian commentaries on the works of some of the earlier prophets of Judaism. In the commentaries on *Nahum* and *Habak-*

kuk some sort of historical sense can be made of their allegorical rendering of their own past, and the indications seem to point back to the time of Simon the Hasmonaean.

If Simon is a highly likely candidate for the "Wicked Priest" in the historical allegories of the Qumran sectaries, then it was his illegitimate assumption of the High Priesthood in the face of a legitimate candidate—the "Righteous Teacher" of the same Dead Sea Scrolls—that must have created this schismatic community. A critical division may have taken place in Judaea at the time of Simon: the earlier Hasidim, at first the allies of the Hasmonaeans and then estranged from them by their willingness to accept Alcimus, appear here to have further divided into a priestly faction withdrawing under their "Righteous Teacher" into an apocalyptic utopia and a moderate branch, the Pharisees, who remained in the mainstream of Judaism, though in increasing opposition to the policies and practices of their Hasmonaean sovereigns.

John Hyrcanus (B.C. 134–105), Simon's son and successor, still had to serve in Parthia as a ruler allied to the powerful Antiochus VII Sidetes, but once Sidetes died, in B.C. 129, there were few further constraints. It is not certain whether Hyrcanus himself adopted the title of king, but he played the role more fully than even Simon had. He was the first to bring in mercenary troops who could be bound to his house by pay rather than the reversible issue of Hellenism versus the Torah. And to pay them Hyrcanus resorted to another Hellenistic practice in some favor with the later Seleucids: he opened and despoiled the tomb of King David. The coinage now appears, glowing with Jewish nationalism on one side and unmistakably Hellenistic on the other.

With Sidetes gone and the uncertain Demetrius II once again in power in Syria, Hyrcanus could put into effect the latent imperialism only cautiously scouted by his predecessors. Earlier the Hasmonaeans had toyed with the notion of bringing all the Jews in outlying settlements into the safe confines of Judaea. As they grew stronger their policy shifted to something closer to an attempt at making Palestine safe for Jews by terrible reprisal raids on their Syrian tormentors. Now under Hyrcanus a new step was taken, to convert the land into an exclusively Jewish state. Hyrcanus and his generals led armies into the Transjordan and Samaria, and south into Idumaea, where Hyrcanus revealed his new policy, the forced conversion of the Idumaeans to Judaism, the token of which was compulsory circumcision. In the same mood the Samaritan temple on Mount Gerezim was razed to the ground.[18]

Hyrcanus ruled as he must and as he could, but his style and, indeed, his success itself raised opposition among the people who had so enthusiastically acclaimed his father in B.C. 140. In the sources, written by the descendants of Hyrcanus' opponents, the differences between the king and his unhappy people appear as ideological and legal ones, but we may be sure that the causes were even more complex. Hyrcanus was in financial difficulty early in his reign, and the Hasmonaean penchant for standing armies, fortresses, grandiose tombs, and an extravagant life style was an expensive habit. The Jewish rulers were now cast in the new role of tax gatherers, and the odium that had once conveniently siphoned off onto Seleucid officialdom now came to rest at their palace.

Cultural Hellenism had been partially checked in Judaea, but political Hellenism was rapidly reviving, and the social and economic chasm that Hellenism had once thrown into relief was as present in the first century as it had been in the days of Bar Sirach in the third. Palestine was a far more prosperous place than it had been a hundred years previous, but it brought the Hasmonaeans no increase; it was they who had politicized the issue of the Mosaic *politeia* and now it was turned against them. They had brought nationalism but not reform.

No new Maccabees rose to confront the Hasmonaeans, for the simple reason that the Hasmonaeans held Palestine in a far tighter grip than the generally tolerant Seleucids ever had used. Opposition took another form. Once one emerges from the pages of the

---

18. The Samaritan temple was not the only Jewish cult center outside Jerusalem; there were at least two in Egypt, at Elephantine and at Leontopolis. But it was the one in Samaria that provoked the most resentment in Jerusalem, and the Judaeans resolutely refused to recognize their northern neighbors as Jews. The Samaritans, the products of an earlier split of the Jewish state into a northern and southern kingdom, resisted attempts of the Judaeans to localize all cult in Jerusalem, but it was not until the time of the Hasmonaeans that the Judaeans could attempt a direct assault. In the fourth century Samaria had been partially repopulated by Macedonian colonists and so became a prime target of both the anti-Hellenist politics and the nationalistic Jewish propaganda of the Maccabees.

Maccabees into those of Josephus and the Gospels, the Jewish landscape is suddenly filled with religious and political parties, factions and sects that have apparently sprung from nowhere. One must conclude that, like the abruptly introduced Hasidim in *Maccabees*, they were there all the time, suppressed by the tendentious historiography of the early Hasmonaeans. In another sense, however, the factionalism that appears with the Hasmonaeans is their own peculiar creation. It was the Maccabean revolt that newly turned Jew against Jew in its relentless pursuit of the Hellenizers in the community. The Maccabees were partisans who thrived on factionalism; every Seleucid attempt at the reconciliation of parties was thwarted by the Maccabees' initial unwillingness to compromise on the religious question. In the end they had to rule under the very conditions they had declared unacceptable. For some the conditions were still unacceptable.

The Pharisees of Josephus were likely the spiritual descendants of the Hasidim, the pietists of an earlier day, who had declared themselves satisfied with Alcimus as High Priest and so had withdrawn from the Maccabean camp. The Pharisees emerge as a group unwilling to accept John Hyrcanus in that same post, but their position was far more complex and, on the face of it, drawn along harder lines than the Hasidic one. The Hasmonaeans' behavior had raised serious questions about the sacredness of the Mosaic Law itself. The current rulers of Judaea were, after all, Jews and could not be written off as impious Gentile intruders as the Seleucids could. The population of Judaea was itself more heterogeneous; in place of the compact temple state of B.C. 200, there was now a large kingdom which embraced not only Gentiles of all varieties but an equally mixed community of Jews, urban and village, soldiers, merchants and farmers, the Hellenized and non-Hellenized, traditional believers and those recently converted at and by the end of a Hasmonaean sword.

After the exile Ezra and other reformers had worked out a version of Judaism viable in the new circumstances of a stateless and templeless Jewish community. Now both state and temple were restored in a milieu filled with the temptations of Hellenism. The Hasmonaeans were now openly committed to all three as the basis and shape of their power and so posed a threat to the Ezran Mosaic *politeia*. The Pharisees were the first reaction to that threat. They were literally "separatists" (*perushim*), not in the sense that they were withdrawing from the state—there were others concurrently taking that course—but in that they were separating themselves from the godless.

The Maccabees had earlier accused the Seleucids and the Hellenizers of godlessness, but in the general and rhetorical manner of a political slogan. The Pharisees were more precise. They were legal purists who were strict in their following of the Law and for whom righteousness was a carefully defined matter of legalistic and ritualistic purity. The chief objects of their pious scorn may originally have been the "people of the land" (*'am ha-aretz*), the careless and uninstructed Jew of the countryside who was indifferent rather than hostile to the Law,[19] a group that included, doubtless, the body of "new Jews" caught up in the Hasmonaean net of conquest and conversion.

Against this neglect of the Law the Pharisees opposed their public teaching in the synagogues and the rigor and precision of their own lives. They were neither a hereditary class, like the priests, nor again a professional one, like the scribes. Many of the Pharisees were by profession scribes, but what constituted them *perushim* was their free choice of an ideology and a manner of life consistent with it; they were a small,[20] self-constituted moral elite, deeply committed to the Torah and its traditional interpretation. Now under Hyrcanus the Pharisees entered for the first time into the political arena.

The Maccabees had come to the people preaching the righteous upholding of the Torah and an end to the social oppression associated with the aristocratic *polis* system. In sixty years they had become the oppressors, supported by foreign troops and given over to whoremongering in their palaces. The old aristocracy had, in fact, been reconstituted, not so blatantly Hellenic as in the days of Menelaus, but closer perhaps to the model of Jason. And in the temple there once again presided the wealthy priestly class known to Josephus as the Sadducees.

Down to the destruction of the temple in A.D. 70 the Sadducees were the ruling class of Palestinian Judaism, deeply involved in the political life of the state and engaged in a running theological battle with the Pharisees. On the surface the Sadducees were scriptural conservatives; they accepted only the five Mosaic

---

19. The *'am ha-aretz* is analogous in both literal meaning and connotation to *paganus*, an inhabitant of the *pagus*, a term Christians later used to describe the last lagging converts to Christianity.

20. Josephus estimates their number at no more than six thousand.

books of the Pentateuch as true and inspired Scripture. In practice it was quite the reverse. The Sadducees' narrow body of Scripture freed them from assent to the evolving form of post-exilic Judaism that was at the heart of the Pharisees' program. The Pharisees for their part possessed not only a more capacious canon of written Scripture, but they accepted as revealed and binding the entire network of oral tradition that by now served as the legal underpinning of the Mosaic *politeia*.

The oral law, the body of unwritten interpretation that had grown up around the Torah and was later to be canonized in the Talmud, had served, since the rise of the scribal teachers at the time of Ezra, as the principle of governance in the Jewish communities. With the exile, history had taken the temple from the hands of the priests. In the place of the temple now stood the Law, and in the place of the priests, the scribes, a new class unconnected with priestly pedigrees. The scribes became the custodians of the new Jewish City of God, whose constitution was set down in the Torah but whose understanding was encompassed in the oral tradition. In favoring the priestly and wealthy Hellenizers, Antiochus IV had jeopardized that arrangement, and the Maccabean revolt was, in a sense, a struggle on behalf of the scribal *politeia* against a Hellenized, priestly one. The support of the Hasidim points in the same direction.

When the latest generation of scribal moralists went into opposition, Hyrcanus betrayed the principles of his Maccabean predecessors by repudiating the Pharisees and their laws, that is, their prescriptions based on the oral tradition, and went over to the Sadducees. The Sadducees as wealthy aristocrats were the natural political allies of the now unmistakably absolutist king. They possessed the resources he needed, and their religious ideology enabled them to move freely through the complex pattern of life in a Hellenistic state without the impediment of the "fences" that the Pharisees erected around human conduct in the name of the law.

The Pharisees delighted in branding the Sadducees as amoral,[21] and when viewed in the light of Pharisaic rigorism, so they may have been. They did, however, follow the Law and were com-

---

21. The historiography of post-Maccabean Judaism was largely in the Pharisees' hands, and one of their sympathizers, Josephus, when he comes to compare Jewish sects with Greek philosophical schools, can think of no better analogue for the Sadducees than the Epicureans.

mitted to the Torah, though not in the fashion of the Pharisees. Their somewhat more relaxed sensibilities, joined to their position of power and wealth in the state, made them vulnerable to another recurring phenomenon, Hellenism. Neither the Hasmonaeans nor their priestly allies the Sadducees were Hellenic ideologues in the manner of an Antiochus Epiphanes, but like all the powerful and well-to-do in the *oikoumene*, whether in Judaea, Bactria, Cappadocia, Cyrene or Pontus, they were exposed to the attractions of Hellenism. Greek names and Greek styles reappeared in Judaea, and even the puritanical Pharisees, who had rendered themselves immune to Hellenic moral values, learned to read Scripture in the nonliteral manner of Greek exegesis.

Hyrcanus died in B.C. 105 and was succeeded briefly by his son Judah, who, like all the Hasmonaeans, was better known under his Hellenized name, Aristobulus (B.C. 104–103). He reigned only briefly but, whatever the custom of his father, wore the diadem in public, openly proclaimed himself king and, perhaps inevitably, "Philhellene." Like Hyrcanus, he was aggressively expansionist and carried the undisguised wars of conquest northward against the Ituraean Arabs in Galilee. As earlier in Idumaea, the inhabitants of Galilee were offered a choice between circumcision and emigration.

At Aristobulus' death his widow Alexandra Salome arranged for the coronation of his brother Alexander Jonathan or Jannaeus (B.C. 103–76) as High Priest and king. The expansion of the Jewish kingdom continued in the face of Seleucid inability to resist. The tribes, peoples and cities of Coele-Syria were now responsible for their own defense, and Jannaeus with his highly trained professional army, including Greek mercenaries from Anatolia, had little trouble taking them in hand. He swept the coastal plain of Philistia from Ptolemais to Gaza into the Jewish state, consolidated Aristobulus' hold on Ituraea and the northern districts, and captured most of the major *poleis* in the Transjordan.

Jannaeus was not invincible. A heavily fortified city like Ascalon or Philadelphia was capable of resisting his siege, and east of the Jordan he found other formidable adversaries, who inflicted his most serious defeat upon him. Transjordan south of Philadelphia, the region of Ammonitis and Moab, was inhabited by a variety of Arab tribes. For the Jews of the early Maccabean days the Arabs of the Transjordan were a refuge and a recruiting ground for allies against the Seleucids. By the time of Jannaeus, however, one confederation of those Arabs had grown to the point where it was capable of contesting the spoils of the Seleucid Empire with the Hasmonaeans.

The Nabataeans of Petra, ethnically and linguistically Arabs, though they wrote in a version of Achaemenian Aramaic, began as nomads but ended by settling into the land as immensely successful agriculturists. More decisively for the affairs of the *oikoumene*, they sat astride a nexus of trade routes that fed from all across Arabia into Petra and thence into Egypt and Syria. Where they went as traders the Nabataeans remained as settlers; the Transjordan, the Negev and Sinai all saw Nabataean trading posts converted, by their advanced hydraulic engineering, into flourishing agricultural communities.

The Hellenes of the *oikoumene* first became aware of the Nabataeans when Antigonus was in Syria. He must have recognized the commercial possibilities of Petra, since he sent troops against it in B.C. 312. They took the fortress of Petra by surprise when it was almost deserted and gave it a thorough looting. The Nabataeans protested to Antigonus, and he assured them it was all a mistake. The credibility of his reply was not enhanced when he sent out another army under his son Demetrius Poliorcetes; but this time the Nabataeans were prepared, and the attack was beaten off.

Antigonus' foray against Petra may have been a random gesture against a rich prize. In Egypt, however, the Nabataeans had a firmly rooted rival of great power and unlimited commercial ambition. For their part, the Nabataeans were more than rapacious camel drivers. Their own enterprise was expanding over the water from their ports at Aila (Elath) at the head of the Gulf of Aqaba and at Leuke Kome farther down the Arabian coast. Ptolemy II Philadelphus and the Nabataeans matched their ambitions on the waters of the Red Sea. The Egyptians ended with control of the waterway to the East, but it had no visible effect on Nabataean prosperity, and presumably the two powers learned not to get in each other's way.

The Nabataeans may have become Hellenized under the auspices of the Ptolemies, but it is vain to search for too specific a point of origin. Their merchants had bureaus in the Hellenized cities of Gaza, Gerasa, Philadelphia and Ascalon in the near vicinity; among their regular ports of call were also Antioch, Alexandria, Rhodes, Delos, and Puteoli in Italy. Greek was the language of trade in the *oikoumene*, and many Nabataeans must have spoken it. During the reign of one of their most powerful kings, Aretas (Harith) III, Hellenization became a matter of state policy, and like many other eastern kings rising from the ruins of the Successors' empires, he officially styled himself "Philhellene."

There was really little need. Nabataean art and architecture bear testimony to that policy as surely as Herod's building program in Palestine. The iconography of the Nabataean gods, for example, is unmistakably Hellenic, not so pure as the Hellenic types found in Gerasa and Pella farther north, but more finely drawn than the Parthian analogues farther east. The styling of hair, dress and posture is Greek, as is the elaborate symbolism. These are, of course, Semitic gods—Hadad, Dushara and Atargatis—but dressed in the borrowed finery of the Hellenic Olympians and prototypes of the eastern deities that would pass so easily into the Roman Empire.[22]

There is little direct evidence on the Nabataeans during the Seleucid hegemony in Palestine. Their first king dates from B.C. 169, and the cause of this reentry of the Nabataeans into the vision of the historians may be in part due to the movement along the overland trade routes of the Parthians under Mithridates. Parthian possession first of the caravan cities stretching eastward from Seleucia on the Tigris and then of Seleucia itself must have led to a reorientation of trade through Arabia into Petra and a new round of prosperity for the Nabataeans.

Some of that prosperity can be measured in terms of political vigor. The first Nabataean king, Aretas I, was allied with the Maccabees in their struggle against the Seleucids, but the alliance came to an end under his successor. By the time of 'Obidah at the turn of the second century, the crumbling of Seleucid fortunes in Syria and Jannaeus' threats north and east of the Jordan brought the two dynasts into conflict in the Transjordan. The Nabataeans had the better of it, and some time about B.C. 90 'Obidah trapped a Hasmonaean army on the Golan heights east of Galilee and inflicted a major defeat on them.

With Jannaeus out of contention the Nabataeans were free to put out their hands for the greatest prize of all, Damascus. A

22. See Chapter XII, pp. 470–79.

welter of petty Seleucids presided over the last years of the empire in Syria, one per city at times. When one such local Seleucid died in Damascus in B.C. 85, the city had to choose its new ruler from among the burgeoning Arab dynasties that surrounded it. Likely but unwelcome candidates for master of Damascus were the Hellenized Arab *shaykhs* of Ituraea, who had their capital at nearby Chalcis. It was not a pleasant prospect; the Ituraeans had a grisly reputation. To avert this the Damascenes issued an invitation to Aretas III, the "Philhellene" (*c.* B.C. 87–62), to receive the city. He accepted and so ruled territories stretching from northern Syria in a wide arc through the edge of the Syrian steppe, Ammonitis and Moab, into the Negev and Sinai. Aretas was still ruler in Petra when Pompey arrived in Palestine in B.C. 64, and in their first brush with Roman arms the Nabataeans were successful.[23]

Before his encounter with the Nabataeans Jannaeus had extended the Hasmonaean kingdom as far as it would ever reach, perhaps to its natural limits, since there were other powerful coalitions of Arab tribes at Edessa, Emesa and Chalcis with greater internal coherence if not the naked power of Jannaeus' expensive imported soldiery. As yet they were a check but not a threat to the Hasmonaean house; Jannaeus' troubles came from within. Twice during his reign he had to take up arms against his enemies in Judaea, and on the second occasion the civil strife lasted six years. The dissidents went to the length of summoning to their side one of the last scions of the hateful Epiphanes, Demetrius III. Jannaeus barely escaped this considerable danger, but once he righted himself he took ample revenge; he had eight hundred of the rebels crucified in Jerusalem after their wives and children had been slain before their eyes. The king himself looked on, feasting and taking his ease among his concubines.

The dissidents can have been no other than the Pharisees and their adherents. Jannaeus realized before he died in B.C. 76 that rule without the kind of religious support represented by the Pharisees was impossible. He persuaded Alexandra Salome of the wisdom of this course, and so when she assumed the throne in her own name she reversed the earlier policy of Hyrcanus and restored the Pharisees to their place of leadership in the state. Their

---

23. They survived as a client kingdom of the Romans until A.D. 106, when Trajan incorporated them as the Provincia Arabia (see Chapter XIV, p. 528).

prescribed temple regulations were put back in force and they themselves took up a commanding position in the Sanhedrin,[24] where the Queen's brother, the Pharisee Simon bar Shetah, played a leading role.

Alexandra Salome could not, of course, hold the High Priesthood; that she bestowed on her elder son, Hyrcanus II. The younger, Aristobulus II, was apparently unconcerned. His ambitions ran higher than those of the rather relaxed Hyrcanus, and even before his mother's death in B.C. 67 he was laying claim to the throne of the Hasmonaeans. Factions were gathering at the sides of both sons, including, in the camp of Hyrcanus, the Idumaean diplomat Antipater and the armed might of the Nabataean *shaykh* Aretas III. By the time Pompey arrived in Coele-Syria, in B.C. 64, the dispute was in full swing.[25]

In Judaea the Romans inherited a state and a people rent from top to bottom with violence and dissent. In Antipater's son Herod they found a ruler who made eminent sense to them, another energetic Hellenic-style king who could bring the blessings of urban Hellenism to Palestine. Their protégé, for all his obvious merits, violated every political lesson to be learned from Jewish history of the preceding one hundred years. He alienated Sadducees and Pharisees alike and succeeded in spawning out of the latter party an even more dangerous faction, the Zealots.

Under Jannaeus the Pharisees had been violently rebellious against the king, and even when restored to power by Alexandra Salome, they took a bloody revenge upon their former tormentors. Herod seems to have quelled them; the Pharisees of the Gospels preferred passive resistance and the power of their moral

---

24. From the time of the High Priest Simon the Just, a contemporary of Antiochus III, the Jewish community in Judaea possessed some kind of a conciliar body, though its name, function and membership fluctuated. At the outset it was a Council of Elders (*Gerousia*), with a membership drawn chiefly from the priestly class, and they served as the chief advisory body to the High Priest in the mixed political and religious life of the temple state. During Jerusalem's *polis* phase the membership was likely even more priestly and aristocratic, and the body's approximation to a Hellenic *boule* drew it more deeply into purely political affairs. The early Hasmonaeans expanded and democratized the council, but since they had less and less need of political advice the Sanhedrin, as it was now called, became the focus of Hasidic-Pharisaic religious and legal activity. Hyrcanus dislodged the Pharisees and replaced them with his Sadducean adherents.

25. See Chapter VIII, pp. 321–23.

authority to their earlier, more violent methods. The new pacifist stance did not suit all of the Pharisees, however, and at least one of their number was among the founders of a new activist resistance that grew up on the Jewish "frontier" in Galilee and burst in upon the Romans in A.D. 6. The census of Quirinus preliminary to the incorporation of Judaea as a Roman province provoked the first violent Zealot sedition under Judah of Galilee. Thenceforward the province was under an almost continuous state of guerrilla siege down to the final apocalyptic suppression of Zealot activity and of Jerusalem itself, in A.D. 135.[26]

Hellenism in the Diaspora

The beginnings of a Jewish dispersion were already implicit in the Babylonian exile when, at the beginning of the sixth century, great numbers of Palestinian Jews were carried off by their Babylonian conquerors and resettled in Mesopotamia. Some of their descendants returned to Judaea under the more tolerant Achaemenians, but many remained in what had become their homeland, and the Jewish community in Babylonia continued to be a force in ecumenical Judaism late into the Islamic Middle Ages. On the eve of the exile other Jews had made their way to Egypt, and though the Egyptian settlements remained small and dispersed, they were sporadically augmented by émigrés from Palestine and Babylonia.

The first great change in the fortunes of the Jews in the era of the *oikoumene* arose from the Ptolemaic conquest of Coele-Syria. For more than a hundred years the temple state of Judaea and the Jews in Egypt were part of a single empire, and a brisk traffic was established between Jerusalem and Alexandria. A massive and enforced migration of Jews into Egypt was set in motion by the Palestinian conquests of Ptolemy I, who carried a great number— one author puts the figure at 100,000—of his Jewish captives into Egypt. Possibly they came as slaves, but under his successor Philadelphus they were free men and the nucleus of a large Jewish population in the land.

The number of Jews in Egypt may have reached one million by Roman times, but whether the figure is accurate or not, the Jewish population of Egypt was considerable. Most of them lived

---

26. See Chapter XIV, pp. 508–16, 530–32.

in Alexandria and grew cultured and prosperous in the curious
Jewish penumbra between citizen and alien. Where they were
not purely a military garrison (*katoikia*), the Jews in Egypt lived
within that peculiar creation of the *oikoumene*, the *politeuma*.
They were not the only ones who lived under that form of
political association; most unassimilated foreigners dwelling in the
Hellenic *poleis* of Asia were gathered into *politeumata*, where
they were granted a degree of self-government under the general
supervision of the *polis* officials.

In one crucial sense, however, the Jews were different from
those other national groups: they were not only unassimilated,
they were unassimilable. Assimilation was within the grasp of any
easterner who stood close enough, in terms of social and economic class, to the ruling Greeks. He had only to pass through
the requisite Hellenic acculturation and be prepared to share in
the life of the *polis*. The Jew could and did avail himself of the
first passage, which lay through the gymnasium of the *ephebeia*.
Until the coming of the Romans there was no overwhelming
objection to this important form of cultural climbing—except, of
course, in Judaea itself, where the issue of Hellenization had
become a political one. Most, if not all, the Jews of Egypt affluent
enough to do so did in fact become Hellenized in this first sense.

Unlike the other Hellenized aliens, the Jew could not take the
second step without apostasy from Judaism. To live the life of a
polites meant to worship the gods of the *polis*, something the Jew
was forbidden to do by a fundamental principle of his own
politeia, the Mosaic Law. The problem for the Jew, as it was later
to be for the Christian, lay chiefly in cult, the actual offering of
sacrifice to the gods of the *polis* or the empire. Neither the Christian nor the Jewish intellectual had any difficulty making identification between his God and the gods of the Hellenes within the
spacious confines of philosophy and in the approved Greek
manner; but offer sacrifice he could not and would not do.

But not all. Some Egyptian Jews, like Philo's nephew Tiberius
Alexander, paid their dues to the *polis*, and they are known to us
because they passed on to illustrious careers in the *oikoumene*.
But the masses of Jews stood firm on the Mosaic *politeia*, and in
Alexandria, the one community where some kind of judgment is
possible, the *politeuma* of the Jews combined its ritual and spiritual Judaism with its cultural Hellenism in a workable fashion.

The accommodation was possible because most of the rulers of the *oikoumene* recognized the special status of the Jews and did not raise the question of their total—that is, religious—assimilation. Epiphanes' abrogation of the Mosaic Law was an extraordinary event; the normal Ptolemaic and Seleucid attitude was to permit their Jewish subjects to "live according to their ancestral laws" within their own *politeuma*, a privilege that was probably certified by a written charter in many places.

Exposure to a mixed environment carried with it special dangers, and almost from the beginning of the Jews' history their leaders were at pains to insulate the fragile Jewish monotheism from the cultic variety that surrounded it. In these latter days too the thrust of most of the Pharisaic legislation was to underline the difference that separated Jew from Gentile. They may have been well advised; at the long established Jewish military colony at Elephantine, far in Upper Egypt, the Jewish soldiers, who had their own temple, seem to have indulged in the worship of a certain unseemly lady at the side of Yahweh.

Syncretism at the remote and isolated Elephantine is curious, but not, perhaps, very important. More significant was the process unfolding in western Anatolia. There were Jewish communities in Anatolia from at least the time of Antiochus III who transported Jewish families there from Babylon to serve as military garrisons. They must have flourished greatly from what can be read of Paul's round of the Anatolian synagogues some two and a half centuries later. The native religious tradition was strong there, and one local version of the god whom the Greeks knew as Dionysus, the Phrygian Sabazius, made noticeable inroads into Jewish cult. Sabazius, Sabaoth, and Sabbath became highly mixed in Anatolia with influences flowing in both directions.

These are exceptions. In the synagogues of the Diaspora it was the Mosaic Law that was preached and taught, though how this was accomplished is a far more difficult question. The Jews of the Diaspora had, no less than the Jews of Palestine, a developing literary tradition from about B.C. 200 onward. Most of its products were written in Greek, the language of the *oikoumene*, but little or none of it gives an impression of what the normative Judaism of the period was like. In Judaea and Babylonia this was clearly something close to the Pharisaic tradition, as can be read in a backward surmise from the two Talmuds produced by the Jews of those regions. But there is no Egyptian Talmud from which one can elicit the modalities of Alexandrian Judaism. Instead there is a translation of the Jewish Scriptures into Greek and the testimony of a later Hellenized Alexandrian who may or may not have been typical of his fellow Jews in the *politeuma* of Alexandria.

According to the Jewish legend produced, perhaps, for Gentile consumption, Ptolemy Philadelphus (B.C. 285–246) summoned together seventy-two Jewish scholars to have them individually translate the Scriptures into Greek. At the end of the work all seventy-two versions were identical, and thus there came into existence the "Translation of the Seventy" (Septuagint). The tale has as its transparent purpose a divine validation for the accuracy of the Greek version of the Jewish Bible circulating in Egypt, a work that was actually done over a period of almost two centuries. What the translation itself signifies, however, is that the Egyptian Jews had lost both their Hebrew and their Aramaic. Nor were they alone. The Septuagint was in wide circulation among the Jews of the *oikoumene* down to the spread of Christianity;[27] Paul, for one, a Pharisee of Tarsus in Cilicia, used it.

It has been suggested that the Septuagint was not merely for the use of the Jewish community, but rather for purposes of enlightening and, ultimately, of converting the Hellenes, somewhat in the tradition of Manetho's work on the manners and customs of the ancient Egyptians and Berossus' on the Babylonians. Measured by the criteria of those latter works, the Septuagint was a crashing failure. One of the few Greeks of the Hellenistic period who had any knowledge of things Jewish, Hecataeus of Abdera[28] was a contemporary of Ptolemy I and so antedates the translation; down to the time of Josephus the Septuagint was a closed book, and Hellenized intellectuals knew little or nothing about the history of those people who caused them so much political discomfort.

If the Septuagint did nothing to convert or even enlighten the Gentiles, it must have had a considerable effect in Hellenizing the Jews. The new version converted the traditional past of the Jews into the currency of Hellenism. The faintly Hebraic rhythms of the Septuagint are of interest only to the comparative reader; for the Jews of the Diaspora synagogues with little or no access to

---

27. See Chapter XIV, pp. 535–36.
28. See Chapters II, p. 112, and XII, p. 450.

the Hebrew original, it was a document in *koine* Greek, and its resonances were those of Greek religious and philosophical attitudes of the third century. Accuracy apart, the fact that the Septuagint was a translation into a language with rich and sophisticated connotations created for its readers a new theological vocabulary whose roots were anchored in a Greek and not a Jewish past.

But to read the Torah, whether in the original Hebrew or in an Aramaic translation (*targum*) or in a Greek version, is not precisely the critical question in the evaluation of Diaspora Judaism. The shape and substance of that reading came from other sources, from the exegesis which the Pharisaic oral tradition gave to the text. Paul of Tarsus, for example, whose Bible was the Septuagint, read it in the full Pharisaic manner. But he was himself a Pharisee who had studied in Jerusalem at the rabbinical school of Gamaliel. It is not at all clear how typical a procedure it was for a pious Jew of the Diaspora to receive his formation at Jerusalem, particularly since the evidence in the case of Philo, the most eminent product of Diaspora Judaism, seems to point in the opposite direction.

Philo of Alexandria (*c.* B.C. 25–50 A.D.), a somewhat older contemporary of Paul's, is a dazzling example of the promise of Hellenized Judaism and a counter to the heavyhanded Maccabean propaganda against the Hellenizers cringing in the Jerusalem citadel. Philo came from the same class that produced the Tobiads, well-to-do Jews drawn into the affairs of the *oikoumene*. The difference between Philo and Simon the son of Tobiah is not only a difference in temperament and training, but of totally different milieus. The latter was an only partially Hellenized financier and landowner in Ptolemaic Palestine, and his career unfolded in the shadow of the temple establishment in Jerusalem. Philo, the intellectual, lived and worked in the open society of Alexandria. There were political differences between the Jews and the newly arrived Roman authorities, to be sure, and though there may have been sectaries in Alexandrian Judaism—Philo describes one such group, the Therapeutae—not one of them had succeeded in putting upon the Jewish community the destructive political edge that followed the Maccabean revolt in Palestine.

Philo was not part of the literary tradition of Jewish Hellenism; the focus of his attention was Biblical throughout. His preserved work contains a number of essays on special questions in philosophy, the eternity of the world, for one, but the great bulk of it is cast in the form of a commentary on the Pentateuchal books of the Mosaic Law.[29] Philo did not, however, read them all in the same fashion. *Genesis,* for example, he explained in the accepted Greek tradition going back to Plato's *Timaeus,* while *Leviticus* and *Numbers* were given a more legalistic treatment.

The ancestry of Philo's philosophical understanding of *Genesis* can be surmised, if not clearly traced in all its details; his legal attitudes have been the subject of a long and complicated debate, since it is precisely there that the question of Philo's relationship with Palestinian Pharisaism rests. That affiliation, if it existed at all, appears slim indeed. Whether Philo drew his legal reasoning from Greco-Roman law, the practices of the Jewish courts of the *politeuma* of Alexandria, or from his own legal theorizing, they do not appear to have come from the Pharisaic *halachoth.*[30]

If Philo was unfamiliar with the oral tradition current in Palestine, was he at least capable of reading Scripture in Hebrew? The two propositions are related, since it appears that it was the negative side of their Hellenism, the Egyptians' loss of Hebrew and Aramaic, that was the most effective barrier between Egypt and Palestine. The Jewish communities in the two lands knew and cared about each other's welfare. The Jews in Alexandria continued to collect and forward money to Palestine for the support of the Jerusalem temple, and the Hasmonaeans propagandized among their co-religionists in Egypt.[31] But whatever

---

29. The focus on the Pentateuch is another striking difference between Philo and the Pharisees, who rested heavily upon the Prophets for their understanding of the Law. The Prophetic books were, of course, in the Septuagint by the time of Philo and were recognized as part of the canon of Scripture.

30. The Pharisees' practice was to extract from their reading of Scripture two kinds of material. The first constituted moral and legal imperatives and were termed *halachoth* (sing., *halachah*). The second, narrative and expository in nature, the *haggadoth* (sing., *haggadah*), might be used for illumination or edification but were not binding prescriptions.

31. II *Maccabees,* which was addressed to the Jews of Egypt in about B.C. 125, may have represented an attempt of Hyrcanus to advance the cause of his new "national"—that is, Hasmonaean—festival of Hanukkah.

communication there was apparently took place in Greek. Philo could manipulate a few Jewish etymologies, but there is little other evidence that this highly cultured Jewish scholar could read Hebrew.

Philo's Hellenism, founded on the Septuagint and nourished by divergent sources in the Greek philosophical tradition, is open and impressive. He stood at the middle of a fertile, if obscure, period of Greek philosophy, when the various Greek schools, particularly Stoicism and Platonism, were coming together in a rich synthesis in the work of men like Antiochus of Ascalon, Panaetius and Posidonius.[32] The work of that generation is largely lost and must be reconstructed from what the eclectic Cicero learned or borrowed from them. Philo, however, is represented by a substantial body of writing and, so, is a major landmark among the ruins of a reviving Platonism.

Philo did not introduce the theological note into later Greek thought; God and ethics reigned supreme in post-Aristotelian philosophy, and the sophistication of a treatise like Cicero's On the Nature of the Gods is an indication that a great deal of thought and concern had been put into the emerging portrait of the God of the Philosophers.

Philo was familiar with that portrait and everywhere reflected it in his own work. But for an extraordinary new end. In the Greek rationalist tradition, philosophy was an autonomous, self-defining, and self-justifying discipline; its principles neither rested upon nor derived from any other. Philo was the first thinker to accept the principles and validity of Hellenic philosophy, and at the same time subject it to a higher source of truth, a philosophy derived from divine revelation. The "natural theology" of Plato's Timaeus and Aristotle's Metaphysics had now to give way to a "sacred theology" of the revelation that Moses had mediated to the Jewish people.

Other revelations would follow; the Old Testament was completed by a New, and both perfected in a Qur'an. The partisans of each had eventually to go the way of Philo and justify their faith in the face of the Hellenes' rationalism. Philo fixed the role of philosophy as the "handmaiden of theology" for those later traditions. But the issue was not as yet sharply defined in Philo. His interest more often appears directed toward synthesis,

---

32. See Chapter IX, pp. 360–70.

to make Moses appear like a Greek sage and otherwise explain the Jewish revelation in terms comprehensible to a Greek of the philosophical tradition,[33] and it is only later, when the Hellenes began to see the drift more clearly, that the battle of faith and reason was fully joined.

In Philo the two theologies are more often reconciled than put in a hierarchical relationship, and here the Greeks themselves had prepared the way. For three centuries before Philo the Greeks had been in close contact with eastern cultures and had come to know, and even to respect, the wisdom of the East. By the time of Philo the notion of an eastern sage was no longer an odd one for the Greeks, and Moses himself had been cast in that role by Posidonius, probably by way of what he had read in Hecataeus of Abdera. Philo seized upon that established notion, the parity of eastern and Hellenic wisdom, and constructed out of it a "Mosaic philosophy."

The conversion of Moses into a philosopher[34] was rendered simpler by another line of speculation being explored by the Greeks. From as early as Plato there had been a recognition on the part of Greek intellectuals that by the side of their own rationalist tradition stood other types of sages with a claim on the attention of men: the poet, the lawgiver and the inspired seer were all privy to the truth in one form or another. As the attack on the traditional Greek mythology mounted in intensity, this multilevel approach to truth could be summoned up, as it was by the Stoics, to reconcile the god of the philosophers with the maligned gods of the poets.[35]

---

33. An attempt along these lines had already been made in the *Letter of Aristeas*, which gives itself out as a letter of a Gentile official at the court of Philadelphus to his brother, but is actually a Jewish pseudepigraph of about 150 B.C. The letter is also the source of the story about the translation of the Septuagint by the seventy-two divinely guided scholars. Another somewhat more substantial and more aggressive predecessor of Philo was Aristobulus, probably a contemporary of Ptolemy VI (B.C. 181–145), whose *Exegesis of the Mosaic Laws* accused the Greek philosophers of purloining their wisdom from older Jewish sources.

34. A process that was to come to full term in a later generation even more impressed by eastern cultures. In Numenius, a Pythagorean of the second Christian century, the philosopher is reduced to Moses: Plato is nothing more than "a Moses speaking Attic Greek" (see Chapter XVI, p. 585).

35. See Chapter XII, pp. 451–53.

Moses, the eastern sage and prophet, was not then an outrageous candidate for a doctor of philosophy, even on the Hellenes' own terms, nor is it odd that his philosophy should turn out to be a version of Platonism; the Stoics, whom Philo knew well, were already accomplished masters at showing that the gods of the poets turned out to bear a remarkable resemblance to the God of the philosophers. It was merely a question of learning how to "read" the poets. For Philo the problem and the solution were similar. The "other reading" (*allegoria*) is all-important in Philo. He did not demean the literal or historical sense of the Scripture texts before him, but there were times when the literal, or "corporeal," sense of the text must yield to a "psychic" or "cosmic" reading, which revealed history in another, more Platonic dimension.

Other Jews were reading under the surface of the sacred texts. The *allegoria* of the Pharisees or the Essenes exposed no Platonic panoramas, however; they were searching instead for a Messiah concealed in typological passages in the Prophets. The search tapered off when their students, the Christians, found their Messiah in those same passages, and when Roman power postponed the hopes of a Messianic deliverance into the distant and unforeseeable future. When rabbinic Judaism had long fallen silent on the subject, Christianity continued to rejoice in its typological discovery, and later Christian intellectuals of Alexandria skillfully combined the Messianic *allegoria* with Philo's Platonic one. To a Christian it was clear that both understandings of Scripture, the Pharisaic and the Philonian, converged on the same point, the *Logos*.

The *Logos* that appears at the center of Philo's system was new to neither the students of Greek philosophy nor a Jewish leadership nourished on the kind of speculation that had lately made its appearance in the Diaspora. Later Jewish literature was already in the habit of hypostatizing the qualities and attributes of God; the "Wisdom" and the "Word" of Yahweh were often portrayed in *Proverbs* and *Bar Sirach* as if they were creatures distinct from Yahweh himself and were even given a role in the creation of the world.

There is no need to read Greek influence here; such a manner of speaking was an indigenous growth in Judaism which paralleled another flourishing in the Hellenic tradition. Already in Aristotle, God's creative activity had been identified as his intelligence (*nous*). The Aristotelian God was, however, a remote being beyond the universe, and in Stoicism he was thrust back into the world as the immanent principle personified as both Zeus and Reason (*Logos*), but operative through the "seedlings of reason" (*logoi spermatikoi*) that permeate the universe and give it coherence, intelligibility and growth.

Between these notions and Philo's own concept of the *Logos*, one other piece had to fall in place. It is present in Philo, though we cannot be sure he originated it: the Platonic *eide* are in the mind of God. For Plato the *eide*, or "Forms," were absolute and perfect spiritual beings that served as both prototype and paradigm for the sensible, material beings of our world. In the *Timaeus* the creator of the universe is described as looking upon these "Forms," which are outside and higher than himself, and fashioning the *kosmos* as an imitation of them. By the time of Philo, or perhaps first in Philo, the *eide* have been gathered together *within the mind* of the Creator God; they are, quite literally, his ideas, a status denied to them by Plato.

The Philonian *Logos* is, in the first place, the complex of *eide* which constitutes the reason (*logos*) of Yahweh and where they serve as paradigms of creation. Further, they are externalized as the "intelligible universe," a *kosmos* of spiritual beings to which our universe materially corresponds, save in perfection. This is the transcendental complex borrowed almost exactly from the Platonic original.[36] For Philo this too is *Logos*, though now more personified as something external and inferior to God, a "Second God" and the "Son of God," expressions at first sight destructive of Jewish monotheism, but well within the hyperbolic and figurative diction that confronted Philo in *Proverbs*. Finally, the *Logos* enters into its Stoic phase: it is the principle of reason and intelligibility immanent in the universe and condensed and glorified in a prophet like Moses.

All of this would make perfect sense to a Hellene in Alexandrian intellectual circles, even though he found it in the still somewhat exotic garb of a "Mosaic philosophy." We cannot be sure for whom Philo intended it—a Hellenized Jewish readership

---

36. Philo can take advantage of the two duplicating accounts of creation in *Genesis*, originally the product of a faulty recension, to show that the Mosaic philosophy had provided a description of the creation of both the "intelligible universe" and an almost identical "sensible universe."

or interested Gentiles. If it was the latter, they must have found other things in Philo to disturb them. Philo, for all his Platonic metaphysics, was in no way willing to accept Hellenic morality. He was still a Jew unmistakably putting forth a claim to a relevant and even superior form of wisdom rather than a convert to Hellenism begging off some outworn creed. The sound of craven cymbals can occasionally be heard tinkling through the lines of Josephus' historical apologia; there is no sound of them in Philo.

Philo is a good example of what Hellenism had to offer the Jew and the Jew had to offer Hellenism. The grandeur of the Pharisees was that they attempted to combine a strict observance of the Law with its spiritualization. That they occasionally failed in this delicate balance is manifest from their portrait in the Gospels; that they more often succeeded finds its testimony in the rabbinical Judaism which was their patrimony. But Philo, no less than the Pharisees, was involved in the same task, though with different premises and methods. The Pharisaic tone was set by the enormous fact of the exile and the later Hasmonaean excursions into power politics; Philo's by his confrontation with Hellenism.

Hellenism taught Philo and other Jews, like the author of the philosophical *Wisdom of Solomon* and the community of the synagogue at Dura Europos with its exquisite Hellenic decoration, how to find new levels of spiritual content in the primitive documents of the Pentateuch. But they had first to discover Hellenism and come to terms with it, just as the once "stiff-necked" Hellenes were coming to terms with the Oriental civilizations that now surrounded them. In the Egypt of the Ptolemies the task was not difficult, since the Jews experienced neither despair nor unfulfilled expectation in Alexandria. In Palestine, Hellenism carried with it a burning political issue and was represented by what Maccabean historiography allows us to see only as a beleaguered minority propped up by Syrian soldiers. The Pharisees were neither stupid nor wicked, but history, first in the form of the Maccabees and later of the Zealots, never allowed them the relaxed appraisal of Hellenism that the Alexandrian Jew had.

Not all the ways were barred, however. The later Judaism of the rabbis turned away from the *oikoumene* that played it false, but in the Pharisees separatism had not yet become closure. However zealous the Pharisees might have been to preserve the ritual purity of the Law-abiding Jew in the face of the Gentiles, they too were caught up in the common Jewish desire to win those same Gentiles to Judaism. Pharisaic piety was revolted at the Hasmonaeans' callously circumcised "converts" in Ituraea and Galilee, but something of that enthusiasm had been communicated to them. In the Gospels the Pharisee is described as someone who is "willing to cross land and sea to make a single convert." In the centuries across the beginning of the Christian era Hasmonaean nationalism and the Pharisees' concept of a universal God came together to make Judaism a missionary religion.

The Gentile found much that was attractive in Judaism: its morality, its transcendent God, even the temple ritual and the Sabbath rest.[37] A total embrace of Judaism must have been a courageous and relatively infrequent act, since it meant the taking on of the entire Law, to the breaking of the social and even familial ties that had bound the convert to the Gentile community. Most of those who show up in the ancient literature as Jewish sympathizers probably belonged to another, less carefully defined class. These "Godfearers" (phoboumenoi) or "reverent ones" (sebomenoi), as they were called, may have adopted certain Jewish practices without, at the same time, leaving the Gentile world or shouldering the full burden of the Law. They existed in considerable numbers around the Diaspora, and when Paul made his rounds of the synagogues of Asia preaching a Christianity that was freed of the Old Law because of its fulfillment in the New, he found a receptive audience among the sebomenoi.

The spirituality that drew the sebomenoi toward Judaism was the common possession of both Diaspora and Palestinian Judaism in the centuries around the beginning of the Christian era; the author of the Wisdom of Solomon, Aristobulus, Philo, Jesus bar Sirach, and the Pharisees were all one in their desire to penetrate under the surface of the Law to the spiritual realities that lay beneath. What separated them was their actual practice and, more ominously, their political expectations. Philo was content to live within the politeuma of Alexandria and protect the rights

---

37. Particularly the social side of the Sabbath. The Greeks of Anatolia, where there were many Jews, found the Sabbath an attractive festival of eating and drinking, and in Cilicia there were clubs of Gentile "Sabbatists" who met every week to celebrate the feast.

and privileges of the community by the legal recourse open to him. In Palestine, where passions were more inflamed, the Pharisees had been pushed into a more passive stance. Nothing could be hoped for from the Romans, nor anything gained by substantial accommodation; the Pharisees held themselves correctly but frigidly aloof from their Roman masters. Others were more violent in their pessimism or more withdrawn in their despair.

VIII

The Romans in the Near East

The successor states of Alexander's empire present a dreary historical chronicle of endless wars provoked by the burgeoning ambitions of enfeebled men and their armies. There was still some vigor among the Seleucids and the Antigonids, but the former had repeatedly shown themselves incapable of protecting both ends of their sprawling, polyglot holdings. The Macedonians too, though their military tradition was intact and their state relatively homogeneous, had to divide their attention. While dealing with the inevitable Seleucid ambitions in the Aegean and the league of petty Greek states in the Peloponnesus, the kings of Macedon had also to observe the struggles between Greeks, Etruscans, Romans, and others of their western neighbors.

Their vigilance was amply justified. Roman aggressiveness upset the balance of power in Italy, and unless Macedon took steps, or Carthage could recover from its savage thirty-year war with the Romans, the new Latin power would control the political and commercial future of the entire western Mediterranean and doubtless eventually raise her voice in the East as well.

Rome, the republic of central Italy that was now paramount in the peninsula and stood poised on the brink of its first excursion into eastern politics, was no rude partner in this fellowship of Mediterranean powers. Its tribal descent from the remote Indo-European past was similar to that of the Greeks themselves, and its language, customs and institutions were parallel to those of the Hellenes across the Adriatic. Indeed Rome had been for some time even closer to centers of Hellenic influence. To the north were the Hellenized Etruscans, and from Naples south into Sicily was a dense pattern of Greek *poleis* dating from the eighth century. Like the Macedonians themselves the Romans were already "second generation" Hellenes, the recipients and, as the passage of time would reveal, the principal heirs of the pervasive and at times almost suffocating powers of transformation that characterized Hellenism's effect on other cultures. Hellenism was to leave its unmistakable marks on almost every aspect of Roman life and thought.

The native Latin tradition did not totally succumb to the attractions of metamorphosis. The Latin language was strong enough (as the Macedonian was not) to hold its ground, and from the time of the wars against Carthage there grew up in Rome a considerable body of Latin literature that owed a great deal of its form and content to Hellenistic Greek models but that was, for all that, unmistakably Latin in tone. The Latin tongue too was worked into some semblance of Greek diction and style, and in the hands of a genius, a Catullus or a Horace, could duplicate the genuine accents of Hellenism without resorting to falsetto.

That this intrusion of another culture was to create a "schism in the soul" of the proud Romans was inevitable and, when it occurred, painfully obvious. Latin poets constantly complained of the poverty of Latin in expressing concepts that had long been domesticated in Greek. The Romans were taught by the later Greeks to reverence the classics, and if a Greek of Alexandria felt embarrassed and awed in the literary presence of Homer, it may well be imagined what occurred in the heart of a Latin.

There was room for self-defense, however. The Greeks were politically impotent by the middle of the second century before Christ, and a Latin nationalist of the stripe of Cato the Censor had no difficulty in contrasting the vitality and virility of the Romans with the decadence of the contemporary Greeks and the Roman Hellenophiles in the circle of the Scipios. It was a melody with many interesting changes to be rung through the long span of Roman history: simplicity versus luxury, rural versus urban, Latin versus Oriental,[1] the doers versus the dreamers, Latin *gravitas* versus Greek *levitas*.

The issue was simple only for a few zealots. The Roman

---

1. For the Romans the "Orientals" began not at Tyre and Sidon but on the eastern shore of the Adriatic.

intelligentsia, the very men who pointed the finger of scorn at Greek decadence, were themselves the products of Hellenic education; Greek was their second language and Athens or Rhodes the goal of their studies. Horace and Vergil gave Greek titles to their works. Augustus and Tiberius were tutored by two of the most eminent Greek rhetoricians of their day, while Germanicus, the heir apparent of Tiberius, wrote Greek epigrams and translated Aratus. Cicero is the perfect example of the intellectual Roman schooled in Hellenism. The translator of Plato, Xenophon, Demosthenes, Homer and the tragedians, he wrote a history of his own consulate in Greek, and even his Latin writings, particularly the philosophical works, bear the stamp of their Greek prototypes. And yet Cicero's speeches and letters are filled with unbelievably harsh judgments about the degeneracy of the contemporary Greek. In Cicero's mind Aulus Gabinius, for whom he reserved some of his choicest vilifications, represented the type of Roman caught up in the company and mores of the Greeks, a rouged and powdered catamite who specialized in nude dancing.

Probably the most thoughtful men would agree with Vergil: the cultural superiority of the Greeks was unquestioned; the Roman talent—and responsibility—was to rule in accordance with justice and equity. The evaluation is a valid one; what it ignored, however, was the painful span of centuries the Romans devoted to mastering self-government.

Like the Greeks and unlike the Macedonians, the Romans had thrown off the restrictions of a monarchy and had developed a system of republican government with legislative bodies representing both the aristocratic (the *senatus*) and the popular (the *comitia*) point of view, and with a graduated system of elected offices whose tenure was gradually extended beyond the narrow circle of the aristocrats. The Romans were at once more tribal, more familial, and more class-conscious than the Greeks, who had managed to blur tribal lines within the *polis* to the extent necessary to ensure upward mobility in the society; in Rome the great patrician families, or *gentes*, clung to their pedigrees and their prerogatives more firmly.

Class strife was tempered in Greece by constitutional evolution, the homogeneity of Greek society or, failing all else, large-scale colonial migration; at Rome it was endemic. Divisions based on wealth and social standing run far back in Roman history, and by the time of Cicero they had become almost institutionalized as political parties: the *optimates*, the social if not the linear descendants of the original land- and blood-based patricians, families celebrated by their claim to generation after generation of Roman magistrates, aristocrats of service; the burgeoning middle-class "Knights" (*Equites*), the rising managerial class of bankers and merchants, who were growing rich on the commercial wealth of Rome; and finally the *populares*, no longer, like their plebeian ancestors, small holders and yeoman farmers, but more and more an urban proletariat.

The Roman Republic attempted to keep these forces in balance in the name of freedom. The constitutional or quasi-constitutional adjustments of the body politic, by the Gracchi toward the left, by Sulla toward the right, were temporary and, in the long run, unsuccessful. The temptations of empire were at hand, and for the last century of its existence the Republic was in that state of political vibration that can betoken only disintegration. Men were more powerful than the institutions designed to restrain them, and private interests triumphed over the common good. The period coincided almost exactly with the Roman entry into the eastern Mediterranean.

A Contested Inheritance

Rome was initially drawn toward the East more by a desire to protect her own security than by imperialistic ambition. The Adriatic was her common boundary with Greece, and piracy there was an immediate and continuing source of concern for the Romans. A Roman protectorate in Illyria on the eastern shore was perhaps a natural outgrowth of that concern, and no one at the time looked upon it as a springboard for a future Roman attempt to overrun mainland Greece. Illyria was eventually to become just that, but the cause was Philip V of Macedon and not Roman design.

Philip was at the outset the promising and attractive monarch of a reviving Macedonian kingdom who won high marks in Greece by curbing the predatory Aetolian League in B.C. 217. An Aetolian conquest was not, however, the limit of his somewhat erratic ambitions, and in B.C. 216 Philip thought to profit from Rome's preoccupation with Carthage by sending his fleet into the

Adriatic and appropriating a slice of the coast. By the next year Philip was in open alliance with Hannibal, and the disaster at Cannae, coupled with Hannibal's occupation of Tarentum, made this apparent closure of Rome's two chief tormentors a source of suspicion and fear.

The Romans were in no position to deal with both these threats simultaneously and so raised up counterweights against Philip in Greece, notably the vengeance-bent Aetolian League and its allies. Among the latter was the Anatolian kingdom of Pergamum.[2] Rome's allies did most of the fighting against Philip between B.C. 210 and B.C. 206, and the war broke off distractedly and indecisively. Philip was still in the Adriatic substantially undamaged. The conflict did reveal to him, however, that the system of alliances that he had put together in Greece was built on sand.

After B.C. 206 Philip's eyes turned toward the Aegean, and though offered the opportunity to serve—profitably, it could be expected—as the protector of Egypt, he chose instead a pact with Antiochus III which had as its object the dismemberment of what remained of the Ptolemaic empire. Philip's share was the Aegean, where he clumsily roused the fears of two of Rome's allies, Rhodes and Pergamum. The two states were caught between Philip on one side and an energetic Antiochus III on the other, and despite their misgivings about the long-range effects, they had little recourse but to summon Rome against Philip.

The Romans dealt with Philip, this time decisively, at Cynoscephalae in B.C. 197,[3] and a year later, after the terms of the peace had been settled, they made a grandiose announcement at Corinth that the Greeks had at last been liberated from Macedonian tyranny. Immediately afterward Rome withdrew her forces from Greece, though not for very long. In chasing Philip from the Aegean, Rome left the door open for Antiochus III. The Seleucids had claims on Anatolia going back to Corupedion and somewhat less substantial ones on Thrace, which Antiochus also

---

2. On the religious aspects of this courtship of the East see Chapter XII, p. 475.
3. Rome was to have further troubles with both the Macedonians and the Greeks of Achaea. Another war was fought against Philip's son Perseus (B.C. 171–168), and after a final outburst against Rome in Corinth in B.C. 146, Macedonia and Greece were incorporated into the Roman provincial system.

occupied in B.C. 196. Rome probably cared little about what Antiochus did with Anatolia, but the occupation of Thrace put the Seleucid in dangerous proximity to Philip V in Macedon.

Antiochus could probably have been bluffed out of Thrace— he had never shown an interest in a confrontation with Rome or in any expansion at her expense, and he had carefully picked his way around Rome's allies, Rhodes and Pergamum, in Anatolia. Not carefully enough, however, to suit Eumenes of Pergamum, who goaded some of the Anatolian *poleis* to take their case to Rome. They did, and provided an issue on which Antiochus felt he could not yield.

The Romans met and defeated Antiochus' Aegean expeditionary force at the hallowed but still strategic pass of Thermopylae in B.C. 191, and an army led by Scipio Africanus pursued him into Asia, where in the following year they delivered the *coup de grâce* to Seleucid pretensions at Magnesia-by-Sipylus. According to the terms of a treaty signed at Apamea in Phrygia in B.C. 188, Antiochus had to surrender all his recent acquisitions north of the Taurus. Rome divided these spoils between the Rhodians and the Pergamenes.

The reward was deserved. In Pergamum, Rome had a powerful and faithful ally in Asia. Under three ambitious but enlightened kings, Attalus I (B.C. 241–197), Eumenes II (B.C. 197–159) and Attalus II (B.C. 159–138), Pergamum had grown from a petty kingdom rising from the wreckage of Lysimachus' holdings in Asia to the premier state in Anatolia, exercising a generally reasonable sovereignty over the Greek cities of the northwest coast, holding the Celtic Galatians of the interior in check, and creating a minor but brilliant culture. Set upon the top of an easily defensible hill, the city itself was supplied with all the public amenities, including a closed sewage system, and was elaborately decorated with the grandiose sculpture of the time. Eumenes' monumental altar still gives some feeling of the wealth and pride of the period's Pergamene kings, who were revered as gods and saviors of Hellenism. There was a state library of some two hundred thousand volumes,[4] and like the similar but larger collection at Alexandria it provided a seedbed for Hellenistic scholarship. A catalogue was prepared, and the Pergamene

---

4. Later given by Antony to Cleopatra. It is not known whether the books were ever delivered.

savants engaged in scholarly dialogue with their opposite numbers at Alexandria on questions of Homeric criticism and grammar.

The sources of the affluence that made these cultural displays possible were varied. There was, of course, tribute from the subject cities, but the kings of Pergamum encouraged and actively supervised their own projects in animal husbandry and textile manufacture. They held a firm grip on the valuable pitch deposits of Mt. Ida. But it was probably an economic *institution* that played the major role in Pergamum's wealth: state-owned factories manned by slaves and serfs. It was these factories that enabled the kings of Pergamum to direct their cattle raising toward the mass production of parchment (which was widely known as *pergamene*) on which they held a virtual monopoly.

This was the complex of culture, trade and imperialism that passed into the hands of the Romans at the death of Attalus III in B.C. 133. Why this rather strange man, who raised poisonous herbs for pleasure, bequeathed his kingdom to the Romans in his will is not entirely clear, but the Romans hastily accepted, becoming, by their acceptance, an Asiatic power. The birth of the Roman province of Asia was not unattended by pain. In B.C. 132 Aristonicus, the half brother of Attalus III, fired up an insurrection against the new Roman presence in Anatolia. After an initial stunning victory over the Roman consul Publius Crassus, Aristonicus sought out new sources of support and worked at stirring up the disenfranchised and dispossessed of Asia, particularly those of Pergamum.

The Pergamenes had apparently scented social revolution; even before Aristonicus began preaching his revolutionary message they had granted full citizenship to all their resident aliens, and raised the serfs and slaves of Pergamum to free, resident-alien status. Social and economic revolution, whether based on cynical *Realpolitik* or ideology,[5] was no match for Roman arms. The consul in B.C. 130, Marcus Perperna, crushed the insurrection and

---

5. The latter supplied by the presence in Aristonicus' army of the Stoic Gaius Blossius of Cumae, a student of the Stoic scholar Antipater of Tarsus and friend and adviser of the Roman revolutionary Tiberius Gracchus. Whatever the utopian ideas of Blossius, it was a period of great general unrest. The slaves on the plantations of Italy were in mass revolt in B.C. 135-132, and there were slave uprisings at about the same time on Delos and in Macedon and Attica.

captured Aristonicus. Both Aristonicus and the treasure of the Attalids were sent back to Rome, the former to be strangled and the latter to be sold at public auction.

At a stroke the Romans fell heir not only to the Attalids' gold and silver but also to the natural and industrial wealth of Asia, its venerable traditions, and its almost inexhaustible pool of rugged manpower. There were richer treasures beyond: the mercantile wealth and millennial cultures of Syria, Mesopotamia and Egypt, and the way to India and the Far East. The Seleucids and the Ptolemies were approaching their end time, and when Rome struck them they fell almost noiselessly. But before that was to be, there was a far more serious threat to Rome—in Asia Minor itself.

At the time of the Roman inheritance of Attalus' domains, inner Anatolia was dominated by the three kingdoms of Bithynia, Paphlagonia and Pontus, each embracing part of the coastal plain and mountainous hinterland along the southern coast of the Black Sea, with Bithynia on the west laying claim to both shores of the Bosporus and the Propontus as well. They were essentially feudal states, but their holdings on the coastland gave them possession of the Hellenic *poleis* founded as trading posts during the Greeks' colonial expansion into the Black Sea region in the eighth and seventh centuries. Thus the kings of Pontus lorded it in their upland fortress at Amasia, while they controlled the considerable coastal trade flowing between and through Sinope, Amisus and Trapezus (Trebizond). About B.C. 120 the ruler of that land, Mithridates V Euergetes, was assassinated, and the kingdom passed into the hands of his wife and his then eleven-year-old son, the future Mithridates VI Eupator.

Even after Corupedion in B.C. 281 the Seleucids were unable to control Pontus, and under Pharnaces I (B.C. 185–157) this Anatolian kingdom began to expand at the expense of its neighbors. Pharnaces' maneuvers brought him into collision with Pergamum and to the attention of Rome. Rome's admonitions little impressed the distant Pontic king, but a coalition army of Pergamenes and Cappadocians proved more persuasive, and in B.C. 180 Pharnaces was forced to evacuate the territories of neighboring Cappadocia and Galatia.

In the aftermath of the war, and after the death of Pharnaces, Rome bound the kings of Pergamum, Bithynia, Cappadocia and Pontus to herself by treaty. The interlocking alliances should have assured peace in Anatolia, and they did for nearly half a century, or until the accession of Mithridates VI in Pontus. This promising young man had murdered his mother and brother to gain the throne before his twentieth birthday. His first excursions into foreign policy were not against the Romans at all. Summoned by the citizens of the Greek city of Chersonesus in the Crimea against the threatening Scyths, Mithridates intervened across the Black Sea and ended by annexing the Crimea and its agricultural riches to his kingdom. At about the same time he extended his control of the southern coast of the Black Sea as far as Trapezus.

Mithridates grew more daring as the Romans became progressively more involved with the Germans to their north. Taking advantage of Rome's distraction he and Nicomedes, the king of Bithynia, partitioned Paphlagonia between them, while Mithridates moved troops into Galatia to the southwest. The situation in Cappadocia, lying in central Anatolia between Pontus and Syria, was likewise promising. The queen there was Mithridates' sister Laodice, and when the Pontic king took the somewhat incautious step of engineering the assassination of her husband, Laodice countered with the retort unforeseen, and married Nicomedes of Bithynia.

The struggle between the two dynasts for the lady's Cappadocian dowry was, however, forestalled by the intervention of Rome, which in B.C. 95 put its own candidate on the throne of Cappadocia. Mithridates was not to be thwarted. He married his daughter Cleopatra to Tigranes, king of Armenia, the eastern neighbor of Cappadocia, and induced him to invade Cappadocia as his surrogate. The Romans were not deceived; in B.C. 92 Sulla was sent out with an army to clear Cappadocia. He performed his commission but, new in the ways of the East, he withdrew prematurely, leaving Mithridates sobered but intact.

Four years later Mithridates was ready to reply. The Romans and Bithynians had massed for a punitive attack on Pontus, but Mithridates went over to the offensive. He swept the Roman forces from western Anatolia and briefly reduced the first proud Roman province of Asia to a heap of fragmented cities. This was no mere war but a genuine anti-Roman crusade. In B.C. 88, in the wake of his stunning conquest, Mithridates bade the peoples of Asia rise up on an announced day and massacre the Romans in their midst. Whether in resentment at the growing burden of

Roman rapacity or fear of the looming presence of Mithridates, the command was carried out, in some places reluctantly, and between eighty and a hundred and fifty thousand Roman and Italian officials and functionaries were murdered. At the same time Mithridates proclaimed the liberation of Greece and sent armies there to cast out the Romans.

The Romans finally bestirred themselves. Sulla took an army to Greece in B.C. 87 and within a year swept out the Pontic forces, though with terrible devastation to the land and the people. Sulla's political problems back at Rome were mounting, but Mithridates' position in Asia was disintegrating even more rapidly. Either because the experience of Mithridates was even less gentle than the Roman occupation or because the eventual victory of Rome was already clear, the cities of Asia began rising up against their "liberator." Once again the kill was averted. In B.C. 85 Mithridates made peace with a Sulla who had almost lost interest in his Asian projects in the face of his mounting troubles at home. Mithridates was allowed to return unscathed to Pontus; the kings of Bithynia and Cappadocia were restored.

In the years that followed, Rome's holdings in Asia grew. At the death of Nicomedes IV in B.C. 74, it inherited his kingdom of Bithynia. It was southern Anatolia, however, where a new kind of enemy had gradually revealed itself and, in time, claimed most of Rome's attention. In B.C. 167, because of a suspicion that the Rhodians had sided with Macedon in the late war, Rome had stripped Rhodes of its possessions on the mainland—notably Lycia and Caria, which became Roman protectorates—and declared Rhodes' island competitor, Delos, a free port.

Either the Romans did not understand the important services performed by Rhodes in southwest Anatolia or they did not foresee how badly they would need those services. It was a strong maritime Rhodes that held the pirates of the Anatolian coast and, indeed, the entire eastern Mediterranean, in check. As the Roman economy grew ever more dependent upon an ample supply of slaves for its huge estates, the free port of Delos became the Mediterranean's chief slave emporium and, no longer protected by the naval power of Rhodes, a source of plunder for the increasingly active pirates who hid in the vastnesses of Cilicia and raided as far west as Italy and Sicily.

Rome made some tentatives at controlling the piracy. Both the grandfather and the painfully inept father of the later triumvir

Mark Antony were given commands against the pirates (B.C. 102–74). In B.C. 78 the general Servilius was sent out, and his campaigns in the south of Anatolia led to the annexation of Lycia and Isauria. At some time previous Caria too had become part of the province of Asia, and at the end of the first Mithridatic War Cilicia was given independent provincial status. None of this appreciably hampered the activity of the pirates, who continued to raid in the eastern Mediterranean from their Cilician bases. In B.C. 74 Lucullus, an earlier associate of Sulla in his wars against Pontus, was given a mandate to clear Cilicia. Before it could be accomplished Mithridates had reappeared on the scene.

Cappadocia was once again the cause, and his son-in-law, Tigranes, was now Mithridates' chosen instrument. Tigranes overran Cappadocia on cue, and Mithridates, ever the opportunist, opened negotiations with the Roman secessionist Quintus Sertorius in Spain, who sent out aides to reorganize the Pontic army on Roman lines. The brand-new province of Bithynia fell quickly, and Mithridates marched on to defeat a Roman army and naval detachment at Chalcedon. But before Cyzicus the Pontic army stalled. Lucullus came up from Cilicia with his troops and the besiegers became the besieged. Within two years (B.C. 74–72) Mithridates' mighty armament was destroyed. Lucullus pursued his prey into Pontus, but in vain; Mithridates escaped to Tigranes in Armenia.

Lucullus had no choice but to take up the onerous task of an invasion of Armenia, which he began in B.C. 69. His position at home was being seriously undermined by political intrigue, and his soldiers were showing signs of restiveness at the prospect of a campaign into what appeared to them at the time as the Far East. But before the ebb of his tide, Lucullus achieved two remarkable victories over the Armenians, capturing the new capital at Tigranocerta and forcing the Armenians to withdraw from their protectorate in northern Syria, where the last tottering Seleucid was restored by the Romans to his tarnished throne.

There was still the question of Mithridates. Tigranes sacrificed hospitality to discretion and sent his lively father-in-law back to Pontus, where Mithridates repossessed his kingdom and inflicted a series of embarrassing defeats upon the Roman occupation forces. Before Mithridates could be dislodged Lucullus was recalled to Rome, and the dubious honor of pursuing this elusive warrior fell to another.

While Lucullus was still in the East the Senate in B.C. 67 passed the Gabinian Law that created an extraordinary command (*imperium*) designed to deal with the pirates. It was similar to the one given earlier to Mark Antony *père*, who had fumbled it away on Crete. This time, however, Rome had found its man, the recent hero of the Spanish campaign against Sertorius, Pompey. He took up his great powers and within three months the pirates were not only swept from the seas but also pursued and destroyed in their mountain retreats in Cilicia. It was a stunning victory that permanently contained the threat of piracy in the Roman Mediterranean and brought Pompey to the center of the stage in the East.[6]

In the following year, B.C. 66, it was proposed by the Tribune Manilius that Pompey replace Lucullus in the East, and the *Lex Manilia* accordingly gave him a new *imperium* against Mithridates and Tigranes. The latter was having his own troubles. His son, also named Tigranes, had raised the banner of revolt in Armenia and when put to flight by the king took refuge with *his* father-in-law, Phraates III, king of Parthia. There was, then, no hope for Mithridates from Tigranes on this occasion. Nor was there even refuge in Armenia when Pompey finally ran the king to ground in Pontus; Tigranes cast Mithridates' messengers into chains when they arrived with his request for asylum. Mithridates finally did escape, fleeing east for Colchis. This incredibly tough old man struggled across the Caucasus to his son's lair in the Crimea, where he finally died in B.C. 63 in the midst of an attempt to raise Danubian soldiers for an invasion of Italy.[7] When the news of his death reached Rome there was a public festival for ten consecutive days.

One understands. For forty years this resourceful old war lord had been provoking the Romans in Asia, defeating or eluding every general sent out against him, raising the cry of nationalism and freedom among the Asians, and yet showing himself the equal of the Romans in repression, almost invincible in the mountains of Pontus, and capable of enormous mischief everywhere from Greece to the Tigris. The Romans never faced

---

6. On its possible religious consequences see Chapter XII, p. 478.
7. An attempt to take poison failed, since the old man had for years been systematically imbibing poison to build up his immunity against this form of assassination. He asked a soldier to run him through with a sword instead.

another like him. And in their forty-year attempt to engulf him they swallowed all of Asia and, by an almost accidental gesture, toppled the Seleucids as well.

The Climate of Judaea

Pompey's punitive expedition in the East turned into a triumphal progress. With Mithridates in flight to the Crimea, Pompey reduced Tigranes' kingdom of Armenia[8] and then marched on to the Caucasus, nearly reaching the Caspian before returning to Pontus in the spring of B.C. 64. The former kingdom of Mithridates became the province of Pontus, and Roman supporters were installed in Galatia and Cappadocia.

Later in B.C. 64 Pompey turned to the south, to Cilicia-on-the-Plain (*Cilicia Campestris*), the flatland south of the Taurus restored to the Seleucids when Lucullus had driven out Tigranes' viceroy. At Antioch Pompey abrogated that agreement. The Seleucid throne, by now the plaything of two local Arab dynasts who removed and restored Antiochus XIII and his cousin Philip II at will, served no useful purpose for the Romans, and Pompey dissolved the line. *Cilicia Campestris* and Syria were thereafter to be Roman provinces; and to serve as a carapace against the power of Parthia and Armenia, local chieftains were confirmed in a series of petty states masking the eastern frontiers of Cilicia and Syria—Antiochus in Commagene, Abgar in Osrhoene, and Aretas in the land of the Nabataeans—extending from Damascus to Petra. Judaea was a special case; there was no tribal chieftain there, and Pompey had to choose between rival claimants of the High Priesthood.

Pompey's involvement in Judaea was involuntary, but nonetheless inevitable. The factions warring there had long been in the habit of appealing to their Seleucid and Nabataean neighbors, who were generally delighted to intervene. The current dispute in Judaea was between the sons of Alexander Jannaeus—Hyrcanus and Aristobulus. Hyrcanus was the heir, but Aristobulus clearly was the more aggressive, and at the death of their mother,

---

8. The younger Tigranes was not put in his father's place as he had hoped, but was featured instead in the triumph Pompey later celebrated in Rome. His father was content, but his father-in-law, Phraates III of Parthia, was not pleased.

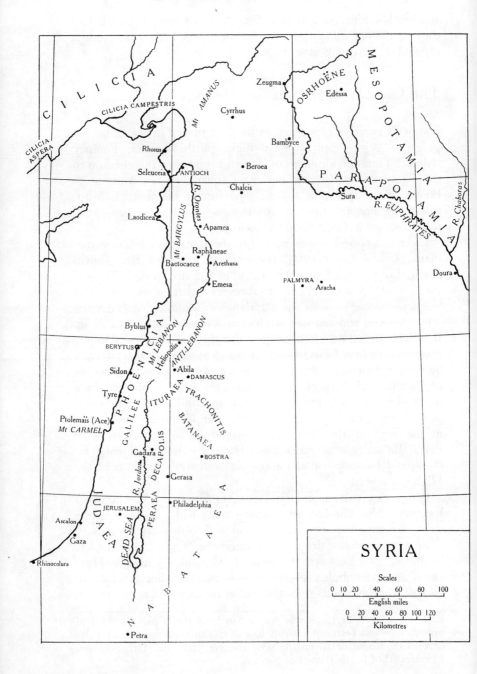

C I L I C I A

CILICIA CAMPESTRIS

CILICIA
ASPERA

Mt AMANUS

Zeugma

OSRHOËNE

M E S O P O T A M I A

Edessa

Cyrrhus

Rhosus

Bambyce

Seleuceia • ANTIOCH

• Beroea

R. Oronies

Chalcis

P A R A P O T A M I A

Sura

R. EUPHRATES

R. Chaboras

Laodicea

Mt BARGYLUS

• Apamea

Raphaneae

Baetocaece • Arethusa

• Emesa

PALMYRA

Aracha

Doura

Byblus

BERYTUS

Mt LEBANON

ANTI-LEBANON

Heliopolis

Abila

Sidon

• DAMASCUS

Tyre

ITURAEA

TRACHONITIS

P H O E N I C I A

Ptolemaïs (Ace)

Mt CARMEL

G A L I L E E

BATANAEA

Gadara

DECAPOLIS

• BOSTRA

R. Jordan

• Gerasa

JUDAEA

PERAEA

JERUSALEM

DEAD SEA

• Philadelphia

Ascalon

Gaza

B A T A N A E A

Rhinocolura

N A B A T A E A

• Petra

SYRIA

Scales

0 10 20   40   60   80   100
English miles

0   20 40 60 80 100 120
Kilometres

Alexandra Salome, in B.C. 67, Aristobulus moved against his brother, and would surely have deposed him permanently but for the arrival of a new figure upon the scene, Antipater the Idumaean.[9] Antipater took up the cause of Hyrcanus and persuaded him to take his case to Aretas (Harith), king of the Nabataean Arabs and an old foe of Jannaeus. This Hyrcanus did, and supported by Arab troops, he had Aristobulus penned up within the walls of Jerusalem when the Roman vanguard arrived.

The Roman in question was Marcus Aemilius Scaurus, Pompey's chief legate in the East, who had just come up from Damascus. Pompey was still in Armenia at the time (B.C. 65), and Scaurus decided, on the basis of a substantial bribe, that justice was on the side of Aristobulus. Aretas, Antipater and Hyrcanus withdrew, but when, in B.C. 63, Pompey himself was in Damascus, Antipater approached the Roman *imperator* to reopen the case. After suitable negotiations Pompey decided for Hyrcanus and went in person to Jerusalem to dislodge Aristobulus:[10] his support apparently did not extend to Aretas, however, since he dispatched Aemilius Scaurus to Petra to reduce the Nabataean capital. According to Josephus, Jerusalem fell on the Sabbath, when the Jews refused to resist. On its fall Pompey gratified his curiosity by entering the Holy of Holies; but the temple treasures he did not touch.

Judaea was now incorporated into the eastern defensive system. Hyrcanus was confirmed as High Priest; no more is heard of Antipater for the immediate present. Aristobulus was carried off to Rome with his family (a son, Alexander, escaped en route) to grace Pompey's triumph. The territories of Judaea were added to Syria so that what, in effect, remained was the temple state of Jerusalem, ruled by a High Priest and under the close supervision of the Propraetors, subsequently the Proconsuls, of Syria. The first of these was Scaurus himself (B.C. 62–59).

Pompey's settlement in Judaea was not so much for the purpose of creating a buffer state, as in Cappadocia or Commagene, but was probably analagous to what he had done with

---

9. Descendants of the Biblical Edomites, the Idumaeans were dislodged from their position in the Transjordan in the fourth century by the Nabataeans and subsequently settled in the lands south of Judaea. They were forcibly circumcised by John Hyrcanus.

10. It was at Jericho on his way to Jerusalem that Pompey heard of Mithridates' death.

the temple state of the Anatolian Great Mother, appropriately called Ma, at Comana in Pontus: its integrity was respected and a native Hellenized prince, Archelaus, was put in charge. Pompey could afford to be indulgent of local traditions centering around an altar and a bank and without an army. That Jerusalem was somewhat more complex than Comana he had no way at present of telling.

The career of the Jews after the destruction of the Babylonian Empire that had held them in thrall was a series of political hopes dashed to disappointment. The liberal Achaemenian Cyrus was hailed as a liberator by the Jewish prophets of the sixth century, but the rule of his successors was not the blessing that was anticipated. The death of the mad Achaemenian Shah Cambyses in B.C. 521 had kindled new hope for a liberator sprung from the line of David, but such was not to be, and the next generation of prophets reflected the growing sense of disappointment. The earlier prophets had immediate and historical expectations; the hopes of their fifth-century successors were postponed into a timeless, eschatological future. The great redemptive warrior charged with the liberation of a historical Israel became a transcendental figure engaged in a cosmic war.

The early successes of the Maccabees did not change these orientations. The "Day of Yahweh," those events in another dimension foreseen by the latest prophets, was not fulfilled in the bloody deeds visited upon Judaea after B.C. 166, nor in Simon's solemn assumption of power in Jerusalem in B.C. 140. The Hasmonaeans lost their own theologians, and with them whatever expectation they may have had of theological justification. Their firmest supporters, the Sadducees, did not even accept the prophetic books into their canon of Scripture. They were immune to Messianic longings.

Few others were. On the testimony of the literature, a large part of the Jewish community had deserted history in favor of an eschatological future when all would be set aright. Writings sounding that theme appear as a mere trickle during the Seleucid era in Palestine, but with the coming of the Romans they were in full flood and did not ebb for a century or more after the beginning of the Christian era.

The characteristic form of the new eschatological literature was the apocalypse, the "revelation" of the events of the last days of human history, when time and eternity come together and the human drama of history is absorbed into a cosmic one. Apocalypses appeared all over the *oikoumene* and in a variety of versions. In its developed form it is most generally cast in the form of a prophetic vision, heavily weighted with both popular and learned lore, numerology, astrology, philosophy and an impressionistic view of history buried deep within an almost impenetrable symbolism. Such were the visions in *Daniel*, one of the earliest of the genre, in *Enoch*, the *Apocalypse of Moses*, the *Testament of the Twelve Patriarchs*, the *Psalms of Solomon*, the fourth book of *Ezra* and the second of *Baruch* and, to cite but a single example from the early Christian literature, the *Apocalypse of Christ*, better known as the *Apocalypse of John*.

According to these visionary accounts, the Messiah, the "anointed one,"[11] will come, sometimes as a preliminary signal of the last days, sometimes during them, and the nation of Israel will be restored. Various mathematical calculations were invoked and signs and portents were described to provide clues to his imminent coming. It was generally believed that the prophet Elias would precede him. Some of the apocalypses saw the Messiah as a transcendent, divine being, but that view was by no means universal; traditionalist Pharisees discouraged such talk, and a transcendent Messiah is curiously absent from the apocalypses of the recently revealed community of Jewish sectaries living at Qumran on the western shores of the Dead Sea.

It was this widespread notion of the "end time" that set the tone of a great deal of Jewish spirituality in the post-exilic period. It also reveals the impressive extent of Greek and Iranian penetration into later Jewish thinking. Even the Pharisees, the guardians of orthodoxy under the Hasmonaeans and the Romans, believed in an immortal soul and, in contrast to the Scripturally more conservative Sadducees, in the resurrection after death, a doctrine that finds its classical formulation in the books of *Ezra* and *Baruch*.

None of this came from a single source, as is clear from the widely diverse forms that these ideas take. Was the resurrection and judgment a function of the fact that *all* men have an immortal soul, or was it part of the exaltation of the nation of Israel? The rabbis disagreed, and it is difficult to determine

---

11. In Greek, *Christos*.

whether one is catching the accents of philosophy or those of nationalism. The same type of ambiguity appears in descriptions of the place of man's eternal reward. In some instances, in *Ezra*, for example, this is a paradise modeled after Adam's abode in *Genesis;* in others, like *Enoch*, it is part of the whole complex of Messianic ideas and so takes the form of a heavenly Palestine and a heavenly Jerusalem. For the evil there is reserved Gehenna, a place that began its career modestly as the city dump of Jerusalem and ended it as the flaming hell of apocalyptic Judaism, replacing in the process the shadowy Sheol of the earlier Jews, which, like the Homeric Hades, had not been connected with any eschatological punishment.

That there were foreign, particularly Greek and Iranian, ideas at work can scarcely be doubted, but the influence is masked, as it frequently is in revelational religions, by the anonymous authors' habit of referring their visions back to older and more orthodox authorities. The post-exilic generations of Judaism produced a considerable apocalyptic literature reflecting the religious preoccupations and political anxieties of their own times, but it was invariably circulated as the work of earlier, and hence more respectable, authors; thus, the *Apocalypse of Moses* and the *Psalms of Solomon.* Or else the new material was inserted into already existing works, as was the case with the apocalypses edited into the writings of nonapocalyptic prophets like Isaiah and Zachariah.

It was also the age of classicism in religious literature. The same piety toward the past and a gradually closing canon of authentic Scripture that impelled some toward forgery directed others to cast their thought in the form of commentaries on the body of recognized Scripture.[12] Philo read the Torah and glossed it as an expression of a "Mosaic philosophy," while from the very same texts the Palestinian Pharisees and the rabbis of Babylonia extracted their legal prescriptions (*halachoth*). The two approaches were widely different, but they by no means exhausted the possibilities. With the discovery of the library of the Qumran sectaries it has become certain that there was also a Messianic and eschatological "reading" of the standard Scripture that was in vogue in Palestine, something that had been suspected from the

---

12. Exactly the same phenomenon was making its appearance in Hellenic philosophical circles in the first century (see Chapter IX, pp. 362–65).

early Christian practice but has now received elaborate confirmation.

The commentaries written or studied at Qumran are not easy going. The scholars there read the texts before them with their own peculiar understanding. Just as the second-century Christian Gnostic saw in the Gospels a symbolic statement of his own cosmic mythology, so the Qumran exegete read all Scripture in terms of his own eschatology, as a guide to the "final days," which were felt to be very close at hand. In *Nahum* and *Habakkuk* he caught veiled allusions to contemporary history, both to the secular events of the day[13] and to the more parochial history of his own community. He scanned the pages for signs of the Messiah.

During the last two or three centuries before the Christian era the premonitions about the end of time were widespread in the Jewish community, not only in Palestine but, as the translation of much of the apocalyptic literature into Greek suggests, in the Diaspora as well. The sentiments they aroused were a curious blend of anxiety and exaltation, since there would soon be at hand both the time of troubles announcing the Messiah and the glorified restoration of the nation of Israel.

The concept of the Messiah was an attractive political instrument, and dissident groups in Palestine availed themselves of it, particularly against the Romans. Jesus of Nazareth was not the first, nor was Bar Kokhba the last, to become involved in the cross fire between apocalypticism and politics, though the magnitude of the latter disaster probably discouraged the later rabbis from lending their prestige to future claimants.[14]

The Pharisees, who from the days of John Hyrcanus stood at the spiritual center of Palestinian Judaism, had embraced Messianism and had high hopes for the Kingdom of God, though not perhaps in full-blown apocalyptic fashion. The Sadducees on the other hand rejected all such notions. They were firmly rooted, politically and spiritually, in the historical present. Nor was that all. The rabbinical version of history, fashioned in the years after the great Roman wars at the academies in Palestine and Babylonia, and set forth in the dense and rich pages of the Talmuds, allowed a great silence to descend upon the incredible profusion

13. See Chapter VII, pp. 285–86.
14. See Chapter XIV, pp. 531–32.

of sects, attitudes and expectations that grew up among the Jews in Palestine and the Diaspora under the uneasy reign of the Hasmonaeans and the Romans. When Pompey came to Palestine, contemporary Judaism had a wide spectrum of belief, which ranged from zealot to quietist and knew every nuance of hope and despair.

Some of the programs and activities of these groups glimmer from the pages of Josephus, but he was writing for Hellenized readers little interested in Jewish sectarianism. Among his other helpful suggestions to these readers was that the chief Jewish sects (*haireseis*) might be compared to the various schools of Greek philosophy. The Pharisees were like Jewish Stoics; the Sadducees were like the Epicureans; and the third sect, the Essenes, most resembled the Pythagoreans. Others had heard about Josephus' latter group. Philo was aware of them, and Pliny knew that there was a community of Essenes at Ayn Geddi, near the Dead Sea. At the beginning of the ninth century the attention of the Nestorian bishop of Iraq was called to some rather remarkable manuscripts from that same area.

Beginning in 1947 Josephus' "Pythagoreans" began to come to light. The chance discovery of the site of the central Essene community at Khirbet Qumran on the western shore of the Dead Sea, quite as Pliny had located it, was followed by other equally spectacular finds, including part of the community's library secreted in nearby caves. The ramifications were immense. New chapters in the history of the Bible could be written and new perspectives opened into the origins of Christianity. But, above all, the discoveries provided nothing short of a revelation in the history of Palestinian Judaism.

Sometime about B.C. 140, when Simon the Hasmonaean was consecrated High Priest of the Jews with the support of the Seleucid Demetrius II, the followers of another, probably hereditary, pretender to the High Priesthood—his name is unknown—followed their leader into what amounted to secession from the Maccabean coalition. They may have been a branch of the Hasidim, but they were far more radical than the others, who remained behind and did not go into overt opposition until the time of John Hyrcanus.[15] Those latter-day opponents of the Hasmonaeans, the Pharisees, though cast from the same Hasidic

---

15. See Chapter VII, pp. 288–89.

mold, chose to fight their battles in the towns; the Essene radicals followed their "Righteous Teacher," as the pretender was called in the oblique language of the sect, into the wilderness, taking up their station at Qumran and at secondary camps scattered through Judaea, where they gathered to await the coming of the "end of days."[16]

Philo and Josephus are in agreement that the sect numbered about four thousand members. The settlement at Qumran seems to date from the days of John Hyrcanus (B.C. 134–105), and on the archaeological evidence the complex there was destroyed by an earthquake in B.C. 31, but was reoccupied in force about the beginning of the Christian era. The community was in full operation until its destruction by the Roman soldiers of Vespasian's *Legio X Fretensis* in the summer of A.D. 68. A Roman garrison lingered on for a while after the fall of Jerusalem in A.D. 70, but the site was finally deserted to squatters and then to silence.

The Essenes were not, of course, Pythagoreans. They were Jews, an apocalyptic and separatist community of Jews, scribal, liturgical and priestly in nature, and leading a life of communal asceticism. The Essenes had, like their more moderate counterparts, the Pharisees, a fastidious regard for the Law, but their perspectives were altered by the fact that they were living under a New Covenant on the threshold of the Last Days. They awaited the imminent arrival of two Messiahs, a priest of Aaron and a Davidic king.

The Essenes' elaborate liturgical life centered around a baptism for the repentance of sins and a communal meal celebrated twice daily. Only the initiated were admitted to this repast, which was a liturgical anticipation of the final eschatological banquet with the Messiah. Ritual purity was of the utmost importance, and another link with their Pharisaic cousins was the scribal complexion of their life. A large number of Biblical texts were copied and commented upon in their own peculiar manner; the "history" of the community, heavily overlaid with an almost opaque symbolism, was committed to writing, as were the rules. At Qumran itself one of the rooms of the complex was a scriptorium.

Other qualities seem to set the Essenes off from the Pharisees.

---

16. The Essene camps are mentioned by Philo and Josephus, but no archaeological trace of them has been found.

Their founder was a priest, and they were dominated by priestly practices and ideals. Some of them may have been celibate, though Philo and Josephus are at odds on this point. There is a similar ambiguity on the subject of war. Despite the marked military tone of their writings and the appointments of the camp center at Qumran, there are grounds for thinking that the war they envisioned was an apocalyptic one. The Essenes saw themselves as priestly soldiers in the army of God, standing at arms for the call to a final Holy War. They could hardly have expected that it would come in the profane person of Vespasian.[17]

The destruction of Qumran by the Romans by no means ended the apocalyptic expectations of the Jews. There were signs and portents seen in the wake of Trajan's Parthian campaigns, and in A.D. 135 the final cataclysmic Roman thrust into the heart of Palestinian Judaism was provoked by still another Messianic figure, Bar Kokhba. Then there was an end to it. Constantly and violently dashed hopes turned instead to the quietism of the rabbinical Pharisee, or perhaps even to a pessimism so deeply experienced that it led to the total rejection of the God of Israel and into the anti-Jewish and anticosmic terrain of Gnosticism.[18] Talk of the end time and of Messiahs was stilled in Judaism.

Before the end, however, one Messiah emerged from the bosom of Palestinian Judaism trailing the apocalyptic and eschatological expectations of the sectarian Jews of the first century into the *oikoumene*. Jesus of Nazareth, once thought to be the creation of the mystery fanciers of later Hellenism, is now at least clearly understood as a typical, if moderate, representative of the same climate that produced the Qumran sectaries, Enoch, Ezra and Baruch, the Zealots of Jerusalem, and Bar Kokhba himself.

The Romans understood little or nothing of this; Josephus had not yet come to enlighten them. Pompey was on a ramble in Syria and stumbled upon the beginnings of another Judaean civil war. What the issues were he probably neither knew nor greatly

---

17. Or perhaps they did. It has been suggested that by the time Vespasian arrived there in the summer of A.D. 68, Qumran was held not by Essenes but by a Zealot contingent. The exact relationship between the apocalyptic and ascetic Essenes and the bellicose and nationalistic Zealots is one of the more intriguing mysteries of the period.

18. See Chapter XVIII, pp. 658–60.

cared. What he did care about was the security of the area in the eastern defensive system and the fate of the Greek *poleis* that the Hasmonaeans had swallowed up into their kingdom. From the outset it was clear that the Romans intended to follow the Seleucid policy of Hellenization in Coele-Syria, and before Pompey left his new possession he unceremoniously amputated all the Seleucids' urban settlements from the bloated Jewish kingdom. Those the Hasmonaeans had not succeeded in razing to the ground he ordered rebuilt and restored to them their free *polis* status within the new Roman province of Syria. The temple state, now reduced to its original modest proportions, was tacked on as a somewhat inglorious appanage.

Republican Governors and Imperial Neighbors

Since the creation of the provincial system in Sicily in B.C. 227, each of the provinces added to the Roman domain was theoretically governed by a charter drawn up by a Senatorial commission. This was done for Asia in B.C. 129–127 under the direction of Marius Aquilius, who was Consul for B.C. 129.[19] In general, the document regularized the relations that formerly existed between Attalus and his subjects, the Roman state standing in place of the king and coming as well into the possession of the crown lands.

The larger provinces were governed by someone acting "for the Consul" (*pro consule*), in practice a Consul of the preceding year whose authority was extended by reason of his being sent out to govern a province. Once he had received his province by lot the new governor took out with him a staff that was in some ways like that of a Consul's at Rome and consisted of a Quaestor to supervise the important question of finance and a number of delegates, or *legati*, to serve as his deputies and advisers. The Proconsul himself had full administrative, judicial, and military

---

19. And the end of whose career illustrates a constant political motif. On his return to Rome Aquilius was tried for extortion (*res repetundae*) and, perhaps typically as well, acquitted. There was a special court set up at Rome under the Lex Calpurnia of B.C. 149 to try such cases. Its constitution varied from the original Senatorial control to Equestrian parity.

command of his province. His normal term of office was one year, though it could be extended.

The administration of the province, civil and military, was supported by a direct tax called "soldier's pay" (*stipendium*), which in Asia took the form of a tithe (*decuma*), or one tenth of the annual yield of the province. This method involved fairly complicated estimates, and the state at first found it more to its advantage to let out contracts for the tax receipts of a province. Bids were submitted by contractors (*publicani*) joined in public holding companies with their chief executive at Rome and the equivalent of an executive vice-president in the province. These tax farmers were drawn from the Equestrian class, which served as their lobby in Rome and so could bring considerable pressure to bear on the provincial governor, with whom they were locked in a death grip of mutual dependence. Since their profits consisted of the difference between their contracted bid and what they actually collected, the *publicani* were forced to exert considerable local pressure. The local communities had, in turn, to resort to another provincial institution, the bankers and money-lenders (*negotiatores*), who charged rates of compounded interest that was on rare occasions as high as 48 percent but was finally stabilized by Lucullus in Asia and Cicero in Cilicia at 12 percent.[20]

Mithridates, the Romans' antagonist in the East for nearly half a century, had been particularly dangerous in that he was constantly poised to take advantage of every misstep in Asia. And the Romans, confronted with their rich new acquisitions, whose working they scarcely understood, showed themselves particularly maladroit on occasion. The politics of Roman Asia pitted the governor, drawn from the Senatorial class and generally interested in good government and public order, against the Equestrian bankers and tax farmers bent on extorting the maximum return from the cities of Asia. The battle between the two was fought in the provinces, but the victory was won in the courts of Rome. Quintus Mucius Scaevola and his legate, Rutilius Rufus, had governed Asia justly and well in B.C. 94, but on his return Rufus was convicted on charges of maladministration in the courts dominated by commercial interests. The verdict granted a license to pillage to those same bankers and tax farmers,

---

20. The former was simple interest; the latter, compounded annually. In the same year the Senate legalized a 12 percent simple interest.

and the immediate consequence was Mithridates' bloodbath of
B.C. 88. In B.C. 85–84 Sulla levied an indemnity on the entire
province of Asia to recompense for the loss of taxes to Rome, and
once again the Asian cities were plunged into debt to the Italian
bankers at ruinous interest rates.

Soon the corruption of the governors began to equal that of
the bankers, particularly after Sulla readjusted the Senatorial
balance in the Roman courts in B.C. 82. At times the rapine was so
great that even a weighted jury could do no other than convict
the miscreant. Such was the case with the governor of Cilicia,
Dolabella, and his notorious legate and treasurer, Verres, who
went out to the East in B.C. 80. Between them they plundered
Asia of its tax and temple moneys. Verres had a particular taste
for provincial art, which he carried off in large quantities.
Dolabella was convicted in B.C. 78, but Verres went on to the
governorship—and the fleecing—of Sicily (B.C. 73–70).[21]

Lucullus tried to govern in the tradition of Scaevola and Rufus,
and he faced similar difficulties. His attempt to reduce interest
rates and indebtedness (the province still staggered under Sulla's
indemnity) was met by the Lex Aurelia of B.C. 70, which
pointedly restored the Equestrian control of the courts, and it
was the growing power of this class that finally deprived Lucullus of his eastern command in B.C. 67. At this juncture Pompey
assumed command, soon to be relieved forever of the presence of
Mithridates and free, as well, to be more randomly adventuresome than any of his predecessors.

Within the provinces Hellenic-type cities, whether going back
to the Greeks or founded by the Romans on Greek models, were
permitted a good deal of self-government. From the very beginning Roman policy encouraged the dismemberment of tribal
conglomerates and movement in the direction of the self-governing polis with its higher sophistication and greater prosperity.
Ideally, the role of the governor was to protect and foster that
growth.

Aulus Gabinius Capito served as governor of Syria, recently
raised to the level of a consular province, in B.C. 57. As Plebeian
Tribune ten years before, he had sponsored the legislation that

---

21. He escaped the first trial by turning state's evidence against
Dolabella, but was finally brought to book in B.C. 70, when Cicero
prosecuted; the case is stated in the latter's two speeches "Against
Verres."

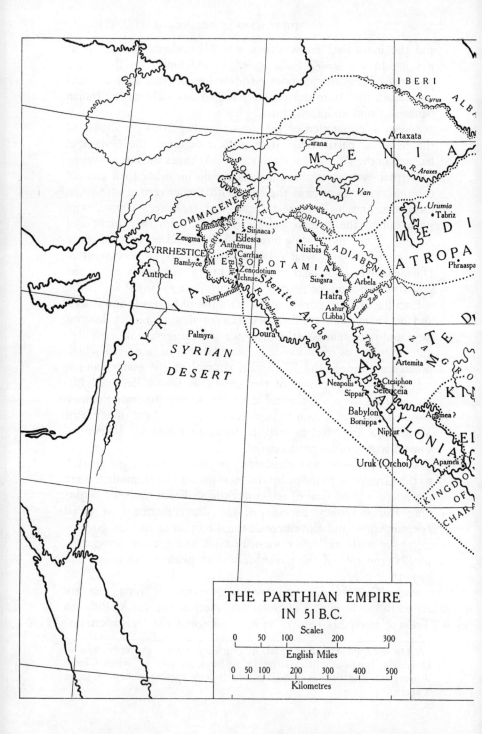

IBERI ALB
R. Cyrus

• Carana   • Artaxata
A R M E N I A
R. Araxes
L. Van   L. Urumia
                              • Tabriz
COMMAGENE   GORDYENE   M E D I
Samosata
Zeugma •   • Sinnaca ?   ADIABENE   ATROPA
Edessa
CYRRHESTICE Anthemus   • Nisibis   Phraaspa
Bambyce •   Carrhae
• Antioch   Zenodotium Singara   • Arbela
Ichnae•   Hatra
S Y R I A   Nicephorium   Ashur   Lesser Zab R.
                            (Libba)
• Palmyra   • Doura
S Y R I A N   P A R T E Artemita
D E S E R T   Skenite Arabs Neapolis
                     B A B Y L O N I A Sippar Seleuceia
                             Babylon Ctesiphon Apamea ?
                             Borsippa
                             Nippur
                             Uruk (Orchoi) Apamea ?
                             KINGDOM OF CHAR

THE PARTHIAN EMPIRE
IN 51 B.C.
Scales
0   50   100   200   300
English Miles
0 50 100   200   300   400   500
Kilometres

CASPIAN SEA

MASSAGETAE

SACARAUCAE

R. Oxus Bokhara

DAHAE

MARGIANE

Merv

YUEH-
CHI

APAVARKTIKENE

Dara

E

R. Ochus of Arius (Tejend)

M   P

ASTAUENE

TAPURIA

ATAUENE

Asaak

TRAXIANE

R. Kasaf-rud

HYRCANIA

COMISENE

P PARTHYENE

Nisa

(Hecatompylos)

MARDI   TAPURI

ELBURZ MTS.

Rhagae

Arsacia

Charax

Caspian Gates

A R I A

Herat

RHAGIANE

CHOARENE

Ecbatana

INDO-PARTHIAN

GDOM

GABIENE

Gabae

Hamun L.

Seistan

KINGDOM

KINGDOM

R. Helmund

Susa

OF

YMAIS

Seleucia?

Charax

Seleucia?

K I N G D O M

Persepolis

OF

P E R S I S

Antioch?

PERSIAN GULF

Portus Macedonum?

Strait of Ormuz

TENE

IA

HIAN

MTS.

NI

deprived Lucullus of his command in Asia,[22] and then introduced the bill creating Pompey's special command against the pirates. It was not unexpected, then, when Gabinius turned up as one of Pompey's legates during his eastern campaign of B.C. 64. He was elected Consul in B.C. 58, and upon completion of his consular year took up the governorship of Syria. According to Cicero, it was a calamitous moment for Rome; he disapproved of Gabinius' politics, his friends, his recreations and his hairdresser. "How much longer," he shouted in B.C. 57, "is that Semiramis going to be kept in Syria?"

During the consulship of Lentulus Spinther in B.C. 55 Rome was filled with talk that Ptolemy XI Auletes, who had been deposed by his volatile Alexandrian subjects, was prepared to buy his way back to the throne of Egypt for an enormous sum. Lentulus fancied the task of restoration for himself, but Pompey too coveted the opportunity, and a stalemate developed when an oracle was produced to the effect that it would be evil medicine indeed if Auletes was restored by force. Gabinius had no such scruples; ten thousand talents were more persuasive than the Sibylline Books. While still governor of Syria, he led an army to Egypt in B.C. 55 only to find enthroned there Archelaus, the erstwhile ruler of the temple state of Comana, who had passed himself off to the Egyptians as a son of Mithridates and married Auletes' daughter, Berenice. He was killed and Auletes was restored.

Both before and after his Egyptian adventure Gabinius was plagued by less profitable disturbances in Judaea. Alexander, the son of Aristobulus, had escaped, as has been noted, from the clutches of Pompey en route to Rome. He inevitably found his way back to Judaea, where he raised an army and an insurrection. Gabinius put down the revolt (his young lieutenant Mark Antony won high marks in battle) and restored Hyrcanus, though with even less political power than before. That was merely the prelude to the escape and return of Aristobulus himself. Again there were disorders, but Aristobulus was captured and once again dispatched in custody to Rome. Afterward Gabinius pursued his Egyptian scheme, assisted by the money and troops of Hyrcanus and his Idumaean vizier, Antipater.

---

22. According to Cicero he stirred up popular dislike for Lucullus by circulating a picture of the latter's sumptuous villa.

Alexander seized upon his absence for another revolt, and Gabinius had to cut short his stay in Egypt to quell this new disturbance.

The Jewish factions of Palestine had shown themselves, from the moment of Pompey's arrival, capable of armed revolt and prolonged resistance in the fortified places in the country, and this was the pattern that was to bedevil the Roman authorities for another century. Under Scaurus and Gabinius the Romans had committed themselves, as a party of the third part, to preserving the peace between the parties of the first and second parts. Their increasing association with the lieutenant of one of these factions, Antipater, led, however, to a deeper level of involvement, wherein Rome was no longer a hapless referee but the immediate object of Jewish discontent.

Gabinius was spared this. His proconsular successors in Syria—Crassus, Cassius and Bibulus—had to face a growing Parthian menace and the threat of civil war, but in B.C. 55 Gabinius was summoned home to stand trial for irregular conduct of his office and for extortion. The business of Auletes' ten thousand talents was still unresolved; Gabinius had also been having increasing troubles with the *publicani*,[23] and so Rome was treated to another of the judicial scandals which her new provinces were casting up with increasing frequency.

Gabinius' trial caused an uproar at Rome. Cicero's years of vilification, the vengeance-minded Equestrians, the flouted oracle, and an avaricious longing for the invisible ten thousand talents of Auletes, all contributed to the feeling of the occasion. But Pompey counted more than all, and Gabinius was acquitted on the first charge of exceeding his commission.[24] In the second trial, for extortion, Pompey made it clear that this time Cicero too would have to back Gabinius. Cicero bowed to the politically inevitable and spoke on behalf of his former whipping boy. The

---

23. Whom he probably treated more severely than his rival Cicero. While still safely in Rome Cicero had wept bitter rhetorical tears for the "wretched *publicani*" whom Gabinius had handed over in bondage to the Syrians and Jews, "people themselves born to bondage." One wonders what Cicero thought after his own gubernatorial experiences with the "wretched *publicani*."

24. In B.C. 57 Gabinius had been granted an unlimited command (*imperium infinitum*) on the motion of Clodius. He claimed that it was sufficiently broad to cover his Egyptian project. It probably was not.

inevitable did not occur; Gabinius was astonishingly convicted and rather pointedly fined ten thousand talents.

The wheels of Roman politics continued to turn, and in B.C. 51 Cicero, as a former Consul, assumed the governorship of the rich and important province of Cilicia. In addition to his Hellenic education at Athens and Rhodes, he had had experience in provincial administration, serving as Quaestor at Lilybaeum in the province of Sicily in B.C. 75. He also knew at first hand the evils of governmental self-aggrandizement from his successful prosecution of Verres, former Quaestor of Cilicia and governor of Sicily. But Cicero was, for all that, an *Eques* by birth and inclination, and, as a member of this commercially oriented class that controlled the syndicates of the *publicani*, he could be trusted not to make too uncomfortable waves overseas.

Cicero had been elected Consul in B.C. 63 and worked for a coalition of the Senatorial and Equestrian classes. His goal was never achieved. His enemies brought about his exile in B.C. 58, but he was recalled the following year and made his peace with both Pompey and Caesar. When he was given the governorship of Cilicia in B.C. 51, he went unwillingly but with sound intent. It was the custom for incoming governors to publish an edict of principle and intent, and Cicero modeled his own on that of probably the best administrator to date in Asia, Mucius Scaevola (B.C. 94–92).[25] He granted to the cities the right to conduct their own courts and, as has been noted, regulated the interest on loans at 12 percent. His administration was frugal and honest to a degree that astounded the inhabitants of the province. He even went to the unheard-of lengths of discouraging local "spontaneous" delegations to Rome to praise outgoing governors. Cicero complied with a recent law of Caesar's that mandated the deposition of copies of the governor's accounts in two cities in the province, even though Bibulus, his contemporary in Syria, refused to do so.

The difficulties of Cilicia were not all internal. During Cicero's term the Parthians broke through the Commagene buffer and were threatening both Syria and Cilicia. This was no mere border skirmish; the magnitude of the danger had been revealed in B.C. 53, when Crassus and a Roman army were destroyed by the

---

25. His uncle of the same name, whom Cicero admired to extravagance and whom he made one of the interlocutors in his dialogue *On the Commonwealth*, had also been governor of Asia in B.C. 120–119.

Parthians at Carrhae. Cicero, who knew nothing of soldiering, marched forth to meet the new threat, and it must have been with a mixed sense of relief and disappointment that he learned that the critical engagement had been won near Antioch in Syria. He exercised himself instead on the local mountaineers.

All in all, it must have been an unpleasant time. On the day his term was up Cicero departed Cilicia leaving the province in the temporary charge of a junior Quaestor who had been there exactly one week. And yet, Cicero, an unwilling governor and a demonstrably honest administrator, left his province with 2,200,000 sesterces in his account with the bankers at Ephesus.[26] This represented his legal share of the booty won by the arms of his province—proceeds of the sale of the captured Cilician mountaineers into slavery, for example. A Roman provincial governor could not help but become rich on a system constructed for his advantage.

The careers of Gabinius and Cicero, very dissimilar men, typify the problems and prospects of the Roman East at a very early stage of its evolution. Rome possessed effective political institutions that showed they could be adapted to local circumstances; the Roman office of Censor, for instance, was frequently grafted onto the local Hellenic Council in the East. It had as well a great pool of highly experienced administrators to assume control of the new provinces, men who had worked their way upward through the various levels, supplied with eager and intelligent assistants and supported by troops which had no equal in the East. Provincial prosperity meant Roman prosperity, and the current opinion was that this could be brought about by encouraging urban Hellenism and economic *laissez faire*.

It was perhaps this very freedom that promoted the evils in the system. Laws might be passed at Rome regulating provincial affairs—Gabinius had sponsored a number of such—but their promulgation and execution depended upon the governor. He, for his part, did not view himself as a mere civil servant. His career had been a political one, and for all his experience in

---

26. The *sestertius* was one fourth of the basic silver coin of the Romans, the *denarius*. For purposes of comparison: it cost one thousand sesterces to keep a Roman legionary in the field for a year. The price of an able-bodied male slave was about two thousand sesterces, and his annual keep amounted to some three to four hundred sesterces.

soldiering and administration he was essentially a highly placed and highly visible politician trailing the usual string of political debts and party ties. As an ex-Consul, the governor had reached the top of the political ladder, and all too often the experience and talent of such men was smothered under the sentiment that provincial administration was a reward for services rendered and not just another service.

A province was for most men a profitable way station in the endless round of Roman politics. For almost all it was part of the spoils to be distributed annually by the current powers in Rome, and an eastern governor had only to resist invasion (the Parthians), quell anarchy and insurrection (the Jews), and show a profit, at whatever cost to the province, to be acclaimed a success. Truly outrageous behavior, the looting of a Dolabella or a Verres, might provoke punitive reaction at home, but if a provincial governor was hauled before a jury it was far more likely to have been the work of his political enemies than of an outraged public conscience. Even then all was not lost. Senatorial juries tended to be protective of members of their own class, and the Equestrians were no less solicitous for their own.

The question of provincial government was a side issue of a larger struggle going on in Rome itself, the fierce battle for privilege and power being waged with increasing ferocity between the patrician *optimates* and their flourishing middle-class competitors. Stability in the provinces obviously demanded some kind of control over the syndicates of *publicani* and *negotiatores* who were fattening on the entire East. But for a governor to repress the rapacious tax farmers and moneylenders was to court political disaster at home where the Equestrian lobby could destroy his career. Probably the only motive strong enough to impel a governor to curb the provincial *publicani* was the prospect of enriching himself with the savings.

The *optimates* narrowly observed Pompey's successes in the East. Like many another politician of the time, the victorious *imperator* had risen to power on the support of the lower-class *populares*, and during his consulate in B.C. 70, an office he shared with another war hero, Marcus Licinius Crassus, he engineered a series of measures aimed at strengthening that support: by his enactments Pompey abrogated the provisions of the Sullan legislation that had reinforced and protected the power of the Senate to control legislation. The aristocrats neither forgot nor forgave, and during Pompey's absence in the East (B.C. 66–63) they acted against his supporters, including both Manilius and the future governor of Syria, Gabinius, who had drawn the laws upon which Pompey's command rested. Crassus, who was Pompey's rival for control of the *populares*, was an interested spectator, as was another newly prominent politician whose ambitions ran in the same direction, Gaius Julius Caesar.

In Pompey's consular year of B.C. 70, the young but accomplished lawyer Cicero was putting his foot upon the second rung up the ladder of political preferment by running for the office of Aedile at Rome. In B.C. 75 he had stood for one of the quaestorships, or junior treasury posts, and had been posted to Lilybaeum. He won his aedileship too, and by B.C. 63 the future governor of Cilicia reached as high as election could carry him, the consulship.

Cicero's own account of his consulship revolves around his brutal or, as some thought, unconstitutional quashing of the conspiracy of the ruined aristocrat Catiline. Rome was concerned about Catiline, but the parties there were far more interested in events in the East, where Pompey was concluding the thunderously successful campaign which had finally throttled Mithridates, enlarged Roman holdings in Asia and Bithynia, and added two entirely new provinces to the Republic, Cilicia and Syria.

The question in B.C. 63 was what Pompey would do with the immense store of troops, booty and prestige that he had accumulated. To the surprise of many he laid down his arms, disbanded his army in a constitutional fashion, and contented himself with celebrating, in September, B.C. 61, the most staggering triumph yet seen at Rome, which featured Pompey, the new lord of Asia, clad in the tunic of his most eminent predecessor, Alexander the Great.

If Pompey really expected to resume the role of a private citizen, he was quickly disabused. He had bought his soldiers, as every ambitious field commander did, with promises of a generous land allotment for the veterans of the campaign. When it became clear that the *optimates* who dominated the Senate would not pass a land bill in the soldiers' favor, or even ratify the administrative arrangements he had made in the East, Pompey threw in his lot with his erstwhile rivals, Crassus and Caesar, and there came into being that informal coalition of power known as the First Triumvirate.

The unlikely political troika won the consulate for Caesar in
B.C. 59, followed by an extended and immensely successful proconsular command in Gaul. It was interrupted three years later,
when the triumvirs reconvened to lay their plans for the future.
It was understood that Caesar would continue in Gaul, while
Pompey and Crassus would share the consulate in B.C. 55 (they
canceled the regular elections of B.C. 56) and then assume five-
year proconsular control of their provinces, Pompey in Spain and
Crassus in Syria.

Crassus, the soldier turned politician and millionaire, had first
come into prominence by crushing the revolt of the gladiator
Spartacus and his malcontents in B.C. 72–71. Though he built up
considerable financial leverage at Rome[27] (Caesar and a large
number of Senators were in his debt), his career seems most
notable for a kind of undirected and unprincipled ambition.
Among his earlier schemes were proposals for the enfranchisement of the peoples north of the Po, so that he could recruit
them into his army, and in B.C. 65, for the Roman annexation of
Egypt, on the grounds that it had been secretly bequeathed to
them in B.C. 80. The Senate found neither suggestion to its liking.

Cheated of Egypt in B.C. 65, Crassus was more than willing to
settle for Syria in B.C. 56. Pompey was by then Rome's most
famous general and Caesar was winning ever fresher laurels in
Gaul, Germany and Britain. Syria would be Crassus' Gaul.
Wealth there undoubtedly was, and the prospect of a triumph
over the Parthians. Both Sulla and Pompey had earlier come into
cautious contact with the Parthian kingdom by their probes into
Armenia, but Gabinius, Crassus' immediate predecessor in Syria,
had had more ambitious designs on Parthia itself before the lure
of Egypt distracted his attention. The recall of Gabinius occurred during the triumvirs' consular year (B.C. 55), and even
before it was over Crassus went out to Syria to replace the dis-
graced Proconsul and to fulfill his dream of eastern conquest.

There was little ground for such. Though relations with
Parthia were watchful, they were not bellicose, and there were
those at Rome who opposed the projected campaign. The will of
the triumvirs prevailed, however, and Crassus mounted his ex-

---

27. Among the other sources of his wealth was his control of Rome's
privately owned fire department. Crassus' real-estate agents accompanied his intrepid, if selective, fire fighters.

pedition. It ended in B.C. 53 in the disaster at Carrhae, one of the most serious and degrading defeats ever suffered by Roman arms. Led on into the deserts of northern Mesopotamia and without the essential support of King Artavasades of Armenia,[28] the Roman troops were cut to pieces by the Parthian archers and heavily armed knights under the command of Surenas, the scion of a powerful Parthian clan in Seistan. The Roman legionary standards were captured, and though he escaped with a remnant of his troops to nearby Carrhae, Crassus too was eventually killed. His head was carried to Orodes, then in Armenia celebrating his new alliance with Artavasades. According to Plutarch, when the grisly trophy arrived the two monarchs were watching a performance of Euripides' *Bacchae*, "for Orodes was not ignorant of the Greek language and literature, and Artavasades was so expert in it that he wrote tragedies, orations and histories, some of which are still extant." The Romans were clearly not the sole heirs of Hellenism in Asia.

How the kings of Parthia came to their easy Hellenism can scarcely be surmised. Parthia is another of the "silent kingdoms" of the East, seen through the eyes of Greek or Roman historians or the even more tendentious regards of the Sasanians, who looked upon their Parthian predecessors in Iran as the lords of a degenerate Middle Ages between the Classical Achaemenians and their own glorious Renaissance. Documentation is sparse; there have been some scrappy finds at Dura Europos and the Soviet excavations at Nisa in Turkmenistan, and, as in Bactria, the coins are helpful. What emerges is, however, a sketch rather than a history.

The people who later came to be called Parthians were originally one part, the Parni, of a Scythian tribal confederation living in the lower reaches of an area between the Caspian and Aral seas. At some time in the middle of the third century the Parni and their confederates made the time-honored move from the steppe to the town, and entered the former Achaemenian satrapy of Parthava where they adopted the local dialect of northwestern Iranian, subsequently called after them Pahlevi, which was to

28. Son of Tigranes the Great whom Pompey had confirmed on the throne of Armenia in B.C. 64. After casting in his lot with Parthia, Artavasades married his daughter to Pacorus, the eldest son of the Parthian king Orodes. Pacorus fell in the Parthian attack on Syria in B.C. 39.

become, by reason of the Parthian expansion, the Iranian *koine* for a thousand years.

The Parthians rose on the ruins of Seleucid disintegration in the East. By B.C. 223 they were firmly in possession of the area between the River Tejend and the southern shore of the Caspian Sea, sitting astride the great east-west road, and, more importantly, interposing a Parthian wedge between the Greeks of Syria and Mesopotamia and those of Bactria. It did not, however, mean the end of Hellenism in the area. The Parthians acted much as the Arabs were to act later in Syria: they kept the local administration intact, ruling from the top in the manner of the petty dynasts who were everywhere springing up behind the receding tide of the Seleucids.

Under Mithridates I (B.C. 171–138) the former nomads of the steppe passed from kingdom to empire. The death of the strong Antiochus IV Epiphanes in B.C. 164 had opened the door for Mithridates, who added to the Parthian holdings all the states so recently detached from the Seleucids. Media was occupied in B.C. 155, and then in B.C. 141 Mithridates crossed the Tigris into Babylonia. The last feeble attempt on the part of the Seleucid ruler Demetrius II to regain his eastern capital at Seleucia led to his capture by the Parthian armies in B.C. 140–139.

Mithridates bequeathed to his successors an empire that stretched from the Euphrates to India[29] and embraced an amalgam of Semitic, Iranian and Hellenistic elements. Politically it was the latter strain that was most important. Mithridates was very conscious of being the successor to both the Seleucids and the Achaemenians, and on his coins he styled himself "The Great King" and "Philhellene" to drive the point home to his subjects.

Though it was not until Mithridates II (B.C. 123–87) that the actual title King of Kings (*Shahan shah*) appeared, his earlier namesake had every claim to it. Mithridates I did rule over what was, in effect, a confederation of kings resting upon the older Achaemenian system of satrapies. In many instances the Parthians bestowed these administrative districts upon their own nobles, thereby converting their own dukes into kings. Set down like islands in the midst of these kingdoms were the Greek *poleis* of Alexander and the Seleucids, Hellenic centers that were by tradi-

---

29. He had taken part of the domains of the Bactrian Greeks; but their final downfall came not at the hands of the Parthians but under assault from the nomads of Central Asia (see Chapter VII, pp. 276–77).

tion autonomous and remained so under the Parthians. The chief such were Seleucia on the Tigris,[30] and Seleucia on the Eulaeus, the former Achaemenian Susa. Mesopotamia in particular was a Macedon in miniature.[31] The Parthians fostered and encouraged these cities, but the forces of Iranian feudalism, temporarily checked by the Seleucids, guided the Parthian evolution in another direction. The power of the satrapy-kingdoms was great and waxed even stronger at the expense of both the Hellenized cities and the central Arsacid monarchy itself.

A strong Achaemenian monarch or a later Sasanian one was capable of transcending his feudal peers, but it did not occur frequently in Parthia after the first Mithridates. The great families like the Suren in Seistan ruled almost unchecked in their own fiefs. It was they who supplied the cataphracts, the heavily armed and mailed cavalry that was to revolutionize ancient warfare, while the lesser nobility provided the mounted archers so successful at Carrhae and eternally impressive to the Romans. The peasants and serfs made up the motley foot soldiery, never an important factor in the Parthian military. The armed might of Parthia reflected its social structure: the great families, the petty nobility, and the peasants, serfs and slaves who made up the bulk of the population.

Two other classes were not reflected in the army muster, officialdom and the priesthood. The scribal and administrative society of the trans-Euphrates was bilingual in Greek and Aramaic. Greek had been introduced by Alexander and his successors and was used extensively by the Parthians in their official documents and for legal and administrative matters.[32] Hellenism penetrated at higher levels of culture as well, as is testified to by the earliest Parthian sculpture and the anecdote about Euripides' *Bacchae* already cited from Plutarch. Hellenism did not, how-

---

30. The Parthians did not take over this center as their capital but built instead a huge military encampment, Ctesiphon, on the opposite bank of the river. It was exactly the procedure of the later Arab conquerors of Palestine and may represent the nomads' residual fear and disdain of urbanism.

31. See Chapter VI, p. 228.

32. There were Greek legends on the coinage down to the time of Vologesus I (*c.* A.D. 55), who replaced them with Parthian. Many of the papyri and parchment documents from Dura Europos on the Euphrates and Avroman in Kurdistan dating from the Parthian period are in Greek.

ever, obliterate the Aramaic legacy of the Achaemenians or suppress the rise of a new Iranian consciousness. When the Parthian tongue finally passed from an oral to a written stage it possessed an alphabet (Pahlavik) that had evolved from Aramaic script and that had embedded in it a great number of words borrowed from Aramaic, a testimony not only to the longevity of the Aramaic tongue but also to the continued vitality of the ancient Semitic communities of Mesopotamia and Babylonia, including, of course, the flourishing colony of Jews in Babylon, who profited from the Parthian toleration of foreign cults.

The Parthians themselves followed the syncretistic religion of Iran—that is, the complex of beliefs and rituals from both Iranian and Near Eastern sources that characterized Iran until the Sasanians created their more monolithic Zoroastrian "Church." All the motifs visible since Artaxerxes II (B.C. 404–359) were present, the temple cults of Ahura Mazda, Mithra and Anahita; the latter two were particularly cultivated in the western parts of the kingdom and had flourishing cult centers in Anatolia that dated back to Achaemenian days.[33] The traditional Aryan priests, the Magi, still held forth, though little is known of their activity. The Sasanian historians did not think very highly of the religion of the Parthians, since they viewed it from their own supposed vantage point as the restorers of both true Zoroastrianism and the genuine Iranian tradition.

We are in no position to judge for ourselves. The Sasanians left behind them their theological books and from them one can reconstruct something of the intellectual substance of Sasanian religious beliefs. For the Parthians, there is little but names and the shattered ruins of their temples. We know whom the Parthians worshiped, but neither their thoughts nor their attitudes, nor even the shape of their rituals, can be traced with conviction.

The discomfiture of Antiochus III by the Romans at Magnesia and Apamea did not end the Seleucids' hope of an eastern restoration. Provoked by the Parthians' capture of Demetrius II in B.C. 139, they may have been encouraged as well by the enthusiasm with which the Parthians' western vassals had earlier greeted Demetrius on his eastern campaign; these latter had not been impressed, it would seem, by the Parthians' protestations of Philhellenism. Demetrius' brother, Antiochus VII Sidetes (B.C.

---

33. See Chapter XII, pp. 474–75.

139–129) once again took the road east, and in B.C. 129 was dealt the final blow to his fortunes by Mithridates' son Phraates II. The Trans-Euphrates was permanently beyond Seleucid redemption and, more, the path into Syria now lay open. For the first time the Parthians were presented with the opportunity of bursting into the Mediterranean *oikoumene*.

The Parthians had, however, inherited the same two-front warfare that had earlier plagued the Seleucids. They now had to contend with increasing pressures from their own eastern steppe, where incursions of the nomadic Iranian Sacae, relatives of the Scythians so well known to the Greeks, and already present on the frontier at the time of Mithridates, were straining the line of defenses along the Oxus. Both Phraates II and his uncle Artabanus II lost their lives defending the eastern frontier between B.C. 128 and B.C. 123 and a disaster of the first magnitude was averted only by the accession of Mithridates II (B.C. 123–87) who recaptured Merv and Herat and stabilized the frontier.

In the west too Mithridates II attempted to repair the damage done by disorder and neglect. Characene at the head of the Persian Gulf was reduced to vassalage and in Armenia he took as hostage the youthful prince Tigranes. Tigranes later came into his kingdom (B.C. 95) to play the role already described as son-in-law and ally of Mithridates of Pontus. It was Tigranes too who anticipated the Parthians' western ambitions and in B.C. 83 took over what was left of the Seleucid Empire in Syria.

The dreams of Tigranes, ruler of an Armenian empire which stretched from the Mediterranean to the Caspian, were rudely shattered by Lucullus in B.C. 69–68. The Parthians too were aware of the new presence in the East, first through the Roman embroilment in Armenia[34] and then, after B.C. 64, by a direct confrontation with Rome across the Euphrates, the frontier breached by Crassus in B.C. 54–52.

Crassus' Roman legions stumbled upon an unsuspected pocket of Hellenism across the eastern frontier. Its dimensions can only be surmised, precisely because it was across the frontier and the Roman sources show little interest in any events, other than military ones, outside the *oikoumene*. But whatever the obscurity

---

34. Which may have saved the Parthians from following Syria into the hands of Tigranes. The Armenian king had already annexed some of the Parthian states in Mesopotamia before he was checked by Rome.

that has settled upon the eastern Philhellenism of Parthia, we are immeasurably better instructed on the progress of Hellenism among the Latins who now held Greece in their political embrace.

The citizen of Rome in the mid-first century had a far broader and deeper strain of Hellenism to draw upon than the spectacular but essentially provincial displays of Orodes and Artavasades. Imperial patronage could doubtless lure a troupe of Euripidean minstrels into Armenia. Rome had its transient Hellenists too, but it had in addition a rich and growing penetration of Greek ideals into its own culture on almost all levels.

Commerce, war and, finally, the business of occupation and administration carried the Romans all over the Mediterranean. At the beginning of the third century they came into contact with the long-established Greeks of southern Italy and Sicily, and one of these western Greeks, Livius Andronicus, who came to Rome after the fall of Tarentum in B.C. 272, introduced the Romans to Hellenic drama and epic; he translated the *Odyssey* into Latin and adapted various Greek tragic themes for the Roman stage. By the next century the Romans were in possession of Greece itself, and there was a heavy traffic in cultured slaves, books and art works from the new province into Rome, while well-to-do Romans went eastward to study at the centers of Hellenic learning.

In the generation after Livius Andronicus, the Umbrian Plautus (*c.* B.C. 254–184) produced his adaptations of Menander, and toward the end of the second century the poet Laevius was trying his hand at some of the Hellenistic lyric meters and erotic themes in Latin. By the time of Cicero's birth in B.C. 106 the intellectual and artistic life among the educated at Rome was substantially Hellenized. Alexandrian poetry was the vogue at Rome in the first century, and Catullus (*c.* B.C. 84–54) stood at the center of a Hellenized poetical circle that was influential well into the days of Augustus. Cicero had some taste for poetry, though little talent at writing it. He was exposed, as were most Romans of his time and class, to Hellenistic poetry and the full range of Greek *paideia*, and occasionally had an opportunity to display his Hellenic culture, as in his defense, in B.C. 62, of the citizenship of the Greek Archias of Antioch, the poetaster who had celebrated, probably unhappily, Lucullus' campaign against Mithridates.

Cicero the lawyer was formed on Hellenic rhetoric—there was

no other kind of training for an orator—but his deep involvement in Roman politics allowed him little time for purely literary or academic pursuits. With the completion of his disappointing year as governor of Cilicia, however, and the failure of his political expectations at Rome, Cicero returned to the Hellenic philosophy that he had studied as a young man at Athens and Rhodes. It was not unnatural for a Roman of Cicero's generation to find solace in philosophy rather than squirehood, however strange it might have appeared a century earlier. In the interval Rome continued to experience its periodic discovery and rediscovery of Greece, but what was new in the period after B.C. 168 was that the objects of this affection betrayed their first significant awareness of the new power in the Mediterranean. The flattering attention of a Polybius and a Panaetius, never lavished on the Iranians across the Euphrates, provided a powerful stimulus to Hellenism at Rome.

IX

The Platonic Revival

With the political absorption of Greece the Romans fell prey to their victims. Roman aristocrats and cultural social climbers courted and were courted by the Hellenic eminences who appeared with increasing frequency in the Latin capital to observe, to teach, and to reap the rewards of their cultural superiority. Before long a well-to-do Roman could get a perfectly respectable education in the Hellenic status fields of rhetoric and philosophy without leaving his native city. A truly serious interest indicated the study of Greek and the mandatory pilgrimage to Athens or Rhodes, such as Cicero had made, but one could make do at Rome, and this was at a time of great vitality and renovation in the history of Greek philosophy. The Romans were privileged to be present, chiefly as observers, at a new turning in Hellenism.

The Academy Without Plato

The history of Peripateticism can be read as a more or less regular genetic evolution; the doctrines of the founder may have been at times modified, corrected, or neglected, but they were still recognizably Aristotelian. The Lyceum was shaken by neither heresy nor schism in its progress from Theophrastus down to the time when Aristotle became a "classic" and so beyond loss and unreasonable distortion.

No such orderly unfolding marked the history of the Academy. Even during Plato's lifetime, Aristotle probably had his disagreements with his teacher, and when Speusippus succeeded to the directorship at Plato's death in B.C. 347, neither piety nor conservatism prevented him from removing the centerpiece of his uncle's metaphysics, the theory of Forms (*eide*). Speusippus flatly denied their existence, substituting in their place the mathematical numbers, "because he saw the awkwardness and fictive quality that surrounded them." This is not to say that all transcendental reality was being rejected. On the contrary, Speusippus posited a single, transcendent One, "beyond being," from which both the numbers and the sensibles derived. There was, however, no place in this transcendental scheme, the prototype of many others in the Platonic tradition, for the transcendental *eide*. They had simply disappeared.

Speusippus' attitude was not singular. Among Plato's students four of the most eminent, Aristotle, Eudoxus, Speusippus, and the latter's successor as scholarch from B.C. 339, Xenocrates, either dropped the *eide* or mathematized them into something quite different. Related to this denial was another curious fact. When Aristotle and Xenocrates come to speak of Plato, they frequently betray a serious doubt as to the exact meaning of his theories, and this after many years in his company in the Academy. No satisfactory answer to this odd situation has been proposed—why Plato did not explain his published work to his advanced students or why they neglected to ask him to do so. Even if, as has been suggested, mathematics was the only subject on which formal instruction was given in the Academy, that fact does not explain the misunderstanding and eventually the silence that fell upon what has seemed to every student of the subject—except Plato's own—the heart of Platonism, the transcendent *eide*.

Aristotle apart, mathematics *was* the chief interest of the immediate disciples of Plato, mathematics and the dialectical division (*diairesis*) that had been illustrated in Plato's dialogue *The Sophist*. Speusippus for one seems to have reduced the essence of an existent to the sum of all its relations to other existents, and to have made a serious attempt at arriving at definitions by an examination of all the *differentiae*. Perhaps the scene from the early Academy preserved in one of the fragments of the comic poet Epicrates was not all satirical fancy: Plato and Speusippus hunched over an unknown plant trying to determine its genus.

In one respect at least, Speusippus and Xenocrates remained faithful to Plato; they shared his faith in dialectic as an autonomous and absolute route to knowledge, a route that Aristotle for his part was already beginning to formulate into a logic. But with

Xenocrates' passing in B.C. 314, a new generation of philosophers took over the direction of the Academy; and under Polemo, Crates and Crantor little was heard of mathematics or dialectic in the school. Instead there was a great deal of interest in ethical questions. The three men appear as unabashed moralists, and it is not difficult to understand what may have drawn their attention in that direction; the dialogue with Zeno, who had attended the lectures of Polemo, was beginning.

Or so it would seem. Here precisely, in the relationship of the Academic Polemo and the Stoic Zeno, the later sources saw a critical issue in the history of philosophy. The later Academic tradition insisted that Zeno, and hence Stoicism, was dependent upon Polemo and wrote its history accordingly. It may very well have been this revisionism that has converted the successors of Xenocrates into thinkers whose prime and almost sole concern was ethics. There is some contrary evidence. We know, for instance, that Crantor took up the task of commenting on the work of Plato, and that his choice was Plato's cosmogony, the *Timaeus*, where at least part of the issue was not the question of man's moral good but the eternity of the *kosmos*.[1]

Under the leadership of Arcesilaus (c. B.C. 315–240) the Platonic Academy took a bold new turn. It completely deserted the a priori dogmatism of Plato for a position of formal skepticism. This new stance, not so much a disregard of dialectic as its denial, is presented in at least some of our sources[2] not as an evolution of Platonism but as a reflection on the by-now dominant Stoicism of the period. Arcesilaus' skepticism was recognized as something new in Platonism, but not until Philo of Larissa, the last skeptic to preside over the fortunes of the school, was any attempt made

---

1. Aristotle, who read the *Timaeus* literally, took the position that the *kosmos* was eternal and did not, as the *Timaeus* seemed to suggest, come into being. The early Academics, including Crantor, were convinced by his arguments, but rather than repudiate the *Timaeus* outright, they maintained that it must be read figuratively.

2. Arcesilaus wrote nothing, but there was an oral tradition deriving from him, and it is preserved in later authors, notably Cicero and Sextus. Most of the history of the Academy from Arcesilaus down to Antiochus must be written from Cicero's philosophical works, chiefly *On the Nature of the Gods*, *Academics* and *Lucullus*, all three dialogues in the form of debates between the representatives of the various philosophical schools.

to relate the position of Arcesilaus to its possible historical antecedents, Academic or otherwise; down to Philo, Arcesilaus appears as nothing more than an opponent of Stoicism.

What we know of Arcesilaus' views does suggest that they had a Stoic point of departure. The Stoic theory of knowledge began with an image presented by the senses to which the will of the sentient could either give assent (*synkatathesis*) or, in cases where the impressed image was not clearly true, withhold it. Arcesilaus extended this principle of withholding of assent (*epoche*) beyond Zeno's doubtful cases to cover every image presented to the mind, since there is no one of them that is so clear that it could not be confused with another. With the systematic suspension of assent the entire Stoic doctrine of true and certain knowledge (*katalepsis*, "apprehension") and of science (*episteme*) would have to fall.

It is unlikely that Arcesilaus was much concerned with the collapse of Stoic physics. He had, however, created a serious problem for himself in the domain of ethics. Knowledge preceded and determined moral activity, and so an epistemological agnosticism necessarily led to action governed either by random choice[3] or, as Arcesilaus preferred, an "educated guess." The Stoics knew of a class of "befitting acts" (*kathekonta*) for which a reasonable defense could be given, but they distinguished them from genuine moral activity wherein the act in question was recognized as a certain good. What Arcesilaus had done, in effect, to the Stoic theory was to remove the absolute epistemological certitude upon which all human moral activity was based and replace it with a fully moral act chosen on the basis of an intellectually reasonable (*eulogos*) probability.

Arcesilaus still located his probability in the realm of reason (*phronesis*); one of his more radical successors at the head of the Academy, Carneades (*c.* B.C. 214–129), took the matter somewhat further. He conceded that we received some images that were more persuasive than others. Such images were not, however, the sole basis for moral action; they must be tested by experience and exposed to the possibility of contradiction, a more

---

3. A contemporary group of skeptics, that founded by Pyrrho, preached just such moral indifferentism based on a radical denial of certitude in either sense or intellectual knowledge. In their view one could neither profess opinion nor make moral choices.

pragmatic and empirical approach to the problem than the intellectually reasonable certitude of Arcesilaus.

Plato would have readily conceded the insecurity of sense knowledge and the impossibility of founding certitude upon it; he explored the question at length in the *Theaetetus*. It was precisely the failure of sensation as a ground for true *episteme* that drove him to the spiritual *eide* with all the characteristics of permanence and immutability lacking in the material objects of the senses. Here once again, however, were Arcesilaus and Carneades arguing as if Plato had never existed. The *eide* appeared nowhere in the discussions with the Stoa. With the implicit denial of the *eide* and the explicit rejection of Stoic sensualism all avenues to certitude were closed to the Academy.

Arguments about the pros and cons of sense knowledge sound exceedingly strange in the mouth of the directors of the Platonic Academy. There is no direct evidence as to how or why this extraordinary change came about, but one may speculate that it had more to do with developments within the Lyceum than with a native transformation of Platonism. Aristotle, once outside the embrace of the Academy, no longer shared Plato's faith in a knowledge that struggled to gain the a priori certitudes of mathematics. Aristotle was an empiricist, even in his derivation of mathematics, and his preference for the inductive generalizing of medicine to the axiomatically derived conclusions of mathematics is particularly evident in his approach to the natural sciences and to ethics.

The Aristotelian leaning to empirical generalization was passed on to Theophrastus, whose work in both ethics and botany was constructed upon a typology, a generalized portrait whose details remained to be worked out on the basis of further research. Theophrastus continued to sound the other complementary Aristotelian themes: the objects of mathematics, numbers and figures, are abstractions derived from sense knowledge; logic is an instrument (*organon*) in philosophical research, not an autonomous branch of philosophy in the manner of Plato. These empiricist attitudes raised other problems, however, with Aristotelian teleology, for instance. Theophrastus sensed it and expressed his doubts on Aristotle's apparent ambivalence between empiricism and a lingering Platonism. Theophrastus' successors in the Lyceum pushed Aristotle's empiricism ever further into the realms of naturalism, until with Strato of Lampsacus even the theological view of the universe, Aristotle's last legacy from Plato, was denied.[4]

A little of this attitude can be detected in Arcesilaus, Strato's contemporary and, like him, a student of Theophrastus; in Carneades the reassertion of the Lyceum's empiricism and naturalism is far more striking. It may be simply a question of our being better informed on Carneades, since his students kept detailed records of his opinions. Cicero read widely in the works of one of those students, Clitomachus, who subsequently succeeded as Academic scholarch (c. B.C. 129–110), and he reproduced out of Clitomachus many of Carneades' positions in his philosophical dialogues. But the difference between the two skeptical Academics, Arcesilaus and Carneades, though explicable in terms of temperament, intelligence, and the state of our sources, probably owed just as much to the presence between them of Chrysippus (c. B.C. 280–205). Arcesilaus had to deal with the former boxer Cleanthes, but Carneades had to take arms against the formidably detailed system of Stoicism's second founder. If there had been no Chrysippus, it was said, the Stoa would not exist; to which Carneades added: "If there had been no Chrysippus, I would not exist."[5]

Like his Aristotelian predecessors Carneades rejected both a theological view of the universe and a tightly knit theory of causality linked to that theological view under the Stoic rubric of "Fate." Carneades accepted the Stoic contention that the universe was an organic and interconnected whole, but he denied that this necessarily led through the cosmological argument to a providential God. Nature coheres by its own powers, but when there is some aspect of it that the Stoic cannot explain he flees, Carneades noted, to the altar.

The New Academy was impressed by neither the Stoic argument from the *consensus gentium* nor the Epicurean gods-in-enclave theory.[6] Both smelled of anthropomorphism, a charge to which the Epicureans were particularly open with their resort to old-fashioned, albeit ineffectual, gods and their pathetic assertions about those gods' "quasi body" and "quasi blood." They cannot,

---

4. See Chapter II, pp. 110–11.
5. Carneades studied dialectic with Chrysippus' student and successor, Diogenes of Seleucia, just as in an earlier day Chrysippus had attended the lectures of Arcesilaus.
6. See Chapter III, pp. 125–26.

Carneades insisted, have it both ways behind the disclaimer of "quasi."

For all their naturalism the latter-day Academics found little to admire in Epicurean physics, epistemology, ethics or theology. Their point of departure was rather Stoic than Epicurean, though they differed with the Stoa on fundamental points. One such was the freedom of the human will. The Epicureans had recognized the difficulty of preserving freedom in a universe dominated by an almost mechanical necessity, and so they had posited in the system the fortuitous swerve (*parenklisis*) of the atoms to provide a kind of physical paradigm for the freedom of choice that men apparently possessed. For Carneades paradigms were not explanations.

The Stoa suffered an equal embarrassment on the subject. Volition appeared, to be sure, in their description of the knowing process as the "assent" (*synkatathesis*) that preceded the final apprehension (*katalepsis*) that constitutes knowledge. But with Chrysippus, particularly, the volitional assent seems to be little more than another act of the intellect. Carneades recognized the essential intellectualism of the schema, a coloration of the internal processes that was no means peculiar to the Stoics; indeed all of Greek philosophy's analyses of the moral and intellectual life were relentlessly intellectualistic. For Carneades the problem was more than one of merely restoring the volitional character of the act of assent in thought processes; the Stoic attitude was connected with the fundamental question of causality.

The causal links in the Stoic organic world view were indissolubly forged; their unfolding was inexorable, though their connection with a provident God guaranteed their working to a good end. Carneades would have it quite otherwise: the universe is governed by causality; some of the causes are the external ones of nature, but there operates at their side the internal cause that is the human will.

How this free and sovereign cause operates vis-à-vis the intellect, our sources nowhere allow Carneades to explain. The position is nonetheless significant, since it marks the first small breach in Greek philosophical intellectualism. Man was freed from the web of causality, naturalistic and theological, that bound him to the processes of the external world, and was, at the same time, constituted as an autonomous cause in his own right, free to cooperate with or countervene the universal causality. No one of the philosophers or moralists had denied the freedom of man's will, of course; all responsibility and the entire moral life rested upon it. Little theoretical attention was paid to it, however, and volitional concerns had constantly to struggle, unsuccessfully, against the overwhelming intellectualism of most treatments of causality. Carneades' achievement was in defending the will as a cause.

Carneades' attacks on the Stoa were struck from all directions with a great variety of weapons. Stoic logic was assaulted by dialectic; theology by logic and history; divination by an appeal to naturalism, heavily spiced with sarcasm; and the carefully constructed Stoic ethic was disquieted by adducing concrete instances of the conflict between wisdom and justice, between "the good" and the "useful," values that the Stoics held to be necessarily congruent.[7]

At the root of the polemic lay Arcesilaus' denial of the premises of Stoic epistemology. According to Arcesilaus, one cannot catch hold of a "kataleptic" presentation of such clarity as to force assent, and so one must rest content with *epoche,* the suspension of judgment. Both thinkers, Arcesilaus and Carneades, could summon up a great number of by-then commonplace examples of defective images; to drive the point home they resorted to the even more persuasive procedure of arguing both sides of the same question.

In B.C. 155 the Athenians somewhat maliciously dispatched the heads of the three great philosophical schools as a political embassy to the impressionable Romans: Carneades the Academic, Diogenes the Stoic and Critolaus the Peripatetic.[8] In the course of their extended visit Carneades treated his Roman hosts to a spectacular display of "arguing both sides." It is not easy to assess the point of this tour de force. Carneades' own student Philo of Larissa later formalized the technique into a rhetorical exercise, but it seems that for Carneades it still belonged to philosophy, that it was not, as Cicero seemed sometimes to have understood it, an attempt at showing that both sides of a question were

---

7. These "cases of conscience" served, much as Aristotle's empirical approach had done, to direct later Stoic ethicians away from theory and into the realm of practical ethics, an evolution that was eventually to carry the Stoics into the streets and into the dangerous toils of Roman politics (see Chapter XI, pp. 416–19).

8. The omission of an Epicurean must have been a calculated snub.

equally likely and so equally unlikely, but rather directed toward the demolition of the dogmatic position of the metaphysicians and the establishment of Carneades' own naturalistic pragmatism.

Carneades created a sensation at Rome, particularly among the young who came flocking to hear Hellenism's premier intellectual perform. Hellenism took Rome by storm once again, but this time it was not literature, art or myth that came garbed in Greek attire, but philosophy. It was Rome's first real encounter with that aspect of Hellenism, and it was to be a momentous one. Not all the Romans were happy with the learned ambassadors. Cato the Censor publicly expressed his disgust at what he construed to be revolutionary notions, and exhorted the Senate to get on with its business and send its eminent guests home. It was really of little consequence; other forces had rendered Cato's protective fears obsolete.

By the time of the famous embassy, Rome was already an eastern power, and through the middle decades of that century she took an increasingly firm grip on Greece. Aemilius Paulus crushed the Macedonian forces of Perseus at Pydna in B.C. 168.[9] In B.C. 148 the Macedonian holdings in Greece were incorporated as a province, and two years later, after the vicious sacking of Corinth by the troops of Lucius Mummius, the Romans dissolved the Achaean League, the last autonomous political body in Greece.

This direct political involvement with Greece had almost immediate cultural effects. In B.C. 167 the Greek historian Polybius was brought to Rome as a political hostage, and there later began to form around his most famous Roman convert, Paulus' son Scipio Aemilianus, a circle of statesmen, jurists, literary men and philosophers who provided the intelligence, support and influence whereby a whole series of Stoic philosophers were given a hearing by interested Latins. The primary mentor of the Scipionic circle was Panaetius; and its finest product Cicero.[10]

---

9. Perseus' Greek library was put at the disposal of the tutors of the young Scipio Aemilianus.

10. Most of the Roman members of the circle were set out, like notable portraits in a museum, as interlocutors in the Ciceronian dialogue On the Commonwealth. The two chief literary members, the dramatist Terence and the satirist Lucilius, were not, however, included.

Philosophy in the Age of Cicero

The general impression that the Stoic Diogenes of Seleucia made upon his Roman hosts in B.C. 155 is not recorded. Diogenes was then nearly eighty years old, and it is unlikely in any event that he could have matched the pyrotechnics of Carneades. His moral earnestness did make one important convert, however, the Roman statesman and orator Laelius, whom Cicero later commemorated in his essay *On Friendship*. Laelius was an important disciple; through him the Stoa gained a hearing in the influential Scipionic circle.

Diogenes' interests extended beyond ethics. As scholarch he had first to meet the polemic of Carneades, and it is clear that the Stoa had to give way to the Academic arguments on some substantial points. They abandoned, for instance, the doctrine of a final cosmic conflagration under the influence of Carneades' critique. They had also to back away, at least by implication, from one of the central tenets of earlier Stoicism, the primacy of an absolute good, and to admit to a share in sovereignty those acts that were formerly held to be merely defensible, the *kathekonta*. Beginning with Diogenes, the Stoics more and more gave their attention to the practical realities of the moral life: poverty, friendship, political power. In this increased emphasis on making the right moral choices one can see the persuasive power of Carneades' "cases of conscience" and the ethical dilemmas they posed to Stoic theory.

Diogenes had a considerable reputation as a grammarian as well as a dialectician. Previous Stoic theory on grammar was organized in his handbook *On Speech*, a book which was carefully read in the Alexandrian schools and provided the basis for grammatical studies there.[11] It was read in Pergamum as well. Crates of Mallus, the founder of the Pergamene school of literary criticism, probably studied with Diogenes at Athens, and his approach to literary criticism and to aesthetics not unnaturally betrays strong Stoic influences. Through Crates Stoic allegorizing

---

11. Dionysius Thrax used Diogenes' system and terminology in his *Handbook* (see Chapter XV, p. 544).

entered literary criticism, up to this point the sole preserve of the Alexandrian grammarians.[12]

Crates was in Rome in B.C. 168, and it is not at all unlikely that he left his mark there as well. Whether instructed by Crates or, as seems more probable, by Panaetius, the first Roman scholar to attempt a Latin grammar, Aelius Stilo, considered himself a Stoic. Cicero heard him lecture, but Stilo's true grammatical and linguistic progeny was Marcus Terentius Varro (B.C. 116–27), whose handbook, *The Latin Language*, is thoroughly Stoic in theory and execution. Thenceforward Latin was studied within —and began to be shaped to—the conceptual framework the Stoics had erected around the Greek language, a Procrustean bed of considerably ampler dimensions than that which Latin in turn engineered for the European vernaculars.[13]

Another Hellenized easterner, Antipater of Tarsus, succeeded Diogenes as head of the Stoa sometime about B.C. 150, but with Diogenes' student Panaetius the school once again came into native Greek hands. From B.C. 129 to his death in B.C. 110 Panaetius served as scholarch and not only opened adventuresome new avenues in theory, but initiated as well the brilliant Roman phase in Stoicism.

Panaetius was born of Greek stock on Rhodes, studied literature with Crates at Pergamum,[14] philosophy with Diogenes at Athens, and was probably well known at Rome before he assumed the directorship at Athens in B.C. 129. He became an important member of the Scipionic circle, perhaps through Polybius, and Scipio Aemilianus took him on his year-long journey around the Near East in B.C. 140–139. Panaetius was not an academic in the style of a Diogenes or an Antipater; he was close

---

12. See Chapter XII, pp. 451–52.

13. The Hellenic manner of dealing with grammar was not limited to the western tradition. The grammar of Dionysius was translated into Syriac by Sergius of Resh Ayna (d. A.D. 536) and proceeded to commit acts of violence against the Semitic Syriac. The Arabs, who came to grammar from the direction of rhetoric rather than philosophy, were more successful in resisting the Stoic blandishments of Dionysius.

14. It may have been due to Crates' influence that in Panaetius' treatment of the traditional cosmological arguments of the Stoa it is not so much the *order* of the universe that is adduced as its *beauty*, a theme not often found in Zeno or Chrysippus.

to the seats of power at Rome and had seen, as Polybius had, Roman imperialistic designs at first hand.

Panaetius followed Diogenes in relaxing the rigorous moralism of the earlier Stoa of Zeno and Chrysippus. A new naturalism is discernible in Panaetius' rejection of astrology and divination. There is a new humanism as well: Panaetius restored the affective life of man and admitted at least some of the previously banned *pathe* as a legitimate basis for moral activity. The new morality relied on the instinctive aspirations of man as an index of the good and stressed the obligations of choosing the good life from among the concrete realities of man's moral environment.[15]

This opening into the world may have been the result of Carneades' criticism of the neat systematizations of Chrysippus, or it may reflect the return of a genuine Hellenic humanism to the Stoa. More than any of his predecessors, Panaetius was aware of the varieties of personality and temperament both in individuals and in social groups, and of the complexity of human behavior. The academic and intellectualistic definition of what it was to be a man and to share that experience with others was modified in the direction of human reality. Humanism, naturalism and realism came together in the philosophy of Panaetius.

Panaetius' realism is evident in his treatment of Rome. Polybius and Panaetius were the first Hellenic intellectuals to give serious attention to the phenomenon of Roman power. Polybius had analyzed it in terms of Greek political science,[16] and now Panaetius made his attempt at understanding Rome and her works in the context of Stoic philosophy. Classical Stoicism, which concentrated its interest on the ideal of the sage (*sophos*), gave scant attention to actual political conditions or institutions: the relative goods of *Realpolitik* held little attraction for the Stoic theoreticians. Panaetius did not, however, share this utopian vision of morality, and so departed from his predecessors' practice and set down a theory of the state that immediately involved him in Roman politics.

Polybius and Panaetius shared a preference for a "mixed" constitution, but differed from Plato and Aristotle in seeing the

---

15. Panaetius' moral teachings, derived principally from his essay *Befitting Acts*, is preserved in the first two books of Cicero's *On Duties*. The third book of that work relied on Posidonius' appendix to the Panaetian original.

16. See Chapter X, p. 400.

mixture of monarchy, aristocracy and democracy guaranteed not by the presence of social and economic classes in the state but by the effective operation of political institutions, the Consulate, the Senate and the Assembly. But if Panaetius' interest in the imperfect institutions of political activity was new in the Stoa, his analysis was not. Where he was more adventuresome, however, was in considering the state—or better, the commonwealth (res publica)—as a kind of social contract entered into by the citizens for the furtherance of their mutual interests, and particularly the protection of their private property.

The subject of private property was a sensitive one at Rome. The Gracchi, who had their own Stoic theoretician in Blossius,[17] were preaching agrarian reform and the redistribution of property. In making the protection of private property a primary concern of the state, Panaetius, who had aristocratic origins himself, came down firmly on the side of the conservative aristocrats of the Scipionic circle. Further, Carneades had attacked Roman "justice," and Panaetius undertook to defend the imperialism of the Roman state by establishing the justice of certain kinds of war, and particularly those humanely fought by Rome for its own security and that of its allies. As for the annexation of conquered territories, Panaetius reached back to Aristotle for the opinion that it was clearly to the benefit of backward nations to be ruled by their natural masters. It is scarcely to be wondered that Panaetius made Stoicism popular among the ruling classes at Rome.

The evidence is obscure, but Panaetius may have fathered another set of attitudes that began to appear during the last century of the Republic, an interest in the history of philosophy. Up to that time scholars had concerned themselves chiefly with noting the succession of masters and students in the academic schools, but after the turn of the last pre-Christian century there was a conscious and definable return to the founders, particularly Plato and Aristotle. And in this more serious seeking out of intellectual antecedents Socrates took on an increasing importance as the genuine beginning of philosophical inquiry. Panaetius' On the Philosophical Schools may have been the source for this new perspective; it is certain, at any rate, that he paid far greater

17. A fellow student of Panaetius' in the Stoa of Diogenes and Antipater, Blossius later joined the revolutionary movement at Pergamum (see Chapter VIII, note 5).

homage to Plato and Aristotle than had any of his Stoic fore-bears.

Panaetius' desire to associate himself with the fourth-century masters opened the way for Plato into the Stoa; it raised as well the question of the antecedents of the Academy itself. Philo of Larissa (*fl. c.* B.C. 88–84) was the last man to preside over a skeptical Academy. His student Antiochus of Ascalon (d. *c.* B.C. 68) repudiated the skepticism that had reigned unchallenged in the schools for two centuries, and the polemic between master and student can be traced across the pages of Cicero's *Academics*.[18] The battle was fought on the grounds of history as the two men struggled for possession of the sacred relics of Plato. Both operated within the same premise, a relatively new one in philosophy: the true Academy was the one that could justify its position out of Socrates and Plato.

The position of Philo was that the Academy since Arcesilaus was fully in the Socratic tradition. He invoked Socrates' own hints of methodical doubt, the testimony of the pre-Socratics, and, less convincingly, Plato himself in defense of skepticism and the withholding of judgment. The Academic tradition, Philo maintained, suffered no lapse with Arcesilaus. Antiochus saw the matter quite differently. He considered Plato as an out-and-out dogmatist and pointed out that the notorious Socratic profession of ignorance was nothing more than the pedagogical technique of irony. Arcesilaus was, then, an aberration from the Academic tradition that he, Antiochus, was restoring by his return to dogmatism.

Both men, then, claimed the bones of Plato. But Antiochus was prepared to go further, and here, perhaps, the hand of Panaetius becomes evident. Arcesilaus not only was a deviate in the Academy but had denied the single great philosophical tradition that flowed down from the past. In Antiochus' view Socrates was the founder of modern philosophy that was systematized by Plato. Plato's students remained generally faithful to the system, and even though Aristotle may have weakened the theory of the *eide* and Zeno may have introduced some corrections into the system, it is nevertheless true that all three schools—the Academy, the Lyceum (Strato excepted) and the Stoa—differed more in terminology than in substance.

---

18. Cicero heard both men lecture: Philo in Rome in B.C. 88 and Antiochus at Athens ten years later.

There is a curious story in a number of ancient authors that suggests that the Lyceum too was engaged in rewriting its history. According to the main version of the tale, Theophrastus bequeathed his own and Aristotle's library to Neleus of Skepsis, who had hidden the books away in a cave so that they would not fall into the acquisitive hands of the librarians of Attalus of Pergamum. The collection, by then in an advanced state of decay, was purchased by the bibliophile Apellicon of Teos, who installed it at Athens and made some well-intentioned but crude attempts at restoring the damaged texts. When Sulla took Athens from Mithridates in B.C. 86 he confiscated the library and brought it to Rome, where the scholarly *grammatikos* Tyrannion, a student of Dionysius Thrax, undertook a complete restoration of the text. Using Tyrannion's text as his basis, the Peripatetic scholarch Andronicus of Rhodes (*c.* B.C. 70) rearranged and catalogued the writings of Aristotle and began the work of commenting upon them.

There is nothing implausible about this story except its tendentious implications. Strabo, one source of the story, made the point quite clearly: between the death of Theophrastus and the time of Andronicus the Lyceum possessed only the Aristotelian *exoterica*[19] and so was reduced to rhetorical inanities; with Andronicus the esoteric school treatises returned to circulation, and so the Lyceum could once again "Aristotelize." Clearly someone, the source of Strabo's story, was intent on reading Strato of Lampsacus and his immediate successors out of the Aristotelian tradition, just as Antiochus sought to repudiate the Academy of Arcesilaus and Carneades.

The beginning and the end of Strabo's narrative are probably true. Theophrastus did bequeath the libraries to Neleus, and Andronicus did mark the beginning of a new scholarly interest in Aristotle, based, in all probability, on a new edition of the school treatises that eventually drove the Aristotelian dialogues out of

19. Scholars of the time of Cicero divided the works of Aristotle into the technical school treatises that began as lectures (*akroatika*) to the students in the Lyceum and then were worked up into treatises (*hypomnemata*), and the "public discourses" (*exoterikoi logoi*) addressed to a wider audience and hence more polished and rhetorical but less philosophically sophisticated than the school treatises. Modern scholarship recognizes the distinction but is more inclined to see Aristotle's passage from dialogues to school treatises as a function of his evolution from an early stylistic and substantial Platonism.

circulation.[20] What happened between those two events is possibly contained in another, less romantic, version of the story: Neleus sold the library to Ptolemy Philadelphus. Whatever the case, the work of Andronicus is another clear piece of evidence for the rising tide of philosophical classicism that characterized the age of Cicero.

This renewed interest in what happened in the fourth century was hardly the product of a disinterested historicism. The sound of axes being ground could be heard everywhere, and nowhere more audibly than in Antiochus' excursions into the history of philosophy. His thesis of one Great Tradition in philosophy blurred the distinctions between the schools, and the intermingling of doctrines was an accomplished fact down to the end of antiquity and beyond, into Islam. Each school invoked this common and distorted past. Stoics did not hesitate to write commentaries on Plato, and Platonists on Aristotle. Philo of Alexandria is indistinguishably a Platonist or a Stoic, and parts of the *Enneads* of Plotinus circulated in the Islamic East as the "Theology of Aristotle." Another Aristotelian pseudepigraph, the treatise *On the Universe,* was the work on an anonymous first-century Stoic.[21]

Did Antiochus' "classicism" extend to a revival of the transcendental Platonic *eide?* One or another version of them is present in the Romans Cicero, Varro and Seneca, in the Alexandrians Arius Didymus and Philo, and in the second-century Platonist Albinus of Smyrna. Antiochus has been suggested as a likely candidate for their common source. If so, Cicero, who provides most of our information on Antiochus, knows nothing of this contribution of his; for Cicero, Antiochus was a Stoic in all but name. For his own part, Antiochus was aware that Aristotle had undermined the Forms, but he does not present himself, nor does Cicero present him, as the philosopher who restored them to their place of honor. On the face of it, it would seem unlikely that someone still so enmeshed in Stoic materialism as Antiochus was capable of reaffirming the spiritual *eide.*

And yet Antiochus must remain the most likely source for that peculiar version of the Form theory that is put forth sketchily in

---

20. This must have occurred sometime about A.D. 200. The Neoplatonists, at any rate, were no longer reading the Aristotelian dialogues.

21. See Chapter XII, p. 465.

Cicero and Varro, but clearly in Philo and Seneca. It was he who saw Platonism, Aristotelianism and Stoicism as a single system, and it was he who stood at the head of the Platonic-school tradition at both Rome and Alexandria. What that school tradition taught was neither pure Plato nor pure Aristotle but a synthesis of the two worthy of an Antiochus. Plato had described the formation of the *kosmos* by recourse to the metaphor of the artisan; Aristotle eschewed the figure and reverted instead to the traditional identification of God with mind. The Platonists of the "middle" tradition, from Antiochus to Plotinus, combined the two.[22] Further, Plato had described the *eide* as transcendent paradigms of the sensible world; Aristotle rejected the transcendence of the *eide* and installed them as principles of intelligibility *within* concrete existents. Once again Middle Platonism syncretized the two notions. The *eide* continued to serve as paradigms, but were now located within the mind of the thinking Artificer-God. They were imperfectly imitated in sensible reality and as such performed the function of immanent intelligibility that Aristotle had assigned to the *eide*. The Platonic tradition thenceforward distinguished between *idea* (the Form in the mind of God) and *eidos* (the form as an immanent principle of intelligibility).

Panaetius was the first of the later Stoics to draw from this mélange, and thereafter Platonism, Aristotelianism and Stoicism drew ever closer together. The Academic Antiochus spoke in Stoic tones in his ethics, while Panaetius' student and successor Posidonius could turn from Aristotelian science to Platonic psychology without the slightest embarrassment. Like his teacher, Posidonius (*c.* B.C. 135–51) was a citizen of the new Roman *oikoumene*. Born of old Hellenic stock at Apamea in Syria, he received his philosophical formation in Athens at the hands of Panaetius, who later introduced him into aristocratic circles at Rome. Posidonius traveled the Mediterranean even more widely than Panaetius had done. In addition to the usual eastern ports of call he visited other parts of Italy, Gaul, the German frontier and Spain. When his studies and travels were over he opened a philosophical school on Rhodes.

---

22. This activist God did not, however, meet the requirements of a later, more demanding transcendentalism and had to take his place as a "second God" beneath the inert and remote High God (see Chapter XII, pp. 464–65).

In B.C. 78, when Posidonius was already a philosopher and teacher of repute, Cicero attended his lectures in the Rhodian school. His fame attracted even the considerably less philosophical Pompey, who stopped off to pay his obeisance at Rhodes in B.C. 68 and again in B.C. 62.[23] Posidonius' influence passed out into the *oikoumene* through his own technical writings on philosophy, science and history.[24] The works themselves have now disappeared, but traces of them can be found lodged in Varro, Strabo, Seneca, Plutarch, Nemesius, Dio Chrysostom and Galen. Secondary reminiscences are spread even more widely. Posidonius, who was interested in the entire sweeping domain of history and nature, introduced into the perspective of philosophy a quality of physical and ethnological information about the world and its workings unsurpassed by any of his predecessors, including Aristotle himself. No one can trace with exactness the career of these fragmentary bits of information that Posidonius had woven into his organic view of the universe, but they appear to have flowed forth from the Posidonian *corpus* into the great mass of diatribe literature and the popular philosophy and ethics so favored by late antiquity.[25]

The question of the innovations introduced by Posidonius into Stoicism is a currently disputed one; the work of the three critical thinkers of the period—Panaetius, Antiochus and Posidonius himself—is, for instance, too ill known to allow for very many definite Posidonian ascriptions to the ideas in circulation in the first century B.C. What are most likely his are some of the emphases that newly appeared in Stoicism. Earlier Stoics had held, for example, that the world was a unified whole, linked together by a universal causality. Posidonius suffused that Stoic Whole with a new vitalism. The universe came alive, became a

---

23. Cicero, who had come as a student and probably was treated like one, sounds exasperated at the glow of celebration given off by the meetings of Pompey and Posidonius, and particularly at the fact that the eminent historian-philosopher had written a monograph on Pompey. Sometime about B.C. 60, after his own never-to-be-forgotten consulate, Cicero sent Posidonius an *aide-mémoire* on his own accomplishments in the expectation that it would be worked up into a fitting Hellenic memorial. Posidonius replied that when he read it not only was he not stimulated to write something on the subject, he was positively discouraged from doing so.
24. On Posidonius as a historian see Chapter X, pp. 400-1.
25. On the diatribe see Chapter XI, pp. 415-16.

genuine organism, because it was now seen in terms of "dynamic powers" (*zotikai dynameis*).

Posidonius' researches into the physical sciences like botany, zoology and geology, as well as history and anthropology, provided detailed evidence that the universe of vital *dynameis* was knit into a system of mutual interdependence. The evidence went even further. The life-giving heat of the sun, the effects of the moon on tides, menstrual cycles and human psychology, all suggested that this growth network (*symphyia*) was also the base for a mutual interreaction (*sympatheia*) between the parts of the organism. All causality depended, of course, on interreaction, but not in the organic sense of Posidonius, wherein even bodies remote from one another could work a mutual effect. Action across a distance held no horrors for Posidonius.

These emphases of Posidonius eventually touched almost all branches of the intellectual life in late antiquity. In science the theory of cosmic sympathy gave encouragement and theoretical support to the new attitudes toward physics then developing in Alexandria. In theology Posidonius' attention to the sun as the center of the material and spiritual vitality of the cosmic organism fostered the growth of the astral theology that became widespread in the Empire.[26] Somewhat less obviously he gave to philosophy a sturdy anchor in nature and humanity to serve as a counter to the rising tide of other-worldliness that also marked contemporary thought. Aristotelian empiricism had exercised just such a check on the Platonic Pythagoreanism of its day, and now that Pythagoras was again coming into prominence in the first century, Posidonius once more supplied the naturalistic corrective. The play of the two, Pythagorean mathematical transcendence and Posidonian empirical humanism, is an almost perfect balance in a thinker like Plotinus, but the philosophical tradition eventually lost its interest in both nature and history. Pythagoras reigns almost unchallenged in the fifth-century Platonist Proclus.

There was, however, one area of obvious Platonic influence in Posidonius, Chrysippus looked upon the human soul as a unity that was essentially rational in its constitution and had gone so far as to reduce the affective life of man, the *pathe*, to a series of judgments. Panaetius had earlier reacted against this monistic and

---

26. For Posidonius' influence on both the physics and theology of the period see further Chapter XI, pp. 441–43.

intellectualistic view of the soul. Posidonius had similar objections, but returned to a more obviously Platonic psychology to make his case. The soul is composed of three faculties (*dynameis*)—the rational, the spirited, the appetitive; they are distinct and all perfectly natural operations of the soul. The affects (*pathe*) are not, then, to be extirpated in the manner of the earlier Stoic *apatheia*, but ought to be brought under the control of the rational faculty.

This tripartition of the soul is clearly Platonic and has led some to suspect that it was Posidonius who stood behind an even more dualistic view of the soul that appears without attribution in Book I of Cicero's *Tusculan Disputations*, in Plutarch and elsewhere. Posidonian or not, there were Platonists in the last pre-Christian century who were holding for Plato's and Aristotle's distinction between an immortal and rational intellect (*nous*) and the less spiritual *psyche*. The former was composed of heated *aither*[27] and born of the sun, to which it returned after death released it from the body. The more material *psyche* is compounded of fire and air from the moon and is joined with the *nous* during the latter's downward progress through the spheres toward birth—that is, the final addition of the gross elements that compose the body.

If this curious mixture did derive from Posidonius, it betrays an attitude remote from the commonplace Stoic materialism with its conviction that the soul was a material substance that perished with the body. In this new view the *nous* and the *psyche* have been distinguished in the manner of Aristotle, and their origins and destiny pictured against a background drawn by someone obviously familiar with the myths of the *Phaedrus* and the *Timaeus*.[28] Platonic psychology, already invoked to undermine the operational monism of Chrysippus, here reopened to the philosophical tradition the broad vistas of the "other world." In these texts the *nous* stands, as it did in the early Academy, as the link

---

27. The fifth element (*quinta essentia*) from which the heavenly bodies were also made. Aristotle proposed this theory of the consubstantiality of the *nous* and the heavenly bodies in his early work *On Philosophy;* the first century was, as has been seen, deeply interested in the Aristotelian *exoterica*.

28. One of the most controverted points on Posidonius is whether or not he wrote a commentary on the *Timaeus*. Whether or not he actually wrote a commentary, it is clear that he knew the *Timaeus* well enough.

between the sensible phenomena of this world and the spiritual realities of the intelligible world that had hitherto been repudiated or ignored. In rediscovering Plato, philosophy rediscovered metaphysics as well.

A Philosophical Education

One of Aristotle's early treatises, the first in which he criticized the Platonic theory of *eide*, was entitled simply *On Philosophy*. Some two centuries later Panaetius wrote his work *On the Philosophical Schools*, and the difference between the two books is an accurate measure of what had happened to philosophy in the interval. Aristotle saw the history of philosophy as a broadly based, progressive and cumulative search for wisdom conducted by priests, mythologers and sages among the Greeks and the *barbaroi*. By the time of Panaetius *philosophia* had come to mean the highly technical and programmatic teaching of the Greek philosophical schools (*haireseis*), and it was Panaetius' chief concern to trace the lineage of these and distinguish them in terms of doctrine.[29]

The progressive scholasticizing of philosophy began, of course, with Plato's founding of the Academy, but any attempt at understanding that process from the inner workings of the Academy is baffled by a simple and almost complete ignorance of what went on within that "institution." We know, for instance, that each of the classical philosophical schools located at Athens was directed by a scholarch normally chosen by his predecessor; we also know that people "studied with" the scholarch or with the director of one or another of the daughter branches of the school located in other places, like Alexandria or Pergamum. But we know little or nothing of the structure of the institution, about the nature and shape of the instruction, what was studied, how and when, and whether there was a curriculum or examinations or assistants. Indeed, it has been suggested, not entirely implausibly, that the only formal instruction given in the Academy was in mathematics.

---

29. Both Plato and Aristotle knew of philosophical "schools" in somewhat the same sense—e.g., the Ionian and the Italian—but they had little or no role in the two men's view of the history of philosophy.

It seems likely that the distinction already noted with regard to Aristotle's works was a valid one, and that there were public lectures, like Plato's notorious one on "the Good" when the audience was treated to a disquisition on mathematics, and, in the Lyceum at least, closed, technical discussions of which the Aristotelian school treatises still bear some trace. The Lyceum possessed a library that was partly archival in nature, and at least some of the students there were set to work on scholarly research projects that produced, in the generation after Aristotle, a spate of Peripatetic histories of the various scientific disciplines.[30]

Aristotle's turning from the earlier Socratic oral and public approach to philosophy and the sciences to a closed, literary manner was mediated by the Platonic dialogue. The dialogues of Plato were, in a sense, an attempt to reproduce in literature the Socratic public conversation. Plato was never entirely easy with the compromise between thought, speech and the written word; and now and again he felt constrained to apologize for his lapse into writing. The Socratic-Cynic tradition generally remained faithful to the tentative and informal discourse of its master, and even some of Plato's more academic successors, Arcesilaus and Carneades, talked rather than wrote.

There is no evidence that Aristotle ever experienced such embarrassment. Indeed, it may have been his own more rigorous method of demonstration that drove the later Plato from dialogue to monologue and sounded the death knell for the dialogue as a vehicle for philosophical discourse. There were some later nostalgic philosophical dialogues—Cicero's are an obvious example—and even an eccentric poet or two, but by and large philosophy followed Aristotle's example and deserted the dialogue for the systematic and undramatic treatises (*hypomnemata*) that bore some resemblance to the lecture notes from which they derived. Aristotle probably worked his notes up into treatises himself, but there are preserved examples of published student transcripts of lectures.[31]

Aristotle's normal method in the school treatises was to pose

---

30. See Chapter II, p. 107.
31. Most of these, the ancestors of the medieval Latin *reportatio*, date from the Platonic schools of the fifth to seventh centuries, and it has been suggested that the professors resorted to the device of publishing their lectures under the names of their Christian students to avoid the unwelcome attention of either the Church or the state.

the question in the form of a Socratic query (*aporia*), then to review the history of the problem by scanning the opinions (*endoxa*) of his predecessors before finally arguing, in what can only be called a rather loose demonstration, his own solution (*lysis*). Elsewhere, however, in somewhat more programmatic treatises like the *Categories* or the *Topics*, Aristotle or one of his students unfolded the material through a series of definitions and distinctions with only a minimum of either argumentation or historical review.

The former method of development is peculiarly Aristotelian, but the latter went back, via Plato and even Socrates, to the first of the Greek literary disciplines to reach the maturity of systematization, rhetoric.[32] The Sophists began the standardization and organization of the means of persuasion around the principles of definition and distinction, and this body of systematic teaching, at first transmitted orally but later committed to writing, constituted the earliest technical handbooks (*techne*, the later Latin *ars*)[33] that the Greeks possessed. Plato knew of them and judged them harshly, even though he used the rhetorician's technique of *diairesis* as the cornerstone of his own dialectic. Aristotle was more respectful; he studied the rhetorical *technai* in preparing his own *Rhetoric*, where, as might be expected, the method of definition-division is more frequently used than in anything else he wrote.

The methods of the rhetorical handbooks, reduced to an increasingly jejune presentation as the oral tradition that lay behind them disappeared, had a profound effect on the teaching of philosophy, and nowhere more markedly than in the Stoa. The Academic practice of division (*diairesis*) was carried on by both Speusippus and Xenocrates, and though it had its effects in the Lyceum, the empirical interests of the Peripatetics inclined them rather in the direction of an inductive collection of data, whether historical or natural, that served as a counterweight to this Academic penchant for analytical unfolding. The Stoa, on the other hand, appears to have succumbed to *diairesis*, and by the time of

---

32. Followed, in fairly short order, by mathematics and medicine, which also began to exhibit a standardized terminology in the fifth century.

33. The word was used indifferently for the craft itself, the systematic statement of its principles, or the manual in which these latter were set down.

Chrysippus there existed systematic statements in abbreviated form of the positions of the school in the three major branches of logic, physics and ethics.[34] The startling success of these epitomes can best be measured by the fact that they eventually drove out of circulation the original works of the masters on which they were based; Zeno, Crates and Chrysippus survive only in compendia.

Where many of the Stoic-school compendia eventually came to rest at the beginning of the third Christian century was in the jerry-built confines of Diogenes Laertius' *The Doctrines and Lives of the Philosophers*. Book VII, dedicated to the Stoics, is patched together from a series of just such epitomes, a few of which can be identified. The compendium of logic is cited verbatim from something called *Synopsis of Philosophers* by Diocles of Magnesia (*c.* B.C. 100–50), the historian to whom Meleager dedicated his *Garland*.[35] Diocles was another compiler and *his* sources carry the reader back to the generation of the great Stoic systematizers: Chrysippus, Diogenes of Seleucia, Antipater, Panaetius and Posidonius. Diocles cites among others Diogenes' *On Speech*, and here one is in the presence of a truly important work, the first Stoic *techne* on grammar and the source in turn of the very first of the Hellenistic handbooks that have been preserved, Dionysius Thrax's *Handbook of Grammar*.

The handbook, whether rhetorical, grammatical, philosophical or arithmetical,[36] was characterized by its unmistakable pedagogic method of defining the basic terms of the discipline in simple and straightforward language and then setting out in brief and schematic form the main points of the subject by a series of distinctions and divisions at one remove from an outline. Since neither argumentation nor evidence was presented, the form was ideally suited to nonprofessional students to be found in the Hellenistic secondary schools, and by the time Hellenism passed into the orbit of Rome very few students on that level approached the subjects of the *enkyklios paideia* through the

---

34. This basic division of philosophy that later became the hallmark of Stoicism—the Lyceum continued to regard logic as an instrument (*organon*) rather than a part of philosophy—went back to Xenocrates but was at least implicit in Plato.
35. See Chapter XI, Note 8.
36. Where the reigning *techne* was the *Introduction to Arithmetic* of Nicomachus of Gerasa (see Chapter V, p. 211).

"Great Books" but resorted instead to the ubiquitous *technai* or their Latin equivalents.[37]

The Lyceum knew such compendia; an extremely popular and influential résumé of Aristotelianism was composed in the first century by Herod's court philosopher Nicholas of Damascus.[38] But Peripateticism was saved from their suffocating embrace by the vogue of classicism that deeply affected philosophy in the same period that saw the proliferation of the *technai*. The handbook might suit the dilettante or the amateur; the professional student within the school needed stronger food and traditionally he had found this in the technical treatises (*hypomnemata*) of his teachers. Philosophical classicism professed to go behind these latter-day pedagogues and find its sustenance in the works of the masters themselves, in Plato and Aristotle, who were once again being seriously read in the first century B.C.

This return to the past first visible in philosophy, though with profound implications in literature and art,[39] had solid scholarly foundations. Mention has already been made of Andronicus' "edition" of the entire school *corpus* of Aristotle. This Peripatetic scholarch was also the first of a long series of Aristotelian commentators who addressed themselves directly to the text. Plato too was carefully read, though selectively. Middle Platonism had its own Platonic "canon," the *Symposium, Phaedrus, Phaedo, Theaetetus,* and particularly the *Timaeus* (the crucial parts of which Cicero translated into Latin), where it devoted its interests and from which it drew its inspiration. Neoplatonism had the same canon, adding only the *Alcibiades* and the *Parmenides* to its range.

---

37. Most of what is known of the ancient handbook tradition comes, in fact, from the Roman examples by Cicero, Varro, Celsus, Vitruvius, the *Poet's Handbook (Ars Poetica)* of Horace, and the *Lover's Handbook (Ars Amatoria)* of Ovid. Varro appears to have been the first to write a multipart *techne* covering all the fields of the *trivium* and the *quadrivium* plus the two crafts of medicine and architecture— in short, a systematic encyclopedia. This has all but completely vanished, but the genre is still represented by the *Marriage of Philology and Mercury* by the early-fifth-century author Martianus Capella.
38. See Chapter X, pp. 402–3. Islamic Hellenism, which was largely unacquainted with the *enkyklios paideia* and knew even less of the Latins, developed *its* encyclopedia tradition out of just such Aristotelian compendia as Nicholas', supplemented by Euclid and Ptolemy.
39. See Chapter XV, pp. 541–42.

None of this touched the handbook tradition, but it did leave its mark on the instruction within the Academy and the Lyceum. The students continued to resort to philosophical compendia for their general orientation, but henceforward the professors offered their advanced instruction in the form of commentaries on the texts of Plato and Aristotle. The scholastic techniques refined in the *technai* were adapted to another set of pedagogic instruments shaped to serve this new textual approach for which the editorial work of Andronicus provided the necessary precondition.

Andronicus' successors in the Lyceum are little more than names, but attached to each is the firm tradition of textual exegesis. It is not until the opening years of the third Christian century, with Alexander of Aphrodisias, that we have any way of judging the results. And they are indeed impressive. Alexander was a commentator of great integrity who did not hesitate to make clarifications and even additions to Aristotle's thought,[40] but was nonetheless concerned to present the unalloyed doctrine of the master without either the mysticism or the syncretism that affected most of contemporary philosophy. With Alexander it is already clear that Peripateticism had set its course in the direction of a scholarly and technical study of philosophy, a narrowing of ambition that served it well in the difficult days ahead.

Not all of Alexander's work was in the form of textual exegesis. He wrote some free-standing essays and a series of "questions" (*aporiai*) on specific problems in Aristotelianism. This latter method of *aporia-lysis* had its origins, as has been seen, in the methods of Socratic discourse, but was soon domesticated in the classrooms of the Lyceum. In the end all the schools adopted it both as a form of composition and as a pedagogical device. Like its later prolific descendants, the medieval *quaestiones disputatae* and *quaestiones quodlibetales*, the *aporiai* of late antiquity were essentially university exercises.

The pedagogical cast of Peripateticism is even more amply illustrated by another device that inevitably accompanied the teaching of Aristotle in the professional schools. As these same

---

40. Much of the later discussions of Aristotle's psychology, and particularly the doctrine of the active and the passive intellect, took as its point of departure Alexander's elaboration of the brief remarks in Aristotle's own work. In this area Alexander's influence on both Latin and Islamic Aristotelianism was primary.

schools became more formalized under the Empire, something of their form and curriculum emerges. We know, for instance, that the discussion of the *aporiai* took place in closed seminars intended for the advanced students. The students "in course"—the course was constituted of the works of Aristotle arranged in a variety of ways—attended formal lectures where the task of the professor was systematically to explicate the entire Aristotelian *corpus*.

The form of this professorial exegesis was thoroughly standardized. There was a general introduction, then a reading of the passage in question, followed by the professor's own clarification of its meaning. A great deal of the later literature of philosophical comment reflected this procedure, even when it was no longer connected with a classroom,[41] but it is in the introductory material that the deeply scholastic character of philosophy reveals itself. Whether it developed out of the schools of rhetoric or was a growth native to philosophy, the "introduction" (*eisagoge*)[42] of antiquity was one of the most popular of the pedagogical instruments fashioned by scholasticism.

The student came to his study of Aristotle with three texts in hand. He had, of course, a copy of the treatise to be read and commented upon. But he possessed as well a biography of Aristotle and a bibliography (*pinax*) of Aristotle's works, and these two formed an important part of the formidably schematized *eisagoge*. Before the student could take up the reading of the *Categories*,[43] he was first given a general introduction to philosophy, its possible definitions and divisions. Thence the professor passed to a discussion of Aristotle's philosophy in particular. The *Life* was read and the *pinax* discussed. How, for instance, were the works to be arranged? By subject, by form, or

---

41. Thus the highly learned commentaries of Simplicius were probably written *after* his expulsion from Athens. The work of the Aristotelian commentators under Islam, where philosophy had no place in the school system, were also creations of the study and not the classroom, but betray the same scholastic characteristics.

42. *Eisagoge* was used both of an introduction to a subject, where it was a general and simplified survey of the field and so indistinguishable from the handbook, or *techne*, and of an introduction to an author. It is used in that latter sense in what follows.

43. Or later, of Porphyry's *eisagoge* to the *Categories*, which became an integral part of the Aristotelian *corpus*.

according to the divisions of knowledge? The philosophy of Aristotle was analyzed under ten heads in all, and only after each of them had been developed could the professor lead the student to the *Categories*, which had, of course, its own *eisagoge*—What is its intent? Its usefulness, authenticity, arrangement, subdivisions?

The entire schema of the *eisagoge* is preserved only in later authors of the fifth and sixth centuries, but there is no doubt that it was being used in one form or another far earlier. It was already suggested in the scholarly edition of Andronicus of Rhodes; and Ptolemy Chennus, one of the obscure Peripatetics between Andronicus and Alexander, prepared an elaborate *pinax* that shows up in the later *eisagoge* literature. The philosophical schools had only to look to Alexandria to find both material and formal precedent for their *eisagogai*.

The scholars at Alexandria had busied themselves with the compilation of the bibliographies of many authors, including philosophers. They had further established a skeleton for the history of philosophy with the chronological studies of Eratosthenes (*c.* B.C. 276–194) and the Stoic-educated Apollodorus of Athens (*c.* B.C. 180–110),[44] both of whom included philosophers in their elaborate chronologies. The Alexandrians, probably under Peripatetic influence,[45] also linked together the chains of scholarchs of the various schools in the genre called Successions (*Diadoche*). That other Peripatetic inspiration, the connection of the ethical biography with this chronological and bibliographical matter, was, as has been seen, somewhat less happy.[46] Unlike the biographies, the latter material rested on fairly solid historical grounds.

None of these projects, historical or imaginative, much bothered with philosophical content. The Alexandrian philologists were little interested in the substance of philosophy; they contented themselves with determining when a scholarch lived, who were his students, and with retailing whatever anecdotal

44. Apollodorus belonged to both the Alexandrian scientific tradition—he was the student there of Aristarchus of Samothrace—and the Athenian Stoa of Diogenes of Seleucia (see Chapter II, p. 116).
45. The practice is connected with the name of Sotion, a Peripatetic at Alexandria sometime between B.C. 200 and B.C. 170.
46. See Chapter II, p. 115.

matter drifted into their biographical nets. Of the internal evolution of philosophy they were completely innocent. The schools themselves did, fortunately, have some notion of this evolution, thanks principally to Aristotle and Theophrastus. At least part of Aristotle's philosophical method was the scrutiny of the opinions (*endoxa*) of his predecessors, frequently set down in simplified and schematized form. In Aristotle the *endoxa* were incorporated into a more elaborate philosophical work like the *Metaphysics* or *On the Soul*, but in Theophrastus they stood alone arranged by subject matter, under the title *Opinions of the Natural Philosophers*.

Here, then, was solid philosophical matter, albeit highly epitomized, and in the course of time later versions and elaborations of Theophrastus' doxography[47] were incorporated with the biographical and bibliographical findings, perhaps first by Diocles of Magnesia in the first century B.C., to produce the very mixed product that is Diogenes Laertius' "history of philosophy."

Later inheritors of Hellenism, with very few original texts in hand, depended very heavily on such handbooks, doxographies and potpourris for their knowledge of the philosophical past. By an odd quirk both the original texts that the handbooks drove out of circulation and the handbooks themselves have all but disappeared. We are not at all sure what an al-Farabi, a Boethius, a Proclus, or even a Plotinus had in hand when he cites his predecessors *outside* the Academy or the Lyceum; Islamic philosophers, for instance, seem not to have known Plotinus by name, because whatever handbooks they were reading left off sometime in the middle of the second Christian century.

Beneath Plato and Aristotle, supported by the filial piety of their own school traditions, the ground was much firmer. Plotinus read both authors with an impressive array of first- and second-century commentators, and at least some of their work continued to be read in the original form, if not in the original language, from the end of the Roman Republic uninterruptedly down to the Renaissance. And the philosophers of each genera-

---

47. Theophrastus' doxography may have formed part of Aristotle's program for an empirical approach to the study of the natural sciences, just as the *Characters* did in ethics, but these collections later found other uses. As a reading of Cicero's philosophical works suggests, they were a rich mine for polemic between the schools in an age that was fond of invoking the past.

tion, in both the Latin and the Arabic traditions, appear to have received their initiation by the identical series of scholastic introductions and handbooks which shaped not only their understanding of what they read but their philosophical production as well.

X

The Augustan Empire

For the inhabitants of the new Roman provinces of Asia and
Syria the Italian struggles of Pompey and Caesar, the two surviving triumvirs, were a distant battle whose echoes were the levies
of money and men in the East. Pompey was a hero there, but
whatever sympathy there may have been for his cause against
Caesar was dissipated by the pressures of his legates. Pompey's
father-in-law Metellus Scipio was particularly active in Syria,
where the legions lately under the command of Cassius and
Bibulus were led off to the final confrontation with Caesar in
Greece, and the *publicani* were pressed to hand over their cash
reserves. The client kings too answered the call for troops.

It was in vain. In B.C. 48 at Pharsalus in Thessaly, Caesar prevailed over Pompey (who had fled to Egypt) and came to the
East to make his own arrangements. Caesar had been in the East
before, but only as a student[1] and an all but unnoticed soldier; he
now came as a conqueror. Unexpectedly he revised the tax
structure, reducing the *stipendium* of Asia and abolishing the role
of the *publicani* in the collection of direct taxes, which would
henceforward be paid directly to the Quaestor by the various
communities. It was an extremely popular measure with the eastern provincials.

Caesar then went off to Egypt in pursuit of Pompey. Ptolemy
XI Auletes had ruled there from his controversial restoration by
Gabinius in B.C. 55 to his death in B.C. 51. He was jointly suc-

---

1. He was another of the distinguished Roman alumni of the Greek
rhetorical school at Rhodes.

ceeded by his daughter Cleopatra VII[2] and his teen-age son Ptolemy XII; the two were also, in the Egyptian fashion, husband and wife. After a few years they had fallen to fighting, and Cleopatra, who had been chased from Alexandria was, at the time of Pharsalus, busy in Syria and Palestine collecting troops for her restoration.

Caesar missed catching hold of Pompey, who was murdered by his own men, by only three days; on landing at Alexandria he was confronted instead by the death rattle of the Ptolemies, the hostility of the young Ptolemy's court, and the charm of Cleopatra VII. The Roman *imperator*, who already had a wife, married her (they had a son, Caesarion) and restored her to the joint rule with Ptolemy. The intervention did not sit well with Ptolemy's advisers, who rose up in revolt. It was a near thing for Caesar; only the arrival of legions from Syria saved him from the army of Ptolemy and the mobs of Alexandria. The chief casualty of the fighting turned out to be a large store of manuscripts sitting exposed on the dockside. Another, younger son of Auletes was placed on the throne beside Cleopatra, and Caesar hastened back to Asia.

The shadow of the redoubtable Mithridates Eupator was once again over the land in the person of his son Pharnaces. Earlier he had been his father's viceroy in the Crimea, and it was he who had thwarted the old man's plans to invade Italy by turning the troops against his father and eventually bringing about his death. Now he profited by the upheavals of the Roman civil war to repossess the ancestral domain in Pontus, since the time of Pompey a Roman province. There were initial successes, but with the arrival of Caesar the opposition collapsed in a remarkably short time. Caesar's comment on the Pontic campaign was very much to the point: "I came, I saw, I conquered." His predecessors in Pontus had not been so fortunate.

Two of Caesar's assassins of B.C. 44 had considerable knowledge of the East. Brutus had been Quaestor of Cilicia under Cicero's predecessor there,[3] and Cassius had been Quaestor and acting

---

2. The "Cleopatra strain" among the Ptolemies went back to Ptolemy V Epiphanes (B.C. 203–181), who had married Cleopatra, the daughter of Antiochus III and Laodice, a princess of Pontus (see Chapter IV, p. 178).

3. And in whose financial affairs Cicero had become inextricably

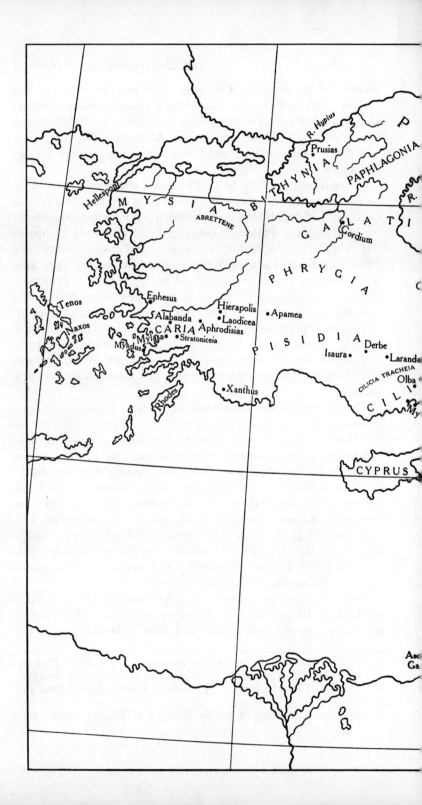

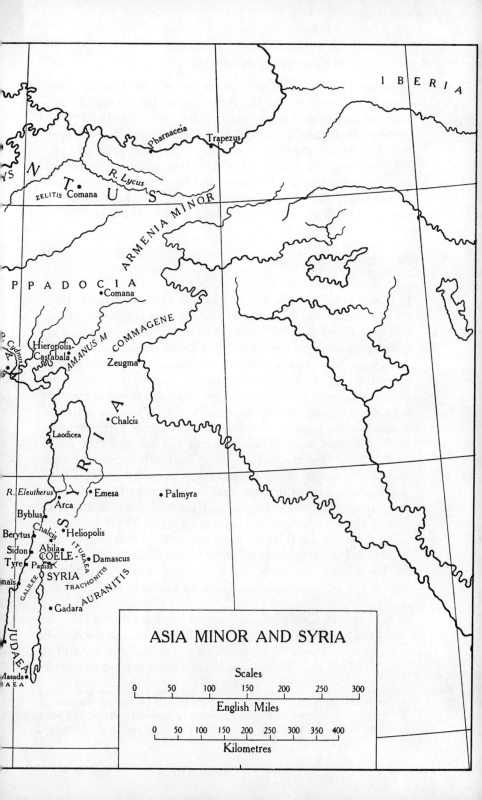

I B E R I A

Pharnaceia • Trapezus

N T U S

ZELITIS Comana

R. Lycus

ARMENIA MINOR

P P A D O C I A

• Comana

AMANUS M

COMMAGENE

Hieropolis- Castabala

Zeugma

Cydnus

S Y R I A

• Chalcis

Laodicea

R. Eleutherus • Emesa • Palmyra

Arca

Byblus

Berytus Chalcis • Heliopolis

Sidon Abila

Tyre Panias COELE-

ITURAEA

• Damascus

GALILEE SYRIA

TRACHONITIS

nais

• Gadara AURANITIS

JUDAEA

Masada •

AEA

ASIA MINOR AND SYRIA

Scales

| 0 | 50 | 100 | 150 | 200 | 250 | 300 |

English Miles

| 0 | 50 | 100 | 150 | 200 | 250 | 300 | 350 | 400 |

Kilometres

governor of Syria after the disastrous end of Crassus. After Caesar's assassination and the formation of the Second Triumvirate of Octavian, Antony and Lepidus, the would-be restorers of the Republic beat about Asia for money and troops as Pompey had done before them. Cassius seized his old province of Syria after deposing the Senate's nominee. Huge advances on the tax revenue were demanded. Rhodes and Lycia were pillaged, and Cassius seized the property of the Jews in Antioch. Again it was all to no end. The triumvirs prevailed at Philippi in B.C. 42.

Antony in the East

In the division of the spoils the East fell to Mark Antony. Both his grandfather and his father had held eastern commands against the pirates, and Antony himself had served with distinction in Gabinius' campaigns against the Jewish insurgents in Judaea in B.C. 57–56. Now as a member of the ruling triumvirate he was given the task of raising funds from the seemingly inexhaustible eastern coffers. The ways were greased by various grants and immunities, which Antony dispensed in B.C. 41 to consolidate his position as the popular liberator from the recent harsh measures of Brutus and Cassius. The provincials too had had their fill of civil war. Antony proceeded through Asia as liberator, governor and judge. Among those summoned to be judged were Herod and Phaselus, sons of the now dead Antipater the Idumaean who had supported Cassius. Antony met them in Antioch and confirmed them in power, leaving Hyrcanus as High Priest and appointing the brothers as civil tetrarchs. Another who had promised, but never delivered, support for Cassius was Cleopatra of Egypt, and she made her spectacular and well-publicized appearance before Antony at Tarsus in Cilicia in the fall of B.C. 41.

Antony, like Caesar before him, was intrigued by the lady and spent the winter with the queen in Egypt. It was a winter ill spent; the Parthians began to attack Syria, and Antony had to return to Italy to collect troops. While he was there the triumvirs

---

entangled. Brutus had made a huge loan to the people of Salamis on Cyprus on the kingly terms of 48 percent compound interest and later brought tremendous pressure to bear on Cicero to retrieve the money.

met once again at Brundisium in the fall of B.C. 40 and renewed their compact. Their spheres of interest were once more de-limited; to Antony fell all the provinces east of Illyria. He married Octavian's sister Octavia in the bargain and returned to deal with the Parthians.

The Parthians had been quiescent since their great victory over Crassus in B.C. 53. Brutus and Cassius had, however, sought their support before Philippi; Quintus Labienus was dispatched to Orodes to persuade him to open hostilities on the eastern front. That was not to be in B.C. 43, but three years later, during Antony's absence in Alexandria, a Parthian army under the prince Pacorus and Labienus, now a full-blown renegade, occu-pied Syria and deposed Hyrcanus in favor of Antigonus, another son of Aristobulus. The agile Herod, ruler of Galilee, escaped to his fortresses in Idumaea, thence to Petra, where he was denied refuge by the Arabs. Finally he made his way to Alexandria and Rome. Both Octavian and Antony were there in B.C. 40, and since he was their only man in Judaea they bestowed upon Herod the title of king, vacant since the death of Alexander Jannaeus. Labienus, meanwhile, had left Pacorus to deal with Syria and had crossed the Taurus, where he was pillaging the province of Asia.

Steps had to be taken immediately. Antony returned as far as Athens and from there directed the preliminaries of what was to be a great offensive against the Parthians. A Roman army under Ventidius cleared Asia. Labienus fell back over the Taurus, where he was defeated, as was a second army sent up in support by Pacorus. Labienus was captured and executed. This was the summer of B.C. 39. The following summer Antony arrived in person to deal with Antiochus, the Parthianizing king of Com-magene. Afterward Antony's legate Sosius and Herod were left to dispossess Antigonus, the son of Aristobulus, who was still holding out in Jerusalem. In the interval Herod had attempted to solidify his claim to legitimacy by marrying the granddaughter of Aristobulus, and when Antigonus was finally deposed, in B.C. 37, Herod's grasp on uncontested rule finally seemed complete.

Until late in B.C. 37 Antony was engaged in assisting Octavian in the west, and when he returned to Antioch that fall, this time to stay, he took the first irreversible steps down a new path. He married Cleopatra, recognized as his children the twins she had borne him in B.C. 40, Alexander Helios and Cleopatra Selene, and gave to their mother as her wedding gift large tracts of Syria,

Palestine and the Phoenician coast that she had coveted at the obvious expense of Herod and Malik, king of the Nabataeans. In her hands these territories reconstituted Egypt in the days of its Ptolemaic glory.

Antony was ready to begin the postponed expedition against Parthia in the spring of B.C. 36; Carrhae was to be avenged. But not at Carrhae. The lessons of Crassus in Mesopotamia had been learned, and Antony's plan called for an assault not through the deserts of Mesopotamia but by way of Armenia. An army was already there, and when Antony joined it they began the transit into Media Atropatene (Azerbaijan). The Armenians were supposed to supply the cavalry support. They did not, and eventually Antony was forced to withdraw with heavy losses as the Parthian King Phraates IV pressed his advantage.

Returning to Syria, Antony carried with him Artavasades, the Euripides-loving Armenian king who had betrayed both himself and Crassus, and the son of Mithridates' old ally and son-in-law Tigranes. In his stead a Roman puppet was placed on the throne of Armenia, and the country took its uneasy place as a buffer state on the spear's point directed at Parthia. It was to remain such after the Romans had become Byzantines and the Parthians were replaced first by the Sasanians and then by the Arabs. Nature had designed Armenia to be the Belgium of eastern militarism.

Antony celebrated his "victory" over the hapless Artavasades by a celebration at Alexandria that marked the final break with Octavian. Caesarion was recognized as Caesar's son and, as Antony's effigy of the dead Caesar, given joint rule with Cleopatra, whose holdings in Syria were, in turn, extended. Octavia was repudiated. His own children by Cleopatra were dowered with all the Roman holdings in the East. Octavian, whose own position in the West had been consolidated, armed to take his vengeance, and Antony and Cleopatra repaired to Ephesus to do likewise. The following year (B.C. 31) at Actium, Octavian broke them. He pursued the pair in an almost leisurely fashion to Egypt, which he annexed to the Roman Empire, whose sole master he now was.

Antony's policy in the East was neither cruel nor repressive. He apparently operated under the shadow of the dead Caesar or attempted to use that hero as a counterweight to Octavian. It was Caesar's plan against Parthia that Antony so unsuccessfully attempted to fulfill, and it was Caesar's son whom he raised up as his candidate for rule in the East. All is overshadowed, of course, by Cleopatra, glimpsed only through the official Augustan portraits of her as a latter-day Oriental Medea. That she was ambitious for herself and her children can scarcely be doubted. But Antony could, when he wished, resist her, as in the case of Herod, whom she wanted deposed. The dismemberment of Syria was not, however, a random, willful gesture to please a queen. Antony had earlier done the same in Anatolia, setting up powerful local kings in Galatia, Paphlagonia and Pontus. It was apparently his intention that Asia and Syria were in large part to be ruled by local dynasts dependent on Rome, Cleopatra and Herod among them, rather than by Republican Proconsuls.

The Augustan Settlement

The constitutional justification of the power that Octavian in fact possessed after B.C. 31 was established in B.C. 27, when a grateful and fearful Senate declined to repossess the extraordinary *imperium* it had granted to Octavian for the pursuit of his war against Antony.[4] Instead the Senate granted him a ten-year mandate over the provinces of Spain, Gaul and Syria and bestowed upon him the title of Augustus by which he was henceforth known. Though it was not obvious at the time, the act marked the end of the civil wars that had been bleeding the state for a century. Nor did many suspect that the Augustan "emergency powers" signaled the end of the republican form of government. Roman conservatism and Octavian's political shrewdness masked the death of the Republic in a veil of constitutional continuity. The Romans dutifully elected their annual magistrates for another five centuries, the Senate bestirred itself upon occasion, and voices might be raised in protest, but it became increasingly clear that beneath the constitutional camouflage the real power in the state rested in the hands of a single man, whether he fancied himself as "First Citizen" (*princeps*), "Father of the Country" (*pater patriae*) or, perhaps most realistically, "Holder of the *Imperium*" (*imperator*).

---

4. Technically the war was against Cleopatra; Octavian was careful not to ask for a declaration of civil war.

From B.C. 27 Augustus was all of these, and as his power became more firmly grounded over the forty years of his reign he could afford to relax his grip on one or another of his constitutional bases, sharing offices that once knew little or no control with men willing to accept *his* control. It was one of the virtuoso performances of history destined to be repeated, with less skill but with equal tenacity, by an unbroken series of Roman *imperatores* reaching down to the fifteenth century.

The settlement of B.C. 27 rested upon the extraordinary *imperium* over Spain, Gaul and Syria; the Senate would supervise the government of the other provinces—for example, Asia and Bithynia—as before. Nothing was said on that historic occasion of Egypt, which was a "province" in a very special sense. Egypt was, and remained, a possession of the *imperator*, used to feed (and control) Italy and jealously guarded against Senatorial or other interference. The land was administered for Augustus not by the usual proconsular governor but by a *praefectus*, and from the very beginning these Egyptian prefects were drawn from among the Equestrians.

The very first Egyptian prefect illustrates some very interesting Augustan motifs. Cornelius Gallus was the commander of one of the armies that took Egypt in B.C. 30. Earlier in his career he had made a considerable name as a poet, the first, in fact, to work in a form in which the Latins could claim some original distinction, the subjective erotic elegy.[5] To this was added the distinction of the prefecture of Egypt, where, within two or three years, an exhibition of his talents for generalship and self-expression brought about his recall and eventually his suicide. Sometime during his term he had led a successful expedition into Upper Egypt "beyond the cataract of the Nile where the arms of neither the Roman people nor the Kings of Egypt had been carried before." It was probably not this military probe that brought about his downfall—one of his successors went the same way with Augustus' approval—but something in the way he described it. According to one account he had it written up on prospects to the Romans. At least since the time of Alexander, a threat to his own position and Gallus was removed, eventually to take his own life.

The occupation of Egypt, of immense economic importance to

---

5. See Chapter V, p. 206.

the state by reason of its agriculture, opened other intriguing prospects to the Romans. At least since the time of Alexander, travelers and merchants had a fairly detailed knowledge of the lands of the farther East and an understanding of the commercial possibilities that they represented. The Mediterranean powers had two means of access to those lands. The first was overland by the great routes that led from termini in Anatolia or Syria across the Euphrates and Tigris, thence through Iran either to Merv (Alexandria) for the trek across Central Asia or to Herat (Alexandria of the Arians) and the Indus Valley. The sea routes began at the Red Sea ports of Egypt, whence once crossed to South Arabia and coasted to Indian ports. A combination was also possible: by caravan to the Euphrates, then down the river to Spasinou Charax at the head of the Persian Gulf for coasting to India.

The Greeks knew all these routes. Alexander had himself reached India through Merv and Herat, and one of his admirals, Nearchus, had cruised the coast west from the Indus to the head of the Persian Gulf. The Ptolemies had explored from the other direction. Philadelphus and Euergetes had shown considerable interest in Red Sea exploration. They founded trade emporia there, and pushed through the Bab el Mandeb to the coasts of southern Arabia and East Africa.

What was chiefly lacking in these enterprises was capital and need. The Romans had both. Rome was wealthy, and her cosmopolitan middle and upper classes had developed a taste for the luxuries of the East. Almost as soon as he inherited the Ptolemaic estate in Egypt, Augustus began to explore the possibilities. The Asian caravan routes were less dangerous, but they depended upon the good will of Parthia, which controlled both land and sea access to Mesopotamia from the east. They were to be developed later; Augustus' first move was from his Egyptian base. Cornelius Gallus' unfortunately advertised expedition beyond the first cataract has already been mentioned. The third prefect, Petronius, had to renew the pressure against the Nubians, and he pushed as far as their capital of Napata in the Sudan. Some kind of understanding was also reached with the Ethiopians, whose queen Candace later maintained diplomatic relations with Augustus.

These may have been expeditions of assault and pacification, but that conducted into western Arabia by the second prefect, Aelius Gallus, had unmistakable commercial implications. Setting

out in B.C. 25, the same year that Augustus was receiving delegations from India, the expedition had to deal, from the outset, with
misinformation supplied by the Nabataeans, who controlled the
north-south overland route through Petra into the Hejaz as far
south as Leuke Kome. To protect their monopoly against the
Roman surveyors they insisted through the guides, whom they
happily supplied, that the northern part of the route was impass-
able and that the Romans would be well advised to sail directly
from Arsinoë at the head of the Gulf of Suez to Leuke Kome.
This was only the first of many missteps. The ill-fated force
stumbled down the coast of Arabia from Leuke Kome and thanks
to their guides never quite reached their goal, the Himyarite
kingdom in Yemen.

The holds that the Parthian, Nabataean and Himyarite middlemen had on the eastern trade were broken in another more
dramatic way. Late in the reign of Augustus, or early in that of
Tiberius, a Greek mariner named Hippalus put together the
geographical and meteorological lore that had accumulated, and
deduced the existence of the monsoon. With this wind behind
him he sailed *directly* from Aden to the Indus. Within the
century the monsoons in both directions had been sufficiently
mastered to permit direct passage from Egypt to the still richer
marts of southern India and Ceylon. Rome had, for the time,
eliminated the middleman and established direct commercial connection with India. The Red Sea was filled with Roman-financed
ships and not until the sixth and seventh centuries did the overland Arabian trade route again become an issue in the Hellenic
oikoumene.

By the terms of the settlement of B.C. 27 Augustus had direct
control of the armed provinces of Spain, Gaul and Syria. A crisis
in his health and the difficulties in managing his vast responsibilities provoked a readjustment in B.C. 23. Augustus was granted a
"greater command" (*imperium maius*) that gave him legal authority over the entire Empire, including the Senatorial provinces, though these were still under the nominal jurisdiction of the
Senate. He now surrendered the consulate, reserving for himself,
however, continuous tenancy of the power of the Tribune
(*tribunicia potestas*). Further, he shared effective command; his
trusted commander and friend Marcus Agrippa was given powers
closely resembling those which Augustus himself held in B.C. 27.
Augustus had apparently settled on the succession.

Agrippa's chief task at this stage was the supervision of the Imperial provinces. Syria received his attention first. It had been governed previously by Augustus' legates, including Cicero's rather unreliable son (B.C. 29–27). Agrippa administered it from Lesbos during the period B.C. 23–21. In B.C. 21 Agrippa departed for the West when Augustus came in person to visit his eastern domains, including, of course, the "Senatorial provinces" of Asia and Bithynia. His eastern policy was not, in fact, very different from that of Caesar or Antony: Hellenization of the provinces, the support of client kings, and the pacification of Parthia, not through arms, but by diplomacy.

Hellenization had always been tied to urbanization. Augustus, like Caesar before him, planted colonies in Asia, and where there already was a *polis* the Augustan policy was to reinforce its Greek physiognomy by elaborate building programs (seen in miniature in Herod's similar program in Judaea, with its crowning glory, Caesarea). Baths, theaters, gymnasia rose all over the face of the Roman East, and the system of roads, begun under Asia's first governor, Aquilius, was extended. As the Hellenization progressed, so too did the granting of local autonomy to communities known somewhat misleadingly as "free cities" (*civitates liberae*), which did indeed have the right of self-government, but were by no means exempt from the ultimate sign of Roman suzerainty, taxation. Here too Augustus followed Caesar in eliminating the *publicani* and making the communities responsible for their own accounts. To this end the census was introduced. Among the first acts, for instance, of Augustus' Syrian legate Quirinus, who presided over the incorporation of Judaea as a province in A.D. 6, was to institute a census.[6]

One instrument used by Augustus to achieve his ideal of limited self-government was an institution already in existence in the East and known as the "Commune (*koinon*) of the Hellenes." There was one such in Roman Asia and a parallel institution in Bithynia and later in Syria. Though religious in origin (its presiding officer was the chief priest in the province; in Asia styled the Asiarch), they performed at least some of the judicial and

---

6. This was undoubtedly the one mentioned in *Luke* 2:11, though there are obvious difficulties in its falling so late. The return of Joseph with Mary to his place of origin for registration is an ominous foreshadowing of the later enserfing of the inhabitants of the Empire, when each man was tied to his birthplace and his father's occupation.

administrative duties of a provincial assembly. Their most important function, however, was the regulation and preservation of the Imperial cult.[7]

The eastern cities had no reservations about paying divine honors (including the establishment of a priesthood to supervise the cultus) to their liberators and conquerors. A number of Hellenes and Romans had received such honors, including Aquilius who was deified by Pergamum, history's first bureaucrat to be so honored. At Ephesus in B.C. 48 Caesar had been hailed "by the people and tribes of Asia" as a descendant of gods and as a god made manifest (*epiphanes*), a common enough title among the Seleucids and Ptolemies. At Rome Augustus was content to use Caesar's deification, styling himself "son of the deified" (*divi filius*), but he resisted his own cultus there. Asia was a different matter, however, and here Augustus allowed his own deification, stipulating only that it be a common cult of *Roma et Augustus*. Cult centers were set up at Pergamum in Asia, Nicomedia in Bithynia, and Ancyra in Galatia, while at Antioch in Syria Augustus was actually the chief priest of his own worship. In Egypt he was Pharaoh and so a god; the millennial tradition was not disturbed by the Romans.

Augustus kept the earlier system of client kings, local dynasts enjoying a tenuous and treaty-regulated autonomy under Roman auspices. Amyntas was confirmed in Galatia, but at his death in B.C. 25 Rome inherited the kingdom and incorporated it as a province. Polemo was king of Pontus, and Agrippa, during his stay in the East in B.C. 17–13, abetted the king's attempt to extend his dominion to Mithridates' old enclave in the Crimea. After initial successes Polemo was killed by the natives, and Pontus was then ruled by his widow, who later married, surely at Augustus' urging, Archelaus, the client king of Cappadocia. Cappadocia was important in that it shielded the upper Euphrates, as Commagene did its middle reaches, against a Parthian invasion of Asia. Both Amyntas and Archelaus had been Antony's men, but Augustus kept them both. After Augustus' death, however, Tiberius haled Archelaus to Rome for trial, and Cappadocia became a province.

In Judaea, Herod continued his precarious rule. Here too, previous support of Antony meant little to Augustus, and Herod found a powerful friend and ally in Marcus Agrippa. Augustus

---

7. See Chapter XII, p. 469.

had completed his visitation of the East in B.C. 19, and two years later Agrippa returned there, while Augustus inspected the western provinces. This time Agrippa remained until shortly before his death in B.C. 13, and during his supervisory travels he was joined by Herod and the latter's cultural attaché, Nicholas of Damascus. In addition to making pleas for various Jewish communities, the King of Judaea scattered his largess far and wide over Anatolia in the manner of the Hellenistic monarch he tried so hard to be.[8] Herod was a valuable man to Rome. He kept order if not peace in one of the most turbulent areas in the orbit of the Empire.

Seen through Jewish eyes, Herod's measures appear as harsh and oppressive as those of Antiochus Epiphanes, and, indeed, the two men operated from similar premises. Like Epiphanes, and like most of the Romans, Herod equated Hellenism with economic prosperity. He attempted to spread Hellenism in Palestine by a magnificent building program, and as Augustus prided himself on the restoration of temples belonging to local religious cults, so Herod in B.C. 20 embarked on the rebuilding on a grandiose scale of the temple in Jerusalem. But he knew his subjects, who read history in other than economic terms, and so the religious complex was abutted on the northwest corner by a fortress that Herod somewhat daringly named Antonia. Herod's jewel was the city of Caesarea, which he had built on the coast on the site of the town known formerly as Strato's Tower and which he outfitted as Judaea's only major port, dominated by colossal statues of the god Augustus and the goddess Roma. To the observer, Judaea was again taking on the appearances of a Hellenistic kingdom.

The appearances were the façade of a violent land that Herod had to struggle to control. He had undermined the Sadducean upper classes, and the Pharisees were slipping into a silent opposition, but to the people as a whole Herod was an alien and a tyrant. His own family, swollen by a multiplicity of marriages and offspring, was in open revolt, struggling for the power that must soon pass to another. The force necessary to hold down the lid on Palestine became apparent after Herod's death in B.C. 4. Even as he grew weaker, Jewish Zealots pulled down the Imperial

---

8. Herod's Hellenic pretensions are most clearly revealed perhaps by his settlement of a permanent endowment on the Olympic Games at Elis.

golden eagle he had placed upon the gate of the temple. At his death the country exploded in revolt. His son Archelaus who succeeded him as king was maintained in power only with the greatest difficulty by Varus, the Augustan legate in Syria, while deputations of Jews went to Augustus and swore they would rather have a Roman governor than Archelaus. So it was to be. After propping up Archelaus for nearly ten years, Augustus finally sent him off to exile in Gaul in A.D. 6, and Quirinus, the new legate in Syria, annexed Judaea to his own province. The Equestrian Coponius was sent out as its resident Procurator.[9] Two of Herod's other sons continued to hold territory, though not royal titles, inherited from their father—Philip in Trachonitis (between Genesareth and Damascus) and Antipas in Galilee and Peraea east of the Jordan.

Augustus' greatest loss, political and personal, was in Armenia. There was a strong and militant anti-Roman faction in Armenia from the time Antony dragged Artavasades into captivity, and the Romans could keep a man to their own liking on the throne there only through constant surveillance. An opportunity to intervene presented itself again in B.C. 20 at the death of Artavasades' Roman-hating son Artaxias, and Augustus entrusted the task of propping up a new claimant to his young stepson Tiberius. Tigranes II was duly installed, and the balance in the East tipped toward the Romans to the extent that the Parthian king Phraates IV surrendered under pressure what Caesar and Antony failed to gain by arms, the legionary standards taken by the Parthians from Crassus at Carrhae. It was one of Augustus' major diplomatic coups.

Tigranes II died in B.C. 6, and Augustus discovered that he could not merely send another candidate to Armenia. Nor would Tiberius, now in self-imposed retirement on Rhodes, consent to escort him there. Augustus took the occasion to try one of his crown princes. The *Princeps* had bestowed his only child Julia on Marcus Agrippa,[10] and she had borne him two sons, Gaius and

---

9. The Procurator was normally a treasury official under the Proconsul of a province, but in the case of some small units like Judaea a Procurator was the chief executive, subordinate to the governor of the larger province upon which it depended.

10. As he had earlier given her to Marcellus (*d.* B.C. 22) and later to Tiberius so that the latter might serve as guardian and protector to the two young princes. He outlived them both.

Lucius. In B.C. 1 Gaius, then nineteen, was entrusted with an *imperium* in the East and put in the hands of an experienced eastern hand, Lollius, the organizer and first governor of the province of Galatia.

All went well at first. Gaius met with the new Parthian king Phraataces at the Euphrates in A.D. 1, and the latter agreed to surrender his claims to Armenia.[11] The way was then open for Gaius to proceed to Armenia and install a suitable king without Parthian interference. The Armenians, however, were not agreeable; civil war broke out in A.D. 4, and Gaius perished from wounds he received in the conflict. Augustus was cheated of another heir.[12]

It may be that Augustus had grown progressively disenchanted with his client kings. The death of Amyntas and the deposition of Archelaus led to new provinces. Under Tiberius, who succeeded to the *imperium* at Augustus' death in A.D. 14, the absorption of the eastern clients continued. Archelaus, king of Cappadocia, was deposed in A.D. 15. The same occurred shortly thereafter in Amanus and Commagene, so that by the end of Tiberius' reign the only client kingdoms left in the east were Pontus[13] and some petty complexes in Transjordan. And the dubious Armenia.

Tiberius had at hand an outstanding agent for eastern pacification, his nephew and heir-apparent Germanicus, who had just celebrated impressive and popular triumphs in Germany. Once again the heir was dispatched to the East with the same kind of extraordinary *imperium* held by Agrippa in B.C. 23 and Gaius in B.C. 1. The situation had deteriorated by A.D. 17. Judaea was in its usual state of disturbance and there were troubles elsewhere, but the immediate crisis was provoked by the necessity of once again securing the Armenian throne for a Roman-sponsored candidate, in this case Zeno, the son of Polemo and Pythodoris of Pontus. There was a king in Armenia, Vonones, the half brother of Phraataces, who had managed to seat himself in Parthia for a while, but was dislodged in A.D. 12 and consoled himself with the

---

11. One unforeseen outcome of the Euphrates meeting was the fall from grace of Lollius who was replaced by another experienced supervisor, Quirinus, the future governor of Syria.

12. Gaius' brother Lucius had died of illness on his way to Spain in A.D. 2. The accession of Tiberius became inevitable.

13. The kingdom of Pontus, the eastern part of Mithridates' much larger holdings, finally became a Roman province in A.D. 64.

throne of Armenia. This was intolerable to the new king of Parthia, Artabanus III (A.D. 12–38), and the Romans considered it scarcely worth their while to support Vonones in the face of Parthian opposition. Vonones bowed to the inevitable and surrendered himself to the governor of Syria in A.D. 15 or 16. It was at this point that Germanicus and Artabanus opened negotiations. Artabanus agreed to Zeno (who assumed the dynastic name of Artaxias), with the proviso that the Romans remove Vonones from Syria. This was done within a year, and Germanicus' mission was a success: a new settlement in Armenia and peace with Parthia.[14]

The history of Egypt under the Roman Empire is written in ledgers and not the annals of war and conquest. Shielded by nature to the east, by provinces to the west, and by client kings to the south, Egypt was free from all but internal war. From the beginning the Emperors took care that the riches of the land should not be a temptation to political ambition or insurrection, and they were generally successful. Economic turbulence was another matter, and the agricultural *fellahin* and the urban proletariat of Alexandria, all members of the gigantic corporation that was Egypt, were not always docile subjects. Economic life was severely and harshly regulated in Egypt, and the strike (*anachoresis*, literally, "withdrawal")[15] was not uncommon along the Nile. From the beginning of Egyptian history the *fellahin's* chief response to repression was to throw down their tools and flee beyond the reach of the Pharaoh's agents.

The prosperity of early Ptolemaic Egypt had disappeared by the time of the Romans' arrival. The decadence of the central government, upon which all else depended in Egypt, had sharpened the rapacity of the higher Greek officialdom, which lay

---

14. Germanicus' own career went no further. First he provoked Tiberius by going to Egypt "to study its antiquities"; no one of Senatorial rank went to Egypt for that or any other reason without the Emperor's permission. He compounded his misstep by returning to Syria and dismissing Tiberius' legate Piso. Shortly afterward Germanicus fell ill and died; Piso was tried at Rome for murder and eventually committed suicide.

15. The same word was later used for the Christian "withdrawal from the world" (see Chapter XVII, p. 640).

like an incubus on the land. The only flourishing element in Egypt was the priestly castes with their enormous and unproductive holdings. The peasantry, unmoved by Hellenism and national glory alike, was ruined.

Ptolemy I, son of Lagos, a Macedonian soldier, had ruled as Pharaoh, and Augustus and his successors continued to do the same. Egypt belonged to the Emperor, and with good reason. Each successive head of the Roman state had bound himself to feed Rome's large population. More than one third of that huge supply of grain came from Egypt alone, most of it as tax but some of it purchased. Without Egypt there was no bread for Rome, and without the bread dole the ruler could not rule. The double chain of politics and economics held Egypt in bondage to the Empire and the Emperor in bondage to Egypt.

At the outset of Roman rule there was some attempt at reforming the Ptolemaic system. The extensive temple holdings were secularized—which in Egypt amounted to nationalization. In exchange for ownership and control, the state would henceforward subsidize religious activities, a gesture that was more than compensated for by the inclusion of the temple lands in the state's tax structure. The prosperity of the other eastern provinces was largely brought about by a growing middle class. In Asia and Syria this was solidly based in the cities, and while there was a mercantile and industrial middle class in Alexandria, the absence of comparable urban centers in Egypt presented a very different kind of economic structure. In Egypt the problem was land, and particularly the conversion of waste land by capital and irrigation into productive acreage. The state was unwilling or unable to put additional capital into agricultural development, and so Augustus opened Egypt for the first time to private capital, Alexandrian and Roman, for land development.

The policy did not achieve its desired ends. Augustus' moves resulted in the rise of large, privately owned (but publicly taxed) estates. What was needed was resident supervision and interest in the reclamation of land; what came about was the possession by absentee landlords in Rome or Alexandria of large estates on what was already arable land. Nor were these highly placed capitalists, who included the Imperial family and members of the Senatorial class, much inclined to pay taxes. Beginning with Vespasian the policy was reversed and the large private estates were dismembered. This proved to be somewhat more successful, and the desired bourgeoisie composed of Greeks, Hellenized Romans and Hellenized Egyptians began to appear and to produce, as one of its secondary social characteristics, modest urban centers on the Hellenic model. But because of the peculiar status of Egypt the quickening breath of political life was never infused into these economic and social pseudomorphs. The vital center of Hellenism, a degree of political liberty, was never achieved.[16]

An Egypt covered with genuine Hellenic *poleis* was, in any event, economically unfeasible. The cities of Asia and Syria lived off the agricultural produce of their own hinterlands. In Egypt, grain was for export; and the more that was needed locally, the less would be available to feed the other parts of the Empire. Alexandria was probably worth what it took to feed its considerable population, since it was the center of Egyptian capitalistic enterprise; the banking trade and the bulk of the manufacturing facilities were located there.

Under the Ptolemies, banking had been a state monopoly. The Romans returned it to private enterprise; and the Egyptian "tables" (*trapezai*), with central offices in Alexandria and branches in the provincial towns, did a thriving business. They took money for deposit at interest, and it was they who underwrote the great shipping trade to India that terminated in the warehouses and factories of Alexandria. Alexandria had a virtual empirewide monopoly on the manufacture of linen and papyrus, the latter, as in Ptolemaic times, state-controlled. The cotton shipped from India was converted into cloth there, and glassware was also produced for export.

Alexandria was also the seat of the Roman power in Egypt, though its culture and tone continued to be Greek. The inhabitants received special privileges; they were, for example, exempt from the poll tax imposed by Augustus on the native Egyptians. What they lacked was the ultimate sign of political maturity, a council, or *boule*, to determine their own affairs; and when they were eventually given one in A.D. 195 it was merely for the purpose of bringing them more firmly under the Roman tax

---

16. A telling illustration of this is the fact that rhetoric, the premier "art" of the Empire, never took root in Egypt. Philosophy and the sciences continued to flourish there under the Roman occupation, but rhetoric, with its intimate associations with the *polis*, aroused no interest.

umbrella. Meanwhile, they had to deal with the Roman prefect, who was, in effect, the commander of the Roman occupation forces, or else to communicate with the Emperor directly through supplicatory delegations sent to Rome.

Easterners in the Service of Rome

The Roman presence in the East served merely to accelerate the Hellenization of Roman culture. From the fourth century Hellenism was everywhere present in Roman religion, art and architecture. In the third century Rome annexed the Greek territories of Sicily and southern Italy, and in the second century Greece itself. Greek teachers came to Italy as slaves and served first as private tutors,[17] and then as instructors in the formal school system. After the conquest of Greece Roman names begin appearing in the lists of the Athenian *ephebeia*, that curious combination of military, civil and literary training that shaped generations of Greek aristocrats.[18] By the end of the Republic, Roman students were seeking out, at Athens, Alexandria, Pergamum and especially Rhodes, the great contemporary masters of Greek philosophy and rhetoric, with deep and permanent effects on the Latin intellectual tradition in those disciplines.

In this meeting of two cultures the archetypal pair is the Latin student Cicero and the professor Posidonius, a Hellenized Syrian from Apamea. In B.C. 78, when he attended Posidonius' lectures on Rhodes, Cicero was a rising Roman lawyer fresh from philosophical and rhetorical studies at Athens. His teacher's horizons were even wider, embracing the entire Mediterranean *oikoumene* in its past and present, and bringing to the study of philosophy a breadth of scientific, literary and historical interest unequaled in anyone since Aristotle. Posidonius represents, as has been noted, another characteristic of his times, the growing interest on the part of the Hellenized intellectuals in the history and achievements of the rising state of Rome.

The first such was the Sicilian Greek Timaeus (*c.* B.C. 356–

---

17. The psychic shock in this confrontation between the culturally deprived Roman and the economically deprived Greek received its classic expression in Juvenal's third *Satire* and Lucian's *Hired Companions*.

18. See Chapter V, pp. 197–98.

260), whose history of Sicily reflected that island's new position in the larger struggle between Rome, Carthage and Greece. But Sicily was only a pawn between more powerful contestants, and by the time of the next major Greek historian the significance of the Carthaginian and Macedonian wars was already clear in the Mediterranean: Rome was the paramount power of the West. Polybius (c. B.C. 200–120) was a statesman in the Achaean League, and was drawn by the events of the Macedonian wars into the orbit of Roman politics. He moved freely in both Greek and Latin circles, in the latter under the patronage and protection of the Scipios. His *Ecumenical History* took as its theme the rise of Roman power. Struck by the unprecedented nature of what had occurred well within his own lifetime, Polybius took up the narrative where Timaeus had left off, at the onset of the Carthaginian wars, traced the rise of Rome and, most importantly, subjected the Roman state to a close political analysis in terms suggested by Greek theory.

Posidonius brought to his continuation of Polybius (from B.C. 146 to B.C. 86) a view that was both more cosmopolitan and more philosophical.[19] Polybius had seen Rome through the categories of the classical theoreticians, Thucydides, Plato and Aristotle. Posidonius, the easterner, the citizen of the mercantile center of Rhodes, politician, traveler, scientist and philosopher, saw events against a much wider background that far more authentically represented the world after Alexander. Polybius' was a universal history because it had as its subject a universal state, Rome. The ecumenicism of Posidonius was rooted not in his subject but in his own eye. For him history was not merely the work of political analysis but must rely as well on the insights of individual and social psychology. The grounds for the first lay ready at hand in the detailed analyses of character and behavior by Plato, Aristotle and Theophrastus.[20] To these Posidonius could add the sophisticated insights of his own age.

As Herodotus bears ample witness, the Greeks had always shown a lively interest in their neighbors. By the time of Posidonius that interest had accumulated a considerable scientific underpinning. The Hellenistic kings, with their widespread political and commercial interests, had drawn to the intellectual

19. On the philosophical context of Posidonius' work see Chapter IX, pp. 366–70.
20. See Chapter II, pp. 108–10.

centers of Egypt, Syria and Asia savants from among the non-Greek peoples, and the information these latter conveyed was widely disseminated in the Greek handbooks of the first century. To cite a single example contemporary with Posidonius, the various volumes of the Milesian scholar Alexander Polyhistor on the culture and climes of the eastern lands were an important source of information for historians of the next couple of generations.

Alexander was a library scholar, Posidonius an observer of phenomena who had the further advantage of working within a Stoic philosophical tradition that enabled him to assimilate this cultural and ethnographical material into his own highly organized—and highly organic—view of the universe. Historical analogy came easily to a man trained in seeing the workings of a universal "sympathy." Milieu, climate and diet are all important in Posidonius' *Post-Polybian Histories*. There is at work, too, the guiding hand of the Stoic providence (*pronoia*). Moses, for instance, in a fragment of Posidonius preserved by Strabo, is treated in a comparative context with other "founding fathers" who operated under the terms of a mandate from God.

Polybius and Posidonius were only the first of the rich spoils of war won by Rome through its conquest of Greece and the East. Not only were there economic riches to be had; there was artistic and intellectual wealth as well. Pergamum, for example, was not merely the hub of a thriving west-Anatolian economic complex; it was an intellectual center that possessed a famous grammatical and medical school. Alexander Polyhistor was on the faculty there and was carried off as a slave pedagogue to Rome, where Sulla finally bought and freed him in B.C. 82. The case of the literary critic Crates has been mentioned, and in a more peaceful day Galen (A.D. 129–199), who had studied philosophy and medicine in his native Pergamum and had done his residency in a gladiators' clinic there, would serve as personal physican to Marcus Aurelius, Verus and Commodus, and spend thirty years in Rome teaching and writing—in Greek—on the practice of medicine.

Galen worked for a Hellenized Roman public, and yet his influence spread in a very different direction. His impact on Roman and then—mediated by Latin translation—medieval and Renaissance medicine is natural and understandable. That he should become the premier authority in Arab medical annals is another matter. His medical and philosophical works were widely read in the East and translated first into Syriac and eventually into Arabic, where they provided the basis of Arab scientific medicine in eighth- and ninth-century Baghdad. This eastern vogue is a distinction shared by Galen with another Hellenized easterner enrolled in the service and interests of Rome, Nicholas, the historian and philosopher of Damascus.

Posidonius had had his influence in the last years of the Republic; Nicholas was a man of the next generation (he was born in B.C. 64, Pompey's year in Syria) and so was part of the new Augustan world. His connection with Rome was not immediate. His first patron was the vigorous Hellenized king of Rome's client Judaea, Herod the Great. Born of a Hellenized family, Nicholas enjoyed the "encyclic education" typical of a Greco-Oriental center and designed to convert Aramaean Damascenes into model Hellenes: grammar, poetry, rhetoric, music and finally, the crown of the work, philosophy.[21] As the student became the professor,[22] it was almost inevitable that the son of a well-known Damascene family should gravitate into the field of vision of such a lavish patron of the Hellenic arts as Herod. Herod's interests certainly reached to Damascus, even though in the Seleucid recession the city may have become a tributary of the Nabataean Arab *shaykhs* of Petra.

Nicholas traveled in the train of Herod and Augustus' Asian Proconsul Marcus Agrippa in B.C. 14 and apparently well served Herod's interests and those of the Asian Jews whose case Herod was representing. He represented Herod before the highest Roman authorities on other occasions as well, as after Herod's death in B.C. 4 he performed the same service for Archelaus. Nicholas was by then well known to Augustus, and on the occasion of a final plea for Archelaus he must have remained at Rome and finished his life there.

Even before Herod's death Nicholas had begun, at Herod's

21. This is the view of someone who considers himself a philosopher. If Nicholas had been a professional rhetorician or sophist, his view of his own education would, of course, have been quite different. We are well informed about his studies, since we possess an autobiographical fragment, a relatively rare literary exercise in the ancient world.
22. Among his first students were the twin children of Antony and Cleopatra who were born in B.C. 40. Damascus was part of the territory that Antony had settled upon Cleopatra in despite of Herod.

suggestion, an *Ecumenical History* from the earliest days down to his own time. It was immense in scope, and though only imperfectly preserved today, the interesting events of Herod's own days in which Nicholas himself shared were incorporated by Josephus into his *Jewish Antiquities.* Elsewhere the standard authorities are in evidence, and Posidonius' touch is visible in the fragments dealing with Roman history. It may have been in the course of writing this work that Nicholas was commissioned for a biography of Augustus, who had no objection to posting his own name on the pyramids.[23] He must have completed it some time after Augustus' death in A.D. 14, when Nicholas himself was seventy-eight years old.

Herod, in addition to his interest in history, was a philosophy buff, and on their trips he and Nicholas "philosophized together." It was probably during this association that Nicholas composed some of his popularized philosophical works; his more ambitious *On the Philosophy of Aristotle* appears to have come from the years of his Roman retirement. Nicholas lived during a period of renewed interest in Aristotle. His *Aristotle,* which is a compendium of the physical works in the *corpus* plus the *Metaphysics* and *On the Soul,* may very well reflect that interest, though it seems unlikely that Nicholas played any important role in the professional philosophical circles at Rome or elsewhere. The work, if used at all, was never very important in the West, and was supplanted by the more learned commentaries of the later Peripatetic tradition. In the East, on the other hand, where Aristotle was at first known primarily as a logician, Nicholas' epitome provided a convenient survey of the lesser-known physical doctrines and so enjoyed great popularity. It was itself abbreviated more than once and split up into its constituent parts for separate circulation. In its Syriac and Arabic translations, *On the Philosophy of Aristotle* was a powerful pedagogical force in the spread of Aristotle in Islam.

---

23. Augustus, the master of official propaganda, left no stone uncut in disseminating official accounts of his deeds. Doubtless every city had a copy of the final authorized version of his *res gestae,* but only the one posted in Ancyra, the metropolis of the province of Galatia, has survived. Nicholas was probably only one of a number of literary figures he had working on similar projects. Augustus also indulged in autobiography, and this interesting if inhibited document was put at Nicholas' disposal.

As has been mentioned, a good part of Nicholas' history found its way into the work of another of Rome's eastern clients, the Jewish historian Josephus, who set himself the far more formidable task of rendering intelligible to a Hellenized audience the heritage and history of a people with whom Rome had just fought a disastrous war. Diaspora Judaism had been producing Hellenized intellectuals for generations, but Joseph bar Matthiah was from the heart of the tradition, a priest and Pharisee of Jerusalem, a brilliant student trained in the Mosaic Law, who in A.D. 64 at the age of thirty-six represented Jewish interests before Nero at Rome. Here he became acquainted with Nero's wife Poppaea, an obviously important Jewish sympathizer.

But whatever future lay in these Jewish circles in Rome was aborted by the outbreak of the Jewish insurrection in Palestine (A.D. 66). Josephus was placed in charge of the organization of Galilee and defended the fortress of Jotapata against a Roman army. Finally captured by the Romans, he predicted Vespasian's rise to the purple, and when this actually came to pass Josephus was freed. Under the name Flavius Josephus he enjoyed Imperial favor, first in Palestine, where he was present among Titus' Roman forces at the fall of Jerusalem in A.D. 70, and then at Rome, for the rest of his life. It was in the capital that he wrote *The Jewish War, Jewish Antiquities,* an autobiographical sketch,[24] and an out-and-out apologetic tract, *Against Apion.*[25]

The Jewish War had a frankly apologetic end, to acquaint a Greek readership with the facts of the recent war. In Josephus' mind, Jewish hotheads had clearly brought the affair upon themselves; but he thought that the importance and seriousness of the conflict had been misunderstood by the Roman public. Originally, we are told by Josephus himself, the work had been composed in Aramaic for the benefit of the Jewish communities in Parthia, which would suggest an attempt at gaining some pro-Roman sympathy—the Romans are by no means the villains of

---

24. The *Life* is not so much an autobiography as an apologia for his behavior in Galilee, directed against another contemporary pro-Roman Jewish historian, Justus of Tiberias, who had accused Josephus of fomenting trouble in Tiberias. Justus, whose work is known only through Josephus' unflattering remarks, appears to have been under the special patronage of Herod Agrippa.

25. An important source, out of which can be reconstructed at least some of the literary anti-Semitic sentiment of the preceding generation.

the piece—at the expense of Rome's enemy Parthia, or even perhaps to intimidate the Parthians themselves. But with the help of some Greek assistants[26] the Aramaic was turned into Greek and directed toward the Roman reader.[27]

The *War* was an enormous success, and Josephus embarked on the more ambitious but less successful project of the *Jewish Antiquities*. This time Josephus may have supplied his own Greek, but the inspiration was undoubtedly a similar work, *Roman Antiquities*, by another easterner, Dionysius of Halicarnassus in Caria. As Dionysius sought to make the Roman past intelligible and respectable to the fastidious intellectuals of the Augustan age, so Josephus set out to explain, defend and glorify the past of a people generally viewed as bizarre, obnoxious and anti-social by the Roman world. For the *War* Josephus had drawn upon the war journals (*commentarii*) of Vespasian and Titus and on his own experience. The horizons of the *Antiquities* are much wider, and so are Josephus' sources—Scripture (both the Hebrew original and the Aramaic and Septuagint Greek versions), *Maccabees*, the Jewish historians excerpted in Alexander Polyhistor, and Nicholas of Damascus.

The immediate effect of the *Antiquities* is unknown, though it was an important addition to the growing body of literature in Greek explaining to politicians, philosophers and historians something of the nature of the Jewish people in terms they could understand.[28] It was to be the last such. The troubles of A.D. 70 were followed by the disaster of A.D. 135, and in the wake of that last onslaught against them the Jewish community repudiated the possibility of a Hellenism tied to Roman politics. Josephus' position was undermined by the closure of rabbinical Judaism.

It was the Hellenic historians who taught the Romans to view

---

26. Modern scholarship has detected at least two such hands of very different quality in the finished work.

27. Perhaps, better, to the Mediterranean intelligentsia, who naturally could read Greek and whose number included not only Romans but Asians and even Josephus' fellow Jews of his own social and economic class. The work, like all the others of Josephus, was dedicated to Epaphroditus, possibly, though by no means certainly, the Greek freedman who served as secretary to both Nero and Domitian and to whom Epictetus originally belonged as a slave.

28. Christians too, as they grew more remote from their original connection with Judaism, drew heavily upon Josephus for their knowledge of Jewish history.

their empire in the expanded context of world history and who connected it with the classical Greek tradition. Latin historians learned techniques and attitudes from their Greek masters, but never quite equaled their breadth of view. As Rome expanded from state to empire to colossus, the measure of this immense political and military achievement continued to be taken by the last arrivals within the Empire, the historians and geographers of the Hellenized East. Strabo (B.C. 63–19 A.D.) was an almost exact contemporary of Nicholas, born during that same period of Pompey's annexation of Syria, but in a very different milieu from the Damascus of Nicholas. His birthplace was Amasia, the Hellenic metropolis of the newly acquired kingdom of Pontus. Strabo's career followed a familiar pattern: education in the Hellenic arts and sciences in the schools of Asia, followed by the inevitable trip to Rome and involvement in court circles and Imperial service.

Strabo's Roman pilgrimage occurred about B.C. 29, and four years later he was part of Aelius Gallus' wretched foray into Arabia. Further travels followed, so that Strabo, like Posidonius, eventually came to see a large part of the Roman *oikoumene* in the Mediterranean. His final years appear to have been spent in Pontus, and the *Geography* was probably written during that retirement. This work of Strabo, conceived along the universalist lines of a Polybius or a Posidonius, both of whom he admired and used, is a geographical *summa* of the Roman Empire in the middle of Augustus' reign. Some of it is based on personal observation, but extensive use has been made of the great Hellenistic legacy of ethnography and descriptive geography and of the more recent work of the Greek historians who had accompanied Roman Republican troops on their eastern expeditions.[29] It is a genuine Book of Empire as no work with purely Roman horizons could be; only a Hellenized Stoic was capable of such.

The mathematical companion piece to Strabo's descriptive geography is the *Geography* of Claudius Ptolemy (*c.* A.D. 100–178), a native of Ptolemais in Egypt and a member of the

---

29. The most interesting of the latter are Apollodorus, a Hellenized author from Mesopotamia, an authority on the Parthian wars, and Strabo's chief source on Hyrcania and Bactria, and Theophanes of Mytilene, who was Pompey's official historian on his eastern campaigns. His important history of the Mithridatic wars was used not only by Strabo but by Livy, Plutarch and Appian as well.

Alexandrian scientific establishment still flourishing after two centuries of Roman rule in Egypt. Ptolemy belonged to a scientific tradition more austerely remote from politics than the rhetoricians and historians of Asia, but his work nonetheless reflects the premise of empire. His credentials were those of a mathematician and astronomer,[30] but in Ptolemy, as in most of his contemporaries, one can detect the unmistakable traces of Peripatetic and Stoic attitudes. His *Tetrabiblos*, for example, is a work of scientific astrology compounded of his own astronomic learning, Posidonian ethnographical theory, and Aristotelian personality analysis.

The Hellenophile dynasts of the Antonine line made their peace with the Greek intellectuals, and henceforward there was no lack of eastern historians to record the deeds of the Augusti and their triumphant march to the ends of the earth. Flavius Arrian[31] (A.D. 95–175) of Nicomedia in Bithynia; Appian[32] of Alexandria under Trajan and Antoninus Pius; Dio Cassius[33] (*c.* A.D. 155–235) of Nicaea in Bithynia; and Herodian[34] (*fl. c.* A.D.

---

30. His *Mathematical, or Great, Collection* (*Mathematike, or Megale, Syntaxis*) was another of the great foundation stones of the heritage of Hellenism in the medieval East. Like the work of Euclid, Galen and Aristotle (frequently through Nicholas) it was translated into Arabic and, as *The Almagest*, was the basis of Arab scientific astronomy. See Chapter VI.

31. Author of a geographical survey of the Euxine, a history of his native Bithynia and of Parthia, some works on Alexander and his successors, and a number of imitations of Xenophon, of whom Arrian was inordinately fond.

32. Originally a civil servant in Alexandria, he pursued his political career at Rome and eventually held high offices in the Imperial treasury. He wrote a history of the growth of Rome from Aeneas down to the campaigns of Trajan, which he arranged ethnographically rather than in strict chronological order. Separate parts have been preserved.

33. His father had been governor of Dalmatia and Cilicia, and Dio himself reached the highest Senatorial offices in the state. He was twice Consul, the second time under Alexander Severus in A.D. 229. His *Roman History*, which was ten years in preparation and twelve years in the writing and was the work of his retirement, covered the history of Rome from its beginnings to A.D. 229. The books covering years B.C. 68–10 have been fully preserved and some of the latter sections in an abridgment.

34. A petty functionary in the Roman government, he wrote a *History of the Empire after Marcus Aurelius*, which reached down to the reign of Gordian III (A.D. 238).

225) of Syria—all gave their varying literary talents and styles to recording the deeds of the Empire, in whose service many of them toiled. Public life and literature were both reflecting the same phenomenon, the gradual displacement of that Empire from its original Roman and Latin center to the Greek East.

XI

Life Styles and Life Sciences

The incorporation of the various states that stretched east and west around the Mediterranean basin into a single, ecumenical Roman Empire changed the face of the ancient world. The provincial system worked the diversified political traditions of the past into a centralized whole that bore on its face the unmistakable stamp of Roman administrative genius. In its bureaucratic aspects and under the rule of a single body of Roman law, the Near East, like all the other parts of the Empire, was Latinized. In another dimension, however, a far more profound and painful syncretism was at work.

The superficial political landscape of eastern Hellenism had been leveled by Rome in the name of *imperium*, but beneath the surface the more deeply rooted and deeply felt traditions of the conquered peoples—Greek, Egyptian, Iranian, Babylonian, Syrian and Jewish—came together in a contest that the Romans largely ignored. Rome had fashioned the body; Hellenism and the East struggled to possess its soul.

The world was different from what it had been. The older forms were changing from within their conservative shells; new mutants with old names were constantly appearing. Under the protective shield of the *Pax Romana* new voices sounded and the dead rose again. Socrates was heard, and Pythagoras. Philosophy, religion and science joined in a bewildering chorus of programs and appeals to the rulers and the ruled, beckoning to the good life and eternal salvation.

Philosophers and Kings

The mainstream of the Greek philosophical tradition after Aristotle is so unrepentantly academic in its form and interests that it seems either to distort or to obscure everything that does not cohere with its own school-oriented point of view. The history of that tradition was written by academicians accustomed to thinking in terms of schools (*haireseis*) and "successions" (*diadoche*) of pupils to master, and they quite naturally made the evolution and teaching of philosophy conform to that pattern, imposing an anachronistic "school" even on the pre-Socratic philosophers, and in general obscuring the existence of a potent nonliterary and nonacademic strain that continued to exist in Greek philosophy even after the founding of the four major "schools" in Athens at the beginning of the third pre-Christian century. This fifth tradition derived, as much else in Greek philosophy, from Socrates.[1]

That Socrates was the teacher of Plato was a commonplace in the philosophical tradition, and yet the portrait that Plato gives of the ideal philosopher in the *Theaetetus* (173c–174a) is an exact measure of the distance between the two men. According to Plato the philosopher does not even know the way to the market and the other places of public assembly; he shows no interest in meetings, dinners and merrymaking, because it is only his body that sojourns in the *polis*. These are strange sentiments from one whose master was a *polites* in the full sense of the word. Socrates spent his days and nights in those same places of public assembly; gadfly or midwife, he lived a life of public service, and the terrible irony of his death was compounded by the fact that it was this same public that executed him. The Platonic ideal philosopher, on the other hand, was a remote academician, disinterested in his city and his neighbors, because he was contemplating truths on a far higher scale than either man or the *polis* could provide.

Plato's own withdrawal from the *polis* was, of course, more than ideological. The public's murder of Socrates, "the wisest and justest man of that time," deeply affected the young Plato, and though he and other members of the Academy were tempted

---

1. For the importance given to Socrates in the history of philosophy from the time of Panaetius, see Chapter IX, pp. 362–63.

back into political consultation on occasion by the prospect of a philosopher-king to be instructed or a constitution to be drawn up, the philosopher himself was no longer willing to exercise his personal role as a citizen; the movement of philosophical discourse away from the *polis* and its pragmatic concerns into a cloistered professional setting had begun.

But the passage in the *Theaetetus* continues (174c–175b). When the philosopher is forced to expose himself to the practices and values of the *polis* he does, after all, have something to say. Far from merely discussing philosophy with his fellow citizens, he confronts, in a direct and dramatic fashion, their values with his own life style, a confrontation that might seem to make the philosopher an object of mockery by the citizens but is calculated to expose the shallowness and pretensions of their own lives.

Here is another and perhaps more authentic side of the Socratic legacy: the touches of the fakir visible in Socrates and some of his contemporaries. It apparently had little appeal to the aristocratic Plato, but his disdain did not lead him to obliterate the trait from his portrait of Socrates. It appears quite unmistakably in the more historical passages of the dialogues, and particularly in Plato's dramatic reconstruction of one who knew Socrates very well indeed. "He cares not at all," said Alcibiades, "if someone possesses beauty; rather he despises such more than you can possibly imagine. He has the same attitude toward wealth and any other honor esteemed by the masses. He treats such possessions as worthless and, let me assure you, all of us too count for nothing with him. He spends his entire life purposely mystifying and making sport of his fellow men."

Socrates' abrasive and provocative critique of the mores of his fellow citizens struck responsive chords at Athens. Chief among his admirers and imitators was Antisthenes (*c.* B.C. 455–360) whose Socratic parentage was obscured by the more striking success of Socrates' other spiritual child, Plato. But with Antisthenes the social criticism of Socrates took on not only the deeper nuances of a class struggle but also the unlovely note of disingenuousness that mars a great deal of the later fakir tradition. Socrates had himself detected it and had scored the touch personally on Antisthenes. The latter had a tear in his cloak, and when he arranged the garment so that people would notice the hole, Socrates wryly observed that the only thing he could see through the tear was Antisthenes' own desire for esteem.

This desire for esteem, perceptible to the eyes of Socrates who was remarkably free of the vice, apparently flowed from Antisthenes' real or imagined social position at Athens. He was the son of an Athenian father but a Thracian mother, and the inferiority of his birth undoubtedly shaped Antisthenes' ethical thinking. The true nobleman, he insisted, was not the well-born but the virtuous man, and it is in accordance with virtue and not the laws of the state that the wise man governs his activity. As for marriage, since it is for the purpose of fathering children, the intelligent man will obviously marry the woman whom nature has best endowed for this end, scorning, one may add as a gloss, considerations of high blood and noble family.

The distance between Antisthenes and the aristocratic, intellectualist and literary Plato was immense. Plato maintained an austere silence on Antisthenes, but the Cynic tradition is filled with anecdotes of Antisthenes' scoring at the expense of Plato's aristocratic ways and fastidious tastes. And yet both men possessed the genuine Socratic strain, even though they stood at the head of two traditions as inimical as themselves. The first found its expression in the Cynic and Stoic ideal of the sage (*sophos*) who is in the world but not, until he becomes a Roman, of it, and who protests against this world and its values by his own eccentric behavior and by alternately preaching and scolding. The other tradition derived from the Platonic and Peripatetic schools, where the sage, for all his excursions near the seats of power as the counselor of kings or as the chairman of constitutional committees, is still the professor on leave, whose natural habitat is the school, where the true business of philosophy can be carried out in a quiet and thoughtful atmosphere. Dialogue, not declamation, remained the ideal of the academic tradition, but it was no longer, as in the days of Socrates, carried out on the streets of Athens but in the cloisters of the Platonic Academy.

The opposition between Plato and Antisthenes was not merely temperamental, and the latter was not the anti-intellectual that the later Cynic tradition was frequently to produce. Antisthenes vigorously opposed the Platonic theory of Forms as a manifestation of extrasensible reality. His intellectual training went back, moreover, to the Sophists, and so the battle with Plato was joined also on the important contemporary issue of philosophy versus rhetoric and dialectic versus eristic. Antisthenes was interested also in myth and religion, an interest which expressed itself not only in exegetical theory but in the use of myth in ethical teaching,[2] which, in the true Socratic tradition, was at the heart of his interests.

These Socratic points of departure received bold new turns in the hands of the Asian who shared with Antisthenes the honor of founding Cynic philosophy, Diogenes of Sinope in Pontus (*c.* B.C. 400–325).[3] The attitudes of Diogenes were, if anything, more ethical in their orientation and more radical in their purport. He shared with Antisthenes his pathetic desire to *épater les bourgeois,* indulging in the classic repertory of insult and crude behavior, living in a cask out in the public ways, and apparently holding nothing and no one sacred.

The portrait of Diogenes, which is today more amusing than it is edifying, comes, like much else in the Cynic tradition, from the *Lives* pasted together by Diogenes Laertius. Antisthenes was an author of some repute among his contemporaries, but the later Cynics had little faith in the written word. Nor was the Cynic "school" organized in the scholastic fashion of the later Academy or the Lyceum, where pious disciples preserved the works of the earlier masters. The Cynics can be reached only through the vagaries of a frequently hostile biographical tradition; their theories must be read off from their lives.

Diogenes did not share Antisthenes' interest in rhetorical and logical questions, but he agreed with him in his insistence on the autonomy of virtue, which was natural and needed no justification from laws, convention or custom. In word and deed he devoted himself relentlessly to "conterfeiting the currency of popular belief and practice."[4] Heracles was once again in the foreground, typifying by his labors the endless practice and exercise (*askesis*) necessary for the acquisition of virtue, an

---

2. The use of Heracles as an archetypal figure of the *struggle* for virtue begins with Antisthenes. In the Cynic tradition the acquisition of virtue was inevitably connected with labor (*ponos*).

3. The ancients were themselves unsure of the origins of the title Cynic ("Dogger"), whether it came from the shamelessly bad manners of the group or from the gymnasium (Kynosarges) at which Antisthenes taught. The history of the tradition was later further confused by the Stoic and Academic penchant for rewriting the history of philosophy.

4. The tale was that Diogenes and his father were exiled from Sinope for counterfeiting the local currency, a practice the son continued on an existential scale in Athens.

askesis that did not, however, derive, as in Plato, from the Pythagorean radical opposition between body and soul, but from an analogy between the excellences of the body and those of the soul, both attainable only by a single-minded athleticism.

Antisthenes was, for all his dubious maternal lineage, an Athenian, but Diogenes appears as the harbinger of a new age. When asked of which city he was a citizen, he replied, in terms later consecrated by the Stoa, that he was a "citizen of the world" (*kosmopolites*), a claim unthinkable on the lips of a Socrates. And yet there was something authentically Socratic in all this. The ethical intensity is his, an intensity run riot, perhaps.[5] Socratic too is the insistence on the autonomy and self-justification of virtue, and while the intellectual corollaries of the "examined life" fall into the background together with its function in the life of the citizen of the *polis,* the supremacy of virtue in the real order is the very instrument that can free a Diogenes from the convention-made and -ruled polity of Athens.

When the Phoenician Cypriote Zeno came to Athens as a young man in B.C. 310, he was immediately drawn to the Socrates that he had read of in Xenophon's *Memoirs.* He could find no better living example of the tradition founded by Socrates than Crates of Thebes (*c.* B.C. 365–285), a disciple of Diogenes devoted to the Cynic life style of poverty and social protest, but less given to theatrical displays than his master in the art. From this apprenticeship Zeno went on to found his own philosophical school, and though "classical" Stoicism developed a highly articulated system of logic and physics in the manner of the Academy, it never lost the mark of its Cynic origins. Zeno's own student Ariston of Chios (*fl. c.* B.C. 250) is almost like a reversion to Cynic type: his repudiation of the "academic disciplines" of physics and logic, his disdain for disputation, and his insistence that the sole object of the philosopher's quest was the life of virtue, all have Cynic antecedents.

Almost from its birth Cynicism was accompanied by a curious literary tradition. Antisthenes wrote dramatic dialogues, and both Diogenes and Crates apparently composed tragedies. We know very little of what to make of these latter productions; both men seem firmly rooted in the tradition of folk literature and rather closer to the satirical and parodic side of comedy than to the

5. Plato is said to have described Diogenes as "a Socrates gone mad."

formalism of tragedy. From Crates we have a few lines of parody preserved, and the indications are that his work entitled *Trifles* also was satiric in intent.

The mockery of values, philosophical, literary and social, so typical of the Cynic viewpoint, obviously lent itself to literary expression, and the earlier Cynics may well have been casting about for the proper instrument to convert this philosophical gold into true Hellenistic currency. Style and substance came together in another of Crates' students, Bion of Borysthenes[6] (*c.* B.C. 325–255), who, though early educated in rhetoric, ended by studying philosophy at Athens, chiefly with Aristotle's student Theophrastus and the notorious Cyrenaic atheist Theodorus.

Bion's debt to his teachers, particularly Crates and Theodorus, is clearly marked, but he never became, even in the attenuated sense that Crates did, a professional philosopher. Bion remained at heart a rhetorician like his first teacher, but his sharing in the world of philosophy had the primary effect of carrying Greek philosophical notions, especially those connected with the Cynicism of Crates and the hedonism of the Cyrenaic Theodorus, to popular audiences. He was the first, as one of his students remarked, to dress philosophy like a whore.

The figure may be attractive, but the claim is surely somewhat overstated. Since the time of the Sophists and Socrates there had existed a popular strain in philosophical or quasi-philosophical discussion of which the Cynics were the direct heirs. Bion's own contribution was the formulation of an appropriate medium and style to give it currency, namely the diatribe, a loosely fitted lecture of high ethical coloring but somewhat low social tone; examples and situations were frequently drawn from life; literary citations abound, frequently in parodied form; the diction is comic, imaginative, vulgar.

The style became immediately popular. It was used by the Cynic Teles (*fl. c.* B.C. 235) and Ariston of Ceos (who succeeded to the head of the Peripatetic school in B.C. 225) and continued to exert a tremendous influence under two distinct but related forms down to the end of antiquity. One was the popular moral discourse that reduced philosophical to popular ethics and as such provided a bridge between philosophy and rhetoric, two disci-

---

6. The Borysthenes was the Dnieper, which the Greeks knew as far north as Kiev. Bion was from Olbia, a *polis* on the joint estuary of the Bug and the Dnieper.

plines frequently at odds in antiquity. The moral diatribe was a form of popular instruction made intelligible by its homely diction and interesting by its use of wit and sarcasm. The content was rarely adventuresome; ethical commonplaces served the modest needs of the diatribe.[7] In this form Bion's creation directly or by intermediaries had its effect across a wide spectrum of literature from the satires of Lucilius and Horace to the Christian sermon, which was its direct descendant.

The other line of the diatribe's evolution emphasized and developed the comic, satiric and parodic side of its nature. Here the creative hand belonged to the third-century Syrian Menippus of Gadara, another student of Cynicism in Greece, who devised a new literary form combining prose and verse, monologue and dialogue. Menippus' works are not extant, but those of his imitators are, written in the same burlesque style and drawing upon the same comic premises that Menippus first popularized: auctions of notable slaves, trips to the underworld, wills, imaginary dialogues between the gods. Running through the whole are Cynic ethical themes and the peculiar Menippean quality that struck his contemporaries and followers, his seriocomic attitude (*speudaiogeloion*). Here too the literary influence was considerable. The Latin Varro (and many generations of Romans after him) and the Greeks Meleager of Gadara[8] (c. B.C. 140–70) and Lucian all wrote "Menippean Satires."

The puzzled Roman heirs of Hellenism did not react with enthusiasm to Cynic eccentricity, and there is little trace of the Cynics' marvelously bad manners in the eager but austere philosophical stirrings of the Republic; Stoicism and Platonism, however, seemed to have fared somewhat better. Both had survived

---

7. The metaphor "All the world's a stage," for instance, though present in Plato, probably passed into the Latin Horace and the Greek *Anthology* through the Cynic diatribe, and thence into Christian moralizing and the body of medieval literature.

8. Meleager's Menippean imitations have disappeared; what have survived are his verse epigrams, which he included in *The Garland*, the first known example of the characteristic late Greek anthologies of epigrams. Much of the contents of the major anthologies from Meleager down to the tenth century were incorporated into the major survivor of the genre, the *Palatine Anthology* of the Byzantine scholar Cephalas under Constantine VII (A.D. 912–959). The best poetry of his own unpoetical century was in Meleager's anthology, including that of the school of eastern poets at whose head he stood. See Chapter VI, p. 207.

their bouts with skepticism and showed increased signs of vitality in the last two centuries of the Republic under the vigorous leadership of Panaetius and Posidonius.[9] Cynicism had to content itself with a pathetic nostalgia for the dear, dead days of Diogenes embalmed in collections of fictionalized letters, and philosophy was apparently once again firmly in the hands of the academic professionals.

In the first Christian century, however, the evolving politics of the Roman Empire brought a relevance not to Cynicism alone, but to the kind of Cynic-Stoic concern with pragmatic ethics typified in the relationship of Crates and Zeno, and very different from the transcendent school Stoicism of the Republic and early Empire that stood aloof in a kind of silent opposition to the demands and vagaries of practical politics; men like Cicero turned to philosophy only as the solace of their retirement or exile. The violent change of mood that thrust both Stoic and Cynic back into the public eye was occasioned by events during the reign of Nero.

Nero, who had been warned by his mother against philosophers, was educated by two of them, first by Chaeremon, a Hellenized Egyptian, and then by Seneca, a Romanized Spaniard. Chaeremon was the mirror of his age: a rationalist Stoic in philosophy, an eclectic religious mystic by temperament, an eminent grammarian by profession,[10] and in the long run the career of Nero may have owed more to this easterner than to the better-known efforts of his other Stoic pedagogue and counselor, Seneca. The first five years (A.D. 54–59) of Nero's reign, the *quinquennium Neronis,* must have seemed like the triumph of enlightened Stoic Hellenism to the intellectuals of the day. But with the death first of Nero's mother Agrippina (A.D. 59), and then of his military mentor Burrus (A.D. 62), and the retirement of Seneca, the forces that conspired to restrain the Emperor disappeared, and the promise of Hellenism degenerated into a mad burlesque. An opposition began to develop, some of it personal, some in search of a return to the Republic, and some apparently philosophical. Nero retorted by exile and execution. Seneca and his nephew Lucan fell (A.D. 65), and in the following

---

9. See Chapter IX, p. 360 ff.

10. At Alexandria he was the successor as head of the school of higher grammatical studies to the same Apion whose anti-Semitic charges were answered by Josephus.

year two eminent Stoic Senators, Thrasea Paetus and Soranus, were condemned. In all of these cases it is difficult to separate philosophy from politics, but at least one well-known Stoic philosopher was sent into exile for his teachings alone, Musonius Rufus, a Hellenized Italian who taught and wrote in Greek.

The banishment of Musonius to the island of Gyaros in the Aegean served only to sharpen the opposition, since he continued to teach in his place of exile. His teaching—or rather, preaching—was essentially in the Cynic tradition: the dependence of virtue on *askesis*, the preeminence of ethical to all other concerns, and the necessity that everyone (even a woman!)[11] become a philosopher in that sense. This was the message that Musonius preached to the masses and which brought him into conflict first with Nero and then with Vespasian and Domitian.

Under the dynasty of the Flavians philosophical opposition was plainly ideological. About A.D. 71 Vespasian banished all the philosophers, in effect the Stoics and Cynics, from Italy, including Musonius (he had been recalled by Galba) and the most eminent Cynic of his day, Demetrius. There was trouble again under Domitian, first in A.D. 89 and then in A.D. 93 or 95. The Stoics and Cynics in opposition to the regime, newly dangerous because of their access to the masses, were exiled or murdered.

Among Domitian's victims were Epictetus (c. A.D. 55–135), a former slave and student of Musonius from Hierapolis in Phrygia, and Dio Chrysostom (c. A.D. 40–112), the Sophist of Prusa in Bithynia, both men illustrations of the contemporary coming-together of Stoicism and Cynicism in the person of the moral preacher. Epictetus, originally the slave of Nero's powerful freedman Epaphroditus, settled in Epirus after his banishment by Domitian, and at this relatively safe distance continued to preach, in his *Diatribes*[12] and in the *Encheiridion*, his characteristic message of virtue as interior liberty under God,[13] a moral state that was dependent on each man's free choice and rendered

---

11. Musonius preached a sexual ethic quite extraordinary in his day and based on the premise that the primary end of intercourse was the generation of children and that such was licit only in marriage; mere pleasure was never an acceptable end of sexual activity.

12. Later collected by his student, the historian Arrian.

13. If the Stoicism of the schools was transformed by its foray into the market place, it is equally true that the cheerful irreverence of the early Cynics was considerably tempered by the later contact with Stoic piety.

him independent of and superior to his immediate external surroundings. It is not difficult to imagine how unpleasantly such teaching must have rung in the ears of a Domitian whose own interpretation of his position as *imperator* bordered on the tyrannous.

Epictetus spent most of his early life as an impoverished and crippled slave; Dio Chrysostom, the scion of a distinguished Bithynian family, quickly made his mark as an orator. In the recurrent debates going on in Roman intellectual circles over the conflicting claims of philosophy and rhetoric, he stood firmly on the side of the latter. But his disassociation from the now dangerous Stoicism did not save him from political involvement, and in A.D. 82 he was compromised and exiled by Domitian. This sudden reversal of fortune prompted his "conversion" to the philosophy of Cynicism, which, unlike most of the contemporary sophistry, had something to say on moral problems, the reality of which the penniless and degraded Dio suddenly understood. As they had for Epictetus, the figure of Socrates and the significance of his mission took on a new meaning for Dio.

For both men their cruel but instructive exile was replaced by the highest honors of the Empire when the liberal Nerva (A.D. 96–98) and his successors came to power. Rome's new rulers sought to conciliate the political and intellectual opposition alike, and both Epictetus and Dio lived to enjoy the fruits of a Hellenic restoration in which the Emperors took upon themselves the trappings of the Stoic philosopher-king and attempted to rule a united mankind with reason and benevolence. The Stoic opposition vanished as suddenly as it had appeared and was replaced by the new Imperial Stoic of which Dio himself serves as the best example, celebrating the union of politics and ideology in his later *Orations*.

There were other Stoics and other Cynics beyond this point—the Stoic Emperor Marcus Aurelius, for instance, and the theatrical Cynic Peregrinus, who burnt himself alive at the Olympic Games in A.D. 165, and whose ashes are somewhat irreverently preserved in Lucian's dialogue *The Death of Peregrinus*. But neither the musings of Marcus Aurelius nor the erratic example of Peregrinus had much to offer to a citizen of the *oikoumene* at the end of the second century. Economic and social crisis, plague, invasions, insurrection and military anarchy descended upon the Empire in the century after the death of Marcus Aurelius in A.D.

180. The orderly *kosmos* of the Stoics, their patience, restraint and refined, if somewhat cold-blooded, cultivation of *humanitas* held out neither cure nor escape for the ills of the third century.

We can never know how deeply the ethical systems fashioned by the Hellenic intellectuals in their academies penetrated the life of the people outside those enclaves. Our histories were written by those same intellectuals, who were far more concerned with the philosophical validity of their beliefs than with their popular acceptance. But even by the modest criterion of what interested the educated upper classes, it is clear that the kind of rationalistic humanism which had been issuing from academic centers into the somewhat larger circles of the educated could no longer sustain itself.

On the testimony of Aristotle it was Socrates who introduced ethics into the business of philosophy, and from that time onward the academics who marched in the steps of Socrates had been fashioning value systems which—however much they might differ in their details—had common premises that ran back to the beginning of Hellenism: man is a being who lives in a world which has a supernatural dimension, but who must, for all that, make his own way, under his own power. Man's bliss is a natural not a supernatural end. It can be achieved here and now by the sole instrument of human intelligence.

There were always some who dissented from that premise; there were times and places in Greek life wherein the supernatural dimension, however it was perceived, proved somewhat more intrusive in its presence and persuasive in its demands than in the academies of the humanists. It is difficult to measure that other world of private fears and private cults, silent prayers, vows, charms and incantations. It was present at Hellenism's birth and never disappeared thereafter. It was present, too, in the academies—rarely, to be sure, in its grosser forms, but cloaked beneath the well-mannered debates about the true character of Pythagoras, the place of Socrates in the history of philosophy, the qualities of the wise man, and the nature of evil. We can trace the issue from the generation after the death of Socrates down through the philosophical circles of the Roman Republic and early Empire. During the troubled years of the third Christian century the debate among the ethicians was in its final stages. Economic, social and political collapse hastened its resolution; the noises from the street were too loud to be ignored.

From Sage to Prophet

Socrates held, it is clear, the central place in the official hagiography of Cynicism and the later Stoa. The schools had historical pretensions in placing him there,[14] and, whatever the validity of these claims of filiation, the reversion to Socratic origins was a natural one for thinkers whose primary interest was in questions of morality. It was, after all, Socrates who had given ethics the rights of domicile among the philosophers, and both Plato and Aristotle, who were very much in the pre-Socratic Parmenidean tradition in other respects, devoted a good part of their theorizing to new questions on the nature and acquisition of virtue.

Not all of their successors shared the Founders' ethical interests; physics, mathematics and logic all possessed, it was well known, a more impressive degree of certitude, and many of the best minds, particularly in the Academy, preferred to go that way. And those who did not were not immune to the longing for a geometrical proof in ethical questions against which Aristotle had warned.

Aristotle, the supreme rationalist, was also one of the few Greek thinkers to attempt to give some weight to inductively derived evidence. Neither he nor his contemporaries were completely at ease with such evidence; the link between the concrete individual instance and the universal essence with which science and philosophy had necessarily to deal remained a difficult one. There was, as Aristotle was fond of saying, no science of the individual.

An ethics without a concern for the concrete problems of the moral life ends in a metaphysics of the good, and Aristotle attempted to balance the natural swerve of rationalism in that latter direction by a number of different techniques. He did pay attention to individual (and actual) behavior by his inclusion of the nonphilosophical universal, the *endoxon*, or "what seems true to most people," and hence a distillation of observed behavior. Again, he took as his norm, as the mannikin against which the garments of morality were to be measured, not the figure of the philosopher current in the Platonic and Stoic traditions, but the

---

14. See Chapter IX, pp. 362–63.

reasonably serious and intelligent man (*spoudaios*), a choice which avoided the unrealized construct on one end of the scale and the pure nonscientific and unintelligible individual on the other. Finally, to facilitate the analysis of behavior, Aristotle and his school paid considerable attention to the study of a typology of character.[15]

The differences between Plato and Aristotle on ethics went far beyond methodology. The other-worldliness that Aristotle had once found attractive in Platonic theorizing yielded increasingly to empiricism, and the results are as evident in ethics as they are in the Aristotelian metaphysic. Plato's thoroughgoing intellectualization found less and less support in Aristotle's ethical treatises, though the full separation—and independence—of moral virtue (*phronesis*) from intellectual virtue (*sophia*) apparently did not occur until Theophrastus had assumed the headship of the Lyceum. The separation can be traced in the debate between Theophrastus and his slightly younger Peripatetic contemporary Dicaearchus, the former holding, with Plato and Aristotle, for the primacy of the contemplative life (*bios theoretikos*), and the latter for the superiority of the active life (*bios praktikos*).[16] The true philosopher, Dicaearchus maintained, was not to be found in the cloisters of the Academy or the Lyceum, but engaged in the mainstream of life; witness the example of the traditional Seven Sages (Thales,[17] Solon, etc.) and, more tellingly, of Socrates himself, all practitioners of the *bios praktikos*.

For Dicaearchus and his followers the active life style found its highest fulfillment in politics,[18] and in addition to his other examples Dicaearchus brought Pythagoras into the lists. Pythagoras, an enigmatic historical person of the sixth century, was a

15. Related to the "New Comedy" of Theophrastus' contemporary Menander and contributing, by way of the Peripatetic Ariston of Ceos, to the later Cynic diatribe.

16. A position at least in part dictated by Dicaearchus' rejection of Aristotle's transcendent and immortal intellectual soul (*nous*).

17. Plato had earlier claimed Thales as an example of the *bios theoretikos* and the conflicting claims for the corpse of the Father of Philosophy account for the exactly contradictory sets of biographical anecdotes current about him in the later tradition, the one showing him as the type of the other-worldly philosopher, the other as the man of affairs in Miletus.

18. A sentiment which later made Dicaearchus popular in Roman philosophical circles, where his works had been introduced by Panaetius.

figure of some importance in the later Academy. His influence, or that of his followers, on Plato was unmistakable, and Aristotle was unkind enough to suggest that "Platonism" was nothing more than a warmed-over version of something that had first been put forward by the Pythagoreans. The Academy itself, for whom Pythagoras was the very founder of the contemplative ideal of life, may have been encouraging just such an affiliation. At least one of Aristotle's contemporaries in the Academy, Heraclides of Pontus, subscribed to it.

The meaning of Pythagoras' teaching was, however, open to other interpretations, and even by the time of the Academic interest in Pythagoreanism there were two versions of such extant, both claiming legitimate descent from the Master. One group, the "hearers" (akousmatikoi), were religious in their intent, practiced the peculiar askesis of ritual purity and taboo, and held the doctrine of the transmigration of souls. The other, the "mathematicians" (mathematikoi), represented the tradition of mathematics, harmonics and astronomy in the "school."

The Lyceum had among its own members a vigorous defender of the scientific side of Pythagoreanism in the person of the eminent musicologist Aristoxenus of Tarentum, another contemporary of Theophrastus and Dicaearchus, and one who wrote a life of another Tarentine scientist, the Pythagorean Archytas whom Plato had visited. Aristoxenus' frankly propagandistic point was twofold: first, that Archytas stood well clear of the tradition of religious Pythagoreanism; and second, that this scientist's restrained and dedicated life contrasted favorably with the licentious and undisciplined behavior of Socrates. What was at stake in this particular exercise in biography was clearly nothing less than the parentage of the entire Platonic tradition.

Dicaearchus was not, apparently, a party to this particular struggle; his interest was in claiming Pythagoras for the bios praktikos. And so a third Pythagoras emerged, the lawgiver and politician engaged in constitutional reform in southern Italy. The respective historical validity of the portraits of Pythagoras the mathematician (Aristoxenus), the wonder-worker (Heraclides), and the political reformer (Dicaearchus) need not, fortunately, be decided here; it is sufficient to point out that about b.c. 300 no one was interested in this as a historical question but rather as a philosophical one, or at very least as a question of academic politics.

The chief weapon in this war of the schools was the *bios*, a word which signifies both a way of life and a "biography"—that is, a literary work describing that particular mode of life in terms of an individual career.[19] Plato and Aristotle saw the possibility of three such general states, the active, the contemplative and the life of pleasure, and later Peripatetic masters devoted themselves to illustrating them, first individually, then in group studies, frequently with specific comparisons of the type later made famous in Plutarch's biographies, and eventually in the form of *Lives of Philosophers* arranged according to the systematic principle of "successions" (*diadoche*) of master and pupil.

The probable innovator of this latter form, the incipient history of philosophy, was Ariston of Ceos, who succeeded to the directorship of the Lyceum about B.C. 225. His interests were not, unfortunately, very philosophical. Both Aristoxenus, who initiated the genre of philosophical biography in his lives of Archytas, Pythagoras and Socrates, and Ariston, who perfected it, wrote from an ethical rather than a historical point of view, and preferred to illumine the *bios* of their chosen subject by maxim and anecdote, frequently tendentious or borrowed or both. From the beginning the scurrilous was more prominent than the analytic, and considerably more space was devoted in these biographies to the will of the deceased than to any philosophical positions he may have chanced to hold while alive. In Ariston the penchant was even more strongly marked by reason of his contact with the Cynic diatribe style.[20]

For reasons that are not entirely clear, the issue of Pythagoreanism disappeared from academic circles after the earliest generation of scholars at the Lyceum. Our sources are silent on the subject from the middle of the third century down to the time of the Roman Republic, and when Pythagoras does reappear, it is the wonder-working sage and religious leader portrayed by Heraclides of Pontus who has triumphed over the scientist and

---

19. See Chapter II, pp. 111-12.
20. The scholarly interest of the Alexandrian scholars in questions of chronology and bibliography did have its effect on the genre, but the only preserved example of an ancient *Lives of Philosophers*, that by Diogenes Laertius (*c.* A.D. 250), is still very much the Peripatetic "biography," a decorative ethical pendant rather than a specialized branch of history (see Chapter II, p. 115). On the other ingredient in the history of ancient philosophy, the doxography, see Chapter IX, p. 378.

politician. Cicero, who was present at the revival of Pythagoreanism, said that it was the work of Nigidius Figulus, the learned contemporary of Varro, who served as Praetor in B.C. 58. Nigidius was a practicing occultist as well as a scholar, and stood at the center of a nascent Pythagorean circle at Rome whose membership included Vatinius and Appius Claudius and which indulged in some rather ominous magical practices.

From this starting point the new Pythagoreanism swelled into a philosophical union with Platonism, eventually debasing the latter into its own magical and superstitious image. The transformation of Platonism from philosophy into theurgy was not an isolated event but part of a sweeping change of tone and texture that worked itself into the fabric of ancient thought, what has been described as the "failure of nerve," "fear of freedom," or "decline of rationalism."

Note has already been taken of the rationalist premise operative in much of Greek thought and life. Expressed in a variety of ways, it was, at root, the belief that unaided human reason was an adequate instrument for both understanding and action. Very few Greeks indeed denied the existence of the gods, and not very many more (e.g., the Epicureans) were willing to go to the lengths of suggesting that they had no effect on human life; what the rationalist premise did suggest was that the operation of these gods was unnecessary for the acquisition of either truth by the intellect or good by the will.

The rejection of that principle by the world of later Hellenism was neither total nor immediate; Plotinus was still operating under it in the third century and Libanius somewhat less convincingly in the fourth. The nature of evil provides a good touchstone for its existence, and Plotinus' insistence that evil is a negative, privative quality is typical of the entire rationalist tradition's equation of evil with intellectual ignorance, formal imperfection or metaphysical privation. The application of the same test to the later Academy, the time when Aristotle and Heraclides of Pontus were in attendance there, reveals, on the other hand, that even at this point the premise was under attack.

Plato's final work, the *Laws*, contains some rather startling departures from the normative doctrine of his middle years. In addition to positing a positive principle of cosmic evil in the form of a second World Soul, Plato had there thrown into unexpected relief the question of a religious piety (*eusebeia, theosebeia*) regulated and severely sanctioned by the state and centered about the cult of the deified heavenly bodies. One need not, perhaps, search very far for origins. Plato's intellectual circle included both the Pythagorean Archytas and the eminent astronomer Eudoxus, the latter of whom, we know, studied astronomy in Egypt and had a more than passing interest in Zoroaster and the Magi.

Like Pythagoras, Zoroaster excited the imagination of the Academy. Aristotle wrote of him in his early work *On Philosophy*, as did Heraclides. The late product of the Academy, the *Epinomis*, had progressed beyond astral theology to astrology. The heavens and the East, singly and in combination, had entered Hellenism not as a mere cultural ingredient, but as agents of destruction of the rationalism that was at Hellenism's heart.

Between Heraclides of Pontus and Nigidius Figulus there was no slackening of the process. Philosophy and science, both of which had the power to resist, were unable to do so, the first because it was in the grip of a paralyzing skepticism, the latter because it was itself infiltrated and under siege by the "new astronomy" and the "new physics." And as a telling sign of the times the sage (*sophos*), the hero type fashioned by the rationalist tradition in the wake of the disappearance of the older epic warrior, was replaced by a new culture hero, the prophet.

The *sophos* was a many-sided figure, but his two chief characteristics were those already noted in connection with the debate on the active versus the contemplative life: he was a *polites* (city founder, lawgiver, magistrate, judge, orator, competent to lead, willing to follow) and a *logistes* (counselor, debater, dialectician, thinker, scientist). There were, to be sure, religious associations here; the Greeks, for all their rationalism, never divorced the human and the divine. But the new type, the prophet, was in essence divine, a religious figure, a wonder-worker (*thaumatourgos*) who was privy to the secrets of life and nature by reason of gift not attainment, an exotic partisan of older, more venerable, and wiser cultures of the East; the Magi of Iran, the priests of Egypt, the astrologers of Chaldea, the Brahmans of India, the wizard sages among the Jews and Armenians, all newly revealed by Alexander's opening to the East.

The Greeks had known most of these people before by report or through their own travels. They had pondered the cultures of the East and detected analogies with their own. What was new in the Hellenistic era was the adulation of eastern civilizations—not, be it noted, as cultural phenomena but as manifestations of a wisdom superior to its own, an attitude scarcely possible to the chauvinistic and self-centered Hellenes of the time of Pericles, or even of Aristotle, who counted all these people as *barbaroi*, interesting perhaps, but culturally inferior and aesthetically distasteful.

New themes were sounded: Moses (or the Magi) discovered philosophy; Plato learned about the immortality of the soul from Pythagoras, who learned it from the Egyptians, who may have learned it from the Brahmans; Pythagoras studied with Zaratas (Zoroaster) under whose name scores of works were circulated in Hellenistic times, as they were for his fellow Persians Hystaspes and Ostanes.

The world after Alexander was filled with gods as never before. These were not the rather quiescent Olympians who had settled into the imposing but ineffectual posture of national monuments, but a more activist breed quick to reveal themselves in epiphanies and to display their not inconsiderable powers (*aretai, energeiai*). The infatuation with the East was simultaneously an infatuation with the wonderful and the exotic, secularized in the romance and divinized in the lives and travels of the wonder-working men, living or dead, who went about preaching the powers of the gods.

Pythagoras was such a one from the past who received the full biographical attention of late antiquity, and not merely at the hands of third-rate literary hacks catering to popular tastes. Nigidius Figulus had, as Cicero reported, restored Pythagoreanism to its former place of prominence among the philosophical schools; and now its founder, invested with a religious aura that neither Plato nor Aristotle could ever possess, was accorded extraordinary veneration.

The recrudescence of Pythagoreanism is a striking symptom of the decline of rationalism operating within the philosophical establishment itself. In the age of Cicero, philosophy in all its branches was entering upon a classicist phase, wherein authority assumed an ever-increasing importance. In the formal schools this meant a new interest in the "founder" and an attempt to legitimatize one's own teaching by connecting it with that of the original school, a process frequently accomplished by the wholesale rewriting of history. Pythagoreanism had no history in the same sense; it did possess, however, a type of "sacred history" in the form of narratives of the maxims and deeds of Pythagoras.

Sayings were far more important in Pythagoreanism than in the older schools, which had been, from their origins, formalized institutions where the preferred manner of teaching was through literary and pedagogical treatises. The more charismatic and religious tradition stemming from Pythagoras had never had the benefit of a succession of scholarchs presiding, with a marked degree of independence, over an academic establishment; indeed, it is unlikely that there was any organization at all in Pythagoreanism after the early collapse of its political power. Pythagoreanism in the first pre-Christian century was engaged not so much in the preservation of a tradition as in the rediscovery of its sainted but nonliterary founder.

Pythagoreanism's primary appeal at Rome was precisely the religious and pietistic strain celebrated by Heraclides. One can observe it in many different ways: Nigidius' fascination with occultism; the dabbling in necromancy by other members of the circle; a strong current of vegetarianism and other dietary restrictions;[21] and the inevitable production of a body of apocryphal literature pretending to go back to Pythagoras or his circle (Archytas, Ocellus) and which included both "sayings" and treatises (*hypomnemata*) in the traditional sense.[22]

From Nigidius to Plotinus the rationalizing Pythagoreans—that is, those belonging to the philosophical rather than the ascetical tradition—attempted to create a Pythagorean school tradition by the expedient of rewriting the history of the early Academy in a manner that made Plato and Aristotle (and their immediate successors) "expropriate" the genuine teachings of Pythagoras. What these latter consisted in was set forth by the great triad of

---

21. Two philosophers involved in this particular tradition were Quintus Sextius, who, in the time of Augustus, attempted to found an ethical philosophy based on native Roman moral values (curiously, he wrote his work in Greek and he included an espousal of vegetarianism), and later Sotion, the Alexandrian Greek who was the mentor of Seneca.

22. The *hypomnemata*, the only grounds for reconstructing the intellectual Pythagoreanism of the period, were excerpted by "authors" like Alexander Polyhistor, Sextus Empiricus, Stobaeus and Photius and so are partially recoverable. The best known of the spurious "sayings" was the collection known as the *Golden Sayings* and those connected with Pythagoras' wife Theano.

Empire Pythagoreans: Moderatus of Gades and the two easterners, Nicomachus[23] of Gerasa in the Transjordan and Numenius of Apamea in Syria.

The mathematical version of Platonism put forth by these
thinkers had a profound effect on a Platonic tradition newly
recovered from its seizure of skepticism. It was quite in the spirit
of the times—and of Pythagoreanism—that the chief elements of
the original Platonic world view, the Forms, should be conceived
of in theological terms; what is more typically Pythagorean is
their conversion into numbers and, in consequence of the serial
nature of number theory, the ordering of these number-Forms
into a chain (*seira*) of transcendental beings derived from the
primordial One and descending, through a great number of
intermediaries, to the terrestrial world of man.

This system was not the work of a mere mathematician turned
philosopher; the sentiments of the theologian were everywhere
present. Numbers were not simple measures of quantity; they
were sacred metaphysical principles.[24] Not only were the principal Forms divinized, but in the material world the planets were
gods and the intermediary region between heaven and earth was
populated with the souls of heroes and demons who mediated the
planetary influences on man. Man himself was bound to the
strictest ritual purity (*hagneia*) and piety (*eusebeia*).

These were the Pythagorean insights that were eventually
blended into Stoicism and particularly later Platonism, by a Philo
with ingenuity, by a Plotinus with restraint and a respect for the
basic premises of the intellectualist tradition, but by a Porphyry
and an Iamblichus with the joy of a religious thinker who had
finally found a philosophical system to his liking.

Mathematical metaphysics was a subject primarily discussed
among the professionals, but Pythagorean morality had its own
popular appeal, and the Pythagorean saint took his place at the
side of the Stoic moralist and the Cynic preacher. The physiognomy of these fakirs of a new age has, however, been heavily
overlaid with legend and literary embellishment. One knows little
or nothing of the "Sextus" who stands behind the collection of

23. See Chapter V, p. 211.
24. To say nothing of pawns in the endless game of numerical symbolism, numerology, and divination by number, the latter an ingenious
method of predicting, for example, the outcome of battles by reducing
the names of the combatants to numbers, which were then analyzed.

aphorisms known as the *Sayings of Sextus,* or of Secundus, the "silent philosopher" of Athens, who lived at the time of Hadrian and under whose name a dubious biography and a kind of catechism of popular Pythagoreanism have been preserved. What is remarkable about both these collections is their later popularity in Christian circles and its natural consequence, the appearance of translations of the original Greek in all the languages of the Roman-Christian *oikoumene* Latin, Syriac, Armenian, Ethiopic and Arabic.

Much of this later material was, of course, projected back upon Pythagoras himself. The best-known of these romantic reconstructions of an almost totally vanished past were the third-century biographies of the Founder by Porphyry and Iamblichus, who had available for their use studies done even earlier by Nicomachus of Gerasa and by the man who was the very archetype of Neopythagorean piety in the Empire, Apollonius of Tyana in Cappadocia, whose own career was the subject of literary distortion. But in the case of Apollonius the manipulation was quite deliberate. His biography, commissioned of Philostratus by the Augusta Dulia Domna but completed sometime after her death in A.D. 217, was an explicit "correction"of earlier—and perhaps truer—portraits of Apollonius. In Philostratus' version, wherein much of the action unfolds in the context of a travel romance that carries the hero to India and Ethiopia, the Cappadocian is indeed a saint of the high-minded Pythagorean type, ascetic, wise, benevolent, constantly doing good and almost as constantly catechizing his traveling companion Damis on everything from the morals of eunuchs to the usefulness of elephants.

Philostratus confessed that in the writing of his *Apollonius* he relied on the journals of Damis and the correspondence of his hero. He knew the hostile sources too, and here the possibility of another Apollonius, the historical one who lived in the middle of the first century, reveals itself. At least some of his contemporaries considered the historical Apollonius a charlatan and a magician. Lucian, who was somewhat later (*c.* A.D. 120–180) and had experience of another such,[25] certainly did, and the contemporary Stoic philosopher, Euphrates of Syria, a student of

---

25. Alexander, the "prophet" of Abonoteichus in Bithynia-Pontus and a student of the "Tyana school" of Pythagoreanism, whom Lucian mercilessly pilloried in his *Alexander, or The Pseudo Prophet.*

Musonius Rufus, made an attempt to combat him as an enemy of rationalism,[26] apparently to no avail, since the wonders achieved by Apollonius at home and abroad brought him a theatrical success in the Empire, a success that Philostratus described in the language and ideals of the new Sophistic of his own times, and which still later propagandists attempted to turn against Christianity.

The career of Apollonius, real or fictionalized, had little in common with either the Stoic sage or the Cynic dissenter, both genuine outgrowths of a tradition going back to Socrates and both thoroughly Hellenic in their sturdy secularism and freedom from the miraculous. Apollonius, however, was the alien eastern *Wundermann* at home in the temple rather than the *agora*, and trafficking in cures, levitations and dream therapy.

Dynamis and Daimon

To a secular age the growth of Pythagorean pietism must necessarily appear as degeneration. Such it may be indeed, in the context of the rationalist tradition in Hellenism. But that tradition was by no means the only characteristic of a vigorous Hellenism; more and more a counterstrain of irrationality has been revealed in the Greeks' life even in the most golden of ages: oracle mongers abounded during the Peloponnesian war, and Socrates was tried on the indictable offense of heresy. Nor is it prima facie evidence that under Roman dominion the Hellenic spirit was any more concerned with the supernatural and Hellenism's new methods of dealing with it. By a curious inversion one can now appreciate primitivism in religion; what is repugnant is science yoked to the service of religion. But what now passes as decadence was in later antiquity nothing more than a "progressive" attempt to create a scientifically based religion to replace the discredited primitivism of an earlier day.

For a Hellene of the Empire, Olympianism no longer sufficed.[27] The culture had, nonetheless, an immense aesthetic, literary and historical investment in that Homeric landscape; and so it was

---

26. Pleading before the Emperor Vespasian, Euphrates characterized the intellectual tradition as "philosophy in natural terms," and that represented by Apollonius as "secret discourse with God."
27. See Chapter XII, pp. 447–49.

not, as has been seen, simply a question of rejecting out of hand an Olympian apparatus that the Greeks had begun to outgrow as soon as they had completed its construction. Out of its ruins the intellectuals had reconstituted a passable version of Zeus who was still capable of addressing one's head; but in the heart only silence reigned. The moral imperatives of Pythagoreanism, with its promise of immortality and its sense of the nearness of God, responded to that silence, as did the other cults that came into prominence in Roman times.

The religious currents of the Hellenistic and Roman periods frequently appear to be flowing in opposite directions. On the one hand the intelligentsia, the philosophers and theologians, were coming more and more to a belief in a remote, unique and transcendent God, highly spiritualized along the lines of development suggested by Aristotle. Popular religion during the same period was, however, enunciating beliefs in quite another species of deity—multiple, activist and immanent. In a sense popular belief had always worshiped such gods; what had changed was that it now had a rationalistic and philosophical justification every whit as imposing as that which supported Zeus Most High. And curiously, its underpinning likewise owed a great deal to Aristotle.

Science has gone so far by the route of quantitative measurement that the peculiar qualitative nature of much of Greek learning has become obscured. Primitive societies are keen in the recognition of the "powers" of things, and the Greeks as primitives paid their share of careful attention to such "powers," considered, as in all such cases, capable of producing quite extraordinary effects and so in a sense wonderful or divine (*theion*). The mythmakers personified such powers into gods, and the philosophers eventually abstracted them into qualities; and though mathematics ignored them, Greek physics was largely the study of the action and reaction of just such qualities.

The triumphs of modern science are a reflection of man's ability to convert all physical properties into quantities measurable by number. There was always the possibility that the Greeks might have anticipated the modern approach and quantified, and so mathematicized, their physics; Pythagoreanism was certainly heading in that direction, and there was some indication that Platonism was willing to follow its lead. But the coming to things through their qualities rather than quantity, the approach that was favored by Aristotle and that relied on techniques of description and analysis instead of mathematical measurement, eventually won out, chiefly through the prestige of Peripatetic science, and henceforth the physical sciences devoted their efforts to studying the activity of qualities in bodies, the circumstances of their appearance and disappearance—in short, the phenomenon of change. Mathematics knew nothing of this; both quality and change were alien to its thinking.

The great war between physics and mathematics was fought in the heavens. Were the celestial phenomena subject to the quantitative laws of mathematics or the qualitative laws of physical mechanics? The struggle was never really resolved to the extent that one side surrendered its claims, but as far as the common man was concerned, it was beyond doubt that astronomy was a branch of physics, though of a very special kind.[28]

The Aristotelian view of nature saw it as an ascending series of species, wherein the individuals within each species were constituted by a union between a passive material substratum and an active system of qualities that made up its specific intelligibility. Each ascending species was in turn characterized by a more sophisticated qualitative system with more complex functions, climaxing in the system known as the intelligent soul whose function is thought. Man possesses such a soul, but the series of ascending beings by no means ends with him; it proceeds upward through more sophisticated souls possessed by the highest species, the heavenly bodies.

The study of all these phenomena was constituted a science for Aristotle by reason of its systematic methodology, but more importantly because their study was theoretic—that is, it had as its end no pragmatic, useful aim in *doing* (like ethics or politics) or in *making* (like carpentry or medicine), but was purely speculative knowledge for the sake of knowing. The glory of science was that it was not demeaned by use.

A few modern critics have found fault with the Greeks' fastidious refusal to turn their considerable knowledge of mathematics and physics to useful ends. But the criticism is not accurately put, and its very imprecision masks the evolution of post-Aristotelian science and religion. Actually it was the demands of religion that converted science into something truly and deeply useful, not, however, for *making*, as in technology,

---

28. See Chapter V, pp. 217–20.

but for *doing*. Astrology was nothing more than an eminently useful astronomy, alchemy a useful form of chemistry, and Hellenistic and Roman "magic" concealed a highly sophisticated and learned theology of physics.

Aristotelian physics was the study of the "activization" (*energeia*) of bodies, and this notion of "activization" owed a great deal, as Aristotle himself readily admitted, to his analysis of function (*ergon*), with all its implications of normative or natural operation. After him, however, physics returned to a somewhat earlier point of view which saw the activity principle not as structure,[29] but as a power (*dynamis*) resident in a body and capable of a far wider spectrum of activities, and so of an even more complex series of actions and reactions than even Plato or Aristotle had suspected.

To this point the new theory was no less scientific than the Aristotelian; where it proceeded to violate the Aristotelian canon of science was in its attempt not merely to understand but to manipulate—that is, to use—these powers in bodies. This pragmatic turn to physics, which can be dated fairly precisely to the second century before Christ, was by no means as revolutionary as it might first appear. Within the confines of Greek science itself an effort had apparently been made in the same direction by the Pythagorean scientists of the fifth century, an effort that was eventually frustrated by the static nature of numbers, which served readily as symbols but only indifferently as wellsprings of activity; the generative power of number was at best an unconvincing metaphor.

Qualities, on the other hand, with the long Greek tradition of vitalism standing behind them, proved far more efficacious, and the "new physics" popularized by Bolus, the "Democritean" of Mendes in Egypt, explored their activities at great length. Bolus, who is described by some of the ancient authorities as a Pythagorean, is unlikely to have been an innovator; his appearance in the second century probably means no more than the literary resurfacing of a tradition already in existence long before Bolus' treatises codified and sanctified it.[30]

---

29. Aristotle himself must have been ambivalent on the subject, since he describes this principle both in terms of a Platonic Form (*eidos*) with its structural implications and as "in-function" (*energeia*) with its activist overtones (see Chapter III, pp. 131–32).

30. On its Iranian connections see Chapter XII, pp. 476–78.

Bolus' most considerable and popular work was that on the "powers" of things, *The Physical Powers*, or *On Sympathies and Antipathies*, but a bibliography of his published treatises shows that his interests ranged widely: agriculture, medicine, alchemy, divination, astrology, ethics and history, the last including a treatise on the Jews. Of some of these little can be said; what is certain is that Bolus was no theoretician, but rather the heir of a great deal of practical information accumulated by the priests and craftsmen of Egypt and by the indefatigable travelers who had been coursing the *oikoumene* since the time of Herodotus. This great trove of lore was now conceptualized and organized under the rubric of immanent and hidden "natures" (*physeis*) or "powers" (*dynameis*), and used to the practical end of bringing men health, good fortune, or knowledge of the future.

At least one of Bolus' treatises was devoted to alchemy, and its title, *Tinctures (Baphika)*, reveals better than the common name of the discipline, *chemia*,[31] the passage of a useful art into the domains of the "useful" sciences. All ancient societies possessed a knowledge of useful techniques, and these were normally guarded as privileged information within guilds, frequently with the added protection of a priesthood. The Greek guilds must have been secularized fairly early, but in Egypt, where the artisans' techniques were highly sophisticated, priestly control was never threatened by the pryings of an open society or the speculations of secular philosophers. One of the most elaborate and valuable of these techniques was that of working the various precious metals, and particularly that of giving base metals the appearance of precious ones by various tincturing processes. These were guarded by the several priestly-artisan corporations and shielded from vulgarization by the regular employment of symbolic or code names for the ingredients and the processes.

It is here that once again Bolus appears in the guise of the scientist converting, like some ancient Diderot, secret guild knowledge into the currency of philosophy and science. Or again, as Pythagoras reputedly did in geometry, he exalted what had been merely technique into science, providing it with theory. The theory derived easily from the Aristotelian view of material bodies being composed of the unity of matter, the substratum of

---

31. Of disputed etymology. The nominal difference between chemistry and alchemy is nothing more than the prefixed Arabic article *al-* in the latter.

change, with the "forms" that pass in and out of that matter. This "prime matter" completely devoid of form and the starting point of all alchemical change was lead, upon which the alchemist could work his knowledge of the various "sympathies and antipathies." In Aristotle one cannot work directly upon the central substantial form but only in terms of its various qualities, and a great deal of alchemical ingenuity was devoted to the extraction of these latter in the form of "spirits" (*pneuma, spiritus*).

Bolus made no attempt to secularize this knowledge. Its priestly and religious associations cling to it in the form of tales of divine origins from Hermes or Isis or of legendary founders, normally easterners like Ostanes the Persian, or his Jewish disciple Mary,[32] or even Cleopatra. As in the priestly guilds the operations frequently included prayers. What eventually resulted was a bizarre blending of Egyptian craft techniques, Aristotelian physical theory and Hellenistic religion, so that by the time of Zosimus, the Hellenized Alexandrian of the third century after Christ who marks the climax of ancient alchemy, the "craft" was more a theology than a science, and the manipulation of the physical elements was merely a kind of dumb show for the awe-inspiring movement of the metaphysical and spiritual principles for which they served as symbols.

This remarkable cultural oscillation whereby the Greeks took eastern religious guild techniques and converted them into secular speculative science, only to have them revert to their theological and pragmatic origins, was repeated more than once in the encounter between East and West, and nowhere more strikingly than in astronomy. The earlier Greeks had constructed the science of astronomy out of Babylonian star lore and then watched its gradual return from Plato onward to the position of a "life science," still bearing unmistakable signs of Greek theorizing but no longer a purely speculative discipline.

The premise of astrology was exactly the same as that of Bolean physics, that the powers inherent in one type of being can affect those in another. What is different about astrology is, first, that the doctrine of affinity (*sympatheia*) is extended to cosmic horizons, so that there is an affective correspondence between the

---

32. Credited with the invention of the piece of alchemical apparatus still called after her the *bain-marie*.

terrestrial and the celestial domains; and second, that the powers in the heavenly bodies are not merely centers of physical dynamism but personalized and intelligent forces—in short, that the heavenly bodies are divine beings. Such a belief was widespread among the peoples of the East in antiquity and not unknown in Greece. It did not, however, play any role in classical Greek astronomy, where the movements of the heavenly bodies were calculated solely in terms of the laws of mechanics.

From the time of Plato, however, the "Chaldean" viewpoint began to make inroads in the scientific and philosophical community. The planets were described as "visible gods," and in Aristotle were credited with souls and intelligences lodged in incorruptible bodies. Aristotle also noted the effect that the movement of the heavenly bodies exercised on terrestrial life,[33] though still in a naturalistic vein.

This new Greek interest in the star gods and their cult was steadily nourished from outside sources. There is some evidence that Plato had admitted a "Chaldean" to membership in the Academy, and it may be he who stands at the source of the Oriental cult of the heavenly bodies urged in both the *Laws* and the late Academic *Epinomis*. But that this cult aspect had not progressed to a serious effort at astral divination is clear from the fact that both Eudoxus and Theophrastus, the associates of Plato and Aristotle, were skeptical of the claims by the devotees of the new cult that they were able to predict human events by casting horoscopes.

The conquests of Alexander brought Babylon into the orbit of Hellenism, a conjunction that affected both cultures. In Hellenized Seleucid Babylon, astronomy came to a remarkable maturity in the third and second centuries before Christ, and it is not always easy to say to whom the priority of genius belongs, Chaldean or Greek. What is certain is that information was flowing westward through the hands of learned Hellenized mediators of the eastern tradition like Berossus, the priest of Bel, who was teaching and writing on Babylonian traditional material

---

33. It was the unceasing revolution of the sun along the ecliptic that was for Aristotle the ultimate explanation for the only experience of immortality on earth, the preservation of species despite the corruption of individuals within that species.

about B.C. 280.[34] The immediate intellectual effects of this blending of two great astronomical perspectives is probably best seen
in the eminent Greek astronomer Hipparchus of Nicaea (*fl. c.* B.C.
161–126) who not only made great strides toward the precision
of astronomical data but also, on the evidence of Pliny, established more fully than any of his predecessors "the relationship
between man and the stars and that our souls are particles of
heavenly fire." He was, in short, a convinced astrologer.

Contemporary with Hipparchus there appeared in Egypt under
the dual—and spurious—authorship of an Egyptian Pharaoh
Nechepso and the priest Petosiris an introduction to astrology
that was to serve as the basic work on the subject for all
antiquity. Its supposed hoary antiquity was, of course, a pretense;
Egypt was as innocent of astrology as were the Greeks until
Ptolemaic times, when the Babylonian influences, mediated by
Greek theorizing, began to gain a foothold there. By the second
century astrology was at home both in Egyptian cult circles and
in the scientific establishment at Alexandria. Indeed, Egypt eventually became the center of diffusion for most of the astrological
learning that inundated the Roman Empire.

For nearly five centuries, from the mid-second century before
Christ to the triumph of Christianity, the ancient world was in
the almost unchallenged grip of this half-religious, half-scientific
phenomenon. It is more than likely that it was precisely its dual
nature that gave astrology its enormous appeal. Its scientific
credentials were of the highest order: Alexandrian mathematics
and the second-century Stoa provided ample material for both
the theory and practice of the art. The premises of astrology
accorded well with the Stoic doctrine of fate (*heimarmene*) and
the world view that saw the universe as an organic whole linked
together by a natural "sympathy." The terrestrial and celestial
spheres were part of the same organism, and events on high both
affected and reflected those on earth. Who could read the
heavens could dispense with all other forms of divination, and
indeed the great variety of divinatory methods practiced by the
Greeks and Romans appears to have been substantially checked
by the spread of astrology.

A true astrological reading was a highly complex affair demanding not inconsiderable mathematical skill. One could, of

---

34. See Chapter VI, pp. 235–36.

course, turn to professional help; there was a great proliferation of *Chaldaei* and *mathematici* under the Empire ranging from highly placed and influential court astrologers down to street-corner sages in the New Mathematics. Or one could attempt to work it out for oneself with the help of a simplified calendar system, and particularly the scheme of the astrological week that came into vogue during the Hellenistic period. This latter schema assigned to each of the seven known "planets" its own influential day in sequence, and there were further attributions of months, years and even longer periods to the influence of the particular planets.[35]

Astrology was, however, more than science or philosophy; it was also a religious phenomenon. The heavenly bodies were first divine and then divinities. About the time of Plato the eastern custom of calling them by the names of gods appeared among the Greeks.[36] Even earlier there had been a mythological "explanation" of the configurations of the constellations, some doubtless mere beast fables, but becoming increasingly religious with the belief in catasterism, the translation of a human hero to a place in the heavens.

Here too philosophy had its word. It is likely that from the beginning the heavens and celestial phenomena inspired primitive communities with the kind of awe that stands at the heart of a genuinely religious experience. When the Greek theoreticians turned their attention to the question of religion they too found in the eternity and regularity of the movement of the heavenly bodies a likely origin for the belief in God. From Plato and Aristotle onward the order and arrangement of the heavens was a staple in every proof for the existence of a God responsible for the obvious sense of order that every quarter of the vault of the heavens betrayed to man.

That the heavenly bodies were themselves gods is, however, quite another matter, and here the argument ran into a ponderous

---

35. The system of time reckoning that finally emerged was a blend of many elements—the solar day, the lunar month, the astronomical week—thrown into considerable disarray by Julius Caesar's conversion of the reckoning from a lunar to a solar year in B.C. 46 and his and his successors' use of the names of the months for political purposes.

36. Earlier the Greeks had used phenomenological designations like "Fiery Star" or "Twinkling Star," which now became, respectively, Ares (Mars) and Hermes (Mercury).

ambivalence. There was no lack of empirical evidence for the divinity of the celestial spheres; the eternity of their motion and their obvious exemption from the laws of decay[37] all suggested that here was something divine. But what nature of gods were these—personalized beings with a will of their own like the prototypes of Olympian mythology, or divine substances locked into an invariable system governed by a superior fate?

It was a difficulty the Greeks never solved. Popular astrology generally followed the eastern antecedents and viewed the heavenly bodies as anthropomorphized gods who had wills of their own and could be pleased or offended and so were suitable objects of prayer and cult. The intellectuals more often sided with the predominant philosophical current of Stoicism that saw all under the sway of a remote, impersonal fate that governed all but deigned to reveal its future plans in a series of celestial "signs." The Stoa believed no less than the masses, though with different emphases, in the practice of divination. For the Stoic it was not so much a question of reading the "will" of the celestial gods as of studying the workings of cosmic sympathy as it pertained to oneself.

Not everyone found this acceptable. Both within and without the Stoa there were those who might be willing to admit a degree of *sympatheia* in the cosmic organism, but not to the extent of obliterating the bases of all moral responsibility, man's freedom of choice. In Roman circles in the middle of the second century before Christ the Academic skeptic Carneades and the Stoic Panaetius devised a veritable arsenal of arguments against both divination and astronomy,[38] but they were overwhelmed by the influence of another thinker, whose interest and learning in celestial matters was considerable, Posidonius.

Time has reduced the work of Posidonius to a memory.[39] What was new in his thought can never be read with certainty in the fragmentary remains of his writings. There are signs, however, that, whatever his originality, his influence was seminal. He was most assuredly not the "inventor" of solar theology, but he was one of its propagators, and after Posidonius the complex of

---

37. Which the philosophers could explain by positing for them a special kind of material, a fifth element (*quinta essentia*), *aither*.
38. Most of which later recur in the works of Christian opponents of the same practices.
39. See Chapter IX, p. 367.

belief and cult surrounding the heavens and centering on the sun plays a far larger role in Greek philosophy and religion than it had theretofore.

The central position of the sun was by no means a corollary of a belief in the divinity of the heavenly bodies. The prevalence of the lunar calendar suggests rather the importance of the moon among many primitive peoples, and for the Babylonians, from whom the Greeks received a great deal of their astronomical information, the moon god (Sin) held a more considerable place than the sun god (Shamesh). For others, including the Greeks, it was the god associated with the sky who held the first place; Zeus, Jupiter, and the Baals of Syria were all nonplanetary universal gods who stood at the peak of the heavens and ruled all.

Much of this had as its basis an agricultural or nomadic economy and a world view which saw the earth as a flat surface covered by the dome of the heavens. Urbanism and Greek science radically altered this backdrop and the more scientific astronomy brought into prominence a new model of the universe in which the earth was a sphere floating free and surrounded on all sides by the revolving planets in the order: Moon, Sun, Mercury, Venus, Mars, Jupiter, Saturn; later, in the second century before Christ, corrected on astronomical grounds to: Moon, Mercury, Venus, Sun, Mars, Jupiter, Saturn.

From this new version of the heavens came a new theology—enriched and encouraged perhaps by the sun worship of Egypt, but essentially the work of Greek scientists, theologians and philosophers—that elevated the Sun to the chief of the celestial gods whom the Sun controlled from its central position in the concentric spheres of the heavens. The other, older theology descended from Aristotle through the Stoic schools, which placed the supreme divinity at the limits of the universe under the rubric *Zeus Ouranios* or *Coelus* or *Jupiter summus exsuperantissimus*, though perhaps more responsive to the monotheistic currents of the time, eventually gave way to the new solar theology. In the end, even the heavenly Baals were converted into solar deities.

Astronomy first brought the sun into religious prominence, but it was Stoicism and politics that consolidated its position. The Stoa from Cleanthes to Posidonius recognized the new importance of the sun, and Cleanthes was the first to draw it into theory by the facile instrument of analogy. Just as man's reason (*hegemonikon*) guided the organism of his body, so, according to Cleanthes, did the Sun direct the members of the larger organic universe. The notion of a cosmic intelligence was certainly not a new one; from Anaxagoras on, a number of thinkers had explored the possibility. What is decidedly new is its identification with the Sun, hitherto, as Helios, leading a modest life in Greek myth as a mere Titan's son.

In Posidonius the analogy was incorporated into the elaborate theory of *sympatheia*, where the Sun, as the central divine fire of the universe, is not only the source of the physical life and movement of the *kosmos* but its spiritual center as well. It is here, in the spiritual role of the Sun and its connection with the origins and fate of the human soul, that Posidonius made his radical break with his Stoic predecessors.

Their materialism had led the earlier Stoics to deny that the soul, composed of matter like all else, could be incorruptible. Zeno had said that it might survive its dissolution from the body, but that in the end the soul too would perish. Panaetius was more direct in his conclusion: the soul, being material, was destroyed with the material body. With Posidonius, however, the Stoa returned, as contemporary religious sentiment insistently demanded, to the spiritualism of Plato and Aristotle, for both of whom at least part of the soul, the intellectual *nous*, was an immaterial, immortal and divine substance that would survive its separation from the body.

Both these earlier thinkers had also developed the idea that the heavenly bodies were animate beings, produced from and feeding upon the most subtle and finest of the elements, *aither*, and Aristotle in his early treatise *On Philosophy* had advanced the theory that the human intellect was also composed of this *aither* and hence, like the heavenly bodies, was divine and immortal. One hears little more of this line of speculation until the generation of intellectuals dependent, in one fashion or another, upon Posidonius. In Cicero, Sextus Empiricus, Plutarch and Galen there is a fully developed theory of "astral immortality." Here the soul, which is consubstantial with the sun, takes on an earthly body at birth and then sheds it at death, eventually returning to be absorbed into its point of origin, the sun.

The *aither* theory served as the philosophical justification of a long-standing popular belief in the translation, by a variety of vehicles, of the great and the near great to a heavenly abode, the "catasterism" noted earlier. Celestial mythology brought forth a luxuriant growth of stories to describe these translations, either the original "fall" from the heavenly abode,[40] or their "return" to their spiritual homeland.

Posidonius was apparently the major force in introducing these spiritualized notions into the previously matter-bound Stoa, whence they passed into the possession of the Hellenized intellectuals of the Empire. Julius Caesar's conversion of the Roman state to the Egyptian solar year was another milestone along the same route. Sun cult and solar calendar are closely related, and as the Republic passed to Empire, the religion of the Sun gained ever wider acceptance among the Romans. The birthday of the Invincible Sun (*dies natalis solis invicti*), which fell shortly after the winter solstice,[41] was celebrated with pomp in the Empire.[42] After Nero, who styled himself the "New Helios," the cult of the Sun and its association with Imperial ideals had a marked vogue. The Severan Emperors openly embraced it as their own, and no one knew or remembered or cared that the Baal of Heliogabalus was originally a sky god not a sun god and that the Emperor's name was Elagabalus. Finally Aurelian constituted the worship of Sol Invictus as the official cult of the Empire.[43]

The belief in the divinity of an omnipotent and universal Sun was but one aspect of the movement, so marked in late antiquity, toward a single, supreme God, a movement which left the traditional gods in a position which was, theoretically at any rate, ambiguous. The solar religion attempted to meet this particular problem in at least two ways. One was to reduce the traditional Olympians to aspects or manifestations of the one, supreme God. The other, more evolutionary, solution was to downgrade the Olympians to the status of *daimones*.

---

40. The "fall" was probably of greater interest to the philosophers, who used it to explain the soul's acquisition of a kind of spiritual body or "mantle" during its descent through the various spheres. These spiritual chromosomes picked up from the various planets in transit provided an ingenious explanation of planetary predominance in the physiological humors; the mercurial or martial temperament was caused by too close a brush with those planets during the fall.

41. That is, during the days after the solstice, when the Sun began once again to triumph with ever longer light over the darkness.

42. And appropriated, about the middle of the fourth century, by the Christian Church as the birthday of Jesus.

43. See Chapter XVI, pp. 582–83.

Viewed in its origin, the *daimon* had a dual nature. In one instance it seemed to be a projection of one or another of the powers of God, the externalization of one of his attributes; in other contexts it was unmistakably a projection of the vital principle of living things, and particularly of man, where the soul-*daimon* is sometimes within and sometimes outside its normal dwelling place, the body. It was the first way of looking at *daimones* that eventually led to their important position as minor gods and messengers (*angeloi*) of the High Gods to men. The second, or soul-*daimon*, was gradually distinguished from the soul, of which it was originally the projection, and evolved into the personal *daimon* of Socrates and Plato, and finally into the guardian angel of the Judaeo-Christian tradition.

The Academy may have inherited its original interest in *daimones* from Socrates' reliance on his "voice," but the later school betrayed a far greater interest in the cosmic version of the species than in Socrates' more personal *daimon*. That testimonial to the inclinations of Plato's immediate students, the *Epinomis*, describes a great chain of beings stretching from the High Gods, down through the "visible gods," the heavenly bodies, then the creatures of the air (the *daimones*), those of water (the nymphs), and finally earth-bound man. The position of the *daimones* as intermediaries, interpreters of the will of God to man and carriers of prayers and vows heavenward, is clearly defined. There is, as well, another pregnant motif: the intermediary position of the *daimones* frees the High God of any necessity of becoming directly involved in the affairs of men. The execution of providence can, in effect, be surrendered to intermediate spirits, thus preserving and encouraging the transcendence and remoteness of God.

This thrusting of God into a remote and august domain beyond the pale of the universe, a reflex of philosophy's search for a spiritual and universalist God free of the gross anthropomorphisms of earlier ages, was in almost direct opposition to other spiritual sentiments at work in the Hellenistic and early Roman periods, the sense not only of the nearness of the gods but also of the working of their all-pervasive powers in both the animate and inanimate worlds. Here too the *daimones* provided a ground for reconciling these two discordant religious themes. They were very close indeed to the world of men, operating and interfering in their mysterious ways, mysterious chiefly to the unlearned, of course; for the intellectuals the *daimon* made possible a personalized and religious approach to the speculations of the "new physics" with its investigations into the extraordinary "powers" and properties resident in nature. Demonism was the religious correlate of cosmic *sympatheia*, and the two were in fact identified as early as Xenocrates.

For the Platonizing Stoic the operation of this organic universe must have been awe-inspiring in its beauty and complexity; for the ordinary man caught between malevolent *daimones* and mysterious *dynameis* it had its terrors as well. The Homeric hero might walk unconcerned in the presence of his Olympians, but by the time of the Roman Empire those powerful but familiar figures had yielded to others less comfortingly defined. The scale and measure of society was now immensely larger, and so too was the fate of man, poised perilously on some unknown fulcrum beyond the intelligible horizon. Religion turned intensively personal. The somewhat casual ritual of the classical *polis* did not serve to calm the anxieties of the new age, which looked to religion for pragmatic remedies rather than gestures of cultural solidarity.

The newly styled religion in league with science had no lack of remedies. Tumbling forth from its newly enlarged domain came a profusion of holy men, quacks, miracle workers, priests, astrologers, magicians, eastern savants, suffering saints, theatrical Cynics, Stoic vegetarians, divinized Emperors, and a rich clutch of charms, tables, recipes, and prayers to whatever god, planet, *daimon* or hero the patient might require. Hellenism had traveled an enormous distance from the tranquil slopes of Mount Olympus.

XII

Old Gods and New

In its discernible beginnings Greek religion appears to have been tied to the entire society rather than to a state. By the end of the Bronze Age the gods portrayed by Homer in the midst of their marvelously anthropomorphized activities had become Panhellenic. Whatever their remote origins, they floated free over the epic Hellenic landscape, dazzling beings larger than life and fixed in their features forever. No one ever quite succeeded in eradicating from the minds of the Hellenes and the Hellenized the Homeric lineaments of the Great Olympians.

Many tried, not from impiety, but by reason of the obvious fact that the Olympian "hypothesis" no longer corresponded with the "phenomena"—in this case, what their reason and their own religious sensibilities told them was the nature of the supernatural. The Olympians were frozen in their Homeric postures like so many golden fossils, while the society that had once cast them in its own image evolved to new levels of awareness and morality. A feudal Zeus was as awkwardly at home in a sixth-century *polis* as a nomadic Yahweh was in the temple of Solomon. Among the Jews, prophetic reformers wrought the painful but inevitable changes in the image of God, but in the more secular, more sophisticated, and yet more factional society of the Greeks, reform had necessarily to come from other quarters.

The End of the Immortals

The sixth-century *polis* had developed a code of behavior derived from its own values. The enunciation of that code was little affected by religious considerations, and yet it drew its ultimate

sanctions from divine forces that were guarantors but not prototypes of the new order. Thoughtful men were aware of the
schism between sixth-century words and twelfth-century deeds,
and some with access to the public did attempt changes in the
substance behind the façades of the Homeric gods. In Pindar and
the Attic dramatists the myths were quietly corrected by new
interpretations and the Olympians emerged more finely attuned
to the best of a contemporary moral thinking. The *Oresteia* and
the *Antigone* might seem to betoken a subtle, painless revolution
in the fifth-century understanding of the traditional myths, but
what passed so smoothly there had necessarily to be preceded by
the smashing of old idols.

Anthropomorphism could stand no serious scrutiny in circles
that were in the process of isolating the notion of the immaterial
from the conglomeration of physical "things" that made up the
Homeric universe. By the sixth century, matter and spirit could
be distinguished, albeit imperfectly, and so questions about the
morality of Zeus were accompanied by pointed queries about the
color of his eyes and hair and the shape of his nose, an exquisite
and painful *reductio ad absurdum* that anticipated many another
such in Judaism and Islam.[1]

Nor was that all. Increased knowledge about their neighbors
brought the Hellenes information about the gods of the barbarians, and that revelation raised the issue of ethnic relativity and
mooted the far more profound question of the relation between
what was natural, like the gods' laws, and what was conventional
and arbitrary, like men's laws. What was unnatural and unholy in
Greece, the exposure of corpses, for example, appeared to be the
height of piety among the Zoroastrians of Iran, and to their credit
the Greeks did not write off the discrepancy to the aberrations of
the *barbaroi*. With the help of the new data, religion could be
placed in the context of social history. What exactly was the
nature of the gods and the origins of this now historicized
phenomenon, religion?

---

1. The Jews quietly eliminated many of the blatant anthropomorphisms and anthropopathisms from their Scriptures in the course of
translating them in the Septuagint, and so the issue of anthropomorphism was pretty much settled by the time Judaism's schismatic
descendant Christianity arrived on the scene. But Islam had to relive
the entire experience, including speculation on the span of Allah's hips
necessary to fill his "throne."

Three remarkable answers to the second question are preserved from the fifth century. The Sophist Prodicus suggested that men originally deified what they found useful in nature, and probably cited in evidence the obvious cases of wine (Dionysus) and grain (Demeter). The responses of the Atomist philosopher Democritus were somewhat more complex. From a moral point of view Democritus was inclined to think that many religious attitudes, particularly toward the afterlife, were the results of a guilty conscience. When he turned to more physical considerations the origins of religion were still seen to be psychological, but the attitudes were now triggered by the presence of phenomena which struck men as inexplicable. Led by their sages, mankind turned to Zeus as an explanation of these awesome forces.

The insightful sage of Democritus was converted to a Machiavellian prince in the theory of Critias, an associate of Socrates and a political reactionary in the dark days at the end of the fifth century. According to Critias, religion had its origins in the deliberate fiction of the politicians, who, to preserve the status quo, took advantage of man's fear and awe of the heavens and filled them with gods to serve as a sanction for their laws.

Prodicus' argument found quick acceptance among the rationalists who, like the Stoics, preferred to mix their physical speculations with a theological awareness. Epicurus elaborated and documented Democritus' suggestions, and at least one Hellenistic observer of the political scene, Polybius (c. B.C. 200–120), saw the Roman Senate as a historical incarnation of Critias' cynical politicians manipulating religion for their own ends.

Another fruitful avenue of speculation that opened into the question of origins found at least implicit support in Euripides. Empedocles had earlier suggested, and the tales of mythology seemed in part to support him, that at least some of the gods were transparent abstractions of human affections. The strongest case, and the one made by Empedocles, was that of Aphrodite, who appeared on the cosmic level as a motive force and in human affairs as love. She plays a similar role in Euripides' Hippolytus.

By the time of Euripides it was perfectly clear that the Olympian pantheon was not as Homer had left it. The traditional gods were rather pointedly ignored in the philosophers' search for ultimate principles, cut down to size by Euripides' penchant for demythologizing, and subjected to all manner of indignity by the Greeks' irrepressible instinct for parody, satire and sheer playfulness. Comedy had been manhandling the Olympians for years before Euripides' bourgeois Apollos appeared on the stage; not even Homer was an innocent in this regard.

But the major force behind the new attitudes was, doubtless, the alternative portrait of God being fashioned by the philosophers. As even his contemporaries suspected, Euripides' new gods were not gods at all, despite their mythological trappings, and led merely into the delightful byways of comedy and parody, where they eventually came to rest in Lucian. Plato's Mind and Aristotle's First Mover, the transcendent force which set the universe in motion, were, however, alternate and competitive ways of looking at divinity. They answered in persuasive but unmythological terms the basic question about the nature of God.

History too had taken a hand in the contest. The new *poleis* had appropriated the Panhellenic Olympians as their special possessions. Each city-state had its own tutelary deities, who were honored by elaborate state cults and who in turn protected and fostered the *polis;* the glory of Athena was the glory of Athens. With the eclipse of these same *poleis* in the fourth century the Greeks who inhabited them wasted little time in commemorating a *Götterdämmerung* or elaborating a theodicy to explain what went wrong. Instead they quietly deserted the slopes of Olympus for new theological landscapes.

The Hellenistic age was a period of makeshift gods. The God of the philosophers had the immense disadvantage of being a God without a cultus, a concept rather than a person, and with little religious appeal save to the rare and rarified soul who could bow the knee to an Unmoved First Mover. Some of the foreign gods made a certain impression, and there were other, not always attractive alternatives. Many of the cultured threw a hasty nod toward something like "the Deity" (*to theion, to daimonion*). There was a considerable vogue for "Lady Luck" (*Tyche*), for the less optimistic "Necessity" (*Ananke*) or "Fate" (*Heimarmene*), and even for the inevitable "Rome" whose cultists could not, at least, be accused of hypocrisy.

All of these rather forbidding abstractions were by way of tertiary prospects. Before the traditional Hellenic piety was finally carried under by the combination of rationalism and eastern cults, some did make a serious attempt at saving the ancestral religion by combining the persuasive and scientific findings of philosophy with the poetical portraiture of the myths. The latter could not simply be dismissed; they carried within themselves the cultural tradition of Hellenism. Homer was the core of every curriculum. Even the Hellene won over to the exclusive claims of Christianity could not bring himself to reject his own past.[2]

The accommodation of scientific truth with the perennial Hellenic verities of the myths was a major intellectual task that absorbed almost every philosopher from Zeno to Proclus. It was also a major accomplishment, and the chief responsibility for its success belonged to the Stoics, whose methods carried the day and the fruits of whose victories were joyfully expropriated by Judaism, Christianity and Islam.

The reduction of the gods to physical phenomena was already apparent in Prodicus, Democritus and, to a somewhat lesser extent, Critias, accompanied in all three thinkers by some suggestion of the psychological state of mind that originally led men to judge such purely natural things as divine. In Hellenistic times another possibility presented itself, perhaps first in Egypt, since it appears in the *Aegyptica* of Hecataeus of Abdera:[3] that the gods were once men.

Though Hecataeus was concerned primarily with Isis and Osiris, an even stronger case for the thesis could be made from Greek mythology, which had the incontestable example of a Heracles raised after his death from man to the status of a god. Just such a case was made shortly after Hecataeus by Euhemerus of Messene, a courtier of Cassander (B.C. 311–298), in his remarkable utopian romance *The Sacred Document*. The document in question was supposedly found on Panchaea, an island in the Indian Ocean then inhabited by Indians, Cretans and Scythians, but once ruled by the royal family the Greeks had since come to worship as gods.

Euhemerus narrates the story as he claims to have read it on Panchaea. The first king was Uranus, so called because he was the first to recognize the divinity of the heavenly bodies.[4] He was succeeded by Cronus, and he by his own son Zeus, not without a great political struggle, which later found its way into the myth

---

2. See Chapter XVII, p. 618 ff.
3. See Chapter II, p. 112.
4. A characteristic of many of the Euhemeristic theories was the acknowledgment that there are genuine gods alongside those that really began as men. These genuine gods were almost invariably the heavenly bodies.

as the wars of the Giants and Titans. King Zeus did not restrict his benevolent activity to Panchaea but traveled extensively to Babylon, to Syria, to Mount Olympus, where he took up residence for a while, and finally to Crete, where he died and was buried. He was a great lawgiver, reformer, temple builder, and inventor, for which benefits men came to worship him and his entire family as gods.

Euhemerism took its place beside the physical reductionism of the fifth-century rationalists. All such theories were at best mocking, at worst impious, and at least suggestively atheistic. None saw much value in the myths, which were, on the face of it, guilty rationalizations, self-serving deceits, false history or the purest fantasy. There was apparently no ground upon which an enlightened and rational orthodoxy might stand.

The Stoics found such a ground. They did not invent allegorical exegesis, but they did perfect its methods and elaborate it into a theory. Plato, who cared only for the morality of the traditional myths as a criterion for their political use, reveals in passing that in his day there were those who saw an "undersense" (*hyponoia*) in the myths. There is reason to suspect that this "other reading" (*allegoria*) was being practiced by Anaxagoras and some of his disciples, and that the hidden meaning was a physical one.

In the fully developed Stoic theory and its Christian derivatives there were many "other readings"—physical, moral and typological—that underlay the literal sense of a "sacred text." The earlier Stoics preferred to allegorize down to physical principles, while the later, more spiritual version of the school after Panaetius used the same methods to elicit moral and ethical allegories; the *Odyssey* became for them a great allegory of the human soul. For both the physicists and the moralists the preferred text was Homer, a choice dictated no doubt by the poet's place at the cultural center of the society and the consequent attention given to his works by literary exegetes at Alexandria and Pergamum. More sacred scripture could serve just as well, particularly since it had the additional cachet of divine inspiration. So Philo read the Torah as a Platonic proof text, the Qumran sectaries saw the Prophets as an eschatological allegory, and Christians searched out the entire Old Testament for a typological foreshadowing of Jesus the Messiah.

In so distinguishing the various senses of a given passage and establishing a rationale for each, it was possible to reconcile and justify all of them. The past could be preserved, the Homeric past for the Stoic philosophers and the Jewish past for the Christian theologians. The Stoics even came to speak of three branches of theology: the physical theology of the philosophers; the mythical theology of the poets; and—with a bow to Critias, Plato and Aristotle, and the obvious example of the Hellenistic monarchies—the political theology of the statesman who used both cult and myth in governing the state.[5]

The cynicism of Critias had, of course, long since disappeared; the Romans used the *theologia civilis* to justify the established religion. In the revelational religions the emphases of controversy shifted away from the theology of the statesman to the relationship between mythical (read "Scriptural") theology and physical (read "rational") theology, and the claim of the philosophers to be the adjudicators of allegory. Could the nonphilosophical discourse of *Gospels* and the *Qur'an* be dismissed, as the Stoics were willing to do with the poets, on the grounds of the enfeebled understanding of the audience to which they were directed? The question was still being violently debated by the Spanish Muslim ibn Rushd in the twelfth century.

Stoic exegesis turns up directly or indirectly in almost every philosophical text from B.C. 200 onward; there is, moreover, a fully preserved school manual on the subject, the *Compendium of Greek Theology* by L. Annaeus Cornutus, a Hellenized Roman—the *Compendium* was written in Greek—from Leptis in North Africa. Cornutus was the teacher of Persius and Seneca's nephew Lucan, and during the difficult days under Nero may have followed Musonius Rufus into exile.[6] His *Compendium* is the very model of a plodding textbook, but it does reveal the extent and the misguided ingenuity of Stoic physical reductionism. It displays as well the awesome exegetic instrument into which the Stoics had constructed the science of etymology.

Nothing betrays the native Hellenic playfulness more convincingly than the Greeks' way with words. But there was high philosophical seriousness here as well. The Sophists' debate over "nature" and "convention" spilled over into the theory of names.

---

5. The tripartite theology can be found explicitly in the Roman Pontifex Scaevola (d. B.C. 82) and Varro (B.C. 116–27), both of whom apparently derived it from Panaetius.
6. See Chapter XI, pp. 417–18.

The Stoics, like Plato and unlike Aristotle, held that the names of things were "natural"—that is, they betrayed the essence of the thing to which they were attached. Their theory served to inaugurate and attend a relentless pursuit of the true meaning (*etymon*) of words.

The root meaning of his name clearly revealed that Zeus was related to life (*zen*), and so immortality; Rhea to flowing (*rhein*), and so to the earth, from which all things flowed; Hera became the air (*aer*); and Cronus, time (*chronos*); Pan, a rather innocuous god of Arcadia, became, on the strength of his name, the All (*pan*). These are but a few passing, though common, examples. Blessed with unsurpassed imagination and untrammeled by a knowledge of the correct etymologies of the names of the gods—many of whom were, in fact, non-Greek—the Stoics performed prodigies of derivation, a virtuoso tradition they passed on undiminished to the Christian Fathers. It was, for both, the single most potent instrument for extracting the "under-sense" from a text.

In this manner the Olympians were shorn of their once proud claim to immortality and reduced to physical forces, just as Anaxagoras had maintained much earlier. The poet and the philosopher were, after all, talking about the same thing. Neither Plato nor Aristotle much cared what the poet had said as long as it was morally edifying; they cared even less about the traditional Olympians. But the Stoics "saved the appearances." Men continued to paint and hymn the gods as Homer had portrayed them, but the believer now had an up-to-date scientific explanation of the substance behind the poetical façade of the gods he no longer worshiped.

Not all the old forms disappeared, however. The cults tied to the *polis* declined into oblivion with the demise of the parent institution, but there were religious complexes of the pre-Alexander era that had managed to transcend the local and the parochial and lay some claim to more universal levels of significance. Such, for instance, were the mystery religions and the great oracular shrines whose Panhellenic status guaranteed their survival into the new age.

There is no dating the great mystery cults; there were sacred buildings at Eleusis as far back as the Bronze Age. Well before Athens' greatness in the fifth century, Eleusis, a modest town with a not untypical cult of the agrarian goddess Demeter, was absorbed by her brilliant neighbor. Linked thenceforward to the premier state of Hellas and supported by her prestige, Eleusis became the focus of a great cult built upon the promise to every Greek, free or slave, of immortality. From all over the Hellenic world men came to be initiated into the mysteries of Demeter and her daughter Persephone, the mythic embodiments of rebirth after death.

The Eleusinian mysteries possessed no theology. There was cult with a priesthood to perform it, and there was myth. The entire Greek world was heir to the myth, but only the initiate who had undergone the ritual purification (*myesis*) was privileged to witness (*epopteia*) that myth converted into sacred drama and offered as a pledge of immortality.

The mysteries of Demeter were beyond the reach of the philosophers and independent of the fortunes of politics. Eleusis became the archetype for similar centers all over the East, and the mysteries celebrated there were adapted in a great variety of forms to other mythic complexes, Greek and barbarian alike. Eleusis itself enjoyed a great popularity in Hellenistic and Roman times; generals, philosophers and emperors[7] flocked there to be initiated at what had come to be regarded as the fountainhead of Hellenism. Claudius wished to transplant the mysteries to Rome. Hadrian lavished the usual architectural tokens of his affection on Eleusis, and the mysteries there flourished, though increasingly the plaything of Neoplatonist theurgists, until the devastation of the Goths and the fierce hatred of Christianity brought them to an end.

The shadow of Eleusis can be seen in a number of centers in the Hellenistic East. Alexandria had its cult and temple of Demeter,[8] and one of the Eleusinian hierarchy, a certain Timotheus, served that indefatigable importer of talent, Ptolemy I, as a kind of Egyptian Pope. Both the Attalids and the later Romans supported mysteries in honor of Demeter at Pergamum. There were similar mysteries at Ephesus and Smyrna, and Greece too had its other Demeter complexes that come into sight only after Alexander.

---

7. Among the emperors were Augustus, Tiberius, Hadrian, of course, twice, Antoninus Pius, Marcus Aurelius and Lucius Verus, Commodus, probably Gallienus, and Julian.

8. Celebrated in one of the hymns of Callimachus, who began his own career as a schoolteacher in an Alexandrian suburb called Eleusis.

Demeter and Persephone were by no means the only gods who had mystery cults. Associated with them at Eleusis was Dionysus, and that popular god had his own cult centers, particularly in Anatolia. The rites of Dionysus had by this time lost most of their orgiastic associations and were celebrated by men as well as women. Alexandria became an important center of the Dionysiac mysteries under the unhappy Ptolemy IV, who took his descent from that god seriously and attempted some sort of convocation-cum-census of the initiates in Egypt. Pergamum too was a center, and the Romans, who received their first unpleasant taste of Bacchic orgies at an early date,[9] found the pacific later version more to their liking. The Phrygian Cabiri also had mysteries in their honor, and the cult spread from the great center on Samothrace all over the Aegean. Other alien deities like Isis, Mithra and the Great Mother all had mystery-type cults attached to their worship.

Unlike the initiates of Demeter, the adepts of Dionysus frequently formed themselves into cult associations (*thiasoi*), one of the most characteristic forms of institutionalization in late antiquity. The circumscribed *polis* provided within its own structure any number of ties linking citizen to citizen via family, phratry, tribe and deme membership. With the *polis'* disappearance into the massive monarchies of Hellenistic times, citizens resorted more and more to private types of self-organization in the form of guilds, clubs and cult associations. Dionysiac *thiasoi* were probably very old, but in these later times, and particularly under the Roman Empire, they multiplied in great profusion.

The Dionysiac and other cult associations obviously offered their members a sense of group solidarity in an age of individual alienation. The mysteries also provided the adept the powerful effect of dramatic ritual, piqued by the sense of secrecy and crowned with the joyous hope of immortality. Beyond that point of generalization it is difficult to go. Quite in the spirit of the times the mysteries borrowed one from another, introduced gods from other cults, and read their myths now mystically in the manner of the Pythagoreans and now philosophically in the manner of the Stoics. Men and women of all classes found the mysteries profoundly attractive.

Despite their widespread popularity, the mysteries never pro-

---

9. Orgiastic bacchanalia were banned by law in B.C. 186.

vided a serious challenge to Christianity when it appeared. In their native, or eastern, versions they offered, it is true, an alternate and competitive route to immortality; but it was a kind of collective immortality rooted in the hope of seasonal harvest, while Christianity held out the unmistakable prospect of personal and individual immortality.[10] More importantly, the mysteries, having once gained Panhellenic status and ensured their survival beyond the *polis*, never had either the unity or the breadth of view to evolve into a universal religion. They left their stamp on the language of Christianity, as they did on the religious vernacular of the entire Empire, but by the fifth Christian century, on the eve of their disappearance, they must have seemed to an intelligent Greek or Roman a curious relic of a long-dead age or the choice vehicle of Neoplatonic magic. Plutarch of Athens, who died in A.D. 431, was both the restorer of Neoplatonism at Athens and the son and heir of Nestorius, one of the last notable hierophants at Eleusis.

At the feet of Plutarch and his theosophic sister Asclepigeneia sat the young man Proclus (A.D. 410–485), who imbibed from this extraordinary pair philosophy, theurgy and mystery lore in about equal doses.[11] Probably from the same source came Proclus' fascination with still another religious phenomenon that had had a remarkable revival in Hellenistic and Roman times, oracular collections.

Oracular sites, like mystery cult centers, go far back into Greek antiquity; their fortunes, however, were far more irregular. Delphi, for example, possessed, almost from the beginning, important political powers which now advanced, now retarded its prestige. The oracle's days of glory in the sixth century were undermined by its pro-Persian stance in the fifth. Philip openly manipulated it to gain his ends. There was a brief revival after B.C. 279, when an invasion of Gauls was checked at the threshold of Apollo's temple, an event that was later invested with a miraculous glow. But Delphi was by then an avowed political pawn, and the priestly establishment there steered a careful course between Seleucids, Ptolemies, Attalids and Romans. To no avail. The rich treasury of Apollo was sacked during the Roman civil wars and Delphi declined into a center of tourism. Pious

---

10. On the basic difference see Chapter XIII, pp. 496–97.
11. See Chapter XVIII, p. 679.

individuals might still consult their fortune there, but the days of glory were gone.

There were fads in oracular popularity in antiquity, and the decline of Delphi was matched by the rise into prominence in Imperial times of the venerable Apollonian oracles at Didyma near Miletus and Claros near Colophon, where Roman emperors could be found consulting the mouthpiece of the god down to the beginning of the fourth century A.D. There were smaller sites too, where more modest clairvoyants held forth to the extent that need demanded and popular credulity allowed.

Most of these sites were long silent by the time of Proclus, whose interest in oracles was, in any event, literary rather than archaeological. The chief object of his attention was the collection of prophecies called the *Chaldean Oracles*. Similar collections had been in circulation in Greece in the fifth century B.C. They seem to drop from sight for awhile, but reappear in Hellenistic times, collected under the names of various Sibyls or ecstatic oracular priestesses.[12]

The content of these collections can be surmised from the Hellenistic material submerged in the later Judaeo-Christian edition of the *Sibylline Oracles*. The substance was historical, the tone apocalyptic, and the point frankly propagandistic. Rome and its political role in the Mediterranean had a central place in these visionary recitals, as it did in the similarly prophetic narrative placed in the mouth of Cassandra in Lycophron's curious poem *Alexandra*.[13]

What had been in the last century before Christ a propaganda struggle between Roman, Greek and Oriental political ambitions became in the course of time more darkly overcast with religious themes. Rome won the political war by the end of that century, but the struggle for men's minds and hearts went on unabated. In the hands of its Jewish editors the basic stuff of the *Oracles*, drawn from a great variety of sources both Greek and non-Greek, was marshaled against the triumphant Roman Empire. Apocalyp-

---

12. In addition to the famous Sibyl at Delphi there were by one count nine others at various sites around the Mediterranean. Aeneas is made to consult the representative at Cumae, and the same lady's utterances figure prominently in the fourth *Eclogue* of Vergil, a happy choice of setting that eventually gained her a place on the ceiling of the Sistine Chapel.

13. See Chapter V, Note 20.

tic visions of the end of the world masked what was some of the most revolutionary literature to be seen in the ancient world.

Antiquity's other major collection of oracles, the *Chaldean Oracles*, belonged to a somewhat different milieu. Their editor was probably the Julian who lived at the time of Marcus Aurelius (A.D. 161–180). Within the oracular setting he has combined elements culled from the new quasi-religious philosophies of the time: Stoicism, Gnosticism,[14] the revived Pythagoreanism that left its deep impress on the philosophy and literature of the second century,[15] and that other fascination of the age, astrology.

The *Sibylline Oracles* were grist for religious propagandists, both Christians and Jewish; the *Chaldean Oracles* became, on the other hand, the preserve, almost the Bible, of the Neoplatonists after Plotinus. From Porphyry in the third century to Damascius in the sixth they were a centerpiece of Neoplatonic speculation. Proclus, who wrote a commentary on them, is reported to have said that of all the texts of the past only two had necessarily to be preserved, Plato's *Timaeus* and the *Chaldean Oracles*, a remark from the fifth century's leading intellectual that reveals better than any other evidence that could be adduced the collapse of the rationalistic premises upon which Hellenism had been constructed.

Spawned in the midst of an apparent Hellenic revival, the *Chaldean Oracles* were more prophetic than they knew. Beneath the Attic embalming of the Second Sophistic, eastern Hellenism received in the second and third centuries the full impact of the eastern tradition that it had at first overwhelmed but never quite destroyed. Now in philosophy, science, religion, ethics and politics the East reasserted its claim to possess an older, more profound wisdom. Many men were convinced that this was so, and the consequent transformations could be read everywhere: from prince to priest, from philosopher to mystic, from sage to prophet and saint, the center of concern was shifting from the mind to the soul as a function of the new theologized view of life.

Some thinkers were swept headlong by this flood from the East; others held at their Hellenic roots. One of the latter was Plutarch of Chaeronea who lived under the Flavians and early Antonines. As the son of a conservative Greek family of priests

---

14. See Chapter XVIII, p. 648 ff.
15. See Chapter XI, pp. 427–29.

and a ranking member of the priestly establishment at nearby Delphi, Plutarch was a Hellenic traditionalist of the old school, and firmly tied to the faith of his fathers (*patrios pistis*). But he was, as well, an intellectual of faultless credentials who had studied at the Platonic Academy at Athens and was himself a teacher and eminent biographer.[16] Finally, Plutarch was a citizen of the wider Roman world; he served in political positions at Athens and Rome and traveled widely in Italy, Anatolia and Egypt. His teacher Ammonius was a Hellenized Egyptian; his friends included Greek and Roman politicians, philosophers, and priests, among others Clea, the chief priestess of Isis installed at Delphi.

The simplicities of the earlier *patrios pistis* were clearly no longer possible to a man of Plutarch's generation living in Plutarch's world. The landscape now included the atheism of Epicurus, Plato's theology, Pythagorean numerology, astrology, Egyptian gods like Isis, and a great host of *daimones*. Plutarch rejected some and modified others of these current trends in religion, but all in the name of the traditional beliefs purified by Hellenic rationalism.

Plutarch attempted to steer a course between atheism and reaction. Some of the most biting judgments in the otherwise mild and urbane *Moral Essays* were reserved for Epicureanism. The evidence for God's working in the world was too obvious to be denied; not, of course, the work of the gods of mythology, but of the God of the philosophers, particularly Plato, remote, transcendent and spiritual. The intellectual Plutarch held for the monotheistic God of later Platonism against the multiple Olympians of myth and the popular religion.

Were the myths, then, phantasy? What of the gods of other peoples with different beliefs and different myths? These latter caused no great difficulty. Plutarch could shuffle the Stoic etymologies with marvelous dexterity, and he was equally at home with the various forms of exegesis, euhemeristic, physical, allegorical. In the *Isis and Osiris* he rang all the changes out of the considerable knowledge of Egyptian religion he had acquired from Clea and Ammonius, from his travels to Alexandria, and from such literary auxiliaries as Manetho's works on Egypt.[17]

---

16. On the antecedents of his *Parallel Lives* see Chapter II, pp. 113-16.
17. See Chapter II, p. 112.

His conclusion was that all the gods, whatever their names and whatever their provenance, were one.

As for the myths, they raised the age-old question of moral propriety in the behavior of the Immortals. Plutarch could deal with this chestnut with new resources, the remarkably proliferating crowd of *daimones* who had taken possession of the middle ground between the philosophically prescribed High God, banned by reason of his transcendence from direct involvement in this world, and the darkling ground beneath the moon. The *daimones*, demigods who are more powerful than men but in the final resort mortal,[18] were immediately useful, for example, to explain the operation of the oracles to which Plutarch's own career was so closely tied. God is no ventriloquist speaking through the raving Sibyl; prophetic inspiration, and indeed all forms of communication from on high, are the work of the *daimones*. Theirs too was all the malicious mischief attributed to the gods of myth.

This solution to the awkwardnesses of anthropomorphism is neat, but it has philosophical extensions that carry Plutarch into the heart of the problem of evil. There is a dimly perceived dualism in Plutarch that seems to be derived in part from Iranian sources and perhaps mediated by what he found in the later Plato. In the *Laws*, Plutarch noted, Plato had come, as the Zoroastrians had, to a belief in an evil World Soul. Souls or Spentas,[19] the two opposed principles accounted for the combination of cosmic blessings and misfortunes that constitute the life of man, all executed, of course, by the omnipresent *daimones*.

The temptation to embrace a totally dualistic universe was, however, generally resisted. Plutarch was a theological optimist and his God a benevolent one. He was credulous in the manner of the times, but attempted, within the limits of his belief, to combat that excessive fear of the divine (*deisidaimonia*) that was the essence of superstition. The same repugnance for *deisidaimonia* had driven Epicurus to a species of atheism, but for Plutarch there was a middle path between the two, a way illuminated by reason. If one holds firm to the conviction that God is good, it is

---

18. The existential states, god, *daimon*, man, were not fixed. Virtuous men could become heroes and eventually be translated into *daimones*. Particularly notable *daimones* like Isis, Osiris, Heracles and Dionysus could even become gods.

19. See Chapter XVIII, p. 660.

possible, Plutarch maintains, to avoid all those ignominious forms of belief and cult that have so marred the history of religion.[20]

One tale in Plutarch's essay *The Obsolescence of Oracles* caught the imagination of his readers as no other. In the reign of Tiberius (A.D. 14–37) the passengers and crew of a boat coasting off western Greece were startled to hear a voice booming across the water the awesome news that Great Pan was dead. The story had provoked great interest when it eventually reached Rome, and when Plutarch retold it somewhat less than a century later he intended it as a proof that even *daimones* die. But for many of his readers and for subsequent generations of Christians the mysterious cry rang out more like an epitaph for the immortal Olympians and a signal for the end of one era and the beginning of another. Plutarch belonged to the old piety, sincerely experienced; it was not permitted to many more to feel the same.

One Lord, One God

For an age that prefers to "read" its texts, sacred and profane, as if they were historical documents, most of the allegorical exegesis of the Stoics must appear as foolishness or fantasy. Much of it doubtless was, but it was born of an effort to give learned voice to a sentiment that found almost universal support in late Hellenic circles: behind the welter of gods inherited from the Greek past or imported from foreign quarters there was an abiding unity, a monistic principle into which all the manifestations of divinity somehow resolved themselves.

The sophisticated syncretism of the Hellenistic age was only the first step in that process of resolution. By it the Greeks merely learned to combine foreign gods with their own, and in so doing they accustomed themselves to separate, however imperfectly they may have expressed the notion, the supernatural essences from their Iranian, Egyptian or Greek externals. As the Stoics saw, Aphrodite, Astarte and Isis were different names for a single reality, as were Zeus, Jupiter, Ahura and Baal. Such resolutions may do violence to the nuances of religious phenomena, but

---

20. One such cited by Plutarch is the Jewish Sabbath rest that led directly to Titus' capture and destruction of Jerusalem in A.D. 70, an event that must have occurred shortly before the young Plutarch wrote his *On Superstition*.

in general the Greeks' instincts were far sounder than those of their neighbors, who syncretized in this manner only after political or military conquest. The Hellenic scholars could identify parallel functions and used them as their touchstone.

The second stage in the syncretism carried the Greeks still further down the path of monotheism. In many quarters—philosophical, astrological, political and popular—the sentiment was expressed that the feeling could proceed further, and that the variously named gods were but different aspects of a single divine force. The poet and the philosopher put it in different ways, but the point was the same: what appeared at different times or different places under different names were refractions of one reality, perhaps functions of a single God.

Both science and theology provided adequate theory for the latter view. Late antiquity saw a revival of an earlier interest in the "powers" (*dynameis, aretai*) of things,[21] and the theologians of Neoplatonism quickly made the identification between such *dynameis* as the operative powers of one God and the multiple gods of mythology: Apollo, already identified with Mithra, was the intelligence of Zeus.

Standing close to the identification of *theoi* and *dynameis* was the downgrading of the Olympians to the role of *daimones* or demigods. Plato had already done something similar in the *Timaeus*, and the philosophers' continuing disdain for the gods of myth prompted many others to take the same approach. Even the traditionalist Plutarch balanced his piety against his conviction that God was one and transcendent, and produced an equation that contained within itself an important role for the *daimones*.

To cast the solution in terms of *dynameis* was the physicists' approach to the problem of monotheism. Put in more philosophical terms, the various gods of tradition could be considered hypostatizations of the attributes of the High God. Late Judaism, which began from a monotheistic premise, had explored this from the other direction. Divine Wisdom (*Sophia*) was one of Judaism's hypostatizations of an attribute of Yahweh, and the *Logos* theory of Philo clearly had affinities with the same way of thinking,[22] now clothed in the conceptual formulae of Greek philosophy.

---

21. See Chapter XI, pp. 431–36.
22. See Chapter VII, p. 304.

Who was this High God who was almost a commonplace figure on the landscape of later Greek theology? He was produced by the concurrence of many forces, but essentially and in his origins he was the God of the philosophers, a figure who was summoned forth to move the universe and stayed on to rule it.

Greek monistic theology properly began with Parmenides' expulsion of process and change from the universe. The position was clearly untenable, but it did force his successors from Empedocles onward to posit an external source of the motion they all agreed was present in the *kosmos*. A Prime Mover was supplied, and an important additional element appeared with Anaxagoras' suggestion that "his"—anthropomorphism died hard —activity was noetic. The Mover, who was also Intelligence, solved two problems with a neat simultaneity: how the motion got into the *kosmos* and why it was a *kosmos* at all. From the time of the Pythagoreans the Greeks had seen the universe as a system of order (*kosmos*), and now it was clear why this was so: it was run by a supreme Intelligence. There had entered the lists of philosophy the question of the nature of God and the two corollaries of (continuous) creation and providence.

Movers are not necessarily single, but lurking in the background of the discourse was the argument, essentially mathematical in nature, of the impossibility of an infinite series. Order suggested *serial* causality, which in turn suggested numbers retrogressing back to the unit (*monas*). God as Mind or Monad; both had their economies, and the question was seriously debated;[23] but once past Plato the philosophers could agree on the resolution back to a single divine principle, whether transcendent in the manner of the Aristotelians and later Platonists or immanent after the Stoics.

The transcendentalists eventually carried the day, even among the Stoics, abetted doubtless by the growing interest in a solar theology. The history of this religio-scientific movement has already been traced; its pertinence here is that the raising of the eyes to the heavens was a gesture shared by professionals and laymen alike. A High God in the heavens who controlled human affairs through his subordinate planetary deities was more than the subject of academic debate, as the passion for popular astrology eloquently testifies. A man's destiny might very well be the

---

23. See Chapter IX, p. 368.

outcome of luck (*tyche*) or of his own prowess (*arete*), but as time passed, more and more people chose to see there the workings of a grand design controlled from on high.

It was precisely the success of the transcendentalist position that prevented the rising tide of henotheism, a belief in a single supreme God, from evolving into a pure monotheism. There were few intellectuals under the Empire who would deny that the operation of religious forces in the universe coalesced finally into a single point of origin; the complex interrelationship of these forces, a theme that every philosopher save the all but vanished Epicurean could demonstrate in exhausting detail, was an even more persuasive proof of One God than the argument from infinite regress, that behind all the metaphysical eggs of this world stood a cosmic chicken that not only started the whole process but superintended its operation.

Where God is Mind, as in Anaxagoras or Aristotle, his executive powers create no great difficulty; but where he is Monad, as the Neopythagoreans were beginning to assert, the immensity of the chasm between the One and the consequent twos inhibited even the passage of the Monad into the universe, let alone his detailed supervision of its operation. Plato's rhetorical outburst about "the Good beyond Being" was the slogan of those who would thrust the High God beyond the limits of the universe, and even of analogy itself. The extent of their success can be measured exactly in the One of Plotinus.

The awkwardness rising out of the conflicting claims of absolute divine transcendence and the immanent operation of divine providence was met by a great variety of solutions of which the daimonism of Plutarch and the planetary deism of the astrologers were but two of the most obvious. Another can be seen in the appearance of the "Second God" (*deuteros theos*) as a species of one-and-a-half to bridge the gap between the One and the twos. Plato resorted to just such a figure in his metaphor of the Demiurge, and later Neopythagoreans urged the necessity of an intermediary being as the middle term in their theological ratios.

For the philosophers the *deuteros theos*, or "the Son," as he was sometimes called, had all the features of the Aristotelian God-as-Mind and conveniently served to explain both creation and providence. But in more religious contexts the Son had another important function. In Mithraism, Gnosticism and Christianity it was just such an intermediary who played the part of the Savior in the providential plan decreed by the God or gods above, but which, by the very reason of their transcendence, they could not themselves fulfill.

Thus a philosophically induced absolute transcendence created in its own wake a second God, who had a philosophical necessity of his own. Even Philo, reared in a tradition of strict monotheism, could not resist the cogency of the argument: his *Logos* was hedged with conditions and disclaimers, but its genealogy is strikingly clear. On this scale an absolute monotheism was impossible; the conflict between transcendence and providence blocked its passage. Theologians solved the conflict with their *deuteros theos* or the less rigorously argued *daimones;* the ordinary man, who sensed the same difficulty, came to essentially the same solution: he held on to his private gods.

When the anonymous author[24] of the altogether typical theological tract of the first Christian century, *On the Universe*, came to speak of the High God he could find no more apt comparison than that of an Achaemenian Shah, a Darius or a Xerxes, remote and inaccessible in his palace at Susa, whose commands were executed over a vast empire by his courtiers and servants, and who was perfectly informed by his elaborate intelligence system.[25] God and ruler, universe and empire, macrocosm and microcosm, the terms of comparison lay readily at hand to any thoughtful citizen of the post-Alexander world. The author of *On the Universe* argued the comparison a fortiori, and so he did not introduce another persuasive ingredient in the analogy, the sacred, almost godlike quality of the ruler that made the comparison with the High God a particularly apt one.

The Achaemenian Shah, for all his autocratic behavior, was no God; the Iranians took their gods too seriously for that. But from Alexander onward the progress toward the divinization of rulers was one of the more striking features of political life in the Mediterranean *oikoumene*, and the policy was pursued recklessly at times by Greek and Roman alike. It was a curious develop-

---

24. The treatise was attributed to Aristotle, but is clearly the product of a milieu heavily influenced by Stoicism. The work was translated into Latin by Apuleius and had an equal vogue in the farther reaches of eastern Hellenism in its Syriac and Arabic versions.

25. The communications system of the Achaemenians, by post and fire signal, struck both Aeschylus and Herodotus and was later widely imitated in the later empires, from the Seleucid and Roman to the Islamic.

ment. One of the attitudes that set the Greeks off from some of their neighbors was the apparently unbreachable wall they raised between gods and men. The pathetic contrast between human mortality and the divine Immortals was first sounded by Homer and never lost its conviction down to the end of the fifth century. The anthropomorphism of the gods was a cruel mirage.

More than one factor worked at eventually blurring the distinction. The cult of Heracles and other heroes, the mysteries' promise of immortality, the belief in an immortal soul all held out the expectation that death was not the critical term in a man's life. And yet this did not quite touch the issue: men still died, as Heracles had, to be heroized *after* death. Before the next step, the recognition of living men as gods, could be taken, a basic shift in attitude on both sides of the equation had to take place: the exaltation of men and the scaling-down of the gods.

The critical undermining of the traditional Olympians has already been described. What began as an attack upon anthropomorphism in Xenophanes ended as radical anthropocentrism in Euhemerus: the gods had once been men. Euhemerus needed neither metaphysics nor anthropology to support his daring hypothesis; the history of his own times, the third century, was filled with examples of men who had become as gods to their fellow citizens.

The earlier belief in the power of the gods had become in the fourth century an almost cynical belief in the power of men. First in Sicily and then elsewhere the citizens of a *polis* paid to their deceased despots—annually elected officials make poor gods —honors formerly reserved to gods alone: temples, altars, sacrifices, cult.[26] No cries of outrage greeted the practice. The cult of chthonian heroes was an old one in Greece, and these same rulers claimed, as did most of the aristocratic families among the Hellenes, descent from a god. Nor were there objections raised when a Lysander or a Dion was granted such honors during his lifetime.

Alexander's deification, then, does not appear extraordinary except in terms of his personal development.[27] The Ionian *poleis* granted him, apparently without solicitation, divine honors and a

---

26. The practice was doubtless abetted by the thin and confused line that separated the cult of a dead hero—the founder of a city, for example—and the cult of an immortal god.

27. See Chapter I, p. 42.

cult on the occasion of his liberating them from their Achaemenian bondage. This was, it will be noted, before he was
greeted at the oasis of Siwa as the son of Amon Re, again a
perfectly normal salutation in the Pharaonic context. And when,
shortly before his death, he requested of the Greek *poleis* of the
mainland that they restore their political exiles and grant divine
honors to himself, it was the first demand that met some opposition, not the deification.

The Athenians on their own initiative far surpassed what Alexander had asked in granting divine honors to Antigonus and
Demetrius Poliorcetes in B.C. 307. Demetrius had freed them of
Cassander and their gratitude knew no bounds; not only were the
two kings divinized and priesthoods set up for their cult, their
images were woven into Athena's sacred cloak, months and tribes
were named after them, and an altar set up on the spot where
Demetrius had first alighted from his chariot. Demetrius found it
much to his liking; he moved into the Parthenon and had his
mistress worshiped as Aphrodite.

The various *poleis* continued the practice in the Successors'
states; they legislated divinity for their kings. What may strike
the modern reader as a flagrant instance of psychopathy had become in reality a very Greek practice governed by specific
juridical procedures and prompted not by megalomania on the
part of the recipient, but by cold political considerations on the
part of the donors. It may indeed have bespoken a progressive
deterioration in the Hellenic notion of what constituted a god,
but at the time deification of the living provoked no theological
crises.

The first of the Successors to recognize the political rewards to
be reaped from constructing this random practice into a full-
fledged state cult was Ptolemy I. The innovation may not, however, be as great as it appears; the history, physiognomy and
organization of the Egyptian state themselves suggest the possibility. Ptolemy did not, at any rate, use himself to this end; he
invoked instead the cult of the dead—and divinized—Alexander,
whose corpse was in his possession. The sacred remains were
buried with pomp at Memphis,[28] and by B.C. 311 Ptolemy I had
constructed around the dead saint, doubtless as a pledge of his
own legitimacy, a state cult with its own temples and its own

---

28. Later moved to Alexandria by Ptolemy II.

priesthood, the latter including the king's own brother Menelaus. The Serapis cult was Ptolemy Soter's face to the international scene; the Alexander cult was intended to consolidate his position in Egypt.[29]

The second Ptolemy was somewhat bolder. He joined his own cultus to that of Alexander, so that the House could share more directly in the glory of the Founder. The priesthoods of Alexander were enlarged to include, during their own lifetime, Philadelphus and his sister-wife Arsinoë.[30] The royal couple shared Alexander's temples at Alexandria and elsewhere and bore the cult name Brother and Sister (*Adelphoi*) while still alive.[31] To cap his policy Ptolemy II instituted in Alexandria in B.C. 279 his own version of the Olympic Games.

In the Hellenistic states divinization was firmly in the hands of the ruler himself. Ptolemies, Seleucids and Attalids alike declared their own apotheosis, instituted their own cults, named their own priests, and led the celebration of their own birthdays. Other gods were not neglected, especially if there were family ties, as with Dionysus in Egypt and Zeus and Apollo in Syria, but the greatest effort was devoted to propagating the cult of the ruler, his wife and family. By the time it reached Roman hands the institution was firmly tied to the office and not the individual.

The arrival of the Romans created an awkward religious situation in the Near East. The Romans came into Asia as republicans, without a king whom the grateful or terrified easterners could deify. There were a number of makeshift solutions like the erec-

---

29. Possibly the Serapis cult was intended to have an effect in Egypt as well; he was, after all, an Egyptian god. All the early Ptolemies were Pharaohs, but they do not seem to have pushed their prerogatives; the first evidence for an enthronement in the old Egyptian style dates from the reign of Ptolemy V (B.C. 203–181), a clear indication of the rising tide of Egyptian sentiment after B.C. 217 (see Chapter IV, pp. 178–179).

30. But not Ptolemy I Soter and Berenice. They were dutifully divinized by their son as "Saviors" (*Soteres*) after their death, but they were not included in the state cult until somewhat later. The aim of Philadelphus was apparently to settle the cult upon the current Pharaoh.

31. Cult names were as common among the Hellenistic monarchs as family and triumphal names were later to be among the Roman emperors. The most common among the Ptolemies and Seleucids were Savior (*Soter*), Benefactor (*Euergetes*), and God Made Manifest (*Epiphanes*).

tion of temples to "Goddess Rome," or the deification of the victorious general, as happened to Flamininus in Greece, or the touchingly naïve apotheosis of Aquilius, the bureaucrat sent out to supervise the transformation of Pergamum from kingdom to province. Republican legates and governors in the East seem to have been given divine cults as a matter of course.

The accession of Augustus made things considerably simpler; the *poleis* then had a proper object for their penchant for divinization. The emperor cult was regularized in the course of time, particularly on the provincial level where it was normally under the supervision of the Commune (*koinon*) of the Hellenes.[32] Augustus acted with what seems to be discretion in the West, where he generally contented himself with the title "Son of the Deified Julius."[33]

The Roman Imperial cult meant different things to different people. The Greek *poleis* granted apotheosis rather freely during life, as they had almost from the beginning; the Senate voted it somewhat more reluctantly, and after death. For a madman like Caligula it was a plaything; for an absolutist like Domitian it was a necessity. Hadrian was greeted as Zeus in the East, but his successor Antoninus had difficulty persuading the Senate to divinize him after his death. Part of the style under the Romans was for the Emperor to compare himself with one or another of the traditional gods: Helios, Heracles, Zeus.

None of this had anything to do with piety and very little with religion. The Imperial cult gave its recipient a convenient propaganda vehicle, suggested in a vague way that God was on his side, justified his possession of power, and perhaps provided the heirs an opportunity to legitimize themselves. The cult was formal and political. No reasonable man devoted any of his time pondering the theological implications of it all, none save the Christians, whose own rather narrow view of what constituted a God left no room for the "worship" of emperors.[34]

Where the Imperial cult did possess some religious significance was in the interpretation put upon it by the Antonines and their Stoic intellectual allies. Stoic emphasis on the organic nature of the universe led directly into Cleanthes' *Hymn to Zeus*, the Stoic

---

32. See Chapter X, pp. 391–392.
33. In B.C. 42 the triumvirs had pushed through the Senate a bill deifying Caesar.
34. See Chapter XVI, pp. 577–81.

anthem to One God as ruler of one world. The topic probably remained the pious possession of the schools until the Stoics' union with the Cynics under the early Empire involved both parties more directly in politics. Seneca and Epictetus were both Stoic henotheists of a type noticeably purified of the earlier materialism, but it was not until the accession of Trajan in A.D. 98 that Stoic theoreticians and moralists like Dio Chrysostom of Prusa had their desired parallelism between microcosm and macrocosm, *unus Dominus et unus Deus*, cosmic Reason and the enlightened Autocrat ruling the City of God and the City of Man.

The dream vanished with the Antonines, swallowed up in the syncretistic and sometimes crude Orientalism of the Severi. Its only echo was in the belated attempt to construct the Invincible Sun into a universal cult rooted in the Emperor. By that time, however, the ecumenical City of Man was itself in danger of collapse.

Gods of the East

The traditionalist Plutarch had espoused a losing cause; it was to his friend Clea, priestess of Isis at Delphi, to whom the future belonged, to Clea and her colleagues serving the gods of Asia throughout the Empire. Despite appearances, the old order was passing. The Olympians continued to be potent cultural symbols, and their *personae* dominated literature and art, as before. There was, however, little religious vitality behind the masks. The telltale marks of genuine spirituality and moral urgency were to be found not in an antiquated Olympianism nor in the politically motivated ruler cult, but in the cults of the East, those of Isis, Cybele and Mithra, to say nothing of a fringe sect like that of the adepts of Jesus the Messiah.

From the beginning Greece knew many foreign gods, and some, like Dionysus and Aphrodite, ended their careers as esteemed members of the Olympian pantheon. Such syncretism was possible in the Bronze Age *oikoumene*, but after the Homeric standardization and with the emergence of *polis* consciousness a different mood prevailed. Hellenism and barbarism were sharply distinguished; pride, self-awareness and nationalism combined to insulate Greece from what it had once embraced. Down to the middle of the fifth century the Greeks judged alien gods as curious but unacceptable, or simply as interesting or amusing.

The Great War against Sparta sapped the earlier Athenian self-assurance, and as their troubles deepened the once incredulous citizens turned to foreign cults. The Phrygian Cybele, her Thracian analogue Bendis, the slain young gods of Phrygia and Phoenicia, Attis and Adonis, and the curious Sabazius[35] all appeared at the center of Hellenism before the end of the fifth century. The reconstitution of the *oikoumene* under Alexander merely hastened a shift in religious sensibilities that was already in progress.

What changed in the century between B.C. 400 and B.C. 300 was that the cults of the East could travel over freshly smoothed paths into Greece. There were, moreover, new forces urging them down those paths. For the Hellenistic monarchs religion was a powerful propaganda weapon in the Successors' endless struggle for political domination. No one used it more effectively than the Ptolemies of Egypt.

In the days of the Roman Empire the Egyptian goddess Isis was celebrated everywhere with an elaborate ritual and a complementary mystery cult. But she was not the first god to come forth from Egypt in Hellenistic times. Before her the eastern Mediterranean was drawn or, rather, summoned to another Egyptian deity, Serapis, who owed his brief but brilliant career to the political astuteness of Ptolemy I Soter.

Some version or other of Serapis was current in Egypt before Alexander arrived there, and probably combined the features of Osiris and the bull-god Apis. The cult center was at or near Memphis, and it was there that Ptolemy came upon it in its native Egyptian form. At this early stage of his career on the Nile Ptolemy may still have been concerned chiefly with consolidating his position in Egypt, as attested to by his interest in the Alexander cult, but with the decisive events of B.C. 312 he stood full center on the stage of Aegean politics.[36] His deliberate involvement in Syria, Cilicia, Greece and the islands showed that his mind had turned to empire. And Serapis was to be his ecumenical god. The cult center was moved from Memphis to the magnificent Serapeum at Alexandria. A Greek sculptor devised an appropriate cult image and the two religious eminences of the time, the imported Eleusinian priest Timotheus and the Hellenized

---

35. See Chapter VII, p. 298.
36. See Chapter II, p. 77.

Egyptian priest Manetho,[37] took a hand at Hellenizing the liturgy and the accompanying myth. The result was a partially Hellenized version of an Egyptian religious phenomenon, intelligible, it was thought, to Greek and Egyptian alike, and eminently suitable for export.

Serapis did take up residence abroad, in Sicily, Athens, and particularly within the Ptolemaic sphere of political influence, on the Aegean islands and in the *poleis* of the Anatolian coast. His personal reign proved ephemeral. The dream of empire dissipated as Ptolemaic power receded into Egypt, and the cult of Serapis suffered the congenital weakness of political religions: they expand and contract in proportion to the political power that supports them. It is likely that Serapis would eventually have retreated back into the tomb of Apis at Memphis had it not been for his connection with a far more potent figure in the same myth complex, his consort Isis.

According to the Egyptian version of the myth, Osiris (Serapis), the son of gods, was treacherously murdered and his limbs scattered abroad by his brother Seth (Typhon). Osiris' wife and sister Isis then began a far-ranging search for the remains, aided by the dog-god Anubis. She was eventually successful. Osiris was restored as Lord of the Underworld, and Seth was defeated in a combat with Horus, son of Isis and Osiris.

From this mythic base grew the great mysteries of Isis commemorating the climactic moments of her search and discovery. As in the parallel case of Demeter's search and discovery of her daughter Persephone, the entire dramatic complex of myth and cult was a token of rebirth for the initiate. And even though the theological center of the myth would seem to be Osiris, the focus of the cult and the primary object of religious veneration was, as it had been from the primitive beginnings, the female figure Isis.

The Greek centers, particularly Corinth, continued to honor Isis and her consort well into late antiquity, but the clearest indications of the power of this Egyptian cult can be seen in Roman circles. The Ptolemaic connection with Sicily introduced Serapis there in the third century. From Sicily the cult spread northward through the Hellenized cities in southern Italy, and by B.C. 150 Isis was a commanding religious figure at Pompeii. A *thiasos* of her priests was instituted at Rome during the time of Sulla.

---

37. See Chapter II, p. 112.

Shortly thereafter a pattern of Roman resistance began to develop. Not only were the mysteries offensive to Roman religious and moral susceptibilities, they were the cult of a hostile political power as well. On a number of occasions the mysteries were legally proscribed and the temples of Isis torn down. In A.D. 19 under Tiberius there was, in addition, a resounding scandal involving the Isiac priesthood and wholesale deportations followed.

This was the last serious difficulty. Egypt was by then a Roman province, and the political associations of the cult had consequently disappeared. From Claudius onward, Isis was supreme among the alien gods who had gained a foothold in the Empire. Caligula, Domitian and Caracalla gave her magnificent temples at the heart of Rome. There were forty-two Serapeums at Alexandria alone. In each was celebrated the *daily* liturgy in honor of Isis; other gods might have occasional feast days in the Roman *fasti*, but Isis was honored every day in her temples.

It is not difficult to understand the appeal of Isis. Constantly before the eye of the believer, she was the protected and celebrated object of a highly organized cult apparatus that had all the appearances of a church. The complex upper and lower priesthoods were almost certainly Egyptian dominated (they involved an at least occasional reading of hieroglyphs), though there is some evidence that the Romans attempted to take control of such a powerful institution. There was, too, an idealized code of behavior that had progressed far beyond what had earlier been simply ritual purity to a genuine moral innocence involving chastity and abstinence. Finally, Isis enjoyed an attractive ritual adorned by hymns, litanies and an impressive pictorial decor.[38]

The public rituals in honor of Isis took place annually between October 26 and November 3, when the great myth of the Seeking and the Finding of Osiris was dramatized with moving splendor. There were, as well, lesser feasts like the Sailing of Isis on March 5. All the holy days were celebrated with public processions in which the images of the Egyptian gods were carried

---

38. Isiac artistic piety is fully represented at Pompeii. A frequent motif was that of Isis and her infant son Harpocrates as "Madonna and Child" in postures providing clear antecedents to later Christian treatments of the same theme. The litanies too, in which Isis proclaims her own all-embracing claims to veneration or in which the adept recited her many titles, must have provided attractive suggestions for the later Marian liturgies.

about the city. Far more secret were the initiation ceremonies proper. Fortunately they are described in some detail (the central core is, of course, suppressed) in the *Metamorphoses* of the second-century Latin author Apuleius, whose hero Lucius is initiated into the Isiac mysteries.

The initiation began with a ritual washing and a protracted fast. Once this was completed Lucius came to the Iseum toward evening. He was given gifts, and the uninitiated withdrew. The ceremonies lasted through the night ("I drew near the confines of death. . . . I was carried through the elements and returned to earth again. . . . I saw the sun shining brightly . . . I saw the gods above and below face to face.") and in the morning, clothed in ceremonial garb, with a torch in his hand and a crown upon his head, Lucius reemerged to celebrate the happy day of his rebirth.

This is the closest we come to an ancient mystery cult. The pledge of secrecy was kept, but from the tone of the passage there is no doubting the genuineness of the experience, its dramatic appeal to all the senses and, through its elaborate symbolism, to the mind of the neophyte as well. Isis proved herself, moreover, the very model of a syncretistic goddess, readily identifiable with all the goddesses of the Olympian pantheon from Aphrodite to Demeter. And behind her stood the venerable authority of Egypt, since Herodotus' time the fountainhead of religious wisdom.

The happy domestication of the Isiac mysteries contrasts sharply with the more barbarous perspectives of another popular eastern cult, that of Cybele, the Great Mother of Pessinus in Phrygia. The worship of Cybele, the mistress of the beasts, and of her young lover Attis was indigenous in Phrygia. The myth of Cybele and the infidelity and castration of the beloved Attis was celebrated by the large priesthood at Pessinus and at other temple states in Anatolia, sometimes combined with other similar cults.[39]

The rites of the Mother must have been awesome to behold. The central feast days, celebrated at Rome between the fifteenth and twenty-eighth of March, reached their climax in a great ecstatic performance where the adepts, incited by drum and cymbal, gashed themselves with knives, smeared themselves with

---

39. In one early version of the myth Attis is crossed with the Semitic Adonis, and Cybele was on occasion identified with the fertility goddess Ma of Comana in Cappadocia, herself syncretized with the Iranian fertility goddess Anahita.

blood, and occasionally even practiced self-castration. Other features of the cult included something that seems like a communion ritual and the curious *taurobolium*. In this latter rite the believer went down into a pit over which a bull was sacrificed in such a way that its blood was shed down upon the adept who was by this process reinvigorated, if not reborn.

The Greeks knew well enough about the Great Mother and had their own considerably tamer versions of her worship. The orgiastic Phrygian lady, however, never gained a practical foothold among the fastidious Hellenes.[40] The Romans, on the other hand, showed considerable interest. The Magna Mater was introduced into Rome in B.C. 204, possibly, as the Romans thought, as a counterweapon to whatever was being prepared for them in the Carthaginian religious armory, but more probably as calculated tender of good will toward the states in Asia to neutralize Philip V in the Aegean.[41] Attalus of Pergamum, who had taken the Mother's fetish from Pessinus, obliged his allies and passed the stone to the nervous Romans.

Once installed at Rome, Cybele suffered the same pattern of opposition that greeted Isis. Here the uneasiness was surely dictated by something other than politics. Roman sensibilities were not yet ready for the ecstatic cult, the public bloodletting, the Galli, or eunuch priests. But even sensibilities harden, and as Caligula had opened the door to Isis, so Claudius accommodated the Magna Mater and her self-castrating Galli. But she never equaled Isis' respectability. In the eyes of most Romans, Cybele was the goddess of the lower classes, of slaves and Oriental immigrants. Their disdain may have been a reflection of the attitudes of the Hellenic intellectuals of the Empire, who found the lady's cult no more appealing than had their fifth-century ancestors. The rule of assimilation continued in force: Hellenism could absorb anything, provided only that it had been previously Hellenized.

The third great cult that came from the East illustrates the same law: Mithraism passed directly from its Iranian centers in Anatolia to the least Hellenized elements in Roman society; Greece, the Hellenic cities of Asia, and the Hellenized intellectuals at Rome were little moved by Mithra or his mysteries. Hellenic nostalgia, pride or pretension might attract intelligentsia

---

40. For the influence of one of her devotees on Christianity see Chapter XVII, p. 629.
41. See Chapter VIII, p. 312.

to Eleusis, but no such motives drew them to the local Mithraeum.

The genesis of Mithraism, a religious movement whose Iranian origins were freely acknowledged by the Romans, was by no means as simple as the ancients would make it. Iranian religion was a complex phenomenon altered by evolution, reform and political manipulation. There was, in addition, an Iranian *diaspora* notably in Anatolia and northern Syria, whose practices and beliefs are not clearly known. Mithra was a god of the oldest Indo-Iranian pantheon, but Mithraism, the mystery religion in vogue in the Roman Empire, was a product of that same Iranian *diaspora* of Parthian times, relatively untouched by either the Zoroastrian reform or political meddling.

The Iranian strain in eastern and central Anatolia went back to the days of the Achaemenian occupation, and Anatolian Mithraism and its priesthood, the *magusaei*, found their later political sustenance in the kingdoms of Pontus, Cappadocia and Commagene, whose lords traced their descent to Darius, and whose political and dynastic fortunes were linked to Parthia. Mithra was their dynastic god,[42] and another member of the Iranian pantheon, Anahita, served as their version of the fertile Great Mother.[43] The Iranian Anahita reigned at Comana in Pontus as the Phrygian Cybele did at Pessinus.

The Mithra of Anatolia was by no means simply his former Indo-Iranian self. In his earlier Vedic and Avestan form, Mithra was a companion and equal of the High God Ahura. Mithraism worshiped him, however, in the context of a well-defined dualism wherein he served as an intermediary between Ormazd of the heavens and Ahriman, lord of the underworld. Though once the lord of contracts and flocks, the latter-day Mithra was also a savior god, the spirit of the light born into this world in a cave and whose soteriological act was the slaughter of a cosmic bull.

Mithra's slaughter of the bull, a theme which holds a dominant place in Mithraic iconography, guaranteed the fertility of the earth. The slain beast's organs and blood are the source from which spring forth all vegetable and animal life. And, in the manner of a fertility rite, the ritual slaughter is also the pledge of man's survival after death, his freedom from the bindings of a

---

42. Compare the frequency of the dynastic name Mithridates.
43. Anahita was worshiped by Artaxerxes II and enjoyed a revival in the Persian homeland under the early Sasanians.

malevolent fate. In one regard the soteriological work is strikingly different from that commemorated in the other mysteries. His male analogues, Osiris, Attis and Adonis, brought life by their own rebirth and rejuvenation; Mithra achieved the same end by the slaughter of another.[44]

Nor is agricultural immortality the same thing as freedom from a cosmic or heavenly fate. The former is born in the annual harvest and reinforced by sexual procreation; the latter is more often spawned at the astrologer's workbench–*prie-dieu*. The Mithraism of the Anatolian *diaspora* had clearly passed through another discernible screen of influences. The Mithraic liturgies in Anatolia were in Aramaic, the Semitic lingua franca of the Achaemenians, and the language points the direction of this other major syncretism. It is probable that Mithraism had come to Anatolia by way of Semitic Babylonia since the later Mithraic cult betrays the obvious marks of an astral theology foreign to the Iranian type. In the *Avesta* Mithra was a sky god and was compared to, though not identical with, the sun. By the time of the developed Mithraism of the Roman Empire the sky associations had become planetary associations and Mithra was drawn within the complex of the Invincible Sun (Sol Invictus) where many another eastern god found his final resting place.[45]

Part of this syncretism took place in the more remote origins of the cult, in Babylonia itself, perhaps, but it is not impossible that the process continued, under somewhat different auspices, in Anatolia. Mention has already been made of the introduction of Egyptian and Chaldean material into the Hellenistic *oikoumene* through the efforts of Manetho and Berossus; works of Iranian wisdom were also in circulation at about the same time, though here the authors preferred the anonymity of attributing their collections to the sages of the past: Zoroaster,[46] Ostanes and Hystaspes.

Some have taken the Iranian origins of this material seriously and suggested the *magusaei* of Anatolia as a likely source for the meshing of the two cultures apparent in the Iranian wisdom lit-

---

44. See Chapter XIII, p. 497.
45. See Chapter XVI, pp. 582–83.
46. According to Hermippus, the imaginative "Aristotelian" who studied and worked under Callimachus (see Chapter II, p. 116), the Library at Alexandria possessed works of Zoroaster totaling no fewer than two million lines.

erature in Greek. If this is so, it is curious that Zoroaster plays no part in Mithraism. What the Greeks knew of Zoroaster points back to Iran,[47] while the Mithra complex was, by all appearances, a quite separate tradition from a different source, almost certainly northeastern Anatolia.

Anatolian Mithraism is a wraith that must be reconstructed, but the Roman inheritance was solid enough. From his Parthian days Mithra was the patron god of warrior guilds, and on the authority of Plutarch it was from the pirate bands of Cilicia that Pompey's Roman campaigners under the banner of the *Lex Gabinia* became acquainted with the cult.[48] After a period of quiescence it began to spread through the military arteries of the Empire along the Rhine and the Danube. Commodus, who liked the virile virtues, was initiated into the mysteries, and in A.D. 307, in the midst of the last frenzied persecutions of Christianity, the retired Diocletian and the new Augustus Galerius met on the Danube to recognize Mithra as the official protector of the Empire.

The choice of patron was an apt one. Mithraism was a militant cult which preached the active pursuit of the manly virtues of courage and fraternity. Its ethos was well suited to camp life, since it saw the moral life as a campaign for justice and righteousness organized along distinctly military lines. The army of believers was marshaled into a tightly run hierarchical organization. The rites were performed in standardized chapels that were stylized representations of Mithra's underground birthplace; in the apse was the inevitable scene of Mithra slaying the bull. The sacramental life of the Mithraic church included baptism for the forgiveness of sins, a sacred meal, and the rite of confirmation in the army of Mithra.

In its Roman phase Mithraism began and ended as the preserve of the military. Its masculine appeal is unmistakable, but whatever its success in the military camps along the frontiers (and its consequent value to the Emperor as commander in chief), the Iranian god said little or nothing to the masses of the Empire.

---

47. Transmitted, probably, by way of Babylonia and Egypt. Most of the substance of the *corpus* of the "Hellenized Magi" pertains to astrology, alchemy and the "new physics" popularized first in Egypt by Bolus of Mendes; the cult of Mithra, on the other hand, was never very popular in Egypt.

48. See Chapter VIII, p. 320.

The sage Zoroaster fascinated the Hellenized intellectuals, but they cared little for the god Mithra, who probably struck them as alien and parochial. For cult they turned instead to Isis, a convincing replica of their own Demeter.

Any treatment of the mysteries, Greek or eastern, must confess defeat almost from the outset. We are fairly well instructed on their myths, but these have passed through so many literary and philosophical hands that their tendentious exegesis leaps up from every page. Plutarch's treatment of the myth in his *Isis and Osiris* is a perfect illustration of the well-meaning rationalist overlay; the standard, to say nothing of the primitive, version of the story is only faintly discernible.

The ritual of the mysteries is even more difficult to lay hold of. One can stand, for instance, in the center of a fairly well preserved Mithraic chapel and be at almost a complete loss to understand the *experience* of those who not so much worshiped as participated there. The tantalizing hints of the ancient authorities, pagan gossips and Christian polemicists, make it clear enough that there was an almost psychedelic assault on the senses and the imagination with sound, light and the highly developed symbolism in which the mysteries specialized. The early Christian liturgy suggests itself as only a mild and relatively public analogue of the dark and fantastic wonders that occurred in a Mithraeum or an Iseum.

And yet it was the restrained liturgy of Christianity that eventually carried the day against its more flamboyant rivals. In the course of the second century the *Christianoi* were just beginning to emerge from their Palestinian habitat into the Hellenized *oikoumene*. Lodged in homes and burrows from Spain to Mesopotamia, the Christian communities were at the critical point of separation from their Jewish matrix. Schismatic talk was stilled in the synagogues, but the first sounds of dialogue with new respondents could be heard in the public places of Rome, Antioch and Alexandria. The last of the eastern cults was moving to its confrontation with Hellenism.

XIII

The Origins of Christianity

Jesus, son of Mary and Joseph of Galilee, was born in Bethlehem in a Roman vassal state in Palestine during the troubled reign of Herod. He preached, taught and worked wonders during the last few years of his life until he was arrested. He was tried by a Jewish court in Jerusalem on charges that are obscure and was executed there by the Roman authorities during the principate of Tiberius when Pontius Pilate was Procurator of Judaea. His followers said that they saw him on a number of occasions after his death. They claimed that he was the Messiah and the Son of God.

The Good News of Jesus

The Gospels as we have them are neither pure history nor pure myth, though elements of both are present in them. Nor are they treatises of theology; and yet their authors had attitudes that must be termed theological. The rather brief works that the Christian Church accepted as the authoritative record of its founder represent two or even three different historical perspectives and a similar divergence of ideologies. There is in all four of the Gospels a kernel of material that is, in the strictest sense, historical in that it represents contemporary eyewitness accounts of the life and death of Jesus of Nazareth. But the "life" of Jesus is described in a peculiar fashion. What appear at first glance to be biographical accounts are rich in detail for the last two or three years of their subject's life, and particularly so for his last days in Jerusalem, while most of what went before is either hagiographical embroidery, as in the haggadic infancy narrative in *Luke*, or is dismissed with a few summary remarks under the general rubric of the "hidden life."

For the evangelists the "hidden life" did not constitute part of Jesus' *bios*, since in retrospect the events of those years had no significance. His biographers took up his career where it became theologically meaningful, and from that point on, from Jesus' baptism by John, the narratives are so filled with what are patently real events that there can be no doubt that a historical person named Jesus really *did* go up to Jerusalem and *was* executed by crucifixion sometime about A.D. 28.[1] There are confusions, to be sure; details of chronology are hopelessly obscure and the legal aspects of the trial were either misunderstood or altered. But the four narratives stand as some form of history based on contemporary witnesses.

What the evangelists actually set down were not, however, biographies, but a form of the "Good News,"[2] the message that was to be preached to Jews and Gentiles and that would bring them to an understanding and acceptance of Jesus and his Messiahship. The Gospels were a proclamation (*kerygma*) based on biographical material but shaped by the certain knowledge that Jesus was and is the Messiah. And it was that conviction, as felt and expressed at the time of the composition of the extant Gospels, that allowed their authors to place the historical kernel of the sayings and deeds of Jesus in a setting that would reveal their "meaning."

There is no question of returning to these accounts in a state of historical innocence of their consequences. The most that can be attempted is the restoration of their original context: how Jesus fitted into his own contemporary setting, namely the Judaism of Palestine during the reign of Herod and the rule of the Romans, and how he was viewed at the later time when the Gospels were composed. The first has already been touched upon;[3] the difficulties of the second are far more severe. For centuries conserva-

---

1. This much at least can be affirmed from the very sparse references to the event in other contemporary historians, Suetonius, Tacitus and Josephus. The references are, however, no more sparse than the event demanded.
2. Thus their titles: "The Good News [*euangelion*] of Jesus Christ according to Mark," et cetera.
3. See Chapters VIII and X.

tive sentiment saw Jesus and the Gospels as synonymous, and it was one of the great achievements of modern scholarship that the two questions, the life of Jesus in its contemporary setting and the composition of the Gospels in their literary and historical context, can be treated separately. On the testimony of the Gospels themselves, the witnesses to the life of Jesus were not at all sure of what he was saying and what he was attempting to do; the evangelists, on the other hand, whether they were identical with those eyewitnesses or not, and the Church of which they were members, did understand, or thought they understood, the claims of Jesus.

The same scholars who separated the question of Jesus from the question of the Gospels frequently pushed their hypothesis to its extreme conclusion: the Jesus of Christianity was the *creation* of the generation that produced the Gospels; the Jesus of history was a simple but impressive rabbi.[4] The hypothesis, once an extremely popular one, has yielded to another, indeed, the original one. After his death—and soon after—the disciples of Jesus came to an understanding of his life and death. The point that he had kept trying to make was that something was *going* to happen, something that they, with their stereotyped Messianic notions, could not conceive of. Their first reaction to the death of Jesus was that it cut off what really mattered, his life and ministry, and the possibility of further exercising his Messianic claim. But it was the *death* of Jesus that was the significant event; the Kingdom of God that he had been incessantly announcing began *then*.

It was an overwhelming discovery, attributed by his disciples to the working of God's Holy Spirit among them, and certified by the appearance of the risen Jesus to scores of witnesses. They immediately set to proclaiming the event. Jesus the healer and teacher was dead. He had died to redeem Israel. It was an act of God, a direct intrusion into human history by a God who was thereby announcing a New Covenant with his people. This was the note struck in the earliest preaching in the Church; it underlay the instruction of Paul; and it was the acceptance of this "tradition from the Apostles" that constituted, from the beginning, the essence of Christianity.

The Gospels, then, are a mixed reminiscence of what it was like

---

4. Perhaps the victim of bad friends, bad advice or bad digestion, depending on which secondary hypothesis one chooses as the bridge between the two Jesuses.

in the days when the coming of the Kingdom was still in the future, preserving Jesus' often enigmatic pointing to it and his disciples' own disbelief. At the same time the narratives are bathed in the *ex post facto* understanding of those living under the New Dispensation. Paul, on the other hand, lived solely in the days when the coming of the Kingdom was still in the Kingdom Come. Neither biography nor history interested him; he was caught up in expounding the present and the future.

The distance that separated Jesus from the Apostles and Paul was not merely that which separated past, present and future; it reflected as well a change in the audience to which the proclamation was being addressed. Jesus taught publicly to Palestinian Jews and gave further private amplification to his disciples, who were drawn from the same milieu; the Gospels and Letters, however, received their final form in quite different settings.

How different were the readers of the Gospels and how different was the Church's understanding of Jesus very much depends on that latter milieu. When and where were the Gospels composed? The tone and feeling of John's work and the tradition relating to him are quite different from those of the other three evangelists, and there is today absolute agreement that John's was the latest of the Gospels, composed, as the ancient tradition maintained, at Ephesus and no later than A.D. 100. Since both Matthew and Luke drew upon material already in Mark, it is generally, though not unanimously, held that Mark's was the oldest of the Gospels. Who Mark was and where he composed his Gospel is suggested in a statement of Papias, bishop of Hierapolis in Asia Minor about A.D. 130. On his testimony, Mark was a disciple of Peter who noted down that Apostle's teaching. It is likely that this occurred at Rome sometime after Peter's death there in the Neronian persecution of A.D. 64 and before the destruction of the temple in Jerusalem by Titus' troops in A.D. 70.

Matthew and Luke, drawing as they do upon Mark,[5] must be later, and their versions of the apocalyptic destruction of the temple in Mark bear some indications that the event has already taken place. The time and place of their composition cannot be determined exactly; about A.D. 80 seems likely, and the Semitic

---

5. And, in some two hundred additional verses they have in common over and above their Marcan base, on another possible but anonymous source called by modern critics Q (for *Quelle*, "source").

coloring in Matthew suggests Syria as a locale for that Gospel. Luke's work is a little different from the other two synoptic Gospels in that it betrays some literary pretensions; there is a book-style prologue, and the work was published in two volumes (*Gospel, Acts of the Apostles*).[6]

These three Gospels of Matthew, Mark and Luke, which give a synoptic view of the life of Jesus, were, then, eyewitness-based accounts composed in Greek,[7] the *koine* or common Greek of the Mediterranean, more than a little crude from a literary point of view, but simple and direct in language, pictorial rather than ideological, and bearing the marks of three broadly distinguished strata of material: (1) the sayings and deeds of Jesus, transmitted orally from two or three different contemporary sources; (2) the collective understanding of the meaning of those words and deeds as experienced by his disciples in Jerusalem shortly after his death, the "apostolic tradition"; and (3) the local redaction of that tradition in one or another of the churches. This latter redaction can be distinguished by its inclusion of local concerns and issues, as, for instance, the prologue of John's Gospel with its reflection of a Hellenized readership at Ephesus, or Matthew's sharpening of the guilt of the Jews in the death of Jesus as part of a general sentiment current in the Christian communities in Syria in the eighties of the first century. Current critical opinion, particularly as it becomes more conservative,[8] is inclined to believe

---

6. Luke's Gospel resembles what in antiquity was an edited book (*ekdosis*), while the remarks of Papias about Mark indicate that his Gospel belongs in the category of the *hypomnemata*, notes and instruction given by a teacher and jotted down in their notebooks by his students. Books were edited on rolls (*volumina*); the *hypomnemata* probably gave rise to the production of "booklets" (*codices*) so closely associated with the spread of the Gospels. See p. 501.

7. It has been suggested that the original of one or another of them was the Aramaic native to Palestine, but the hypothesis has not found a great deal of support. The oral tradition upon which they were based could be none other than Aramaic. The literary Gospels themselves, however, despite an unmistakable Semitic cast to some of their idiom, were almost certainly composed in Greek.

8. Scholarly criticism has tended to take a far more conservative view of oral traditions and ancient literary texts than it did in the last century. Both the Old and New Testaments were once defoliated as ruthlessly as the Homeric poems. The "restoration" of Homer has led to a similar respect for the integrity and historicity of Scriptural texts.

that the apostolic tradition rests firmly upon the words and deeds of Jesus and did not, as once thought, create them, and that the actual writing down of the Gospels does not imply a redaction of major proportions.

Jesus taught in the manner of a first-century rabbi; the use of parables, to cite a single example, was a rabbinic commonplace. The technique, the images, the language and rhetoric of the message were all familiar. Perhaps all too familiar. Jesus' chief pedagogical problem seems to have been the avoidance of stereotyped responses to such familiar concepts as "Messiah" and "Kingdom," with their current military and political overtones. His well-known reticence about his own Messiahship probably arose from just such a concern, as did the constant doctrinal corrections given even his own disciples. But whatever the corrections of specific points, there lay behind the Gospels, including both Jesus' teaching and the apostolic understanding of that teaching, a coherent ideological frame of reference that furnished the premises of the proclamation and shaped its physiognomy.

One of the most pervasive elements of that Gospel tradition was later Judaism's highly developed sense of the *eschaton*, or end time, the period of tribulation associated with the coming of the Messiah and culminating with the coming in of a New Age marked by the judgment and exaltation of Israel. It was a recurrent theme in the Old Testament *apocrypha*, and the *eschaton* was endlessly and enigmatically detailed in the many apocalyptic visions in circulation in Palestine and the Diaspora.[9] It is normal that Jesus should preach the end time, and he did, in the mood and terms current in the apocalypses.

The earliest community of his disciples was not quite certain what to make of this particular eschatology. Jesus' death and resurrection made it clear that in some sense the end time was *now;* the appointed time had come; the Kingdom of God was at hand. But there were confusions; not all the apocalyptic signs of the *eschaton* had been fulfilled. What of the restoration of Israel? Paul, for instance, was convinced that the end time had broken in, but he and the membership of the churches which had received the apostolic tradition from him were equally convinced that there would be a Second Coming (*parousia*) in the not too distant future, and that this would mark the final end. Paul's

---

9. See Chapter VIII, pp. 324–27.

Letters to the Thessalonians are filled with such speculations. What of those believers who had already died? Were they cheated of the glories of the End? They were advised to relax their expectation somewhat; certain very visible conditions would have to be fulfilled before the second and final *parousia*. The early Church had a not very practical handbook of such signs, the *Apocalypse of John*.

The relaxation of expectation proceeded naturally and inevitably. Doubts arose about the authenticity of John's *Apocalypse*, and the *parousia* faded into millennial distance. *"Maran atha!"* ("Lord, come!") was intoned with diminishing urgency as the whole eschatological complex that lies so close to the surface in the thinking of the apostolic age was replaced by the sanctification of the present through the process of life in the Church.

And yet this message, the true meaning of which was so little understood by Jesus' own disciples, so provoked the authorities that they put this particular rabbi to death. One can surmise reasons, though without absolute certainty that they represent the whole truth. During the short span of his public teaching Jesus made few permanent disciples but did occasionally manage to attract the attention of large crowds. Their enthusiasm never lasted very long, but the speed with which they were willing to proclaim the immediate kingship of this teacher showed the danger of the situation. Palestine was politically explosive. Jesus' listeners knew it and never hesitated to put political questions to him. Various *provocateurs* did the same. His answers were cautious, and he never showed any inclination to assume the political role that the inflamed crowds offered him. The Romans for their part were officially uninterested in miracle mongers. But when Jesus shifted his activity from Galilee to Jerusalem and entered the city in what was clearly a provocative manner, the Procurator's office could no longer afford to ignore this oddly reluctant Messiah.

Jesus, Pontius Pilate, the Sanhedrin, the Pharisees and Sadducees, "the Jews." The characters who played their part in the arrest, trial and execution of the man who "would make himself King of the Jews" are all set in their places in the Gospels. That there was an arrest, trial and execution is beyond reasonable doubt. Equally clearly, the Romans executed the sentence; it could hardly have been otherwise. But the instigators, the connivers and the issues themselves are hopelessly buried under the sentiments of the Christian editors. Pilate and the Romans come off relatively untarnished in the Gospels; were their roles retouched by the Church that had to live, for good or for ill, in the Roman Empire? The Jews, sometimes the Chief Priests, sometimes the Pharisees, sometimes "the whole people," appear to bear a heavy responsibility for the deed. Does this reflect the mutual disenchantment between Christian and Jew that was becoming very clear in the East at the time the Gospels were reaching their final form? Was Jesus crucified for theological blasphemy or for political sedition?

No one can be certain. Resurrection followed execution, and the passion and death of Jesus took on a new appearance to those dispirited few who had followed to the end. The end, it appeared, was not yet.

Jewish Christianity: The Church of Jerusalem

The Jewish followers of Jesus the Messiah, at first huddled together in terror at Jerusalem, gradually emerged from hiding as there grew among them the slow understanding of what had happened and what it signified. Galilee was forgotten, and there was no attempt on the part of the original twelve to return to their former callings. They and their followers were joined together in a community whose common experience of Jesus united them forever. In the words of the *Acts of the Apostles,* "They met constantly to hear the Apostles teach and to share the common life, to break bread, and to pray." They sold their possessions, and the proceeds were distributed in the community according to the need of each. Daily they preached through the city and attracted a great deal of attention, including the Sanhedrin's. The Jewish authorities did not, however, interfere; they judged that this movement, like others before it, would eventually disappear. There was not, apparently, a great deal to fear. The followers of Jesus had no political aspirations; they were scrupulous in their observance of the Law and the temple ritual.

The crisis, when it came, arose inside the Christian community. Jerusalem was not a provincial town. As the center of Judaism, it was filled with transient and permanent residents from the Diaspora, Hellenized Jews from Egypt, Syria and farther afield. Converts to Christ had been made from this group too, and the

"Hellenists" among the Christians thought they were being discriminated against in the community's primitive welfare program, a charge that the leaders attempted to put to rest by transferring this work to the sole administration of the Hellenists while they, the Aramaic Christians, devoted themselves to the spiritual side of the ministry. A committee of seven was appointed to direct the social program: Stephen, Philip, Prochorus, Nicanor, Timon, Parmenas, and Nicholas of Antioch.

The decision marked a fundamental change in policy, an opening outward, and the results were quickly felt. Stephen had been preaching publicly in the synagogues of the Hellenized Jews in Jerusalem, but now he began openly to attack the Law and the temple: the Covenant had been abrogated; the temple would be destroyed as Jesus said it would. He had gone too far. Stephen was summoned before the Sanhedrin where he repeated his allegations. Death by stoning followed.

This startling rupture of the peace had two long-term effects: the creation of a Christian *diaspora* by the flight of the Hellenists from Jerusalem after the death of Stephen in A.D. 34, and the turning of the original Jerusalem body of disciples, now unwittingly purged of its Hellenic elements, to a more conservative— that is, a more Judaizing—view of the message of Jesus and its meaning. It could not be otherwise in the light of the now serious opposition on the part of the Jewish authorities.

Of the original board of seven, Philip went to Samaria, an attractive place for dissidents, since the Samaritans too rejected the Jerusalem temple cultus, and began to preach and make converts among the *sebomenoi* there. Peter came up from Jerusalem to investigate. He approved, and it may have been at this point that Peter himself decided that the future belonged not to the Judaizers of Jerusalem, for whom the outcry after the death of Stephen could only mean the greatest circumspection in their activities, but rather to the Hellenizers and *sebomenoi* of the diaspora. It was, at any rate, soon after his trip to Samaria that Peter converted, on his own initiative, the Roman *sebomenos* Cornelius at Caesarea.

The other Hellenists had gone their own way, into Syria, Phoenicia and Cyprus, where they avoided the orthodox and preached successfully to Hellenized Jews and *sebomenoi*. Nicholas probably returned to Antioch, and here the results of Christian activity were spectacular. Antioch, like Alexandria, had a highly mixed and cosmopolitan population reflecting every shade of belief, conviction and cult in the *oikoumene*. Judaism was in a flourishing state there, free of the dangerous political and social climate of Palestine, and there the Hellenists took the final, consequential step in their proselytizing: they preached Christ crucified and risen to the Gentiles,[10] those who were neither circumcised Jews nor uncircumcised sympathizers with Judaism but worshipers of Mithra, Astarte or Zeus. It was here too, in Antioch about A.D. 40, that the followers of Jesus were called Christians; "Jew" would no longer serve to describe the new phenomenon.

It is uncertain what immediate reaction this provoked in the Jerusalem community. The elders there had already investigated in Samaria, and they sent another commission under Barnabas to Antioch about A.D. 38. Apparently they were satisfied. But there were others at Jerusalem who were not. At a later date some members of the Jerusalem Church went to Antioch, where the mission of Barnabas, who had since been joined by Paul, was enjoying considerable success. They announced to the Antiochene Christians that salvation was for the Jews who followed Christ and that therefore circumcision and the Law were binding upon the Christian. It must have been a stunning blow to the Church there. They dispatched Barnabas and Paul to Jerusalem— a clear indication of the leadership of the Mother Church—to plead their case before the leaders, Peter, John and James, "the brother of the Lord." The defense proved successful, and the elders at Jerusalem accepted the principle that at least for the Gentile followers of Jesus circumcision and observance of the Mosaic Law were not necessary for salvation; the only obligation of the "mission to the Gentiles" was to contribute to the support of the Church at Jerusalem.

This was not the end of the matter. Sometime after this, Peter went to Antioch and mixed freely with Jewish and Gentile Christians alike. The news of this must have come to the ears of James at Jerusalem, and he sent a delegation to Antioch to object:

---

10. The *ethne* (Latin, *gentes*) was the Septuagint designation for the "peoples" who were not part of Israel and hence were not true believers. The Christians adopted the same usage, using *ethne*, or simply "Hellenes," to describe those who were not Christians or Jews.

though Gentile Christians might be granted a share in salvation, as previously decided at the conference at Jerusalem, their intermingling with the Jewish Christians at common meals constituted a ritual defilement for the latter and so was forbidden. Peter was convinced by the argument, as was Barnabas; not so Paul. We hear no more of the business, but the Jewish view of the separation of Jewish and Gentile Christianity must have prevailed in Syria. Paul maintained relations with Jerusalem, but he never again preached south of the Taurus.

In the days before A.D. 70 the fissure in the community must have seemed of no great consequence. Peter, whose position in the controversy had been a moderate one, left Jerusalem, where James thus became the undisputed head of the Church. The Jerusalem group probably tried to make peace with the authorities, but the temple faction at least was not to be appeased. In A.D. 62 Ananus the High Priest, son of the Annas who had tried Jesus, took advantage of a change in the Roman command in Judaea and had James arrested and executed on grounds of transgressing the Law. Its position in Jerusalem had clearly become untenable so the Judaeo-Christian community migrated across the Jordan to the free city of Pella in the Decapolis; it must have been the very eve of the great revolt. At least some of them trickled back after the terrible destruction of A.D. 70, only to be savaged anew by Bar Kokhba and his followers in the uprising of A.D. 132–135.[11] It was the end. Henceforth Jerusalem, then Aelia Capitolina, was a bishopric of the Gentile Christians.

The fate of the other Judaeo-Christian communities, the remnant of Pella, is not easy to trace. They must have suffered from the increasingly violent polemic between the Jews and the Gentile Christians. The Gospels themselves, and particularly Matthew and John, products of the same era, reflect the growing antagonism, but it is most marked in documents like the *Letter to the Hebrews*, the *Letter of Barnabas*, and Justin's *Dialogue with Trypho*. The Jews for their part introduced a curse on the Christians into the synagogues and an anti-Christian oath into the liturgy. Caught in between were the Judaeo-Christians, rejected by the Jews and looked upon by Gentile Christianity as "half-Jew, half-Christian." When ambivalence passed into rejection we

---

11. The reasons are not difficult to suspect: The Christians' predictions of the destruction of the temple, their political withdrawal, as in A.D. 68–70, and their rejection of Bar Kokhba's Messianic claims.

cannot say,[12] but later writers at the time of the complete triumph of Gentile Christianity knew of obscure Judaeo-Christian sects in Syria which may have been descendants of the once proud Jerusalem Church. Such were the Nazoraeans and the Ebionites,[13] the latter characterized by the fact that they observed the Jewish Law and the Sabbath and practiced circumcision, demanding essentially the same things that James's legates had in Antioch. They repudiated Paul as an apostate from the Law. Their view of Jesus was that he was indeed the Messiah, a man born of intercourse between Joseph and Mary and so of unimpeachable Davidic descent. Of Paul's preexistent *Kyrios* or John's *Logos* they knew nothing. The groups likewise had their own Gospel, the *Gospel to the Hebrews*, possibly an Aramaic version of *Matthew* touched up to give a greater role to James.

The Christians at Jerusalem constituted the first Church (*ekklesia*),[14] and as such give an interesting picture of the earliest ecclesiastical organization. Jesus had appointed "apostles," twelve in number (the defector Judas was replaced by Matthias), to act as his representatives, with a position of special eminence given to Peter. Paul for his part understood "apostle" as a somewhat wider term, and his dealings with Jerusalem reveal that from an administrative point of view it was not the Twelve who governed the Church there, but rather Peter, James and John, and a body of elders (*presbyteroi*). It was only with the departure of Peter and the disappearance of John that James presided alone over the *presbyteroi*.

On their missionary travels Paul and Barnabas appointed "elders" in the churches of their ministry; in other places the same men are called "overseers" (*episkopoi*, bishops). The appointment of the seven Hellenists to serve as temporal administrators in Jerusalem has already been mentioned, the beginning of

---

12. Perhaps after Simeon, the successor of James as head of the Jerusalem Church.

13. Whether they were identical is uncertain, as is the derivation of the names of each. Throughout the Gospels Jesus is called a *Nazoraios*, traditionally interpreted as "man of Nazareth," a town mentioned frequently in the Gospels and, curiously, nowhere else. According to Jerome, the Jews used the term "Nazoraeans" to denote all Christians.

14. Very early the word had all its later connotations; a local community, the building in which it met, the total body of Christians (*ekklesia katholike*), both as an earthly and a heavenly institution.

the function and the office of deacon (*diakonos*). There were other proto-offices as well, though their function is not always clear; "prophets and teachers," for example, are mentioned in the early Church at Antioch.

The first disciples of Jesus in Jerusalem frequented the synagogues and participated in the temple ritual.[15] The baptism of initiates was practiced, as it was in Judaism. The center of the early Christian life of prayer, ritual, preaching and charitable activity was the celebration of the *eucharistia*. The earliest description of the Eucharistic banquet celebrated in commemoration of Jesus' Messianic banquet is that in Paul's first *Letter to the Corinthians*, and the text there, taken in conjunction with others in *Acts*, suggested that there were two different rituals originally celebrated at the same time, but later separated: the fellowship meal, or *agape* (and it was probably this that caused the dispute about ritual purity at Antioch), and the Eucharist proper, the latter present in kernel from the beginning of the life of the Church and gradually developed into a highly articulated form. The *Didache*, an ecclesiastical handbook from the second century, describes what is already a fairly sophisticated Eucharistic liturgy.[16] There was no question of church buildings at this point; the rites were celebrated in private homes. Public churches suggest public worship, and before the community could move in that direction it was forced underground by increasingly malevolent attention from Rome.

Gentile Christianity: The Churches of Asia and Antioch

Jesus died somewhere near the end of the third decade of the first century—the chronological carelessness of the evangelists makes exact computation difficult—and within twenty years of his death there were communities which had "received" and "held fast" to the tradition (*paradosis*) of his Messiahship not only in Palestine but at Alexandria, Cyprus, Antioch, Damascus and

---

15. It was Paul's participation in such that led to his arrest.
16. There were, of course, a great many local variations. The later standardization of the liturgy was a function of the growing centralization of the Christian Church.

Rome as well. The earliest preaching was done in synagogues and the converts were Jews, either Pharisees or Sadducees of strict observance or from the ranks of the *sebomenoi*, God-fearing Gentiles who worshiped the All High God but who were not bound to the more stringent observance of the Law or to circumcision. The Jews of the Diaspora were the first great instrument in the Christianization of the *oikoumene*.

The Hellenized synagogue was also the door to the wider world of Hellenism, and when certain of the Christians essayed the passage at Antioch it provoked first doubt and then recrimination in Judaeo-Christian circles. The missionary Paul was, as has been noted, involved in the controversy. He and Barnabas, his co-worker in Antioch, won, with the support of Peter, acceptance of the idea of a Gentile Christianity, but James and the elders at Jerusalem would not consent to the sharing of rites. The two Christianities would perforce have to go their own ways; Gentile Christianity to the conquest of the Roman Empire; Jewish Christianity to oblivion, as Gamaliel, the moderate Pharisee and Paul's teacher had predicted to the Sanhedrin that it would.[17]

Gentile Christianity was not the creation of Paul; it was he, however, who provided it with its theoretical justification. Paul, formerly Saul of the tribe of Benjamin, was born at Tarsus of Cilicia in the Diaspora, a Pharisee by persuasion, a student of Gamaliel of the rabbinical school of Hillel, and an early savage persecutor of the Jewish Christians. Pursuing them to Damascus he was converted en route by a vision of Christ, and devoted the rest of his life to spreading the "Good News" of Jesus, until his death in Rome, possibly during the Neronian persecution of A.D. 64.

The "Good News" disseminated by Paul in synagogues and public meetings from Antioch to Rome was not the canonical Gospels extant today (the earliest of them, Mark's, did not receive its final form until after Paul's death), but a highly per-

---

17. To support his proposal, which is reported in the *Acts of the Apostles*, Gamaliel cited the example of the earlier uprisings provoked by the incorporation of Judaea as a Roman province in A.D. 6. Gamaliel's choice of paradigm was not a happy one: guerrilla activity did *not* cease with the death of Judah the Galilean in A.D. 6, but was progressively organized by the Zealot party and was still a major threat to the peace of Palestine at the very time that Gamaliel was addressing the Sanhedrin.

sonalized view of the same tradition upon which the Gospels were based. His transmission was mediated by a personal revelation of Jesus, not "in the flesh," as was that of the eyewitnesses who passed down a picture of Jesus tied firmly to biographical detail, but rather "in the spirit." Paul's "Gospel," then, lies somewhere under the surface of the letters that he addressed to the churches to which he and others had carried the "Good News." The *Letters* are not themselves a Gospel; they confirm or correct a Gospel that had already been proclaimed in those churches.

The early Church recognized Paul's claim to Apostleship and included his *Letters* in the canon of the New Testament. It placed them, however, for all their chronological priority, after the four Gospels. As far as the synoptic Gospels are concerned, the arrangement is correct. The synoptic tradition, whatever the place and date of its final redaction, represents a view of Jesus that is Palestinian, a more primitive and more immediate tradition than that of the Pauline *Letters*. Mark, Matthew and Luke may have had some shaping at the hands of the several churches, but this is minimal when compared to the direct stamp of Paul's own personality on his Gospel. There is very little sign of the anonymous, self-effacing oral tradition in Paul. In the Gospels the Church had seen Christ; in the *Letters*, the individual, Paul, had. There is no question but that they saw the same reality; Paul saw Jesus, however, in a perspective that was personally narrower but intellectually wider.

Paul was a Pharisee, a Jew of the Jews, and his approach to Christianity was not, as some once thought, that of an Athenian philosopher or of some adept of a Hellenistic mystery cult. He accepted the Torah and the other writings of the Jewish Scriptures, which at this stage still included everything in the Septuagint version, and as a Pharisee he sought to interpret them in the light of the oral tradition, the *mishnah*, that he had "received" from Gamaliel. Paul's break with Judaism was one of substance, not method. There could be, of course, no new Torah, but the breaking-in of the Messiahship of Jesus provided a new *mishnah*, a new "handing down" (*paradosis*), which Paul had himself received,[18] and which he then transmitted orally to the churches;

---

18. Perhaps not so charismatically as first appears. After his conversion, Paul eventually went up to Jerusalem where he "conversed" with Peter for two weeks. It was his first contact with the Church and the

his *Letters* are his exegesis of it. Again one is confronted with the difference between the Gospels and the *Letters;* the Gospels are the *mishnah* of Christianity in written form; the Pauline *Letters* form part of its *talmud.*

That Paul operated within the same general lines of the Christian tradition as its other proclaimers can be seen in one of the few places in the *Letters* where the original *paradosis* lies close to the exegetical surface. I *Corinthians* 15:1–11 appears to be a schematized summary of the "Good News": Christ died for our sins, according to the Scripture. He was buried. He rose on the third day, again in accordance with Scripture. He was seen by Peter, then by the Twelve, then by more than five hundred of the Brethren (most of whom were still alive), then by James. Paul concludes with the cachet of authority, ". . . and last of all by me."

This is the heart of the New Dispensation as expounded by Paul in letters to his Churches of the Christian *diaspora*. His instruction sweeps over a variety of topics, ethical behavior, Church order and discipline, liturgical usage, all highly revelatory of the life of the early Church, and each characterized by an assurance and authority in teaching that betrays Paul's confidence in his sharing of the apostolic tradition. And of his new grasp of Scripture: an essential part of the *kerygma* cited from I *Corinthians* is that the death and resurrection of Jesus took place *according to Scripture*. This imposed another obligation on the early community, to reexamine the Scriptures in the light of their new understanding. Jesus had constantly referred himself back to the Torah tradition, and the Church (and Paul) continued the practice.

Paul's position vis-à-vis the Law and the Scripture was a paradoxical one. He continued to view the Jewish Scriptures—as Jesus had regarded them—as the words of God, and at the same time to preach, in the face of opposition from Jerusalem, the Christian's freedom from the Law promulgated in those same Scriptures. Others were to go to even greater lengths and proclaim freedom from both the Law and the Old Testament. For the Jewish Paul the later position, a product of Gnosticism not of Judaism, was probably unthinkable. The abrogation of the Law

---

Apostolic College, and it may also have marked his reception of the *paradosis* and a rabbinic "laying-on of hands."

was difficult enough. "Are we using belief in Christ to rob the Law of its force?" asked Paul. "No, we are setting the Law on its right footing."

The guarantee of a true understanding of Scriptures was a special knowledge (*gnosis*) given to the Apostles; its implementation was the exegesis of those Scriptures. Much of this latter Paul could work out in accordance with contemporary rabbinical rules of hermeneutics, which he doubtless knew well enough.[19] But the *spirit* of his approach to Scripture owed a great deal as well to the modes and expressions visible among the sectaries of later Judaism, the Hellenizers of the Diaspora, and such local groups as the Qumran community.[20] The former came to the Scriptures allegorically in the manner of the Hellenistic schools, and the latter as foreshadowing in an apocalyptic fashion the coming of the Messiah. Paul drew from both. His allegorical interpretation of the children of Sarah and Hagar in *Genesis* is worthy of Philo, and the *Letters* are filled with typological readings of the Old Testament, including the apocalypses. But a Hellenizer like Philo read the Torah allegorically to justify its integration with the best of the Hellenic tradition; Paul used the Torah (and, unlike Philo, the Prophets) to convince the Jews from their own Scripture that the Law had been abrogated.

This penchant for allegory, shared by the later Church even after the immediate Pauline point was unnecessary, was not Paul's only connection with the Diaspora version of Judaism and with the Hellenic milieu that surrounded it. In *Colossians* and *Ephesians* there are references to what appears to be a full-blown Gnosticism at work in the Christian community.[21] There are, of course, Greek ideas in the *Letters* themselves, clad in a far more sophisticated language than that found in the Gospels, but it seems likely that the bulk of such concepts, apart from the jargon terms current in the cities of Asia, were already present in Hellenistic Judaism. Paul is far less the Hellene than he at first appears; it was Judaism itself that was Hellenized.

For Paul the drama of the Incarnation was the final revelation of the "mystery" of God, that divine plan for salvation conceived by God from all eternity and now put before men. The Gospels

---

19. Particularly the arguments of the "school" (*beth*) of Hillel to which he had belonged.
20. See Chapter VIII, pp. 328–30.
21. See Chapter XVIII, p. 654 ff.

themselves had used the same expression, *mysterion*, in an almost identical sense: "the *mysterion* of the Kingdom of God." The Hellenized reader of Paul or of the Gospels in the third or fourth century of the Christian era would doubtless have been reminded of the *mysteria*—always in the plural—of Isis or Mithra. It is somewhat less likely that the first-century authors of those works had the same things in mind.

The once popular inclination to see in Christianity a highly derivative mystery religion rested upon two major premises, which have since crumbled away. The first was that where Christian Scripture and the pagan mysteries used a term in common, the term was a technical one in the mysteries and was used knowingly as such by the Christians. The presumption generally ignored two important pieces of linguistic evidence: the Greek terminology already present in and popularized by the Septuagint, and the free currency of many of the terms used in the mysteries in the common speech of the Mediterranean.

The second premise, which at closer inspection proved illusory, was that the mysteries were as popular and as widespread in the first Christian century as they were in the third, from which most of our evidence on them derives, or that they had at Christianity's beginnings the same form and implication they later possessed. By the time Peter died at Rome the mystery cults were only beginning to lodge themselves in the capital. They were still very much disreputable foreign religions with notoriously lax moral standards. The more spacious and enlightened mysteries that converted Isis from a whore to a saint were the creation of a later time, and it is not unlikely that the obvious spiritualization of their moral teaching, far from providing a paradigm for Christianity, may have itself been a result of the mysteries' being influenced by Christianity.

Students of the origins of Christianity have given over the pagan mysteries as an understandable but essentially incorrect choice of matrix. Jesus of Nazareth and his immediate followers knew and cared little for vegetation gods. Jesus belonged to history, not myth, a fact that made his death and resurrection almost totally incomprehensible to a Greek rationalist, for whom the gods died seasonally in mythic time and certainly not during the Passover of A.D. 28. The breaking into history of the *mysterion* of the Kingdom of God was absolutely alien to every ancient religion except Christianity—and Judaism.

Jesus and Paul were both Jews; their historical and religious antecedents and their frame of reference was the Judaism not only of the Torah and the Prophets but the Septuagint transformations, the *apocrypha*, the Messianic apocalypses, the sectaries, known and unknown, of Palestine and the Diaspora. Jesus' claims were Messianic, not Adonisiac. His baptism and his last supper with his disciples owed nothing to the remote *taurobolium* or the vaguely realized meals of the mysteries; they were rather direct continuations of practices current in Palestine during Jesus' own lifetime.

Paul's vocabulary was somewhat more sophisticated in the manner of one who grew up in Tarsus and preached in the *oikoumene*. But he betrays no great curiosity in the mystery religions, and there is no suggestion in the *Letters* that these cults were so unavoidably present that one could not help but form Christianity in their image.[22] Paul understood enough about the intellectual currents of the times to address the Athenians on the Areopagus with the Stoic commonplace arguments they understood, but he preached in the first instance to Jews, and with them he employed the syncretisms of ecumenical Judaism. His approach appears clearly in his treatment of the Messiahship of Jesus.

In the Gospels Jesus is presented as the Messianic Son of David who had triumphed over death and whose Second Coming was expected. He is the Humbled Servant of Isaiah, but also the transcendent "Son of the Living God." Paul moved forward. His *one* Lord (*Kyrios*) is Jesus Christ, as contrasted to the many gods and *kyrioi* of this world.[23] The contrast between the Humbled Servant and the transcendent Jesus is worked out in detail in the second chapter of *Philippians:* Christ Jesus, existing in the condition of God, "emptied himself," taking on the condition of a slave by assuming the likeness of man. He debased himself to a

---

22. Christians of a later generation, when the mysteries *did* appear to be everywhere, could not help but see the resemblances between those rites and their own developing sacramental system. Justin and Tertullian knew far more about Mithra than Paul did, and they could see the analogies that never occurred to Paul. They had no explanation to offer except that Satan had maliciously concocted the pagan forms in the image of Christianity to lead souls astray.

23. *Kyrios* was the translation of Yahweh in the Septuagint, but Paul's paralleling it here with the deities of the Greek world is significant.

death on the cross, wherefore God raised him up above all creation, giving him a name above all names, *Kyrios*. Further, his reign is cosmic; just as he rules over the *ekklesia* on earth, Jesus Christ is also the Lord of Creation reigning over the powers and principalities of the cosmic world.

The climate here not only is that of a Messianic King come into his Kingdom,[24] but owes something as well to late Jewish speculation on the Wisdom (*Sophia*) of God as a quasi-hypostatized entity that both reveals God[25] and is an instrument in God's creation of the *kosmos*. All of this is familiar from Philo, but the gap between the two men is equally apparent, underlined by Paul's strong language in describing the second act of the redemptive drama, the "emptying" and "humiliation" of the Christ in becoming man.

The dramatic change of existential state implicit in the incarnation of the Son of God and described by Paul in *Philippians* and elsewhere received its classic theoretical formulation in one of Paul's successors in the Asian churches, the author of the fourth of the canonical Gospels, John,[26] who died at Ephesus during the reign of Trajan (A.D. 98–117). In the prologue to his Gospel, John describes Jesus as the Word (*Logos*) of God which became flesh (*sarx*). The Word, like the Jesus of Paul, is both the revelation of God in the world and the instrument of its creation. Again the context is the wisdom literature of Judaism, particularly *Sirach* and *Proverbs*. But John reached in another direction for his designation: it was not the female *Sophia* he was describing, but the male *Logos*, a word and a concept with a long history in Greek speculative thought and a short but spectacular

---

24. This was the image that was to dominate the portrayal of Christ in eastern religious art. *Christos Pantokrator*, Christ the Ruler of All, enthroned in majesty, was pervasive in Byzantine fresco and mosaic. It was not until the early Middle Ages that the western Church began to turn to the image of the Humbled Servant and to depict the crucified Jesus in realistic terms.

25. Compare Paul's use of Jesus as an image (*eikon*) of God.

26. The identification which became traditional from the time of Irenaeus (*c*. A.D. 180) was with the "beloved disciple" of the Gospels. Modern scholarship, however, leans to another author, perhaps the "John the Elder" of the letters under that name. But the fourth Gospel, which stands apart from the synoptic tradition in other regards, does show strong evidence of at least some eyewitness material and a considerable knowledge of Palestinian geography.

one in the system of Philo. The *Logos* of John was not, however, that of the Stoics, which was by nature immanent in the world, nor that of Philo, for whom the *Logos* had a metaphysical condition intermediate between God and man and was quite incapable of "becoming flesh" in any sense understood by John. And yet the prologue may have owed something to both lines of thought and stood, at any rate, as an open invitation to a Gentile reader to understand the Christ, a title which had become for the Greeks, who knew nothing of Messiahs, a name, within the philosophical cadres familiar to them.

Such an invitation, no matter what the Jewish antecedent of John's Gospel, was but another sign of the changing fortunes of Christianity. Judaism's rejection of its progeny was an accomplished fact by A.D. 100. Paul had been thrust from the orthodox synagogues of Asia and Greece in the middle of the first century. James was executed by the Sanhedrin in A.D. 62. Matthew's Gospel, probably a product of Syria in the eighties, shows characteristic anti-Jewish additions to the narrative it had inherited from the synoptic tradition,[27] and by the time of John the parties responsible for Jesus' death were simply "the Jews."

Judaism's refusal was compensated by the eastern Gentiles' ready acceptance of the Christ. There were churches all over Asia, many of them founded upon Paul's *paradosis*, and the venerable Polycarp, a disciple of the Apostles themselves, governed the Church at Smyrna until his martyrdom in A.D. 155.[28] Formal catechetical instruction was begun at Alexandria before A.D. 190. But it was, after all, at Antioch that the "Mission to the Gentiles" had begun and where it flourished most richly.

An early tradition made Peter the first bishop of the Church of Antioch, before Evodus and Ignatius. The tradition is not impossible, and that Peter worked there on occasion is almost certainly true; but it is difficult to reconcile a lengthy stay there with the Roman tradition of a twenty-five-year-long episcopacy in the capital before his death there in A.D. 64. In Jerusalem James governed in concert with a collegium of elders, and there is no visible distinction in being between the bishop and the presbyters. The same was probably true at Rome. But at Antioch by

---

27. Including the terrible *demand* for collective guilt put in the mouth of "all the people": "His blood be upon us and upon our children."
28. In the account of his martyrdom the anti-Jewish element is still present.

the time of the leadership of Ignatius (d. A.D. 116) the principle of a monarchial as opposed to a collegiate bishop was firmly established, as was the distinction of Church orders into *episkopos, presbyteroi* and *diakonoi*. The responsibilities of the bishop were clearly set forth: to supervise the liturgy and the sacraments, and, in general, to preside over the life of the Church. At about the same time, the notion that these same bishops held office as successors of the Apostles was taken for granted. The shape of the early Church had all but completely emerged.

The Spreading of the Good News

On the basis of the manuscript tradition alone, the works that made up the Christian's New Testament were the most frequently copied and widely circulated books of antiquity. The proliferation had little to do with readership; each community had to have at least one copy for use in the liturgy. There are some sixty-eight preserved papyrus fragments that date from the second to the fourth century, the oldest written about A.D. 120, a very short time after the redaction of the Gospels. The four great manuscripts embracing almost all of the Old and New Testaments, and upon which all modern editions of the Gospels are based are likewise surprisingly early:[29] the *Codex Vaticanus*[30] from the beginning of the fourth century, the *Codex Sinaiticus*[31] from the middle of the same century, and the two fifth-century manuscripts, the *Codex Alexandrinus*[32] and the *Codex Ephraemi rescriptus*.[33]

Each of these is a *codex,* a manuscript in book form, a fact

---

29. The first completely preserved text of Homer, for instance, another widely read author, dates from the thirteenth century, and the oldest complete Hebrew manuscripts of the Bible from the tenth century.

30. In the Vatican Library since 1475.

31. Discovered in 1844 in the monastery of St. Catherine in Sinai and preserved in the Leningrad Museum until 1933, when the Soviet government sold it to the British Museum.

32. From 1098 to 1751 in the Patriarchal Library at Alexandria and now in the British Museum.

33. So called because parts of the original Scripture texts were erased and written over with some treatises of Ephraem the Syrian. The manuscript is now in the Bibliothèque Nationale in Paris.

which may explain the explosion of New Testament manuscripts over the ancient world. Since the seventh or sixth century B.C. the Greeks had written on papyrus and gathered the single or joined sheets into rolls.[34] But between the second and fourth centuries of the Christian era there was a sudden and radical displacement of these *volumina* by the *codex*, whose papyrus pages were bound at one edge and leaved in the manner of a modern book. The papyrus was shortly replaced by parchment, a material more suitable to the *codex* form, so that from the fourth century down to the introduction of paper in the eighth the standard form of the eastern book was the parchment *codex*. Such books seem to have been known at Rome at a somewhat earlier time— Martial refers to them—but by all appearances their prodigious spread over the Mediterranean was due to the Christians' adopting the format to make copies of their Bible, whence the use spread to non-Christian literature as well.

Another feature of these early Christian manuscripts is their inclusion of the Old Testament. The juxtaposition of the two Scriptures, a perfectly natural one for later Christians, was by no means as easy or as obvious in the second century. What is implicit in such a combination is the affirmation of continuity with a Jewish tradition that had already rejected the affiliation. Christianity had rejected Judaism as well; Paul preached a freedom from the Law for his Gentile converts, a freedom which the Jewish branch of Christianity had denied to itself and others.

The position eventually taken by the Church was a compromise between the Judaeo-Christian acceptance of the Law and another view that was gaining ground in the middle of the second century, and which was associated with the Gnostic Marcion. Son of a Christian bishop of Pontus, Marcion was already a wealthy man when he came to Rome about A.D. 138 and gave generous gifts to the Church there. Apparently there were strings attached, and the gifts were later returned. But Marcion was no mere dabbler in ecclesiastical politics. Marcion showed that logic demanded that if the Law of the Old Testament was abrogated by the coming of Christ, then the Old Testament itself had been voided and should be discarded. There was, moreover, internal

---

34. The Latin *volumen;* the Greek term was either *biblion* (from Byblos, the Phoenician point of import of the papyri) or *chartes.* Liturgical copies of the Torah are still preserved in roll form in synagogues.

evidence for the correctness of his position. In his work *The Antitheses* Marcion picked over the Old Testament to show the moral and ethical contradictions between it and the Gospels. The Jewish Scripture was merely the record of the works of the God of Hate, canceled and contradicted by the message of the God of Love.

A retort to this had been developing in the churches for some time. Jesus himself had interpreted the Old Testament typologically, and the same kind of nonliteral approach to the Jewish Scriptures was taken up and developed by Paul. Marcion had, of course, to reject allegorical interpretation as an unnecessary attempt to "save" what was at root alien to the Christian tradition. He could accept the Paul who had announced the abrogation of the Law, but not the other tendentious documents that described Jesus as an outgrowth of Judaism. The Marcionite Church—a mirror image of the Christian Church—thus set itself to delimiting the apostolic tradition, the first Church to have done so, and promulgated a canon of authoritative Scripture: the "non-Jewish" Gospel of Luke (with deletions) and some of the *Letters* of Paul.

Marcion's talents were not as a theologian—metaphysics was probably secondary in his considerations—but his earlier success as a businessman presaged his real abilities, those of an organizer and a propagandist. Marcionite churches multiplied rapidly. At the beginning of the third century Tertullian commented that they had "filled the whole world," and in the fourth century Epiphanius found them lodged in Italy, Egypt, Palestine, Arabia, Syria, Cyprus, the Thebaid and Persia. Part of the reaction of the orthodox was to hasten the enunciation of their own canon, in which they definitely accepted the Old Testament as a work of divine inspiration and admitted, by implication, the corollary of its allegorical interpretation.

Other pressures were at work as well. At a synod held at Jabneh sometime after A.D. 70 the rabbinic leadership had drawn up a list of books considered genuinely Scriptural by the Jewish community.[35] Much of the apocalyptic literature was omitted. The first Christians who preached in the Diaspora had followed the earlier Jewish example and used whatever they found in the Septuagint version of the Scriptures. But when, after Jabneh, the

---

35. See Chapter XIV, pp. 535–36.

Jews narrowed their Scriptural base—doubtless as a reaction to the Christians' constant use of the convenient Messianic predictions—it posed a problem for the eastern Christians, whether to go along with the Jews and remove from the canon such things as *Enoch* (they did) and *Tobias* or *Maccabees* (they did not). In the end the question of canonicity was taken up by a series of local church councils beginning with Laodicea in the fourth century and extending down to the Council *in Trullo*, which in A.D. 692 drew up a definitive canon for the eastern churches.[36]

For most Christians, whether Judaizers or Hellenists, the inclusion of the Old Testament in the Christians' world view created no insuperable difficulties. The logic of Marcion might dictate its discard together with the Law, but the habit of treating it allegorically was a firmly rooted one. Philo had done so for the Hellenists of his day, and two hundred years later Origen was continuing the practice in Alexandria, this time under Christian auspices.[37] But Origen had problems that had confronted neither Philo nor Paul. By the beginning of the third century there were in circulation new Greek versions of the Jewish Scriptures, and the Jews themselves were casting doubts on the reliability of the Septuagint text.[38]

The problem probably would not have bothered Paul; his attitude in purely textual matters was rabbinical rather than Hellenistic. Origen belonged to a different milieu. As a scholar, he deemed texts important, and to provide a sounder base for his own work, chiefly commentaries on Scripture, he attempted to correct and reestablish the Septuagint text by subjecting it to the kind of comparative collation that had been going on in the secular schools of Alexandria for centuries. The outcome was the *Hexapla*, or Sixfold Bible, arranging in parallel columns the Hebrew text of the Old Testament, its transliteration into Greek characters to clarify the pronunciation, and then the four current translations into Greek, all done under Jewish auspices: Aquila, Symmachus, the Septuagint and Theodotion. The Septuagint could then be annotated with the various diacritical signs used by

---

36. This Council still did not accept the *Apocalypse of John*, the only purely apocalyptic work with a claim for inclusion in the New Testament. The western churches canonized it, but the eastern Patriarchates did not follow suit until the fourteenth century.

37. See Chapter XVII, p. 627.

38. See Chapter XIV, pp. 535–36.

the Alexandrian editors of Homer to denote additions or lacunae. From it emerged a sounder text of the Greek Old Testament.

Marcion's limitation of the apostolic tradition to the Gospel of Luke raised similar questions regarding the New Testament canon. But what may have been even more pressing than the Marcionite exclusion of certain books was the rapid growth of a body of apocryphal literature within the Church itself. Like Judaism, Christianity was constructed upon the notion of a "handing down" of tradition from authentic "fathers," in the case of Christianity from the original Apostles, whose authority rested upon their witnessing of the risen Christ. Very quickly there began to circulate under just such apostolic titles a number of Gospel narratives that proposed to fill in the gaps in the life of Jesus or describe the deeds of the Apostles after Pentecost. Some were surely the product of a popular and pious desire to know more of Jesus, and where authentic tradition failed, folk or literary imagination did not hesitate to supply details.[39] Others, however, were of somewhat more disingenuous origin and were constructed to support, by supplying an authentic apostolic base, a particular doctrinal point of view. The Gnostics in particular availed themselves of the "silent Apostles" to write their own Gospels.[40]

Though a complete New Testament canon did not immediately appear, there was early agreement on the authoritative claim of the four Gospels of *Matthew, Mark, Luke* and *John*, the Pauline *Letters*,[41] and the "Catholic Letters" of I John and I Peter. There were lingering doubts about the *Letters* of James and Jude, II Peter, and II and III John, and, particularly in the East, about the *Apocalypse of John.*[42]

Many of the apocryphal "Gospels" circulated in languages

39. Such, for instance, was the *Protoevangelium of James*, a Gospel of the infancy of Jesus that had an enormous influence on Christian art.
40. See Chapter XVIII, p. 653.
41. Modern criticism doubts that everything included in the canon under his name is really by Paul. *Titus, Timothy* and *Hebrews* are all suspect, though doubtless they are early.
42. Most of this information goes back to Papias and Irenaeus, bishops in the middle of the second century, and has been preserved in Eusebius' *Ecclesiastical History*. Another testimony is the *Muratorian Canon* written down in Latin in the eighth century but from a second-century Greek original.

other than Greek. Shortly after their foundation the Christian Churches of the Diaspora began speaking in a variety of tongues. The original Greek of the New Testament was undoubtedly the single best vehicle of transmission in the Mediterranean *oikoumene,* but the *koine* did not penetrate very deeply into the native cultures outside the large cities. The native population of Egypt, for example, where the knowledge of Greek was constantly shrinking, had need of their own version of Scripture; and, on the testimony of the biography of the first hermit Anthony, there was a fairly complete translation of the Gospels into Coptic in circulation about A.D. 250. There must have been a similar Latin version in use before A.D. 200, not for the Roman Church (which was still Greek-speaking until later in that same century) but for the African churches, which were more directly the products of a purely Latin culture.

A major focal point of non-Hellenic Christianity in the East was Edessa in the former kingdom of Osrhoene, where there was a native—and cultured—community of Christians at an early date. What was in use there was not simply a translation, but a Syriac "harmony" of the Gospels—that is, a blending of the separate accounts into a single continuous narrative, a type of text that suggests that the need of these early churches was a liturgical one. This Syriac "combination of four" (*diatessaron*) was the work of Tatian, the eccentric Syrian scholar who had worked at Rome in the middle of the second century.[43] Whether he originally composed it in Syriac is unknown,[44] but the *Diatessaron* was, for all practical purposes, *the* text of the Gospels in Syria into the fifth century. Beginning in the fourth century there was as well a Syriac version of the separate Gospels that gained ground in the Syrian monastic communities, and held there, even in the face of the version that was to become the vulgate of the Syrian Church, the *Peshitta.*[45]

---

43. See Chapter XVII, p. 621.

44. Tatian's other theological works are in Greek, though doubtless he knew Syriac. There are versions of the *diatessaron* extant in almost all the European languages, but the original is no longer at hand.

45. There were at least two translations or revisions subsequent to the *Peshitta,* both done under Monophysite sponsorship. One, at the beginning of the fifth century, was under the direction of Philoxenus, bishop of Mabbugh, and the other, done in A.D. 616, was the work of Thomas of Heraclea, an eminent product of the school of Greek studies at Qennesre on the Euphrates.

The continuing series of Syriac translations from the *diatessaron* down to the Harclean version at the beginning of the seventh century throws an interesting light on the spiritual and intellectual life of the Christians in Syria. The earliest versions are almost paraphrases, a retelling of the Gospel narrative in Syriac. Progressively, as the notion of a sacred text grew stronger, the translators came closer and closer to the original, first *translating,* as in the *Peshitta*, and finally *reproducing* the original Greek in Syriac, as in the Harclean, with little regard for either the syntax or the style of the Syriac tongue. And yet it was a valuable experience; the Syrians were the most accomplished and sophisticated translators in the East, fully in command of the Greek original, whether Scriptural or theological, and it was they who mediated the passage of Hellenism into both their native culture and that of their eventual conquerors, the Arabs.

By the time Christianity passed into the Syrian hinterland, Trajan's Roman legions had already taken up their position there. The imperialism of Trajan had, however, far less an impact on the consciousness of early Christianity than events somewhat closer to home, the destruction that visited Jewish Palestine under Titus and Hadrian, and the Christians' own growing involvement with the legal and political arms of the Roman state. From Jesus' own execution by order of Tiberius' Procurator in Judaea the fortunes of Christianity were bound to those of the Empire.

XIV

Violence and Growth under the Pax Romana

Tiberius' (A.D. 14–37) administration of his eastern provinces was neither timid nor adventuresome. Parthia was the chief danger, and Armenia usually the issue. Tiberius was content to show the flag when necessary, as in his sending out of Germanicus in A.D. 17–19, or again in A.D. 34–35 when Artabanus III thought the occasion ripe (the occasion being, as usual, the death of an Armenian king) to test Rome's resolve in Armenia. Tiberius' man on this occasion was Vitellius, who as legate in Syria not only managed to seat the Roman candidate in Armenia but so weakened the power and prestige of Artabanus that the Parthian king was forced to send one of his sons as a hostage to Rome. But Tiberius' successes with Parthia served merely to distract from what was to be a major source of Roman discomfort for the next century, Palestine.

Toward a Solution in Palestine

In Judaea the Roman authority was represented since the removal of Archelaus in A.D. 6 by a series of Procurators dependent upon the Imperial legate in Syria. It was a position that required both firmness and tact. From Hellenistic times the Jews had been granted royal privilege, and the Romans from Augustus on confirmed the privilege of "living according to their ancestral laws." What this meant was in some instances spelled out, the right to observe the Sabbath (and the corollary exemption from military service), to collect and send money to Jerusalem, to preserve the ritual purity of the temple.[1] In other important areas, however, the privilege remained vague. There was, for instance, no *specific* exemption from Emperor worship, though this would seem to recognize and legitimize the entire High Priest establishment in Jerusalem. A Roman governor, then, in dealing with the Jews was bound by statutes that were couched in general terms and faced by a people jealous of their rights.

The deposition of Archelaus and the Roman assumption of direct rule held other hazards. During Herod's early career as governor of Galilee he had tracked down and destroyed a certain Hezekiah who had been terrorizing the area between Galilee and Damascus. At the death of Herod in B.C. 4, Hezekiah's son Judah made his appearance, taking advantage of the disorders of the times to break into the royal armories. By A.D. 6 Judah was preaching open revolt against the Romans. His issue was the payment of the Roman poll tax that had been vividly heralded by the tax census taken by Quirinus in A.D. 6. Around Judah grew up the party of "Zealots,"[2] whose program was complete independence from Rome to be achieved by violence if necessary and not excluding assassination.

The career of Pontius Pilate as Procurator of Judaea covered the last ten years of Tiberius' reign (A.D. 26–36)[3] and witnessed not only the turmoil surrounding the trial and execution of Jesus,[4] but troubles arising from his own desire to assert Roman authority in the face of the "ancestral laws." In an incident involving the introduction into Jerusalem of Roman standards with their offensive icons of the Emperors, Pilate backed off in the face of stiff Jewish opposition. Another of his projects was the construction of an aqueduct, for which he expropriated some of the temple funds. The Jews again resisted, but here Pilate had his way, violently. His violence led to his undoing, and Pilate was

---

1. A number of these statutes have been recorded by Josephus in his *Jewish Antiquities*.
2. There was probably a party member in the entourage of Jesus, Simon (*Matt.* 10:4), whose presence may explain the test question on the tax put to Jesus by the Pharisees and Herodians in *Matthew* 22:15–22.
3. Long tenures in these posts was a feature of Tiberius' administrative policy.
4. Where his role has almost certainly been retouched in the Gospels to shift the principal onus from the Romans to the Jews.

recalled by Tiberius in A.D. 36 for a massacre of some Samaritans. Tiberius died before a trial could take place.

The brief reign (A.D. 37–41) of Germanicus' son Gaius (Caligula, "Bootsie") appears to be constructed of half madness and half design, or perhaps madness born of a design which his contemporaries traced to the influence of his two youthful eastern friends, Herod Agrippa of Judaea and Antiochus of Commagene.[5] Agrippa, grandson of Herod the Great, grew up in Rome and was eventually granted by his friend Gaius the territories formerly ruled by his uncles Antipas and Philip as tetrarchs; Agrippa, however, ruled them as a king. This was a curious reversion to the Republican policy of client kings, and though it may be construed as a design of state it is equally likely that Gaius in his derangement preferred to rule as an emperor over kings rather than as a *princeps* over governors.

Gaius labored at his own deification, claiming brotherhood with Jupiter. The eastern Hellenes could take this claim in stride as they had all other such, but it was quite otherwise in the Jewish communities, which had had other troubles with Roman effigies. There were outbursts of violence between the Jews and the citizens of Alexandria and Antioch,[6] and an incident in Judaea that could have caused, except for the prudence of the governor of Syria, open insurrection or a mass slaughter. Gaius' conviction of his own divinity prompted him to dispatch Petronius, his legate in Syria, to Jerusalem in A.D. 39 with orders to set up his image in the temple, by force if necessary. A great number of Jews went out to meet Petronius in Galilee and managed to convince him that he would be forced to kill them to carry out the Emperor's command. The governor held off and fortunately Gaius died before he could force the issue further—which he apparently had every intention of doing.

The events in Alexandria and Antioch were of a more sinister

---

5. Another member of Gaius' set was Ptolemy of Mauretania, grandson of Mark Antony by way of a marriage that Augustus engineered between Antony's daughter Cleopatra Selene and Juba of Mauretania.
6. One reads "Alexandrians," "citizens of Antioch," et cetera, in the sources. It would be interesting and important to know on each occasion whether the groups referred to are the local Hellenes, the local Egyptians, or whatever. The physiognomy of these riots is very obscure.

kind. Both cities had large and thriving Jewish communities that were attacked by local groups all during the days of Gaius' reign. The worst outburst in Antioch occurred in A.D. 40, and though it started as a squabble among the always volatile factions at the hippodrome it quickly turned against the Jews, many of whom were killed and whose synagogues were burned. The exact cause is not known. There must surely have been turmoil in the Jewish community, not only because of the previous winter's events in Jerusalem but because of its own schisms brought on by the activity there of Jewish sectaries of Jesus, an increasingly difficult problem in the synagogues of Asia. Or the rioting may have been a ground swell of the even more serious disturbances in Alexandria.

In A.D. 37, Agrippa I, friend of Gaius and now ruler of a petty Jewish kingdom in Palestine, visited the Egyptian capital and provided the spark to ignite the combustible ingredients that had always been there. Egypt had long been a breeding ground of a particularly virulent strain of anti-Semitism, but on this occasion there were constitutional issues at stake as well. As far as the events can be reconstructed, the Jews of Alexandria had been raising, from the time of Augustus, the question of their civil rights. Since the days of the Ptolemies they had lived in their own *politeuma* and exercised a degree of self-government without any notable disabilities. But with the coming of the Romans a new fiscal ingredient was added in the form of a poll tax (*laographia*)[7] of the type the Palestinian Jews had to pay, under protest, from A.D. 6. The Jews of Alexandria, it would appear, did not enjoy what was termed *isopoliteia* and which amounted to municipal citizenship. In many places there was a financial condition for the holding of this privilege, but such was clearly not the problem in Alexandria, where the Jews were generally well off. Nor were the Egyptian Jews unwilling to take the classic route to civil rights, the one that led through the gymnasium of the *ephebeia* and Hellenization. What was unspoken in the entire controversy was the degree to which a Jew, even had he been granted isopolity, could participate in municipal life without worshiping the gods of the state. The Jews were already exempt

---

7. The normal distinction was between the *demos*, the citizenry who had civil rights in a community, and the *laos*, the "people" who did not. The head tax was levied on the latter.

from this as one of their "ancestral customs"; apparently they considered the rights of isopolity worth having in themselves.[8]

The other Alexandrians, faced with the loss of the poll-tax revenue and agitated by their own considerable dislike for the Jews, seized on the visit of Agrippa to practice political blackmail on the Roman prefect of Egypt, Flaccus—he had backed Gaius' rival for Emperor—to stir up trouble against the Jews. Various provocative gestures were made against both the person of Agrippa and the synagogues of the Jews. Provocation led to riot and finally to massacre, all with the acquiescence of Flaccus.

Both Flaccus and the unfortunate Gaius disappeared from the scene, but as soon as Claudius succeeded in A.D. 41 the dispute was resumed in his presence. A copy of his decision has been preserved and in it he reaffirms the privileges granted to the Jews of Egypt since Augustus, but quite clearly denies the petition for isopolity. The Jews were forbidden to go through the gymnasia and become citizens. Presumably the poll tax stood. Rome appeared to be raising the price of isopolity beyond Hellenization to defection. The Jews of the Diaspora might be willing, and even eager, to embrace Hellenism, but the latter price was too high,[9] as Philo had attempted to explain to Gaius earlier.

According to Philo's account, Flaccus had hoped that the attacks against the Jews would spread to other lands and perhaps the disturbances at Antioch were a fulfillment of his wish. In both Antioch and Alexandria, however large the Jewish population of the latter might be,[10] the Jews were in a minority. In Palestine, on the other hand, they were the majority, and so there the possibilities of disaster, already foreseen by Flaccus, were close at hand should the Jews attempt to test the limits of Roman authority.

---

8. As they were to Paul, who claimed them for his own juridical protection in *Acts* 21. That Paul could possibly have been a full "Roman citizen" is quite another matter.

9. Not, of course, for all. How far and how high one could go by that route can be seen from the career of Philo's nephew Tiberius Julius Alexander who was Procurator of Judaea (A.D. 46–48), then on Corbulo's staff in Armenia, Prefect of Egypt where he was among the first to acclaim Vespasian Emperor, and on Titus' staff before Jerusalem in A.D. 70. He had, of course, defected from Judaism.

10. Philo says that there were one million Jews in Egypt out of a total population reckoned by Josephus at seven and a half million. Philo's figure seems quite high.

The Roman Emperors could scarcely be called indifferent to Jewish affairs. At Rome their attention was not always benevolent, since the unassimilable colony of Jews there had its occasional troubles, and the Emperor, who was charged with the responsibility for good order in the capital, would take the normal repressive steps against the Jews as against others. On at least two occasions, under Tiberius and Claudius, Jews were deported from Rome, and on the second of these occasions the unrest may well have been a result of schismatic struggles with the Christians. Claudius may have lumped them together; but by the time of Nero, the Emperor could distinguish well enough between Jews and Christians,[11] and the first great persecution specifically directed against Christians broke out in Rome in A.D. 64. The problem of Jewish disorders in Rome was, however, a criminal problem; in Palestine it had become a political issue.

Immediately upon his accession in A.D. 41, Claudius had to deal with Jewish disturbances in both Egypt and Palestine. In Egypt, as has been seen, he confirmed Jewish privileges but denied their claim to isopolity in Alexandria. His policy in Palestine was somewhat more compromising. Since the procuratorial system was proving unpopular with the Jews who had originally asked for it, Claudius reverted to a Herodian kingdom and from A.D. 41 to A.D. 44 Agrippa I ruled not only the Galilean tetrarchies as previously, but was made king of Judaea as his grandfather Herod had been before him. The Jews seemed content, but Claudius apparently was not, and at the death of Agrippa I in A.D. 44 he reverted to the old system: a Roman Procurator in Judaea with Agrippa's son, Agrippa II, restricted to a kingdom in the northern regions.[12]

In their rule of Palestine the Romans could count on the

---

11. He almost certainly had help. Nero's wife Poppaea Sabina had some kind of connection with the Roman Jewish community and may even have been a quasi proselyte of the type known as *sebomenos*. Her influence on Nero's attitude toward the Christians is unknown.

12. The Herodian blood was still flowing strong and black. Agrippa I's daughter Berenice married or was sleeping with in succession: Philo's nephew Marcus; her uncle Herod, king of Chalcis; her brother Agrippa II; Polemon II, king of Olba in Cilicia; and finally Titus, whose mistress she was both in Judaea and in Rome after he became Emperor. Her more modest younger sister Drusilla contented herself with Aziz, the Arab dynast of Emesa, and Felix, the Roman Procurator of Judaea.

support of Agrippa II as well as that of the Sadducean party and a certain number of important Hellenized Jews. Against them were ranged principally the Zealots, who since the time of Herod had been resisting the Romans and their Herodian clients. Under other circumstances it might have been possible to control the Zealot nationalists; in Palestine of the first century the social and economic circumstances were far too incendiary for the show of Roman force that normally sufficed. The Palestinian Jews had shown before that there was a point where they would choose to resist the Romans to the end. The lesson was apparently lost on Nero's Procurators, Felix, Festus, Albinus, and Gessius Florus, who between A.D. 52 and A.D. 66 mercilessly suppressed the Zealot guerrillas, while exacting the last *sestertius* of tax from a land that in addition to the normal tribute was saddled with a poll tax (*laographia*) of the type that had stirred discontent in Egypt.

The Jews in Caesarea and the other *poleis* seem to have sought the same type of redress as that petitioned for in Alexandria, the right of isopolity that would put them on an equal footing with the Greek residents and free them from the *laographia*. In these cities Jewish isopolity meant, of course, increased burdens for the non-Jewish citizen, and economically inspired attacks against the Jews broke out in Caesarea. The Jews retaliated with pillaging in the Hellenic show places of Palestine and Transjordan: Philadelphia (Amman), Pella, Gerasa, Scythopolis, Sebaste in Samaria. The vengeful reaction of the Greeks spread over an even wider area in Syria and on to Alexandria. In the fall of A.D. 66 Cestus Gallus, the governor of Syria, was forced to intervene. Taking a Roman army supplemented by troops from the client kings (including Agrippa II), Gallus marched through Palestine dispersing the insurgents, who then fell back upon Jerusalem. That too could easily have been his, but after a brief siege he inexplicably withdrew. The guerrillas took advantage of the unexpected turn of events and turned the Roman withdrawal northwest to the coast into a rout.

Nero received the news of what had happened during his famous concert tour of Greece during the winter of A.D. 66–67, and as the Jews prepared for the blow that must inevitably fall upon them Nero appointed to the Palestinian command his best general, Vespasian, whom he judged to be sufficiently experienced and sufficiently obscure to crush the Jewish revolt without duly magnifying himself.[13] Vespasian bade his son Titus bring a legion from Alexandria while he marshaled the forces of Syria: two Roman legions, provincial auxiliaries, both infantry and horse, and the armies of Agrippa II and the client *shaykhs*—Antiochus of Commagene, Sohaemus of Ituraea, and Malchus of Petra.

The campaign was protracted but not difficult. The Jews took refuge in their cities and they had to be reduced one after another. One of them, Jotapata, yielded up the future historian of the war, Flavius Josephus, then still modestly known as Joseph bar Matthiah. By A.D. 69 Vespasian had all but accomplished his task, only Jerusalem remaining, when the news came of Nero's murder. Vespasian held off the armies until his own position was confirmed from Rome. What he heard instead was that in the course of a few months the Praetorian troops had made and unmade two Emperors, Otho and Galba, and now a third, Vitellius, had been uncertainly placed upon the throne by the legions of the Army of the Rhine.

Jerusalem was now forgotten. Vespasian and Licinius Mucianus, governor of Syria, with the open support of the eastern legions decided that the time was ripe to put forth the claims of Vespasian. The first overt gesture came from Egypt, where the Prefect Tiberius Alexander administered the oath of allegiance to the troops in the name of Vespasian on July 1, A.D. 69, followed, three days later, by his acclamation by the legions of Caesarea.[14] Within two weeks the eastern army corps had come over to the sixty-year-old general; it remained only to take formal possession of the provinces. Vespasian went to secure Egypt, Mucianus marched against Vitellius, who fell even before Mucianus' troops arrived in Italy, and Titus was left with the task of reducing Jerusalem.

As it turned out this was the most difficult task of all. The

---

13. Vespasian was on tour with Nero at the time, and the general frequently fell asleep, as generals will on such occasions, during Nero's concerts. The Emperor was not amused, but in this case his need for a general was even greater than his vanity.

14. Moved doubtless by the terrifying rumor that Vitellius intended to transfer them from the Oriental delights of Syria to the more rigorous German frontier on the Rhine.

natural strength of the city had been bolstered by extensive defenses constructed by Agrippa I. The Jews within the city understood full well that the final hour had come, and they met it with a courage and intransigency that baffled the Romans. Fighting among themselves and racked with famine and disease, the defenders held the closely invested city against a Roman army of sixty-five thousand men from May 10 to September 26, A.D. 70. Finally Titus entered the ruined city, where the captives were either slain or sent into slavery. Rich spoils were sent to Rome to adorn the double triumph of Titus and Vespasian; included was the temple paraphernalia, still visible in the dramatic scenes depicted on Titus' Roman arch of triumph. The land was confiscated and sold at public auction, and a colony of Roman veterans was planted at Emmaus. As a final indignity the Jews were commanded to pay the annual temple tax of two *denarii* directly to the Emperor for the maintenance of the temple of Jupiter Capitolinus.

The capture of Jerusalem and the destruction of the temple was not quite the end of the war. Titus left in the hands of the succeeding Procurators, Lucilius Bassus and Flavius Silva, the difficult task of reducing the great Herodian wasteland fortresses of Machaerus and Masada, which the Zealots still held. This took another three years. And yet, when it was all over nothing had been solved and nothing cured. The fund of ill will that was born of the disparity of right and privilege between Greeks and Jews in the Diaspora remained. Isopolity had not been granted and now perhaps never could. While the other provinces of the East grew rich in the shelter of the *Pax Romana*, agricultural Palestine, already pressed by a heavy tax burden, had been devastated by another war. All that the Romans had accomplished was the destruction of the temple establishment, men whom the Empire could manage and control, and the creation of a dangerous political vacuum.

Roads of Silk and Spice

As one surveys the peasant culture that is dominant today in Anatolia and Syria it is difficult to imagine the prosperity of those areas under the first two and a half centuries of the Roman Empire. Egypt the Romans had not greatly changed; they used it as a kind of agricultural brood mare, fecund, abused, protected. It had but a single genuine *polis*, Alexandria,[15] and so no tradition of self-government and no provincial councils; there is no record of a "*Koinon* of the Egyptians" such as those that were found in Asia or Syria. In these latter two areas, on the other hand, flourished the finest fruits of urbanism shielded by the *Pax Romana*.

In Asia the Greek cities of the littoral that antedated Alexander became thriving industrial and commercial centers from which spread the tendrils of the original Achaemenian road system. In the hinterland were the later city foundations of the Seleucids. The Romans pushed their roads still farther into the interior of the country carrying urban settlements in their wake. Some parts of the interior remained wild and uncultivated for centuries, like the fastnesses of Pontus and Isauria, but the primary urban civilization of Asia was and is unmistakable, though today it is represented chiefly by ruins, some scarcely accessible.

The decline is even more striking in Syria, where neglect has been accompanied by desiccation. Under the Romans the Transjordan was filled with flourishing Hellenic *poleis* graced with sumptuous public architecture and well-appointed private dwellings. A fair-sized eastern *polis* possessed a *curia* for the meetings of the Municipal Council, a *basilica* or law court, an *agora* or public market with meeting halls for the various commercial guilds (*collegia*), a theater and/or an auditorium, and possibly a library and a picture gallery. Even the smallest had temples, altars and a gymnasium. Today many of them are merely piles of magnificently dressed stone surrounded by desert and steppe.

In some of these areas the number of inhabitants has actually declined since Roman days. Population figures from antiquity are notoriously difficult, but some estimates have been made. During the Empire the population of the Anatolian provinces was probably near thirteen million, of Syria near six, and of Egypt perhaps seven or seven and a half million. The largest cities were Alexandria and Antioch (about six hundred thousand), then Ephesus and Smyrna (about four hundred thousand), with Pergamum somewhat smaller. Before the destruction of the temple Jerusalem may have had about one hundred thousand inhabitants. For

---

15. Technically there were others, the old Greek trading station at Naucratis, Ptolemais, and Hadrian's settlement of Antinoöpolis. None bore any comparison to the *poleis* of Asia, Syria, or even Palestine.

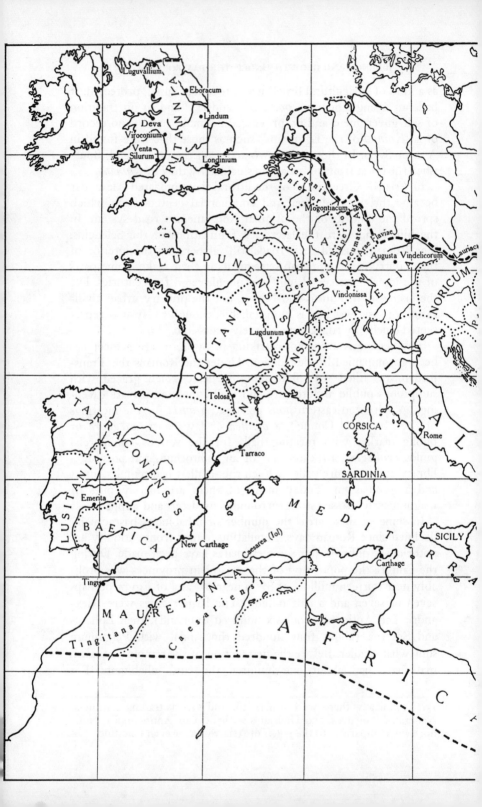

THE ROMAN EMPIRE
UNDER HADRIAN

Scales

0   100   200   300   400   500

English miles

0   100 200 300 400 500 600 700 800

Kilometres

Carnuntum

Aquincum

Pannonia Superior

Pannonia Inferior

DACIA

Potaissa

Sarmizegethusa

Viminacium

ILLYRICUM

DALMATIA

Moesia Superior

Moesia Inferior

Durostorum

BLACK SEA

THRACIA

MACEDONIA

Thessalonica

Byzantium

Nicomedeia

Sinope

BITHYNIA ET PONTUS

Trapezus

EPIRUS

ACHAEA

Athens

ASIA

GALATIA

CAPPADOCIA

LYCIA ET PAMPHYLIA

CILICIA

Antioch

CRETE

CYPRUS

SYRIA

Palmyra

NEAN

SEA

Damascus

Bostra

SYRIA PALAESTINA

Alexandria

Gaza

Jerusalem

CYRENAICA

EGYPT

ARABIA NABATAEA

purposes of comparison, Italy had a population of some twenty million and Rome stood near the million mark.

Urban industry was supported by the carefully irrigated local agricultural complex, and the Roman control of the entire area ensured the safety and stability necessary for commerce. Roman arms secured the highways, both the land roads and the internal maritime ones of the Mediterranean, from the center at Rome to the frontiers of the Empire. The frontiers themselves were held against hostile incursions. Manufactures and produce passed easily from one end of the Empire to the other. Syria imported pottery and dried fish from the western provinces and exported in return olive oil, wine, timber and hides. The textile industry of Tyre and Sidon was famous throughout the Mediterranean. Asia too exported timber from Pontus and Cilicia, as well as wine and fish, but in the highly industrialized Asian provinces local commerce was far more important than in the Syrian emporia which were engaged in international trade.

Syria was the gateway to the only higher civilizations that the Romans knew beyond their own, and Roman interest in what went on in these other cultural centers was neither historical nor philosophical nor anthropological but unabashedly commercial. As has already been noted, there was a considerable maritime trade with India from the time of Augustus and the discovery of the monsoon. Ships departed from Red Sea ports like Myos Hormos and Berenice, sailed down to the Roman colony at Aden, whence they could sail without stop (and intermediary customs) to India. The overland route had, of course, to pass through Parthia, whether to reach Spasinou Charax at the head of the Persian Gulf or to trek farther overland.

Augustus had already expressed an interest in these routes. His colleague Marcus Agrippa made an elaborate survey of the entire Empire that resulted in a map and a geography. During Gaius' negotiations with Parthia, Isidore of Charax surveyed the Persian Gulf, and Greek merchants[16] traveled to the eastern borders of Parthia at Merv and Kandahar, but not beyond. They brought back information about the world beyond, the land of the

---

16. The Romans generally supplied the capital for these commercial ventures while eastern Greeks did the actual traveling and trading. A merchant speaking only Latin would probably not survive beyond Campania, much less Bactria.

Seres,[17] whom the Bactrian Greeks knew of from the second century before Christ.

Interesting information was flowing in the other direction as well. Sometime after the descent of the Yüeh-chih on the Bactrian Greeks in B.C. 130, the Chinese Han Emperor Wu Ti sent his ambassador Chang Ch'ien to the Yüeh-chih to investigate the possibility of an alliance against the Huns. He traveled as far as Sogdia and Bactria, and returned to China in B.C. 126, bringing with him data about the southern trade routes to India and information which amounted to the Chinese discovery of the West: Parthia (An-hsi), Babylonia (T'iao-chih), Seleucid Syria (Li-kan) and then, later, Roman Syria (Ta-ts'in). The return of Chang Ch'ien was followed by Han offensive action in Central Asia, and by B.C. 100 Wu Ti had taken Ferghana and stood abreast of Alexander's easternmost penetration at Alexandria Eschate (Khojend). Shortly thereafter silk began arriving in the West, transmitted by the Parthians.

The Han dynasty could not hold Ferghana across the formidable desert of Taklamakan in the Tarim river basin, and this profitable trade was soon taken over by Yüeh-chih or Kushan middlemen who, for a price, passed on the silk to the Parthians, whence it passed, again for a price, up through northern Mesopotamia, where the Parthians' Arab clients in Osrhoene took their share before allowing the final passage across the Euphrates at Zeugma.[18]

The trade to India grew immensely from the first to the second century after Christ. Outgoing Egyptian ships from Berenice carried glass, metal ware, and linen that had been shipped up the Nile from Alexandria to Coptos and then brought by caravan east to the Red Sea ports. On their return voyage from India the ships were filled with spices and cotton, the latter turned to goods in the factories of Alexandria. The route was guarded at its critical

---

17. This was the common Greek and Latin word—derived from the Chinese word for silk (ssu)—for both the Chinese and the various Siberian middlemen in the silk trade. "China," from Ch'in, a dynasty of the third century before Christ, appears somewhat later in various forms: Sina (Latin), Thin (Greek), Sin (Arabic).

18. Since the silk was ultimately destined for the textile mills in Berytus (Beirut), Tyre and Sidon, a more direct route developed. Instead of mounting into Mesopotamia, the caravans left the Euphrates at Dura Europos and crossed the desert to Damascus by way of the oasis city of Palmyra.

points by a Roman squadron on the Red Sea and by caravan police on the overland haul from Coptos.

Most of this trade was locally owned. The Roman state adopted a general laissez-faire attitude, and the Italians so prevalent in Asia during Republican times had long since departed. The Roman Imperial treasury or *fiscus* may have been the single largest purchaser of eastern produce, but the production and sale of the goods and the attendant risks of trade were in the hands of the merchants of Ephesus, Antioch and Alexandria. The opportunities for profit were obviously great. Self-sufficiency might be the economic ideal of the Empire, and most of the municipalities probably could support themselves under normal circumstances. But the larger urban areas, particularly Rome, had developed such an insatiable appetite for luxury items from *outside* the Empire that international trade was a lucrative if dangerous business for the private entrepreneur. There were alarming consequences, however. By the time of Nero the drain of gold and silver to support the unfavorable trade balance became noticeable. The Indians with their less highly developed economy much preferred to bury their Roman gold than spend it on linen shirts.

There was no simple cure for this new disease attendant upon sophistication, though Nero tried a variety of them. He devalued the gold and silver coinage.[19] He may also have contemplated reaching behind the Parthians in one fashion or another. At one point he commissioned a probing expedition through the Caucasus to the north of the Caspian Sea, but the plan aborted because of the new presence of the nomad Alans on the Caucasian steppe.[20] In the south Nero extended Augustus' survey into Nubia; his men reached as far as Meroë in their search for

---

19. The Roman coinage was bimetallic, and at its best period there were forty-two pieces (the *aureus*) to the pound of gold, and eighty-four silver pieces (the *denarius*) struck from a pound of silver. There was also a brass (*sestertius*) and a copper (*as*) coin and the entire system was correlated at: 1 *aureus* = 25 *denarii* = 100 *sestertii* = 400 *asses*. Nero not only struck more *aurei* and *denarii* to the pound (forty-five and ninety-six respectively), he also debased the silver coinage by the addition of 10 percent alloy, a move which eventually undermined the silver coinage.

20. The southern end of the passes through the Caucasus was secured by Vespasian in A.D. 75, but the actual exploration of the northern reaches of the Caspian and the mouth of the Volga was not done until the time of Marcus Aurelius.

new trade routes. From the time of the Ptolemies the fate of partially Hellenized Meroë had been linked with that of Egypt, and as Rome flourished in the first and second centuries so did Meroë. They went into decline together in the third century, and Meroë fell to the Negro tribes around her, the Blemmydes and the Nobades, who then had free access to the frontiers of the debilitated Empire. Meroë was later to find a new "protector" in the rising power of Axum in the south; Axum annexed Meroë and her port Adulis replaced Meroë as the emporium for Central African trade.

The Romans and the Chinese both understood the role of Parthia as intermediary and impediment to direct contacts between their Empires. In A.D. 97 a Kan-ying was sent from China to Roman Syria (Ta-ts'in). He reached as far as Babylon, where the Parthians discouraged him from taking ship to Egypt, adding not a word of the easy overland trip that the Chinese learned of only later. About A.D. 120 the Romans received permission from the Parthians to travel in the eastern regions, and the silk merchant Maes Titianus sent out parties that reached as far as Kashgar on the western edge of the Tarim basin and brought back with them information on trade and commerce that was later incorporated into Ptolemy's *Geography*. Direct contact between the Romans and the Chinese did not come about by the overland route, however. The Chinese records reveal that in A.D. 166 a commercial mission sailing in the name of An-tun (Marcus Aurelius) came to China by the sea route around India, Malaysia and Vietnam. Roman maritime commerce, which had been creeping even farther east, had finally reached China.

The Parthian Empire, unaffected by these attempts at encirclement, continued to be tested by assault. Toward the end of Claudius' reign a new Shah ruled in Parthia, Vologesus I (A.D. 51–80), under whom there was a marked internal shift in emphasis. Philhellenism as a state policy was on the wane in the East, and the Iranian factions were being heard in Parthia. This need not be invoked, however, to account for Vologesus' traditional attempt to put his brother on the throne of Armenia as Tiridates IV. Circumstances defeated him, but only temporarily, and almost immediately after Nero's accession in A.D. 54 Vologesus returned to his project, and this time came close enough to success to send Armenian delegates scurrying in panic to Rome. Nero acted promptly, fashioning an extraordinary command for the general

Domitius Corbulo and rearranging his eastern clients to ensure maximum security. But Corbulo had first to train troops, and so it was not until A.D. 58 that the campaign got under way. It was rousingly successful: at the end of the year both Artaxata and Tigranocerta were in Roman hands, and by A.D. 60 the erstwhile Tiridates IV was back in Parthia temporarily cheated of his royal expectations. To replace him, the Romans reached into the complex Herodian family and came up with Tigranes, a great-grandson of Herod. Corbulo was rewarded with the governorship of Syria.

Tigranes displayed some of the old Herodian madness and proceeded to an invasion of the Parthian client kingdom of Adiabene. Vologesus had kept his peace to this point, but now he could no longer ignore the situation and made ready to intervene. Since Corbulo now had the responsibility for Syria, Nero appointed a new commander for Armenia, Caesennius Paetus. His campaign of A.D. 62 was a disaster, and it was only the timely arrival of Corbulo that saved the remnants.

Neither Corbulo nor Vologesus was a fool. Both realized that Rome had superior strength in the East but that, short of annexing Armenia as a province, the effort at holding a Roman candidate on the throne there exceeded Rome's powers. A compromise was worked out: Rome would accept the Arsacid ruler Tiridates IV as the legitimate king, but he would have to receive his crown from the hands of the Roman Emperor. In A.D. 66 Tiridates came to Rome and was crowned there in splendor by Nero.

Nero's Near Eastern policy was aggressive and energetic; Vespasian's work there was one of consolidation. He created in the heart of Asia the huge province of Galatia (the kingdoms of Pontus and Lesser Armenia disappeared into it), which provided a unified frontier to Armenia marked by the natural boundary of the upper Euphrates. Legionary garrisons were stationed at Satala and the Euphrates crossing at Melitene. The client kingdom of Commagene that had been enlarged and restored to his friend Antiochus by Gaius was incorporated into Syria, where too the Euphrates provided a natural eastern frontier. The river crossings at Samosata and Zeugma were held by legionary garrisons.[21] From

---

21. The legionary deployment along the frontier as it is known from the time of Hadrian was as follows: at Satala, the *Legio* XV *Apollinaris;* at Melitene, the XII *Fulminata;* at Samosata, the XVI *Flavia firma;* at Zeugma, the IV *Scythia,* with another, the III *Gallia* at

the Black Sea to Damascus the Empire had a natural defense: the Caucasus, the Euphrates, and the Syria desert. Beyond lay the Parthian clients and buffers: Iberia, Armenia, Osrhoene, Adiabene, Palmyra. None save Armenia was capable of independent mischief, but some were temptingly wealthy.

Rome Beyond the Euphrates

Nero, a scion of the Julio-Claudian line, was the first Philhellene to come to the supreme power in Rome. At all periods such men abounded among the Romans, antiquarians, sentimentalists, romanticizers of the Greek past, and intellectuals of genuine Hellenic culture. Nero's Philhellenism was of the grossly romantic type crossed with a streak of despotic madness. His notorious concert tour of Greece (only the Greeks deserved to hear him) in A.D. 66–67 that climaxed in his proclamation of tax immunity for Greece was not the signal for the triumph of Hellenism in the politics of Rome, but rather a symptom of unbridled self-indulgence that, when carried out on an imperial scale, could ruin an empire.

The revolutions of A.D. 69 were a cry of "enough," and even Vespasian with his restrained manners and cautious policy provoked serious resistance from a people who had had their first real taste of despotism. It is not easy to sort out the forces of opposition in the Empire. Much of it was popular and mute, and almost all of it was complex. The classic struggle of the haves and the have-nots was complicated by the issues of Republic versus Principate, the Hellenized versus the native, the local versus the central—that is, Roman—authority with, in the large urban centers, the Jews thrown in as pawns.

Roman policy, which was directed toward prosperity, favored the already prosperous and so indirectly fostered economic class struggle everywhere in the Empire. The prosperous were the urban middle and upper class; in the East, the Hellenized. And more and more they bore the brunt of Imperial demands in the form of discriminatory taxes. During the course of the second century they responded to these demands responsibly and even generously. But then they too became exhausted.

Emesa. Palestine was garrisoned by the *Legio* X *Fretensis* and after A.D. 106 Arabia by the VI *Ferrata* at Bostra.

They were not, however, the revolutionary class. Below them stood the disenfranchised peasantry and the urban proletariat of the East, which, like their counterparts at Rome, had less and less to do with municipal government. Both these much abused groups were in a constant state of agitation, and in Egypt the condition was very nearly endemic; from Gaius to Marcus Aurelius the Roman authorities had constantly to intervene against popular strikes and rioting. Nor was Asia much quieter; the letters of Pliny the Younger and the speeches of Dio Chrysostom graphically illustrate the same kind of economic and social unrest there.

At the other end of the social scale stood the Hellenized intellectuals of the Empire. It may be that for all his tyrannous behavior Nero represented some kind of promise to them. It was he, after all, who introduced one of their own, Seneca, into the seats of power, and during those years at least there may have been some sentiment that the narrow Roman and Italian cast of officialdom had been broken. If such hope there was, it was dashed by Vespasian. Though carried to power by Syrian troops, he was an Italian general and a far cry from a philosopher king. The Cynics read him out as a tyrant. But there were changes; during his reign the provinces did count for more than they had previously, and the Roman aristocracy gave way to a provincial one. These latter, the new faces in the Senate, were still, however, Latins of the West; the ascendancy of the East was still a generation away.

Nerva (A.D. 96–98) instituted a line of Emperors reaching down to Marcus Aurelius (A.D. 161–180) who changed the pace and texture of Roman rule. Trajan was the first Emperor born in the provinces (Spain), the sign of the triumph of a Latinized provincial aristocracy moving up through the Equestrian and Senatorial ranks. Under Trajan and Hadrian the Greeks and Orientals put their feet upon the same path, and the purely Roman character of the Empire, though embalmed for eternity in its laws and institutions, began its gradual disappearance from the living tissue. The polarity of Italy and the provinces disappeared too. The Italian peninsula was in serious economic trouble from the time of Domitian (A.D. 81–96), and, despite the attempts of Nerva and Trajan to shore it up, the flight of capital and the ravages of depopulation had gone too far. Hadrian abandoned any pretense that it was the center of the Empire. Previously the Empire had been a loose confederation of city-states ruled by Rome. By the time of Hadrian it had become a group of provinces ruled by the Emperor through his bureaucracy. The bureaucracy was still at Rome, but more and more the Emperors were not. Previously they had gone into the provinces only for conquest, to lend some credence to their claim to the title "Germanicus" or "Parthicus"; now they ruled from the provinces, which were in turn drawn more and more into the central administrative system. *Laissez faire* was abandoned.[22]

With the coming of the Antonines the Stoic and Cynic intellectuals had their ideal rulers,[23] and, in the person of Hadrian and Marcus Aurelius, as close an approximation of the philosopher-king as would ever wield power at Rome. Personal tyranny had given way to an enlightened rule, which avoided Oriental despotism on the one hand and romantic dilettantism on the other. There was an attempt at social reform: the cancellation of debts, the distribution of land to the *fellahin* in Egypt, the protection of the lower classes (*humiliores*) against the provincial establishment (*potentiores*). But nothing of this amounted to a reversal of the class distinction inexorably deepening all over the Roman East.

At the top of the pyramid were still the Senators, politically feeble, and no longer distinguished by lineage nor solely Italian in origin, but chosen by the Emperor on the basis of wealth and service (the two were increasingly inseparable). Below them were the wealthy *Equites*, the candidates for future Senatorial dignity. Again service was the key to success, and from the time of Vespasian it was men of the Equestrian order who manned— and directed—the Imperial bureaucracy. The *Equites* were, in turn, drawn from the upper ranks of the urban middle class, the provincial aristocracy to which access could be had, in an eastern

---

22. Trajan sent Pliny to Bithynia-Pontus in A.D. 110–111 to scrutinize and report on the finances of the entire province. Their correspondence is extant in Book X of Pliny's *Collected Letters*. This was followed by the institution of the office of *curator*, or *logistes*, a kind of Imperial Accountant to watch over the finances of a single municipality.

23. Whose portrait, sketched by Dio Chrysostom in his speeches *On Kingship*, is remarkably like that of Trajan. See Chapter XII.

city, by wealth derived from commerce, industry or agriculture, and by a veneer of Hellenization. Below was the petty bourgeoisie of the arts and crafts and minor officialdom. At the bottom stood—or repined—the urban proletariat, free and slave, and the agricultural peasantry, impoverished, largely illiterate, whose contact with Hellenism was its urban monuments, and whose link to the Empire was the tax collector or the military police.

The Empire had become stabilized along its eastern frontiers (from the time of Augustus, the Euphrates), and since the days of Nero the troublesome question of the Armenian succession had been settled to the satisfaction of both Parthia and Rome. And it was well within the lines of traditional policy that Trajan annexed, apparently without resistance, the kingdom of the Nabataeans as the *Provincia Arabia* in A.D. 106. Vespasian had already straightened the provincial line in Anatolia by incorporating Pontus and Lesser Armenia into a Greater Galatia and had extended the line south by annexing the client kingdom of Commagene. Further links southward fell into place with the absorption of Emesa; and then, at the death of Agrippa II, his kingdom too reverted to provincial status. The new province of Arabia with its metropolis at Bostra extended the frontier down through the desert to Aqaba, and over the Nabataean caravan trail Trajan built a Roman road, with protective forts, from Damascus to Aila. It is significant that the road terminated in the port; the Nabataean holdings that reached southward into Arabia as far as Leuke Kome on the coast and Madain Seleh inland were abandoned. Trajan was interested only in the maritime trade to India and the Far East.

From the Parthian side of the frontier these moves must have appeared alarming. Roman buffers were being replaced by provinces. Palmyra was already half encircled, and the Parthian clients were exposed, particularly Osrhoene and Adiabene across the Euphrates from the Roman jumping-off point at Zeugma. But the Parthians were not seeking war, and if they did fumble the protocol of Corbulo's settlement in not getting Roman acquiescence in a change of monarch in Armenia, Osrhoes, the Parthian king (*c.* A.D. 109–128), showed his willingness to negotiate. Trajan had other plans, namely, the annexation of Armenia, which he accomplished with only the slightest effort in the summer of A.D. 114.

Trajan did not return the way he had come. He stood at the head of a large and experienced army, much of it tested in his Dacian campaigns north of the Danube in A.D. 101–106; resistance was minimal. Instead of returning to Melitene and Cappadocia he moved his legions south into Mesopotamia, where the Parthian clients west of the Tigris quickly pledged their allegiance to Rome. By the time Trajan arrived back in Antioch in the winter of A.D. 114 he had added a second new province to the Empire, Mesopotamia.

The Parthians had shown themselves almost impotent to resist, largely due to Osrhoes' troubles with a rival claimant, Vologesus II. Weighing this, Trajan decided that all the stakes could be won with just one more throw. In A.D. 115 two Roman armies descended the Euphrates and the Tigris, Trajan commanding the latter force which started from Nisibis. There was resistance from the satrap of Adiabene, but the Romans broke through and converged on Ctesiphon which fell after a short seige. Osrhoes had escaped, but the heart of western Parthia was in Trajan's hands. During the winter he descended in triumph to Spasinou Charax, the India trade emporium at the head of the Persian Gulf.

With little or no difficulty Trajan had carried off a tremendous commercial coup. The crowds at Rome might be impressed by their Emperor's annexation of three new provinces, Armenia, Mesopotamia (the Parthian lands west of the Tigris), and Assyria (the satrapy of Adiabene), but they were probably of less value than the troops needed to garrison them. What was more impressive was that he had eliminated the Parthian middleman from the India trade. Or so it seemed; the moment of exaltation was brief indeed. At the very time that Trajan was in Babylon calculating his future profits the news came to him that the Parthians had launched a counterattack from Media into Armenia and Adiabene, and that there were revolts, not only in Ctesiphon and up and down Mesopotamia, but in the home provinces as well. Only with the greatest effort were Seleucia and Mesopotamia held, but the ephemeral province of Assyria was lost forever. The Romans retrenched. Convinced that he could never hold Babylonia, Trajan was willing to settle for Armenia and northern Mesopotamia.

Babylonia was quickly and unconvincingly erected into a client kingdom and an appropriate Parthian puppet was found. Trajan then turned his attention to new disturbances in the Mediterranean.

Beginning with Cyrenaica in A.D. 115 and followed by Egypt and Cyprus, the Jewish communities of the eastern Mediterranean were in full revolt, probably over the recurring issue of isopolity. Revolt against the municipal aristocracy was also revolt against Rome, and the fighting had far surpassed the level of mere disorders. Indeed, Cyrenaica never recovered from the massive destruction visited upon it first by the Jews and then by the Romans in suppressing them. The fighting never seems to have spread in any serious degree to Palestine; the memories of A.D. 70 still doubtless lingered there. What was probably of greater concern to Trajan were the possibilities of disaster in Mesopotamia and Babylonia with their large Jewish populations. It is by no means certain that the Jewish insurrections were in fact unconnected with the Roman invasion of Parthia in the first place.

Trajan took vigorous action. The Mediterranean countries were takan in hand by a naval man, and for the pacification of Mesopotamia the now ailing Emperor designated the Libyan Moor Lucius Quietus, who had begun his career as the somewhat unruly *shaykh* in charge of a detachment of Libyan irregulars and had risen to the position of Trajan's most competent and unrelenting general. Mesopotamia was dealt with promptly and ruthlessly, and the efficient Lucius was then installed as governor of Judaea, another reason why the fighting in Egypt did not spread there. By A.D. 117 all was quiet once more, but before he could try Parthia again Trajan died.

In his place stood his adopted heir,[24] Hadrian, another Spaniard with a long and varied experience including the governorship of Syria and the staff command of his uncle's Parthian campaign. But unlike Trajan whose evolution ended at his Romanization, Hadrian had become, in his formative years, a Hellene whose spiritual home was in Athens rather than in Rome. Earlier in his

---

24. One of the policies that caused trouble for Vespasian was his dynastic plans. From Nerva to Marcus Aurelius the more reasonable procedure of selecting a competent successor and then "adopting" him was followed. Marcus reverted to the dynastic principle and the result was Commodus.

career he had been elected an Archon of Athens, and after his accession as emperor he returned there to be initiated into the Eleusinian mysteries. His official portrait on his coins breathe an idealized Hellenic glow. In the East he was Zeus.

Almost immediately he renounced Trajan's imperialistic pretensions. He could and did quell insurrections, as in Judaea, and keep a violent peace on the frontiers, as in Britain and along the Danube, but he saw that he could not hold Armenia and Mesopotamia. They were returned to their client kings. Hadrian reverted to the Augustan ideal of the Euphrates as the frontier, to which he added his own of the rebirth of the *polis*. Hadrian was a conscious apostle of Hellenism, and while this might have on occasion its romantic or sentimental side,[25] his promotion of Hellenic urbanism was genuine and effective. He even attempted the impossible, the founding of another *polis* in Egypt, Antinoöpolis.[26]

Hadrian's Panhellenism was not everywhere successful. Antiochus Epiphanes had pursued the same policy in Palestine some three centuries earlier and had provoked the Maccabean revolt. Now in A.D. 130 in passing through Palestine Hadrian decreed the revival of Judaea by his favorite instrument, the construction of a Greco-Roman city named Aelia Capitolina on the ruins of Jerusalem, with the temple of Jupiter Capitolinus on the site of Herod's temple. It would have been sound policy anywhere else in the Roman world; in Judaea it brought on Armageddon. Trajan's wars of A.D. 115–116 had seen the rise of Messianic figures, and now another appeared, Bar Kokhba. Once again, as in A.D. 66, the population was torn by doubt, but now as then events carried them along with the Zealot leader. The most prestigious figure in contemporary Judaism, Rabbi Akiba, the elderly head of the academy at Jabneh, affirmed Bar Kokhba's Messiahship and proclaimed a Holy War. Before it ended, three and a half years later in A.D. 135, another half million Jews had perished. The pitiful

---

25. His villa at Tivoli near Rome reproduced with exquisite style, but somewhat in the manner of a miniature golf course, various locales in Greece.

26. Named for the Bithynian youth after whom Hadrian sighed, in the Greek style, for some years. Antinoüs died in Egypt in A.D. 130, and Hadrian had him declared Hermes and Pan. He gave his name to a city and his likeness to thousands of coins, statues and monuments. Antinoüs was the symbol and the fetish of the Hadrianic era.

remnant was driven from the land, and Hadrian, who had directed the war from Gerasa during its final year, clamped upon the community a series of restrictions against cult that were designed to suffocate it.

The Closure of Rabbinical Judaism

With the obliteration of Jerusalem and Judaea from the life of the Jews a great stillness seems to descend upon Palestinian and Diaspora Judaism. There was an almost unbroken official silence in the face of the great event of the age, and one that particularly touched the Jews, the incredibly rapid growth of Christianity. From a mere dissident sect in the Jewish community in A.D. 70 it had become by Hadrian's time a phenomenon of the *oikoumene*. The rabbis, however, maintained a discreet silence on their schismatic offspring, adjusting in a significant way their now disappointed Messianic hopes, but otherwise contenting themselves with building the structure of a new Talmudic Judaism.

The old political divisions of Palestine had no meaning in the new circumstances of A.D. 135. The Christian wing had withdrawn. The Essenes were destroyed when the holocaust of A.D. 70 reached Qumran. The Sadducees had held themselves aloof from the struggle against Rome with whom they were in principle willing to cooperate. But Roman success brought them no increase, since they could not survive the destruction of the temple to which they were so closely linked.[27] The Pharisees alone survived, and it was their institution of the synagogue, combined with the judicial function of the Sanhedrin, that provided Judaism with the instruments of survival. Pharisaism turned inward and began to take on the scholastic, learned aspect that was to characterize Judaism thenceforward.

The learned tradition among the Jews went back as far as the scribes (*soferim*) who had been one of the outgrowths of the years of exile. Its rebirth during this period is connected with a significant event. Even before the destruction of A.D. 70 Johannan

---

27. An ideological if not a historical link with the teachings of the Sadducees was maintained by the later Qaraites (*Qara'im*, "Readers"), a Jewish sect founded in Islamic times by Anan ben David (*c.* A.D. 754-775) which held to the Saducean position of rejecting the oral tradition of the *mishnah* in favor of the written one of the Torah.

bar Zakkai left Jerusalem and founded a school (*beth ha-midrash*) at Jabneh on the coast. The type was absolutely new in the Mediterranean. There had been scribal schools before, in Mesopotamia and elsewhere; there were, too, the institutions of higher learning in Athens and Alexandria from the time of Plato and the Ptolemies. What was novel in Johannan's institution was the combination of a learned and a religious tradition, and whatever the title—theological school, catechetical school or *madrasah*—it was to have an impressive history. The loose association of pupils and teachers in the manner of the early Athenian Sophists that characterized the "schools" of eminent rabbis like Hillel and Shammai was replaced by something of far greater permanence and formality.

The *beth ha-midrash* also abrogated to itself most of the prerogatives of the *beth ha-din*, the "House of Law" that regulated the external affairs of the Jewish community. The repressive measures taken by Hadrian in the wake of his capture of Jerusalem aborted the work of the *beth ha-din* at Jabneh, but in the more tolerant atmosphere of Antoninus Pius a new body was formed, not now in devastated Judaea, but in the northern province of Galilee, which had stood outside the revolts and so escaped with little damage. An academy was founded there under the direction of Simon bar Gamaliel of the school of Hillel. The Romans chose to deal with the Jewish community through him, and this unofficial recognition established Simon as the acting head of the Jews, the office which was designated as Patriarch and guided Jewish affairs in the Empire down to its lapse in A.D. 429. Galilee, and particularly the towns of Tiberias and Sepphoris,[28] which were almost entirely Jewish in population, took the place of Judaea at the heart of Judaism. For the Jews, Jerusalem was a ruin and a prohibited place. They were allowed to resort there on one day a year to gather at the only remnant of the temple, the Wailing Wall.[29]

After the war the Jews were allowed to make their own internal arrangements, which they proceeded to do in terms of the Torah and the oral tradition (*mishnah*) connected with it, but they had also to live under the prescriptions set down by the Romans to regularize their position in the state. Vespasian had

---

28. Later destroyed in the wake of a Jewish revolt against Constantius.
29. How strictly this Hadrianic proscription was observed is a matter of some doubt.

imposed a special discriminatory temple tax (*fiscus judaicus*) on all the Jews of the Empire after the war of A.D. 70—it was rescinded by Nerva—and Hadrian went even further in making circumcision a capital offense[30] and forbade the public teaching of the Law and the observation of the Sabbath, by far the most serious restrictions ever placed upon the Jews. Hadrian, like Antiochus before him and Heraclius after, may have been attempting to impose unity upon his Empire by the forced assimilation of his most separatist minority. The Jews' cult center at Jerusalem was destroyed and deliberately rebuilt as a city of Jupiter, with the expectation, doubtless, that the end of the cultus would mark the end of the cultists. But his prohibition against the teaching of the Law seems to indicate that Hadrian understood that there was more than mere cultus involved. And Hadrian's Hellenism had even less of a retort to the Torah than it did to the Gospels.

Antoninus Pius lifted the restrictions on circumcision somewhat, allowing it only to the offspring of Jewish parents and thereby effectively limiting the possibilities of conversion. Septimius made the prohibition of proselytism specific. Judaism was to be contained, and the policy needed no other justification than what political self-interest dictated. For the Jews, however, the destruction of the temple was a theological event that cried for explanation. A theodicy of guilt lay close at hand, and if the rabbis' explanations lacked the poetic fervor and imagination of a Jeremiah, they shared his attitudes: Yahweh was once again punishing his chosen people for their sins, in this instance for their neglect of the Torah. Somewhat more pragmatic historical considerations were indulged in as well. Bar Kokhba was execrated in the rabbinical writings of the period, and the Talmud considerably tempered the more militant Messianism of the earlier period: the Messiah, whose coming was by no means to be considered imminent, was a figure of peace.

Life had to go on, however, and the scholars and teachers in whose hands now rested the responsibility of preserving "the remnant" in some integral form addressed their attention to its regulation. Primary here was the calendar. On the computation of the appearance of each new moon depended all the liturgical feasts of the year, and to allow each community to follow its own

---

30. This applied to Arabs and Egyptians as well.

peculiar system of reckoning would have added to the forces of particularism already evident in the Diaspora. There was privilege at stake as well; who controlled the calendar exercised a degree of hegemony over the entire body of Jews. Despite an abortive attempt on the part of the Babylonian communities to make their own computations, the fixing of the dates remained in the hands of the Palestinian academies, whence the information was transmitted to the Diaspora.[31]

The outer tensions that beset the Jewish community left relatively little trace in the Talmud. The Jewish merchant or farmer had to live in a world that was increasingly Christian and to suffer the harassment of monk and bishop alike, but the scholarly reflections of the academies echo little of this. A heavy veil of pietism seems to have dropped over Judaism, disconnected from and disinterested in the alien affairs of an *oikoumene* that held out tantalizing promise but ended by playing it false. The rupture with Hellenism gave place to disenchantment; after A.D. 200 there is nothing but silence from the Hellenized Jews of the Diaspora. The vital center was once again in Palestine and then increasingly in Persia, where the religious work of a Jew was, above all, Scriptural and exegetical.

A corresponding change in the Jewish attitude toward Scripture itself can be detected. The Septuagint had originally served the Greek-speaking Jews as a translation of the sacred texts. In the second and third centuries of the Christian era the need for a Greek version still existed,[32] but it was becoming increasingly clear that the Septuagint would no longer do. Every translation bears, in its understanding of the text, the mark of its own times, and the mood of early rabbinical Judaism, with its repudiation of grandiose Messianism and its adherence to the literal sense of the

---

31. This arrangement continued in force until A.D. 358–359, when the Palestinian Patriarch Hillel surrendered the privilege and with it the waning Palestinian preeminence. At least part of the pressure to do so came from Christian quarters. The Council of Nicaea had decided in A.D. 325 that the date of Easter was to be calculated independently of that of the Jewish Pasch, but there were Christian churches which continued to keep the Jewish usage. It was felt that the annual publication of the Jewish dates by the Palestinian Patriarch would only serve to abet the heretics.

32. The bulk of the Jews of the Empire still spoke Greek, Latin or Aramaic. Despite an uninterrupted nostalgia for Hebrew, it remained a dead language.

text, was not that of Ptolemaic Alexandria. The Christians, moreover, whose point of departure vis-à-vis the Jews was the fulfillment of Messianic prophecies, had expropriated the Septuagint as their common translation of the Old Testament, and this too was a factor in the growing Jewish disdain for the Septuagint. New Greek translations appeared in the second century. One such was that done by Aquila, a Jewish proselyte from Pontus who during the reign of Hadrian prepared an extremely literal translation from Hebrew into Greek, and somewhat later in the century Theodotion of the Judaeo-Christian Ebionites provided that sect with its own translation. A final second-century Jewish version was the one done by Symmachus. For the Aramaic-speaking Jews there were the various Targums, and there are some small traces of Latin versions.

Judaism's turning in upon itself after the destruction of Jerusalem is also evident in the acceleration of other processes, begun earlier but brought rapidly to a conclusion during this period, the fixing of both the canon of Scripture and its definitive Hebrew text. By about B.C. 130 Jesus bar Sirach, writing in the Egyptian Diaspora, knew of a collection of the Scriptural books under the headings of "the Law, the Prophets, the Writings." The constituents of this last category, the *Ketubim*, were still in some doubt when, some time after A.D. 70, a convocation at Jabneh debated the inclusion of "the Rolls" (*Megilloth*) in the canon. The books of the *Megilloth* (*Song of Songs, Ruth, Lamentations, The Preacher* [*Qoheleth,* or *Ecclesiastes*] and *Esther*), were eventually accepted, despite the obvious Greek tinge to the thought of "the Preacher." But no succeeding generation of rabbis ever saw fit to accept, as to a certain degree the Christians did, the great mass of apocalyptic literature in circulation among the Jews (the Essenes, for example, read such works avidly) at the beginning of the Christian era. The Jewish community at Alexandria had had a much more liberal view three centuries earlier when the Septuagint was being prepared. The three intervening centuries had seen, however, a new phenomenon, Christianity, that made use of the same material and so rendered the preservation of an "authentic" tradition imperative.[33]

---

33. The rabbinical—or, better, the Pharisaic—view of Scripture was still more liberal than the fundamentalist attitude of the Sadducees and Samaritans, that the true canon was the pentateuchal Torah and nothing more.

The Alexandrian tradition was rejected in another way. One of the self-imposed tasks of rabbinical Judaism was the fixing of a standard text of the Hebrew Scriptures, a work of considerably greater difficulty in Hebrew than in Greek. Greek orthography is adequate in that both the vowels and consonants are written; the Semitic scripts have signs for the latter only, and so the exact "vocalization" of such an imperfectly written text may be the matter of some dispute. As with the canon, the text tradition of the Hebrew Scriptures had narrowed down in pre-Christian times to one text in general use in Alexandria (the base of the Greek Septuagint) and another in Palestine.[34] It was the Palestinian text, already in use in a fairly standardized form by the time of Qumran—it was the basis, for instance, of the text of *Isaiah* found there—that was chosen by the rabbis to serve as the authorized text. The traditionalist scholars (*masoretes*) of the academies of both Palestine and Babylon worked to standardize the text even further, finally adopting in the seventh century a system of diacritical marks to establish for the reader just how the consonantal text was to be vocalized.[35]

Neither the savagery at Jerusalem nor the subsequent desecularization of a culture interested even the most curious of Hadrian's Hellenized contemporaries. The events in Palestine and indeed the withdrawal of the Jews from the *oikoumene*, where they had long played a notable part, were overshadowed by another drama being played out with infinitely more grace and elegance at Athens, Antioch and Smyrna, where the Empire itself was passing, with a final burst of brilliance, into its own crisis of survival.

---

34. Both, of course, the object of modern reconstruction, since the oldest complete Hebrew manuscript of the Bible dates from the middle of the tenth century A.D. There are papyri fragments that go back to the second and third centuries, but the greatest windfall for the reconstruction of this prestandardized text was the coming to light of the manuscript hoard in the storeroom (*genizah*) of the old Jewish synagogue in Cairo and the discovery of the Scriptural library of the Jewish sectaries at Qumran.

35. The Syrians had already in the fourth century worked out a similar procedure for their vowelless text in Syriac, using a system based on the vowels of the Greek alphabet.

XV

Classic and Baroque

Gibbon's favorable verdict on the Antonines is well known and, despite our heightened ability to see the historical warts on the fairest of faces, still defensibly true. Their age does appear to be one in which intelligent men ruled reasonably and well a generally flourishing populace. Chance and process produced the Antonines, and it was that same unpredictable and erratic combination that brought new rulers to the Roman state. Old debts fell due. Even philosopher-kings have heirs, and it was they who had to observe, piously or distractedly or desperately, the toll of Trajan's imperialism, the inexorable decline of Italy's population and productivity, and the final collapse of constitutional government and the perilous economy upon which it had so long rested, all accompanied by the last sad music that Roman Hellenism was to produce.

The Autumn of Eloquence

Discourse (*logos*) was the lifeblood of Hellenism. The Homeric warrior took as great pride in the eloquent telling of his deeds as in their doing, and from that point forward there was no ebbing of the Greeks' fascination with the "word." The change from the military feudalism of the Bronze Age to the urbanism of the eighth and seventh centuries served merely to add another dimension to the function of communication in the new literate *polis* society, where political power was paramount and oratory the increasingly useful instrument for its acquisition.

It was the special achievement of the Greeks that they fashioned a powerful and flexible form of prose discourse to rival the considerable poetic tradition that they possessed in common with other early cultures of the Aegean *oikoumene*. The *polis* orators forsook the verse forms favored by their bardic predecessors and chose instead to express themselves in the new prose style. The philosophers had already been experimenting with prose forms, and it was probably this connection with philosophical specula-tion that led to the rapid development of a body of theory under the auspices of the Sophists, who had begun a systematic study of the techniques and ends of public discourse. The result was the emergence of the first Greek literary discipline, the "art of speaking" (*rhetorike techne*).

Its success in the assembly-oriented states of fifth- and fourth-century Greece was immense, and by the generation of Plato rhetoric in the person of its most eminent practitioner Isocrates was challenging the position of philosophy as the crown and climax of an ideal education. Isocrates, who had broadened and deepened the limited technical goals of the earlier Sophists, made a strong case for a sophisticated and informed culture rooted in oratory and based on the technique of the imitation of models.

The debate was abruptly and ironically ended in favor of a philosophical culture by the very man, Philip of Macedon, who fulfilled Isocrates' political ideal of a unified Greece. Unity of a sort was achieved, but the price was the freedom of the Greek *poleis*. Under the Macedonian protectorate oratory lost its politi-cal point, and the serious study of rhetoric went into a steep decline. Oratory, however, did not; the stream of words flowed unabated in the Hellenistic kingdoms. For Athens Philip and Alexander marked the end of meaningful autonomy, but to the *poleis* of Asia the new order meant the end of Achaemenian repression. The arrival of Alexander signaled the beginning of a great new urban age in Asia that lasted half a millennium, and at its beginning there was a remarkable outpouring of oratory in Asia, and in a style particularly its own.

Hellenistic literature and art, freed of the self-imposed re-straints of Periclean classicism, had created a new baroque style, and the same characteristics—and many of the excesses—that typify that style were present in the oratory of the period. Gone was the restraint of a Demosthenes and the depth of an Isocrates. Detached from the confinements of political reality, the Asian style, as it came to be called, converted the careful classical balance of phrase and idea into jingling and grotesque bombast, and relied as heavily as the contemporary art on effects created by pathos and sentimentality. The spirit of Isocrates lingered on only long enough to suggest to these rhapsodists that the same techniques were also valuable for history. Hegesias of Magnesia, an eminent Asianist orator of the third century B.C., for instance, wrote a "historical" treatment of that magnet of the baroque, Alexander the Great, and he had no lack of imitators.

The philosophical schools showed no great interest in formal rhetoric. The Peripatetics continued to do some analysis after the example of Aristotle and Theophrastus,[1] but rhetorical theory as such played little or no part in contemporary speculation, since most of the philosophers took the position enunciated by Plato in the *Gorgias:* rhetoric was not an art (*techne*), but a pastime (*tribe*) comparable to cooking. The professional orators (*rhetores, sophistai*), it was maintained, were innocent of political affairs, and the point was strongly underlined when in B.C. 155 the Athenians sent not professional speakers but three eminent philosophers to plead their case before the Roman Senate: Carneades the Academic, Diogenes, a Stoic, and Critolaus who, though a Peripatetic, had little regard for rhetoric or rhetoricians.

Rhetoric, bereft of theory and completely overshadowed—and ignored—by the flourishing establishments of Hellenistic philosophy and science, remained in the category of show oratory until the time of Hermagoras of Temnos (*fl. c.* B.C. 150), who undertook to claim a legitimate field of inquiry for rhetoric and to construct the beginnings of a theory. His work was neither brilliant nor profound, but he did succeed in staking out a small area of legitimacy and concern for what had been a moribund discipline.

Oratorical methods and interests reached Rome as part of the general wave of Hellenism that flowed westward. By the first century the Asian style was firmly rooted in Rome and found a facile and formidable advocate in the lawyer Hortensius (B.C. 114–50). There was more than a touch of Asianism in Cicero's oratory as well, but his theoretical writings on the subject show evidence of new currents. Cicero had had his rhetorical training at Rhodes under Apollonius Molon of Alabandra in Caria,[2] and

---

1. See Chapter II, p. 111.
2. Also the author of a treatise *Against the Jews*, known from Josephus' retort in *Against Apion* (see Note 9 p. 544).

the Rhodian school had already begun to move from the excesses of Asianism in the direction of a more restrained and scholarly approach to the theory and practice of public speaking.

What was occurring in Greek intellectual circles of the last century before Christ was, however, far more than a mere exercise in restraint. That was a symptom of a far more general movement, the discovery and formulation of the doctrine of classicism, which, put in its most general terms, states that the artistic and intellectual standards of fifth- and fourth-century Greece are the norm against which all subsequent activities—literary, artistic, political, intellectual or linguistic—are to be measured. It was to become one of the dogmas of the western and eastern intellectual tradition.[3]

The motives for a return to a supposedly purer and more authoritative past were various. In part it was reaction, the reaction to a philosophical skepticism that led back to the more assured masters of the fourth century,[4] and the reaction against the literary and artistic excesses of the Asianist baroque. In part, too, the new classical attitude must have reflected a defensive reaction against the Roman conquest. Eventually this reflection on and veneration for the past would degenerate into archaicism, but in the first century its effects were still salutary. There was a revival of interest in Plato and Aristotle, while the rhetoricians looked with new eyes on the orators of the "classical age."

The restoration of rhetoric in the first century was also part of a more general rethinking of the problems of Greek style. Even in Aristotle's day there had been concern for "Hellenism" in literary expression, and now, after three centuries' exposure to the most diverse cultural and linguistic elements, the problem of correct usage, to say nothing of grace and felicity of expression, had obviously become far more serious. Here the rhetorician and the stylist made common cause with the philologist in the work

---

3. The chief refinement contributed by the western Hellenic tradition was due to the loss of Greek. The Latin Middle Ages had their own "classics," the authors in the standard school curriculum, usually chosen on moral rather than aesthetic grounds, and all Latin. The Renaissance reintroduced both the aesthetic criterion and Greek, but it never dislodged the notion that there were Latin "classics," an idea that would have amused the Hellenes of the Roman Empire, very few of whom bothered to translate Latin works into the current Greek or even to learn Latin at all.

4. See Chapter IX, p. 365.

of literary criticism, preliminary, in the case of the rhetorician, to remodeling his own style on that of the great masters of the past—Plato, Demosthenes, Lysias, Thucydides.

A leader in the revival of literary and critical studies in the first century was Dionysius, a Greek of Halicarnassus in Caria who came to Rome, like many others, in the wake of Octavian's victory at Actium, and remained there for twenty-two years as an influential teacher and scholar. An admirer of Demosthenes and a student of Aristotle and Theophrastus, Dionysius instructed a generation of Romans on matters of style by his analysis of the "classics"—particularly the Attic orators—and his insistence on imitation of their style. And in the tradition of Isocrates and Hegesias he brought his rhetorical studies to bear on the writing of history. To the same movement and era belong the two anonymous treatises[5] *On the Sublime* and *On Style*, both concerned with the mimetic approach to stylistic elegance and based on both analytical and comparative methods.[6]

All these critics had insisted upon sublimity and purity of style, but none made a fetish of purism. It remained for the generation of the Antonines to convert classicism into archaicism. At its best, classicism suggested the easy mastery of sophisticated forms that are recognized as normative; the mastery *by* form and the triumph of the letter over the spirit or of nostalgia over reality are the degenerative symptoms of neoclassicism. Under the Julio-Claudians, Hellenism and Latinism existed in equilibrium and produced the moderately Hellenized Latin of a Vergil and the literary but nonpedantic Greek of a Philo or a Strabo. But the passage from the Julio-Claudians and Flavians with their sense of Roman tradition and imperial correctness to the Philhellene Antonines had quite different effects. The shift of the economic and administrative bases of the Empire to the Hellenized East was undoubtedly necessary and, as the sequel showed, ensured the survival of the Empire for another thirteen centuries. It was

---

5. Falsely attributed to Longinus and Demetrius of Phalerum.
6. The comparative method (*synkrisis*) was popular in contemporary rhetorical and critical studies and went back at least to the time of Posidonius, who wrote a *Comparison of Homer and Aratus*. Caecilius, a Hellenized Jewish freedman of Kale Akte in Sicily and a contemporary of Dionysius, introduced a new turn with his *Comparison of Demosthenes and Cicero*, and it became, of course, an essential part of Plutarch's biographical method.

inevitable too that the shift of political emphases should be reflected in the cultural life of the state.

Hellenism was never a foreign quantity at Rome from the time the first Greek pedagogues arrived in Italy, and the higher a Roman youth mounted in the educational system the more Hellenized became the instruction; the most advanced study, rhetoric, was almost totally Greek in both its ideals and its expression. And as time passed, the Roman state's attitude toward this system more closely approximated that long pursued by the Greek *poleis*. Under Vespasian, for example, secondary-school teachers and professors of the higher studies were granted immunity from the onerous civil responsibilities of the ordinary citizen, and the same Emperor founded, out of state funds, chairs of Greek and Latin rhetoric at Rome. Marcus Aurelius extended the tradition of the Imperial professorships to Athens, founding a chair of Greek rhetoric and four in philosophy. By the time of the Christian Empire every good-sized *polis* in the eastern provinces had schools of secondary and even higher (rhetorical) studies supported from municipal funds or private endowments,[7] and frequently interfered with by the Imperial administration.

All of this was merely the continuation of a Hellenistic practice which the Romans assimilated. Vespasian's interest was more administrative than cultural, and he had, as has been seen, his difficulties with the Hellenized cultural establishment. It was the atmosphere that changed with the Antonines. Hellenism was not merely acceptable; it was the hallmark of the new regime. Imperial policy and the political philosophers made common cause in proclaiming the rule of the Imperial Sage over the Ecumenical Empire. Encouragement was followed by patronage; the Imperial salon became a commonplace. The old forms in sculpture, architecture, literature and language were revived. The games were celebrated; the oracles spoke once again.

Rome shared in this Greek revival, but the finest fruits of the renaissance were to be seen in Greece and the East. The Antonine Emperors actively fostered municipal life, and the *poleis* entered a period of unparalleled prosperity under their tendance. Local pride joined with public spirited affluence to produce a flowering of eastern Hellenism, and whatever architectural

---

7. This is not to say there was no private education. Private tutors continued to ply their trade, though faced with increasingly heavy competition.

wreckage is still visible in the Near East today was largely the creation of the Antonines and the Severi, who followed them. In the van of this civic exuberance were the *rhetores* and *sophistai* who served as civil officials, teachers, or sometimes merely as highly paid public performers, honored by their municipalities and lionized by their fellow citizens. And both their lectures and the honors heaped upon them were couched in the most exquisite Attic Greek.

The Hellenized intellectuals took eagerly to this new order of things, and their political difficulties with the regime disappeared in time, to be replaced by an unconcealed enthusiasm. The literary results of this union of politics and the arts were not, however, uniformly happy. Hadrian's was not a classicism but a romantic archaicism, more moderate and restrained than the Philhellenism of Nero but based, nonetheless, on a past that was irrevocably dead and whose revival displayed all the disconcerting hues of a skillful act of embalming.

The foundation upon which the second-century Greek literary revival was reared was the work of the grammarians, who had been engaged since Hellenistic times in the study of the language from a syntactical and morphological point of view, a work which continued under Roman domination.[8] Lexicography was an important complementary study initiated by the later Alexandrian master Didymus (*c.* B.C. 80–10) and his student Theon,[9] both of whom compiled lexicons from the works of the great authors of the classical and Hellenistic age. Still other scholars studied the dialects.

Thus by the first Christian century there was available a great deal of information on the literary Attic tongue as well as innumerable editions and commentaries on fifth- and fourth-century authors. When coupled with the rhetoricians' insistence on purity of style and the Hadrianic nostalgia for an earlier Hellenism, it produced the literary movement known as the

---

8. Grammatical studies at Alexandria had their true founder in Aristarchus (*c.* B.C. 215–145), and the work done in his school, which betrays marked Stoic influences, is preserved in the extant grammar of Dionysius Thrax (*c.* B.C. 170–90), one of his students who later taught at Rhodes. See Chapter V, p. 195.

9. Another student of Didymus, and Theon's successor in the chair of Classical Philology at Alexandria, was Apion whose *History of Egypt* was a common and unfavorable source of information on Jewish history. Josephus attempted to answer him in his *Against Apion*.

Second Sophistic whose primary agent, the *sophistes*, provided the leadership and the ideals that dominated the entire literary culture for the century after Hadrian's accession.

The point of departure for the new sophistic was rhetorical, though it cared little for rhetorical theory.[10] The culture of the times was literary, and it was the wandering orators who doubled as teachers and statesmen who were the great apostles of the word. Improvisation was highly valued, but skill in it was won only at the price of long and dedicated immersion in and imitation of the classics; works of the Hellenistic period were disdained. The new sophist's medium was speech; his material, history; his ideal, purity of diction.

Oral speech alone, however, did not do justice to the studied techniques of these orators, and so most of them turned to literature as well. They published their speeches or letters or turned to a variety of literary forms—history, biography, the diatribe, the novel, the dialogue. Material could be drawn from any source, but the favored subject was the history and myth of the past.[11] The enemy and competitor was philosophy, but the sophist, who once had to beg crumbs from the table of the philosophers, was now triumphant; he claimed all as his domain.

Though he had predecessors,[12] the official founder, teacher, and propagandist of the new sophistic was the rich Athenian Herodes Atticus (A.D. 101–177), the student, significantly, of a pleiad of grammarians, philosophers, and sophists, and in turn the teacher of most of the great sophists of the next generation. He was honored with every political laurel the Philhellenic Empire had to bestow, and he responded by adorning his native Athens and the rest of Greece with every architectural ornament a cultured man of immense wealth could provide.

---

10. There was one great theoretician of the period, Hermogenes of Tarsus who flourished in the second half of the second century. His body of rhetorical treatises, derived chiefly from analyses of the classics (Plato and Demosthenes) and owing little or nothing to philosophy, was influential in the Neoplatonic schools and served as basic texts into Byzantine times.

11. One sophist cited the battle of Marathon so often in his speeches that he was referred to simply and pointedly as "Marathon."

12. Most notably the *sophistes* Dio of Prusa surnamed "The Golden Mouthed" (*Chrysostomos*) who outlived the difficult days of Domitian to experience the joys of the Hellenic revival under the Antonines (see Chapter XI, pp. 418–19).

Herodes' literary work is lost, but his eastern counterpart, Aelius Aristides (A.D. 129–189), a native of Mysia who studied at Pergamum and at Athens with Herodes, is considerably better known. As a young man he traveled the panegyric circuit,[13] where he made a name for himself and, after a romantic visit to Egypt, was introduced in A.D. 156 into court circles at Rome. Somewhat later he was afflicted by a serious nervous illness and spent the rest of his life between the temple-hospitals of Pergamum and his adopted city of Smyrna, which regarded him as its greatest citizen since Homer.

Aristides' own contemporaries and later generations considered him the preeminent stylist of his times. His fifty-five preserved discourses give some support to this claim, but he would perhaps have been surprised to learn what part of his work has most recently attracted attention. Most of the discourses, which exhibit a variety of literary forms from showpieces (*meletai, declamationes*) to prose hymns, are on predictable and time-worn themes: the greatness of Rome, praise of Athens, the superiority of rhetoric to philosophy, a lament for Smyrna. What are considerably more interesting, however, are his *Sacred Discourses*. From the beginning of his illness Aristides kept a daily dream diary of his curative and religious experiences. These notes were incorporated into the *Sacred Discourses* and provide an almost unparalleled source on the personal religious life of a cultured and intelligent Greek of the second century.

Aristides' belief in Asclepius was personal and immediate, supported by a number of visions and epiphanies of the god to whom he attributed all the skill and talent that he possessed. But this intimate relationship with one god did not inhibit his acceptance of the syncretism of the times. The half-Egyptian Serapis appeared to Aristides at the side of Asclepius, and he composed hymns to Zeus, Dionysus, Athena and other of the traditional Olympians. They were no longer, however, clearly distinguished individuals; the philosophically inspired henotheism had worked its effects on Aristides too: all the gods are One.

The unfortunate reign of Commodus and the transference of power to the Severan dynasty brought no slacking in the rule of the sophists. Antipater of Hierapolis in Syria played a diminished

---

13. A feature of Antonine Hellenism was the revival of the Greek games, normally accompanied by an oratorical contest and a great deal of scheduled and nonscheduled public declamation.

Herodes to Septimius Severus' Hadrian,[14] and Herodes' own pupils continued to dominate the scene.[15] And yet a shift in emphases can be detected. The ecumenical Hellenism of Hadrian was yielding to the eastern Hellenism of the Severi that, for all its imperfections, more nearly reflected the actual culture of the times than the essentially artificial concoction of the Hadrianic era.

It was one of Antipater's students who dominated the life of the court from the time of Septimius Severus. Antipater's was a political role, played out in the councils of state of Septimius; his student Flavius Philostratus ruled in the circle of the Syrian Augusta Julia Domna, who had surrounded herself with the leading sophistic wits and astrologers of the day. The best of them were second rate, Claudius Aelian, the Hellenized Italian raconteur and moralist, and Athenaeus of Naucratis in Egypt whose *Sophists at Dinner* literally tells all;[16] Philostratus himself, however, is of considerable interest. The sophistic movement found in him its historian,[17] and it was at Julia Domna's request that he composed his major work, *The Life of Apollonius of Tyana*, a description of the career of the wonder-worker of the time of Nero and Domitian.[18]

The biography of Apollonius is no religious testament in the manner of an Aristides; it is highly unlikely that Philostratus had any particular devotion to Apollonius. The initiative came from Julia, and what she had in mind may be surmised. Could not this

---

14. Antipater began as Greek Secretary to Septimius and tutor to the princes Geta and Caracalla, later became Consul, and eventually governor of Bithynia.

15. Aristides was a notoriously bad teacher (his seven students were later said to include the four walls and three benches in the classroom) and founded no school.

16. The format, a series of set topics on which the dinner guests discourse, gave the author an opportunity to display a fund of knowledge as staggering as it was pointless. As a piece of literary amber it is, of course, priceless, since Athenaeus cites only the best poets to illustrate his trivia. Almost everything we know, for example, about Greek comedy apart from Aristophanes comes from Athenaeus' citations of comedians to illustrate points about food.

17. His *Lives of the Sophists* was dedicated to his student Gordian sometime before that erstwhile epic poet became Emperor in A.D. 238 at the age of eighty. Gordian's taste for the heroic is further illustrated by the fact that he attempted to rewrite the poems of Cicero.

18. See Chapter XI, pp. 430–31.

eminent Hellenic sophist perform the same function for the
Oriental wonder-worker Apollonius that Josephus had done for
Judaism? To render him intelligible and attractive to an audience
not yet ready to embrace outright magic? The tones of the his-
torical Apollonius were muted in Philostratus' literary portrait.
And whether Julia intended it or not, the life and career of
Apollonius became a weapon in paganism's later, more deter-
mined stand against Christianity.[19]

It was a triumph for the Antonines and the Severi that they
had harnessed the literary energies of the Second Sophistic to
their own dreams of Empire. From Dio of Prusa to Philostratus
the most prominent members of the intellectual establishment
praised and served their Imperial patrons. Philosophy had either
vacated the political platform (as in the case of Platonism and
Aristotelianism, the former turning toward a union with the
mysticism of the new Pythagoreanism, the latter constructing a
technical-school tradition of imposing importance) or was in full
decline; Epicureanism and Stoicism were moribund by the second century. For at least one man, however, there was nowhere
to go.

Lucian (*c.* A.D. 120–180) was a Syrian of Samosata in Commagene, who learned Greek as a second language (Aramaic was his
mother tongue) in his adolescence. From this provincial Syrian
backwater he made his way as a lawyer and a rhetorician,
traveling extensively in the manner of the times, and even
holding a chair of Greek rhetoric in Gaul. To this point his
career matched any described in Philostratus' *Lives;* his style was
refined Attic and his mastery of the classics was complete,[20] a
celebrated orator with some good light literary pieces to his
credit. What followed cannot be pieced together with any great
certainty, but his subsequent works, whatever their exact order,
show that at some point Lucian left behind him the banalities of
the sophists, their philosophy, and their cynicism. His evolution
reads like a commonplace tale from the autobiography of antiquity

---

19. Apollonius was used as a foil for Christ, for instance, by Hierocles, the Neoplatonic governor of Bithynia who played a role in
Diocletian's persecution of the Christians. Hierocles' charge of religious plagiarism was answered by Eusebius.
20. So complete, indeed, that Lucian was the past master of parody.
He could ape the manner of Homer, Herodotus or Thucydides at
will.

("I went first to the sages . . .") without at the same time having the obligatory ending of peace restored (". . . until I came home safe to the harbor of . . ."). There was no harbor. The complete cynic ended taking a government job in Egypt, and a later sophist wrote his epitaph, "Very good at getting laughs." Not even Lucian knew what was behind the laughter.

A great many works of this Hellenized Syrian have been preserved, and in them one may see pilloried not only human failings but the all too naked foibles peculiar to that vulnerable time: the pathology of Atticism (*Lexiphanes*),[21] the vanity of a career in rhetoric (*A Professor of Rhetoric*), the Greek lackey in the hire of Rome (*Hired Companions*), the emptiness of contemporary philosophy (*Philosophies for Sale*), and of the traditional religion (*Zeus Declaims*), religious charlatanism (*Alexander, or The False Prophet*), and perverted Cynicism (*The Death of Peregrinus*). Each shows a great deal of cleverness and a certain degree of feeling. The times provided material for the high comic talent of an Aristophanes or the savage anger of a Juvenal; they produced instead, almost exactly in their own image, a Hamlet-like Menander.

On two occasions Lucian turned his not inconsiderable gift for parody to a contemporary genre of popular literature, the romance. The origins of the form went back to Hellenistic times, when the basic ingredients, a recitation of adventures drawn from the legendary or historical past, were already present. The basic "historical" material was frequently combined with those other products of a suddenly enlarged *oikoumene*, fabulous travels and tales of the exotic and the bizarre. The integration of these motifs probably owed something to the exercises in the late Hellenistic schools of rhetoric, where a typical exercise was to take just such material and render it in a dramatic—and sentimentalized—form.

The rhetorical parentage of these works is evident enough in the first fully preserved examples of the genre that date from the time of the Second Sophistic. There is, for example, a marked ambivalence about the language. Some of the romances were composed in the common dialect of the time, the *koine*, a fact that unmistakably attests to their circulation as entertainments

---

21. Lucian's own style was, of course, impeccably Attic, but like many contemporary sophists he could adeptly switch into one of the classical dialects, as he did in his Ionic *On the Syrian Goddess*.

for the Hellenized middle class, while others have adapted an
Attic style that betrays the pure hand and pedantic heart of the
sophistes. There was apparently an evolution in the subject
matter as well. The "historical" romance gave way to a purely
fictional form, wherein the subject matter was supplied by a
variety of traditional motifs and the imagination of the author.

The complete genealogy of the finished romance is highly
complex; the mime, New Comedy, the picaresque Milesian tale,
the fable, all had something to contribute to the finished product.
Mention has already been made of two examples of the historical
romance: Philostratus' romance-biography of Apollonius of
Tyana and the most widely diffused piece of secular literature
from the ancient world, the *Alexander Romance*,[22] the first the
work of intellectual pietism, the latter the work of many hands,
learned and unlearned. There were others, known only from
citation or from Latin reworkings of the original,[23] but the two
earliest completely preserved romances, the *Chaereas and Calli-
rhoë* of Chariton of Aphrodisias in Caria and the *Ephesiaca* of
Xenophon of Ephesus, both show by their quasi-historical subject
matter and the *koine* diction that they belong to the earlier stage
of the genre, when it was still relatively untouched by sophistic
attitudes. The slightly later works (they must all be before A.D.
300), the *Aethiopica* of Heliodorus of Emesa, the *Leucippe and
Clitophon* of Achilles Tatius of Alexandria, and the *Daphnis and
Chloë* of Longus of Lesbos, are pure fiction, highly stylized and
polished. Heliodorus, for example, was a cultured man who could
use not only Homer and Euripides but the new Christian literature as well.[24] The *Aethiopica* uses, as do all the others, the motif
of the young lovers who are separated or in flight and are, after a
series of adventures, finally reunited. The *Daphnis and Chloë*,
however, adds a new motif, the pastoral idyll.[25] The two lovers
are converted, via the convenient machinery of infant exposure,

---

22. See Chapter I, Note 17.

23. The Latin Middle Ages made wide use of three such romantic
revisions of ancient history drawn from Greek originals of Roman
Imperial times: the "eyewitness" reports of the Trojan War by Dictys
and Dares, and the history of Apollonius, King of Tyre.

24. A persistent and not entirely unlikely tradition makes this "Gift of
the Sun" (*Heliodorus*) from the cult city of Emesa a convert to
Christianity and eventually a bishop in Thessaly.

25. On the poetical antecedents of this, see Chapter V, pp. 201–3.

into shepherds and their sweet innocence survives even the moral rigors of sheep herding.

Lucian's two excursions into the genre do not take as their subject young love thwarted and fulfilled. The *True History* belongs rather to the category of the "fabulous journey," while *Lucius, or The Ass* is an example of the "realistic" romance or novella that descends from a slightly different tradition. Only a master could have constructed such telling parodies of a popular genre, and the *True Story* in particular, where Lucian clearly states his mocking intentions in the preface, betrays the sophist's touch: the skillful but contrived dialect, the literary and historical reminiscences, the learned trivia.

The literary renaissance of the Antonines and the Severi fell upon hard days in the latter half of the third century. Hellenism had, in a sense, failed to bind the state together in the semblance of a Hellenic Ecumenical Empire, and the years between Gordian and Constantine measured off the ebb of Greek letters and learning in the western regions, despite the well-meaning philhellenism of a Gallienus or an Aurelian. Even the Christian communities of the West eventually deserted their "native" Greek and wrote and prayed in Latin. But within its own sphere, from Dalmatia to the Euphrates, the literary culture fashioned by the new sophists revived with the fortunes of the Empire. Diocletian's strenuous efforts saved the East, and as the despair of the late third century gave way to the hope of the new *Pax Romana Christiana* of the fourth, the Second Sophistic blossomed forth once again in the eastern provinces of an Empire that was Roman only in name. By A.D. 350 not only the gods but even the politicians had abandoned the Old Rome for the New Rome on the Bosporus.

Orientals Enthroned

The road from Rome to Constantinople was paved by war. Even in Gibbon's golden age of Empire there was no such thing as permanent peace. Under Hadrian's Gallic successor Antoninus Pius (A.D. 138–161), less energetic and less the cosmopolitan Hellene than Hadrian,[26] there were more Jewish troubles,

---

26. Unlike his predecessor he spent most of his reign in Rome.

peasant revolts in Egypt that threatened the vital grain supply, and the danger of Armenia's once again reverting to Parthian control, this time through the agency of the Parthian client-king of Osrhoene, Abgar VIII. The Parthians were additionally disturbed by the fact that the Roman vassals who were supposed to serve as wardens of the marches in the Caucasus had allowed the passage of the Alans into Media Atropatene. Antoninus dealt with all these problems, forcibly where necessary, peacefully if possible, as in Parthia and Armenia, but the morbid character of the pressures along the periphery of the huge Empire was unmistakable.

The haze of a Golden Age continued to dissipate under Marcus Aurelius (A.D. 161–180). The Parthian Shah Vologesus III (A.D. 148–192) had probably been awaiting the transfer of power in Rome, and when it occurred his army promptly crossed the frontier into Armenia, destroyed the Roman legion that moved in from Cappadocia, and installed a new king. Another Parthian army met and defeated the Romans in Syria. Marcus as the new senior Emperor appointed his co-ruler and adopted brother Lucius Verus to command the punitive expedition. He did this from Antioch, leaving the field command to his generals, Statius Priscus and Avidius Cassius. Priscus regained Armenia for Rome and installed there still another Roman vassal, in this instance Sohaemus, a scion of the Arab kings of Emesa, who had been raised to Senatorial dignity. The success of Avidius Cassius was even more spectacular. He crossed into Mesopotamia and in combination with Priscus fought his way down the Euphrates past Sura, Nicephorium, and Dura Europos, finally reaching Babylonia, where he took both Seleucia and Ctesiphon from the Parthians. The reversal of fortune that followed was as sudden as it had been in Trajan's day. In the fall of A.D. 165 the Roman troops contracted their first cases of smallpox. The disease spread rapidly back to Syria and thence over the entire Empire. The troops drew back from Babylonia, and the joint triumph celebrated at home by Marcus and Lucius in A.D. 166 was marred by the chill of death.

The first easterner to attempt the seizure of supreme power in Rome was the same ambitious Syrian who had been the instrument of Lucius' victories in Mesopotamia. Avidius Cassius had earlier (A.D. 162) been governor of Syria, but in the wake of the Parthian campaign he was given an extraordinary command (*imperium maius*) of the entire East. It was a well considered appointment. Marcus Aurelius had stripped the eastern provinces of troops for his war against the Germans, and when in A.D. 172–173 there was still another peasant revolt in under-defended Egypt, Avidius crushed it with dispatch. The time seemed ripe for a bolder stroke. Lucius had died in A.D. 169, and by A.D. 175 Marcus was heavily and dangerously committed on the northern frontiers against the Germans and the Sarmatians. Imperial prestige was on the wane, and it was even said that the Augusta Faustina, anticipating—prematurely—the death of her husband, was contemplating marriage to Cassius to preserve the throne for her son Commodus. Cassius, with an easy control of his native East and particularly of the all-important Egypt, had himself proclaimed Emperor and set up a rump government in Syria. Only Cappadocia held firm for Marcus. Cassius' usurpation, like his marriage plans, was decidedly premature. At the mere news that Marcus was heading east in person to quell the revolt Cassius was murdered by his own lieutenants.

Cassius' was the failure of a merely political bid for power. Had he succeeded there is every reason to believe that the Syrian-born but Roman-trained disciplinarian would have hastened to the Dalmatian frontier to take up his Imperial duties as protector of Rome against the barbarian. But a general, Syrian or otherwise, could change the Empire no more swiftly than it was changing itself. Eastern aristocrats were rising through the Equestrian and Senatorial ranks, and it would merely be a matter of time until one of them came to power legitimately. There were other avenues that led from East to Rome. The Empire was an *oikoumene*. Merchants traveled it from end to end; troops were shuttled from the Rhine to the Danube to the Orontes and back, carrying with them native brides, a taste for the local delicacies, and a bewildering variety of eastern cults. The generally tolerant religious attitudes of the Antonines (Hadrian's repression in Palestine was a political act) permitted and even encouraged this trade in deities. Oriental cults had been in Rome for centuries but now they were the vogue.

The change was already observable in Marcus' son Commodus (A.D. 180–192, co-ruler with his father from A.D. 177). The Stoic sage, an image judiciously cultivated, and occasionally even fulfilled, by his predecessors, disappeared in the miasma of another Nero, who specialized not in music but in athletic prowess, a gladiator with a mystical streak. His coins are crammed with all the gods the times held sacred: Magna Mater, Serapis, Helius, Jupiter of Dolichene, Mithra. Commodus was strangled to death by his private sparring partner in A.D. 192.

The various political powers of the Empire, the army, Senators, the Pretorian Guard, all moved into the vacuum. The eastern candidate was Pescennius Niger, governor of Syria from A.D. 190 or 191. He was immediately acclaimed by the legions in Syria, Palestine and Egypt, Asia and Bithynia. Another claimant emerged in the West, Septimius Severus, and when the minor figures in the drama had been disposed of, Severus brought his Dalmatian legions to Asia to confront Pescennius. Their forces met at Issus in A.D. 194, and Severus was triumphant. Since Pescennius was the second Syrian pretender in twenty years, Severus took immediate steps to reduce the possibility of there being another at his own expense. Syria was divided into two provinces: Coele-Syria[27] and Phoenician Syria, the northern and central heartland and the Phoenician coast,[28] to reduce the army commands to more modest proportions. Nor did he overlook Antioch's support of the rebel; Septimius deprived it of its position as capital of Syria and made it a "village" dependent on nearby Laodicea.[29]

What equally disturbed Severus was the support Pescennius received from the Parthian clients in Osrhoene and Adiabene, and here he resorted to force. In two expeditions across the Euphrates, in A.D. 195 in Mesopotamia and in the more bitterly fought campaigns of A.D. 197–199, the tottering Parthian Empire was once again brought to its knees by Roman arms. On the surface it seemed like another punitive war, but doubtless the figure of Trajan loomed large in the ambitions of Severus. Since

---

27. The area around the central depression which runs north from Aqaba and is represented in Palestine by the Jordan valley and in Lebanon by the central valley of the Biqa (see Chapter IV, Note 3).

28. Coele-Syria was later to be divided once again and so too Phoenicia, the latter into Phoenicia-by-the-Sea (*Parhalos*) and Lebanese Phoenicia.

29. Its normal position of preeminence was restored by Caracalla, who raised Antioch from the rank of *municipium* to *colonia*, a distinction that not even contemporary politicians perfectly understood, though they knew that it was more advantageous to be a *colonia* than a *municipium*.

that earlier Emperor's day the triumphant title of "Parthicus" exercised its fascination at Rome. Severus thought as Trajan had thought: the east bank of the Euphrates could be held. He annexed the area between the two rivers down to the edge of the Syrian desert as the provinces of Osrhoene and Mesopotamia, with the respective capitals (*metropoleis*) at Edessa[30] and Nisibis. What Severus and his son Caracalla, who also conducted a senseless campaign against Parthia,[31] did not perceive was that at each new blow Parthia was being pushed closer to her doom. At the assassination of Caracalla near the fatal Carrhae in A.D. 217 the end was only ten years away.

The Roman Empire almost resists analysis of change. Conservative institutions and ways of thinking mask the foment beneath them. The Imperial coinage was frankly propagandistic, and contemporary history—exceedingly sparse in the third century—was as tendentious as it was anecdotal. But there are signs to be read. Commodus marked a change from the central stability of nearly a century of orderly, almost impersonal rule. At his death the principle of succession was once again in doubt, and ambitions were excited. The army came more and more to be recruited locally—so that, for instance, the Syrian army corps came to represent both a potential emperor-maker and a force representing a Syrian point of view. Power had fled from Rome to the armies of the frontiers, and they in turn had taken on a marked parochial tone.

The frontiers were long and difficult to hold, stretching from Britain, along the Rhine and the Danube, across the Caucasus and Anatolia, along the Tigris and the Syrian desert to Aqaba. And from Egypt to Morocco there were ominous pressures against the advanced Roman positions in Africa. There appears to have been a growing feeling that the Empire was beyond the powers of a

---

30. The Abgars were allowed to sit at Edessa a few years longer.
31. Caracalla, whose Trajanic fantasies were complicated by visions of himself as Alexander, offered a dynastic marriage to the daughter of Artabanus V of Parthia (A.D. 213–224). When she declined to play Roxane to his Alexander, Caracalla took up arms. Like Alexander he had in his army a Macedonian phalanx, a military antique of dubious value at this point. But he improved Alexander's scenario at Troy: where Alexander had been content to weep, Caracalla had the body of one of his servants, who opportunely died at the time, burned on a truly Patroclan funeral pyre.

single man to administer. From Marcus Aurelius there had been co-emperors on occasion, and though their respective administrative responsibilities were not clearly set forth, a basis for the division of authority, geographical or otherwise, had been established. The subject of an eastern and a western ruler had been broached at the accession of Septimius' sons Caracalla and Geta in A.D. 211, but it came to nothing when Geta was murdered by his brother in the following year. More importantly, Caracalla's mother was opposed to it.

Each new Emperor strove to restore the dynastic principle that would ensure the survival of himself and his family in the seats of power. The Severi were successful both in holding their own line of succession and relating themselves back to the Antonines; their successors were not. The Severan connection was, of course, spurious (Commodus had no heir), based as it was on the contention of the Antonines' posthumous adoption of Septimius into their family. Septimius was himself born in Leptis, a former Phoenician colony in Africa, where Punic was still spoken in his day. But he was no barbarian; indeed his rise was in the best Imperial tradition: Romanized in the army, Hellenized in Greece, brilliant service rewarded by a Senatorship, and finally governor of Pannonia on the Danubian frontier, where his troops had acclaimed him Emperor; all in all, an intelligent and cultured provincial[32] who was neither a revolutionary nor an Oriental tyrant.

The rule of Severus rested upon a military foundation, and his most important measures were devoted to strengthening that base. Both he and Caracalla raised the army pay, to unsound heights as it later turned out. Further, he paid off his veterans with grants of land that formed colonies with special rights and privileges. In Egypt they may have been intended for economic ends, the reclamation of land for instance, but in Syria and Mesopotamia their function was more clearly military. Carrhae, Edessa, Nisibis and Dura were all *coloniae*, and all had either Roman army veterans living in them or regular army detachments stationed there. There was even a garrison in the caravan city of Palmyra, even though it was not constitutionally part of the Empire, and regular army detachments were recruited there.

---

32. Not nearly cultured enough, however, to win over the intellectuals, the hearts of most of whom still belonged to the Antonines.

The network of forts and *coloniae* and the presumed good will of the sovereign *shaykhs* of Palmyra were the Severan shield against Iran.

Severus' lavish treatment of the army put an additional strain on the faltering economy of the Empire. To reward, cajole and bribe the military establishment, and at the same time conduct wars and embark on huge public works projects—Severus adorned his home province of Africa as no one before him and few since—required enormous sums of money that could be gained only by greater and greater pressures. And the well was beginning to run dry. In Egypt, normally the first to feel the pressure and the last to succumb to it, confiscation and the flight of the peasants from the estates grew to an alarming pitch. Collapse was imminent.

Caracalla, while indulging in the most unrestrained financial prodigality, cast about for palliatives. He continued to tamper with the coinage,[33] but more spectacular was the "Antoninian Constitution," an edict which extended Roman citizenship to all the free population of the Empire.[34] In other times it might have been a liberal gesture recognizing the unity of the human race under Roman rule; for Caracalla it represented the extension of the inheritance tax—which was paid only by Roman citizens and which he had just doubled—to everyone in the Empire. Whatever its financial motivation and value, the Constitution did end once and for all any claim to prerogative by Romanism. It did not, needless to say, erase the chasm between the social and economic classes, the urban provincial aristocracy and the *humiliores*.

Severus had come from that aristocracy and had taken a wife from an even more potent segment of it in Syria. Julia Domna, his second wife, whom the credulous Severus married for her royal horoscope, was the daughter of Julius Bassianus, hereditary priest-king of the cult of Baal of Emesa. Severus and his wife appeared on their coinage as the Sun and the Moon. She was also portrayed as Cybele, and her titles included "Mother of the Army Corps,

---

33. The *aureus* slipped up to fifty to the pound of gold, and there was a new silver piece, the *antoninianus*, designed to pass as a double *denarius* but weighing no more than a *denarius* and a half.

34. Or nearly all. One Greek papyrus which reproduces the edict excludes one class, the *dediticii* ("surrendered"). Who they were is still, after many attacks on the problem, not clear.

the Senate and the Fatherland." Emperor worship became exceed-ingly outspoken in the third century, and the Imperial women were given their own place in the "Divine Household." The cult of the *dominus deus* who was the Emperor was introduced into and supported by the army. Oaths were sworn in the name not of the gods but of the Emperor.

The tide that had been rising since the time of Augustus through the agency of the municipal cultus and the eager politi-cal pieties of the army now reached the Imperial level, and the worship of the sovereign could be blatantly proclaimed abroad. Everything that was connected with the person of the Emperor or with his government came to be called sacred, and the official protocol inevitably reflected the new attitude. Subjects ap-proached their lord with the kissing of hands or feet (the *proskynesis* that caused Alexander so much grief) and remained standing in his presence. The Emperor was portrayed with diadem, scepter and orb, and seated on a throne, all symbols and signs of the monarchy that the Romans had once found so hateful but was now, in the course of the third century, accepted by the people of an Empire whose most sophisticated and important subjects were from eastern lands where monarchy was not only accepted but expected.[35]

This was the mood of the times from the beginning of the third century, and the ascendancy of the Syrian sisters, Julia Domna and Julia Maesa, was a harbinger of those days. Like Severus, they were Hellenes, but while his Hellenism was grounded in the Roman tradition of Africa, their own had Oriental roots. During her reign as Augusta Julia Domna presided over a literary salon in the capital where the luminaries of the Greek revival held forth. Philostratus received her particular patronage, and his life of Apollonius of Tyana was, in a sense, a monument to her spirit and interests. But her interest in litera-ture, religion and philosophy was only her second choice; access to political power had been barred by the ascendancy of others. When Severus died, however, Julia was in the center of things, pushing her favorite son Geta at the expense of his brother Caracalla, only to have him murdered in her own arms by the vicious Caracalla.

---

35. It should be noted, however, that the *imperator* never styled himself by the obnoxious title of *rex;* and its Greek equivalent, *basileus,* was not adopted until the time of Heraclius, in A.D. 629.

When Caracalla too was assassinated in A.D. 217, it was Maesa's turn. The Imperial power had been usurped for a few months by the instigator of the assassination plot, Macrinus, a Mauritanian lawyer serving with Caracalla and the first non-Senator ever to wear the Imperial purple. Macrinus had sent Maesa back to Syria, where she now produced one of her grandchildren, the fourteen-year-old son of Maesa's daughter Soaemias and the Syrian Senator Varius Marcellus. Neither mother nor son promised well, but so strong had grown the dynastic attachment that, at Maesa's suggestion that he was the illegitimate son of Caracalla, the boy Varius Avitus was acclaimed Emperor by the Syrian troops. Macrinus was deserted by his men and eventually slain.

The Empire, formerly the occasional pawn of both fools and knaves, never experienced anything quite like the four-year reign (A.D. 218–222) of Varius Avitus, who reigned over the Senate and the Roman people under his sacerdotal name of Elagabalus. Others, Nero, Commodus, Caracalla, had yielded to their own fantasies; Elagabalus was genuine. The depraved priest of an orgiastic cult, he openly celebrated the rites of his solar god in Rome. The Romans knew solar religions, as they knew almost every other conceivable religious phenomenon, but they had never experienced one in this raw local form, complete with attendant eunuchs and a conical black stone which was the god's presence and which Elagabalus had thoughtfully brought to Rome. Elagabalus converted no one but his political sycophants, some of whom took to wearing hair nets in emulation of the Emperor, and perhaps also the Vestal Virgin he insisted on marrying, to the great scandal of a Roman populace, who thought they had seen all. Finally even Maesa was disenchanted. And she had another candidate.

At his murder in A.D. 222,[36] Elagabalus was succeeded by the son of Maesa's other daughter, Mamaea, and this new scion of Emesa reigned under the name of Alexander Severus. He too was only fourteen at his accession, but had been carefully educated at a healthy distance from the infectious Elagabalus. Alexander was quietly affiliated back to Caracalla under the careful governance of the two Augustae, Maesa and Mamaea. The latter guided her son skillfully, and his reign was marked by only one major crisis;

---

36. His mother, Soaemias, perished with him; the black stone was sent back to Emesa.

Mamaea could not play the soldier for him and it brought about Alexander's ruin.

On the subject of religion mother and son were of the same mind, an inquisitive tolerance. In his private chapel Alexander had statues of Jesus, Abraham and Orpheus.[37] It was a gesture typical of a syncretistic age—and worthy of a cousin of Elagabalus[38]—remarkable only for the presence of Jesus. The earlier Severi had treated the Christians rather harshly, and the change in Alexander is almost certainly due to the influence of Mamaea, who betrayed more than a passing curiosity about Christianity. During a stay in Antioch about A.D. 231, for instance, she had summoned Origen from Caesarea to consult with her there. Mamaea was not herself converted, but there were almost certainly Christians in the "divine household."

The Iranian Renaissance

The degeneration of the line of the Severi was the prelude to the more disquieting shocks the Empire was to receive as the third century wore on. In other days Rome's internal disorders might have drawn careful attention across the eastern frontier, but at the beginning of that century the Parthians were approaching their own end time, and so it was not they but others who harvested the Empire's discomforts in the name of a new Iranian consciousness. The Parthians, ever uncertain as to whether they were the heirs of Alexander or of Iran, turned to their Iranian past with Vologesus I (c. A.D. 51-80). From his reign onward the Imperial coinage bore Parthian and Aramaic inscriptions instead of the earlier Greek ones, and the cities in the eastern part of his realms reassumed their native Iranian names.

Politically the policy was no more successful than the earlier Parthian philhellenism. The Romans in their strength breached the frontier on three different occasions, under Trajan, under Marcus Aurelius and under Septimius Severus. The Parthian

---

37. In the same room were portraits of the "deified Emperors," an interesting juxtaposition. In a smaller chapel Alexander paid his dues to Roman pretensions with portraits of Vergil and Cicero.
38. A connection which the Antiochenes, never very gentle with their Emperors, did not allow Alexander to forget. On a visit there he was derided as "a Syrian synagogue keeper."

confederation began to atomize into a series of petty kingdoms that appropriated more and more power to themselves. Indeed some of these Parthian "provinces," in reality semiautonomous states under loose Parthian suzerainty, had never been under the close jurisdiction of Ctesiphon. Fars, for example, the home province of the Achaemenians, had had local princes in control since as far back as the Seleucids, an arrangement in which the Parthians too were constrained to acquiesce.

The Parthians' difficulties with Roman arms through the second and early third century were magnified by the dangerous condition of their own eastern frontier. At about the same time the Parthians were first consolidating their power in Iran, the great confederation known in the Chinese sources as the Yüeh-chih were settling in Bactria where they destroyed the Greek kingdoms and thrust the Sacae south and east of the Hindu Kush.[39] One part of the Central Asian confederation, the Kushans, perhaps Scythians in what must have been a very mixed horde, won supremacy over the rest of the Yüeh-chih, and from the first century A.D. there rested upon the eastern frontiers of the Parthians a powerful Kushan Empire that stretched from the Indus to the Oxus. The aggressive mercantile policies of Nero brought him in contact with these new masters of the eastern trade routes, a relationship conducted to the obvious disadvantage of the Parthians. The Iranian turnings of Vologesus doubtless nodded in the same direction.

The founder of this mighty tribal state was a king known as Kajula Kadphises, but it was under one of his successors, Kanishka (A.D. 144–173), that the Kushans' role as commercial middlemen in the complex of routes running overland from the Mediterranean to India and China was expanded into the dimension of ideas. Kanishka was a convert to the Mahayana Buddhism that had been moving steadily northward in India, and through the agency of the Kushans it spread still farther along the trade routes, making its first substantial contacts with the West and passing even more easily into the Chinese protectorates of Central Asia and eventually China itself.[40]

The Kushans, little known and little understood, were the true propagators of Hellenism in eastern Iran. The earlier Greek

---

39. See Chapter VII, p. 276.
40. It was a Kushan who translated the Buddhist scriptures into Chinese in the first half of the third century A.D.

THE SASANIAN EMPIRE

Scales

0   50 100   200   300
English miles

0 50 100   200   300   400   500
Kilometres

kingdoms were parochial and limited; the Kushans controlled an empire. And among the debris of that empire are the coins and artifacts with Chinese and Hellenistic motifs, the gods of India and Rome, the alphabet of the Greeks and the language of the Iranians. Especially fertile was the contact of Greco-Roman art and Buddhism in the kingdom ruled by Kanishka. In the territory of Gandhara between the upper Indus and Kabul the two came together to form a school of art that had a profound influence on the iconography of Buddhism. The earlier unrealized figures of Buddha yielded to new Apollo types derived directly and demonstrably from Hellenistic prototypes. The artists were probably Greek sculptors from the Roman province of Syria carried eastward along the open lines of commerce.

The Kushans showed themselves more interested in India than in whatever enticements the tottering Parthians might offer. The distractions of India may have saved the Parthians from extinction, but it did not prevent the Kushans from enriching themselves at Parthian expense in the eastern caravan cities of Iran which were detached from Parthian suzerainty and added to the Kushan holdings. The Parthians stood by as helplessly as the Seleucids had done when their vast empire fell to pieces.

The Parthians were permitted one final strike against Rome. Caracalla had designs against Parthia, encouraged doubtless by the protracted civil war between the brothers Vologesus V and Artabanus V. The latter's refusal to grant his daughter in marriage to the *imperator* sealed matters in the uncertain mind of Caracalla. An expedition was mounted in A.D. 215, and Roman armies penetrated into Media. As a renewal was being planned for the next season of campaigning Caracalla was assassinated at Carrhae by order of his pretorian prefect Macrinus. Artabanus was quick to seize the opportunity presented by the violent change of rule on the other side of the Euphrates and the battered Macrinus had to sue for an expensive peace.

Artabanus' success was short-lived. His eastern vassals were restive and the province of Fars was in open insurrection. The instigator there was Ardashir, the descendant and successor of Papak and Sasan, vassal kings of Fars who were members of a family descended from the Achaemenians and important functionaries in the temple of Anahita at Istakhr. Ardashir may have been attempting to extend his hereditary power outside the province of Fars; he attracted, at any rate, the unfavorable attention of Artabanus V, who marched out to chastise his rebellious vassal. The battle between their forces in A.D. 224 cost Artabanus his life and brought to an end the Parthian hegemony of Iran. Ardashir's troubles were not yet over. A coalition of Parthians, Armenians and Kushans, probably with Roman support, confronted Ardashir anew. He was once again successful. Ardashir, now styled "Shah of Iran," had placed the dynasty of Sasan firmly in control of all the lands once ruled by the Parthians.

In their official hagiography the Sasanians pictured themselves as restorers of the genuine Iranian tradition that had fallen onto ill times under the Greeks and Parthians. In language, style and religion they connected themselves back to the glorious days of the Achaemenians. The claim was mostly propaganda. The state remained the feudal conglomerate it had been under the Parthians, though the Sasanians attempted to curb the power and number of the noble families that had gathered enormous strength at the expense of the enfeebled Arsacid monarchs. Their language was not the Old Persian of the Achaemenians, but the Pahlevi of the Parthians. Only their claim to have effected a religious renaissance will bear scrutiny.

Under the Achaemenians the Iranian religion had undergone a reform and purification at the hands of Zarathustra, or Zoroaster (c. B.C. 628–551). The old Indo-Iranian paganism was reduced to a monotheistic religion of great force wherein the High God Ahura Mazda ruled over his two powers, the Spenta Mainyu, the Spirit of Holiness, Truth and Light, and the Angra Mainyu, the Spirit of the Lie, Destruction and Darkness. According to the reform, man must choose between the Lie and Truth; that choice is the essence and point of the moral warfare that is life. The other gods of the old Aryan pantheon Zoroaster dismissed to the rank of *daevas*, lower spirits not unlike the Greek *daimones*.

The reforms of Zoroaster found favor with Darius and Xerxes, and thereafter the Achaemenians were officially worshipers of Ahura Mazda and followers of the religion of the Truth. But Zoroaster no more than Muhammad could totally suppress the polytheism inherent in the religion he sought to reform. Under the later Achaemenians some of the derogated *daevas* returned to their original preeminence at the side of Ahura Mazda. The sun god Mithra and the fertility goddess Anahita were once more abroad,[41] and it eventually came about that Ahura Mazda, transformed into Ormazd, was identified with his Holy Spirit and set against the Evil Spirit, Ahriman, in a system of radical dualism that struck the later Greek observers, Plutarch for example, as the most distinctive characteristic of Iranian religion as they knew it.

This broad, eclectic version of Zoroastrianism must have been the one that flourished under the Parthians, even though the new rulers were not as noticeably interested in religion as either their Achaemenian predecessors or their Sasanian heirs. Anahita was popular—the family of Ardashir were wardens of her fire temple at Istakhr—and the Philhellene Parthians displayed little scruple in assimilating to her various ladies from the Greek pantheon. And somewhere in the midst of this the tradition of orthodox Zoroastrianism must also have been preserved.

There is much made in the Sasanians' books of Ardashir's reconstituting the text of the Zoroastrian Scripture, the *Avesta*, that had allegedly been destroyed during the dark days of Alexander's conquest. Whatever the truth of this, the veritable restorer of the strict Zoroastrianism was not at all the Shah but the Magus, or *mobadh*, Kartir, who came to the fore under Shapur I and who, as Chief Priest (*mobadhan mobadh*) of the realm, lorded it over his weak successors Ormizd I (A.D. 272–273), Bahram I (A.D. 273–276) and Bahram II (A.D. 276–293). The years after the death of Shapur I in A.D. 272 were filled with crises and reaction for the Sasanians. Shapur's dazzling successes against the Romans were in the long run countered by the rise of Palmyra,[42] and his flirtation with syncretistic Hellenism and Manichaeism found no support among the stubborn and conservative Magi, whom Kartir represented.

The *Denkart* is a ninth-century Pahlevi book on religion that provides, together with the imperial Sasanian inscriptions, most of what is known of the history of Zoroastrianism.[43] The

---

41. It was, for example, the Anatolian worship of Mithra, untroubled by Zoroastrian reform, that infiltrated the Roman Empire as a mystery religion (see Chapter XII, pp. 475–79).

42. See Chapter XVI, pp. 596–601.

43. The *Denkart*, which is only partly preserved, was the work of the theologian Aturnfarnbag, who spent at least part of his days at Baghdad under the Caliph al-Ma'mun (A.D. 813–833) arguing on behalf of a failing Zoroastrianism.

Denkart's narrative of the religious activity of Shapur says nothing of that Shah's dalliance with Manichaeism,[44] an evil word
after the purges of Kartir, but makes note of his collection of
those writings on Zoroastrianism "which were dispersed throughout India, the Byzantine Empire, and other lands," writings on
the subject of medicine, astronomy, physics and cosmology.
What exactly is meant is not entirely clear; perhaps Shapur had
translated, or, as he may have thought, retranslated into Pahlevi
and incorporated into the *Avesta* the body of literature current
in Hellenic circles under the name of Zoroaster and other Persian
sages. Whatever the channels of transmission, the Iranians knew
well enough about the Greek sciences. Another ninth-century
Pahlevi book, the *Bundahishn,* a religious cosmology, is shot
through with Hellenic learning introduced into Zoroastrianism at
an earlier date, through the influence of either Shapur or the later
Hellenophile Shah Khusrau (A.D. 531–579).

Shapur's imperial ambitions may have urged him toward the
conversion of Zoroastrianism into a broadly based world religion
on the style of Christianity or Buddhism. The Magi, the traditional priestly caste in Iran, had other notions. Kartir appears to
have headed Shapur off from imminent Manichaeism, but the
accession of the Shah's weaker descendants provided the *mobadhan mobadh* with an opportunity for purges at home and
missionary activity abroad, both based on what Kartir read as the
true Zoroastrianism. Kartir's zeal cost Mani his life, and after A.D.
273 the ascendancy of Kartir at court was felt not only by the
daeva-fanciers among the Iranians but by Manichaeans, Christians, Jews, Mandaeans and Buddhists as well.

Kartir strengthened the hand of the Magi in Iran and created
the semblance of an orthodox Zoroastrian Church, but he signaled the end of neither the manifold sects that held the ground
there nor of the call to syncretism that was as strong in Iran as it
was within the Roman Empire. Judaism had been entrenched in
Babylonia since the sixth pre-Christian century and in the days of
Ardashir and Shapur stood on the brink of that academic renaissance that was to produce, within another three centuries, the
finished monument of the Babylonian Talmud. Christianity
passed effortlessly across the frontier, assisted by Shapur's policy

---

44. See Chapter XVIII, p. 664.

of resettling his Roman captives in Sasanian territory, and constituted another important and vocal minority in Iran. Manichaeism
did not disappear with the execution of its founder. Greek and
Indian ideas continued to circulate along the periphery of Iran in
the Roman West and the Kushan East to a degree that can be
read most clearly in the annals of early Islam. The Arab masters
of Iran found there a soil whose earlier Hellenic richness must lie
concealed beneath the poverty of the Sasanian sources. Islamic
Hellenism was not solely the fruit of the conquest of Alexandria
and Antioch; it derived in large part from what was already
present within the Sasanian realms.

Despite this open acceptance of the cultural and religious ideas
of others, the Sasanians remained what they claimed to be, the
latter-day successors to a millennial Iranian tradition. The literature in Pahlevi is very imperfectly preserved, but there are more
impressive monuments to the depth and strength of that tradition. Within Islam, in the permissive climate of the petty principalities of the East, the Iranian spirit began to revive in the ninth
and tenth centuries, nourished by the strain of ideas, forms, and
motifs going back to Sasanian times.

Sasanian literature, like its art, centered about the person and
court of the Shah. His deeds, and those of his courtiers, were
recorded, together with the feats of the earlier Achaemenians, in
a rich epic tradition compounded equally of myth, folklore,
legend and history. Some of this can still be read in Pahlevi, in the
Book of the Deeds of Ardashir, for example, but far more perfectly in the *Book of Kings* of the later Persian poet Firdawsi (*c.*
A.D. 934–1020), a national history of early Iran in verse form.
Eventually Islam was to erode the Zoroastrian bases of Iranian
sentiment and produce the skeptical and mischievously immoral
note characteristic of later Persian poetry. During Sasanian times,
however, the tone was still relentlessly moral, if not pietistic. The
Iranians took their religion seriously, almost defensively. Zoroaster's own emphases on truth, justice and morality dominated
the Iranian feudal epic, as well as the other Sasanian literary
forms, collections of aphorisms, advice to princes, and precepts
of the faith.

Zoroastrianism, although it felt the influence and control of
the cult-oriented Magi, was under constant pressure from Manichaeism, Christianity and finally Islam, to produce a learned and
scientific theology on the model of those other religions. By the

ninth century there was something approaching such a theology, illustrated, as has been noted, by the *Denkart*, the *Bundahishn*, and the *Shkand Gumanik Vičar*, the "Elucidation That Removes Doubts." Not all doubts were removed, however; Zoroastrianism had little future under Islam.

XVI

Crisis and Survival

When the childless Alexander Severus and his mother Mamaea were murdered by his disenchanted troops in A.D. 235 it signaled the end of another dynasty. The Empire had survived such crises before. On three previous occasions Vespasian, Nerva and Septimius Severus had shown that it was possible to raise up a new house from the chaos of an interregnum. This time, however, no new founding father emerged. For half a century the Empire was at the mercy of its problems, which neither good will nor energy were able to overcome and which, by the death of Alexander, seemed to threaten the very survival of the state.

The Crisis of the Third Century

Between A.D. 235 and A.D. 284 Rome was governed by a procession of soldiers and Senators, peasants, lawyers and civil servants, and the son of a Transjordanian Arab *shaykh* who, by an exquisite irony of history, wore the Imperial purple in A.D. 248, when the millennium of Rome's founding was celebrated with pomp in the capital. Philip the Arab was neither the best nor the worst of these Emperors. He rose through the ranks in the normal Roman fashion of preferment, and once come to power, he dutifully played his Imperial role on the frontiers. He tried hard to found a dynasty but reigned only five years and fell.

Philip's reign was longer than most. The twenty legitimate Emperors who ruled from A.D. 235 to A.D. 284 averaged two and a half years in power. One died of plague, two at the hands of the enemy, and the rest in the clutches of their subjects, usually their successors. Men were overmastered by events, no one surviving long enough to confront, much less to solve, the complex of problems threatening the Empire. Two vigorous new peoples had appeared on the frontiers: the Goths had broken through the Danubian defenses, and the Sasanians had replaced the moribund Parthian Arsacids in Iran. Internally it appeared to be merely a question of whether bankruptcy or civil war would be the first to destroy the state. Both Romanized Gaul and Hellenized Syria appeared ready to secede and be reconstituted as separate kingdoms. Or perhaps it would be the treason of the Christians that would hasten the end.

The end did not in fact come, and though no single man saved the Empire from its imminent dissolution, the most effective and imaginative action was taken by the Dalmatian soldier Diocles, who, as Marcus Aurelius Valerius Diocletianus, guided the destiny of the Roman state from A.D. 284 until his voluntary abdication in A.D. 305. Even before he came to power it was clear that the Gothic and Sasanian threats had been at least temporarily checked,[1] but not before the Goths had overrun most of Greece and conducted extensive sea raids along the Asia coast, where in A.D. 263 they destroyed the temple of Artemis at Ephesus. The stabilization of the eastern frontier was the work of Aurelian (A.D. 270–275), the most effective of the post-Severan Emperors, who put down the insurrections in Gaul and Syria, and held the Sasanians in check. What still confronted Diocletian, however, was the internal collapse of the Imperial system initiated by Augustus.

With the gradual decline of the Italian economy during the days of the Julio-Claudian line, the prosperity of the Empire rested squarely on the provinces. Italy could still, down to the time of the Severi, provide the manpower for the legions, but goods and land came from other quarters, from the great estates of Africa and Egypt and from the industrial and commercial complexes in Syria and Egypt.

Ancient states led their financial lives almost from day to day. There was normally enough income from taxes to satisfy operat-

---

1. The Goths were defeated in a series of campaigns under Gallienus (A.D. 253–268) and Claudius (A.D. 268–270).

ing expenses, and if with careful management or opportune booty a surplus was accumulated, it quickly disappeared into public works, entertainment or extravagance. Wars fought by such states might involve the loss of men or damage to the crops but rarely huge outlays of money, since the armies were essentially citizen militias willing and able to take up arms at notice.

Rome, on the other hand, was a complex political and economic entity with a professional standing army whose payment in either money or land was a recurrent and serious problem. The Roman Republic had possessed millionaires capable of floating, from their own resources, enormous government loans. By the time of the Empire most such large fortunes had been wiped out, and the state had to turn to new sources of extraordinary income. One such was the banks of the temple states of Asia, but such tempting sources of ready gold did not long survive. As war grew endemic and armies ever larger (and more difficult to control) there had to be a regular supply of ready money to pay the troops and at the same time continue the extravagances which the Roman people had come to look upon as their birthright. The provinces were flourishing; they were tapped next.

The Greek East had two distinct economies since the days of Alexander: the *fellahin* state of Egypt and the *polis* economy of Asia and Syria. The Romans ran the first as the Pharaohs and Ptolemies had. Egypt was administered from its combined *polis*, trade mart and bureaucratic headquarters at Alexandria. And in the end the Romans failed as the Ptolemies had failed before them. Neither centralization nor decentralization, neither estates nor small holdings served to keep the workers in the fields or the managers at their posts. It was frequently the *immediacy* of their needs that led the Romans to resort to various forms of that ancient eastern practice well known on the Nile—the *corvée*, or forced labor. In theory, and in Egypt in practice, the individual belonged to the state. And the state, more and more impotent of its needs, exacted goods and services on demand. Under a variety of names (*indictio, annona*) the Romans demanded from Egyptian individuals and guilds, in addition to the regular taxes, the compulsory delivery of goods—sometimes paid for, sometimes not—of food and of means of transportation. Requisition and confiscation were the order of the day. The manager, the farmer, the peasant-serf had only one recourse, flight (*anachoresis*). It was more and more frequently taken.

The statist approach to the economy of Egypt left untouched the municipal aristocracy of Alexandria. This *polis* was a sport in the structure of Egypt, and it was not the policy of Rome that Alexandria possess a normal city government on the Greek model with its attendant degree of autonomy. Various petitions had been addressed to early Emperors requesting a municipal council or *boule*, but such was the Roman fear of insurrection in this most vital of provinces that even this modicum of self-government was denied. But the decision, taken on political grounds, also had the effect of depriving Rome of revenues which derived from municipalities. By the time of Septimius Severus the economic need outweighed the political fear, and in A.D. 197 Alexandria was given its *boule*—and its new taxes.[2] Caracalla's extension of citizenship in A.D. 212 had much the same motivation: it brought everyone into the tax structure.

The essence of the *polis* was that it was an autonomous unit, and from the time of their foundation in Asia such states were allowed to preserve that autonomy. Under the Persians, Alexander, and the Romans, the *poleis* retained all their original rights but two: they had to surrender control of their foreign policy to their new masters—in effect they could no longer on their own initiative make war—and they were obliged to pay tribute.[3]

Both the Republican governors and the early Emperors fostered these *poleis*, pushing new ones farther into the hinterland or founding their Italian equivalent, the *colonia* of military veterans. The municipalities, in turn, spread Hellenic culture, anchored the Roman presence in the area and, flourishing under the peace and security of the *Pax Romana*, provided a sound tax base. The provinces in which they were found might have a Roman governor, greedy or responsible as character or circumstances dictated, but the *poleis* themselves were self-governed. In the ideal Hellenic *polis* all the free men of the city were enfranchised citizens and constituted the *demos*. But, as at Rome itself, the *demos* of these latter-day *poleis* had surrendered most of its

---

2. There were probably other towns in Egypt which received this "privilege" at the same time.
3. On occasion some *poleis* were exempted from the tribute for reasons of gratitude or sentiment. Under the Romans those motives gave way to economic necessity, though even the Romans were capable of the random grand gesture—e.g., the immunity of Troy (Ilium).

legislative powers, and during the greater part of the period of Roman control the effective government of the eastern cities was in the hands of its council (*boule*).[4] This was a body composed of ex-magistrates, and since the council controlled the nominations for magistrates, it had an effective say in who would eventually join its membership. These local senators (*bouleutai, curiales*) became the provincial aristocracy of the Roman East, wealthy men, cultured and public spirited.

One had to be wealthy to be a *curialis*. Not only was a public donation expected upon the assumption of this dignity,[5] but the magistracies themselves frequently entailed dipping into one's own pocket. The actual government of the *polis* was in the hands of an executive board of magistrates termed "generals" (*strategoi; archon* was also used on occasion) who supervised the various specialized magistracies: the market inspector (*agronomos*), who regulated the commercial life of the city, its mercantile dealings and the buildings; the grain suppliers (*sitones*), who were responsible for an adequate supply of food at reasonable prices; the "chief of peace" (*eirenarch*), who saw to good order and public morals; the public prosecutor (*ekdikos*); and, finally, the "ten first men" (*dekaprotoi, decemprimi*), the wealthy citizens in charge of remitting the assessed tax to Rome.

Many of these offices were, for all their honor, expensive to hold, since the *polis* expected the official to make good any deficiency from his own resources. To be an *agronomos* or one of the *sitones* might be a costly office indeed, particularly at times of drought or harvest failure. More expensive and even dangerous was the office of *dekaprotos*. In the Republic taxes were contracted and collected by private corporations of *publicani*. But so great was the corruption of the system that the Romans gave it up,[6] choosing instead to make the citizens themselves responsible

---

4. The *curia* of the Italian *municipium*. There are general correspondences between the *municipium* of the West and the *polis* of the East, and though Roman legislation naturally used the Latin terms, the Greek ones appropriate to the East will be used here, with occasional notations of correspondence.

5. And it was, at its best period, a dignity. It was frequently bought for wives, children and even the dead.

6. At least for direct taxation; many indirect taxes were still collected by *publicani*.

for the taxes, and specifically those citizens capable of making up the arrears out of their own fortunes. As the taxes grew larger and the ordinary citizen's ability to pay proportionately smaller, the *dekaprotoi* were slowly crushed beneath the burden. By the third century the honor of holding a magistracy disappeared beneath the difficulty of fulfilling it.[7]

The holding of public office was originally conceived as a privilege, and a distinction was drawn between those offices and the duty that every citizen owed to the state. To pay one's taxes and to serve in the army were clearly the obligations attendant upon citizenship; but for their extraordinary needs the Greeks, Latins and Egyptians resorted to somewhat different versions of an identical practice. The Greeks of the classical age imposed a *leitourgia* or special assessment upon their wealthier citizens, normally in rotation and with safeguards against injustice. The Romans felt that every citizen of the municipality had certain obligations (*munera*) toward the upkeep of the community and thus could be called upon by the magistrates to bear his share in the maintenance of roads, aqueducts, et cetera. The Egyptian *angareia* has already been described, amounting to seizure of goods, vehicles, and even one's person for the work of the state.[8] It was a bludgeon frequently wielded by the military and petty officialdom.

The *poleis* of Asia began in the Greek tradition of the *leitourgia*. A wealthy citizen might be appointed a gymnasiarch or an *agonothetes* and be charged with the responsibility of maintaining the public gymnasium or producing the annual or special athletic contests. The inscriptions found in these cities show that there was no lack of wealthy and public-spirited men willing to come forward and put part of their wealth at the disposal of their fellow citizens. But as the Greek system closed with the Roman and the Egyptian, the distinction between the *honor* of public

---

7. The case of the Jews is instructive. Banned from the *curia* when it was an honor to belong, they claimed this exemption when it became a burden. The state disallowed the claim for exemption under Constantine and held the Jews bound to curial obligations but incapable of holding any of the offices which might make such expenses worthwhile.

8. It was probably just such an *angareia* that Simon of Cyrene was forced to perform in carrying Jesus' cross to Golgotha.

office and the *munus* of public service disappeared; all became *munera*, painful and expensive, as the Romans persisted in their efforts "to get public work done at private expense."

The breakdown of the Roman economic system began with the excessive pressures put upon it by the imperialistic designs of Trajan. The results were not immediately visible, though Trajan himself was forced to tamper with the essentially laissez-faire character of the eastern economy by installing Imperial agents to act as overseers (*correctores, curatores*) of municipal finances. Hadrian's retrenchment to the Augustan frontiers was only a temporary solution to the overextension, since the Severi soon afterward involved themselves in important new obligations.

Septimius Severus stands at the beginning of the militarization of the Empire. Far from being prompted by purely strategic considerations, the bond between the Emperor and his soldiery was forged by political necessity. Septimius was not the first to be carried to power by the arms of legions; but he was the first to regularize the alliance. Thenceforward the donative of money, originally a gift to the soldiers on the Emperor's accession, became a matter of state policy, a frequent and expensive bribe to the troops.

To pay for these donatives and to underwrite the relentless rhythm of war and civil strife the Imperial government exercised closer and closer control over the municipal economies, squeezing the *dekaprotoi* and the guilds (*collegia*) of artisans and merchants who provided the services essential for the functioning of the Empire. Concurrently there was spawned an army of police and petty officials charged with seeing that the new obligations were met. Most significantly of all, the Emperors continued to tamper with the coinage.

The debasement of the silver *denarius* had begun with Nero, and by the third century it had reached such proportions that a serious inflation set in. The Imperial mints squeezed more and more *denarii* out of the same pound of silver so that this basic silver coin became little more than a disguised copper that not even the government that minted it would accept at the tariffed value. The precious golden *aurei*, which oddly were never significantly debased, disappeared into private hoards.

The inflation had serious results. As the sound coinage was driven out of circulation, the government continued to pay standard wages—to the army, for instance—in the debased coin.

There was some attempt at rectifying this by supplying troops with double rations,[9] and the soldiers scrambled to make up the rest by plundering. Unwilling to accept its own coinage, the state began to exact a tax in kind. A barter economy was very near.

A great part of this grim picture must be credited to the failure of economic and political institutions. Parallel with this institutional failure ran a broad current of personal and social disaffection; in the words of a contemporary historian, the age of gold had turned to iron and rust. Everywhere men struggled to escape the omnipresent tax collector and police. The Imperial troops, increasingly barbarized, fattened off a land once rich and fertile but now almost a desert. Earlier in Judaea political and economic opposition had taken the form of brigandage; in the third century it was endemic. Outlaws and fugitives banded together from desperation and for their own self-protection. And within society itself there was another growing army of fanatics who appeared to constitute an even greater social threat to the Empire, the Christians.

The Emperors were soon enough alerted to this latter group, though they may originally have thought them another branch of the troublesome Jews. Certainly Nero could distinguish the two, and according to Tacitus,[10] Nero used the Christians, whom Tacitus describes as "a class hated for their abominations," as scapegoats for the great fire at Rome in A.D. 64. Many were executed, not so much for arson, Tacitus explained, but because they "stood convicted of hatred for the human race."

Leaving aside the question of the fire, there are grounds enough for thinking that the Christians at Rome were in trouble with both the populace and the authorities for the very same reasons the Jews were: the strangeness of their cult, which prompted talk of dark and unholy rites, and their exclusiveness and apparently antisocial behavior. The Emperors took seriously their obligation to preserve order in the capital, and both Tiberius and Claudius had expelled Jews from Rome for the sake of peace. But what may have been different in the case of Nero's activities against

---

9. An ordinary soldier of the second century received six hundred *denarii* annually, about half of which was deducted for rations, clothing, weapons, et cetera.

10. But strangely by no other contemporary. Some have doubted the authenticity of the passage in question (*Annales*, XV, 44).

the Christians is the possibility of Imperial legislation forbidding the existence of the sect.

There is no direct evidence that Nero enacted such legislation, and the executions of A.D. 64 may have had no other juridical base than the will of a half-crazed autocrat. But certainly by the time of Trajan there was legislation on the subject, and there is no good reason to doubt that Tertullian is correct in asserting that it went back to the time of Nero. The law making the admission of Christianity a capital offense remained in effect until the time of Septimius Severus and was enforced with varying degrees of vigor. When the younger Pliny went out to Pontus-Bithynia in A.D. 111 he found many Christians there and corresponded with Trajan on the exact application of the anti-Christian laws. Trajan's attitude was in the nature of a compromise: the state was not to search out Christians, but if someone were publicly denounced as such (anonymous pamphlets were to be ignored, however), the case would have to be tried and the death sentence rendered on the basis of whether the accused admitted to being a Christian then and there; it was possible to recant up to the last minute and thus escape the penalty. Hadrian, writing to his Proconsul in Asia somewhat later in the century, took essentially the same view, though he tightened the procedure of denunciation; false denunciations were to be subject to stiff penalties.

The application of the law may also be read in the Christian tradition, where the measured tones of a Pliny and a Trajan ring somewhat differently. The Christians preserved some of the court proceedings against their early martyrs, and even though the accounts are subject on occasion to hagiographical embroidery, the historicity of the prosecutions and deaths is firmly established. To speak only of the East, Ignatius, bishop of Antioch, was prosecuted in A.D. 105 under Trajan, and Polycarp of Smyrna under Antoninus Pius in A.D. 155. These were heads of their churches and pillars of their communities; doubtless there were a considerable number of lesser figures who perished with them.

Septimius Severus, apparently alarmed at the growing number of conversions, tried a new approach, forbidding by law conversions to either Judaism or Christianity. The ban on Judaism was an old one, but the inclusion of the Christians at this point may have been due to the open and successful Christian proselytizing in Egypt, where, only a few years before, a catechetical school had been opened. If this was the object of Severus' restrictive legislation of A.D. 201, it was successful; the school was closed and several Christians lost their lives, including Origen's father. Septimius was not typical of the later Severi in this matter. Their religious syncretism has already been noted, and if Septimius executed Origen's father, another member of the family, Mamaea, summoned the Alexandrian scholar himself to Antioch for discussions about Christianity.

Though little official attention was given to the Christians in the first part of the third century, the Neronian legislation was still on the books, and any sudden burst of ill will or civil strife could be immediately turned against the Christians in the community, now, doubtless, more exposed to identification by reason of their growing numbers and the apparent Imperial indifference to their technically illegal status. Indeed Philip the Arab seems to have shown a positive benevolence. Suddenly, with his successor, the mood changed.

Decius (A.D. 249–251) was no Oriental provincial in the style of Philip or Alexander Severus. A stern disciplinarian who married into the Italian aristocracy, he was a stubborn devotee of the Empire and a partisan of the renewed vigor of the Senate. Soon after Decius' accession Fabian, the bishop of the Roman Christians, was seized and executed. This was merely the first move in a widespread campaign to eradicate Christianity. Up to this point persecution had been local and sporadic; in the summer of A.D. 250, Decius embarked upon a program to submit every man, woman and child in the Empire to a loyalty test whereby Christians could be identified and, if they did not recant, be destroyed.[11] The test was some form of worship or sacrifice to the Emperor or the gods, even the most symbolic, and upon its completion the individual was given a certificate (*libellus*) attesting to his loyalty and dismissed. These were not trials; what Decius attempted was nothing less than a scrutiny of everyone in the Empire.

Many Christians offered the sacrifice and were certified,[12] but as many or more refused. Some of these latter may have escaped the

---

11. The test might include torture, even to the point of death, although it seems clear that what Decius wanted was apostates not martyrs.

12. What to do with these "certified" who wished to return to the Church after the persecution died down raised a serious and difficult problem.

peril through the leniency or connivance of local magistrates, but thousands of others died in the bloodbath, until Decius himself perished a year later defending his Empire against the Goths in the Balkans.

There is no simple reason why this episode should have occurred at this time. The personality of Decius and his analysis of the woe that beset the Empire, the social odium that continued to be attached to the name of Christianity both locally and generally, their own insistence that the Kingdom of God transcended the Empire itself, the "failure of nerve" on the part of populace and officialdom alike, all doubtless contributed. Decius was correct enough in perceiving that the Imperial cultus was the one cohesive factor in the Empire that was linked by little else than its universal fear of the tax collector. The Antonines and Severi had fostered Emperor worship, without at the same time doing anything against the largest single segment of the population that refused to have anything to do with it, the Christians. Decius proposed the test on political grounds, and the Christians refused it from religious motives; it, of course, occurred to neither that the two could be separated.

The Christians were by now quite distinct from the Jews. The Romans dealt with the Jews as a juridically constituted body, the continuation and extension of what had once been a political entity. The Christians had never been such, and in a sense this worked in their favor, since they suffered no major civil disabilities. But the Romans were never either aware of or willing to deal with the Church as a whole; each Christian stood individually before the law.

When Valerian (A.D. 253–260), Decius' former lieutenant, came to power it was merely a question of time until he would resume his mentor's religious-political policy. The inevitable came after a series of disastrous defeats in the Balkans and elsewhere. The Sasanians too had taken Antioch and were threatening to do so again. In rage and frustration Valerian turned against the Christians (A.D. 257), striking now not at individual members but at the heart of the Church. Valerian's officers swept down upon the Roman catacombs. Church property was seized, assemblies were forbidden, the upper clergy were executed; Christians in the Imperial household were deported. Only the capture of Valerian by the Sasanians in A.D. 260 brought the violence to an end.

Valerian's son Gallienus, who shared his father's Imperial position and command,[13] assumed sole rule after his father's capture. Gallienus belonged to the Hadrianic tradition rather than to the Decian, and he reversed his father's policy on a number of counts, including a published edict of toleration toward the Christians and the restoration of their property. It was neither the attractiveness of Christian doctrine nor despair that he could ever check the movement that prompted the Emperor's unusual move; Gallienus may have felt that he had more potent weapons at hand.

The Stoics had long dreamed of the restoration of a Hellenistic kingdom under the rule of an enlightened *basileus*, and Hadrian was perhaps the first with the disposition and effective power to put the dream into operation: mankind would live in the glow of Stoic harmony and Hellenic grace protected by the shield of Roman arms. The times of Hadrian were such that the visionary ideal could be indulged and even, perhaps, briefly and fitfully attained. But the temper of the third century was quite different. Not only had the military and economic situation deteriorated, but the Greek gods of Hadrian had been put to flight by a bewildering array of eastern dieties, each with its own alien and often bizarre cultus. One aspect of Hellenism, however, still betrayed a great deal of spiritual vitality—the revived form of Platonism—and it may have been the presence in Gallienus' circle of the high priest of that revival, Plotinus, that inclined the Emperor to the new approach of pitting a spiritualized Platonism against Christianity, instead of attempting to destroy the latter by main force.

If such were Gallienus' intentions,[14] he was cheated of his role as a third-century Julian by the collapse of his Empire. Gaul and Syria were in secession; the Goths had broken the frontier defenses. The times had no need of another Hadrian[15] with

---

13. But whose differing position in policy led in A.D. 258 to a distinction in commands: Valerian's in the East, Gallienus' in the West.

14. Perhaps their only immediate fruit was the treatise directed against Christianity by Porphyry, who studied at Rome with Plotinus in A.D. 263–268; Plotinus had himself entered into discussions with Christians, but they were of the Gnostic variety.

15. Like Hadrian, Gallienus had himself elected *archon* of Athens and inducted into the Eleusinian mysteries. Most curious is his appearance on his own coinage as Demeter under the stupefying legend *Galliena Augusta*.

visions of a utopia in Campania, and Gallienus perished in still another civil war (A.D. 268).

Julian had one other third-century predecessor, the energetic Aurelian (A.D. 270–275), who styled himself, with some justice, "Restorer of the World," and who, more than any other ruler since Septimius Severus, assembled the elements of Diocletian's fundamental work of restoration. By force of arms he won back Rome's secessionist provinces in the West and the East, and he applied himself as well to the more difficult task of constructing some kind of unity that might bind the Empire from within. His choice marked an important departure from what had been, since the time of Augustus, Imperial policy. The deification of the Emperor was an accomplished fact, and he was on occasion assimilated to one or another of the gods of the Greco-Roman pantheon, or even, with the Severi, to the gods of Africa or Asia.[16] The Severi gave, however, a place of special importance to one deity, a Syrian one, which, as the "Invincible Sun" (Sol Invictus), was to be the object of the Roman Empire's first established religion.

The cult of Sol Invictus was a product of the unrestrained religious syncretism of the post-Alexander age. At its roots was a primitive Semitic sky god, the god of storms, thunder and weather, visible in the genealogy of the various Syrian Baals, Hadads and even Yahweh himself.[17] For all his celestial activities the Baal of the East was also an earth-bound deity, connected to the earth and the plowed fields by virtue of his rain-giving and fertilizing functions. What eventually sundered him from this lowly domain was his association with Babylonian astrological ideas. The probing of Greek astronomy and Oriental astrology had pushed the limits of the heavens beyond the rain clouds on the horizon to the outermost limits of human speculation. Baal fled outward through the spheres to take up his new place as master of the universe and lord of the heavens, exercising through his intermediary stars and planets a profound influence on human life. Baal was metamorphosed into the supreme deity, and in various Greco-Syrian syncretized forms took his increasingly important

16. Usually under a Hellenized form; the enormity of Elagabalus was that his Baal was nakedly and unashamedly foreign.
17. The type is not exclusively Semitic. The Greeks had the cult of Zeus "the thunderer" (*keraunios*), and the same type is represented in the Hittite pantheon by Teshub.

place in the pantheon of the Roman Empire as Heaven (*Coelus*), the Most Transcendent God (*Zeus hypistos, Jupiter summus exsuperantissimus*), Jupiter of Dolichene (in Commagene), Jupiter Belus of Palmyra, Jupiter Hadad of Heliopolis, Elagabalus' Baal of Emesa, the Helios and Sol Invictus of the Severan coinage, and even affected the Iranian Mithra.

Aurelian avoided the crudeness of Elagabalus' attempt to prescribe his local Baal. The Greek and Roman associations of the divinity of the Sun were now stressed and its universality underlined. In A.D. 274 a magnificent temple to Helios was erected in Rome and, more significantly, a *collegium* of pontiffs of Sol Invictus was instituted. The cult was officially introduced into the army, and Aurelian was presented on the coinage as "Lord and God," restorer of the universe under the patronage of the Invincible Sun with whom he was identified. Imperial policy had at last drawn apace with the Stoic-Platonic speculation that had been developing a learned theology of the ruler (*hegemonikon*) of the universe whose outward manifestation was the sun. This new religious attitude had the added advantage of easily assimilating not only most of the major Baal cults to which it was related, but the protean force of Mithraism as well. And Aurelian had the wisdom to institute the cult in a manner which was redolent of ancient Roman forms.

Whereas former Emperors had been gods in the Hellenic mode, Aurelian had himself proclaimed something quite different, *deus et dominus*, not a god from the fertile Olympian pantheon, but the God of the universe and master (*dominus*) of all. The assimilation to the eastern model of the god-king was now complete, buttressed by the learning of the Greek theologians, themselves Orientalized. Augustus, Aristotle and Yahweh had all converged in the person of Aurelian. Only the figure of Christ was missing to make the Emperor a Byzantine.

The Last Rationalist: Plotinus

As the reign of the Severi drew to a close amid the first palpable symptoms of disintegration in the Empire over which they had presided, the Greek philosophical tradition was approaching an unexpected moment of synthesis that would determine the course of its history over the next millennium. The two protagonists in this transformation, Origen and Plotinus, are well known; a third, Ammonius Saccas, is little more than a shadowy eminence.

After Origen and Plotinus the variegated philosophical tradition that had come into being at Athens immediately after Aristotle was reduced to a single, imposing structure; from the death of Plotinus in A.D. 270 every philosopher and every theologian was in some sense a Platonist. Both the Epicurean and Stoic schools had by then all but vanished, and if Aristotle survived in considerable quantity, it was chiefly by reason of his inclusion in the Platonic curriculum.[18] Christian and pagan alike labored up through an elaborate Aristotelian course of studies compounded of logic and physics, eventually to reach the sublime heights of a Platonic theology.[19]

Plotinus was the major creative force in this final version of Platonism, and Origen was its somewhat unwitting propagator in Christian circles. Both men studied with Ammonius at Alexandria: Origen during the period A.D. 205–210, and Plotinus for eleven years beginning in A.D. 232, a year after Origen, already a prominent member of the Alexandrian Church, was forced to leave Egypt.[20] Like his two students, Ammonius was himself likely an Egyptian, born there about A.D. 175, but apart from the fact that he was originally a Christian and then later embraced paganism, little or nothing is known of his life or his teaching.

Ammonius Saccas wrote nothing; his teaching was communicated orally in the "seminars" (synousiai) conducted with his students. There remains, however, the stubborn evidence that someone at a later date knew an impressive amount about the doctrines of Ammonius,[21] and so the search for traces of his

---

18. After Plotinus most of the great "Aristotelian commentators" were actually Platonists who had reason enough to dissimulate their Platonic theology (see Chapter XVIII, pp. 679–80).

19. Perhaps the clearest illustration of this is the fact that the Aristotle-smitten scholastics of medieval Islam paid their final prostrations before a so-called Theology of Aristotle which was, in reality, extracts from the Enneads of Plotinus. But for all that, the philosophers in Islam were more convinced Aristotelians than any of the Alexandrian savants whose commentaries on Aristotle they knew so well.

20. See Chapter XVII, p. 624.

21. Chiefly Hierocles, who studied with Plutarch (d. A.D. 432) at Athens, and sometime about A.D. 420 was teaching philosophy in the Platonic school at Alexandria.

the soul.

the one

the Spirit

Whenever talking about mysticism — Get into a language of Plato obscure.

students' notes (*scholia*) has continued. On one reckoning of the evidence a likely candidate for their transmission is Porphyry, since he, like the Christian Origen, appears to have held more closely than Plotinus to what can somewhat hesitatingly be construed as a more genuinely Ammonian position. It was Porphyry, for example, who was credited with having introduced Aristotle into the Neoplatonic school curriculum.[22] Plotinus explicitly resisted the syncretizing of Plato and Aristotle that Porphyry was promoting, but we know, or rather, suspect, that Ammonius had earlier subscribed to the argument that Plato and Aristotle were in essential agreement.

If the role of Ammonius in the formation of Plotinus remains obscure, we are somewhat better informed on another important influence. According to his biographer Porphyry, Plotinus paid particular attention to the work of Numenius, to the extent that it suggested to some of Plotinus' contemporaries in Athens, who likely saw themselves as the guardians of the "pure" Platonism, that their eminent rival in Rome had plagiarized the earlier man. Plotinus found his defenders within his own circle, but the charge has served to direct attention further back in the Platonic tradition, and more precisely, to the Pythagoreans of the second century, among whom Numenius, a native of Apamaea in Syria and a teacher at Rome toward the middle of the second century, was reckoned.

Numenius' "Pythagoreanism" was more likely a Pythagorean "reading" of Plato, reinforced, in his case, by a revival of the historical quarrels that had earlier taken place over Pythagoras, Socrates and Plato in the Academy and the Lyceum.[23] Numenius attempted to integrate all three in the same line of descent, a line broken by the skeptical interlude in the Academy. The Academy did not exhaust Numenius' historical perspectives. As many had been doing since Alexander first opened the new, cosmopolitan *oikoumene*, Numenius cited supporting evidence for his version of the history of philosophy from the wisdom and cults of the East, the Brahmans, Jews, Magi and Egyptians. He knew both Jesus and *Genesis*, and at one point made the remark that has attracted almost as much attention as his alleged use by Plotinus: "What else is Plato but Moses speaking Attic Greek?"

---

22. See Chapter XVIII, pp. 678–79.
23. See Chapter XI, pp. 422–24.

The *mot* had led some to see the Syrian Numenius—himself Jewish perhaps?—as a somewhat sinister promoter of Orientalism at the heart of the Hellenic philosophical tradition. That sentiment has abated somewhat with the realization that a sophisticated awareness of the wit and wisdom of the *barbaroi* was not new with Numenius, and that his Orientalism, if any, must be sought in the body of his teaching and not in the rhetorical comparisons with eastern sages that were by then commonplace in the schools.

The firmest case for the presence of non-Greek substance in Numenius can be made in connection with his holding for two souls in man, a rational soul and an evil and irrational one, the latter acquired, it would seem, during the descent of the rational soul through the spheres. No previous Greek appears to have held this duality of soul, though there is evidence for it among the Gnostics, Zoroastrians and Manichaeans. Nor was any Greek likely to have admitted to the proposition that there was evil in the superlunary world, while the heavens as a place of evil was close to the heart of both the Gnostics and Babylonian astrology.[24]

Plotinus subscribed to neither of those propositions, but there are other things in Numenius with which he obviously agreed. Over and above the sensible world Numenius posited three *hypostases*, or grounds of being, one descended from the other, but not yet as distinct as Plotinus would later make them, since in Numenius the higher "used" the lower as its instrument, in this instance for the creation of the world, much in the way that Philo's God the Father used his offspring for the work of creation.[25] Numenius' removal of the demiurgic function from the High God was, perhaps, new in the later Platonic tradition, as was his tentative backing off from the position of earlier Platonists like Albinus who, in the wake of Platonic-Aristotelian syncretism, identified their High God with the Aristotelian "thought

---

24. Numenius' career at Rome must have taken place during or near the time that the Gnostic Valentinus was preaching there, and from what we know of his theories Numenius may have been listening attentively.

25. But differently from the Gnostic view, where creation is indeed taken out of the hands of the High God and entrusted to an evil demiurge who can hardly be said to be the "instrument" of the High God (see Chapter XVIII, p. 649).

thinking itself"[26] in favor of a more genuinely Platonic position where the first principle is more properly the transcendent Good or, in the Pythagorean style, the Monad. Numenius still called the High God Intellect (*nous*) but significantly removed the act of thinking itself to the Second Intellect, or Demiurge.

This was a central point in the history of later Platonism. In accepting the Numenian *hypostases* and a demiurge distinct from the transcendent Good, Plotinus was apparently departing from the positions of his teacher Ammonius, who still held for the identification of the Good and demiurgic function in the High God. And Origen, despite a powerful movement within the Church to disassociate Jesus from the demiurge Yahweh in *Genesis,* followed Ammonius in seeing both the goodness and sometimes severe justice of God as the corollaries of a single principle, that of creation, and not, in the manner of the Gnostics, the functions of two separate gods,[27] nor, in that of Plotinus, of two different *hypostases.*

At the death of Ammonius in A.D. 243, Plotinus left Alexandria to join the expedition of the Emperor Gordian III against the Shah, to investigate, as his biographer would have it, something of the Persian and Indian systems of philosophy. It is unlikely that he learned anything more than the vagaries of political fortune, and at the assassination of Gordian, Plotinus extricated himself with difficulty from the dangerous circumstances in Syria and made his way to Rome. He arrived there in A.D. 244; he was then forty years old.

Plotinus remained in Rome until his death in A.D. 270, surrounded by a circle of friends and disciples that included, from A.D. 262, Porphyry. Porphyry left for Sicily in A.D. 269 on Plotinus' advice and so was not present at his master's death, but out of their six-year association came Porphyry's edition of Plotinus' writings and a reliable biographical memoir, both published in A.D. 301, after Porphyry had returned to Rome. Plotinus

26. As even earlier Antiochus of Ascalon had converted the Platonic transcendent Forms into "thoughts" present as paradigms in the mind of God (see Chapters VII, p. 305, and IX, pp. 365–66).
27. See Chapter XVIII, pp. 659–61. Origen's position was the same as that of another of Ammonius' students and an early associate of Plotinus, a pagan Origen who was quickly confused with his Christian namesake in the ancient sources.

had not begun writing until he was nearly fifty,[28] and Porphyry collected this late literary harvest, ordered the essays roughly by subject matter (though he thoughtfully appended information on their original chronological order), titled them, and then grouped them into six books of nine essays each.

The "Nines" (*Enneads*) as put together by Porphyry have not been much tampered with—Porphyry did break up some of the longer essays and scatter their parts—and from them and the *Life* emerges what is doubtless the clearest and most accurate portrait of a philosopher that antiquity has transmitted. Plotinus led a spacious and well-connected life at Rome. He had friends among the Roman aristocracy, was on familiar terms with the Emperor Gallienus and the Empress Salonina, and managed to combine and reconcile the remote and contemplative self-containment of the *bios theoretikos* with the businesslike conduct of the *bios praktikos*. Not only did he teach philosophy in the professional sense, he gave spiritual guidance to intimates like Porphyry and the Senator Rogatianus, and practical advice and assistance to a wide circle of friends and dependents. There was even a scheme for some sort of Platonic utopia to be constructed on the site of Pompeii, and even though Plotinus may have envisioned it as a community with an ascetical and monastic rather than a political orientation, there was political opposition and the Emperor Gallienus was forced to veto the plan.

Like Ammonius, Plotinus conducted seminars or discussions (*synousiai*) rather than the formal lectures that were the normal fare in the Platonic schools. Some of the participants took notes (*scholia*), but it must have been a difficult business, since there was, in the words of one of the members, "a great deal of futile and wandering talk."[29] Sometimes pieces were read, either of

---

28. According to Porphyry, the students formerly in Ammonius' seminar agreed not to publish, possibly because it was impossible to distinguish individual contributions to the conglomerate of Ammonius' philosophy. When others violated the agreement Plotinus no longer considered himself bound.

29. This was the judgment of Amelius, the Tuscan who had been with Plotinus almost from the beginning and who later, when he was teaching philosophy at Apamea, gave his transcriptions and notes to his adopted son Hesychius Hostilianus. It was also the industrious Amelius who undertook to defend Plotinus against the charge of plagiarizing Numenius, a task for which he was specially fitted, since he had all but memorized the works of Numenius.

members of the circle—Porphyry once read one of his poems, whose mysticism the others thought somewhat overdone, though Plotinus spoke kindly of it—or some of the older literature from the schools, the Platonists Gaius or Atticus, Numenius, or Alexander of Aphrodisias on Aristotle, and there is no doubt that Plotinus himself read deeply and well, whether in the seminar or privately, in the works of Aristotle and particularly of Plato.

Plotinus considered himself a Platonist, but an immense distance of time, temperament and history separated the two men. Though Plotinus was possibly closer to the seats of power than Plato, he was infinitely more remote from the realities of politics. The state concerned him neither personally nor as a philosophical problem. We know little of Plato's private life, but Plotinus appears to be quite another type of personality: deeply and piously immersed in his own interior life, other-worldly in a far deeper and more genuine sense than Plato, a Platonist of the dialogues without the occasional mathematical and dialectical formalism that appears in the Platonic ideal, a personal embodiment of the poetry and warmth that shine through passages in the *Symposium* and the *Phaedrus*.

The piety of Plotinus was strangely untouched by the rising tide of astral mysticism and magic that was threatening to engulf the Empire in the third century. Plotinus was no cynical scoffer in the style of a Lucian a century earlier; he was simply disinterested, professionally and personally, in his own age's fascination with the exotic and the occult. Plotinus was himself a mystic, but in the classic—and Hellenic—Platonic mold: the highest aspiration of man was assimilation to God, the one and ineffable source of Being, a *homoiosis* that was accomplished by the highest use of *theoria*, the transintellectual culmination of the Platonic dialectic.

The route to this union with God was an arduous one and was accomplished only by the most rigorous intellectual and moral training (*askesis*). Plotinus thus remained faithful to both the Platonic and the Socratic sides of his legacy. He added, however, his own emphases in filling out the largely uncharted area in Plato where the *process* of dialectic (which Plotinus understood in its Platonic existential sense rather than as the formal logic of the Aristotelian dialectic) yielded to the immediate *intuition* of the Good. For Plotinus the passage into those higher regions was a question of attention. The activities of the universe are a descending series of progressively more degenerate turnings away from the source of Being. Thus man, by a kind of distraction that has its cosmic antecedents, allows his intelligent thought to degenerate into sense knowledge, and even into the still more debased form of activity known as action (*praxis*). For Plotinus the return (*epistrophe*) that is, as it had been for Plato, the heart of the ethical life, is the reversal of that process of distraction, the concentration of one's attention on the essentials to bring into prominence and operation the true modes of activity and being. The thrust of the Plotinian spirituality is *inward* toward the progressively simpler and more authentic levels of being, back past action, sensation, discursive thought, and even intuition, to that point of unity that is the One, "the flight," as Plotinus called it, "of the alone to the Alone."[30] On the testimony of his biographer, Plotinus experienced this union on four occasions during the six years that Porphyry was with him in Rome.

This introspective focusing of attention as the method of discovering the One is possible, in Plotinus' view, because every being resumes within itself the history of the metaphysical descent of which the difficult return is the ethical correlate. In the formula already enunciated by Plato, "all things are in each thing, but in each according to its own proper way of being." The fulfillment of being consists, then, in retracing upward, by acts of the intellect and will, what had come forth from the One by metaphysical necessity.

Long before Plotinus the Platonic tradition had been exploring Plato's somewhat opaque hints that there was a hierarchy among the transcendental Forms (*eide*) that constituted the Intelligible Universe and that one or more of those Forms held a place of special importance. Among what might constitute Plato's candidates, One, Beauty, or the Good, for example, there was no place for Intellect (*nous*),[31] and Plato's tardy discovery of a place for *nous* beneath the Forms went no further than to allow *nous* to "craft" (*demiourgein*) the sensible universe in imitation of the higher Forms.

There was, however, a powerful pre-Socratic tradition behind *nous*, and Aristotle's restoration of it as his supreme being was well within that tradition. Aristotle did go to some pains to meet

---

30. The phrase had earlier been used by Numenius.
31. Plato's disqualification of *nous* rested on the fact that intellection somehow involved process, something that had been excluded from the unchanging reality of the Forms.

Plato's objections against process; his *nous* was not an acting cause at all but a final cause that moved things "like an object of love." The thought that constituted its essence was, moreover, the perfect self-identity of thought about oneself where knower and known were one. The later Platonists apparently were convinced, and among Plotinus' predecessors like Albinus it was a commonplace that the highest being was, as Plato seemed to suggest, the Good, but was also, as Aristotle maintained, Intellect.

Plato, and behind him Parmenides, still lingered in the background, however, and the uneasiness over compromising the simplicity of the One by attributing either function or plurality to the highest being led first Philo (who probably derived more of his inhibitions from *Genesis* than from Plato) and then Numenius to give over the demiurgic function to a secondary *hypostasis*, and to make it, in addition, the *locus* of the plural Forms. Ammonius, as has been seen, apparently disagreed and stood with Albinus; but his student Plotinus followed where Numenius led.

For Plotinus true being is the One which transcends all function, thinking, and even being itself, and the last suggestions of noetic activity still present in Numenius were removed. Plotinus' One is absolutely simple and totally good, the ground and starting point of all the more diffuse and less perfect forms of being that flowed from it, in its simplicity doubtless Platonic, but in its uniqueness unmistakably the product of a more transcendental point of view. The One does not, however, remain isolated in its uniqueness; it "produces" a secondary *hypostasis*, the *nous*, an image of itself in all but its absolute perfection, and the beginning of the serial slide into plurality.

To explain this "production" Plotinus had frequent recourse to the metaphor of emanation (*eklampsis*), whereby the sun gives out heat and light without at the same time suffering diminution of its own powers. The figure was rather too physical for Plotinus' unqualified liking,[32] but it did justice to a principle already well established among the Middle Platonists and Numenius: the law of undiminished giving whereby the production of an effect in no way alters the efficient ontological status of the cause. Thus

---

32. Another objection felt by some of Plotinus' successors was that emanation was essentially a figure of *descent* and was not suggestive of the important *ascent* that was its ethical correlative. Proclus for one preferred the figure of a mathematical series from 1 to *n* along which one could pass in either direction.

Plotinus' One can be both final and efficient cause without the embarrassment of either motion or change in that cause.

In this way there came into being as the necessary effect of the superabundant goodness of the One, Plotinus' second *hypostasis*, Intellect, with clear affinities to Numenius' "Second God" and Philo's *Logos*. Here too is Aristotle's self-thinking thought in a more vital and dynamic form, a kind of noetic externalization or "energizing" of what is the essence of the One. Within the *nous* the system of Forms is realized in all its unity and variety, and in that total present simultaneity that is eternity (*aion*).

At this point there occurs a somewhat curious break in the regular dialectical and necessary procession of the lower manifestations of the One. Plotinus introduced into his system a certain restless willfulness or, as he calls it, audacity (*tolma*), whereby something within the *nous* desires to be its own master. The procession of the *nous* from the One had been described in terms of the goodness of the One, but here there is almost a "fall from grace"—that is, a *chosen* descent from the intelligible world to the sensible world—that brings into being the third *hypostasis*, the Soul.

There are Platonic antecedents for this and, behind Plato, an even older religious tradition. In the *Phaedrus* the soul commits some undefined sin whereby it falls into the sensible world and is imprisoned in the body, even though by nature it is akin to the divine Forms. Plato used the "fall" for his own philosophical purposes, to explain recollection (*anamnesis*) among others, but in its earlier form the account wore full mythological trappings and formed part of the religious complex of Orphism. Empedocles knew it, and in his version the sin is specified: one of the *daimones* whose natural condition was immortality committed a blood crime (bloodletting or flesh-eating) and as a result was thrust into this world and condemned to successive reincarnations over the span of a "Great Year."[33]

The Soul is the activist among the *hypostases*. The marvelous unity within the *nous* was shattered into moments that follow upon each other in succession rather than being present simultaneously and so there came into existence time. The self-identical

---

33. Here thirty thousand seasons; the length of the Great Year, the span of time required for all the heavenly bodies to make a circuit of the heavens and return to a fixed starting point, varied in other calculations (see Chapter III, Note 17).

and intuitive thought of the *nous* lapses progressively into discursive reasoning (*dianoia*), then sensation, and finally action. The degeneration visible in the Soul is present because of its extreme ambivalence: in one direction it is turned upward toward *nous* and thus it reasons, its imitation of the intuitive *noesis* of the Intellect; in another it is turned, or better, distracted downward into the darkness that is matter. This lower part of the soul eventually dissipates itself in individual souls enmeshed in matter.

For Plotinus the material world is like a twilight zone wherein the rays of the One's goodness peter out into absolute darkness. This is man's abode, whose bewildering complexity and debased forms of activity are like a parody of the higher echelons above it. Yet man's soul is also an effect of the One, linked upward by an unbroken chain of preceding causes, and so has within it all of those same causes, not excluding the One itself. Like its immediate parent, the World Soul, it can turn inward and so upward, and thus begin the reconstitution of its origins. The human soul is not evil; it is merely degenerate. And its degeneracy is not by essence or by design of a malevolent creator, but merely by position.

Plotinus was well aware that there were present at Rome and elsewhere others who had very different views on the universe and man's place in it. He had little sympathy for the Gnostics, whose dualism led them into extreme anti-cosmic positions, and some of the strongest language in the *Enneads* is to be found in the special treatise (II, 9) that Plotinus devoted to a refutation of the Gnostics. He opposed not only their multiplication of *hypostases* into endless and empty Aeons, but their profound repudiation of Hellenism by the secrecy and superstition that surrounded their doctrines, their denial of the order and beauty of the universe, for Plotinus no less than for Plato a "visible God" whose living forms still betray the presence of Soul, Intellect, and the One within it, and their casting-over the entire system of moral virtues that had been constructed by the Greek tradition.

Plotinus' insights were correct; in withstanding the Gnostics he was resisting a powerful attack on Hellenism. But there were other forces working unwittingly to the same end. If Plotinus saw them in his own circle they were allowed to pass without comment or went unreported by Porphyry. Though he had no way of knowing it, Plotinus was himself the last major figure capable of assenting, without reservation or distinction, to the premise of Hellenic intellectualism that the good life for man can be adequately achieved by the unaided use of the human intelligence. From one side and the other the partisans of theurgy and revelation were narrowing in on what was once a powerful and attractive postulate. That postulate never totally disappeared, but in the future it would run in harness or in competition with its alternates, for the Platonist Iamblichus as the *ancilla theurgiae* and for the Christian Origen as the *ancilla theologiae*. Piety was never alien to Hellenism, but the notion that the life of the mind, the autonomous and sovereign *philosophia*, could be made to serve, as "handmaiden" or other, some higher end, would have been incomprehensible to philosophers in any but the third century. By the fourth there was no one to defend the contrary.

An Arab Empire

Ardashir, whom the Sasanian sources style "*Shahan shah* of Iran," had in fact exceeded the traditional boundaries of that land. During the disorders that followed the death of Alexander Severus in A.D. 235 he probed the frontiers of the Roman Empire and captured the two key fortresses of Carrhae and Nisibis. Shapur, who succeeded him in A.D. 241, had even wider ambitions. Ardashir may have already chastised the Kushans for their part in the coalition against him, but it was Shapur who put an end to the continuous existence of a Kushan Empire. After a series of campaigns an Iranian dynasty once again controlled the non-Iranian lands (*Aniran*) east of Merv as far as Ferghana and the Indus. Shapur's armies also crossed the Caucasus and imposed Sasanian suzerainty through Armenia to the tribes of the Georgians and the Albanians.

Master now of his own house, Shapur turned his attention to Rome. Sasanian forces drove directly to Antioch, and the city was saved only by the prompt defensive action of Gordian III, or better, of his pretorian prefect Timesitheus. The Romans quickly lost their advantage. Illness carried off Timesitheus at Nisibis during the winter of A.D. 243–244 as preparations were being made to follow up the previous summer's success. His successor as praetorian prefect, Philip the Arab, had his own ambitions and they spelled the doom of the boy Emperor Gordian, who was murdered by his troops while his guest Plotinus fled toward

Rome. The military situation turned dangerous, but Philip bought his way out at the price of the surrender of Armenia and Mesopotamia.

Shapur was not to be denied. The sources are confused on the details, but Cappadocia and Syria appear to have been under almost constant Sasanian siege from A.D. 251, the same year in which a plague began to sweep the Roman Empire. Disaffection may have been spreading as well. With the help of a pro-Persian faction within the city Shapur in A.D. 256 put his hand upon the show place of the Roman East, Antioch. The city was taken by surprise—according to one account, many of the people were in the theater at the time and could not believe their eyes when the Persians appeared—and the Sasanian troops sacked and burned their prize. Captives were carried off and resettled in Iran, the first of many such deportations, and their number included the Christian bishop of Antioch, Demetrianus.[34]

Thus the stage was prepared for the unfortunate Valerian, ruler of the shattered Empire from A.D. 253, who came east to inspect the damage in A.D. 256 or 257. What he found was Antioch in ruins, the eastern trade routes disrupted, and their fortresses occupied by Iranian troops. Valerian set about rebuilding Antioch, but whether from the failure of funds or of morale, the work did not progress very far. Nor did the reorganization of the army. When Shapur struck again in A.D. 260 he scattered a Roman army of seventy thousand troops, captured an Emperor in the field, and once again had Antioch in his possession. High up on the cliffs of Bishapur in the home province of Fars, Shapur had depicted the scene of high triumph: the Roman *imperator* Valerian bending his knee in subjection to the *Shahan shah-i Eran.*

Valerian's son and Caesar, Gallienus, was apparently unable to restore order, and what was left of the province of Syria took advantage of Gallienus' deep involvement in the West to acknowledge the insurrectionist claims of rivals to the throne. It seems likely that Gallienus had the strength eventually to deal with the Syrian usurpers, if not with Shapur. Relief on both

---

34. Shapur is said to have resettled seventy thousand Roman soldiers after his successes in A.D. 260. Most were located at Jundeshapur in Fars, the city that was to be Shapur's answer to Antioch, but there were other colonies elsewhere.

accounts came, however, from quite another source, the Arab *shaykh* of Palmyra, Odenath.

The oasis at the place called by the Semitic peoples Tadmur, located midway in the Syrian desert between Damascus and the crossings of the Euphrates, was probably a primitive stopping-off place on the trek across central Syria. The oasis was known in Assyrian times, but it was not until the great age of international trade inaugurated by the Roman Empire that the caravan city, now known as Palmyra, grew to major economic and political importance. By the beginning of the second century A.D. it was firmly within Roman jurisdiction, though not occupied by the Romans in the same sense as the cities of the arable "mainland" of Syria. Rome was its suzerain, but Palmyra governed itself under its native Arab dynasty.

The native population of Palmyra was predominantly Arab, though its location and role dictated that it wrote and spoke the commercially more useful Aramaic. Arabic might serve the bedouin of Syria and Arabia in the second and third centuries, but its value in the *oikoumene* was limited. Aramaic, on the other hand, was the lingua franca of the Parthians and the native tongue of the populated centers of northern Syria.[35] Though the language of Palmyra was Aramaic, the culture was thoroughly Hellenized, probably as early as Seleucid times, if the Hellenization of nearby Dura-Europos is any indication. Within the city the preserved inscriptions are chiefly Greek and Aramaic doubles, shading off into Aramaic alone in the environs. The dress was Greek and Parthian. Palmyrene religion also reflected the mixed character of the place. A variety of Semitic deities were worshiped, with a place of eminence granted to the sky gods Bel and Baal Shamin, later inevitably identified with Zeus and eventually drawn into the complex of Sol Invictus.

Nowhere in the East did the Romans succeed in replacing a Hellenic culture with their own Latin one. Latin was known at Palmyra, enough to deal with the Roman civil and military authorities, and some Palmyrenes, probably those granted citizenship, began to adopt Roman surnames as was the custom elsewhere in the eastern provinces. But Palmyra retained its cosmopolitan, Hellenized air, and when the Roman Emperors,

---

35. Aramaic was successfully resisting Greek in the province of Osrhoene, though the dialect in use there was slightly different from that spoken and written at Palmyra.

particularly Septimius Severus, began to lavish their attention on the important city, it was in the form of monuments in the "Empire Hellenic" style. Palmyra showed forth her proud temples, colonnades, porticoes, and public buildings, including a massive temple enclave dedicated to the cosmic god Bel. The splendor of Palmyra was enhanced by the fact that the inhospitable desert stretched away on all sides.

This display of patronage and wealth rested on solid commercial foundations. The Palmyrenes guarded and serviced the great complex of trade routes passing between the Parthian Empire and the Roman hinterland. As soon as the westbound caravans left the Euphrates they were under the protection of Palmyrene troopers, a formidable cavalry that had in the past added its cohorts to the Roman regular army. A price in the form of customs duties was exacted for this protective service, and despite the intermittent wars between the two great empires, Palmyra grew fat on the Roman-Parthian-Kushan overland trade during the two centuries between Nero and Valerian.

Rome allowed her vassals the privilege of growing fat, but had little patience with the waxing of political ambition. The Emperors bestowed titles freely, but they were intended as compliments for services rendered and not incentives to future action. The *shaykh* of Palmyra, a certain Septimius Hayran, was honored with the title of Senator about A.D. 250, and eight years later his son and successor Odenath was raised to consular rank by Valerian, perhaps in anticipation of some service expected in the approaching confrontation with Shapur. Odenath's help came too late, but as Shapur was withdrawing from Syria with the captured Valerian, Odenath's Syrian and Arab troopers fell upon the Sasanian army and inflicted considerable damage; they could not, however, gain the release of Valerian.

Gallienus took a dangerous and, as the sequel showed, fortunate gamble. He had his own troubles with insurrections and Germans in the West; the Goths were bursting into Greece and becoming increasingly bold in the Asiatic provinces north of the Taurus. South of the Taurus things were not much better: insurrection in Syria and the Sasanians once again poised at the frontier. Gallienus' solution there was to appoint Odenath as *Dux Orientis* (Commander in Chief of the East), uniting under his sole charge the Roman military forces in the Near East. The arrangement worked marvelously well for both sides. Odenath put down the Syrian rebels, drove the Goths out of Asia, and twice drove deep into Sasanian territory, impelled as much by his desire to open a Palmyrene corridor to the head of the Persian Gulf as by his defensive obligations to Rome.

The assassination of Odenath in A.D. 267 occurred under suspicious circumstances. The Romans were blamed, but the king's second wife was not above suspicion, particularly since Odenath's elder son of his first marriage perished with him. The ambitious queen was Zenobia, but if she expected Odenath's considerable Roman perquisites to descend automatically upon her young son Wabhallath, she miscalculated Gallienus' uneasiness with his earlier eastern arrangement. Odenath had grown far beyond the modest prescribed dimensions of a vassal king, and so, what had been granted in desperation to the father in A.D. 260 was denied to the son in A.D. 267. The rebuff did not materially alter the situation. Though no longer officially *Dux Orientis*, Wabhallath and his mother still had a *de facto* grasp on the east, since neither Gallienus nor any other was strong enough to dislodge them.

There were other forces that put Palmyra's control to an indirect test at Antioch. Demetrianus, the bishop of Antioch who had been carried off by Shapur, died in captivity in A.D. 260. The Palmyrenes then elected as their bishop Paul of Samosata, who, if not then, was later appointed the fiscal procurator of the city. This combination of civil and ecclesiastical power was already extraordinary, particularly in the third century, but Paul's theology was to prove even more curious. He took the position, not entirely unfamiliar in Antiochene Christianity, that Jesus was an ordinary man with a mortal soul—better than us, but still a man—and not the divine *Logos* beloved of Origen and the Alexandrians.

The position ill squared with the apostolic tradition, and Paul's own life suggested that his theology was no sounder than either his fiscal policies or his morals. There was talk from his opponents, it is true—of extortion and bribery, of personal bodyguards, of strange goings-on during the liturgy, and of unnecessarily attractive lady deaconesses. But there was more than this. Paul's doctrine of the Messianic humanity of Jesus had been heard earlier in the East, among the Judaeo-Christian outcasts of the primitive Church dispersed in Syria after A.D. 135. The Jewish cast to Christianity remained strong in Syria in the early days, encouraged and enhanced by the large Jewish colonies at Antioch and elsewhere in northern Syria. There was an obstinate tradition that Zenobia was either herself Jewish or a Jewish sympathizer. Nothing can be demonstrated, but it does seem reasonably certain that Paul, whatever the origins of his theology, was the "Palmyrene bishop" of Antioch, in league with and supported by the authority of Palmyra, an anti-Roman and anti-Hellenist figure in a complicated game of political and theological chess.

In a synod convened in Antioch by the bishop of Tarsus in A.D. 264, Paul was threatened with condemnation, and at another synod, which met there in A.D. 268, he was actually deposed and the son of Demetrianus elected in his place.[36] Paul, secure in his Palmyrene support, refused to budge, and the proof of Zenobia's strength in that capital of a Roman province is indicated by the fact that no one could make him. Paul ruled in Antioch until Zenobia herself fell.

Gallienus was assassinated in A.D. 268, and the stalemate between Rome and Palmyra continued under his successor Claudius, who spent most of his brief reign checking the Goths on the Danube. Wabhallath's titles were still not granted, and Zenobia was still the mistress in what passed as the eastern provinces of the Roman Empire. But when Claudius died of the plague in A.D. 270 and was succeeded by Aurelian, Zenobia made her move. First Wabhallath apparently assumed the forbidden titles and then in the next year proclaimed himself as Augustus and his mother as Augusta. Sometime in the interim, perhaps during the brief period of disruption after the death of Claudius, Palmyrene troops occupied Egypt, Syria and parts of Anatolia. The ancient historians did not miss the instructive parallels with Cleopatra.

It took Aurelian two years to free his hands in the West, and then he turned to Zenobia. Probus was sent to reclaim Egypt. Aurelian himself retook Anatolia and then proceeded to Syria, where Zenobia awaited him at Antioch. The queen was simply outgeneraled. Defeated near Antioch, she fell back on Emesa, where she took heavy losses. A forced march and pursuit to

---

36. The charges against Paul were formulated by a certain Malchion, "principal of a school of rhetoric, one of the centers of Hellenic education at Antioch," phrases of Eusebius that have been construed to make Malchion the founder of the school of Christian theology for which Antioch later became famous.

Palmyra followed. The city was besieged and finally taken; the queen was herself captured as she attempted to slip across the Euphrates to her Sasanian allies. This time no asp cheated the *imperator* of his triumph. Zenobia was paraded in chains at Rome, and then Aurelian, apparently satisfied, pensioned the former Empress of the East to a villa at Tivoli. Palmyra lay in ruins; it never recovered.

Zenobia had had little time to consolidate her hold on the East before superior Roman forces dislodged her. Whatever success she did have can be credited at least in part to Roman distraction elsewhere. Her Palmyrene base was too narrow; the later Muslim invaders of those same provinces quickly deserted their caravan city of Mecca and ensconced themselves in the urban centers to a degree never attempted by the Palmyrenes. The occupation of Antioch and Alexandria in A.D. 263 instead of 270 might have produced far different results for a regime whose Helleno-Semitic credentials were far more impressive than those of the generals of distant Rome or the ragged bedouin of the seventh century who were confronted by an enfeebled Roman state and an adolescent Christian Church.

Only conjecture is possible on Zenobia's long-range plans. Did her support of Paul of Samosata mean that Palmyra was willing to put its weight, forty years before Constantine made his decision, behind a Christianity that was still in difficulty with the Roman political authorities? The evidence does not extend that far. And there is the countering evidence of Longinus, the only other clearly defined individual connected with the Palmyrene aspirations. Cassius Longinus (*c.* A.D. 213–273), probably a native of Emesa, was Plotinus' fellow student in the Alexandrian school of Ammonius Saccas and later studied and worked at Athens until the Gothic invasions of A.D. 268 drove him back to Syria and into the orbit of Zenobia. Longinus had philosophical aspirations, but his contemporaries thought more highly of him as a literary critic.[37] Porphyry, who studied rhetoric with Longinus for some years at Athens before joining Plotinus' circle in Rome, judged him the best critic of the time. Despite their philosophical differences, Plotinus would probably agree; but Plotinus and Longinus had more than their mutual respect in common. Both stood close

---

37. But he was almost certainly not the author of the treatise *On the Sublime* that later circulated under his name.

to the sources of Imperial power, Plotinus by his ill-starred presence in the train of Gordian III in A.D. 243,[38] and by his long and close association with Gallienus, Longinus by his involvement with Zenobia.

The details of that relationship are unknown except for the fact that Longinus taught the Palmyrene Augusta Greek literature and was executed by Aurelian because of his support for the rebel regime. Longinus' value to Zenobia may have been chiefly propagandistic. The presence at her court of one of Hellenism's premier intellectuals must have enhanced her stature at Antioch and Alexandria. Nor was Longinus alone. Amelius, one of Plotinus' disciples, was in residence at Apamea in A.D. 270, possibly at Longinus' invitation, since at about the same time he was attempting to persuade his former student Porphyry to quit Sicily and join him in Syria.

Whatever the political and ideological ambitions of Zenobia and her minister of culture, they came crashing down on the battlefields of A.D. 272–273. Rome did not yet relax her grip on the Near East. Neither the Shah of Iran nor the Arab queen of Palmyra was strong enough to detach those rich and tottering provinces from the Roman Empire, even in the ruinous circumstances of the mid-third century. The weakness of the Romans' eastern defenses was obvious enough, and when Diocletian came to power later in that same century he doubled the number of troops along the eastern frontier and anchored the line with a series of roads and fortresses. Three and a half centuries later, neglect and poverty undid Diocletian's work, and once again the Shah's troops were in possession of Antioch, followed, in short order, by the Arab legionaries of another caravan city, Mecca in the Hejaz.

The Reforms of Diocletian

The all but audible crumbling of the foundations of their Empire in the mid-third century swung Romans alternately to a desire

---

38. Though the alleged reason for Plotinus' presence with Gordian was his desire to learn something more about Indian philosophy, it is interesting to note that after Gordian's death the rebels attempted to lay hold of Plotinus, a strange attitude toward a disinterested philosopher on a research leave.

Maxima
Caesariensis

XII
Britannia
I et II

Flavia Caesariensis

Belgica
II

Belgica
I

Germania
II

Germania
I

Lugdunensis
II

Lugdunensis
I

XI

Sequania

Raetia

Noricum
ripense

Pannonia
superior

Valeria

Aquitanica
II   I

Viennensis

Alpes Graiae
et Poeninae

VII

Noricum
mediterraneum

VI

Pannonia
inferior

Novempopulana

Narbonensis

X

Aemilia et Liguria

Alpes
Cottiae

Alpes
Maritimae

Venetia et Histria

Flaminia et Picenum

Savensis

Dalmatia

Tarraconensis

Gallaecia

Corsica

Tuscia et Umbria

Rome

Lusitania

IX

Carthaginiensis

Baleares

Campania et
Samnium

Apulia et Calabria

Lucania et Bruttii

Sardinia

B a e t i c a

M E D I T E R R A N E A

Sicilia

Mauretania
Sitifensis

Proconsularis
Zeugitana

Mauretania
Tingitana

Mauretania
Caesariensis

VIII

Numidia
Cirtensis

Valeria
Byzacena

Tripolitana

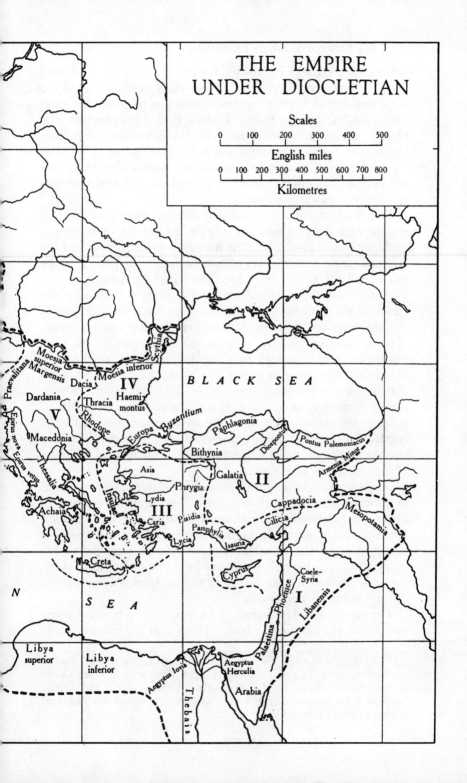

THE EMPIRE
UNDER DIOCLETIAN

Scales

0   100   200   300   400   500

English miles

0   100 200 300 400 500 600 700 800

Kilometres

Moesia
superior
Margensis Moesia inferior
     Dacia   **IV**   **B L A C K S E A**
Dardania   Haemi
       Thracia montus
V   Rhodope
Macedonia   Europa Byzantium   Paphlagonia
                         Pontus Polemoniacus
Thessalia   Bithynia   Diospontus
         Asia   Galatia **II**   Armenia Minor
             Phrygia
Achaia   Lydia   Cappadocia
   III   Pisidia   Cilicia   Mesopotamia
    Caria   Pamphylia
        Lycia   Isauria
   Creta
              Cyprus   Coele-
N   Syria
S E A   **I**   Libanensis

Ad Praevalitana
Epirus nova Epirus vetus

Libya
superior   Libya
        inferior   Aegyptus
               Aegyptus Iovia Herculia   Palaestina
                     Thebais Arabia Phoenice

Scythia

for scapegoats, for palliatives and for reform. Religion was bound up in all three, and its fascination suggested remedies and at the same time spread further the disease that was progressively paralyzing the body of the Roman Empire. Behind the measures of a Decius, a Valerian, a Gallienus or an Aurelian was the firm conviction that both the problem and its solution had to be faced in terms of religion, to excise the unhealthy forms and to renew, on the basis of the old or the new, a religious sentiment that was politically and socially sound.

This preoccupation with religion did not mean that men entrusted with the responsibility of rule ignored the more prosaic problems of administration. The pressure on the frontiers and the economic ruin visible everywhere were far too painful to be swept under a prayer rug. The Sun King Aurelian (A.D. 270–275), the most energetic and resourceful of the rulers during the "time of the troubles," had attempted to meet the problem of disintegration on all fronts, but neither Aurelian nor his immediate successors[39] had the time or the inclination to see these visionary reforms through to a conclusion. The Illyrian soldier Diocletian, who came to power in A.D. 284, had, however, more than twenty years—the longest reign since Antoninus Pius—to put the Roman house in order. There is no reason to think that he came to the throne with any more of a master plan than what Aurelian's work had already suggested, but over the following two decades of his rule a vast adjustment of the internal structure of the Empire did take place.

Diocletian faced the normal difficulties of third-century rule as he proceeded to the work of reform. The Arabs of the eastern desert were restive in A.D. 290, and Diocletian directed the punitive measures in person. In A.D. 296, while the Caesar Galerius was occupied along the Danubian frontier, Egypt burst into open revolt. A certain Domitianus assumed the title of Augustus there, probably abetted by the new sect of the Manichaeans with its disturbing Persian resonances.

The use of the Manichaeans as an extension of Sasanian interests outside the frontiers of Iran, a policy that the Sasanians were

---

39. The elderly Senator Tacitus, then another Illyrian soldier, Probus —followed, after an army mutiny, by the Praetorian Prefect Carus. Carus was murdered by *his* Praetorian Prefect, Aper, and briefly succeeded by his sons Carinus and Numerianus. All of this occurred within a span of nine years.

shortly to discover could cut two ways, would have seemed highly unlikely some twenty years earlier. The death of Rome's great antagonist Shapur I in A.D. 272, while it brought relief to Aurelian, signaled the outburst of a religious reaction in Iran that was directed in the first instance against Mani and his adherents.[40] The pogrom must have lasted until the accession of Shapur's youngest son Narseh, in A.D. 293.[41] Both the motives and the details are unclear, but Narseh reverted to the more tolerant attitudes of his father, and friendly relations were restored between the Manichaeans and the rulers of Iran.

Whether instigated by the Shah or not, the Manichaean agitation in Egypt provided Narseh with an opportunity for profiting at the expense of Rome. As insurrection flamed in Egypt Sasanian troops occupied Armenia and began an invasion of Syria. Galerius was quickly summoned from Illyria. His first season of campaigning ended disastrously at the Euphrates crossing at Callinicum, but in the following year more careful preparations were made and the reverses of A.D. 297 were erased in an overwhelming victory in Armenia. Narseh suffered the same indignity as his Achaemenian predecessor Darius when his queen and the entire harem were captured by the Romans. Galerius' troops drove south into Mesopotamia, overran Nisibis, and marched in triumph into Ctesiphon.

The terms of the peace that followed were harsh, as befitted the size of the victory. Rome took back all of Mesopotamia and carved the Sasanian satrapy of Adiabene east of the Tigris into new provinces. Armenia was restored to the Roman sphere of influence under yet another Tiridates. Narseh's misplaced ambitions brought Rome forty years of peace on its eastern frontiers. Diocletian used the time well.

His first move was toward a solution of the most serious failing in the Imperial system, the problem of succession or, to put it more bluntly, the ease with which military commanders could and did usurp the supreme power of the state. The history of the second and third quarters of the third century was little more than a catalogue of such usurpations, preceded or followed by varying periods of civil war. It had been obvious to every Em-

---

40. See Chapter XVIII, p. 664.
41. If it was not discontinued earlier. The earlier Arab disturbances along the frontier may have been connected with the Sasanians' reconciliation of their Manichaean Arab allies.

peror since Augustus that some attempt should be made to guarantee succession, and of the two systems generally followed it was clear that the Antonine practice of adopting the "best man" was superior to the alternate of filial succession. Every Marcus Aurelius had at least one Commodus in his loins, and the problem of minor succession had never satisfactorily been solved.

Diocletian, who had no direct heirs, invoked the Antonine precedent by adopting, shortly after his accession in A.D. 284, Maximian as Caesar and junior colleague and entrusting him with the pacification of Gaul. His plans matured swiftly. Maximian was soon raised to the position of junior Augustus with full Imperial authority, followed in A.D. 293 by the appointment of two Caesars with the rights of succession, Constantius and Galerius. The Caesars were later linked by bonds of dynastic marriage. Galerius married Diocletian's daughter, and Maximian in turn gave his daughter to Constantius, who had to divorce Helena, his first wife (and Constantine's mother), before taking his new Augusta.

What Diocletian had created was an administrative tetrarchy whereby a *collegium* of four men shared, in graduated order, the administrative power and burdens. The duties were divided along geographical lines: Maximian and Constantius in the West, Diocletian, the senior Augustus, and his Caesar Galerius in the East. There may have been an even further subdivision of authority, with Galerius in the Balkans and Diocletian responsible for the rest of the East. But even though Diocletian frequently operated from Nicomedia in Bithynia and Galerius from Sirmium in Pannonia, the geographical distinction was not stringently observed. Whatever the niceties of the system, Diocletian had managed not only to reduce the bulk of the Empire to sizable administrative limits but to put the various areas under the jurisdiction of men least tempted to abuse their powers for political ends. All of this was publicly proclaimed; there was no doubt as to the succession. And the crown upon the work was to be the voluntary abdication of the two Augusti and the promotion of the Caesars. The decision was taken in A.D. 303 and fulfilled two years later.

After the executive responsibilities had been delegated on the highest levels Diocletian pursued the same principle down through the provincial structure. All through the third century the provinces had been growing smaller in size and larger in number, a division dictated more by political fear than by admin-

istrative philosophy, until by the time of Diocletian they numbered about fifty. He drastically increased the number, reducing
them to administratively viable size, but checked the progress
toward atomization by grouping the new smaller provinces into
progressively larger units. The entire Empire was divided into
four great prefectures—Gaul, Italy, Illyricum and the Orient—
each under a praetorian prefect.[42] The prefectures were in turn
divided into dioceses; there were three of these in the East, the
Asian, Pontic, and Oriental dioceses, each under the government
of a vicar. The dioceses were subdivided into provinces, the
eastern dioceses embracing thirty-three of these new smaller
provinces, each headed by a governor, or *praeses*.

A provincial governor now had a far smaller area to administer.
Nor did he any longer have to concern himself with military
affairs; the provincial armies were now under the separate administration of a military commander (*dux*, duke). Despite these
rather obvious restrictions in responsibility the tasks of a provincial governor were still, however, considerable. The municipalities were no longer allowed to go their own autonomous way.
By A.D. 300 the hand of the central government was everywhere
visible, particularly in economic and tax matters, and the burden
of the detail work fell upon the governor, who still had to serve
as chief executive and supreme judge.

He did not, of course, work alone. Every executive official,
high and low alike, had his own bureaus (*officia*) which served as
his staff and were located in the metropolis of the province.
There were *officia* right up through the ranks of the vicars and
praetorian prefects to the Imperial level itself. Since the Emperor
was frequently in transit his entire staff was prepared to travel
with him. This was his "retinue" (*comitatus*) comprising his personal household (*cubiculum*), his personal guard (*scholae*), the
praetorian prefects and *their* staffs, the Imperial council (*con-
silium, consistorium*), and several secretariats (*officia*).

The state claimed by Diocletian had long had the appearance
of an economically starved beast that ate when it was hungry,

---

42. Neither this office nor that of the vicars (*vicarii*) were new ones.
Before Diocletian the office of the prefect of the Praetorium had
evolved from that of commander of the Imperial guard to that of a
representative of the Emperor who possessed not only military responsibilities but wide-ranging judicial powers. The *vicarii* were rov-
ing commissioners appointed to assist the praetorian prefect.

which was often. The new Emperor did nothing to diminish the hunger—indeed, his expansion of the administration must have increased expenses—but he did regularize the feeding times. The single greatest achievement of the entire Diocletianic age was the reform of the tax system: predictable expenses were matched by predictable income, and for the first time the Roman state had what approached a modern national budget. Expenses could be predicted; the hierarchized chain of command enabled the praetorian prefects to prepare fairly reliable estimates of production. Diocletian accomplished this by nothing short of assessing the productivity of every person and every foot of land in the sprawling Empire by a series of careful censuses which were still being taken in A.D. 311.

Each administrative unit, province, diocese, and prefecture was divided into ideal productive units of land (*juga*) and "heads" (*capita*), the latter including men, women, children and cattle. The ideal unit, each with an ideally identical production capacity, was constituted of varying real units. Thus in Syria a *jugum* embraced twenty acres of first-quality land or forty of second quality, or five acres of vine land, or a grove of two hundred and fifty trees. A *caput* was only one man but two women or a variable number of animals. At first the land tax (*jugatio, annona*) was payable in kind and the head tax (*capitatio*) in money, but in the end both were assimilated into a single system of payment in kind. The tax schedules were originally reassessed every five years, but then, after A.D. 312, every fifteen years.[43]

These were the rural and agricultural taxes. City taxes came from a variety of import-export (interprovincial and international) and customs duties, and special "anniversary" taxes were payable in the increasingly precious gold and silver by city councils, Senators and merchants. The chief municipal burdens came, however, from quartering and provisioning the ever-growing army. The arrival of an army corps was rarely the occasion for a parade.

For this carefully calculated system to work, everyone had to be what and where he was assessed. The departure of a real "head" from an estate to the more congenial climate of the city (or the wilderness) did not subtract an ideal *caput* from that

---

43. This fifteen-year assessment period was called an "indiction" (*indictio*) and constituted the normal method of calculating chronology in the later Empire.

same estate's tax rolls. As a consequence men were increasingly "frozen" in their class, and three major segments of the population soon found themselves locked in a hereditary caste system: members of the city councils (*curiales*) and members of the trade, business and artisans' guilds (*corporati*),[44] both groups responsible for the tax load of the *poleis* and the long-suffering tenant farmers on the estates (*coloni*). Each group was absolutely necessary for the functioning of the state, and in these hard times every exit from the clutches of enforced service was blocked;[45] the *coloni*, now full-fledged serfs, were sold with the land.

Progress was made in stabilizing the coinage. Provincial issues were suppressed and a uniform Imperial coinage was maintained. The *aureus* had held firm for most of the preceding period, and Diocletian fixed it at sixty to a pound of gold. More impressively, he was able to mint *denarii* (this silver coin was now called the *argenteus*) at the old Neronic standard of ninety-six to a pound of silver. It was a paper triumph, since the issues were in fact small ones. Most of the money transactions were conducted through the small billon (silver-washed bronze) coins which were wildly unstable and pushed up prices to ever more inflated levels. To counteract the galloping inflation Diocletian published, in A.D. 301, his Edict on Prices, fixing the maximum price on a thousand goods and services. On contemporary authority it did little good and was finally rescinded by Constantine.

Diocletian's religious policy was unconsciously paradoxical. The Hellenism of a Hadrian or the Greek-veneered Orientalism of a Gallienus or an Aurelian was not his style. He was a somber, efficient administrator in the classic Roman mold,[46] a soldier by training and a propagator of Roman law by inclination and instinct. Aurelian had pushed the divinity of the Emperor to bold new limits, and the coinage of Diocletian and his tetrarchs shows an ideological retrenchment. The Emperor was still the recipient of divine favor, and his authority and rule were protected by divine sanction. But Diocletian never called himself a god, con-

---

44. The guilds, finally known as *collegia*, were at this point called *corpora*.

45. The chief immunities were restricted to the Senatorial order, the Imperial civil service, the army, and later the clergy.

46. It is interesting that it is increasingly the Latinized Balkan provinces that spawn these "Roman" types. The last great "Roman" to direct the destinies of the Empire was another Illyrian, Justinian.

tenting himself with the epithet "Jovian," while his co-Augustus Maximian was officially designated "Herculean." Thus each man had a divine progenitor and paradigm which also clearly underscored the seniority of Diocletian.

This conservatism may have gone unnoticed by the majority of the people since the whole texture of imperial protocol was not to be reversed by the mere slipping from "Jove" to "Jovian." The process of converting the Augustan *princeps* into *dominus et deus* had been going on for half a century; the Imperial authority rested heavily upon the divine character and associations of the person of the Emperor as reflected in the court ceremonial. There was no retrenchment here. Access to the Emperor's person was even more severely limited and was preceded by the now normal ritual prostration (*proskynesis, adoratio*). His rare public appearances were calculated, hieratic and splendid. The Emperor's court, his councilors, his appurtenances were all "sacred"; around his head in the official portraits was the supernatural nimbus. Unfriendly contemporaries thought it bore a striking and sinister resemblance to the protocol of the Persian court.

By all the evidence, Diocletian's relations with the Christians during the first years of his rule preserved the peaceful conditions that had prevailed since the time of Gallienus.[47] Then quite suddenly in A.D. 303 an Imperial edict was published: the Christian churches were to be destroyed, their sacred books burnt, assembly forbidden. Christians were no longer to be granted the protection of judicial process.

Two contemporary Christian writers, Lactantius and Eusebius, place the responsibility for the new outburst squarely upon the eastern Caesar, Galerius, with Diocletian serving as a somewhat reluctant accomplice. Galerius may have had considerable encouragement. The numbers of Christians, for some years now flourishing in the open, continued to grow, and the Neoplatonic philosophers and intellectuals had not relented in their opposition. One of their number, Hierocles, was governor of Bithynia and played a provocative role in the events of those years. Or it may have been that Galerius was simply trying to build up his own position for the coming political struggle. The trouble seems to have broken out on religious rather than political grounds, but

---

47. Aurelian may have been planning a persecution, but it was forestalled by his death.

the sequel suggests that political considerations were not entirely lacking.

Some time before the edict, perhaps in A.D. 302, Diocletian and Galerius were attending an augural ceremony, at which the omens could not be read. The chief augur complained that Christians were interfering by making the sign of the cross. Diocletian was enraged at the incident and ordered that the Christians should be removed from the army unless they performed the sacrifices. These were the visible antecedents of the edict. What followed were two mysterious fires in the palace at Nicomedia. Galerius made the inevitable accusation of Christian complicity, and Diocletian was then determined that the edict be enforced in all its vigor.

It clearly was enforced in the East, though Constantius may have held off in Gaul and Britain. Events followed swiftly. There were civil disorders in Cappadocia and Syria, again attributed to the Christians, and a second edict was forthcoming: the clergy was to be imprisoned, a move that struck, as Valerian's had, at the nerve sinews of the Church. Diocletian's twentieth-anniversary celebration was approaching (September 304), and he used the occasion to move off on another tack. The jails were emptied by the expedient of forcing the imprisoned clergy to sacrifice.

By the spring of A.D. 304 Diocletian was ill to the point of incompetence, and Galerius was in full control. A final edict was promulgated, and it was the most radical of all: every Christian, without exception, was to sacrifice or die. Thus began, at least in the East, a sustained and concerted attempt at eradicating Christianity. Diocletian's abdication in A.D. 305 served merely to aggravate the situation, since Galerius was thereby promoted to Augustus and had as his Caesar in Egypt and Syria his nephew Maximin Daia, whose zeal in enforcing the edicts was even greater than his uncle's. Thousands must have died in Egypt, where the Christian population was fairly large and the fanaticism of the natives well known. Maximin's alternatives to execution were in the spirit of the times: mutilation or servitude in the mines.

Then in A.D. 311 the pogrom ended as suddenly as it had begun. Galerius contracted an exceedingly vile disease. Christian authors saw it as an unmistakable divine sign of displeasure, and Galerius himself may have been persuaded that it was such, since shortly thereafter (April 30, A.D. 311) he published at Nicomedia an edict of toleration: ". . . in virtue of our extreme clemency and our immemorial practice of dealing gently with all men, we have decided to extend our indulgence even to them and allow henceforth that Christians should exist and restore their assemblies, provided they do nothing against good order." Further instructions would follow.

They never came; Galerius died in May of the same year. Maximin, who had refused to publish the edict of toleration in the eastern provinces, occupied the dead Augustus' territories and proclaimed himself Emperor of the East. His position was in fact perilous, since he had no place in the plans of the two new Augusti, who had emerged in the political scramble in the West: Constantine, son of Constantius, and Licinius, a former associate of Galerius. The two had agreed in Milan in A.D. 313 on a policy of complete religious freedom, and Maximin's reaction to this move was not only to continue his repression of the Christians (in A.D. 311–312 the bishops of Alexandria and Antioch had been executed, as well as Lucian, the celebrated Antiochene theologian), but to foster the creation of a pagan Church on the model of the Christian one. Priesthoods were created and vicious anti-Christian propaganda was circulated. Finally Licinius marched against him, scattered his troops at Adrianople, pursued the unfortunate Maximin to Tarsus, where he died (A.D. 313). In June A.D. 313 Licinius promulgated the agreement of Milan in the eastern provinces of which he was now Augustus.

Licinius' promulgation signaled the end of the final persecution that the Christian Churches suffered at the hands of the Roman Empire. Roman thinking about the Jews was always colored by the political fact that there once had been a Jewish national state in Palestine and that there were Jews bent on restoring that state. The Christians, once separated from their Jewish origins, had neither national connections nor political aspirations. The Christian "Way," as their religion was called in the early days of the first century, cut across both ethnic and class lines, and so held no promise of either social revolution or national insurrection.

The issue of the Christians had something to do with loyalty, loyalty to the Empire realized in the person of the Emperor to whom the Christians would not offer sacrifice. Loyalty had never been an issue in the Empire, but in the third century the Romans made it one in the case of the Christians. It is unlikely that any intelligent Roman official of the time seriously believed the old allegation that the Christians practiced cannibalism and incest. They may have perceived, however obscurely, in the fashion that Socrates' persecutors had, that here was more than the introduction of a new God into the overcrowded Roman pantheon; here was rather the revolutionary reorientation of the life of man. The Christian "Way" led into a different dimension, away from the City of Man into another Kingdom, ruled by another Lord, who was neither Hellene, Roman nor Jew, but ruler of the *kosmos.*

The Romans had heard of cosmic archons before, and the report had not set them to trembling. But these other Lords of the Universe ruled in the distant realms of mythic time; the Christian Kingdom of God was grounded in history. Its herald, Jesus of Nazareth, the Romans themselves had crucified in Judaea in the first century, and his disciples were preaching his physical resurrection. He would come again, they said, and the world would be restored in him.

Meanwhile, the faithful kept vigil, recalling his life and message and trying to live by his precepts. They did not threaten the state; they ignored it as irrelevant. It would be difficult to state the seditious quality of Christianity any more clearly than did the anonymous Christian author of the *Letter to Diognetus,* written sometime before the great persecutions of the third century: "They [the Christians] spend their days on earth, but hold citizenship in heaven. They obey the established laws, but in their private lives they transcend the laws." Pericles would have found the notions of a "citizenship in heaven" and "transcending the laws" as little intelligible as Decius and Diocletian did.

Whatever their personal views, Constantine and Licinius ended the persecutions because they valued public order more than they feared ideological revolution. But the Christianity whose toleration they officially sanctioned was already different from that which had confronted Nero, Trajan and even Decius. Though they were still a minority, the number of believers had grown, and they were now to be found at all levels of society, from slaves to highly placed members of the court, including men whose intellectual credentials could no longer be dismissed or ignored. In the days of Paul the issue had been whether a Gentile Christian was bound to the Mosaic Law; in the third century it was whether a Gentile, now that he had rejected his Mosaic past, was constrained to disavow his Hellenic heritage as well.

XVII

Christianity and the Hellenic World

By the second century Christianity had grown to that state of maturity where it could no longer be ignored or dismissed. Its Jewish past was fading, and what had occurred almost symbolically in Paul's own lifetime, the passage from Jerusalem, to the synagogues of Asia, to the Areopagus of Athens, was being reenacted on an ecumenical scale. In Asia Paul spoke of the Torah; with the Athenians he discussed the "unknown God." A Hellenized Greek or Roman who knew or cared nothing for Jewish prophets could not be convinced of Jesus by a typological reading of the Bible. Nor could a sophisticated polemicist be answered with parables. Christianity was drawn by its success onto the grounds of Hellenism and had, from the second century onward, to cope with the new threats and new aspirations posed by that change in perspective.

Spoliatio Graecorum

A passage in *Exodus* records the justification that their God had given the Hebrews for making off from Egypt with the gold and silver ornaments of the Egyptians. In the course of his exegesis of *Exodus*, Origen, the brilliant Hellenized Egyptian who directed the Christian school at Alexandria, used this "spoliation of the Egyptians" to justify the Christians' own expropriation of the cultural wealth of Hellenism for its own purpose. The *spoliatio Graecorum* had begun once again. Judaism in the past, now

Christianity, and in the future Islam—each availed itself of the intellectual and artistic treasures stored up by Hellenism over the course of two millennia. The manner was as simple as the temptation was alluring; it is only the price that each paid that is difficult to calculate.

Christianity began with Jesus, a Jewish carpenter's son from the rude district of Galilee, who went about Roman Palestine preaching his message of salvation. He had a varied audience, peasants of Galilee, the middle classes of the towns, members of the religious establishment in Jerusalem, even Hellenized Jews from the coastal cities, but the message seems not to have varied: fervor mixed with gentleness, exhortation, correction, metaphor, parable.

Jesus' message can be read only indirectly through the preaching of it by his followers as they proclaimed the "good news" of his birth, death, resurrection and Second Coming. The preaching of the Gospels was at once, however, more sophisticated than the message they announced. Their language was not the Aramaic of Palestine but *koine* Greek, the language of the *oikoumene*, and their manner more studied and more argumentative. The events in the life of Jesus, particularly the sacred history of his passion and death, were projected against a complicated background of Messianic and eschatological motifs understood with a new clarity.

The evangelical tradition was still preaching (*kerygma*), intended in the first instance to move; but it had moved forward to explanation and argumentation as well. The argumentation was still, despite the Hellenization of the language, directed at a Palestinian, or at least a Judaicized, audience whose points of reference were the Torah, the Prophets and the contemporary apocalypses. Beyond Palestine and beyond the synagogue was, however, another audience, which was equally capable of being moved by the preaching of the Gospels, but had other forms of discourse and other modes of proof. *Kerygma* spoke to the hearts of men; what had also begun with the extension of Christianity into the *oikoumene* was a struggle for their minds, conducted, as all such controversies in the Hellenic world, according to the rules of rational discourse, *logos*.

Put simply, *logos*, the beloved "word" of the Hellenes,[1] was, in

1. See Chapters VII, pp. 304-5, and XV, pp. 539-40.

its more technical acceptance, the rational process that used abstract intellectual concepts, expressed in propositional form, and in accordance with certain procedural rules, for the acquisition, description and defense of truth. Its pioneers of the sixth century B.C. had discovered that it was possible to explain the *kosmos* and its workings in new terms. There had been explanations before, chiefly of the type called *mythos*, and plentiful descriptions of physical phenomena. But *logos* created a new world picture that had the advantage of self-extension; based on certain postulates and implemented with highly manipulable terms, the system could be enlarged to absorb and explain extremely diverse phenomena in accordance with a set of principles that could be enunciated and tested. And unlike *mythos*, the new method was dialectical; it could respond.

Mythos was far from dead. The Stoics made an effort, as has been seen, to save it for the intellectualist tradition by applying their special "reading" to the traditional narratives. It was not the Stoic rationalists, however, who revived the more primitive religious functions of myth. Greek contacts with eastern mythologies led in some fashion or other to the production of Gnosticism, a strange amalgam of Cosmic pessimism that Hellene and Christian alike had to face in the second and third centuries.

Christianity could deal with Gnosticism, because it could confront it as a religion; philosophy could speak to both but compete with neither, except in the refined and secularized atmosphere of the schools. Philosophers had been attempting to deal with the question of God and his operations in the world almost from the beginning, and, though the horror and awe characteristic of a primary religious experience were but ill served by the methods of rational discourse, philosophy could and did conceptualize God for service within its cadres. There was a certain amount of uneasiness about the "God of the philosophers"; but discourse about God, *theologia*, became a standard part of the problematic of Greek philosophy, and in the interval between the first major treatments of the subject by Plato and Aristotle and Cicero's comprehensive *On the Nature of the Gods* a considerable literature had grown up on the subject.

Christianity, rejected by Judaism and rejecting it in turn, followed the example of Paul and carried its message to the Gentiles. It found that the objects of its zeal dwelled in a world that was doubtless in the throes of a deep-seated religious anxiety but that was, at the same time, highly sophisticated on the subject of both gods and God. Christianity could and did address itself to the anxiety, and with increasing success. Its very success carried it into wider circles and new quarters until, inevitably, it came into contact with the Hellenic theologians.

The problems faced by the nascent Christian Church in its passage from the narrow confines of a Palestinian milieu into the more spacious realms of a cultural Hellenism dominated by the political presence of Rome were considerable. The political confrontation with Rome gave rise, as has been seen, to a series of savage persecutions in which the Christian, caught in a tension between Caesar and Christ, was faced with either defection (*apostasis*) from the body of the Church or the bearing of a bloody witness (*martyria*) to his fellowship with his redeemer.

These tensions yielded, both before and after the violent interludes of persecution, to resolutions of considerably greater complexity. The mild docility that seems to characterize the *passiones* of the early martyrs, the kissing of Caesar's sword, was not the only possible reaction to pressure, particularly for the new generation of intelligent and thoughtful men reared in the very tradition that sought to bring them down. These Christians had, in the first instance, to resolve the incompatibility between being a good Roman or Hellene and being a good Christian. Was the option so clear-cut? And could the politicians and intellectuals of the Empire be convinced that any other course was possible? An attempt at explanation and reconciliation in the form of dialogue was taken up by the Christians of the second century, who added to their willingness to bear witness a more aggressive spirit of defense (*apologia*)—not, as originally, in the form of speeches before his judges by the Christian approaching martyrdom, but in closely reasoned treatises that betray both the Hellenism and the growing confidence of their authors.

The attack mounted on Christianity was not the work of Roman politicians only. The Hellenic intellectuals of the Empire had also discovered Christianity, and they too had identified it as the enemy. Some of the literary broadsides were doubtless prompted by official attitudes, like the one leveled against the Christians by Fronto, the philosophical tutor of Marcus Aurelius. But the new sect had caught other observant eyes as well. The satirist Lucian (*c.* A.D. 120–180) had noted the bizarre Christians and their practices, and though he was somewhat uncertain about the difference between a Christian and a Jew, he introduced a "Christian phase" into the life of one of his more theatrical charlatans, the Cynic Peregrinus. This was one reaction to Christianity: Christianity was another form of Oriental humbuggery, unfit for the serious attention of a Hellene. But with the increasing sophistication of Christian dialectic the attack began to veer off in another direction. It was no longer the cult that attracted attention; it was the intellectual pretensions. Shortly after Lucian's *The Death of Peregrinus* the eminent Platonist Celsus mounted a full-scale attack on the *substance* of Christianity in his *True Discourse.*

This was the context within which the work of the Christian apologists unfolded: a turning on both sides, Christian and pagan, from the deed to the word, not merely, as in Christianity's first confrontation with this world, to the word of the "good news," but to an accounting (*logos*) of Christian belief, an explicit comparison of it with both Judaism and the prevailing religious sentiments within the Roman Empire, and, finally, to a joining of issues with the partisans of the religious Platonism that was then on the rise and that was, in its final effort, to wrest one last Emperor after Constantine from the grasp of the Church.

The Christian "apologies" indicate that their authors had given a close and attentive reading to the staples of Hellenic culture. And no wonder. These second-century defenders of the faith were not converted products of Judaism but citizens of the *oikoumene.* Justin was born of pagan parents in Samaria, was converted to Christianity at Ephesus, taught and was martyred at Rome. Tatian was a Hellenized Syrian who also migrated to Rome. Athenagoras was an Athenian; Theophilus served as bishop of Antioch. All were to some extent products of a Hellenic education, for whom Christianity represented a conversion to a new life.

The Hellenized Christian was, however, a new phenomenon in the Church and created new problems. Did the acceptance of ethical and cultic Christianity imply the rejection of cultural Hellenism? This was precisely the question that was to torment the Christian intellectual for another two centuries. The extreme responses to this question are perhaps best illustrated later by Clement and Origen in the East and Tertullian and Cyprian in the

West,[2] but the same ambivalence was already present in Justin and his pupil Tatian.

Justin (d. *c.* A.D. 165) reached Christianity through the study of Greek philosophy, and he retraveled his spiritual and intellectual odyssey in his *Dialogue with Trypho,* an example of the contemporary polemic with the Jews, from whom the Christians were now increasingly distinguished.[3] For Justin the acceptance of Christ did not mean the rejection of his own Hellenic past. He explained that the Greeks too had a vision of the truth, fitful and obscured, to be sure, but the truth nonetheless. According to Justin, reason (*logos*) is given to all men, and so they share in the truth; but the integral *Logos* is Christ, and it is only with his coming that the entire truth is revealed. Even Socrates had a partial knowledge of Christ.

By his skillful playing on the various meanings of *logos* Justin created a kind of theology of knowledge and had, in effect, opened for Christianity the extraordinary vistas of Greek culture and learning to be appropriated for its own ends. Hellenic *paideia* was a revelation before revelation, so that eventually one could scrutinize the pagan past not merely to scout what might be salvaged from it, but to trace there the foreshadowing of Christianity. This was later made explicit by Clement of Alexandria, who maintained that philosophy served the Greeks in the same function as the Torah did the Jews, to foreshadow the coming of Christ. This is also the same premise of Eusebius of Caesarea's *Preparation for the Gospel* and lies behind the later Christian notion of the *anima naturaliter Christiana,* the Christian before Christ, applied preeminently to Plato for his recognition of the

---

2. The *locus classicus* for the problem remains the passage in one of Jerome's letters wherein the humanistically trained Latin Father, having departed Rome for the more austere monastic atmosphere of Syria, was troubled by the fact that he could not give up his library of pagan classics. The *crise* of this particular fever occurred when he was dragged before the throne of God in a cold sweat and accused of being a "Ciceronian" and not, as he claimed, a Christian. A good flagellation exorcised his qualms for the moment, but there are other passages that indicate that the stylist within the Father never felt quite at home with the un-Ciceronian language of Scripture.

3. The earliest known example of the genre is the now lost *Discussion* of Ariston of Pella, a Jew by birth, which dated from about A.D. 140. It was Ariston's flair for allegorical interpretation that provoked the *True Discourse* of Celsus.

immortality of the soul and to Vergil for the Messianic insights of his fourth *Eclogue*.

Justin's attitude toward Hellenism, though eventually to become the standard one in Christian circles, was opposed by his student Tatian.[4] His *Discourse to the Greeks* is marked by a violence of tone and an unswerving conviction that Hellenism had nothing to teach the Christian but folly and immorality. Bridling under the charges that he had lapsed into a kind of Oriental barbarism, Tatian was at some pains to defend Christian belief on the grounds of its (Moses') great antiquity, and that its sacred books, by reason of their simple and straightforward character, their high moral quality and their monotheistic doctrine, had led him to belief.

These were mere protestations; interlined in Tatian's diatribe against Hellenism was the Christian point of view, and here the Platonic and Stoic strains appeared straightway. Jesus is the *Logos,* existing in the beginning as a potency (*dynamis*) of the Father, who is the *hypostasis* of all. He is *pneuma.* Tatian was as enmeshed in the Hellenic framework as Justin, as he himself perhaps eventually realized, since his career ended on a very different note far from the philosophical schools of Rome. He returned, sometime after A.D. 172, to the Syrian East, where his personal tensions were resolved in a radical asceticism.[5]

We have little or no idea of the nature of a Christian education at Rome in the circle of Justin. Justin's own formation had been under strictly secular auspices at Ephesus, where he had come into contact with Stoics, Pythagoreans (he did not, however, follow their course, since it involved the study of music, astronomy and geometry, in which he had no interest), Peripatetics and Platonists before his conversion to Christianity about A.D. 130. But even if he had not noted down the main lines of his education, it would be clear enough from his works themselves that someone with a considerable background in contemporary phi-

---

4. For Tatian's role in the dissemination of Scripture, see Chapter XIII, p. 506.
5. According to Epiphanius, Tatian founded the heretical sect of the Encratites, or "the Abstemious," a group of radical ascetics with Gnostic associations who abstained from marriage, the eating of flesh and the drinking of wine. They even substituted water for wine in the celebration of the Eucharist.

losophy was attempting to bring the apparatus of Hellenism to bear on the enunciation of Christian belief.

Justin was no rationalist; he could and did correct the findings of Greek philosophy in the light of revelation: Plato was right in holding that the *kosmos* was created (an interpretation of the *Timaeus* rejected by most of the Platonic tradition) but was incorrect in his belief in the transmigration of souls. Justin's defense of Christianity rested heavily on a typological interpretation of the Old Testament, a method of reading texts by then a commonplace in both Judaism and Hellenism, rather than on purely philosophical reasoning; but when it came to explanation he had no hesitation couching his discourse in terms borrowed from the conceptual world of Hellenism. He provided a Platonic explanation of the transcendence of God and related God's immanence to the Stoic doctrine of the *logoi spermatikoi*, all this while attempting to keep faith with the historicity of the *Logos* made flesh.

This was doubtless Justin's intent. What he could in no way have foreseen was that by adopting such terminology he was setting the stage for the great Trinitarian and Christological disputes of the following centuries that hinged precisely on the question of how to express in philosophical terms the relation of Father to Son and the nature of the Son.[6]

The work of expropriating Hellenism was continued by Clement, who sometime before A.D. 200 succeeded Pantaenus[7] as head of the Christian catechetical school in Alexandria. Born and trained in Athens, Clement was drawn to Alexandria by the reputation of Pantaenus, and though he spent only a few years there before the Severan persecution drove him to Cappadocia, the influence of the Hellenistic intellectual center left strong traces in his work. Clement's perspectives were different from Justin's; they were broader and at the same time less defensive, looking to attracting the intelligent Hellene to Christianity down the broad avenues of his own culture.

Clement's program was to be set out in a series of works in

---

6. See Chapter XIX, p. 691.

7. Before his conversion Pantaenus was a Stoic philosopher, described by Clement as "a Sicilian bee gathering the spoils of the flowers of the prophetic and apostolic tradition."

rough trilogy form: the *Protreptikos* (or *Exhortation*), designed, on the model of similarly titled works in the philosophical tradition, to attract and prepare the reader for conversion from paganism to Christianity; the *Paidagogos* (or *Tutor*), a treatise on the conduct of a Christian life; and the *Didaskalos* (or *Teacher*), presumably an instruction for the convert on the rudiments of Christian belief. The third work was never undertaken, but was replaced instead by the *Stromateis* (or *Miscellanies*), in which Clement took up a great number of diverse topics in a highly unsystematic fashion.

The *Exhortation* differs very little from the *apologiae* of the earlier generation of Christian writers. If the defense against cannibalism and incest is no longer deemed necessary, all the other commonplace themes of the *apologia* are still present. There is, moreover, the same development of the *logos* doctrine visible in Justin: the transcendence of God is mediated by one *Logos* that proceeds from him. There is perhaps a growing sophistication in philosophy, and a greater confidence in its use, but there is something else as well. With Clement the Christian intellectuals began to turn from defenses of the faith in terms of Hellenic rational discourse for the benefit of the non-Christian community to the more demanding task of enunciating for the Church itself a coherent and systematic statement of its own beliefs.

Both the *Paidagogos* and the *Stromateis* were directed within, to the body of Christians at Alexandria, still the intellectual focal point of the *oikoumene* after five centuries of existence. Indeed, it was somewhat more than that: Alexandria of the second and third centuries was also the mixing bowl for most of the religious currents—scientific, arcane and prophetic—swirling about the Roman Empire. One of them, Gnosticism, was particularly strong in Egypt, and it lay close to the heart of Christian belief.

Clement was well instructed on Gnosticism and on the Christian reaction to it. The Gnostic blending of Christianity with the theses of Greek philosophy and eastern myths struck some believers as so treasonous to the witness of the Gospels that there was already developing within the Church a kind of simple fundamentalism that advocated "simple faith." The same kind of "simple faith" was being practiced in the Egyptian deserts by increasing numbers of monks in Clement's own day, but this thinly veiled rejection of the Hellenic intellectual tradition did not recommend itself to one raised in that tradition. Instead,

Clement proposed to join what the Gnostics had set asunder: faith (*pistis*) and knowledge (*gnosis*). According to Clement the two are closely connected: true knowledge is unobtainable without faith, while knowledge is the perfection of that faith. The Gnostic separation is explicitly denied.[8]

Natural knowledge had, then, a part to play in the life of the Christian, and particularly its highest manifestation, philosophy. Thus there lay open before the Christian theologian the whole range of the Hellenic philosophical tradition to be drawn upon. Clement did so, but his preferred source was his fellow Alexandrian Philo, and nowhere more markedly than in his exegesis of Scripture. It is Philo, for instance, whom Clement followed in basing his defense of Hellenic culture on an allegorical reading of the story of Abraham, Sara and Hagar. Sara is sacred wisdom; Hagar the profane sciences of the *enkyklios paideia*. Hagar had to bear children to Abraham before Sara became fertile.

We do not know how Clement put this allegorically derived educational theory into practice, but with Origen, his successor as the head of the school, we can trace the first steps in the construction of a new *paideia*. According to Eusebius, Clement directed a catechetical school, that is, an institution directed toward teaching the rudiments of Christian faith as a preparation for baptism. With Origen it became a school of higher education.

If Cicero is the type of the Hellenized Roman, Origen is that of the Hellenized Christian. A native Egyptian, Horigenes, the child of Horus, he was educated in both Scripture and secular learning by his father, whose own devotion to the new faith led to his martyrdom in the Severan persecutions of A.D. 202. Origen's education did not end there; he was, along with Plotinus and others,[9] the student of the most eminent Alexandrian philosopher of his time, Ammonius Saccas.[10] At seventeen on his

8. Clement also knew, and was attracted to, a *gnosis* close to the Gnostic understanding of that term: the secret tradition of knowledge handed down orally from James, John and Peter and given to a few in the Church. This defense of the "apostolic tradition" was doubtless appealing, but was never accepted by the Church as orthodox.

9. Apparently Ammonius numbered two Origens among his pupils, the Christian theologian and the Neoplatonic philosopher in the circle of Plotinus. The two men became hopelessly confused in the later accounts.

10. See Chapter XVI, p. 570.

own initiative he restored the disrupted Catechetical School and took over its direction. By this time Origen was already a professional teacher of literature. He may have given this up for a time because of his new responsibilities, but his own temperament, training and commitment to the intellectual life of Alexandria did not long permit him to restrict his teaching to the rudiments of the faith. A curriculum of higher studies began to develop at the new school, and it reached the point where Origen delegated the purely catechetical work to another.

His lectures attracted the attention of the secular philosophers. Psychologically it signaled his reacceptance by the intellectual community. Origen accepted it as such and gave himself over to a more intense study of both philosophy and Scripture. He even learned Hebrew to that end. Thanks to a wealthy convert, there was a full staff of stenographers and copyists to serve his increasingly prolific literary output. All the while he taught geometry, arithmetic, philosophy and theology, and later, as described by his student Gregory the Wonder-Worker, who went through Origen's version of the *enkyklios paideia* at Caesarea in Palestine between A.D. 235–238, what was an even more elaborate course progressing from logic to astronomy.

This life, begun so prosperously, ended in trials. Origen fell from the favor of the bishop of Alexandria and was excommunicated in A.D. 231. He found refuge at Caesarea for a number of years, but was eventually caught in the net of the Decian persecutions, was tortured, and died in broken health at Tyre in A.D. 253. The controversy over some points of his teaching, particularly that of the preexistence of the soul of Christ, raged on after his death and played a part in the Christological disputes of the sixth century. His positions were anathematized at a local synod in Constantinople in A.D. 543, and again at the Fifth Ecumenical Council in Constantinople in A.D. 553. But for all the shadows in his career, he left behind two enduring foundation stones that were incorporated into the rising edifice of Christianity: his Scriptural commentaries and the systematic treatise *On the First Principles*.

If his projected *Teacher* is understood correctly, Clement had promised but not executed a systematic treatment of Christian principles. The work was in fact achieved by his successor Origen sometime after A.D. 220, and Christianity came into possession of its first *summa theologica*. Compared to its more imposing successors, *On the First Principles* is a treatise of modest proportions. It was, however, no mere *apologia* directed toward a specific opponent, as Origen was himself to do in a treatise directed against Celsus,[11] where the retort matches the points made by Celsus and is drawn from the same sources. The *Principles*, on the other hand, began with the basics of the Christian faith as found in the apostolic preaching. But Origen had no sooner summarized these than he stated that in many cases the apostolic tradition did no more than announce *that* a thing is so, without explaining the *how* or the *why*. The voice was that of Origen, but the tone was that of the authentic Hellenic tradition in its analytical pursuit of causes.

According to Origen the task of the theologian was to begin from these same Scriptural principles (*archai*) and form a systematic body of truth developed through arguments and illustrations. Thus the manner of procedure was not merely the exegesis of a sacred text of revelation, but the movement toward the explanation and development, in the methodical and systematic form already highly developed in the secular schools, of Christian dogma. Like his contemporaries in the philosophical schools, Origen too was guided by current controversy, particularly that surrounding Gnosticism. But that steering mechanism is somewhere beneath the surface; what appears in the *Principles* is not a heresiology but a theological *summa* treating of God, the Trinity, the spiritual world, the physical world, God's activity in it, sin, redemption and Sacred Scripture.

The influence of Origen on subsequent theological literature has been somewhat obscured by reason of the suspicion of heterodoxy that fell upon some of his opinions, as well as the fact that the more familiar tradition of western scholasticism stems more immediately from Boethius (*c.* A.D. 475–525). It is true that Boethius' theological treatises—his *On the Trinity*, for example—betray a more highly developed scholastic methodology, and the later Latin author was far more conscious of being an innovator because he was pioneering the translation of Greek conceptual

---

11. *Against Celsus*, written when Origen was over sixty, was directed against an attack leveled by the Platonist philosopher against Christianity more than half a century earlier.

terminology into an alien tongue.[12] But whatever the relative claims, what sets both men apart is the progressive intrusion of a distinctly Aristotelian methodology into Christian discourse. Origen stood at the beginning of that process; Boethius at its flood.

In the Jewish tradition theology had its modest pre-Hellenic beginnings in the reading, collation, and expounding of Scripture in the scribal society of the post-exilic age. After Ezra the interpretation of the Law became increasingly important, and to this was joined, during the Maccabean period, a new eschatological way of reading the Sacred Books. The early Christians too, as is clear from the Gospels themselves, read Scripture in the same light, and a good part of the debate between Christian and Jew in the first two centuries of the Christian era had to do with the question of a typological reading of passages in the Bible and whether Jesus fulfilled them, a dialogue made extremely difficult with the Jewish repudiation of the Septuagint.

Origen operated within this same exegetical tradition, and the great bulk of his work is devoted precisely to commentaries on Scripture, two hundred and ninety-one different studies on practically every book of the Old and New Testaments.[13] And if the influence of his *summa* was considerable but indirect, that of the commentaries was massive and immediate.[14] Origen the exegete was important in the life of the early Church not only by reason of the tremendous breadth of his work, but primarily because of the methodological possibilities that he exposed.

Early on, within the Jewish tradition itself, it was understood that Scripture was not a homogeneous whole but embraced various genres—history, law, prophecy, liturgical prescriptions. Approaching this premise from one direction, the early Hellenized Christians worked out a correspondence between the various parts of Scripture and the divisions of Greek philosophy, an ap-

---

12. Boethius did, in fact, a great deal to domesticate Greek philosophical terminology in Latin, but he was not without eminent and creative predecessors, notably Lucretius and Cicero. But both the earlier men worked at a time when the full scholastic quality of philosophy was only beginning to emerge (see Chapter IX, p. 374).

13. To say nothing of his preliminary textual work (see Chapter XIII, pp. 504–5).

14. Even in the Latin West where they were known chiefly through the revisions of Jerome and Rufinus.

proach that had as its not too distant corollary the position that
Greek philosophy derived, by a primitive plagiarism, from
Moses.[15] This is essentially the view of Clement: the historical
and legal sections of the Torah correspond to Greek ethics, the
liturgical sections to physics, and those that deal with God to
theology, or metaphysics, or to Platonic dialectic.

With Origen, however, there was a new point of departure
that led into an investigation not of the genres of Scripture but of
its *senses*. His understanding of Scripture was based on an analysis of man, a composite being of body, soul (*psyche*) and spirit
(*pneuma*). Scripture was given for the perfection of man and so
necessarily corresponds to this division: for the simple there is a
literal and historical sense; for those who are somewhat more
advanced, a moral or psychic (later tropological) sense; and for
the perfect, an allegorical or spiritual sense that reveals "the
wisdom of God hidden in mystery."

The importance of this was immense. Origen was not the first
to introduce a nonliteral interpretation of Scripture. The Greeks
read their myths as allegories, and the later Jews scanned the
Prophets for a Messiah. Christianity adopted this latter method of
typological reading, and, despite Gnostic pressures to disassociate
the two Testaments, continued to argue Christ from the Jewish
Scripture. What Origen did was to connect the two traditions,
the "Christianizing" of the Old Testament, and the secular exegetical tradition mediated through Philo. The first is represented
by Origen's "spiritual sense," the second by the tropological reading as practiced by Philo and the secular Greek tradition before
him, particularly by the Stoics and Platonists.[16] To Philo's "natural history" of the soul Origen added the Christian "supernatural history" of the soul, and the combination passed intact—
and in a highly refined form—into the main body of the Christian
tradition.

---

15. The opposite opinion could also be held, that Moses studied the
books of Egyptian wisdom before composing his own work. By an
ingenious twist it could be had both ways: Abraham taught the
Egyptians their sciences, which they, in turn, taught to Moses.
16. Eusebius cites the charge of the Neoplatonist Porphyry that
Origen learned his allegorical method from the Stoics, specifically
Chaeremon and Cornutus (see Chapter XII, p. 452). The charge is
doubtless true, though Origen's application is unmistakably Christian.

The Eastern Church Before Nicaea

The obvious intellectual sophistication of these Hellenized Christians stands in marked contrast with the still somewhat primitive organization of the Church. Relations between individual metropolitan churches and between their bishops were loose and sometimes uncertain. Origen was excommunicated from the Alexandrian Church but found support in Palestine and Athens, an incident that sharply differs from the events of the sixth century, when his teaching was anathematized by the *ecumenical* Church. Between the two condemnations the bishops had obviously learned to make common cause against common dangers. The instrument they devised for this concerted action was the synod, and it first appeared in connection with a doctrinal problem of the second century, Montanism.

The problem that provoked the summoning of a council of bishops was generally that of heresy, a deviation from the traditional practice or belief of the Church. That there should be such was almost inevitable. Though all had received their apostolic tradition from a common source and so were members of a shared Christian experience, the difficulties of communication and the absence of a central authority left the Christian churches of the Mediterranean with only their own instincts to guide them in the unfolding of that tradition. The times too were disjointed by the increasing pressure from the state, attacks from the intellectual establishment of the *oikoumene*, and the churches' uncertainty about their own future. The earliest Christians had a strong sense of an imminent Second Coming, but as the *parousia* faded into the distant future profound adjustments in attitude and practice took place, not without doubts and false steps.

Even in Paul's day the churches of Asia had their difficulties with some of their own members, and as those same churches passed out of the shadow of the Apostolic Age and the relatively homogeneous atmosphere of Diaspora Judaism, their internal troubles multiplied. The earliest converts shared, by and large, in the common heritage of that Judaism and brought to their understanding of the Gospels a sense of Scripture and of the Messiahship of Jesus. Their successors brought far more, a knowledge of Greek philosophy and of that rather indeterminate mélange of

Greek and eastern ideas that was to issue in the tremendous crisis of Gnosticism. They brought as well a bewildering variety of local custom and sentiment, and it was this latter ingredient that was at the base of one of the most threatening of the pre-Nicene heresies, Montanism.

Montanus was converted to Christianity sometime about A.D. 170 from the cult of Cybele that had spread from its native Phrygia as far as Rome itself.[17] Montanus came from the borders of Phrygia, and though there is no evidence that he attempted to introduce into Christianity some of the more exotic practices of the cult of the Magna Mater he did begin to preach a vital prophetism in Anatolia. There were grounds for prophetism within the apostolic tradition; "prophets" constituted one of the recognized orders of the primitive Church, and the *Acts of the Apostles* frequently adverts to individuals filled with the Spirit of God and speaking as prophets. Indeed Jesus himself had promised to send his prophetic Paraclete.

Prophetic enthusiasm was very much a part of the eschatological excitement of the first Christian century. The excitement gradually passed and the individual charismata of the imminent end time yielded to more institutionalized means of salvation: the sacramental system of the Church and its hierarchical rule; the bishops alone taught with the authoritative voice of the Spirit. Montanus rejected this premise. For him the *parousia* was still nigh,[18] and in the grip of an ecstatic transport he and his followers—notably the two Phrygian ladies Priscilla and Maximilla —spoke in and of the Spirit.

Montanism was the reassertion of eschatological prophethood in an age when it had almost disappeared from within the Church. Unlike the rationalist heresies spawned by Christianity's contact with Hellenic philosophy, Montanus did not put himself forward as an interpreter of the apostolic tradition, but rather as a mere passive mouthpiece through which God still spoke directly to the Church. Montanism in effect undercut the apostolic tradition, preserved and transmitted by the bishops, and by them alone, in favor of a continuing private revelation.

Religions with systems of "closed" revelation have never been

---

17. See Chapter XII, p. 475.
18. The Heavenly Jerusalem was expected to descend at Pepuza in Phrygia.

completely at ease with such private visionaries. Judaism gave a hearing, not always willingly, to her latter-day prophets, but to a noticeably lesser degree after the institutionalization of the rabbinate in the years after A.D. 70. Christianity was experiencing just such an institutionalization in the second century, and so the appearance of visionaries, monks, dervishes, or otherwise, in Phrygia, where the phenomenon was indigenous,[19] threatened the emerging structure of the Church.

The hierarchical reaction to Montanism led to the summoning of the first synods of the Church, wherein bishops of more than one jurisdiction sat to consider a problem of common interest. The bishops of Thrace and of Asia met to resist the threat posed by Montanism, and their common front of opposition seems to have been effective; Montanism lingered on in pockets of Anatolia but could no longer summon up the kind of popular support it had evoked before the bishops convened in synod and condemned the doctrine as heresy and its adherents to sacramental outlawry.

The synod proved to be an effective weapon against deviations from the apostolic tradition which passed beyond the boundaries of a single Church, and they occurred with increasing frequency through the third century. But the gathering together of bishops raised questions as pressing and as complicated as the ones they were intended to solve. Eusebius described one such convened at Antioch in A.D. 268 to discuss the doctrinal problem raised by the bishop of Antioch, Paul of Samosata. The substance of the dispute was Christological, a forerunner of the great debates of the fifth century, but Paul was deeply involved as well with the imperialist pretensions of Palmyra and may have been serving as a kind of theological stalking-horse for Palmyrene designs on Antioch itself.[20] All of this made for a highly complex finding, but when the bishops finally condemned Paul's position as heretical they declared their decision in a letter addressed to the bishops of Rome and Alexandria but actually sent to all the provinces of the Empire.

---

19. Phrygian prophets caused no difficulty for the Greeks or Romans with their "open" revelation, but later in Islam, where prophethood was explicitly "sealed" by Muhammad, Anatolian dervishes raised the identical problems for the Islamic "apostolic tradition" that the Phrygians had raised for the Christians.

20. See Chapter XVI, pp. 598–99.

The synod of A.D. 268 is interesting in far more than its first, tentative confrontation with the problems attendant upon a philosophical and theological approach to the person of Jesus. It marks in an unmistakable fashion the growing importance and jurisdiction of Antioch as a Christian center: represented at the synod were bishops from Cappadocia, Pontus and Cilicia in Asia, Caesarea and Jerusalem in Palestine, and Bostra in Arabia— seventy or eighty in all. There were, as well, the ecumenical overtones; the crisis was more than a provincial matter, and so the results were communicated to the entire Church, but with a careful recognition of the primacy of certain Sees within that ecumenical body, namely the Sees of Rome and Alexandria.

There would be more hard going on some of those issues, but not until Christianity's second great confrontation, that with the Roman political authority. Between A.D. 150 and A.D. 250 the Church had faced and begun to master the challenge of Hellenic intellectualism. The same pattern of conflict, resistance, resolution and assimilation was destined to be repeated in the following century's dealings with the Roman political authority. And just as post-Origen theological treatises resembled, to an ever greater degree, the contemporary philosophical works, so the organization of the post-Nicene Church came more and more to look like its "parent" organization, the Roman state.

Though this final impression of an external form was still in the future, the Church of the third century continued its spread across the East, radiating from the primitive centers of Jerusalem, Alexandria and Antioch. There were thriving Christian communities in the Hellenized cities of the Mediterranean littoral, like Tyre, Beirut and Caesarea, and some progress was made in the hinterland as well. The new creed flourished in Cyrenaica, and Christians were found in Lower Egypt, Arabia, and particularly in inner Syria where the conversion of Roman client king of Osrhoene, Abgar (c. A.D. 179–214), signaled the birth of a Syriac version of Christianity that prospered down to the fifteenth century.[21] There was a vigorous Christian life in Anatolia from the time of Paul's activity there, and these Asian communities, not yet fallen under the jurisdictional shadow of Constantinople, continued to play an important and sometimes disturbing part in

---

21. It was the Syrian version of Christianity, frequently under suspicion of heresy by the Hellenized Church, that spread to the Sasanian Empire and prospered there under both the Shahs and the Caliphs.

the life of the Church, most notably in the great controversies on the date of Easter that broke out at the end of the second century.[22]

Most of the details of this sketch must be pieced together from remarks let fall by Eusebius in his *Ecclesiastical History,* written sometime about A.D. 325. What is more immediately known from Eusebius' account is that the period in the Church's growth down to Nicaea was dominated by locally autonomous bishops, men elected by the Christian community, and frequently for their learning as much as their piety. A good example is provided by the three scholars who governed the Church at Laodicea in Syria in the latter half of the third century: Eusebius, Anatolius and Stephen. Anatolius is particularly interesting in that he founded a school of Aristotelian studies at Alexandria before his elevation to the bishopric, and is probably the same man who was the teacher of Iamblichus, another religiously inclined scholar with a very different career. In the next century, as the bishops were falling more and more under the control of the great Patriarchal and Metropolitan Sees, their own effective jurisdiction was progressively delegated to the presbyters and priests within a parochial (*paroikia*) system. Before Nicaea, however, the local bishop was still supreme. He exercised control over the liturgical practices of his Church, regulated catechetical instructions, and safeguarded the tradition (*paradosis*) passed on from his apostolic forebears.

When, where, and how the activity of the Christian community unfolded in the third century depended on the political climate. During times of peace the Christians of the East served in the Imperial or the local government and otherwise shared in the life of the cities; Origen, as has been noted, was a public celebrity in Alexandria, and this despite the fact that his father

---

22. The Roman usage celebrated the Pasch as the resurrection of Jesus on the Sunday following the fourteenth day of the lunar month of Nisan; the eastern Churches observed the Pasch as the death of Christ on whatever day of the week the 14th Nisan chanced to fall. Victor (A.D. 189–199), the first aggressively Latin Pope in what had been a mixed Greek-Oriental Christian community at Rome, attempted to force the Roman practice on the entire Church and elicited a highly "nationalistic" defense of the eastern way in reply from the bishop of Ephesus. The same controversy also brought to the surface a Judaizing movement centered at Laodicea. Peace was restored through the good offices of Irenaeus, the Greek bishop of Lyons, and the Roman practice eventually prevailed.

had been executed there for his Christian beliefs not many years before. There must have been a fairly substantial number of Christians in the army as well, though some moral theorists opposed this. Public churches were built in the intervals between persecutions; but when the pogroms broke out anew, Christian cult practices once again became domestic, private or clandestine. There were catacombs in the East as well as in Rome, and they served as centers of refuge and liturgical assembly. They were decorated, probably in imitation of the Jewish pictorial art of the Diaspora, in the Hellenistic mode, with frequent resort, as in the writings of the contemporary apologists, to a typological appreciation of scenes from the Old Testament.

The oldest form of self-expression properly Christian was the hymn, again modeled on Jewish prototypes from the Septuagint, and serving, like the psalms and songs of the Old Testament, liturgical ends. Testimony to this goes back to the time of Pliny at the beginning of the second century. These earliest hymns probably had little or no genuine metrical content and belonged rather to the category of rythmical prose. Genuine metrical hymns eventually did develop, frequently under the instigation of the more innovative heretical groups,[23] and the genre reached its artistic and literary height in the sixth century.

The early Christian hymns marked the creation of a new art form in that they broke with the older, closed-verse forms based on the quantitative measure of syllables. Instead of the regular succession of long and short syllables the prosody of the Christian hymn rested upon word accent and the number of syllables in a line, and, like the parallel development in the West, codified in literary form the passage of the ancient tongue into the medieval vernaculars. The future belonged to this new type of vernacular, stress verse, but there was also the adaptation of the classical mode of poetry—now in its final stage—to Christian ends. Such are the anapestic hymns to Christ at the end of Clement's *Tutor* and the far more ambitious antiphonal hymns at the end of the *Symposium* of Methodius of Olympus in Lycia (*d.* A.D. 311). The entire latter work was intended as a frank imitation of Plato, but the choral hymn at the end, sung by the virgin Thecla and alternating choruses of girls, owes more to Alcman and Pindar.

---

23. Two well-known examples are the Gnostic *Odes of Solomon*, originally written in Greek, but preserved in Syriac and Coptic translation, and the lost *Thalia* of Arius, a drama in verse.

Late pagan antiquity had its own liturgical hymns, though their disappearance is almost complete. Philosophers adapted the type to other, nonliturgical uses and some of these latter are extant. We possess Aristotle's *Hymn to Virtue*, the Stoic Cleanthes' celebrated *Hymn to Zeus*, and the hymns of the best exponent of the tradition, the Neoplatonist Proclus. The eighth of these latter, the *Hymn to God*, was long attributed to another practitioner in the genre, Gregory of Nazianzus in Cappadocia. The confusion is understandable since by the fifth century Christians had appropriated the literary, nonliturgical hymn, and with some success. Proclus' two most eminent predecessors in the field were the Christian bishop Gregory (Patriarch of Constantinople in A.D. 380) and Synesius of Cyrene (*c.* A.D. 370–415), the former a student of Libanius, the latter trained in the Neoplatonic schools of Alexandria. Both were products of the best Hellenic culture of their times and deeply imbued with the rhetorical and philosophical principles of the contemporary schools. Their poetry is what one might expect from citizens of two cultures—a blend of the old and the new, of the sacred and the profane, theologians in verse but still sufficiently convinced of the validity of the classical heritage to adhere to the quantitative verse forms.[24]

In the course of the third century Christianity had encountered Hellenism and been transformed, at least intellectually. In the next century the process was to continue with the constitution of an ecclesiastical organization on the model of the morphology of the Empire in which it had become domesticated. Both were to remain part of the life of the Church, attacked, one or the other, by the forces of reform and of separation. The alarums of the reformers were in vain. What the Church had done in the third century was to join itself to the contemporary Hellenic intellectual (and artistic)[25] tradition. Judaism too, though it had earlier apparently declined this step, was more quietly moving in the same direction. And Islam was to follow as well. All three religious bodies suffered anxieties in making this choice, because each realized that in the desertion of kerygmatic fundamentalism there was implicated some kind of loss—of inno-

---

24. Gregory also wrote a few pieces in the new accented style; he was one of its pioneers.
25. Objections to the Church's assimilation of the Hellenic artistic tradition were relatively mild until the Iconoclastic controversy in eighth-century Constantinople called this too in question.

cence perhaps, if nothing else. But each also understood that in a world created by Hellenism the fundamentalist position, the "that" without the "how" and "why" of Origen, was ultimately indefensible in intellectual terms.

Theology did not, however, exhaust the content of the Gospels, any more than it did that of the *Qur'an*. Christianity was also, in terms of Hellenism, a *bios*, a mode of living, a life style, and here the Christian went his own way. Hellenism had its own *bioi* to offer as paradigms, but if Christianity appeared on occasion to approximate those prototypes, it was more by reason of a common ground of asceticism present in many religious cultures than from any deliberate desire to imitate a Socrates or a Pythagoras. Quite the contrary, Christian asceticism and the various institutionalized forms that developed out of it served as a kind of rallying point for much of the anti-intellectual and anti-Hellenic sentiment in the Church.

Athletes of God

There is no beginning of asceticism; the contrast between the this-worldly and the other-worldly is implicit in any religious experience from the outset, whether expressed in taboo or flight or the more activist exercise known to the Greeks as *askesis*. In its most general form asceticism mandates that certain things are to be done and others avoided, and not merely on an occasional or random basis but as part of a fixed pattern of life. The Greeks saw such patterns in the regimen of the soldier and the athlete and used the word *askesis* to describe their training.

Genuine religious asceticism, the adoption of the *askesis* pattern for supernatural ends, appeared among the Greeks with Pythagoreanism, which, with its elaborate taboos on food, its distinctive dress, probation of initiates, formation into closed brotherhoods (*hetaireiai*), and a desire to reform the society in which it was a part, illustrates all the motifs that characterize Jewish, Christian and Islamic asceticism. Contrary to most Greeks nourished on the traditional anthropomorphism, the Pythagoreans had a highly developed sense of the other-worldly apparent in the often expressed tension between the earthbound body and the divine and spiritual soul.

The postulates of Pythagorean asceticism were embodied in

their myths, but neither the myths nor the actual *askesis*, both subject to elaborate retouching in late antiquity, are very reliable witnesses to what was felt or done in the sixth century B.C. Philosophy had discovered Pythagoreanism and its congener Orphism and constructed their insights into something quite different. Plato's *Phaedo* reads like a philosophical commentary on Pythagorean *askesis*, connecting its tension between soul and body with his own more metaphysical dualism of intelligible and sensible, eternal and temporal, spiritual and material. The proverbial Orphic identification of the body as the prison of the soul is repeated by Plato, but the perspectives have changed: the *askesis* that will liberate man from this prison is no longer immediately connected with ritual purity or taboo but with the practice of philosophy.

Plato intellectualized the nascent Pythagorean asceticism, both in his teaching and in his own way of life; the testimony of some of his contemporary adversaries, Antisthenes for one, makes it very clear that Plato was far more interested in horse breeding than in self-denial. There did exist in the Greek tradition, however, a genuine current of secular asceticism descending from Socrates and owing little to either Pythagorean piety or Platonic intellectualism. Its practitioners were fakirs who operated from social rather than religious premises, who wanted to reform society rather than save its soul. Greek religious asceticism had to await the rebirth of Pythagorean ideals at the end of antiquity.[26]

Where the asceticism of the East differed most markedly from that of the Greeks was in its comparative poverty of philosophical theory and the presence in its midst of a type alien to the Greeks, the solitary saint. Greek society never valued the lone eccentric, the *idiotes*. Most *poleis* were highly urbanized, and their cohesiveness was founded upon an individual's willingness to submit to some type of political contract. The East, with its more diffuse organization and its tradition of supernatural contract, of private revelation transcending merely human society, encouraged the individual who had "seen God" to go his own eccentric way. Such men leave little trace behind them. The lives of holy men living in communities are preserved and revered by the piety of their communities; the solitary lives and dies alone and, except for the truly exceptional saint or wonder-worker

---

26. See Chapter XI, pp. 428–29.

whose charisma has gone out into the world, the drama of his life, played out within himself, perishes with him.

No such oblivion has settled upon the great holy men of Israel. The words of its prophets, addressed to a community that eventually heeded them, have been preserved, and it is possible to fill out in some detail a rich chapter on the mantic tradition in Judaism. But it is a chapter in the history of enthusiasm; only on the fringes of Jewish prophetism can there be detected the traces of a complementary ascetical tradition.

As early as the days of Samuel, prophets (*nabis*) or seers lived together in some kind of guild, roaming the countryside and indulging, as did their Canaanite counterparts, in a variety of psychic and enthusiastic activities. In the crisis provoked by the Omrids in the ninth century B.C. they seem to appear once again as the "sons of the prophets." There are, however, differences of behavior that suggest these latter are not the same confraternities. They lived a common life of some privation, but in fixed locations (Bethel, Jericho, Gilgal), and there is little or no trace of the ecstatic phenomena that characterized the earlier *nabi* guilds. Elias, though not one of their number, was connected with them, and his work was completed by his disciple Eliseus with the aid of another similar group known as the Rechabites.

With the Rechabites one has arrived at what seems to be a genuine ascetical tradition in Israel. According to the account in *Jeremiah*, they lived in a community, probably tribal, under a rule given them by their founder. They refrained from wine and lived in tents, not houses. Another group, the Nazirites, also refrained from wine and did not cut their hair. Here is what appears to be a strong if symbolic protest against urban agriculturism, associated in the minds of these purist groups with the Baal cult of the urbanized Canaanites. The Jewish *experience* of Yahweh had been as nomads in the desert; the Rechabites were not practicing a simple withdrawal, as later the Egyptian Christians were to do, but were returning to their origins. They were resurrecting, in the sixth century, the nomadic life of their ancestors and at the same time making a social and religious gesture of opposition to what Israel had come to be.

One looks in vain among these groups for Pythagoras' or Plato's rejection of the flesh. Jewish asceticism, at this juncture at least, did not flow from any such radical dualism as that preached by Plato. The only impurity was ritualistic impurity, a concern of the entire community and not merely of the purists who sought the Jewish past in the desert. Nor is the evidence any stronger for the latest of the Jewish ascetics revealed by archaeology. In none of the documents from Qumran is there any hint of a Platonic disdain for the body.[27] Josephus would have his Hellenized readers believe that the Essenes were a species of Pythagoreans who thought the soul was imprisoned in the body. The analogy may have clarified things for those readers, but there is no trace of such an attitude in what we read from Qumran. Qumran asceticism was eschatological and its dualism was of the complementary Iranian type, wherein the forces of good and evil are locked in a cosmic conflict reflected here on earth; the metaphysical type visible in Plato and the Pythagoreans, wherein spirit and flesh are contrasted as principles of good and evil, is foreign to the Jewish tradition. If there was any ambivalence on the subject, it arose from the conflicting exhortations to remain ritually pure on the one hand and increase and multiply on the other.[28]

It is now beyond a serious doubt that the wide sectarian phenomenon represented by Qumran was at least a part, and perhaps the most important part, of the milieu from which Christianity came forth. The Essenes' eschatological asceticism, for example, is echoed in the New Testament texts on marriage that set the question of celibacy in the context of the "appointed time" and the "new age." But the most important bridge between the two worlds, that of the Gospels and that of Qumran, is clearly the figure of John the Baptist, who, like those other saints of the desert, was connected with a priestly family, baptized "for the remissions of sins," preached that the end time was at hand, and led a life of celibacy and asceticism at the Jordan ford no more than two miles north of the Qumran community. Was John an Essene of some unknown solitary type? It is difficult to say.[29] Whatever the case, for John, as for the Christians them-

---

27. See Chapter VIII, pp. 329–30.
28. Archetypically illustrated by the Talmud's story of the rabbi who had intercourse with his wife only five times in his life, and produced five sons, all rabbis! Rabbi Ben Trovato?
29. The Gospels do not identify him as such, but they are curiously and totally silent on the Essenes. No student of the subject finds this accidental.

selves, Essene eschatology was in a sense transcended, dissolved, since the Messiah *was* at hand: *"This* is the Lamb of God."[30]

Interwoven in the fabric of Christianity were still other strands that played no part in Essenism. The priestly note was absent in primitive Christianity, and if the early Christians lived in closed communities, they bore little resemblance to the Qumran model. Did the Qumran model, on the other hand, have any influence, either directly or through intermediaries, on those Christians who *did* live in closed communities, such as the Egyptian founders of monasticism? On the archaeological evidence, the Qumran Essenes disappeared about A.D. 70; the first Christian ascetics took up residence in the Egyptian desert exactly two centuries later. Clearly if the Essenes influenced Christian monasticism, it must have been through some extension of themselves. There have been those—and their number includes Eusebius—who have seen just such an extension in the Therapeutae described by Philo in his essay *On the Contemplative Life.*

According to Philo, the Therapeutae were a community of Jewish contemplatives living on the shores of Lake Mareotis near Alexandria. The group was constituted of men and women who had renounced their property and retired to a community to read and study the Scriptures. They lived in small, separated houses and spent most of their time in a solitary room (*monasterion*), where they passed their time in reading and study. They were ascetics, eating infrequently and poorly, and taking little thought of their dress or dwelling. Nothing more is known about the Therapeutae than is in Philo's sparse report; and having learned from Josephus and the Essenes what a Hellenized author can do to a native Jewish sect, one finds even the evaluation of that bit difficult. Despite certain similarities, however, Christian monasticism does seem to have sprung from other circumstances.

About A.D. 250 Egyptian Christians were already fleeing to the desert to escape the Decian persecutions,[31] and indeed the tradi-

---

30. The figure of John does not disappear from history as completely as he did from the Gospels. There exists to this day in Iraq a sect, the Mandaeans, who trace their origins back to Palestine and John the Baptist. Their rich Gnostic system of ritual and myth is compounded of Mesopotamian and Iranian elements, some of great antiquity, but there is no reason to doubt the authenticity of their "baptist" tradition. See Chapter XVIII, pp. 668–69.

31. They were frequently harassed, then and later, by the bedouin, whom Eusebius calls the *Sarakenoi* the first occurrence of that word.

tion of flight (*anachoresis*), for a variety of reasons but chiefly
economic ones, was a long and honorable tradition in Egypt,
where the *corvée* was a way of life.[32] There were ample grounds
for taking up a solitary life of asceticism, even in the Egyptian
wastes, in the third century. First and foremost there was both
the preaching and celibate example of Jesus himself in the Gospels, an example that must have borne early fruit, since Paul
knew Christian Greek celibates, both men and women,[33] at
Corinth. Later Hellenism knew both the solitary ascetic[34] and
Pythagorean communities of holy men, and Egyptian religion
was not without its own examples. Life in Alexandria, the second-
largest metropolis in the Mediterranean world, was economically
grinding in the difficult third century and, for the pious Christian, unspeakably sinful. One or more of these motives drove the
illiterate Copt Anthony from Alexandria to the desert sometime
about A.D. 270, an event that marked, by the Christians' own
reckoning, the beginnings of monasticism.

The pioneering feats of Anthony have been preserved in
Athanasius' *Life of Anthony*, and his motives are plain to read.
He was neither poor nor needy; it was simply that a Christian life
was impossible in Alexandria, so he betook himself to the desert
to work out his own salvation. Philosophy had no part in the
decision; in fact Anthony expressed his dislike of Hellenic philosophy (and theology) in the same fundamentalist terms to be
heard again and again in Christianity: the Gospels alone sufficed.
Once in the desert, Anthony had to face new threats. He was
plagued with a cloud of evil spirits, the same *daimones* that were
a common feature of all the literature and religious practice of
the day, whether that of the Hellenic theologians or simple
Christians living in mud villages. Demons were not the only
distraction. The fame of his holiness soon reached back to
Alexandria, drawing crowds of would-be disciples and the curious into the wilds. Anthony retreated farther into the wastes

---

32. See Chapter X, p. 396.
33. That communities of virgins played an important part in the early
Church is clear from the literature they provoked, the earliest of
which is probably the pseudo-Clementine letter *On Virginity* dating
from about A.D. 250 in Palestine.
34. The Cynic Peregrinus was one such (see Chapter XI). Lucian
calls Cynicism an *askesis* in the sense of a fixed manner of life, just as
Josephus uses the same word of the Essenes.

lying to the east of the Nile, toward the Red Sea, but eventually he relented somewhat, emerged from his solitude, and began the instruction of the imitators who had camped around him. Thus the charisma of holiness transformed the life of the solitary (*heremos*) into the kind of encampment later known as a *laura*, an arrangement like the one described by Philo in which the monks continued to live alone but close enough to come together on fixed occasions for instruction and liturgical practices.

Christian monasticism was constructed upon the ascetic ideal that preceded it, taking as its premise the conviction that solitude, or at least separation from the world, provided the most suitable context for awaiting the end time. That eschatological longing so apparent at Qumran ran deep and strong among the first Christian ascetics, far stronger than it did among the Hellenic Christians of the cities, where the expectation of the *parousia* had already largely yielded to other ideals. The eschatological virtues of poverty and celibacy burned fiercely in the desert from the beginning, but there eventually came, even into the remote fastnesses of Egypt, the realization that salvation rested not on the imminent arrival of the end time but on the sanctification of the present. More stable and institutionalized forms of life appeared. About A.D. 318 Pachomius, another native Egyptian, a convert who had already served his time in the Roman army before embracing Christianity and the desert, received an angelic call to found the first community (*koinobion*) of ascetics at Tabennisi on the west bank of the Nile near Dendera. Pachomius' monasteries, the first one at Tabennisi and its later offshoots, were more than collections of hermits under one roof; they were genuine communities, governed by a common rule, order and discipline. To the eschatological virtues was added the social one of obedience.

Some form of regularization was clearly in order. The deserts were being converted into vast cities of monks. Pachomius' foundations had seven thousand monks in the fifth century, and the even more forbidding deserts of the Wadi Natrun south of Alexandria had other thousands. The cities too began to fill up. Palladius numbered two thousand monks in Alexandria; and Oxyrhynchus had a remarkably high monastic population. There were even ascetic immigrants: travelers joined the movement from Syria and Palestine, and black Christians from Nubia and Ethiopia were not an uncommon sight in this new Christian

utopia. The monks were highly active in a number of ways—
Therapeutic contemplation was quite alien to them—but not
notably given to intellectual pursuits. There was some small
gardening or modest cottage industry like basket plaiting, but for
the most part the literate monks read Scripture and the others
recited it. Learning was for them, as it had been for Anthony, a
form of worldliness.

Like Anthony, most of the Egyptian monks were native Copts
untouched by Hellenism, simple men wrestling the demons and
the elements for their salvation. Their main weapon in this
warfare was the arduous *askesis* that tradition, the environment,
and their own competitive zeal imposed upon them. Imitation
was a powerful force among the monks, and rivalries developed
wherein zealot competed against zealot for the palm of athletic
asceticism. Contests of fasting and penance became veritable
Olympiads of chastisement. The most terrible kind of physical
pain must frequently have masked a delicious sense of spiritual
self-indulgence.

A brake was applied, first by the various monastic legislators,
who sought to maintain discipline from within, and then, after
Constantine, by the civil and ecclesiastical arm. Pachomius'
koinobion was governed by a rule that dictated a highly organized regimen and a strict, unquestioning obedience to a monastic
superior. Basil the Great, whose own spiritual formation was in
the unorganized ascetical environment of Pontus and Cappadocia,
visited Tabennisi in A.D. 358, and five years later produced his
own elaborate rules for the governance of cenobitical monasticism. His rules, set down in catechetical form, were widely
adopted in the East and set the tone and style of Byzantine
monasticism. They serve as well to illustrate the immense difference between the mature version of Christian asceticism and the
Qumran type. The militant apocalypticism was absent in Christianity. Gone too was the wild-eyed fervor of some of the earlier
Christian hermits; Basil spoke with the voice of moderation and
restraint. He was neither an Essenian Messiah-crier nor the
compleat Copt à la Pachomius, but a Hellenized theologian of
considerable sophistication. The refinement of Basil in discussing
monks was not, however, the Platonizing of Philo in describing
the Essenes. Basil was, at least to some extent, part of the
phenomenon he was describing; Philo was an observer, and
perhaps an indirect one.

The growing number of monks and their accumulation of property and influence made it imperative that their position vis-à-vis the central Church administration be defined. Local synods had passed legislation on the subject, but the first successful ecumenical effort in this direction was at Chalcedon in A.D. 451, where it was made explicit that the monasteries in a given area fell under the jurisdiction and control of the bishop of that province. The monks were further required to remain in the place where they first took up the monastic life, and their participation in commercial and civil functions was restricted. The state addressed itself to the same task. Justinian's legislation moved to bind the monk even more closely to the organized Church. Stringent restrictions were placed on the various hermits and anchorites who lived on the fringes of the monastic movement. The *laura* was assimilated to the *koinobion*, and the jurisdiction of the bishop confirmed. Further internal reforms were introduced in the ninth century by Theodore of the monastery of Studius in Constantinople. The norms enunciated by Theodore in his writings, essentially a reworking of Basil's ideals, shaped the classic form of Byzantine monasticism, set forth in each monastery's foundation charter, or *typikon*, and executed by its head (*hegoumenos;* larger communities were governed by an *archimandrites*).

Monasticism radiated from Egypt into the rest of the Christian world. Athanasius tried to interest the West in the institution during his exile at Trier in A.D. 340, apparently with little success. Even earlier a certain Hilarion had visited Anthony and carried his practices to Gaza, whence they spread into the fastnesses of Judaea. Mar Awgin (Eugenius), a monk at Tabennisi, led a troop of seventy ascetics in Syria and established a monastery at Nisibis in upper Mesopotamia.[35] Palestine favored the *laura* type of community, and a great number of them grew up between Jerusalem and the Dead Sea, not far from where the Qumran community practiced its earlier form of Jewish *askesis.*

Within the larger context of eastern asceticism Palestine monasticism, like the Essene movement before it, betrayed a strong

---

35. It is by no means certain, however, that Syrian monasticism was merely an outgrowth of the Palestinian or Egyptian variety. There was a strong native tradition of asceticism in Syria, and both Christianity and Manichaeism may have drawn from it.

theological and literary bent. Its great *koinobia* and *laurae* were founded in the fifth and sixth centuries and quickly became embroiled in the revival of certain teachings of Origen on the preexistence and transmigration of souls that led to the condemnation of the latter in A.D. 543 and 553. Again in the eighth century the Palestinian cloisters were in the center of the Iconoclastic controversy. And there flowed from Palestine a great deal of the type of literature most closely associated with monasticism, biographies of the saints.

Christian hagiography had its antecedents in pre-Christian literary forms, some of them secular, others connected with the religious movements of the day. The "acts" of the Christian martyrs, accounts of the trials of the earliest sufferers for Christ and the likeliest starting point of the entire genre, began as fairly straightforward narratives, frequently based on official documents. The "acts" soon gave way to the "passions," which detail, in almost epic fashion, the sufferings of the saint, and not merely in the final moment of his life. It is clear that here, in the "passions" at least, not merely religious ends were being served by their composition and diffusion. The anonymous authors of these accounts had their eye upon the reader as well. A highly developed love of the marvelous is everywhere evident in late antiquity, and these "passions of the martyrs," bedecked with rich—and legendary—details borrowed from contemporary romances, hero-sagas, and the writer's own imagination, served as the beginning of a new Christian folk literature. In briefer and more sober form they and their hagiographical descendants played an important role in the liturgy as well. They found their way into what were known in the East as synaxaries or menologies, collections of brief biographical notes on martyrs and saints arranged by months of the year and suitable for insertion into the liturgy celebrated on the saint's feast day.

Martyrdom eventually gave way to other forms of sanctity in the Church, and the monk replaced the martyr as the object of biographical interest. Athanasius' *Life of Anthony* is a prime example, and here, perhaps because Athanasius' own Hellenic education made for a more refined taste, the literary antecedents can be traced somewhat more clearly. Athanasius' literary roots run deep back into the pagan biographical tradition, back to the encomia of Isocrates and Xenophon, and more immediately to the *bioi* of pagan saints and sages that had first come from the

Lyceum and were widely read by the marvel-devouring audiences of the third century.[36]

Athanasius' imitators were many, composing either single lives or, more frequently, collections of such *bioi*. About A.D. 420 appeared the most important representatives of the latter type, Palladius' *Lausiac History* and the somewhat earlier *History of the Monks of Egypt,* whose frame-narrative is an account of a trip from Jerusalem to Egypt. Somewhat different in form was the gnomonological collection entitled *Sayings of the Fathers.* All three had a great vogue in the East, not only in the Greek original, but in translation in Coptic, Syriac, Armenian, Arabic and Latin.

Palestinian monasticism was the subject of a series of biographies written by Cyril of Scythopolis (*c.* A.D. 524–560), including lives of the monastic giants of the time, Euthymius (d. A.D. 473) and Sabas (d. A.D. 532). Wider in its scope, but with a general Palestinian orientation is the work of John Moschus (d. A.D. 619), who with his friend Sophronius traveled the Near East during the chaotic days of the Persian invasions at the beginning of the seventh century,[37] and who put together a collection of biographies in his *Spiritual Meadow.* Both Cyril's and John's biographies are works of high art, far removed from the folk hagiography of the earlier period. They also differ from the earlier edifying lives in that they are filled with doctrinal echoes of contemporary theological controversies. They give, as well, brief but vivid pictures of life on the frontier where the ascetics chose to live. By A.D. 600 the eastern borders of the Empire were in a state of serious disarray, more dangerously so than any time since the third century, and the growing temerity of the bedouin, exercised in the first instance against the remote and unshielded monastic establishments on the fringe of the desert, is witnessed on almost every page of Cyril and John.

It has already been suggested that there is a choice between fundamentalism and the intellectual tradition bound into the Hellenization of religious bodies. The choice was never absolute, however, since each of the three religions which eventually Hellenized themselves—Judaism, Christianity and Islam—pre-

---

36. See Chapter XI, pp. 429–31.
37. Sophronius lived long enough to experience the Muslim invasion as well. He was Patriarch of Jerusalem when the Arabs took it in A.D. 638.

served within itself a prophetic, charismatic and ascetical strain, frequently anti-intellectual, that continued to reflect, in the midst of a rising Greek-style theology, that body's kerygmatic origins. The theoreticians of asceticism came, of course, from the ranks of the Hellenized theologians and so are poor witnesses to the phenomenon; their explanations normally reflect motifs present in the Platonists and Pythagoreans of late antiquity.

The legislators, canonists and administrators of the Great Church never ceased their attempts to exercise some measure of control over the monks. Western monasticism, for instance, was for the most part regularized by the rules of Saint Benedict, brought under the jurisdiction of the bishops, and thus "saved" for orthodoxy. The eastern version of asceticism, on the other hand, though there had been an even earlier attempt at regularization by Basil of Caesarea, proved far less tractable. The eastern monks continued to go their own idiorhythmic ways and served, on a number of occasions, as counterweights to the Hellenized theologians.

The monasticism of the Latin West was centralized and activist; that of the East was born in the wastes of Egypt and Syria and never lost what has been called its "nostalgia for the desert." It looked to the solitary "athlete of God" as the archetype of the monk, and indeed of the Christian, and had a marked preference for the contemplative over the active life. The eastern monastic ideal was quietism (*hesychia*) and the unaffected state (*apatheia*) that bore little resemblance to the philosopher's desired state of emotional equilibrium but was born rather of a lifetime of the most savage *askesis*.

XVIII

Eastern Philosophies

The other-worldly *askesis* of the desert solitaries in Egypt and Syria would have seemed alien in the world of Pericles and Plato, but in the third century after Christ it was merely another piece in an extraordinary religious mosaic that had been in the making for centuries. The evaporation of the Homeric pantheon, the collapse of the *polis*, the creation of the cosmopolitan *oikoumene* in the wake of Alexander's conquests, Rome's imperial ambitions and commercial aggressiveness in the East all contributed to the new religious sensibility.

The signs of the times can be read everywhere, in cult and style, in the new heroes and the old schools, but nowhere more clearly than in the transformation of Hellenism's most impressive intellectual monument, *philosophia*, the pursuit of truth by human reason. Religion had attended the birth of philosophy through the agency of myth, and the early evolution of the philosophical tradition fell under the influence of Pythagoreans, whose aspirations were unmistakably religious. But Socrates, Plato and Aristotle successfully secularized that tradition and confined their undiminished interest in God within the severe limits of a rational *theologia*. God became the object of a speculation freed from the subjective associations of cult, national strivings or personal piety. It was an endeavor crowned, as has been seen, with remarkable intellectual success, but marked as well by an equally remarkable failure. The God of the philosophers, an entity as intellectually astonishing and as emotionally unappealing as the geometry of Euclid, made his academic progress through a world that was distracted elsewhere.

The Syrian and Egyptian monks were part of that distraction, as were the mystery devotees, astrologers, wonder-workers, and other ascetics that swarmed in the Roman Empire. The academics were not untouched by what was occurring about them. Hellenic science had begun to direct its attention to the same eastern riches from which the ascetics drew their inspiration,[1] and it was inevitable that philosophy should follow in the same way. The earliest indication that something new was stirring in the philosophical schools was the revival of Pythagoreanism during the closing years of the Roman Republic.

At first the influence seemed healthy. Platonism, the school where Neopythagoreanism had its chief impact, was vital and active in the first and second centuries after Christ, as Plotinus, the heir to that development, still testifies. But the chief danger to the intellectual premises of the philosophical tradition was approaching from another direction. Outside the formal and even classical atmosphere of the schools the new Platonism made other, more exotic but poorly documented liaisons, whose oddly tinted offspring excited both interest and horror on the part of the intellectuals in the schools and the guardians of orthodoxy in the Christian Church.

Gnosticism

Gnosticism was first identified by the Church's heresiographers as an aberration of Christian doctrine originally put forward by Simon Magus and then elaborated in various systems of which the best known are those of Marcion, Basilides and Valentinus. Since then a great deal of attention has been paid to this intriguing but amorphous phenomenon, and evidences of identical or similar movements have been found as far afield as the teachings of Pythagoras and the tenets of Mahayana Buddhism. Recently scholars have concentrated on a more careful delimitation and description of what is understood as Gnosticism, and as a result that term has been restricted to something very close to its original meaning.

Accepting this delimitation, Gnosticism can be defined as those

---

1. See Chapter XI, pp. 436–38.

systems that came to maturity in the second Christian century and were characterized by certain common premises and typological similarities. A Gnostic system was one that was rooted in a fundamental, dualistic opposition between the transcendental world of the "fullness" (*pleroma*) embracing the High God and the Aeons, his inferior emanations,[2] on the one hand, and, on the other, the "emptiness" (*kenoma*), the planetary and terrestrial world inhabited by man. The *pleroma* is good because it is divine in its source and unfolding; the *kenoma* is evil because it was the creation of an evil spirit or spirits, the rulers (*archontes*) who lord it over the planets, the earth and man. The two worlds are alien and opposed to each other.

The *kenoma* came about because of some crisis in the *pleroma,* whereby the lowest of the Aeons on the emanation scale, a female figure known variously as Wisdom (*Sophia*) or Thought (*Ennoia*) lapsed out of the *pleroma,* and in her consequent state of confusion and disaffection, she produced the angel archons, generally seven in number, who created and then ruled the world. One of these archons is Ialdaboath, or Yahweh, and it is his Law, the Torah, that holds the world in thrall.

This state could not be allowed to persist, because by Sophia's fall there came into this world some spark of the divine *pleroma,* its spirit or *pneuma,* that must be regained and restored to its rightful place on high. Thus another Aeon is sent down to redeem the *pneuma* that is the innermost part of every man. The Aeon Jesus does this by apparently suffering,[3] but the actual work of redemption is accomplished by *gnosis,* knowledge, the awakening in man of the recognition of his consubstantiality with the *pleroma* world. By this secret and special knowledge man can return to that divine home where at least the spark of the *pneuma* lodged within him destined he should be.

Gnosticism, then, was a theology in the form of a myth, a

---

2. The mechanism of emanation, with its clear affinities with later Platonism, appeared particularly strongly in the system of the Alexandrian Valentinus who was later active at Rome sometime about A.D. 140–160.

3. Thus Gnosticism shared the attitude of the somewhat wider movement known as docetism, an affirmation that Jesus was only *apparently* man. All Gnostics were docetists, but docetism appealed to almost anyone who had his difficulties with the human side of Jesus.

partially optimistic view of the nature and destiny of man, but a deeply pessimistic view of the universe. It knew a creation, not by a good God but by a malevolent demiurge identified with Yahweh; a "fall," not of man but of the Aeon Sophia; a redemptive act, not of suffering and death but of a special revelation effected by Jesus, no longer the Jewish Messiah but a transcendental Aeon. At its heart it was mythological, dualistic and anticosmic.

This cosmogony and soteriology, and the many variant versions of them, were the heart of Gnosticism, the substance of the revealed *gnosis* that would save man, or at least some men. The Gnostic theoreticians viewed man as a tripartite composite of the divine element of the *pneuma*, the natural spirituality of the *psyche*, and the base ingredient of matter, *hyle*, and thus divided mankind according to the predominance of one or another of these elements into the Pneumatics, the Psychics and the Hylics. The first group, the Gnostic elect, had need only of the *gnosis* for their salvation, while the Pneumatics, who operated on the basis of faith (*pistis*) rather than true knowledge (*gnosis*), had to work out their doubtful salvation by good works and the observance of the Law. The Hylics, irredeemably enslaved by the cosmic demiurge, could anticipate nothing but their own damnation.

The Gnostic caste system had its attractions to the early Christians, who cherished a suggestively elitist "apostolic tradition" and who guarded their mysteries from the unbaptized or the "middle" grade of the catechumens. Clement, for one, attempted to promote a variation of this Gnostic theme, but orthodox sentiment eventually moved off into more open attitudes. Beyond this distinction within itself between the predestined Elect and the doubtful Psychics, Gnosticism betrayed little internal organization and is probably more accurately characterized as a movement rather than a Church, a religion of ideas almost entirely without cult or institutionalization, where one group was distinguished from another chiefly by the variations in its central myth or in the *askesis* peculiar to its members.

Its external formlessness made Gnosticism a somewhat difficult adversary for the guardians of orthodox Christianity, since believers were seduced by Gnostic ideas rather than drawn into outright schism. Gnosticism was essentially a state of mind, and the destruction or disappearance of its manifold sects was no guarantee that the orthodox remnant was totally free of Gnostic ways of thinking. The Gnostic had little or no quarrel with what then passed as Christian dogma; his subversion was couched rather in terms of *understanding,* the possession of which rendered the initiated, elitist center of Gnosticism absolved of the externals of the Law.

In its general thrust Gnosticism appears to have been a beguiling temptation rather than an outright rival of Christianity, but in at least one instance there existed within the Empire something that can fairly be called a Gnostic Church that presented itself as a fully articulated alternative to the Christian Church. Marcion, the son of an Asian bishop, had been condemned at Rome in A.D. 144, but the Churches he founded spread east and west over the face of the Empire and contested the ground with Christianity well into the fifth century.[4] According to Marcion, the Old and New Testaments were discontinuous despite the allegorists' attempts to read Jesus back into the Old. The Yahweh of the Jewish Bible was the creator of the world, as *Genesis* accurately described him; but his creation, this *kosmos,* if not essentially evil, was the domain of severe justice and retribution. Jesus came into this world as the messenger of the Alien God of Love whose goodness prompted him to redeem mankind, but not, as in "classical Gnosticism," because there is some divine spark in man, some kinship with the *pleroma;* the God of Love had and has nothing to do with this world and its demiurge. In Marcionism there was no "fall" and no devolution; the polarity of the two realms and their two lords was absolute; they existed side by side from all eternity.

Marcion's disinterest in an emanationist cosmogony, in Aeons and angels, or in an allegorical reading of Scripture sets him off from the mainstream of Gnosticism. His dualism was more rigorous than that of his Gnostic contemporaries in that he severed all genetic connection between the transcendent world of the Alien God and the material world of our *kosmos.* The sudden appearance in the world of the demiurge had no cosmological antecedents; it was arbitrary and unwarranted. Similarly, man's reaction to Jesus' revelation of the God of Love was not that of someone preparing himself to return to his spiritual homeland, but of a son to whom a stranger inexplicably offers better lodg-

---

4. See Chapter XIII, p. 503.

ings than his parent can provide, and who, before departing, repays his father by sabotaging his home: the Marcionite initiate had to disengage himself from the *kosmos* that had formerly been his natural habitat, holding himself aloof from its pleasures, from marriage and procreation.

The Gnosticism of Basilides and Valentinus gives the appearance of a perverted Hellenism onto which had been grafted the sacred history of the Torah and the Gospels. Marcion was little interested in emanationist metaphysics or myth; the theological problem of Yahweh and Jesus stood at the front of his concerns, and he attacked the problem of their relationship through the historical instruments of textual criticism and exegesis inductively applied, and not by the reconstruction of the transcendent circumstances that served to explain both. The strength of his appeal to the ordinary Christian was that he began with the Gospels and hewed sensibly if selectively to them without resort to the imaginative Gnostic reconstructions that aroused admiration among the Hellenic intellectuals but must have seemed remote from evangelical Christianity. And if Marcion led the believer to a repudiation of the Jewish antecedents of Christianity, there was ample support for that position in the East, where in Marcion's own lifetime the Roman state unleashed its full power against Palestinian Judaism and where the struggles between Christian and Jew had gone on unabated for nearly a century.

The origins, single or multiple, of this complex tissue of Gnostic beliefs that was fully visible in the second century after Christ has been the source of almost endless speculation. In its developed form Gnosticism appears as a Christian heresy, the creation, according to the early Fathers, of Simon of Samaria, the *magus* who first appears in the *Acts of the Apostles*. But taken at large, Gnosticism betrays so many syncretistic qualities that few modern scholars have been content to accept this simple explanation. Failed apocalyptic Judaism has been put forth as its origin, and there have been others who have advanced the candidacy of Greek philosophy, specifically later Platonism as transformed by Hellenistic religious sensibilities. The appearance of later Gnostic systems under the patronage of Bar Daisan in Syria and Mani in Iran opened two more possible seed beds. Finally, the recent discovery of a large Gnostic library in Egypt has focused attention there.

Most of the Gnostics' own writings were formerly known from excerpts preserved in the orthodox Fathers, but in the nineteenth century Gnostic writings in Coptic began to turn up among the Egyptian papyri. Even as these were still being edited and studied, a major discovery was made in Egypt. In 1945 at Nag Hamadi near the Pachomian monastery of Chenoboskion in Upper Egypt there came to light the remains of an extensive Gnostic library in Coptic, including among its forty-six different treatises the central *Gospel of Thomas*, a Valentinian *Gospel of Truth*, and a *Secret Book of John*. The presence of the collection in Egypt was more than merely a function of climate. Gnosticism arrived in Egypt at a very early date, possibly even before the orthodox Church was well established there. Simon Magus may have studied at Alexandria. Basilides, who had worked with Simon's disciple Menander in Antioch, came to Egypt some time in the first half of the second century, and Valentinus was teaching there in the latter half of the same century. All of this occurred before the orthodox Church of Egypt produced its first major theologian, Clement, who was obviously well instructed on the subject of Gnosticism.

According to a Christian heresiographer, one Gnostic sect, the Egyptian Carpocratians, venerated images of Pythagoras, Plato, and Aristotle,[5] but if the Gnostics found attractive the Greeks' speculation on the nature of man and his place in the universe, they were remarkably reticent about it in what has been preserved of their own writings. There was no Plato in the library at Nag Hamadi, nor is there any reference to him; there were, however, other "secular" works which, if not purely the product of Greek philosophy, stand somewhere between the Hellenic tradition and the theological myths of the Gnostics. Whoever owned the Nag Hamadi library was reading in the *Corpus Hermeticum*.

The *Corpus Hermeticum* is the generic name given to a collection of treatises preserved chiefly in Greek—the last work in the *corpus*, the *Asclepius*, is in Latin—from an Egyptian milieu of perhaps the second century A.D. Hermes, or, in his Egyptian identification, Thoth, was the patron of much that went on in

---

5. And one of Jesus made by Pontius Pilate. Apart from the obviously unique character of this last artifact, one is reminded of a similar eclectic oratory set up by the Emperor Alexander Severus (see Chapter XV, p. 560.

Egypt at the time, including a great deal of alchemy, astrology and magic. The nineteen treatises of the *Corpus Hermeticum* stand somewhat aside from that occultist tradition. They are quasi-philosophical dialogues on cosmogony, prophets and the nature and fate of man, expressed, under their Egyptian surface coloring, in the language and style of intellectual Hellenism of a Stoic or Platonic type. And at least one of them, the *Poimandres*, is thoroughly Gnostic in its views.

The *Poimandres* is a revelation of the creation of the universe by the demiurgic offspring of God and of the creation of a Primal Man by God himself. The universe, after the demiurge withdraws from it, is equated with darkness, and it is into this darkness that the Primal Man sinks. Eventually he redeems himself by progressively stripping off his acquired human nature and returning to the realms of Light. The system is patently Gnostic, and yet there is no suggestion that the demiurge is evil or that he is identified with Yahweh. Jesus is nowhere mentioned, and indeed the saved one and the savior are identical, as in the myth of Gayomart, the primordial man of the Iranians.

There must have been, then, a kind of "secular" Gnosticism popular in some circles, though it was not demonstrably earlier than the more familiar Judaeo-Christian variety. The rabbis, as always, are silent on the subject, and secular hermeticism is certainly not what the Christian Fathers understood by Gnosticism. The evidence remains, however, that these hermetic treatises were being read at Nag Hamadi by a sect, probably the Sethians, who were Gnostics of the Christian type.

The official and orthodox version of the origins of Gnosticism blamed the heresy on one Simon the Magus of Gitta in Samaria. Who he was or what his "magic" was about is not very clear from the *Acts of the Apostles* where he is described as a convert of the Hellenist Christian Philip who later attempted to bribe Peter to pass on some spiritual gifts. Simon passes out of the *Acts* narrative after expressing sorrow at his rather unimaginative request, but by the time he reappears in the antiheretical works of Justin (*c*. A.D. 150), also a Samaritan, and of Irenaeus (*c*. A.D. 180), he is no mere inventor of the unlovely art of simony but the father of a full-blown Gnostic system.

According to his Christian opponents, Simon claimed that he was God the Father come down into this world to rescue his Thought. His Thought was a certain Helen, in her latest manifestation (earlier she had been Helen of Troy) a prostitute of Tyre held captive in the flesh by the angels and powers whom she had in fact mothered and who then turned against her. It was thus that Simon, at the same time Father who had become a stranger to this world and redemptive Son, came into this world and seemed to suffer in Judaea in order to free Helen-Thought and bring salvation to men.

Though emphases were to change and various grace notes added, this is, in its essence, Gnosticism, apparently more anti-Christian than anti-Jewish,[6] and perhaps not so much a heretical version of Christianity as an alternate to it. There is as yet no evil demiurge here, no "fall" on the part of Helen. Unlike every other Gnostic teacher except Mani, Simon and his successor Menander both gave themselves out as divine beings who enjoyed immortality. And the radical anticosmic quality of fully developed Gnosticism is only lightly touched upon in Simon's system: the ambitions of the angels who held Helen captive prevented them from ruling the world well; they were, for all that, creations of Helen and so of God.

The contemporaries and immediate successors of Simon are all shadowy figures. One intriguing prospect is opened by the information that Simon was the disciple of a certain Dositheus, who founded some sort of religious movement in Samaria, and was also connected with John the Baptist. A third Samaritan was Simon's own disciple Menander, who later taught at Antioch, but not, however, the original doctrine of Simon. Menander, who also claimed to be the Savior, did not identify himself with the Father or the High God as Simon had done. Indeed, there was no talk of Simon at all, nor of Helen. Salvation was through baptism.

Menander carries us down to the time of Trajan (A.D. 98–117), though not with a great deal of illumination. What seemed to occur at this point, however, was both a burst of energy in the movement and a radical turn in the direction of dualism. The great Gnostic systematizers appeared in Egypt under Hadrian,

---

6. Possibly because both Justin and Irenaeus were describing a Roman version of Simonianism. The *Recognitions*, a kind of historical novel spuriously attributed to Clement of Rome (*c.* A.D. 100), likewise has a great deal to say about Simon and his supposed conflict with Peter at Rome. Legend had Simon attempt to fly over Rome only to be mortally grounded by a prayer from Peter. One of Simon's later legendary transformations was as Doctor Faustus.

and their contemporary in Antioch, Saturninus (or Satornil), had taken the step of identifying the evil archon-angel-demiurge with Yahweh and the Savior-Son with Jesus. By the middle of the second century classical Gnosticism was essentially in place as an anti-Jewish, dualistic interpretation of the redemptive work of Jesus.

The ancient world knew many shades of dualism: the Pythagorean-Orphic tension between spirit and flesh; the Platonic distinction between the intelligible and the sensible world; the Zoroastrian ethical dualism between a good and evil spirit, later converted into gods. The dualism of the Gnostics, relentless in their powers of syncretism, may have owed something to all of these, but its own peculiar version of dualism sounded a note unheard in those other varieties: this world, the *kosmos*, is, in its creation and its government, something by nature evil.

In the *Timaeus* myth Plato attributed the creation of this world to a demiurge who was good and who wished to make the *kosmos* as good as was possible under the circumstances, the circumstances being the relatively intractable state of matter. Later Platonism substituted for the artificer myth a theory of emanation, but the theme remained the same: this world is an imperfect reflection of the intelligible world, imperfect only because it was precisely a reflection, an approximation. From the beginning to the end of the Platonic tradition matter was never endowed with a positive quality of its own, however malevolent. The world was deficient but never radically evil. Platonism never really knew a true dualism in the sense of equal and opposed principles.

In Christianity, whatever evil there was in the world was introduced there by the sin of man. In Gnosticism the perspective was quite different: the *kosmos*, planetary and terrestrial, is at root evil. It was created by an evil demiurge born of *Sophia*'s fall from the *pleroma;* and all in it, with one exception, is evil. That one exception is the *pneuma* in man, the divine spirit that is the point and object of the soteriological drama played out by Jesus. Unlike Platonism, where the One is unspeakable here below because of its transcendence, the High God of the Gnostic *pleroma* is an alien in this world, unspeakable here below because it is nothing to him. The Jesus of Gnosticism came not to redeem this world, which is unredeemable, but to reveal to the human *pneuma* its essential *otherness*. This is the *gnosis* that saves.

To ask whether this strong anticosmic sentiment was an original creation of Gnosticism is merely to repose the question of the origins of Gnosticism. There is, perhaps, a hint of an answer in the person of the evil demiurge. In the Gnostic texts he is never called Zeus or Ahriman; after Simon and Menander down to the end of the Gnostic tradition he is identified with one form or another of the creator in Judaism, the Yahweh of *Genesis*. We know fairly accurately at what point this first occurred. Saturninus taught that the world was a creation of seven archonangels, of whom Yahweh was one. Simon and Menander seem to have been almost emanationist on the Platonic model; Saturninus was a creationist of the Judaeo-Christian type, but unlike the orthodox traditions in both those systems, he was anticosmic.

Saturninus was teaching at Antioch during the reign of Hadrian (A.D. 117–138), and he could likely have been either of two things: a Jewish apostate driven from the historical expectations of apocalypticism to the mythic panoramas of Gnosticism by the disaster of A.D. 135, or a Christian bent on drawing as far as possible from Judaism.[7] The presence of Jesus as a redeemer in the system suggests the latter, but the currents of speculation in late Judaism render the first possibility equally attractive.

The interesting possibility presents itself, then, that in Gnosticism one is confronted with another schismatic (Samaritan?) offshoot of Judaism, far more vehement than either Christianity or Essenism, which, for all their separatism, did not entirely reject their Jewish past. Roman armies put an end to the Qumran community before it came to the term of its evolution, but in Christianity at least it is clear that the mutual rejection of Christian and Jew was not an accomplished fact until the second century. Even Paul's reading of the Law, revolutionary as it was from an orthodox Jewish point of view, did not seek to destroy the Torah. Gnosticism, on the other hand, had within itself a violent anti-Jewish strain revealed by its denigration of the creator in *Genesis* to the rank of an ignorant or malevolent demiurge.

That Gnosticism was deeply influenced by Judaism cannot be seriously doubted. But whether the students of Jewish specula-

---

7. Like his contemporary in Antioch, the bishop Ignatius, who took the lead in opposing a Christian observation of the Sabbath, a custom that was all but eradicated by the middle of the second century.

tion elaborated their Gnostic systems before or after their own
break with Judaism cannot be decided on the present evidence.
The closest one can come in bringing the two traditions together
is in the work entitled *Baruch*, whose author, a certain Justin, was
not a Christian, and whose book is a strange mixture derived
from elements in *Genesis*, the Gnostic biblical text par excellence, and motifs and figures from Greek mythology: Priapus,
Aphrodite, Heracles.

It has been suggested, not implausibly, that Gnosticism represents the final disappointment of Jewish apocalypticism, a profoundly pessimistic disbelief that this world is redeemable in time
or history. Philo had accepted the historical and literal reading of
the Torah but had burrowed down deeper into the *hyponoia*, the
"under sense," that revealed a spiritual history. This hypothetical
Jewish gnosticism rejected the Torah as a lie and a deception, and
saw it not as the ultimate revelation but as one piece in a larger
cosmic drama, just as the Yahweh who stood behind the Torah
was one malevolent actor in that same drama.

There is much more in later Judaism that reappears in Gnosticism. The figure of *Sophia* is a familiar one from the post-exilic
apocrypha. In *Enoch* and *Proverbs* she descends from her proper
place in heaven to dwell among men. Philo makes her an analogue
to the creative *Logos*,[8] and she is called the mother and nurse of
the world. Even her Hebrew name *Chokhmah* appears among the
Gnostics as the curious plural Achamoth. There is little doubt
that the Gnostics were reading *Enoch* and *Proverbs* as well as
Genesis, and that they found there a prototype of a hypostatized
emanation of God who descended into the world and was, in a
sense, its creator. Philo had read them in Alexandria; there is no
reason to think that Valentinus could not have done the same a
century later.

The developed angelology of Gnosticism is another point of
possible Jewish influence. The Jews of the post-exilic age were so
notoriously infatuated with angels that more than one Christian
author accused them, probably without foundation, of worshiping angels. The four archangels at the throne of God, Michael,
Uriel, Raphael and Gabriel, appear in *Enoch*. Others turn up
elsewhere in the *apocrypha*, in *Tobias*, for example, and though

---

8. In some of the Gnostic systems too the place of the female Sophia
is taken by a male Logos.

the names vary from place to place, there was clearly a tradition of four (or six or seven) archangels that stretched through this literature into the Qumran scrolls, the Gospels and Paul, down to the *Apocalypse of John,* and into Gnosticism, where they appear as the seven Archons of the Universe.[9]

There was nothing particularly unorthodox about this. Later Judaism, like contemporary Hellenism, filled its intermediary regions with a multitude of *daimones,* and in much the same way that the henotheistic philosophers of the Greeks explained away the traditional gods in terms of *daimones,* so the Jews used the angels not only to explain natural forces but to guide the destinies of peoples. The "angels of the nations" had each the fate of a people; to Yahweh alone was reserved the destiny of Israel. In all these cases, however, the angels were creatures of God, made by him and subordinated to his will. In dualistic Gnosticism, on the contrary, the archon-angels, one of whose number was Yahweh, are the adversaries of God, the evil creators and governors of the universe.

At least part of this notion was domesticated in Paul and the Gospels. Both spoke of the "ruler(s) of this world," and Paul particularly seems to have a highly articulated picture of this world under the power of the "archons of this age." The *Letters* are filled with "principalities," "dominations" and "powers" against whom the Christian must struggle and over whom Christ triumphed. Already here the mood is more pessimistic and the dualism more pronounced than in the Jewish sources that preceded. There is a subtle but meaningful distinction between the Jewish *apocrypha*'s regard for the angels as the frequently fearsome and sometimes overenthusiastic instruments of God's will and the Christian view of Satan and his cohorts as the adversaries of God.

But Satan was not a creation of the New Testament. The degree of his powers appears to be more limited in the Old Testament, but there are not lacking traces of his ascendancy in Judaism. As Belial, in the Qumran scrolls, he seems to have gained power over Israel in the contest between the Angel of Light and

---

9. In Gnosticism they are associated with the planets, the astrological rulers of the world. But it is by no means certain that their association was planetary in Judaism. There the archangels are equally likely to have been connected with the seven days of creation, which is not the same thing as the planetary week.

the Angel of Darkness. That there were evil angels was also a standard part of the Jewish tradition, again under the direct control of Yahweh. They were not, however, evil by nature; they chose evil by their sin. Nor is there any trace in that variegated Jewish tradition that the angels created the world.

The somewhat mitigated dualism visible in post-exilic Judaism, at Qumran, for instance, has itself been traced to another source, one that has also been advanced as a point of origin of Gnosticism, the religion of Iran. It is not, of course, a question of Manichaeism, already in a sense a product of Gnosticism, but the common Indo-Iranian base ranging from the archaic *Upanishads* of India and the Iranian *Avesta* down to the developed Mazdaism current in parts of the Near East in the last couple of pre-Christian centuries. There are grave problems in this inquiry. The post-Avestan Iranian literature is late (ninth century) and extensively reworked by scholars who knew Gnosticism in its mature Manichaean form. Despite that basic disability of method, there is evident a basic dualism in both Iranian religious theory and in Gnosticism that suggests syncretistic borrowing by the latter.

In the original version of Zoroastrianism, the High God, Ahura Mazda, created two spirits, one good, the Spenta Mainyu, the partisan of the Truth, and one by choice evil, the Angra Mainyu, the partisan of the Lie, a view similar to the one put forth in the Qumran *Manual of Discipline*. But as the religion evolved Ahura Mazda was identified with his Good Spirit, and in this fashion what had originally been two ethically opposed spirits subordinated to a supreme God were converted into two opposed Gods, Ormazd and Ahriman. Just as the original Ahura Mazda was surrounded by the Bounteous Immortals, so now Ormazd and Ahriman each had six such, the latter the suggestive prototype of the wicked Ialdaboath and his six fellow archons.

This later version of Zoroastrianism, however far it may be from the reformer's monotheistic intentions, expressed an unmistakable form of ethical dualism, but its extension into the realm of matter and spirit is by no means as convincing. Mazdaism did draw a polar distinction between the heavenly realm (*menok*) and the earthly domain (*getik*). But the *getik,* though tormented by Ahriman, is not completely his creature, nor is it totally evil; rather it is an ambiguous mixture (*gumečišn*). In later Manichaeism it was quite otherwise, but in Iranian Mazdaism at least the ethical dualism present by suggestion from its origins did not come to full term in the anticosmic spirit so typical of Gnosticism.

Nor did Greek philosophy share this disdain for the *kosmos*. At one stage in its development, from Pythagoras down to Plato, there was present in that tradition a sentiment which appears at base religious rather than philosophical, and which posited a tension between the essence of man, his soul (*psyche*), and the enveloping and imprisoning body in which it was locked. This attitude, clear enough in Pythagoreanism, Orphism and the early Plato, was doubtless born of the same self-alienation that later produced Gnosticism and its Manichaean offspring, but it did not long survive unmodified in Greece, because it contradicted other, more deeply felt realities about man and the universe. Even Plato surrendered his earlier view of a simple soul set at odds with the body, for a more realistic psychology of a tripartite soul with clear somatic resonances. Nor could he sustain his projection of the soul-body dichotomy onto the cosmic level. His later dialogues backed off from the strict separation between the noetic world and the sensible world, as soul, mind and movement were granted some share of the "true reality" once denied them. Finally, in the *Timaeus* Plato further closed the gap between the two by describing the fashioning of the sensible, material *kosmos* by a benevolent demiurge bent on making it "as good as possible."

Their essential optimism never permitted the Greeks to philosophize matter into a positive principle of evil. From Plato to Plotinus matter is privative rather than positive, amorphous and so anarchic, but always more properly the place where there was no form—that is, intelligibility—rather than an operative principle. Indeed, matter as such did not really exist at all. Even the somewhat uncertain "matrix" of the *Timaeus* was further blurred by the later Platonists into a species of penumbra. For the philosopher, matter was like the void, a not very intelligible postulate necessary to make the system work.

The *kosmos* was itself one of the earliest of the Greek philosophical concepts, a place, as the etymology suggests, of order and beauty. Whatever alienation a man may have experienced within himself on the testimony of Orphism, he clearly felt at home in the universe onto which generations of speculation had projected an exquisite and detailed order. The Greeks found the *kosmos* one of the most persuasive proofs for the existence of

God and the origins of religion itself. And with the collapse of the traditional religion of the *polis* and the erosion of the Olympians, it was the *kosmos*, with its governing planets and stars, its transcendent majesty and its promise of immortality, that was increasingly the center of both cult and aspiration.

There may have been poison in this. The pious Stoic was affably at home in the *kosmos*, even one dominated by an invincible fatalism. Fate (*heimarmene*), the Stoic explained, was just the chain of causality fashioned by the providential plan of an intelligent and benevolent God. Fatalism accompanied by confidence may yield optimism, but there are signs that some experienced the determinism as oppressive, particularly as the late Hellenistic skyscape was progressively infiltrated by Babylonian astrology. Eastern astrological fatalism did not share Greek optimism, and the cheery Stoic was yielding, toward the beginning of the Christian era, to darker moods and more anxious feelings.

Greek philosophy took no official cognizance of Gnosticism until the third century, but there can be no doubt that it undermined the very premises of the Hellenic tradition. And the one branch of that tradition that bears the most superficial resemblance to Gnosticism—Platonism—was so little convinced of the affinity that Plotinus devoted a full-scale refutation to the contemporary Gnostics, because they "rejected the ancient philosophy" and interjected a "tragedy of terrors" into the universe. The context is secular in Plotinus, but in Celsus the Gnostics were lumped with the Christians, while Porphyry appears to have envisioned something considerably more Iranian.

The emergence of Gnosticism is the most impressive possible evidence of the bewildering complexity of the spiritual and intellectual climate in the *oikoumene* of the first and second centuries of the Roman Empire. Gnosticism simply had no single progenitor. One emphasis or another can be traced, perhaps, to a single origin, but the whole, the reality that was Gnosticism, is obviously and convincingly a composite. Some themes had doubtless come together earlier—the confrontation of Platonism with Zoroastrianism, for example, or Jewish Messianism with Iranian eschatology—and the other elements lay ready at hand in the inquisitive, tolerant and anxious atmosphere of the Empire awaiting only the peculiar set of circumstances provided by the tension of Christian and Jew in first-century Syria-Palestine.

The Prophet of Iran

In April of A.D. 297 the Augustus Diocletian issued from Alexandria an edict directed to Julian, the Proconsul for Africa, calling his attention to the recent and unexpected appearance within the Empire of a seditious movement originating in Persia and known as Manichaeism. At about the same time the Christian bishop of Alexandria, possibly Theonas (A.D. 282–300), alerted his flock there to the same movement, now portrayed as attacking the sacrament of marriage.

The sect that exercised both Christian bishop and anti-Christian Emperor was by then less than fifty years old. Its founder Mani had been executed by the Shah Bahram I, probably in A.D. 277, after a turbulent ministry that had begun under Ardashir (d. A.D. 240) and had spanned the glorious reign of Shapur I (A.D. 240–272) and that of his weak successor Ormizd (A.D. 272–273). He left behind him his own fully articulated formula for a world religion of the dimensions of Christianity, a Gnostic Church equipped with all the missionary zeal, the instruments of propaganda and diffusion, and the same intellectual, spiritual and ascetical *élan* of the Ecumenical Christian Church that it clearly set out to rival and surpass.

Christianity began with a Gospel, a kerygmatic presentation of the life and teaching of Jesus; Mani, who served as the Jesus, John and Paul of his own revelation, likewise composed a *Great Gospel* that contained his teaching, though perhaps not his biography, most of which must be reconstructed out of the Christian and Muslim heresiographers who had to contend with his followers. The future "seal of the Prophets," the same title later adopted by Muhammad, was born about A.D. 216 in southern Babylonia and called Kurkibios. According to the Christian sources, he had Persian parents, who sold him when he was still a child to the widow of an itinerant religious eccentric named Bados. Among other things, Bados claimed that he was born of a virgin, had studied Greek and Egyptian learning and, more importantly, was the real author of some of the books that Mani later said were his own. According to these same versions, Kurkibios was educated on those books and later, having come to manhood and taken the name Mani, joined a Christian docetist sect to which Bados had belonged, perhaps at Jundeshapur.

This pat explanation of how Mani "stole" his doctrines and how they were nothing more than reworkings of Plato, Pythagoras and Empedocles is quite different from the official Manichaean account of their founder's career. In the authorized version Mani received his "call" under Ardashir and soon thereafter journeyed to India. At the accession of Shapur he returned to Iran, where he made an impression on the new Shah to whom he addressed his sole writing in Pahlevi, the *Shahpuhrakan*. Mani possibly served as one of the court physicians,[10] and accompanied Shapur on his Syrian expeditions against the Romans (A.D. 256–260).

Whatever success Mani may have had with Shapur was fiercely countered by the Shah's reactionary *mobadhan mobadh* Kartir,[11] who came into the ascendancy with Shapur's immediate successors Ormizd and Bahram I. Under the latter the *magus'* power was such that he could demand and be granted the execution of Mani. The archheretic was crucified and beheaded, and his head was hung over one of the gates of Jundeshapur. Even as this was occurring in Iran, probably in A.D. 277, Mani's disciples were carrying his Gospel east into Khorasan and west into the Roman Empire.

The discernibly Christian versions of Gnosticism within that empire generally contented themselves with developing the "true understanding" of the canonical Gospels and some of the *apocrypha*. Mani, who went back to the old tradition of Simon Magus and Menander and identified himself with the Paraclete, found all other Gospels unacceptable and offered his own, the *Great Gospel*, which together with some four other books from his own hand constituted the Scriptural revelation of Manichaeism. Mani's was a paradoxical public Gnosticism, in later Muslim terms a "religion of the Book," like Judaism and Christianity. The message was set forth for all to hear and be converted.

Manichaeism was a missionary religion with a zeal shared only by Christianity, and it surpassed Christianity in its use of pictures

---

10. The frequent references to Mani as a "physician" may refer to his spiritual activity, but at least some of them argue for a literal interpretation. There is another persistent tale that Mani fell out of favor with the Shah for killing instead of curing one of his ailing sons.

11. See Chapter XV, pp. 566–67.

and illustrations as adjuncts of the Word. In the Manichaean canon was the *Ardahang,* or *Book of the Drawing,* which carried Mani's message in pictures, and his apostles were accompanied by scribes and artists. In Iran he wrote, except for the Persian *Shahpuhrakan* addressed directly to Shapur, in Syriac, the lingua franca of eastern Christianity. In Turkestan fragments of the Manichaean Scriptures have been found in all the major Iranian and proto-Turkish dialects in use on the eastern trade routes. In Egypt other exemplars have turned up in Coptic, the somewhat remote survivors of what was certainly a large body of *Manichaeica* in circulation in Latin and Greek and eventually destroyed by orthodox Christianity.

The combination of zeal and method, yoked in the service of a single but demanding morality, worked marvelously well. In its birthplace Manichaeism survived well into Islamic times to baffle the orthodox guardians of the Caliphate.[12] In its eastern course Manichaeism was widespread among the eastern Iranians by the eighth century, had been adopted by the Turkic Uighurs, and was a sufficiently potent force to be banned in China as a secret society in A.D. 732. In the West the Prophet's doctrines were current in Egypt even before his death, spread there by his disciple Adda. Cyril was preaching against them in Jerusalem in A.D. 350, and between A.D. 373–382 Augustine belonged to the sect. Checked in the western Empire, Manichaeism surfaced once again in the East in the ninth century as Paulicianism, spread to the European provinces of Byzantium, engendered a parallel form in Bogomilism and eventually returned to the West, where, as the confraternity of the Albigensians, it converted most of the south of France to its ways.

In its later forms Manichaeism was only indifferently centralized, but its founder had made some provision for a successor, a head *(archegos)* who presided over the Manichaean communities in direct succession from the Prophet. Each community, probably ruled by a bishop, was composed of the two classes already familiar from Valentinian Gnosticism, the Elect and the Hearers; both were privy to the Manichaean *gnosis,* but the former alone assumed the full burden of Manichaean asceticism:

---

12. Some of the most illuminating notices on Manichaeism come from Muslim heresiographers, particularly Ibn al-Nadim (*c.* A.D. 987), the cultured bookseller of Baghdad whose catalogue, the *Fihrist,* provides equally priceless information on the course of Hellenism in Islam.

celibacy, abstention from meat and wine, inhibition from either the growing or the preparation of food, and a commitment to a life of wandering without property and clad only for the moment. The Hearers might marry and own property, but they too were forbidden meat and had to undergo long and rigorous fasts in the course of each year. Their life was one devoted to obedience and service to the Elect and to that reverence for all living things that opens into the heart of Mani's teaching.

Manichaeism began not, as the other Gnostic systems did, with a cosmogony but with a cosmology. The division of reality into the realms of good and evil did not come about through any "fall" or other disruption of the *pleroma*. As in Marcion's view, the two worlds, that of the Father of Greatness and that of the King of Darkness, existed side by side from all eternity. The cosmic crisis, provoked in the Syrian forms of Gnosticism by a lapse from above, is here brought on by an attack from below. The Darkness, Matter (*Hyle*), Ahriman, lusts for the greater perfection of the Light. Alerted to the possibility of attack, the Father of Greatness fashions his own weapons, his "first Creation": the Mother of Life, her son, the Primal Man (Ormazd), and his five sons who are his soul. They went forth to meet the King of Darkness and his Aeons.

The battle was joined and the forces of Light were defeated, then consumed by the Aeons of Darkness. The Primal Man was eventually freed by the "second creation" of the Father, the Living Spirit, but he left behind his soul-sons. They must somehow be saved as well, and to simplify the task the Father of Greatness bade the Living Spirit separate the now "mixed" part of the Darkness from that untouched by soul, and thus came into existence the material *kosmos*, some of it still deeply imbued with Darkness, with other parts, the heavenly lights, relatively free of matter. Then follows the "third creation," that of the Messenger, whose first act was to set the heavenly lights in motion, thereby providing a paradigm and magnet by whose revolutions other parts of the entrapped Light are drawn heavenward to freedom. As a further enticement the Messenger reveals his male and female form to the world below, but this provoked a convulsive response from the Darkness, the counterfeiting of these forms in the person of Adam and Eve, the final repository of most of what was left of the Light in the realms of Darkness.

The drama of salvation now enters its final stage in the struggle for the redemption of Adam. To win him in a manner even more convincing than that of the cosmic circulation of the heavenly bodies, the Messenger sends down his own emanation Jesus to reveal to Adam his true "psychic" nature and to encourage him to free himself from the grip of Hyle. At first Adam was convinced, but finally he yielded to the seductions of Eve and begot upon her Seth (Cain and Abel were offspring of her intercourse with the Aeons). Thus the dismal progress of human propagation was initiated and the Light continued to be dissipated through generations of men.

The revelation was not, however, ended. Other prophets of the Messenger came to mankind, Buddha and Zoroaster among others, and finally Mani himself, inspired by and identified with the Paraclete, the "Apostle of Jesus Christ," the "Seal of the Prophets," who has delivered to man the final revelation in his Scriptures. Manichaeanism offered the means of salvation founded on this *gnosis* and on the exacting ascetical regimen that has as its object both a veneration for the spark of Light that is life and a pointed refusal to cooperate with its further dispersal in this earthly, fleshly form. Vegetarianism was the Manichee's form of life affirmation; their refusal to marry or propagate children, a pointed example of their material negation.

Both the Elect and the Hearers shared in the life of the Church: a baptismal liturgy, confession, psalms, fasting and penance, and the celebration of the annual *bema* feast, the analogue of the Christian Pentecost. Each year on the anniversary of the Prophet's death the faithful, the Elect and the Hearers, gathered around a raised throne (*bema*) on which was placed a lighted and garlanded figure of Mani. The *Hymn of the Foundation* was sung, recalling the great cosmological history that was the Manichaean *gnosis*, and summoning Mani, the Paraclete, to redescend in spirit upon his Church.

At a later date Islam too was to invoke a series of "prophets" that came to term in Muhammad. The significant difference between the two chains was the absence in Mani's world view of any Jewish affiliation; and, given the Gnostic context of his thought, this was surely an omission rather than an oversight. There was not, to be sure, any evil, demiurgic Yahweh in Manichaeism; the King of Darkness was called, in the Iranian style,

Ahriman, or in the Greek fashion, Hyle. But the realm of Darkness was not created in the same sense that it was in the Gnostic systems of the Roman Empire; the Darkness was eternally preexistent at the side of the Light.

Mani's system was more strictly and radically dualistic than anything the West knew, with the possible exception of Marcion's *gnosis*. But Manichaeanism was obviously more than merely a reworking of Iranian motifs. The clear Iranian origins of the Primal Man (Gayomart) are overshadowed by the central and critical role of the docetist Jesus who under the guise of the man from Nazareth first revealed the *gnosis* to Adam and whose prophet Mani stoutly proclaimed he was. It is not impossible that Manichaeism was born of some Christian Gnostic sect, perhaps the Marcionite version. Ephraem's *Prose Refutations*, written at Edessa sometime about A.D. 370, reveal a north Syrian milieu impregnated with the Gnostic or near-Gnostic ideas of both Marcion and the Syrian Christian Bar Daisan,[13] and, by that time, those of Mani as well. Indeed the Syrian Church, or those elements of it least exposed to the influence of Hellenism, seems to have pursued an ascetical ideal remarkably similar to Mani's own, based on a common exaltation of celibacy and a repudiation of marriage.

Mani's views had their origins, however, not in northern Syria but in southern Mesopotamia where the consistent testimony of the heresiographers makes him an early adherent of some Christian sect. The evidence for who or what they might be converges on the shadowy tribe of the Mandaeans, literally the "Gnostics," remnants of which are still in existence in Iraq, and whose Aramaic Scriptures and liturgy, of great and unshakable antiquity, provide a clearer and more illuminating vision of ancient Gnosticism than even the Nag Hamadi library, the Coptic and Central Asian fragments of the Manichaean Scriptures, or the treasures of the *Corpus Hermeticum*.

If the identification of the Aramaic *manda* and the Greek *gnosis* is transparently satisfying, the other name of the sect, the Nazoraeans, is temptingly suggestive. "Nazoraean," once the term used by the Jews to designate all Christians,[14] was replaced by

---

13. Bar Daisan (A.D. 154–222) is the author of the oldest non-Scriptural texts preserved in the Syriac dialect of Edessa.

14. See Chapter XIII, p. 491.

the name that became current at Antioch, "Christian," and ended by becoming the specific designation of groups of Judaeo-Christians that were progressively isolated from the Hellenic Church. These orphans of history are obscurely attested to in the regions east of the Jordan, and, indeed, the latter-day Mandaeans/Nazoraeans of Iraq possessed a rich Jordanian tradition centering around the figure of John the Baptist.[15] What the Mandaeans likely represent, then, is a community of Jews, possibly like the Qumran one, located somewhere on the fringes of pre-Christian Jewish orthodoxy and which in the early days somehow cast in its lot with the Christians only to find itself disassociated from the future growth of the Church by the events of history, if not by choice. Other such Judaeo-Christian groups were eventually swallowed up in Syria, but the Nazoraeans managed to preserve their integrity during their wanderings through northern Syria before finally coming to rest in the more peaceable climate of Parthian Mesopotamia.

It was in Mesopotamia, perhaps in contact with the traditions of Iran, that the Nazoraeans became Mandaeans, that is, more identifiably Gnostics, and into one of whose communities Kurkibios came and assumed a form of one of the Mandaean technical terms, *mana* ("vessel"), as his new name. This is surmise; the simple fact is that, while there is an obvious Christian milieu in northern Syria from about A.D. 200, the evidence for the spread into Mesopotamia of a Christianity that might influence a man born about A.D. 216 is slim indeed, and that the Mandaeans represent the single most convincing foothold on otherwise slippery ground. But there were other Christians besides the Mandaeans present in Mesopotamia, as is testified to by the edict of Kartir published sometime after Shapur's death in A.D. 272 which proscribed "Jews, Buddhists, Hindus, Nazoraeans, Christians and Manichaeans."

Kartir's text is an accurate enough description of the religious milieu in which Mani taught, and, in the case of Buddhism, one element of that milieu in which Mani expressed a particular interest. Mahayana Buddhism was established on the Indus from the time of the Mauryan King Ashoka, and during the reign of its Kushan devotee Kanishka a century before the lifetime of Mani it

---

15. See Chapter XVII, pp. 638–39.

spread into eastern Iran.[16] Buddhism's progress eastward from the Iranian emporia into Central and East Asia is well documented, and its contemporary presence within the Sasanian Empire is doubtless cloaked under the pious Zoroastrian orthodoxy of the Pahlevi sources. This is the implication of Kartir's edict; even if Mani's journey into India never took place, and there is no reason to doubt that it did, he could have learned of Buddhism well enough at home.

What Mani may have learned from Buddhism awaits the resolution of another invincible question: was Gnosticism a movement sprung from a single source and diffused from that source, or was it a phenomenon that occurred independently but in parallel forms in different religious and philosophical contexts? Mahayana Buddhism shows marked resemblances to certain features of Greek philosophy, even though there are no demonstrable historical connections between the two. It possesses as well unmistakable Gnostic elements. Buddhism knows, for instance, a salvation through enlightenment (*jñana*)[17] and recognizes a threefold division of men that corresponds to the Gnostic Pneumatics, Psychics and Hylics. There was even a cult of a transcendent and hypostatized Wisdom (*Prajña*), a vision of an absolute and remote God distinct from the demiurge of the *kosmos*, and a contemptuous view of the material world that held it was at best an illusion and a counterfeit.

All or some of this Mani knew, or could have known, and in his address to Shapur in his *Shahpuhrakan* he explained his position in contemporary Iran by expressly comparing himself to other prophets in other times: Zoroaster earlier in Iran, Jesus in the western lands, and Buddha in India, a comparison that presumably made some sense to the curious and eclectic Shapur. Invocations of other Indian authorities are scattered through the preserved fragments of Mani's work. But for all that, Buddha and Jesus did not hold analogous positions in the Manichaean system. Jesus was central in the redemptive work of the Messenger, and Mani clearly signaled himself as the "Apostle of Jesus," while a similar claim was never made regarding either Buddha or even Zoroaster.

---

16. See Chapter XV, p. 561.
17. The word is even etymologically related to the Greek *gnosis*.

Magicians and Schoolmen

From A.D. 300 Manichaeism contributed its share of turbulence to the anticosmic tempest that was assaulting the premises of Hellenic rationalism in late antiquity. Christianity had itself undermined that tradition by opening into it the paths of revelation, a channel of knowledge that challenged in its veracity and certitude the truths ascertained by dialectic. The developed position of Christianity eventually accepted philosophy as an ally, rather than a rival, with whom it shared, as did classical Zoroastrianism, a regard for this world as a kind of neutral ground, where man had to work out his salvation. Gnosticism, on the other hand, with its absolutist claims for a secret *gnosis* at the expense of both rational discourse and an open revelation, had enemies in both the philosophical schools and the Christian Churches, where neither its elitism nor its radical pessimism found much sustained support.

But if the schools resisted the anticosmic sentiments of Gnosticism, they appeared willing to compromise their own absolutist claims for dialectic and to admit to the legitimacy of other forms of knowledge and action that neither Plato nor Aristotle would have recognized. And though Plotinus resisted them, both revelation and sacramentalism became part of the Platonic tradition as handed down by even his most immediate disciples.

Mention has already been made of the *Chaldean Oracles*, the collection of religious texts put together by Julian at the time of Marcus Aurelius.[18] More and more they came to serve as the Book of Revelation for the later Platonists and a short cut across the dialectic of philosophy. Dialectic had never been the sole cognitive process recognized by the philosophers. In the *Symposium* and again in one of his *Letters* Plato had exposed other vistas that lay beyond philosophical dialectic, a point at which the *process* of dialectic yielded to an immediate, nondiscursive vision of the truth.[19] This suggestion of a unitive and intuitive *unio*

---

18. See Chapter XII, p. 458.
19. Aristotle too had admitted the presence of an intuitive knowledge into his cognitive schema, but his concession appears to have been born of the logical necessity of somehow grounding a knowledge of the first principles of syllogistic reasoning rather than of any firm

mystica was more deeply internalized and expanded in Plotinus' treatment of *noesis* and played an important part in that philosopher's own experience, or so it seemed to his biographer and editor Porphyry, who noted their occurrence in his *Life of Plotinus*.

The desire for assimilation (*homoiosis*) to God lay near the heart of Platonism, but it was a goal made arduous by man's material condition and achieved only intermittently, even by philosophers. Purely religious sentiment urged man even more insistently to the same end and contrived other, somewhat more direct means of attaining it. Ecstasy, enthusiasm, revealed but secret knowledge, and magic all promised to put man in close contact with God, and without the intellectual rigors of the Plotinian regimen. Plotinus himself was well aware of these competitive appeals. In the *Enneads* he attacked the devotees of *gnosis* and magic, though he was once prevailed upon to attend a séance conducted by an Egyptian priest at a Roman Iseum.

The attitude of his student Porphyry was at once more complicated. Plotinus, though an Egyptian, was apparently immune to the hermetic traditions of his native ground. Porphyry, born Malchus, had, however, to fight his way clear of the equally attractive enticements of Syria. Born about A.D. 232, he spent his youth and early manhood in his native Phoenician Tyre before falling under the influence and tutelage of Longinus at Athens.[20] If the provisional chronology of his work holds true, he composed in Syria his *Philosophy from Oracles*, while the work *On Statues*, the treatises of Homeric exegesis like his *Cave of the Nymphs*, and at least the plan of his *Philosophical History* were conceived at Athens.

Philosophy from Oracles is a revealing illustration of the beliefs and attitudes of an educated eastern Hellene in the third century. Oracles, according to Porphyry, are useful because they provide, from an unimpeachable source, directives for the cult of the gods, how each class of the swarming pantheon is to be dealt with. Porphyry's notion of cult is, naturally enough, far different from the stately Panathenaia of fifth-century Athens. The social resonances of the old *polis* religion had by now almost totally

---

conviction that such knowledge played a part in the experience of man.

20. See Chapter XVI, pp. 558–59.

disappeared, to be replaced by a variety of magical prayers and practices whereby the gods might be manipulated for the bene-fit—and protection—of the individual.

Protection loomed large in the religious views of Porphyry, for whom the world and its upper air was populated by a horde of *daimones*, frequently malevolent, who must be controlled by man, a view not unlike that of Plutarch a century earlier—with-out, however, the restraints of Plutarch's conservative Hellenic background. Even at Delphi Plutarch felt the eastern influence of the Isis cult and was well informed on Iranian dualism. Porphyry had the same points of reference, all the cults and wisdom of the East from Babylonian astrology to the work of the learned and probably apocryphal Persian sage Ostanes. But a new dimension had been added: Porphyry was prepared to acknowledge the wisdom of Jesus too, though not, as his later writings show, that of Jesus' followers, the Christians.

Porphyry's progressive steps into the rationalist tradition, probably under the guidance of Longinus, can be traced across the pages of the treatise *On Statues*. He had discovered at Athens the work of Apollodorus and Nero's tutor Chaeremon that reflected the Stoic method of allegoresis. The somewhat crude theurgy of his earlier work was dropped in favor of Stoic symbolism.[21] Images of the gods were valuable only insofar as they were understood symbolically rather than literally. The traditional gods were themselves interpreted in the accepted Stoic fashion as personified representations of natural powers (*dy-nameis*), with perhaps somewhat more of an astral emphasis than an earlier Stoic might have deemed appropriate.

Porphyry was reaching for the rationalist position but never quite grasped it, or rather, never quite surrendered his grip on the other gods and practices that passed for the ordinary religious practice in his day. Plato and Aristotle were assured enough in their intellectualist convictions to ignore or disdain the traditional Olympianism, but their assurance was not Porphyry's, nor indeed anyone else's since the first pre-Christian century. The third was a god-ridden century, caught between either the cool henotheism of the philosophers or the calculating version of the same urged

---

21. *On the Cave of the Nymphs* is a model work of the genre in which Porphyry puts forth his exegesis in terms of nature symbolism of a passage in the *Odyssey*. See Chapter XII, pp. 451–52.

by the imperial propaganda and the agitated polytheism of the general citizenry of the *oikoumene*.

Porphyry's own uncertainties appear in a whole series of works composed after the essay *On Statues:* the *Letter to Anebo, On the Return of the Soul,* and *On Abstinence.* How does one reconcile, Porphyry inquires, the intellectuals' henotheism with the masses' polytheism, theurgy and magic, contemplation and prayer, bloody and unbloody sacrifices, flesh eating and vegetarianism? In the end he resorts to a map of the complex spiritual landscape of the Empire and beyond[22] to find a niche for the divergent elements of contemporary religion. The High God of the philosophers is a pure spirit whose only appropriate worship is purity of thought and who can be approached only through philosophical contemplation (*theoria*). Beneath the High God are the intelligible gods to whom verbal prayers and hymns may be offered. By a further descent one comes to the visible gods, the heavenly bodies and particularly the sun and the moon, who are to be worshiped by tasteful sacrifices of such things as fruits and flowers. Beneath the sphere of the moon is the haunt of the *daimones,* some benevolent, but others unmistakably evil. These lower regions constitute the area within which the traditional religion operates and where theurgy has its validity.

Porphyry was not prepared to accept all forms of contemporary theurgy.[23] The student of Plotinus was constrained somehow to distinguish between the true theurgy and its bastard, magic (*goëteia*). The former is the imperfect but useful means of sanctification for the masses incapable of the contemplative prayer of the philosopher; the latter is the work of the evil *daimones,* who are the source of physical and moral evil for man, frequently in the disguise of the benevolent gods, and who, from

---

22. Porphyry was well instructed on the eastern religions. Egyptian religion was by then a commonplace; he had read, as well, of the Essenes, Brahmans and Buddhists, and he cites Bar Daisan as his source on the latter.

23. *Theourgia,* action upon a god, was probably coined as a deliberate contrast with *theologia,* talk about a god; it was, at any rate, a form of action directed toward the achievement of supernatural effects and generally took the form either of manipulating certain tokens (*symbola, synthemata*) or using a psychic medium.

a liturgical point of view, delight in blood and flesh offerings. They had moreover a leader, a type of Iranian Prince of Darkness who aspired to be the High God. Though Porphyry at one point identifies the chief of the evil *daimones* as Serapis, it is more likely the shadow of Ahriman at work, probably as seen through Jewish or Christian eyes, for whom Satan was already a standard piece of cosmic furniture.

In A.D. 263 Porphyry came to Rome and took up a position at the center of the Plotinian circle there. A few years later he was seized by fits of depression that drove him to contemplate suicide. Plotinus recommended that he travel, and Porphyry voyaged to Sicily, where the news of Plotinus' death reached him in A.D. 270. Eventually he returned to Rome, where he directed Plotinus' school until his own death sometime between A.D. 301 and 306. The Plotinian turns are evident in Porphyry's later work. In addition to serving as his teacher's posthumous editor and biographer, he gave himself over to the exegesis of Aristotle and the explication of problems of the Plotinian metaphysic.

His religious focus may also have grown sharper. From as early as A.D. 178, when Celsus wrote his *True Discourse* against them, the later Platonists had begun to identify the Christians as a new and dangerous species of enemy. There were some among the Greek intellectuals, like the Pythagorean Numenius, who, as has been seen, were willing to give all the eastern sages rights of domicile at the side of the Greeks, including Moses and Judaism. But the Platonists saw Moses' offspring the Christians as something different from merely another eastern cult, and so their admiration of Moses was an occasional thing. Celsus' polemic was extremely wide-ranging, encompassing as it did everything from the philosophical nonsense of the "incarnation" of a transcendent God, the crude anthropomorphisms of the Old Testament, the Christian abuses of allegoresis, the objectionably *secret* nature of their teaching, to, finally, the patent absurdity of their claim to originality when the Roman Empire was filled with dying saviors and both Phoenicia and Palestine abounded with prophets and enthusiasts of all types.

Plotinus curiously knew little or nothing of orthodox Christianity, though he was acquainted with Christian Gnosticism and condemned it. Porphyry was better informed, and while he was in Sicily he wrote his *Against the Christians*. Little of it remains,[24] but it seems to have been less philosophical and more historical than Celsus' treatise, directed perhaps against a typological reading of the Old Testament by undermining the validity of the documents in question. We do know that Porphyry took this tack against the *Book of Daniel* and demonstrated its late authorship.

Porphyry apparently had no such critical qualms about the *Chaldean Oracles*, since he wrote a commentary on them. His later, more rationalistic work did not repudiate his belief in oracles, but was rather an attempt to integrate the three traditions amid which he now rather hopelessly stood: the Greek intellectualist tradition from Plotinus with its insistence on contemplation and the intellectual virtues as the way to God; the folk tradition shared by the Greeks and others that expressed itself in mythology and cults; and, finally, the eastern ecstatic and oracular tradition with its emphasis on action (*praxis*) rather than speculation (*theoria*). The reconciliation of the first two had been undertaken much earlier, and in accepting the Stoic resolution through allegory, Porphyry was merely following a course trodden by many others. But the resolution of *praxis* and *theoria*, though it had been lurking in the schools at least since the debates over Pythagoras in the early Lyceum,[25] assumed a new urgency in the second and third Christian centuries as the *praxis* took on deeper and deeper religious associations. In Porphyry's day the debate was clearly on the merits not simply of *praxis* but of *theourgia* versus *theoria*.

Porphyry's conciliatory position was not destined to prevail unchallenged for long. Iamblichus (*c.* A.D. 269–330), a Syrian who studied with Porphyry at Rome and later taught philosophy at Apamea in his homeland, took up the difficulties posed by Porphyry in his *Letter to Anebo* and responded to them in his own *On the Mysteries*. Here Porphyry's ordering of theurgy beneath *theoria* as the necessary religious activity of the uninstructed masses was reversed. For Iamblichus theurgy and philosophy were separate categories, unlinked by any association. Philosophy dealt with intelligible causes, while theurgy, since it was a mode whereby the remote High God who was beyond

---

24. It was consigned to the flames by a decree of the Council of Ephesus (A.D. 431) which was confirmed by an edict of Theodosius II in A.D. 448.

25. See Chapter XI, pp. 422–23.

EASTERN PHILOSOPHIES / 677

understanding communicated with men, had to do with essentially incomprehensible causes.

Porphyry had attempted to work out, much as Plotinus had done, a theory of action based on the Stoic notion of *sympatheia*, the natural interdependence of the powers of things. For Iamblichus this constituted nothing more than a rather uninteresting natural magic. Theurgy, on the other hand, operates not through *sympatheia* but through *synthemata*, the marks and seals set down upon things by God and through which he governs them. Theurgy, then, is the activization of the *synthemata* system in a manner necessarily incomprehensible to man. It is, moreover, the most effective means of uniting oneself to God.

With Iamblichus the rationalist tradition was dealt a fatal blow, at least in its promise to bestow upon man a felicity born of assimilation to God. This had been the religious attraction of Platonism, but its fulfillment there had been connected with contemplation. In one sense the blow fell from the increasingly uneven encounter between Hellenism and the religious cultures of the East, but in another it was self-inflicted. The theology of transcendental Platonism had removed its object beyond its own grasp. Plato himself had sensed it, and his successors continued to thrust the unknowable and unspeakable God further beyond the ultimate categories, beyond Intelligence, Good and Being. The Unknown God (*agnostos theos*) did not, however, lead to agnosticism, but rather to other means of attaining the still strongly desired assimilation.

The gods of the East were untouched by the structures of a critical philosophy, and their cult was surrounded by the irresistible musk of antiquity. Earlier thinkers had put the wisdom of the East next to the Hellenic version, but Iamblichus was prepared to go further. No longer was it merely a question of eastern wisdom; as a partisan of *theourgia* he found the cults and practices of the eastern religions not only the equal of Hellenic cults but even superior; the Greeks were notoriously dazzled by novelty and constantly changed things, while the easterners held to the older and purer forms of religious cult. In matters of religion both the Egyptian and the Babylonian manners of expression were preferable to Greek. Iamblichus' almost casual rejection of Hellenism's most revered fetish, the Greek language, bespeaks its own enormity.

And yet Iamblichus was no magician or Oriental wonder-worker in the style of Apollonius of Tyana, but the head of a Platonic school. His treatises included not only *On the Mysteries* and yet another elaborate treatment of the *Chaldaean Oracles*, but commentaries on Plato and the logic of Aristotle, and the latter runs back to another side of the Porphyrian legacy. It was doubtless Plotinus who, together with Longinus, won Porphyry to academic philosophy and away from his earlier temptations to theosophy. And in that mixed milieu in which Plotinus had received his own philosophical formation Aristotle was an important part. In his *Life* Porphyry describes Plotinus' careful studies in the Aristotelian *corpus*, studies that the *Enneads* themselves reveal at every turn. Plotinus had serious reservations about a great deal of what he found in Aristotle: he knew very clearly, for example, the differences between what Plato understood as dialectic and what Aristotle understood as logic. But the syncretizers of Middle Platonism, particularly Albinus (*c.* A.D. 150), seemed unaware or unconcerned with most of the distinctions, and Platonists continued to study the Aristotelian psychology, ethics and logic.

During his therapeutic stay in Sicily, Porphyry turned to philosophy in the manner that was rapidly becoming the standard one in that increasingly conservative tradition; he wrote commentaries on various Aristotelian treatises ranging from the logic to the *Metaphysics*. They were likely elaborate productions on the scale introduced earlier in the century by Alexander of Aphrodisias. It was not, however, those scholarly works of exegesis that survived, but rather the pedagogically more significant *Introduction to the Categories of Aristotle* and the *Explanation of the Categories of Aristotle in Question and Answer Form*.[26] Both had the obvious intent of providing a simple but informed introduction[27] to the Aristotelian logic which was, at this point, at least, an important part of the Neoplatonic school curriculum. In a broader context the two works, but particularly the *Introduction* (*Eisagoge*), signaled the development of another side of the Platonic tradition that stands in sharp contrast to the obvious theosophic inclinations of some of its adherents. At the very moment that theurgy was settling into the schools, the

---

26. The catechetical form of the latter corresponded—deliberately, one sadly concludes—to the manner in which philosophical examinations were posed in the schools.

27. On the evolution of the genre see Chapter IX, pp. 376–77.

Platonists of Rome, Athens and Alexandria were turning toward a more technical and analytical view of philosophy, typified here by the growing importance of Aristotle. In an odd but genuine sense the rationalist Plotinus' real legacy to his heirs may have been his enlightened and informed opposition to Aristotle. The consequences of this paradoxical clash of interests were immense. The Platonic theurgists, who themselves ranged from the still moderate Iamblichus to the notorious Maximus who instructed the Emperor Julian in theurgy,[28] had triumphant moments under Julian, and though disappointed in their hopes, never retreated from the pietism first scouted by Porphyry and sanctified by Iamblichus. The later Neoplatonists of Athens may have vacated some of the theosophic crudities of Iamblichus' disciples, but they kept up their interests in Pythagoreanism,[29] the *Chaldean Oracles*, the wonders of prophetism, and the kind of philosophical polytheism that got them into deeper and deeper trouble with an Empire daily more Christian. They somehow escaped the baleful eye of Theodosius I, and in the fifth century had a modest renaissance under the scholarchs Plutarch (d. A.D. 431), Syrianus, and Proclus (d. A.D. 485), men who faithfully followed the example of Iamblichus in deriving their logic and psychology from Aristotle, their mathematics from the Pythagoreans, their speculative theology from Plato, chiefly the *Parmenides* and the *Timaeus*, and their sacred theology from the *Chaldean Oracles*. This mélange was not a particularly savory one in the fifth Christian century and even less appetizing in the sixth. In A.D. 529 Justinian ordered the closing of the Athenian school.

The program was not completely unviable, however. By stressing the other side of the Porphyrian legacy, the technical and

---

28. And who, nonetheless, wrote a commentary on Aristotle's *Categories*.

29. Both Porphyry and Iamblichus wrote biographies of Pythagoras, the former as the sole surviving part of his *Philosophical History* that reached from the beginnings to the death of Plato, the latter as part of a larger whole as well. Iamblichus composed a ten-volume work entitled *Collection of Pythagorean Doctrines* of which the extant *Life of Pythagoras*, drawn chiefly from such impeachable sources as Nicomachus of Gerasa and Apollonius of Tyana, formed the first part. Other parts of the same general work were Iamblichus' *Exhortation to Philosophy*, large sections of which were, happily, lifted verbally from Aristotle's lost work of the same name, and his *On Nicomachus of Gerasa's Introduction to Arithmetic*.

scholastic Aristotelianism that pursued texts and, in the manner of philosophical classicism, gave the impression of adding nothing personal to the ancients, a quite different and inoffensive image could be presented. Sometime in the same fifth century of Athens' Platonic brilliance another school of Platonists in the latter more conservative and technical style emerged at Alexandria. There had probably been a school there continuously since the time of Ammonius Saccas, but it fell upon violent days at the time of Hypatia[30] and afterward demonstrated a less aggressively pagan outlook and, doubtless as a result of that, had in residence a growing number of Christian students.

Ammonius, a student of both Syrianus and Proclus, assumed the directorship at Alexandria sometime in the latter half of the fifth century, and due to his prudent management[31] the school there was not included in Justinian's edict and survived to pass its version of scholastic Aristotelianism to the Arabs. "Aristotelianism" does not quite describe what was being taught at Alexandria. Among Porphyry's other works was one entitled *On the Agreement of Plato and Aristotle*, a formal treatment of a theme current in the schools since the days of the Stoic eminences of the Republic, Panaetius and Posidonius, and Plato and Aristotle continued their tandem passage through later antiquity, transforming each other as they went, long after Stoicism itself had fallen by the wayside.

If Porphyry is responsible for introducing Aristotle into the Neoplatonic curriculum and of providing, with his *Eisagoge*, the standard introduction to the *Organon*,[32] to Iamblichus, the defender of theurgy, belongs the credit—or shame—of turning

---

30. See Epilogue, p. 716.
31. Including the somewhat disingenuous practice of the pagan professors' publishing their work under the names of their Christian students.
32. The Porphyrian *Eisagoge* became a permanent feature of both eastern and western scholasticism. As a permanent preface to the *Categories* it was translated into Latin by Marius Victorinus in the middle of the fourth century and again by Boethius at the beginning of the sixth, the latter the chief western representative of the brand of philosophy taught at Alexandria by Ammonius. The *Eisagoge* was translated into Syriac no fewer than three times, was epitomized in the eighth century and then fully translated into Arabic in the tenth by Abu 'Uthman al-Dimashqi. As late as the nineteenth century a version of Porphyry's work was in the curriculum of Muslim universities in the form of al-Abhari's (d. A.D. 1265) *Kitab al-Isaghuji*.

Neoplatonism from the genial, essayists's approach favored by Plotinus onto the track of a determined and systematic scholasticism. With Iamblichus something of the deductive rigor of mathematics returned to the Platonic metaphysics, which now unfolded in a remorseless system of triads. Athenian Platonism carried the systematic stamp of Iamblichus down to the time when it found its Euclid in Proclus.

XIX

The Triumph of Christianity

Diocletian stiffened the fabric of the Roman Empire in the face of the accumulating disabilities he had inherited. The earlier policy of *laissez faire*, successful as long as it was sheltered by the *Pax Romana*, was abandoned for a rigidly controlled economy. The institutions of the executive branch were expanded into a formidable bureaucracy to deal with their new responsibilities. The provinces were reorganized and the armies assigned to their defense strengthened.

The verdict of later historians has been generally favorable; the eastern Empire did, after all, survive for another millennium. But the judgment is ringed with uncertainty. Diocletian's reforms were accompanied by the last serious persecution of Christianity, a persecution in which he at least connived, and it may have been to the reversal of that policy by his successors more than to any well-intentioned doubling of troop commitments or the publishing of price controls that the Empire owed its survival. Constantine's embrace of Christianity, though it appeared to be a remarkably dangerous gamble at the time, paid off handsomely in the sequel. Byzantinism, the combination of Roman political institutions, Hellenic cultural ideals, and the religious aspirations of Christianity, proved to be far more effective than either Romanism or Hellenism alone in winning the commitment of men of all classes and all origins.

Constantine the Great

The two unchallenged Augusti of the East and West, Licinius and Constantine, were a somewhat uneven match. Constantine's Imperial pedigree went back to the origins of the tetrarchy through his father Constantius Chlorus, the Illyrian who was Maximian's original Caesar for the West. And it was Constantine's shrewd foresight and ambition that aborted the elective principle upon which the tetrarchy had been founded. Both he and Maxentius, the son of Maximian, were passed over in the original plans for the succession, but Constantine was prudently available at his father's deathbed in A.D. 306; and, as expected, the legions, whose sentiments were dynastic rather than constitutional, proclaimed him Caesar. Galerius, who had another candidate, did not acquiesce. Maxentius soon followed Constantine's example,[1] and, as in the last days of the Republic, the Roman state of the dawning fourth century was faced with the grim prospect of powerful and ambitious men struggling for rule.

During the marches and countermarches of the dreary days between the abdication of Diocletian in A.D. 305 and the victory of Constantine and Licinius over Maxentius and Maximin Daia in A.D. 312, the issue of the Christians was a peripheral one in the power struggle going on at the heart of the Empire. But on the eve of the battle of the Milvian Bridge Constantine declared he had been given a vision of his own triumph over Maxentius under the sign of the Cross. "In this sign," he had been told, "conquer"; and his troops carried into battle shields emblazoned with the Christians' Cross. Under that sign they had, indeed, conquered.

There is little to explain this crucial turning in history. Galerius had granted toleration to the Christians shortly before his death in A.D. 311, but there is nothing in the background of Constantine or of his family that reveals why he should so outstrip his predecessor in his enthusiasm for the new faith. Up to this point Constantine was probably, like his father before him, a

---

1. Maxentius' plans were somewhat complicated by the fact that the father on whom his dynastic ambitions were founded was still very much alive.

somewhat eclectic worshiper of Sol Invictus,[2] and if his mother, Helena, showed herself to be a most pious Christian, it was probably only after her son's own conversion. It is even difficult to credit Constantine with a cynic's view of some "wave of the future." In A.D. 312 Christians were still very much a minority in the Empire, and the power bases were still firmly in the hands of devotees of other faiths.

And yet there was no wavering in the new senior Augustus' commitment to the cause of Christianity. From A.D. 312 until his death a quarter of a century later Constantine attempted to translate his new faith into a program of political action absolutely without precedent, and in so doing unwittingly set down norms of action that guided a centuries-long sequence of his successors. At Milan in A.D. 313 he and his colleague Licinius promulgated their acceptance of Christianity into the fellowship of creeds and cults of the Empire. Confiscated Christian property was restored, the clergy was excepted from the burdensome and expensive service in the municipal *curia*,[3] and vast donations were made to the churches as the state became heavily involved in the Church's welfare program.[4] Out of his own pocket Constantine embarked upon an ambitious church-building plan, and nowhere more splendidly than in Palestine and Rome, which he and his mother turned into Christian show places.

For reasons that are not entirely clear, relations between Constantine and his brother-in-law Licinius steadily deteriorated. Constantine's ambitions left little room for a colleague on the throne, and Licinius for his part may have been growing uneasy over Constantine's obvious construction of a Christian power base. A growing list of favors, powers and immunities were being granted to Christians. Churches were magnificently endowed;

---

2. A cult Constantine never quite repudiated. It is very likely that Constantine made no very sharp distinction between the High God worshiped by the Christians and the Invincible Sun. His proclamation in A.D. 321 of the "Sun's day" as a weekly holiday is ambiguous enough, and he continued to issue coins in honor of the solar deity.

3. The richer Christians soon discovered this tax advantage and offered themselves for ordination. Constantine was later forced to restrict ordinations to the clergy to plug this fiscal gap that he had himself created.

4. Here too Constantine overreached himself, and Jovian had to reduce the payments by two thirds.

bishops were given the right to manumit slaves and to hear, on appeal, civil lawsuits; Christians were promoted above their pagan counterparts; and Christian soldiers were ostentatiously given the day off on Sunday. Given such inducements the number of converts swelled so that the Church waxed stronger not only among the middle and lower classes, where it had always had its primary appeal, but among the upper classes. Licinius countered by dismissing Christians from the court, and a rupture became inevitable. After some preliminary skirmishing the two men, marching under the sign of Christ and the emblems of the traditional gods, clashed near the ancient city of Byzantium on the Bosporus. Licinius was defeated, captured and executed; Constantine reigned as sole Augustus, more securely in control than any Emperor for over a century.

Immediately after his defeat of Licinius in A.D. 324, Constantine embarked upon a construction scheme that was almost as consequential as his conversion. At the outset the rebuilding and rededication of Byzantium as the "City of Constantine" may have been prompted by nothing more elaborate than the desire of the Emperor to provide himself with an Imperial residence that would rival if not surpass those that had served his predecessors at Milan and Nicomedia and that was to be immaculately Christian. What resulted—if not in Constantine's lifetime then shortly thereafter—was that the city on the Bosporus did what none of the other places of Imperial resort had managed to do: Constantinople rivaled and eventually usurped Rome's position as capital of the Empire. Power was where the Emperor was, and the economic and cultural center of the Empire had been slipping eastward for over a century. But Rome, deserted by the Imperial presence and bypassed by the prosperity of the East, remained the center of the web of constitutional toils that was still somehow part of the Roman Idea. Constantine, as it turned out, had built more than a residence; he had, perhaps unwittingly, perhaps deliberately, constructed another capital, a second, Hellenic and Christian Rome.

Constantine's city, bristling with churches and bedecked with the spoils of what was already a classical antiquity carried off from Greece, was dedicated on May 11, A.D. 330. There were no omens at the time, but history can detect the political, cultural and eventually ecclesiastical dislocations suffered on that day, not only by Rome but by Antioch and Alexandria as well. In the next three centuries, power, wealth and learning were drawn into Constantinople at the obvious expense of her older and more mature rivals. There was no future for a Roman West except in the hands of its heirs, and the burden of maintaining Roman privilege and honor fell not to the Roman aristocracy, still pleading for the traditional but pagan Romanism at the end of the fourth century, but ironically to the Christian bishop of Rome who struggled against the combined forces of Constantinopolitan Emperor and Patriarch for as long as there were such. In the Greek east, Antioch and Alexandria did not appear immediately threatened, but after Justinian their fate too was plain. Their Arab conquerors found the two cities already in a decline, from which they never recovered. The Arab masters of the Near East preferred Damascus and Cairo.

A Christian Constantine and his Christian sons reigned for just short of half a century, and their rule changed the fortunes of Christianity. It was their support—moral, financial and political—coupled with the subtle but firm discouragement of an already moribund paganism, that transformed the followers of Jesus from a troublesome growing cult into the masters of the Empire. Numbers are difficult to come by,[5] but the shift in balance is unmistakable. The freedom of conscience of the non-Christian was as yet unaffected, but temple lands, money and plate were confiscated, and very likely, sacrifices were prohibited. The blood was being drained from the corpse in preparation for its burial by Theodosius.

The new role of the Emperor as protector and nourisher of the faith did not free him from his older and less satisfying obligations. Neither the Goths in the West nor the Sasanians in the East beat their swords into plowshares during the marvelous goings-on among the *Romaioi*. The Sasanians were as yet constrained by their own internal difficulties from attempting to avenge the disasters visited upon the unfortunate Narseh. But there was a new Shah on the throne of the Sasanians, Shapur II (A.D. 309–379), destined to outlive Constantine and all his sons, and the new appearance of an old *casus belli*, Armenia. The Tiridates restored by Diocletian to the throne of Armenia became his own land's

---

5. It has been estimated that at this point perhaps one tenth of the population of the Empire was Christian.

Constantine sometime very early in the fourth century and his countrymen followed him into the Christian fold. Once again the balance in Armenia was tipped in favor of the Romans—intolerably so, to the mind of Shapur II, who intervened and dethroned the Armenian king.

Constantine, who had hastened the hostilities by some rather intemperate remarks to the Great King, never had to deal with the protracted war that broke out between the Empire and the Sasanians in A.D. 338 and continued intermittently until A.D. 363. The heaviest price was doubtless paid by the Christians within the Sasanian Empire. In A.D. 339 Shapur, who doubted the loyalty of his Christian subjects in the light of Constantine's provocative statements about the power of his new God, initiated a savage persecution of Christianity that lasted over a number of years and provided the Persian Church with its first martyrs. On the Roman side of the frontier the responsibility for the war rested with Constantius, with Julian, whose life it claimed, and with Jovian, who brought it to an end only at the price of ceding to Shapur the trans-Tigrine provinces seized by Diocletian, large parts of northern Mesopotamia, including the fortress of Nisibis, and the Roman claim to eastern Armenia. It was a high price, and Jovian, a neophyte in the game of international politics, probably thought he had little choice.

A closer reading of events in Iran might have counseled a harder bargain. Shapur was not without his own difficulties. Early in his career he was threatened by a resurgence of the Kushans, who had dominated Iran's eastern frontier until Shapur I had reduced them to vassalage.[6] It was to be their last threat. As soon as the young Shapur II had fortified his own position, he completed the work of his older namesake by attacking and dismantling the Kushan states which were then incorporated into the Sasanian Empire. As always the clearing of the frontier created a dangerous vacuum, and into it, on this occasion, the first elements of the nomadic Chionites began to move. There was more fighting, and Shapur eventually had to settle in much the same fashion that the Romans had to do with the Goths: the Chionites were domesticated on the frontier and incorporated in the Sasanian army.

All this lay beyond Constantine's immediate horizon, though

6. See Chapter XV, pp. 567–68.

not beyond his concerns. It is not easy to separate the defense policies of Diocletian from those of Constantine, but it seems clear that a major reorganization of the Roman army was under way, based on the new distinction between the mobile elite troops, infantry and cavalry, the *comitatenses*, and those legions and *vexillationes* of cavalry settled at fixed points along the frontier. Diocletian had devoted some of his closest attention to the frontier defenses. At the time of the Severi there were twelve legions stationed along the *limites* from the Black Sea to Egypt. Diocletian doubled their number. In addition there were seventy cavalry detachments and a large number of irregular units of cavalry (*alae*) and infantry (*cohortes*), a total of over two hundred thousand troops serviced and protected by a network of roads and fortresses through the deserts and mountains.

Constantine apparently placed greater faith in the more mobile field army of the *comitatenses* which he strengthened, probably at the expense of the frontier forces (*ripenses, limitanei*). Diocletian's distinction between the military and civil authorities was further reinforced. The Imperial bureaucracy was expanded under the increasing influence of the Master of the Offices,[7] and new, inflated titles were created to satisfy the growing Imperial aristocracy.

The monetary inflation continued apace. The small alloy coins were progressively debased and drove what was left of the gold and silver deeper into private hoards. Prices galloped far out of sight of the scale set down by Diocletian in his Edict of A.D. 301. A barter economy lay directly ahead. By a variety of means, special taxes payable only in gold or silver and the confiscation of temple hoards, Constantine managed to pry loose enough gold to mint a new coin, the *solidus*, at seventy to the pound of gold. The *solidus* went undebased until the eleventh century, and its stability and credibility held the Empire at the hither edge of the gold standard.

The Emperor, whom his Church called "the Great," approached death in A.D. 337, and in the manner of those times requested Christian baptism from Eusebius, bishop of Nicomedia,

---

7. Who had under his jurisdiction the interesting *agentes in rebus* who began as simple couriers and ended as the Byzantine Intelligence Agency.

as a final remission of sins.[8] It must have been an interesting confession; the Emperor had had both his wife Fausta and his eldest son Crispus executed in A.D. 326 under circumstances both sordid and cruel. The character of Constantine has been debated and the motives and sincerity of his conversion endlessly discussed. To little or no point. Nothing was expected of a Christian Roman Emperor in A.D. 312, because there had never been one; the absolutist ruler devoted to an absolutist creed was a combination still to be tried. Nor can any judgment be passed on his relationship with the Church, because here too there was no precedent. An Ecumenical Church in the institutional sense did not come into existence until after the Ecumenical Council of Nicaea.

The Council of Nicaea

The picture of the Christian Church rising triumphant around the bier of Constantine is at best only partially correct. The very bishop who baptized the dying Emperor, Eusebius of Nicomedia, was embroiled in a controversy which at that very moment (A.D. 337) was threatening the Church in a manner that neither Decius nor Diocletian nor Maximin had found within their capacities. Some twelve years before, in A.D. 325, between two hundred and fifty and three hundred bishops of the Church had come together at Nicaea, a town near what was still the Imperial residence at Nicomedia, to deal with the question of the theology of Arius, a priest of Alexandria whose doctrines they subsequently judged heretical. Arius was not the Church's first theologian so judged; what made him unusual was that he came at a point in the Church's history where heresy could have unforeseen but explosive consequences.

The history of Arianism falls into three phases: from its origins to Arius' condemnation at Nicaea; the period from Nicaea to the death of Constantine; and finally, from the reigns of Constantius

---

8. There were some, perhaps the Novatians, who claimed that only baptism could forgive a mortal sin, and they may have influenced Constantine's late baptism. But the practice of late baptism was still common enough to require little explanation in the case of Constantine.

and Valens down to the accession of Theodosius. During its first phase Arianism was almost purely a theological controversy, rendered complex by a new court of final appeal; during the second it gathered into itself the unlovely overtones of ecclesiastical politics; followed, during its final period, by the complexities of Imperial politics on an ecumenical scale.

With the possible exception of Gnosticism, the beginnings of all heresy lie in the Gospels, which, by their assertions or their silence, provided for succeeding generations of Christians an understanding of the life, nature and mission of Jesus. The presentation of Jesus to be found there was, as has been noted, heavily Messianic and eschatological in the manner of Palestinian Judaism. But quickly, within the next half generation, the portrait of Jesus was opened out by both Paul and John to include the perspectives of a more Hellenized Diaspora Judaism. There was talk of a preexistent Jesus as *Kyrios* or *Logos*, dwelling with the Father "in the beginning" and then "becoming flesh." Such expressions, as alien as they might have seemed in the immediate circle of Jesus, provoked no visible opposition in the *oikoumene* where they were uttered; possibly those who might have found them most objectionable, the Judaeo-Christians of Jerusalem, were drifting off into schism and eventually into oblivion.

Paul and John were mere naïve pioneers in a field of infinite complexity. They had brought Christian *mythos* to the edge of Hellenic speculative theology, and others were left the exciting but dangerous task of converting the impressionistic lines of the original *kerygma* into a detailed explanation that would square with what the Christian community, speaking through its bishops, judged as orthodoxy, and what the Hellenes, speaking through their philosophers, judged as making sense. That bishop and philosopher were sometimes the same man merely added to the complication.

The difficulties of the task did not deter the brave or the imaginative. Across the third century there were a great variety of such "explanations" of the Gospels. A number of them have already been touched upon, those of Justin, Tatian, Clement and Origen, for example, but those that centered more precisely upon the person of Jesus and his divine status may be reduced to three general types reported under many different names by the Christian heresiographers: monarchianism, emanationism and adoptionism.

The first two patterns of explanation, monarchianism and emanationism, were essentially Hellenic in their inspiration and technique. Both were defenses of monotheism, the first on a plan favored by the Stoa, the second in the manner of Platonism. Monarchianism, known in two of its historical manifestations as modalism or Sabellianism, put heavy emphasis on the unity and simplicity (*monarchia*) of God. The Father and his *Logos* were one—one substance (*substantia*), as the Latin Tertullian expressed it, or of the same substance (*homoousios*), as it appeared in the formula of Paul of Samosata. What, then, was one to make of Jesus in this stringently monotheistic view? A variety of responses were possible. According to Tertullian, Father, Son and Holy Spirit were three different "persons" displayed by the one, unique substance. A more extreme view, and one judged clearly unorthodox, was that the three were merely different modes of the single God, modifiers or attributes, much in the way that the Stoics explained away the gods of myth as different manifestations of the One God. Paul of Samosata, whose monotheism was apparently closer to the Jewish variety than to the Stoic, explained Jesus as a human Davidic Messiah whom God raised up among men, the position that came to be known as a form of adoptionism.

Emanationism had, of course, a prior history in later Platonic theology, where the procession of the lower *hypostases* from the original divine Monad was set out in terms of the metaphor of the sun and its rays. Origen, who was opposed to monarchianism, had found this explanation attractive and used it to describe the procession of the *Logos* from the Father, though with the precisions he thought necessary to safeguard the witness of the Gospels. The *Logos* was, in the accepted Platonic terminology, an "image" (*eikon*) of the Father, and so, in some sense, on a lower plane of reality. The *Logos* did not, however, belong to the order of time but, like the Father, to that of eternity. They differed in that they were distinct *hypostases*.

All of these suggestions and concepts had been offered before Arius appeared on the scene. Some had been rejected outright, while others were still part of the continuing dialogue on the nature of the Trinity. The dialogue was not always conducted in the most peaceable of circumstances: the persecutions, intermittent until A.D. 311, had created apostates from Christianity; bishops fled their sees and others took their places, raising questions of succession and legitimacy. One such dubious case was that of Meletius, bishop of Lycopolis in Egypt, who came to Alexandria and discovered that there was no bishop in residence there. To care for the pastoral needs of the metropolis he ordained two men, one of them the Libyan Arius.

In the easier atmosphere after Galerius' edict of toleration, Arius was appointed pastor of one of the district churches of Alexandria, and sometime later, about A.D. 321, his preaching began to attract attention, not all of it favorable, in the always excitable atmosphere of the Egyptian capital. What Arius was exposing in his sermons was an outgrowth of Origen's emanationism, but without the earlier theologian's careful protection of the full divinity of the *Logos*. Arius stood closer to Platonic orthodoxy. He subordinated the *Logos* to the Father in an unmistakable sense and held that he was created and not merely, as Origen maintained, "begotten." The Father alone belonged to eternity; the habitat of the *Logos* was time. Arius made it clear that he worshiped Jesus, but essentially as a wonderful creation of God.

Alexander, the bishop of Alexandria, was cautious in dealing with these novel views. What constituted orthodoxy in this area had never really been defined, and, more pragmatically, Arius had allies who were, like him, former students of Lucian of Antioch, who had come to high estate in the Church. Lucian's own teaching is not very well known, nor is his career in Antioch, where he was an important Christian teacher until his death at Nicomedia in the last convulsive persecution under Maximin Daia in A.D. 312. Lucian's most genuinely attested accomplishment was an edition of the Septuagint revised on the basis of the Hebrew Bible, a text that became the standard one at both Antioch and Constantinople.[9] It is not unlikely then that it was Lucian, no matter what the role of the ambiguous Malchion at the time of Paul of Samosata,[10] who gave the theology of Antioch its Scriptural orientation toward historical and literalist exegesis. The great defenders of the humanity of Jesus, whether orthodox or unorthodox, were products of the Antiochene school.

---

9. Another contemporary student of Hebrew at Antioch was the priest Dorotheus, perhaps Lucian's associate in his Scriptural labors. Dorotheus ended his career in charge of the state-owned dyeworks at Tyre, a post given him by Diocletian.
10. See Chapter XVI, Note 36.

Among their number was the historian Eusebius, who was born about A.D. 260 in Caesarea, the capital city of Roman Palestine and the see over which he would one day rule as bishop. From the days of Herod Caesarea was the intellectual center of southern Syria, and in Eusebius' youth there was already a Christian school there, as well as an extensive library that Origen had used during his exile from Alexandria. Eusebius studied in the school and was caught up in the nets of Maximin Daia's persecution, first in Caesarea in A.D. 309 and two years later in Egypt. In A.D. 314 he became bishop of his native city and soon came to the attention of Constantine, whose adherent he remained until the Emperor's death. Eusebius himself died no more than two or three years later, in A.D. 339 or 340.

Only about a third of Eusebius' total literary production in dogma, polemic and history is preserved, and among the extant works it is his *Ecclesiastical History*, on which most of our present knowledge of the early Christian Church rests. It takes up the story of Christianity from the days of Jesus and follows the trials and triumphs of Christianity down to the fall of Licinius in A.D. 324.[11] Arius plays no part in the story, and the *Ecclesiastical History* ends before the bishops gathered at Nicaea, but in another work, the *Life of Constantine*, written shortly after the Emperor's death in A.D. 337, Eusebius gave his own somewhat impressionistic account of the proceedings at Nicaea. Neither it nor a letter that Eusebius addressed to his church at Caesarea at about the same time are of much help in understanding Arius' position; Eusebius was far more interested in Constantine than in the troublesome Alexandrian cleric whom he had at first supported.

Eusebius of Caesarea, a figure of learning and prestige in the Constantinian era, eventually followed where his Emperor led and subscribed to the acts of the Council of Nicaea, but among Arius' "co-Lucianists," as they were called, was another Eusebius,

---

11. Eusebius' *Ecclesiastical History* is the work of an impressive and lively historian with access to a wide range of early Church documents. Its pages are dense with verbal citations from the letters of bishops, archival material from churches in every corner of the *oikoumene*, Imperial edicts, works of theologians like Philo, Porphyry and Origen, historians like Josephus and Julius Africanus, and the whole range of the New Testament, including the apocryphal Gospels. Most of what we know about the heresy and orthodoxy in the Church before Constantine comes from these same pages.

who was to prove far more tenacious and useful to the cause of Arianism. Eusebius, formerly bishop of Beirut, now bishop of the Imperial residence of Nicomedia, and later to assume the first episcopal charge of Constantine's new capital of Constantinople, had the ear first of the Emperor's sister, the Augusta Constantia, and eventually of Constantine himself, and never relaxed or relented in his support of Arius.

Alexander's caution, then, was well founded. He convened a local synod to investigate Arius. It found against him, and Arius was forced to withdraw, first to Caesarea, and then to the side of his strongest ally, Eusebius of Nicomedia. Alexander circularized his fellow bishops as to what was going on; Eusebius and Arius retorted,[12] and the conflict escalated into something far more serious than another Alexandrian quarrel. And since the protagonists were conducting their counteroffensive in the Imperial city itself, it was not long before Constantine, freed at last of Licinius, prepared to intervene. He dispatched his personal envoy, Hosius, bishop of Cordova in Spain, to look into the affair at Alexandria. Hosius judged that Alexander had acted correctly.

The noise and excitement did not abate. Constantine, who was more interested in the unity of the Church and of his Empire than in the theological niceties involved, decided to resort to an institution that had proven useful in the past, a convocation of bishops. In the past such had occurred on the provincial level, normally summoned by the metropolitan bishop of the province. Now, however, the Empire possessed an ecumenical authority with a legitimate claim to the power of convoking all the bishops of the Great Church. No single bishop, metropolitan or other, could or did make such a claim at that point, and so there was no ecclesiastical opposition when Constantine summoned the bishops of the *oikoumene* to gather for the purpose of restoring unity to the Church as he himself had restored unity to the Empire. The original site for their convocation was to have been Ancyra in central Anatolia, but for a number of reasons, not least of which was Constantine's desire to observe the proceedings somewhat more closely than would have been possible in Galatia, the Council finally met in May of A.D. 325 at Nicaea, in the shadow of Nicomedia.

---

12. It was this occasion that produced Arius' verse drama *Thalia* (see Chapter XVII, Note 23).

Constantine presided over the bishops, who numbered somewhat more than two hundred and fifty and who were overwhelmingly easterners. The bishop of Rome sent two deacons to represent him, and there were perhaps a few other Latin bishops in attendance. Arius was there, both Eusebiuses, and Alexander of Alexandria, attended by his future successor and heir of the controversy, Athanasius. The issues were settled quickly. Both sides were heard, and Arius' support suddenly vanished. Only two Libyan bishops refused to sign the final declaration against him, and they probably had other objections to the Council's findings.[13] Eusebius of Caesarea was cleared of any complicity in the matter, as Constantine wished, but Arius was discharged into exile.

The Council did one extraordinary thing. In drawing up its declaration of what constituted orthodoxy, its creed, or *symbolon*, it reached for a term that already had a history in the controversy. The Father and the *Logos*, the Nicaean Creed affirmed, were "of the same substance" (*homoousios*). In the middle of the previous century the term *homoousios* was being bruited in theological circles; it had been rejected by Origen's disciple Dionysius of Alexandria because it seemed to blur the distinction between Father and Son, the principle and its image, and affirmed by the adoptionist Paul of Samosata because he read it as the strongest possible affirmation of his own monarchian monotheism. And Nicaea, which condemned Paul, reaffirmed *homoousios*.

Unaccountably Arius was back on the scene shortly after the Council, and Eusebius of Nicomedia, the most powerful prelate in the eastern Churches, had withdrawn his signature from the Acts of Nicaea and was casting about for ways to restore his dishonored colleague. Eusebius' attacks were directed against the Council's three chief defenders, Athanasius, who succeeded Alexander at Alexandria in A.D. 328, Eustathius of Antioch and Marcellus of Ancyra. Eustathius was a simple matter, as it turned out. He had fallen personally afoul of the Dowager Augusta Helena and was deposed, apparently with Constantine's acquies-

---

13. The council addressed itself to other matters. It fixed the date of Easter, dealt with the problems of Meletius' free-wheeling ordinations in Egypt and of Paul of Samosata in Antioch, and recognized the broad jurisdictional powers of Rome, Antioch and Alexandria outside their immediate provinces.

cence. Constantine, who was persuaded to accept Arius back into communion, tried to convince Athanasius to do likewise at Alexandria. Athanasius refused, and the matter passed for the time. But only for a time. At a synod held at Tyre in A.D. 335 serious charges were lodged against the Alexandrian bishop, and Athanasius, who was not the gentlest of men, had created enough disturbance in the Egyptian metropolis to convince the Emperor that his outspoken bishop was better off in Gaul.[14]

Once Athanasius was removed to Trier it fell the turn of Marcellus of Ancyra. Eusebius was now triumphantly in control of Constantine, and Marcellus was summoned to a synod convoked in Jerusalem in late A.D. 335 to celebrate the Emperor's thirtieth anniversary in the purple. Marcellus must have suspected what was in store and refused to attend. He was deposed the next year and followed Athanasius into exile in the West. Arius died about the same time, almost unnoticed by the controversialists contending in his name.

Constantine's death persuaded the refugees that they might regain their sees. But Eusebius, now bishop of Constantinople, was as firmly in control of Constantius as he had been of his father, and the exiles were once again rebuffed. This time, however, the refugees found a new and more powerful haven with the bishop of Rome, a see that considered itself a court of appeal in such cases and had the additional advantage of not fully comprehending the issue. By Nicaean standards Athanasius was orthodox, but in eastern eyes Marcellus was a thinly disguised monarchian of the Sabellian variety, for whom the reality of Jesus was swallowed up in the Nicaean *homoousios* formula. Rome for its part disliked talk about three separate *hypostases* and was, moreover, convinced that Eusebius was an Arian of the most obvious and unacceptable type.

Eusebius died in A.D. 341 and a major stumbling block to détente was removed. What actually brought about the reconciliation was more likely due, however, to events on the larger stage of Imperial politics. In the original settlement at the death of

---

14. One of the charges at Tyre, the most serious one that could be lodged against an Egyptian, was that Athanasius had disrupted the grain trade by threatening a dockers' strike. That single accusation probably impressed Constantine more than all the others, many of them purely malicious.

Constantine, the West was to be shared by his eldest and youngest sons, Constantine II and Constans, while the middle son, Constantius, ruled in the East. The arrangement apparently galled Constans, even though his sphere of authority was far greater than his eldest brother's and included Africa, Italy and Illyria. He announced his independence of Constantine II, and while Constantius busied himself against Shapur II, the western Augusti had the matter out in Italy in A.D. 340. Constantine II was killed and Constans assumed sole rule in the West. Constantius raised no objections.

Constans, as firm an adherent of Nicaea as Constantius was of Eusebius of Nicomedia, had now to be reckoned with. After an exploratory ecumenical synod at Sardica (Sophia) aborted in even further schisms in A.D. 342, the two brothers moved out of the public forum to settle an issue that was threatening to dismantle their inheritance. Marcellus of Ancyra was flatly unacceptable in the East, but Constantius undertook to allow Athanasius back into his see at Alexandria in A.D. 346, and both Constans and Rome expressed themselves as content.

If Constans had some success with Constantius, he had considerably less in his own territories. The Emperor was personally unpopular, and the economic slide, fitfully arrested in the eastern provinces, was accelerating in the West. Constans was deposed and executed by his own troops who recognized one of their Frankish officers, Magnentius, as Augustus (A.D. 350). This time Constantius did not dally on the eastern frontier. Magnentius' troops were defeated in Illyria in A.D. 351, and the usurper himself relentlessly pursued into the embrace of suicide.

Relieved of both Constans and Magnentius, Constantius returned to the Arian issue. This time he found the western bishops somewhat more compliant and extracted from many of them the desired condemnation of Athanasius. The Alexandrian bishop, now stripped of his Latin allies, was once again forcibly deposed from his see (A.D. 356). Radical Arian bishops who denied any similarity of essence between Father and Son took over at both Alexandria and Antioch as Athanasius fled into the Egyptian desert.

The radicals found little support among the eastern bishops, and their extreme position may have had the effect of drawing the Nicaean Athanasius and the adherents of the compromise formula of "similar in essence" (*homoiousios*) closer together. Athanasius spent his years of exile in arguing Nicaean orthodoxy in a spate of theological treatises, and once the ominous jurisdictional question of Rome was cast into the background, they began to have their effect. By the death of Constantius in A.D. 361 theological reconciliation was already in sight, only to be postponed once again by another violent turn of Imperial politics.

Arianism was the Church's first bitter harvest of Origen's profound Hellenizing of the kerygmatic Gospels or, on a longer view, of Philo's similar ventures with the Torah. Porphyry had already experienced the collision of faith and reason from the other side: how to integrate into his philosophical Platonism the practices of popular piety and the utterances of divinely inspired oracles. But no Hellene had ever died for his mythology or suffered the wounds of persecution still exhibited by some of the delegates at Nicaea. There was no issue in the philosophical schools capable of dividing an Empire, and no Emperor had ever seen fit to intervene in the debates there. The articulation of a Christian theology was clearly of another order.

The Church never retreated from the work of Origen nor shrank from the painful consequences on full display at Nicaea and every subsequent Ecumenical Council. The work of fashioning a Hellenic but Christian *theologia* out of the Gospels was just beginning, and the tools were still somewhat crude. At the beginning of the fourth century the Christian theologians stood about a generation behind their pagan counterparts. Through Origen they had discovered an adaptable version of Ammonian Platonism, but the upper vistas of Plotinus' mysticism were still ahead, and, more significantly from a pedagogical point of view, the solid Aristotelian foundation that Porphyry and his successors had cast under Ammonius and Plotinus had not as yet had its full effect on Christian theology. Both came in due course in the generation after Nicaea, and Aristotelianism particularly gave a facility and sophistication to theological discourse that became increasingly apparent in the fifth century. There were Christians in attendance at the Platonic school at Alexandria in the fifth century, commenting, at the side of their pagan masters, the school *corpus* of Aristotle, and even out in the Syrian hinterland, where Greek had never displaced the native Aramaic, these same logical treatises were being read in Syriac translation by the neophyte theologians of Nisibis and Edessa.

Sons and Heirs of Constantine

When Constantine died in A.D. 337 his contemporary in Iran, Shapur II, had been Shah for twenty-eight years, crowned, according to the Iranian tradition, before his birth, and still had another four decades of rule stretching before him. He had inherited an empire disturbed by the reactionary reforms of Kartir and the failed ambitions of Narseh, who had not only lost Armenia and Mesopotamia but had been forced to concede to Diocletian provinces in the satrapy of Adiabene on the east bank of the Tigris. His own father, Ormizd II (A.D. 302–309) was forced to buy time in the east by a dynastic marriage with a Kushan princess, but with the accession of an infant Shah ruled by his regents time ran out and the Kushans, who had been reduced to vassalage by Shapur I, seized the opportunity to reassert their power. They likely occupied eastern Iran as far as Merv and the southeastern provinces to the border of India.

When Shapur came of age the timidity of his regents was replaced by a far more aggressive foreign policy. The provocation against the Romans may have come, as has been noted, from the conversion of Armenia to Christianity, whereby the sword once brandished by Narseh in the form of Manichaeism was now turned against Shapur II. It was now the Christian Roman Empire that had an extension of itself in the Christians of Armenia and of Iran itself.

Christianity may have spread naturally to Iran in the third century, at the beginnings of Sasanian rule, from north Syrian centers like Edessa. But Shapur I had himself unwittingly contributed to the process by his policy of resettling Roman prisoners within his realms. The group sent eastward after Shapur's campaigns in A.D. 260 included the Christian bishop of Antioch Demetrianus and doubtless numbers of his flock as well. Nor were these Roman citizens in exile dissipated over the Shah's empire. They preserved their identity in centers like Jundeshapur.[15]

Shapur II continued his namesake's practice of deportation and ironically added to his crop of Hellenized Christians in A.D. 363

---

15. See Chapter XVI, p. 595.

by winning back from Rome the trans-Tigrine provinces ceded by Narseh. Such was not his intention, since in Shapur's eyes a Christian Armenia was intolerable and a Christian Iran was unthinkable. To combat the first his troops occupied Armenia in A.D. 334, while his response to the second was to initiate, from A.D. 340, a persecution of the Christians in Iran.

A Sasanian Armenia was equally intolerable to the Emperor of the Romans, and shortly after Shapur's move Constantine prepared his counterstroke. A large force was raised,[16] and the Emperor's nephew Hannibalianus was groomed to rule as king over the new Christian Armenia. Death caught the Emperor in the midst of his plans, and in A.D. 337 his three sons inherited their father's growing Arian difficulties, while Constantius II, as his father's successor in the East, had to take up as well the incipient war against the Shah. On both fronts his successes were limited. Constantius was capable of breaking neither the adherents nor the opponents of Nicaea, though it was clear enough that he would have personally preferred to go the way of his Arian mentor, Eusebius of Nicomedia. Against Shapur too the Imperial forces had not the power to break through into Iran in the fashion that Galerius had, while the Sasanians for their part had their own distractions elsewhere. The Roman-Sasanian campaigns of A.D. 338–362 were a series of brutal slugging matches around Nisibis and Amida.

The Sasanian distraction lay in the East, where Shapur II had to deal not only with his old foes the Kushans, but with other hordes that were thrusting across the Caucasus, the Qara Qum, and the Oxus. Shapur seems to have settled with the Kushans first, and by about A.D. 340 they were reduced to the tributary status in which the first Shapur had left them. A Sasanian prince was restored in Bactria, while the southeastern portions of the former Kushan holdings were annexed by the Indian Guptas.

Shapur had gained a respite in the East but not, it would seem, peace. Between A.D. 350 and 358 he was once again on the frontier. The events there are clouded in obscurity, but in A.D. 359, when he appeared before the fortress of Amida, the Shah was accompanied by a new allied people, the Chionites. Subsequently the Kushans appear principally south of the Hindu Kush, and it

---

16. This army and its frequent successors over the next three decades created serious food shortages and an equally dangerous inflation all over the eastern provinces.

seems probable that the instrument for their eviction from Bactria was the newfound ally of Shapur, the Chionites.

The arrival of the Chionites and their dynastic successors, the Hephthalites, from the steppe in the mid-fourth century marks the first appearance of a Turko-Altaic people in the Near East, the first in a long series that did not end until the last Mongol invasions of the fifteenth century. The Chionites appear to have been the first mixed wave of the people known in the western sources as Huns.[17] At first they were useful and docile allies of the Sasanians, but the servants grew into the role of masters, and through the fourth and fifth centuries the Chionites-Hephthalites, or White Huns, became an increasingly difficult problem for the Sasanians. They killed one Shah (Peroz) and deposed another (Kavad) until the time of the powerful Khusrau who in A.D. 563–567 caught them in a vise between himself and the Turkish people on the steppe behind them.

The Chionites in Shapur's army amazed the Romans with their ferocity, but they did not win the war for the Shah. Frontier cities changed hands but neither Shapur nor Constantius could deliver the final blow. Like Shapur, Constantius had his own distractions. The Franks and Alamans were pressing in Gaul, and the partisans of Nicaea stubbornly refused to yield to the Emperor's desire for an Arian Church, even after they lost their most powerful political support by Constans' death in A.D. 350.

The dynasty founded by the worshiper of the Invincible Sun, Constantius Chlorus, now seemed firmly committed to Christianity. His grandsons continued along the ways of their pious father, Constantine, and exerted increasing pressure on the external forms of the old pagan cults. In A.D. 356, as sole ruler of the Empire, Constantius decreed the death penalty for all those found sacrificing or otherwise worshiping idols. The temples tumbled in growing numbers, and on his only visit to Rome in A.D. 355 the Christian Emperor ordered the Altar of Victory removed from the Senate house. In the same year members of the court were

---

17. The West chiefly knew the Western, or Black, Huns, who displaced the Goths from South Russia in A.D. 376 and who themselves arrived within the Roman Empire in the middle of the next century under their khan Attila (d. A.D. 453). Even earlier, in A.D. 395–396, their advance bands crossed the Caucasus, broke through the Sasanians' northern defenses, and pillaged Cappadocia and Syria.

forbidden under the severest penalties to consult oracles, augurs or soothsayers.

New favors were granted to the Christians. Constantine had freed the clergy from curial duty. His son extended the exemption to include extraordinary taxes and all forms of forced labor (*sordida munera*) so common in the later Empire. The clergy apparently wanted complete exemption from all tax, but Constantius had enough fiscal responsibility to go no further than exempting Church property, though not the private property of the clergy, from the land tax.

In questions of Imperial reform Constantius followed rather than led. The Empire designed by Diocletian and Constantine, in almost all its particulars the medieval Byzantine state, was firmly in place by the death of the latter Emperor in A.D. 337. Under Constantius there were some changes of emphasis, but the outline remained as before. He did, however, complete the organization of his father's capital by calling into existence, shortly after A.D. 337, a Constantinopolitan Senate to rival its centuries-older predecessor at Rome. The Roman Senate continued to be the senior in aristocratic prestige; Constantius was forced to create new Senators from his own retinue (*comitatus*), most of whom were provincials of rather recent prominence.[18] Some Roman Senators resident in Greece or the East had their membership transferred to the eastern capital, but by and large Constantius' new Senators lacked the aristocratic lines and sense of tradition of their western counterparts.

On the death of Constantine the Empire experienced a violent bloodbath perpetrated in the name of the dynastic principle. Constantine's army, faithful from the day they crowned him until his death, vowed they would have no others but the sons of Constantine rule them and executed all the likely candidates who did not so qualify. Among those who perished were Constantine's nephews Dalmatius, since A.D. 335 one of the officially designated Caesars, and Hannibalianus, the recently crowned king of Armenia. Two of Constantine's half brothers were also killed, Dalmatius, the father of the Caesar, and Julius Constantius. The

---

18. One somewhat unexpected effect of opening the rolls of the eastern Senate was the further depletion of the local aristocracies, the tax foundation of the Empire. The Senatorial honor was hereditary, and once the father reached the Senate both he and his sons were lost to the ranks of the *curiales* forever.

only ones to escape were the latter's two sons, Gallus and Julian, and Constantius kept them under close scrutiny for as long as he lived.

Gallus' enforced obscurity lasted until A.D. 351, when the Augustus had to deal personally with the usurper Magnentius and appointed his young cousin as his Caesar with jurisdiction over the entire East. Gallus, then twenty-five and married to Constantine's daughter Constantia, betrayed his fair promise in a remarkably short period of time. The suspicious, sadistic and intemperate Gallus and his equally unattractive wife, who played out most of their brief career in Antioch, converted the eastern province to turmoil and sedition. Within three years Constantius was disenchanted. He gradually stripped the Caesar of his troops and finally summoned Gallus to the West and to his own execution in A.D. 354.

In the following year it was Julian's turn. He was hastily summoned from his studies in Athens and married to the Augustus' sister Helena. Constantius, who was by then deeply involved in the East, handed over the western frontier against the Franks and Alamans to the last surviving male of the house of Constantine. At first Julian surpassed all expectations, even though surrounded by the spies and minions of Constantius. In his five years in Gaul he cleared the province of intruders, pacified the east bank of the Rhine, and put the finances of the prefecture on a sound basis.

A young second in command with the absolute confidence of his troops and the gratitude of a population for whom he had, by his careful management, reduced taxes by 80 percent had necessarily to create suspicions in the mind of Constantius. The Augustus began to unfold the procedures that had worked on Gallus, the gradual recall of the troops assigned to the Caesar. This time, however, it did not work. The army in Gaul mutinied, and in February A.D. 360 they proclaimed their Caesar as Augustus. Julian hesitated, then accepted, and only the death of Constantius in the following year prevented a confrontation between their forces. But in the end the dynastic sentiment held firm; on his deathbed Constantius appointed Julian his successor.

From Constantius' death in November A.D. 361 Julian reigned as sole Augustus until June of A.D. 363. His first five months were spent in Constantinople and the last four in the field against Shapur II; in the interval Julian was in Antioch, where his extraordinary program of religious reform unfolded—and failed. Julian was by nature and temperament a sophisticated cynic who was paradoxically committed to the most lost of causes, and he chose to play out his ungainly role to an audience that savored his inevitable defeat from the moment he appeared before them. Antioch destroyed Julian with the kind of mocking laughter that would have best been heard from his own lips.

Julian was asked to survive the murder of his father and a childhood spent under the shadow of a rival in a lonely and enforced isolation. He had also to survive the teachers that he himself had excitedly embraced in his adolescence. Earlier Julian had been given the obviously ambivalent education of his day. He was instructed in the Christian rudiments by no less than Eusebius, Constantius' confidant and the Arian bishop of Nicomedia. Thence he passed into the hands of Mardonius, who taught him Greek literature. These earliest studies were pursued in Constantinople and then in Nicomedia, where Julian read Libanius but was forbidden to attend the celebrated sophist's lectures. In A.D. 345 the suspicious Constantius remanded his two young cousins to a remote spot in Cappadocia, where Julian was to all practical purposes immured with his books from his fourteenth to his twentieth year. In A.D. 351 he was allowed to pursue his studies in Pergamum, while Gallus took up his unfortunate post in Antioch. At Gallus' execution Julian was at first held under house arrest at the court in Milan, but at the intervention of the Augusta he was finally allowed to continue his studies at Athens over the summer of A.D. 355.[19] In November he was appointed Caesar.

Julian's contact with Christianity—into which he had been baptized while still a boy—was through the fanatic Arian Eusebius or the palace eunuchs set to guard him, and was likely dominated by the ominous figure of Constantius. But his exposure to the higher reaches of Hellenism was considerably wider, from the degenerate students of Iamblichus to the most cultured and eloquent Hellenist of his day, the sophist Libanius.

Julian's religious reforms betray a close observation and admiration of the techniques of Christianity, but the general tone of what he attempted to do owed more in its execution to the

---

19. And probably to be privately initiated into the Eleusinian mysteries.

Neoplatonist Maximus than to the balanced and moderate Libanius. Julian was nineteen or twenty when he arrived in Pergamum, an intelligent if fearful and sheltered student. In A.D. 351 the chief philosopher in residence there was one of Iamblichus' students, Aedesius, then approaching the end of his days. Julian was drawn to his school and into the muted crisis that gripped the progeny of Iamblichus. Some of Iamblichus' students had moved off toward the scholarly Aristotelianism that had become part of the Platonic tradition,[20] but at Pergamum there were gathered the more openly theurgic Aedesius and his like-minded students. Even here the issue of theurgy still troubled some. When the curious Julian arrived Aedesius somewhat nervously passed him on to his students Eusebius and Chrysanthius. Julian was obviously avid for the marvels of theurgy, but Chrysanthius, who was a theurgist and yet scented some danger in the young man, was reluctant to talk, and Eusebius, who believed in philosophy and not magic, warned him against the charlatanism of theurgy and especially against its chief practitioner, Maximus, another student of Aedesius then in Ephesus. It was enough for Julian; he set out for Ephesus in hot pursuit of Maximus.

The man Julian was seeking, whom he thenceforward kept at his side and with whom he had his last conversation in a field tent on the eastern frontier, was one of the odd clutch of sophists, magicians and professors assembled in Eunapius' (c. A.D. 346–414) *Lives of the Sophists and Philosophers*, a gallery of eastern savants of the fourth century. Eunapius' subjects, the hybrid offspring of Iamblichus and the Second Sophistic, shuttled between the Imperial courts at Constantinople and Nicomedia and their own schools at Athens, Pergamum and Smyrna, but no one of them ever gained the degree of favor that the infatuated Julian accorded to Maximus. Another student of Iamblichus, Sopater, had earlier made a certain impression on Constantine but over-reached himself and was executed. Maximus, an outright and unabashed theurgist who animated statues and brought torches flashing into flames, suffered no such setback. Julian never flagged in his devotion to him.[21]

Libanius (c. A.D. 314–393) was the antithesis of Maximus. He

---

20. See Chapter XVIII, p. 680.
21. After a number of narrow escapes following the death of Julian, including a suicide pact with his wife wherein the lady died alone, Maximus was finally executed by Valens at Ephesus in A.D. 371.

trained as a sophist in his native Antioch, then in the turbulent academic atmosphere of Athens.[22] The brilliant student matured into the brilliant teacher, first at Constantinople and Nicomedia, and finally, from A.D. 354 to his death, in Antioch.

Libanius was the last, inexplicably powerful reflection of the Second Sophistic from the days of the Antonines in whom eastern Hellenism found its final serious defender. His students were the great Christian churchmen of the next generation, John Chrysostom, Basil of Caesarea, Gregory of Nazianzus, and Theodore of Mopsuestia, but Libanius himself was a convinced Hellene, culturally and religiously, though without the stylistic compulsions of his sophistic predecessors or the religious obsessions of Julian. For Libanius Julian was the last hope of Hellenism after the destruction wrought upon it by Constantine, but the sudden death of the Augustus in A.D. 363 ended neither the hope nor the effort of Antioch's premier intellectual. Under Valens (A.D. 364–378) and particularly Theodosius (A.D. 379–395), Libanius continued to plead the case of the old Hellenism before the new Christian Emperors.

Libanius and Julian came to the same ideal of a pagan restoration from two different directions, Libanius from that of the traditional *enkyklios paideia* and the humanistic aspirations of Hellenism, Julian by the route of Iamblichan Neoplatonism. The sophist was the purer type of the old cultured Hellene, relatively untouched by the mysticism or the magic of the day and fastidiously free from the slightest touch of Latin culture. Like his model Aelius Aristides he cared little for and knew little of philosophy.

Libanius was sincerely attached to Julian and read his death as a disaster. And while the Emperor admired and respected the sophist in return, the two men were separated by a wide gulf of temperament and position. Libanius was a popular teacher, a respected and influential figure among both the pagans and the

---

22. In the fourth century, students at Athens apparently were assigned to professors on a national basis, but there was a lively trade in kidnaped and shanghaied students delivered to the teacher's classroom by main force. By the normal procedures Libanius should have studied with the eminent Christian sophist Prohairesius, but on his arrival in Athens he was "captured" for the class of Diophantus, the sophist who instructed the Arab students. It made little difference, as Libanius attended none of the lectures.

Christians of Antioch, the same city that laughed the stubborn and fanatical Emperor to scorn. The teacher operated in the realm of ideas, where a strong case for a humane Hellenism could be made; his protégé had unfortunately to transfer sentiment into action and perform the rites that were nostalgic in the telling but somehow outlandish and even comic in the doing.

The Julian who came to the throne in November of A.D. 361 had long been a convinced pagan, and once he passed from beneath the shadow of Constantius he asserted his conviction by word and deed, by law, subsidy and example.[23] Except on certain quite specific occasions there was no persecution of Christianity as such. Ecclesiastical exemptions were ended, Christians were removed from public office, subsidies were discontinued, and in general the association of the Roman state with Christian cult was sundered. Julian preferred to encourage his competitive version of Hellenism rather than to attempt to obliterate Christianity.

One of Julian's first moves was to proclaim an open and all-inclusive tolerance of religion in the Empire. As he probably intended, it was the signal for the suppressed animosity of decades to spill forth. When it became clear that the government would intervene only mildly or not at all, pagans began to pull down the Christians' churches, while in other places the no longer complacent Christians attacked newly opened temples. The Nicaeans, kept in close check by Constantius, fell upon their Arian opponents.[24] Though he saw little to admire in Judaism except its welfare program, Julian assiduously courted the Jews as a counterweight to the Christians; he actually began the reconstruction of the temple in Jerusalem until some unfavorable omens discouraged him. This was the background against which his own program unfolded.

If Julian was a visionary, his line of sight was directed con-

23. Julian, the most literary Emperor since Marcus Aurelius, left behind a considerable legacy of letters and orations, all highly interesting for the insight they provide into the philosophy and personality of this complicated man.

24. The murder of George of Cappadocia, the unpopular and ultra-Arian bishop of Alexandria, once again opened the way for Athanasius to return from exile to the see he had been forced to vacate in A.D. 356. Julian tolerated him for only eight months, and once again Athanasius resorted to the desert. He was restored by Jovian and once again exiled for four months by the Arian Valens. He died in A.D. 373.

sistently backward, to the theology of third-century Platonism, the political ideals of Plato and the Stoics, the moribund pieties of the Second Sophistic, and the extraordinary if unwitting accomplishment of Constantine in uniting state and Church. His only observance of the contemporary scene lay in his close attention to the Christian organization of that Church.

What Julian attempted was to play Aurelian in the guise of Constantine. Aurelian had sought to establish the worship of the Invincible Sun as the religion of his Empire, but in the manner of the third century could do little more than associate it with the Imperial cult and broadcast it through the normal channels of Imperial propaganda.[25] Its competitors were absorbed rather than dislodged. Perhaps Constantine had begun with some such ideal for Christianity, but the new absolutist creed resisted both rivals and fellows. The cult of the Sun, no matter what its origins, offered for Julian, as it had for Aurelian, an elaborate and spacious framework for the philosophical ideals of transcendental Platonism[26] and the Romanized version of Stoicism, which provided a model and a justification for the Empire. Christianity had just begun its flirtation with that same Platonism in the schools; and in the generation of Julian, the Church's political ideals still appeared profoundly anti-*polis* and anti-Empire. Julian ignored Origen and could see no Augustine on the horizon. Instead he beheld a suffering and bleeding God, disreputable and life-denying monks, theological warfare, and a value system that subverted, as Plotinus accused the Gnostics of doing, the carefully wrought system of values constructed by Hellenic humanism.

The sequel indicates that he saw something more. Julian intended to "establish" the cult of King Helios in somewhat the same fashion as Constantine had done with Christianity. The temples were reopened and refurbished in the style and decor of the churches; the old cults were reformed along lines suggested by the Christian liturgy, and they were served by a regular and hierarchical priesthood that Julian constantly exhorted to lead an impeccable and exemplary life. Julian railed against monks, but

---

25. See Chapter XVI, pp. 582–83.
26. Julian's Helios was, of course, a nonsensible, intelligible Sun, identified with the Platonic transcendental Good.

he fully understood the impressive accomplishments of a morally committed clergy.

Julian's analysis of the success of Christianity underlay his own program. His version of a Hellenic Church featured not only a clergy dedicated to more than the mere performance of rites, but a social-welfare program that had as its unmistakable model the one that had been in operation first among the Jews and then within Christianity since the early days in Jerusalem. With Constantine's financial support it had grown into a practical attempt to alleviate the social ills that Hellenism's political institutions had largely ignored for centuries. In Julian's version too the Hellenic clergy and the state were to cooperate in feeding the poor and dispossessed.

Closer still to the heart of the Christians' success, Julian reformed the Empire's educational system and took direct issue with the Christian appropriation of the Hellenic classics as a *praeparatio evangelica*. Christians were forbidden to teach in the state-subsidized public schools; all teachers were to be licensed by the municipal *curia* and verified by the Emperor; private schools were outlawed. The grounds for the exclusion of Christians from the schools were, in the light of Hellenism's own evolving view of its Homeric legacy, extraordinary: to teach the classical authors one had to subscribe to their values and particularly their religious beliefs; otherwise, "let them enter the Galilean churches and there study Matthew and Luke."[27]

Julian's position was highly reactionary. Both the Hellenic and the Christian intellectual were drawing together in the belief that in the classics there were humane values which transcended the antiquated Olympian machinery that had become an embarrassment in the sixth century before Christ. Julian's decree obviously excluded Christians from the schools, but short of the most flagrant hypocrisy it must needs have cast out most of the Hel-

---

27. There were other alternatives. Two Christians of Laodicea in Syria, a father and son both named Apollinaris, undertook to construct some Christian "classics." They rewrote the various parts of the Old Testament in the form of Homeric epic, Euripidean tragedy, Menandrian comedy and Pindaric ode. The New Testament they converted into Platonic dialogues. Julian must have died shortly after this extraordinary tour de force was completed and so their labors went for nought.

lenic intelligentsia as well. His intent was, however, clear enough: to force the Christians who wanted to follow the ordinary route to preferment in the Empire, that through the schools and the *enkyklios paideia,* to be subjected to a totally pagan indoctrination.

The shrewdness of Julian's insights was clouded by his almost complete lack of understanding. He had accurately measured the success of Christianity and perceived some of its weaknesses. Where he failed was in attempting to put in its place a body of practice and belief that was in many of its details faithful to Hellenism,[28] but was, for all that, a corpse. It was precisely that prior failure of much of what Julian attempted to resurrect that had opened the door to Christianity. Platonic theology was still a viable quantity, as Christianity was brilliantly to show, but the careful Stoic ethic was not, nor were the rituals that Julian obsessively encouraged and that must have appeared, even in the fourth century, like exotic curios from a remote past.

Upon it all lay the dead hand of Maximus the theurgist. The enlightened Julian, who was to restore the supremely rational Hellenism, was in the grip of the most flagrant of magicians, who inspired doubts even in the minds of some of his colleagues. "Superstitious rather than truly religious," was the verdict of one of Julian's more objective non-Christian contemporaries,[29] and Julian, whose fears are comprehensible enough in the light of his personal history, never shook his fascination with oracles, portents and dreams, paraded on public display before the mocking laughter of the citizens of Antioch.

From the moment of his arrival in the city, presumably a more appropriate setting for his reforms than the totally Christianized Constantinople, disaster dogged the Emperor's heels. At the

---

28. But like most of the contemporary intellectuals Julian suffered from the usual philorientalism and had nothing but praise for the wisdom of the Chaldeans and Egyptians.
29. The historian Ammianus Marcellinus (*c.* A.D. 330–391) who, though a Greek of Antioch, chose the unusual course of writing his *Res Gestae* in Latin as a continuation of Tacitus. The original work began with the accession of Nerva in A.D. 96 but the preserved books start at A.D. 353 and continue to A.D. 378. Together with the orations and letters of Julian and Libanius, Ammianus, who stood close to the events he describes, provides an almost unparalleled portrait of the mid-fourth century, richer in detail than any comparable period back to the age of Cicero.

annual feast of Apollo he hastened to the god's famous shrine in the suburb of Daphne to be greeted not, as he expected, by a large throng of devotees prepared for the traditional sacrifices, but by the solitary figure of Apollo's priest clutching one of his own geese. The incident set the tone for all that followed, and not even the prestigious figure of Libanius, who was called upon to lend support, could make the Emperor, who affected the beard and dress of a philosopher, a popular figure in Antioch.

At the very time when Julian was subsidizing the old rites in Antioch, the city was in the grip of a food shortage that produced an almost uncontrollable inflation. The lavish sacrifices sat ill with a populace hungry for grain, and the Imperial troops could scarcely restrain themselves until the end of the rites to wolf down the sacrificial meats.

Antioch was filled with troops during most of Julian's stay there—another source of discontent—in preparation for new campaigns against the Shah. The war was of Julian's own making, since in A.D. 362 Shapur sent a conciliatory letter suggesting a conference. Julian, who labored under the recurrent imperial incubus of Alexander the Great and Trajan, rejected the offer and persisted in his plans, which at this point were to sail down the Euphrates, join with his ally Arsaces, king of Armenia, and invest Ctesiphon. After the city was reduced, Julian planned to put on the Iranian throne Shapur's younger brother Ormizdas, who had fled from Iran to the West in the time of Constantine. In March of A.D. 363 all was prepared, but before he departed Antioch Julian addressed to its citizens a remarkable piece of self-mockery entitled *The Beard Hater* (*Misopogon*), in which he vented all his pent-up feelings of anger and frustration against the city that he had doubtless expected would hail him as its liberator from Christian tyranny but that regarded him instead as a curious and eccentric theologian with some dangerous economic ideas. Julian then gathered his Etruscan soothsayers and Syrian theurgists and left Antioch forever.

Julian did, indeed, reach Ctesiphon, but was unable to take the city. During the slow and dangerous withdrawal the Persian forces attacked from ambush, and in one such the unarmed Julian was wounded by an errant spear.[30] He slowly expired on June 26,

---

30. According to Libanius' version, Julian was assassinated by one of the Christians in his own army.

A.D. 363, attended by the Praetorian Prefect Sallustius[31] and in the midst of a discussion with the ever-present Maximus on the nobility of the soul.[32] He was thirty-two years old.

Julian was the last male of the house of Constantine and made no provision for a successor, and so at his death his senior officers met in conclave to select their own candidate. Their first choice was the elderly Praetorian Prefect Sallustius, a close associate of the Emperor and a Neoplatonist of a moderate type. He declined, and a compromise choice was the young officer Jovian, a Nicaean Christian who reigned just long enough to buy the army out of Persia and reestablish the religious *status quo ante*. Shapur's price for peace was now severe: the cession of the trans-Tigrine provinces won by Galerius and Diocletian, Sasanian occupation of the border fortresses of Nisibis and Singara and of eastern Armenia. In addition, Rome was to contribute to the defenses of the Caucasus passes against the Hunnish nomads already stirring in the south of Russia.

With Jovian Christianity returned to the Empire, but no longer under the aegis of Constantine and his heirs. New dynasties were in the wings, Christian, and eventually Nicaean.

---

31. A long-time friend of Julian and probably the author of the exemplary catechism of Neoplatonic theology called *On the Gods and the Universe*.

32. According to another, obviously tendentious account found in the Christian historians, Julian's final words were, "You have won, Galilean."

Epilogue:
The End of Paganism

If the Council of Nicaea was the harbinger of difficult days ahead, it was as well a triumphant symbol of the Church at home in its own house, dealing on its own terms with its own problems. The terror had passed, never to return. But as the program of Julian had made painfully clear, the conversion of Constantine did not mean the end of the old ways in religion, what the Imperial legislation called the *gentilicia superstitio*. Very few of the incredible variety of cults and beliefs followed in the Empire possessed much vitality in the fourth or fifth century, but the difference between a dying religion and a dead religion is considerable, and to achieve this latter, a constant ideal from the time of Theodosius (A.D. 379–395), increasingly stringent measures had to be taken. The ideal was, of course, the Church's, but it was shared and executed by the state. As the resources of the Roman state were once directed toward the extirpation of Christianity, so they were now turned against heretics and pagans.

The chief weapon in the long struggle against the nonbeliever was legislation, and law followed law down to the time of Justinian in the sixth century. The non-Christian was gradually stripped of his civil and legal rights. Nor was that all. The laws were accompanied by a series of practical measures, some official and others not, designed to blot out the last traces of the cult of the old gods. The mere number of these laws and their increasingly fierce execution suggests that the task was not a simple one. Who were these last tenacious adherents of an outworn creed? They probably reduced themselves to two classes: the professional pagan of the educated upper classes and the rural believer of the countryside, the *pagus,* whose inhabitants, the *pagani,* gave their name to the phenomenon.

The first class was considerably the smaller and more visible, and so, easier to contain. It included the old Roman aristocracy for whom *pietas* in the old style was a way of life and a symbol of solidarity with the Empire. The antiquarian rites, now merely curiosities, had to be performed for the sake of continuity and stability. The type of this late Roman pagan was Symmachus, the city prefect of Rome in A.D. 384–385 who, in the measured tones of the scion of a Senatorial family, pleaded with the Emperor Valentinian II for the restoration of the Altar of Victory to the Senate house. The altar was first removed in A.D. 357 by order of Constantius during his visit to Rome on the occasion of the twentieth anniversary of his rule. Julian naturally restored it, and the altar became the subject of a running debate between Symmachus and the bishop Ambrose at the Imperial court in Milan in the early eighties of the fourth century, when Gratian, the last Emperor to bear the title of Pontifex Maximus, had it removed again in A.D. 381.

Boethius later married into the same Senatorial family, and his own spirit stands not too remote from it: the aristocratic Roman caught between his conservative politics and his new religion. This Symmachan type of patriotic paganism could be dealt with easily enough, even though the methods of suppression may have excited inner qualms on the part of those charged with dismantling the huge and impressive structure of a millennial past. Here belief was tied irrevocably to public cultus; it served no end for the old-guard Senators to go underground, and so the closing of the temples and the legal abolition of the remnants of state cult necessarily marked the end.

Patriotic and historical paganism was a phenomenon to be found chiefly in Roman circles. In the East the old religion took another form, which is perhaps better designated as cultural paganism. This was not the reflection of the solidarity of Empire or of Romanism, but rather the last self-protective gesture of Hellenism. Neoplatonism provided its ideology and the accession of Julian its last desperate political hope. Traces lingered on into the fourth and fifth centuries. Libanius played his part in Julian's plans, and twenty years later he was still lobbying for the restoration of pagan cultus. Perhaps in the same year that Symmachus was making his appeal in Latin to Valentinian II, Libanius was addressing a similar plea in Greek to Theodosius who, for all his Catholic zeal, could resist on occasion the even fiercer determination of Ambrose. *For the Temples,* as Libanius' oration came to be known, struck the same low-key, somewhat sorrowful note as Symmachus' speech. But where Symmachus appealed to history, Libanius spoke for culture, the ancient Hellenism that Christianity was threatening to destroy.

Libanius' protestations had little effect in the partisan atmosphere of the late fourth century. In A.D. 391 Theodosius enacted, perhaps under pressure from the militant Ambrose, the first general edict forbidding sacrifice and closing the temples throughout the Empire, and he followed it in the next year with a law that made even private, non-Christian cultus illegal. This was the official attitude expressed through the normal legal channels, but even earlier crowds in the cities and the countryside took matters into their own hands and destroyed pagan temples, frequently with a great deal of bloodshed, since the temples also had their defenders. Probably the most spectacular of these incidents was the destruction, sometime about A.D. 390, of the great temple of Serapis in Alexandria. For the Egyptians it seemed like the end of an era, and indeed it was, and in more senses than one. Along with the temple, the crowds put to the torch the great library that had been gathered there since the days of the first Ptolemy.

Not all the temples were destroyed. Many were converted into churches, the Pantheon at Rome, for example, and the Athenian Parthenon, just as the Muslims later converted some of those same churches in Syria and Egypt into mosques. Some few even remained open for the benefit of the various non-Christian tribes on the frontiers, like the temple for the Nubians at Philae on the upper Nile which continued functioning until the time of Justinian (A.D. 527–565). But there was little else to show, at least in the public sector. The Olympic Games dragged on until A.D. 393, but thereafter the magnificent complex in the Peloponnesus was little more than another nostalgic way station in a generally bedraggled Greece poised at low ebb between the decline of its native Greek population and the sixth-century arrival of the Slavs and Avars.

But merely closing the temples was not enough. The *pagani* were dug in throughout the countryside, where the zealous Antiochene bishop John Chrysostom had to send expeditions to root them out. The difficulties here were immense, because the authorities were now dealing with a bedrock *private* practice. Justinian made one final and savage effort at suppressing the hideaways: in A.D. 528 a law was passed requiring every pagan to present himself and his family for baptism. A purge was carried on in Constantinople itself, and in A.D. 542 a monk of Amida, John, was commissioned to cleanse Asia of the recalcitrants. There were mass baptisms in his wake, and he seems to have accomplished his task. Against this, however, must be placed the evidence of a place like Carrhae-Harran, which flagrantly and notoriously harbored a community of pagans down into Islamic times.

The mountains and the countryside were not the only refuge for the non-Christian. The intellectual progeny of Libanius were still cultivating a kind of philosophical Hellenism through the fifth century at the university centers, particularly Alexandria and Antioch. Hypatia, the daughter of a mathematician and herself a mathematician and head of the Neoplatonic school at Alexandria, was murdered by a Christian mob there in A.D. 415, but the school managed to remain in operation right down to the eve of the Arab conquest, and with both Christian and non-Christian professors. Athens too had its Neoplatonist pagan professors: Plutarch, the son of an Eleusinian hierophant; Proclus, whose favorite reading was the *Chaldean Oracles;* Marinus, by birth a Samaritan; Damascius and Simplicius. In A.D. 529 Justinian forbade the teaching of philosophy at Athens. Damascius and Simplicius and some other philosophers who were then in residence there migrated to Iran, where for a brief time they were in residence at the court of the Sasanian Shah.

The Jews of the Empire, unlike the pagans, survived, though they too were subjected to ever fiercer pressures. Judaism, for all its problems under the Romans, had a privileged status in the Empire that neither the wars of Vespasian nor those of Hadrian materially altered. They did not have to share in the Imperial cultus and were exempt from military duties and other civil responsibilities. Conversion to Judaism was forbidden, but the Jewish community itself, widespread in the Mediterranean, suffered no overt hostility.

With the coming of a Christian Empire the atmosphere began to change. Under Theodosius the construction of new synagogues was expressly forbidden, as was intermarriage between

Christian and Jew. In the fourth century Jews apparently began entering public life in somewhat larger numbers than at any time since A.D. 135, and this movement provoked a new series of crippling edicts from A.D. 438 to 527 barring Jews from holding public posts or even from practicing the law. Finally, under Justin (A.D. 518–527), a Jew was juridically disabled for the performance of any legal act.

The eastern Jews eventually found respite under Islam, but the *pagani* had all but disappeared; the later Arab conquerors of Egypt and Syria were the inheritors of a culture that was remote from the old Hellenism. Its physical monuments still dotted the landscape, but the life within the body had been changed. The Muslim Arabs attacked neither a Seleucid or a Ptolemaic kingdom, nor the Roman Empire of Augustus or Hadrian, but the Byzantine state where the ghosts of those earlier polities had come to rest.

The successors of Julian ruled an eastern Empire where political traditions were still recognizably Roman, but whose religious ideals were Christian and whose language and culture were Hellenic. The *pagani* were not the last dispirited carriers of Hellenism in the *oikoumene*. Hidden in their peasant villages deep in the countryside, they knew nothing of Homer or Pericles or Aristotle; their crime was that they continued to worship their folk gods instead of the Christian High God. Long before the *pagani* disappeared, however, Hellenism had passed into Christianity and transformed it. Plato and Aristotle were alive within the Christian *paideia*.

The Christian Hellenism of the fourth century was very different from the Periclean version of more than eight hundred years earlier, but so too had been the Hellenism of the Second Sophistic under the Empire, of the Scipionic circle in the Roman Republic, of Herod in Palestine, of Antiochus IV Epiphanes in Syria, and of Ptolemy II Philadelphus and his scholars at the Museum. Christianity added neither God, scholasticism, nor eastern influences to Periclean Hellenism. Alexander, not Constantine, had created the *oikoumene*, and its other political architects, Seleucus I, Augustus, and Diocletian, were long dead. It was Trajan's fortresses that still held the eastern frontier against the Arabs.

The Stoics had first theologized the *kosmos*, and Aurelian, not Constantine, was its first God-king. Origen learned his theology from Platonists, and the Cappadocian Fathers their ethics and mysticism from the Stoics and Plotinus. Christian legal theory was Roman and so Stoic. Their odd theological manner of reading Homer and the poets came from the same sources, from the Stoic scholars of Pergamum via Philo, the Hellenized Jew of Alexandria. The Christian monk, whose life was commemorated in a Hellenic-style *bios*, still trailed his Cynic antecedents, just as his Christian Emperor bore the imprint of Achaemenian Shah and Stoic *basileus*.

None of this would have been recognizable, perhaps, to a Pericles *redivivus*, but it was, nonetheless, his offspring. There were still those, even in the fourth Christian century, who struggled to see Homer whole across the haze of the centuries. They were few, however, and their scholarly instruments were too feeble to permit that integral resurrection of another, dead age that the archaeologists and philologists of the nineteenth century first accomplished. For the rest, they had to be content with an evolved but living version of Hellenism that saw Homer only across the rich distortion of their own past.

Central and Western Asia
During the Greco-Roman Period
B.C. 338 to 393 A.D.

B.C.

338: Philip defeats Greek coalition at Chaeronea; death of Shah Artaxerxes III; Xenocrates succeeds Speusippus as head of Academy

337: Congress at Corinth; organization of Philip's Greek League

336: Philip's advance forces cross into Asia; assassination of Philip and accession of Alexander as King of Macedonia

335–330: DARIUS III, Shah of Iran

335: Aristotle returns to Athens from Macedonia, founds Lyceum

334: Alexander crosses Hellespont; battle of the Granicus

333: Battle of Issus

332: Fall of Tyre; conquest of Egypt and foundation of Alexandria

331: Battle of Gaugamela; Alexander winters at Susa and Persepolis; insurrection of Agis III at Sparta

330: Pursuit and death of Darius; at Athens, Demosthenes' speech "On the Crown"

329: Campaigns near Kabul; crossing of Oxus and campaigns in Sogdiana

328–327: Bactria; execution of Cleitus and conspiracy of the pages

326: Alexander descends to India; Porus; mutinies and beginning of return; fall of Lycurgus' government at Athens

325–324:   Land and sea return to Susa; flight of Harpalus and exile of Demosthenes; death of Cynic Diogenes

323:   Death of Alexander; uprisings at Athens repressed by Antipater, suicide of Demosthenes; establishment of regency for Alexander's sons

322:   Death of Aristotle; Theophrastus head of Peripatetic school

321:   Dramatic debut of Menander at Athens; Perdiccas attempts to seize Egypt from Ptolemy, repulsed and murdered

319:   Death of regent Antipater

318–317:   Antigonus unites holdings in Asia; Demetrius of Phalerum Cassander's governor at Athens

316:   Cassander executes Olympias and gains control of Macedonia

315:   Beginnings of Mauryan Empire: Chandragupta

314:   Death of Xenocrates

312:   Battle of Gaza; bid of Antigonus and his son Demetrius for Asian domination foiled

311:   Seleucus restored as satrap of Babylon

310–308:   Ptolemy on prowl in Aegean; Seleucus in India

310:   Zeno arrives at Athens

307:   Demetrius Poliorcetes liberates Athens from Cassander and Demetrius of Phalerum; Epicurus opens school there; Antigonus' inconclusive attempt against Egypt

306–305:   Alexander's successors assume royal titles

305:   Demetrius Poliorcetes takes Rhodes after spectacular siege

302–291:   Voyages of Megasthenes

301:   Battle of Ipsus, death of Antigonus and flight of Demetrius; Lysimachus ruler of Anatolia (301–281) and Seleucus gains northern Syria; Duris of Samos

300:   Beginning of Stoic school at Athens; founding of Antioch; Seleucus campaigns in East; construction of Great Wall of China

298:   Death of Cassander; struggle for succession in Macedon

297:   Accession of Pyrrhus in Epirus

294:   Demetrius Poliorcetes establishes himself as King of Macedonia; organization of Museum and Library at Alexandria by Demetrius of Phalerum

292:   Death of Menander; Seleucus associates his son Antiochus in his rule

291: Romans complete conquest of Samnites in Italy
290: Aetolians occupy Delphi
288: Joint invasion of Macedonia by Lysimachus and Pyrrhus; Ptolemy harasses Demetrius' governors at Athens and Corinth
287: Landing of Demetrius at Miletus; death of Theophrastus and succession of Strato as head of Lyceum (to 270); birth of Archimedes
285: Greatest extent of kingdom of Lysimachus in Macedonia, Thrace and Anatolia; death of Cynic Crates of Thebes; Ptolemy adopts Berenice's son and associates him in his rule as Ptolemy II
283: Death of Ptolemy I and Demetrius Poliorcetes
283–246: PTOLEMY II PHILADELPHUS: Callimachus, Theocritus
283–239: ANTIGONUS GONATAS of Macedonia
281: Battle of Corupedion: Seleucus defeats Lysimachus and occupies Anatolia; assassination of Seleucus by Ptolemy Ceraunus
281–261: ANTIOCHUS I SOTER: Berossus of Babylon; Aratus' *Phaenomena*
280: Pyrrhus of Epirus intervenes in Italian politics (driven out in 274); Ptolemy II proclaims divinity of his father and mother
279: Galatians fall upon Macedonia, defeat and kill Ceraunus
277: Gonatas defeats Galatians in Thrace
276: Perseus, Menedemus, Bion and Aratus at Gonatas' court at Pella
275: Antiochus defeats Galatians in Anatolia; Ptolemy II repudiates his wife and marries his sister Arsinoë
274: Antiochus opens campaign against Ptolemaic holdings in Coele-Syria
272: Pyrrhus invades Peloponnesus and is killed
271: Ptolemy II proclaims his own and his sister's divinity
269–232: ASHOKA, Mauryan Emperor
268–241: Arcesilaus head of skeptical Academy
267–261: Chremonidean War between Athens and Gonatas
265: Death of King Areus of Sparta
264–241: First Carthaginian War of Rome
264: Death of Zeno; Cleanthes heads Stoa
263: Death of Philetaerus of Pergamum; accession of Eumenes
261–241: EUMENES I of Pergamum
261–246: ANTIOCHUS II THEOS

261: Gonatas starves Athens into submission; Ashoka converted to Buddhism

c. 260: Apollonius of Rhodes becomes chief librarian at Alexandria; death of historian Timaeus

259: Gonatas' fleet defeats Ptolemy II off Cos

255: Ptolemy II concludes peace with Antiochus II and is forced to cede Ionia, Cilicia and Aegean islands; death of Bion of Borysthenes

252: Antiochus II repudiates Laodice and marries Ptolemy's daughter Berenice

c. 250: Appearance of Parthians of eastern steppe; Diodotus of Bactria proclaims independence of Seleucids

246–221: PTOLEMY III EUERGETES (I); Eratosthenes chief librarian at Alexandria

246–226: SELEUCUS II CALLINICUS: struggle of Laodice and Berenice for possession of Syria; Ptolemy III occupies Antioch

245: Aratus captain of Achaean League; death of poet Aratus; Gonatas defeats Ptolemy III off Andros

244–241: Agis IV's reforms at Sparta

243: Achaeans liberate Corinth from grasp of Gonatas

241: Reaction at Sparta; exile and death of Agis IV

241–197: ATTALUS I of Pergamum

c. 240: Death of Callimachus

239: Death of Antigonus Gonatas, succession of Demetrius II in Macedonia

239–229: DEMETRIUS II of Macedonia

238: Seleucus III defeats his seditious brother Hierax near Ancyra; Galatians roam Anatolia

232–206: Chrysippus head of Stoa

230: Alliance of Pergamum and Rome; Pergamenes check Galatians in Caicus valley, drive Hierax from Anatolia; Seleucus campaigns against Parthians in East

229–221: ANTIGONUS DOSON of Macedonia

227: Reforms of Cleomenes III at Sparta

226–223: SELEUCUS III SOTER

225: Ariston of Ceos becomes head of Peripatetic school

223: Doson reconstitutes Hellenic League

223–187: ANTIOCHUS III "THE GREAT"

222: Doson and Aratus crush Cleomenes at Sellasia, occupy Sparta

221–205: PTOLEMY IV EUPATOR

221–179: PHILIP IV of Macedonia

220–219: Antiochus III puts down insurrection in Babylon

219–218: Antiochus retakes Seleucia Pieria and Phoenicia from Egypt

219–201: Second Carthaginian War of Rome (Hannibal in Italy; Cannae, Trasimene)

217: Battle of Raphia: Ptolemy repulses Antiochus from Egypt; Philip represses Aetolian League

217–214: Antiochus puts down insurrection of Achaeus in Anatolia

215: Alliance of Hannibal and Philip IV against Rome; career of Roman comedian Plautus

214–129: Carneades, head of Academy

212–204: Antiochus' eastern *anabasis* exacts tribute from Parthians and confirms Euthydemus in Bactria

212: Death of Archimedes in Roman siege of Syracuse

205: Death of Chrysippus

204: Introduction of cult of *Magna Mater* at Rome

203: Fall of regents Arsinoë, Sosibius and Agathocles in Egypt

203–181: PTOLEMY V EPIPHANES

200: At behest of Rhodes and Pergamum Rome issues ultimatum to Philip V; Antiochus III defeats Egyptian army under Scopas at Panium; final Seleucid occupation of Coele-Syria; careers of Euclid and Apollonius of Perge

198: Antiochus dislodges Ptolemaic faction from Jerusalem, occupies Lysimachia in Thrace

197–159: EUMENES II of Pergamum

197: Romans defeat Philip V at Cynoscephalae

196: Flaminius proclaims liberation of Greece at Corinth; inscription of Rosetta stone

192: Antiochus III lands in Greece at request of Aetolians

191: Romans defeat Antiochus at Thermopylae

190: Scipio Africanus pursues Antiochus into Asia and defeats Seleucid army at Magnesia

189: Death of Euthydemus in Bactria; succession of his son Demetrius; Achaeans and revolutionary regime at Sparta

188: By treaty of Apamea Seleucids relinquish claims in Anatolia; expansion of Pergamum; future Antiochus IV hostage at Rome

187–178: SELEUCUS IV

184: Demetrius invades India; death of Plautus

c. 183: Suicide of Hannibal

181: Ptolemy V poisoned; regency of his widow Cleopatra I (to 173)

c. 180:	*Wisdom of Jesus bar Sirach*
179–167:	PERSEUS of Macedonia
175–164:	ANTIOCHUS IV EPIPHANES
175–172:	Jason High Priest in Jerusalem
174:	Yüeh-chih in Sogdia
173–145:	PTOLEMY VI PHILOMETOR: Aristarchus of Samothrace
172:	Jerusalem converted to *polis* status; Menelaus High Priest
171–138:	MITHRIDATES I of Parthia
170:	Egypt attempts to retake Coele-Syria; Antiochus IV counter attacks, takes Memphis and captures Ptolemy VI
169–116:	PTOLEMY VII EUERGETES (II) in Cyrenaica to 145, then Egypt
169–168:	Antiochus despoils temple treasury at Jerusalem; fighting in Palestine; rise of Nabataeans
168:	Romans destroy Macedonian army at Pydna; Roman ultimatum forces Antiochus to evacuate Egypt; Stoic Crates at Rome
167:	Antiochus IV abrogates Mosaic Law in Palestine; Seleucid Eucratides sent against Demetrius in Bactria; Polybius and Perseus hostages in Rome
165–164:	Antiochus campaigns in Armenia; Lysias assumes command in Palestine; Menander checks Eucratides in India
164:	Maccabees seize Jerusalem and purify temple
163–162:	ANTIOCHUS V of Syria
162–150:	DEMETRIUS I SOTER of Syria
161:	Demetrius I regains eastern provinces from Parthians; Hasidim accept Alcimus as High Priest; Maccabees continue guerrilla warfare in Palestine
159–138:	ATTALUS II of Pergamum
159:	Eucratides destroyed by Parthians
155:	Embassy to Rome of philosophers Carneades, Diogenes of Seleucia, and Critolaus
153:	Balas, Seleucid pretender, lands at Ptolemais with Egyptian and Pergamene support
152:	Jonathan accepts High Priesthood from Balas
150:	Demetrius I trapped and killed by Balas' forces; *Letter of Aristeas;* career of rhetorician Hermagoras
150–145:	BALAS of Syria
149:	*Lex Calpurnia* sets up special courts at Rome to try cases of extortion

147–145: Ptolemy VI once again intervenes in Syria, killed near Antioch, replaced in Egypt by his brother Ptolemy VII; appearance of Demetrius II in Syria, receives Egyptian support and destroys Balas

146: Romans destroy Carthage and Corinth

145: DEMETRIUS II of Syria

142: Death of Jonathan; Seleucids recognize autonomy of Judaea under his brother Simon

140–70: MELEAGER of Gadara

140: Great Assembly in Jerusalem recognizes Simon as King and High Priest; separation of Essenes

140–130: SIMON of Judaea

139: Demetrius II campaigns against Parthians and is captured

139–128: ANTIOCHUS VII SIDETES of Syria

138–133: ATTALUS III of Pergamum

135: Assassination of Simon the High Priest; Seleucids reoccupy Jerusalem; Panaetius teaching at Rome

134–105: JOHN HYRCANUS of Judaea; opposition of Pharisees; composition of I *Maccabees;* community at Qumran

133: Death of Attalus III and Rome's inheritance of his kingdom; resistance of his half brother Andronicus (132–130)

131: Euergetes II forced to flee Egypt under pressure from his wife, Cleopatra II

130: Sacae overrun Greeks in Bactria

129: Death of Antiochus VII on campaign against Parthians in East; return of Demetrius II; death of Phraates II of Parthia at hands of Sacae; Roman constitutional organization of province of Asia

128–125: DEMETRIUS II of Syria

128: Chinese embassy to Central Asia

126: Euergetes II restored in Egypt; death of astronomer Hipparchus of Nicaea

125: Parthians sack and burn Babylon

123: Death of Artabanus II of Parthia fighting Sacae

123–86: MITHRIDATES II "THE GREAT" of Parthia

121–63: MITHRIDATES VI EUPATOR of Pontus

c. 120: Yüeh-chih enter Bactria at heels of Sacae; death of historian Polybius

120–119: Mucius Scaevola Roman governor of Asia

120–110: Panaetius head of Stoa

116–27: Varro

104–103: ARISTOBULUS of Judaea

103–76: ALEXANDER JANNAEUS of Judaea

94-92: Mucius Scaevola the younger, Roman governor of Asia

92: Sulla arrives in East to clear Cappadocia

90-55: Lucretius

90: Revolt of Pharisees against Jannaeus

88: Asia rises up against Romans; Mithridates invades Greece

87-62: ARETAS (HARITH) King of Nabataeans

87-86: Sulla clears Greece of Pontic forces

85-84: Sulla imposes indemnity on province of Asia

85-69: Antiochus of Ascalon; height of philosophical eclecticism

83: Tigranes of Armenia occupies Seleucid holdings in Syria; forced by Romans to withdraw

82: Sulla restores Senatorial control of courts; death of Pontifex Scaevola

80-51: PTOLEMY XI AULETES

80: Verres and Dolabella in East

78: Romans annex Lycia and Isauria; Cicero attends lectures of Posidonius on Rhodes and Antiochus at Athens

76-67: ALEXANDRA SALOME of Judaea; her sons Hyrcanus and Aristobulus struggle for High Priesthood, ascendancy of Idumaean Antipater

74: Romans incorporate Cyrenaica as a province; death of Nicomedes of Bithynia; Romans inherit his kingdom; Lucullus arrives in East to clear Cilicia

74-72: Mithridates Eupator and Tigranes of Armenia overrun Cappadocia; driven off by Lucullus

72-71: Gladiatorial insurrection in Italy

70: *Lex Aurelia:* Equestrians regain control of courts; Pompey and Crassus Consuls; career of Andronicus of Rhodes, editor of Aristotle

69: Lucullus invades Armenia

67: *Lex Gabinia* granting command against Cilician pirates to Pompey; introduction of cult of Mithra to Rome

66: *Lex Manilia:* Pompey replaces Lucullus in command against Mithridates, campaigns in Pontus and Armenia

64: Pompey annexes Cilicia and Syria; birth of Nicholas of Damascus

63: Death of Mithridates in Crimea; Pompey confirms Hyrcanus as High Priest and Judaea placed under control of Roman Propraetors; Consular year of Cicero

60: First triumvirate: Pompey, Caesar, Crassus

59: Caesar Consul, then takes up command in Gaul

58: Nigidius Figulus Praetor

57–37: ORODES of Parthia

57–55: Gabinius governor of Syria; attempts to restore Ptolemy XI in Egypt; revolts in Judaea

55: Trial and conviction of Gabinius; Pompey and Crassus Consuls; Crassus takes up governorship of Syria

53: Parthians destroy Crassus and Roman army at Carrhae (Harran)

51: Cicero governor of Cilicia; death of Ptolemy XI, succeeded by Cleopatra VII and Ptolemy XII

48: Caesar defeats Pompey at Pharsalus in Thessaly; Pompey flees to Egypt, Caesar pursues

46–44: Death of Pompey; marriage of Caesar and Cleopatra VII; campaigns against Pharnaces in Pontus

44: Assassination of Caesar

43: Death of Antipater the Idumaean

42: Second triumvirate of Octavian, Antony and Lepidus prevail over Brutus and Cassius at Philippi

41: Antony in Asia; Parthians invade Palestine and depose Hyrcanus

40: Triumvirs consolidate gains: Antony given eastern provinces, marries Octavia; birth of Alexander Helios and Cleopatra Selene; Herod confirmed as King of Judaea

39–38: Antony clears Parthians from eastern provinces

37: Antony marries Cleopatra VII

36–32: Antony campaigns against Parthians; repudiates Octavia; breaks with Octavian

31: Octavian defeats Antony and Cleopatra at Actium; Egypt absorbed as Roman province (30)

27: Strabo in Rome

27: Senate confirms Octavian as Augustus with a ten-year *imperium* over Spain, Gaul and Syria; death of Varro

26: Death of erotic elegist Gallus

25: Expedition of Aelius Gallus in Arabia, accompanied by Strabo

23: Augustus granted *imperium maius*

23–21: Marcus Agrippa administers eastern provinces for Augustus

21–19: Augustus' visitation of the East

20: Augustus negotiates return of standards lost to Parthians at Carrhae
17–13: Agrippa in East; consultations with Herod and Nicholas of Damascus
13: Death of Marcus Agrippa
c. 7: Birth of Jesus
6: Execution of Herod's sons Alexander and Aristobulus
4: Death of Herod; Archelaus ethnarch of Judaea, Antipas tetrarch of Galilee and Peraea; activity of Zealot Judah

A.D.

1: Augustus' grandson Gaius' *imperium* in East
2: Death of Augustus' second grandson Lucius
6: Deposition and exile of Archelaus; creation of Roman province of Judaea; census of Quirinus
12–38: ARTABANUS III of Parthia
14: Death of Augustus; accession of Tiberius; absorption of eastern client kings
14–37: PRINCIPATE OF TIBERIUS
16–18: Germanicus' negotiations with Artabanus on Armenian question
19: Death of geographer Strabo; scandal of Isiac priesthood at Rome
26–36: Pontius Pilate Procurator of Judaea
28: Arrest and crucifixion of Jesus
34–35: Artabanus III contests succession in Armenia; embassy of Vitellius
34: Execution of Stephen in Jerusalem
37–41: PRINCIPATE OF GAIUS; visit of Agrippa I to Alexandria and disturbances there
39: Demonstrations against Gaius in Judaea
40: Anti-Jewish riots in Antioch
41–54: PRINCIPATE OF CLAUDIUS
41: Judaea reverts to kingdom; Agrippa I confirmed as king (to 44)
44: Judaea restored to procuratorial control; Tiberius Alexander Procurator (46–48)
46: Death of Philo of Alexandria
50–64: Letters of Paul
51–80: VOLOGESUS I of Parthia; Iranization of policy of the Shahs; edition of the *Gathas* of the *Avesta*
54–69: PRINCIPATE OF NERO; careers of Cornutus and Apollonius of Tyana
54–66: Repression of Judaean guerrillas

58–60: Roman invasion of Armenia to prevent the accession of Vologesus' brother there

59: Death of Agrippina

62: Arrest and execution of James, head of Christian community in Jerusalem; composition of *Acts of the Apostles*

64: Josephus pleads Jewish interests before Nero at Rome; persecution of Christians there; death of Peter and Paul; Pontus becomes Roman province

65: Fall of Seneca and Lucan

66: Nero's banishment of opposition; Romans accept Herodian Tiridates IV as King of Armenia; Roman army in Palestine to repress insurrection, defeated

66–67 Nero on concert tour of Greece; Vespasian dispatched to pacify Palestine; redaction of Gospel of Mark

68–70: Christians withdraw from Jerusalem to the Transjordan; destruction of Qumran; Vespasian invests Jerusalem

69: Death of Nero and disorders in Rome; Vespasian delegates Jewish War to his son Titus and is proclaimed Emperor

69–70: PRINCIPATE OF VESPASIAN

70: Fall of Jerusalem to Titus; Vespasian imposes special tax on Jews; Jewish synod at Jabneh

71: Vespasian banishes philosophers from Italy

75: Josephus' *Jewish Wars;* Romans secure southern passes of Caucasus

75–102: Chinese protectorate of Tarim basin

79–81: PRINCIPATE OF TITUS

81–96: PRINCIPATE OF DOMITIAN

85: Schism of Hinayana and Mahayana Buddhism

89–93: Domitian's measures against philosophers; banishment of Epictetus and Dio of Prusa

93–94: Josephus' *Jewish Antiquities*

95–175: Flavius Arrian

96–98: PRINCIPATE OF NERVA, rescinds Vespasian's *fiscus Judaicus*

98–117: PRINCIPATE OF TRAJAN

100: Earliest date for Gospel of John; Kushans occupy eastern provinces of Parthian Empire

101–177: Herodes Atticus

102: Death of Josephus

106: *Arabia Petraea* of Nabataeans erected into Roman province of Arabia

109–128: OSRHOES of Parthia
110–111: Correspondence of Trajan and Pliny on Christians in Bithynia
114: Roman annexation of Armenia; invasion and annexation of Mesopotamia
115: Trajan takes Ctesiphon and annexes Adiabene
115–117: Jewish revolts in Cyrenaica, Egypt and Cyprus
116: Death of Ignatius of Antioch
117–128: PRINCIPATE OF HADRIAN; activity of Christian Gnostics in Egypt
c. 120: Roman commercial mission of Maes Titianus reaches Kashgar; death of Plutarch; birth of Galen and Lucian; spread of Mahayana Buddhism into central Asia; oldest papyrus (P52) of New Testament
129–189: Aelius Aristides
130: Hadrian founds Aelia Capitolina on site of Jerusalem; death of his favorite Antinoüs; conversion of Justin to Christianity
132–135: Holy War of Bar Kokhba in Palestine
135: Crushing of Jewish revolt; anti-Jewish legislation of Hadrian
138–161: PRINCIPATE OF ANTONINUS PIUS
138: Marcion arrives in Rome
144–175: KANISHKA King of Kushans
144: Condemnation of Marcion by Roman Church
c. 150: Careers of Alexander of Abonoteichus and Nicomachus of Gerasa; birth of Clement of Alexandria; Christian community at Edessa
155: Death of Polycarp of Smyrna
c. 155–235: Dio Cassius
156: Aelius Aristides at Rome
c. 160: First Buddhist missionaries arrive in China
161–180: PRINCIPATES OF MARCUS AURELIUS and LUCIUS VERUS; edition of the *Chaldean Oracles*
165–166: Roman War against Parthia, fall of Ctesiphon; beginnings of plague in Empire
166: Roman commercial mission reaches China by sea
169: Death of Lucius Verus
c. 170: Conversion of Montanus to Christianity; Tatian's *Diatessaron*
172–173: Peasant revolt in Egypt
175: Insurrection of Avidius Cassius
176: Marcus Aurelius founds chairs of philosophy at Rome
177: Investiture of Marcus Aurelius' son Commodus as co-ruler with his father

249–251: PRINCIPATE OF DECIUS; major persecution against Christians; Egyptian Christians flee to desert
251: Beginning of Sasanian invasion; plague in Empire
253–260: PRINCIPATES OF VALERIAN and GALLIENUS
253: Death of Origen
256: Sasanians take Antioch, carry off captives
257: Persecution of Christians
258: Valerian divides eastern and western commands
260: Sasanians invade Syria; capture of Valerian; foundation of Jundeshapur; career of Kartir, *mobadhan mobadh* of Iran
c. 260–330: Iamblichus
260–268: PRINCIPATE OF GALLIENUS; rescinds edicts against Christians and restores confiscated property; Paul of Samosata, bishop of Antioch
260–262: Odenath of Palmyra restores Roman position in East
262: Porphyry joins Plotinus' circle at Rome
263–270: Goths in Greece and Asia
264–340: Historian Eusebius of Caesarea
267: Assassination of Odenath; Wabhallath demands his father's titles
268: Church of Antioch deposes Paul of Samosata; Longinus joins court of Zenobia
270: Death of Plotinus; Wabhallath and his mother Zenobia assume royal titles at Palmyra; Anthony takes up monastic life in Egypt; career of mathematician Diophantus of Alexandria
271: Palmyrene troops overrun Egypt, Syria and parts of Anatolia
271–275: PRINCIPATE OF AURELIAN
272: Aurelian defeats and captures Zenobia near Antioch; execution of Longinus
272–273: ORMIZD, Shah of Iran; ascendancy of Kartir at court
273–276: BAHRAM I, Shah of Iran
277: Execution of Mani
284–305: PRINCIPATE OF DIOCLETIAN
290: Diocletian crushes bedouin revolt in Syria and Arabia
293–302: NARSEH, Shah of Iran
293: Tetrarchy established
296–373: Athanasius of Alexandria
296: Insurrection in Egypt; Manichaean activity there; Sasanians occupy Armenia and invade Syria
297: Galerius overwhelms Sasanians in Armenia, takes Ctesiphon; Romans regain Mesopotamia and Adiabene

301: Porphyry publishes *Enneads* and *Life of Plotinus;* Diocletian's edict on prices
302-309: ORMIZD II, Shah of Iran
303: Roman Imperial edict against Christians; persecutions
305: Abdication of Diocletian and Maximian; Caesars Constantius and Galerius promoted to Augusti
306: Death of Constantius; his troops proclaim his son Constantine Caesar
309-379: SHAPUR II, Shah of Iran; destruction of the Kushans
311: Galerius rescinds edict against the Christians and publishes edict of toleration; Maximin Daia, eastern Caesar, proclaims himself Augustus and continues persecutions; death of Methodius of Olympus
312: Constantine defeats Maxentius at battle of Milvian Bridge under banner of Christianity; death of Lucian of Antioch
312-324: PRINCIPATES OF CONSTANTINE and LICINIUS
313: Death of Diocletian; Licinius defeats Maximin Daia at Adrianople; Licinius now eastern Augustus, re-promulgates edict of toleration
314-393: Libanius
318: Pachomius founds first cenobitic community of monks in Egypt
318-320: Abrogation of Augustus' laws against celibacy; haruspicy and magic banned; Sunday rest imposed
321: Arius preaching at Alexandria
324: Defeat of Licinius near Adrianople; Constantine sole Emperor
324-337: PRINCIPATE OF CONSTANTINE
325: First Ecumenical Council of Nicaea
326: Execution of Crispus and Fausta
328: Athenasius succeeds Alexander as bishop of Alexandria
330: Dedication of Constantinople; death of Iamblichus
330-379: Basil of Caesarea
330-391: Ammianus Marcellinus
330-390: Gregory of Nazianzus
334: Sasanian troops reoccupy Armenia
335: Synod of Tyre hears charges against Athanasius, who is exiled to Gaul
336: Marcellus of Ancyra deposed and exiled; death of Arius
337: Baptism and death of Constantine; massacre of collateral branches of Imperial family
337-340: PRINCIPATES OF CONSTANS, CONSTANTIUS and CON-

379–395: PRINCIPATE OF THEODOSIUS
380: Theodosius establishes Nicaean Christianity as the religion of the Empire; the *Apostolic Constitution*
381: Second Ecumenical Council of Constantinople; Emperor abandons title of Pontifex Maximus
384–385: Symmachus City Prefect at Rome
c. 390: Burning of Serapeum at Alexandria
391: Wide edicts against pagan worship; death of Ammianus Marcellinus
393: Last celebration of Olympic Games

A Guide to
Some Further Reading

What follows is not a bibliography in the usual sense. An exhaustive survey of the literature is obviously out of the question, and so I have attempted to be helpful in lieu of being complete and to avoid the middle ground of a perfunctory list of titles. The emphasis is on more recent work, but I have not hesitated to reach farther back for something fundamental or interesting. Books and articles in languages other than English have been cited on the same principle. Finally, I have designedly been dense where standard history books are thin on bibliography: on the eastern material, later Greek philosophy, and non-Christian religions. There is no need to rehearse titles on Roman history and the Gospels, and I have not done so.

ALEXANDER

Note has already been made in the text of the two major Alexander sources, Plutarch (pp. 55–56) and Arrian (p. 407), but the eyewitness memoirs filtered down into other historians as well. They have been evaluated in Alexander's major interpreter in English, W. W. Tarn, *Alexander the Great*, 2 vols. (1948; r-p. 1956). The personality of Alexander is very much an open question, but Tarn's views on his ideology, and particularly Alexander's commitment to a theory of the "unity of mankind," have been carefully scrutinized and criticized by E. Badian, "Alexander the Great and the Unity of Mankind," *Historia* VII (1958), pp. 425–444, and R. Andreotti, "Die Weltmonarchie Alexanders des Grossen in Überlieferung und geschichtlicher Wirklichkeit," *Saeculum* VII (1957), pp. 120–166, the latter with a full bibliography. For further orientation the reader should consult G. T. Griffith, ed., *Alexander the Great: The Main Problems* (1966).

PRIMARY HELLENISTIC SOURCES

For the world created by Alexander the major literary source is the *Ecumenical History* of Polybius (p. 400), whose focus was chiefly Greece but who knew the *oikoumene* and its workings. The preserved sections of his work reach from B.C. 221 and have received detailed explication in F. Walbank, *A Historical Commentary on Polybius,* 3 vols. (1957–1968). For the earlier period there is only the Greek compilation of Diodorus of Sicily, whose account of the years B.C. 323–302 did, however, draw from the work of a major contemporary historian, Hieronymus of Cardia (p. 90). Other, lost parts of Polybius were a major source for the account of Greek affairs in the preserved sections of Livy, where we can follow events from B.C. 220 to 167. A number of Plutarch's biographies of both Greek and Latin leaders of the *oikoumene* fill in some of the gaps.

NONLITERARY SOURCES

None of these authors showed a great deal of interest in the internal affairs of the eastern kingdoms, and here the work of historical reconstruction rests more heavily upon archaeology, the evidence of inscriptions, papyri and coins. These latter have been published and studied in a number of places, including, most importantly, W. Dittenberger, *Orientis Graeci Inscriptiones Selectae,* 2 vols. (1903–1905); H. Mitteis and U. Wilcken, *Grundzüge und Chrestomathie der Papyruskunde,* 4 vols. (1912); and C. Seltmann, *Greek Coins. A History of Metallic Currency and Coinage down to the Fall of the Hellenistic Kingdoms*[2] (1955).

THE OIKOUMENE

The material on the Hellenistic *oikoumene* has been collected, sifted and evaluated in Vols. VI, VII and VIII of the *Cambridge Ancient History,* and in M. Rostovtzeff, *The Social and Economic History of the Hellenistic World,*[2] 3 vols. (1959); M. Cary, *Greek World from 323 to 146 B.C.,*[2] (1951; r-p. 1963); P. Jouguet, *L'Impérialisme macédonien et l'hellénisation de l'Orient* (1961); E. Will, *Histoire politique du monde hellénistique,* 2 vols. (1966–1967).

POLITICAL FORMS

The period was an important one for political innovation, and attention has been concentrated on some of the new forms: V. Tcherikover, *Die hellenistischen Städtegrundungen* (1927); H. Bengston, *Die Strategie in der hellenistischen Zeit*, 3 parts (1937–1952; r-p. 1964); A. H. M. Jones, *The Greek City from Alexander to Justinian* (1940; r-p. 1966); H. Hammond, *City-State and World-State in Greek and Roman Political Thought until Augustus* (1955); V. Ehrenberg, *The Greek State* (1960; r-p. 1964); and J. Larsen, *Greek Federal States* (1968).

THE MILITARY AND COMMERCE

Most Hellenistic states rested on the twin supports of their armies and commerce. Primary for the first is M. Launey, *Recherches sur les armées hellénistiques*, 2 vols. (1949–1950). The perspectives are narrower in W. W. Tarn, *Hellenistic Military and Naval Developments* (1930; r-p. 1966); G. T. Griffith, *The Mercenaries of the Greek World* (1935; r-p. 1968); and F. Adcock, *The Greek and Macedonian Art of War* (1957). Hellenistic travel and its commercial motivation has been studied within their general contexts in L. Casson, *The Ancient Mariners: Sea Farers and Sea Fighters in Ancient Times* (1959), and M. Cary and E. H. Warmington, *The Ancient Explorers* (1929; r-p. 1960).

EGYPT

Some, though not all, of Alexander's successor states have received individual treatment. For the earliest period there is P. Cloché, *La Dislocation d'un Empire: les premiers successeurs d'Alexandre le Grand* (1959). The evidence is best for Egypt, and its histories are the most complete. The older *Histoire des Lagides*, 4 vols. (1903–1907), by A. Bouché-Leclercq, and *A History of Egypt under the Ptolemaic Dynasty* (1927; r-p. 1968), by E. R. Bevan, are still sound but should be completed by C. Préaux, *L'Économie royale des Lagides* (1939). There is a more comprehensive but far less detailed treatment in H. I. Bell, *Egypt from Alexander the Great to the Arab Conquest* (1948).

THE SELEUCIDS

The Seleucids are surveyed in A. Bouché-Leclercq, *Histoire des Séleucids* (1913), and the important E. Bickerman, *Les Institutions des Séleucids* (1938). Their capital has received a detailed and fastidious treatment in G. Downey, *A History of Antioch in Syria from Seleucus to the Arab Conquest* (1961), and there are monographs on two of their most important monarchs: H. Schmitt, *Untersuchungen zur Geschichte Antiochus des Grossen und seiner Zeit* (1964), and O. Morkholm, *Antiochus IV of Syria* (1966).

BABYLON

Among the Seleucids' subjects the mathematical studies of O. Neugebauer, particularly his *The Exact Sciences in Antiquity*[2] (1957), have directed new attention to Seleucid Babylonia; E. Schmidt, "Die Griechen in Babylon und das Weiterleben ihren Kultur," *Jahrbuch des Deutschen Archaologischen Instituts* LVI (1941), pp. 786–844; W. Wetzel *et al.*, *Das Babylon der Spätzeit* (1957). On Berossus there is P. Schnabel, *Berossos* (1923).

BACTRIA

Farthest east Tarn pioneered the study of the Greeks in Bactria and India in a difficult historical reconstruction based almost solely on the evidence of their coinage: *The Greeks in Bactria and India*[2] (1951; r-p. 1966). Since then the evidence has been reexamined and reevaluated by A. K. Narain, *The Indo-Greeks* (1957); compare A. M. Simonetta, "A New Essay on the Indo-Greeks," *East and West* IX (1958), pp. 154 ff.

THE PARTHIANS

Beyond the Seleucid heartland lay the emerging empire of the Parthians, neighbors to both the Seleucids and Romans to the west, and the eventual buffer against the nomads after the fall of the Bactrian kingdoms in the east. The Parthian succession to the Seleucids is studied by J. Wolski, "The Decay of the Iranian Empire of the Seleucids and the Chronology of Parthian Beginnings," *Berytus* XII (1956–

1957), pp. 35–52. On Parthian history as a whole there is only N. Debevoise, *A Political History of Parthia* (1938), and for the language, A. Ghilain, *Essai sur la langue parthe* (1939). As a steppe people the Parthians left little archaeological trace. Their best-surveyed site was the former Greek colony of Dura-Europos. The remains have been published over three decades by Yale University, and the literary evidence gathered by C. B. Welles *et al.*, *The Excavations at Dura Europus, V: The Parchments and Papyri* (1959). The artistic evidence is weighed in M. Rostovtzeff, "Dura and the Problem of Parthian Art," *Yale Classical Studies* V (1935), pp. 155–304. Many of the other Parthian sites are currently within the borders of the Soviet Union and work there is reported in A. Mongait, *Archaeology in the U.S.S.R.* (1961).

The sum of what is currently known about the Parthians may be surveyed in the appropriate chapters of R. Ghirshman, *Iran* (1954; r-p. 1961), and R. N. Frye, *The Heritage of Persia* (1963; r-p 1966). For the views of the Sasanian historians and theologians, on whom the Iranian traditions concerning the Parthians depend, see below.

EASTERN IRANIANS

Apart from the Bactrian Greeks, the Parthians' eastern neighbors were, like themselves, Iranians and nomads. The Khwarazmians have left archaeological tracks in their delta culture south of the Aral Sea (see Mongait, cited above), but the traces of the Sogdians are chiefly linguistic, in most cases in the form of Manichaean Scriptures written in the Sogdian lingua franca of the steppe. For a general orientation there is R. N. Frye, "Soghd and the Soghdians," *Journal of the American Oriental Society* LXIII (1943), pp. 14–16, and M. J. Dresden, "Bibliographia soghdiana concisa," *Ex oriente lux* VIII (1942), pp. 729–734, and *Bibliotheca Orientalis* VI (1949), pp. 28–31. The Sogdian linguistic material is analyzed in I. Ghershevich, *A Grammar of Manichaean Sogdian* (1954).

SACAE AND KUSHANS

The problem of the Sacae/Yüeh-chih/Kushans is extremely complex. There is a survey in both G. Haloun, "Zu Ue-tsi Frage," *Zeitschrift der Deutschen Morgenlandischen Gesellschaft* XCI (1937), pp. 243–318, and O. Maenchen-Helfen, "The Yüeh-chih Problem Re-Examined," *Journal of the American Oriental Society* LXV (1945), pp. 71–82. On the Kushan period in India R. Ghirshman has resumed his earlier studies in "Le problème de la chronologie des Kouchans," *Journal of World History* III (1957), pp. 689–722, and other points of view are expressed in J. Marshall, "Greeks and Sacas in India," *Journal of the Royal Asiatic Society* (1947), pp. 3–32, and J. H. van Lohuizen-de Leeuw, The *"Scythian"* Period. *An Approach to the Art, Epigraphy, and Palaeography of Northern India from the 1st Century B.C. to the 3rd Century A.D.* (1949).

KANISHKA AND GANDHARA

On Kanishka and the related problem of Gandharan art, see A. Deydier, "La date de Kaniska, l'art du Gandhara, et la chronologie du Nord-Ouest de l'Inde," *Journal Asiatique* CCXXXIX (1951), pp. 135–152; A. Maricq, "La grande inscription de Kanishka," *ibid.* CCXLVI (1958), pp. 345–440; and, finally, D. Schlumberger, "Descendants non-méditerranéens de l'art grec," *Syria* XXXVII (1960), pp. 131–166, 253–319. Some of the illustrative material is easily available in T. Rice, *The Ancient Arts of Central Asia* (1965).

GREECE

Mainland Greece during the rule of the Successors receives full treatment in the general histories of Hellenistic times cited above. Attention may be called here to a number of special monographs: W. S. Ferguson, *Hellenistic Athens* (1911); W. W. Tarn, *Antigonus Gonatas* (1913; r-p. 1969); F. Walbank, *Aratos of Sicyon* (1933); *idem, Philip V of Macedon* (1940; r-p. 1967).

MINOR KINGDOMS

Among the minor kingdoms of Anatolia only Pergamum has received adequate historical treatment in recent times: E. V. Hansen, *The Attalids of Pergamum* (1947), and R. B. McShane, *The Foreign Policy of the Attalids of Pergamum* (1964). For Syria there is O. Eissfeldt, *Tempel und Kulte syrischer Städte in hellenistisch-romischer Zeit* (1941). The two chief Arab states, where the bulk of the evidence dates from Roman times, have been studied in A. Kammerer, *Petra et la Nabatène*, 2 vols. (1929–1930); and, for Palmyra, J. Starcky, *Palmyre* (1952), and I. A. Richmond, "Palmyra under the Aegis of the Romans," *Journal of Roman Studies* LIII (1963), pp. 43–54.

PALESTINIAN JUDAISM

Palestine stands alone, of course, in both evidence and the historical attention paid to events there. Both the Maccabees (pp. 263–64) and Josephus (pp. 404–5) present a continuous literary account of Jewish history under the Greeks and Romans, an account which must with difficulty be filled out from the apocryphal and pseudepigraphical literature edited and translated by R. H. Charles, *The Apocrypha and Pseudepigraphica of the Old Testament*, 2 vols. (1913). For the Maccabean period particular attention is called to two important works: E. Bickerman, *Der Gott der Makkabäer* (1937), and V. Tcherikover, *Hellenistic Civilization and the Jews* (1959). Two special studies have been devoted to Hellenism in Palestine: S. Libermann, *Greek in Jewish Palestine* (1942), and *idem, Hellenism in Jewish Palestine* (1950).

DIASPORA JUDAISM

The Judaism of the Diaspora forms an important part of Tcherikover's work already cited, and there is further material in H. I. Bell, *Jews and Christians in Egypt* (1924); L. Fuchs, *Die Juden Agyptens in ptolemäischer und römischer Zeit* (1924), E. Breccia, *Juifs et Chrétiens de l'ancienne Alexandrie* (1927). The same subject has been studied from an iconographical point of view in E. R. Goodenough, *Jewish Symbols in the Greco-Roman Period*, 11 vols. (1952–1964), with a great deal of evidence drawn from the Hellenistic synagogue at Dura Europos; *compare* E. J. Bickerman, "Symbolism in the Dura Synagogue," *Harvard Theological Review* LVIII (1965), pp. 127–151. There is now a full-scale treatment of the Jews in Babylonia: J. Neusner, *A History of the Jews in Babylonia*, 4 vols. to date (1965–1969), covering the Parthian and early Sasanian period.

ANTI-SEMITISM

The question of anti-Semitism is touched upon in many of the works already cited, but there are special studies as well: H. I. Bell, "Anti-Semitism in Alexandria," *Journal of Roman Studies* XXXI (1941), pp. 1–18, and R. Marcus, "Antisemitism in the Hellenistic World," in *Studies in Antisemitism*[2] (1946), pp. 61–78. For Philo, see below.

HELLENISTIC CULTURE

On the general culture of the Hellenistic age the best over-all view is provided in the various chapters of W. W. Tarn, *Hellenistic Civilization*[3] (1952), and M. Hadas, *Hellenistic Culture. Fusion and Diffusion* (1959). The academic base is described in H. I. Marrou, *History of Education in Antiquity*[3] (1956), and the work of the literary establishment is now traced in R. Pfeiffer, *History of Classical Scholarship to the End of the Hellenistic Age* (1968). The standard survey of the literature is W. von Christ, W. Schmid and O. Stählin, *Geschichte der Griechischen Litteratur*, Part II: *Die Nachklassische Periode der Griechischen Literatur*,[6] 2 vols. (1924). For the poetry there remains U. von Wilamowitz-Moellendorf, *Hellenistische Dichtung in der Zeit von Kallimachos*, 2 vols. (1924), and the revision of A. Körte, *Die Hellenistische Dichtung*[2] (1960).

SCIENCE

For the scientific culture of the period a general orientation is provided in the second volume of G. Sarton, *A History of Science* (1959), with more specialized studies by O. Neugebauer (cited above); J. O. Thomson, *A History of Ancient Geography* (1948, r-p. 1965); T. Heath, *A History of Greek Mathematics*, 2 vols. (1921); the opening chapters of W. Stahl, *Roman Science. Origins, Development, and Influence to the Latin Middle Ages* (1962); and the second volume of C. Singer *et al.*, *A History of Technology* (1956).

PHILOSOPHY

The chief texts of post-Aristotelian philosophy have been gathered in C. J. de Vogel, *Greek Philosophy. A Collection of Texts, III: The Hellenistic-Roman Period*[2] (1964). Aristotle's immediate successors can be followed in the texts and commentaries in F. Wehrli, *Die Schule des Aristoteles*, 10 vols. (1944–1959; r-p. 1968–   ). Epicurus has been studied in detail by C. Bailey, *Epicurus* (1926), to be supplemented by the same author's elaborate commentary on Lucretius' *De Rerum Natura*, 3 vols. (1947); A. J. Festugière, *Epicurus and His Gods* (1956); and the important *L'Aristotele perduto e la formazione filosofica di Epicuro*, 3 vols. (1936) of E. Bignone.

STOICISM

The basic texts of Stoicism, collected in H. von Arnim, *Stoicorum Veterum Fragmenta*, 4 vols. (1903–1924), have generated a large bibliography. M. Pohlenz, *Die Stoa*, 2 vols. (1948–1949), is fundamental, and various special questions are treated separately in S. Sambursky, *The Physics of the Stoics* (1959); E. Brehier, *Chrysippe et l'ancien Stoicisme* (1951); M. E. Reesor, *The Political Theory of the Old and Middle Stoa* (1951); E. V. Arnold, *Roman Stoicism* (1911); and J. Bidez, *La Cité du soleil chez les Stoiciens* (1932). On the Cynics there is D. R. Dudley, *A History of Cynicism* (1937).

LATER PLATONISM

A great deal of attention has recently been given to the revival of Platonism and Pythagoreanism in late antiquity. The best detailed introduction is the somewhat misnamed *Cambridge History of Later Greek and Early Medieval Philosophy* (1967), edited by A. H. Armstrong and chiefly concerned with later Platonism. Individual problems and figures are studied in the published symposia (III and V) conducted by the Fondation Hardt: *Recherches sur la Tradition Platonicienne* (1957), and *Les Sources de Plotin* (1960). There are complete bibliographies in the *Cambridge History*, but of fundamental importance is W. Theiler, *Die Vorbereitung des Neuplatonismus* (1934; r-p. 1964).

POSIDONIUS AND PHILO

The two central figures in that revival, Posidonius and Philo, have each received elaborate treatment. For Posidonius it is enough to call attention to one of the latest, the survey of K. Reinhardt, *Poseidonius* (1953), an offprint of his article in the Pauly-Wissowa *Realencyclopädie der classischen Altertumswissenschaft*. The bibliography on Philo, whose works are all available in English translation in the Loeb Classical Library, has been collected in E. R. Goodenough, *The Politics of Philo Judaeus* (1938), and L. Feldman, *Scholarship on Philo and Josephus* (1963), where the issues, philosophical, religious and legal, raised by Philo have been thoughtfully analyzed.

PLOTINUS

Plotinus has been translated into French by E. Brehier (1960–1963), into German by R. Harder (1956–   ), into English by S. Mackenna (1917–1930), and newly into English for the Loeb Classical Library by A. H. Armstrong. The chapter on Plotinus in the *Cambridge History* is likewise by Armstrong and is excellent and accompanied by a full bibliography. The author's earlier work, *The Architecture of the Intelligible Universe in the Philosophy of Plotinus* (1940; r-p. 1967), remains valuable.

ROME IN NEAR EAST

The Roman arrival in the Near East brought that area into the mainstream of Latin historiography, and after Livy the Imperial historians from Nicholas of Damascus (pp. 402–3) to Ammianus Marcellinus (p. 710, note 29) included the East in their treatment of the affairs of the Roman *oikoumene*. The Republican phase of Roman intervention is the subject of a number of secondary works: M. Holleaux, *Rome, la Grèce, et les monarchies hellénistiques au III siècle av. J.C.* (1935); E. Badian, *Foreign Clientelae (264–70 B.C.* (1958); *idem, Roman Imperialism in the Late Republic*[2] (1968); F. Walbank, "Polybius and Rome's Eastern Policy," *Journal of Roman Studies* LIII (1963), pp. 1–13; G. Bowerstock, *Augustus and the Greek World* (1956); and the more general and interesting H. Fuchs, *Der geistige Widerstand gegen Rom in der antiken Welt* (1938; r-p. 1964).

ADMINISTRATION

G. H. Stevenson, *Roman Provincial Administration*[2] (1949), and F. F. Abbott and A. C. Johnson, *Municipal Administration in the Roman Empire* (1926), may serve as a general introduction to Roman administrative practices in the provinces. The eastern Roman provinces, Republican and Imperial, have received rather unequal treatment. The basic survey is the second volume of T. Mommsen, *The Provinces of the Roman Empire*[2] (1909; reprint in preparation), and on the municipal level there is A. H. M. Jones, *The Cities of the Eastern Roman Provinces* (1937). Both surveys can be read against the texts provided in translation in N. Lewis and M. Reinhold, *Roman Civilization*, 2 vols. (1955; r-p. 1966), accompanied by an excellent bibliography.

EASTERN PROVINCES

The Roman treatment of Anatolia has been painstakingly documented in D. Magie, *The Roman Rule in Asia Minor*, 2 vols. (1951; r-p. 1966), and analyzed in W. M. Ramsey, *The Social Basis of Roman Power in Asia Minor* (1941; r-p. 1967). Egypt, with its rich documentation, has likewise been well served: G. Milne, *A History of Egypt under Roman Rule*[3] (1924); A. C. Johnson, *Egypt and the Roman Empire* (1951); S. L. Wallace, *Taxation in Egypt from Augustus to Diocletian* (1938); R. Taubenschlag, *The Law of Greco-Roman Egypt in the Light of the Papyri*[2] (1955); and the general history of H. I. Bell already cited. For Syria most of the illumination comes from G. Downey's *History of Antioch*, cited above, taken in conjunction with some older studies, such as E. S. Bouchier, *Syria as a Roman Province* (1916); G. M. Harper, "Village Administration in the Roman Province of Syria," *Yale Classical Studies* I (1928) pp. 105–168; and L. C. West, "Commercial Syria under the Roman Empire," *Transactions of the American Philological Association* LV (1924), pp. 159–189.

JUDAEA

The narrative of Josephus, available in a variety of English translations, illuminates Judaea during its days as a Roman province. It has, of course, its disabilities and biases, but they can be at least partially corrected from other sources, the literary evidence of the Gospels, the various contemporary apocalypses and the later Talmuds, and particularly the archaeological evidence. A full bibliography on Josephus will be found in the work by L. Feldman cited above in connection with Philo.

SECTS AND PARTIES

The general landscape is surveyed in M. Simon, *Sectes juives au temps de Jésus* (1960). Political complexities began with the Herodian family: A. M. H. Jones, *The Herods of Judaea* (1938; r-p. 1967); S. Perowne, *The Later Herods: The Political Background of the New Testament* (1958). The origins and history of the Pharisaic opposition have likewise been set out, first by R. T. Herford, *The Pharisees* (1924; r-p. 1962), and then by L. Finkelstein, *The Pharisees. The Sociological*

Background of their Faith[3] (1962). The spiritual climate has been studied by G. E. Moore, *Judaism in the First Three Centuries of the Christian Era*, 3 vols. (1927), and J. Bonsirven, *Le judaisme palestinien au temps de Jésus-Christ, sa théologie*, 3 vols. (1935).

ZEALOTS AND QUMRAN

Most recently scholarship has concentrated its attention on the nationalistic movements that led to the events of A.D. 135: W. R. Farmer, *Maccabees, Zealots, and Josephus* (1957); S. Brandon, *Jesus and the Zealots* (1967); M. Hengel, *Die Zeloten* (1961). The Zealots are connected with Qumran in C. Roth, *The Historical Background of the Dead Sea Scrolls* (1956), though not with much general assent. Qumran has by now its own immense bibliography. Reference will be made here only to a few major works in English: M. Burrows, *The Dead Sea Scrolls* (1956); H. H. Rowley, *The Zadokite Fragments and the Dead Sea Scrolls* (1959); F. M. Cross, *The Ancient Library of Qumran and Modern Biblical Studies*[2] (1961); and G. R. Driver, *The Judaean Scrolls* (1965).

ORIGINS OF CHRISTIANITY

Zealots, Pharisees and Essenes are all connected with the career of Jesus and the origins of Christianity, as most of the above-cited works testify. This is the point of D. Daube, *The New Testament and Rabbinic Judaism* (1956), W. D. Davies, *Christian Origins and Judaism* (1962), and many others, among them, from three very different points of view, S. Mowinckel, *He That Cometh* (1956); S. Brandon, *The Fall of Jerusalem and the Christian Church*[2] (1957); and S. Gerhardsson, *Memory and Manuscript* (1961).

HELLENIC BACKGROUND

Behind the Gospels also stood the *oikoumene*, visible in the texts collected and translated in C. K. Barrett, *The New Testament Background: Selected Documents* (1956; r-p. 1961), and in A. N. Sherwin-White, *Roman Society and Roman Law in the New Testament* (1963). The same conflation of Jewish and Greek influences arises in the study of Paul: A. D. Nock, *St. Paul* (1938; r-p. 1963); *idem, Early Gentile Christianity and Its Hellenistic Background* (1928; r-p. 1964); and W. D. Davies, *Paul and Rabbinic Judaism* (1948).

EARLY CHURCH

Three surveys of the earliest Church are given in P. Carrington, *The Early Christian Church*, 2 vols. (1957); J. G. Davies, *The Early Christian Church* (1965; r-p. 1967); and H. Chadwick, *The Early Church* (1967), each with ample bibliographies. There is a special emphasis on the Jewish wing of Christianity in H. J. Schoeps, *Theologie und Geschichte des Judenchristentums* (1949), and J. Daniélou, *Théologie du Judéo-Christianism* (1958).

LATER GREEK RELIGION

The religious attitudes of the world into which Gentile Christianity eventually moved were new and complex. Basic to its understanding is M. Nilsson, *Geschichte der Griechischen Religion*, Volume II, *Die Hellenistische und Romische Zeit*[2] (1961), and compare his masterly survey article: "Problems in the History of Greek Religion in the Hellenistic and Roman Age," *Harvard Theological Review* XXXVI (1943), pp. 251-275. There are two interesting and impressionistic views in A. D. Nock, *Conversion* (1938; r-p. 1963), and E. R. Dodds, *Pagan and Christian in an Age of Anxiety* (1965). More detailed and more intellectualized is A. J. Festugière, *La Révélation d'Hermès Trismégiste*, 4 vols. (1944-1954), which covers far more ground than its title indicates. Easily available are two provocative older studies by F. Cumont: *Oriental Religions in Roman Paganism*[2] (1911; r-p. 1956) and *Astrology and Religion among the Greeks and Romans* (1912; r-p. 1960).

RISE OF SASANIANS

Sasanian history is surveyed in the works of Ghirshman and Frye cited above in connection with the Parthians. The rise of the dynasty has been traced in S. H. Taqizadeh, "The Early Sasanians," *Bulletin of the School of Oriental and African Studies* XI (1943), pp. 6-51, and some chief historical sources studied in W. B. Henning, "The Great Inscription of Shapur I," *ibid.*, IX (1939), pp. 823-849, and E. Honigman and A. Maricq, *Recherches sur les Res Gestae Divi Saporis* (1953). The standard over-all treatment of the Sasanians remains A. Christensen, *L'Iran sous les Sassanides*[2] (1944), now to be completed by F. Altheim and R. Stiehl, *Ein Asiatischer Staat: Feudalismus unter den Sasaniden und ihren Nachbarn* (1954). The older study by T. Nöldeke, *Geschichte der Perser und Araber zur Zeit der Sasaniden* (1879), is still important.

PAHLEVI LITERATURE

The problems of literary history, as they concern Parthians, Sasanians, and the evolution of Zoroastrianism, are considerable. The field is surveyed in Part I of J. Rypka, *History of Iranian Literature* (1968), and the point is made more precisely in H. W. Bailey, *Zoroastrian Problems in the Ninth Century Books* (1943). Many of the critical Pahlevi texts have been translated in R. C. Zaehner, *Zurvan, A Zoroastrian Dilemma* (1955), and in his more general *The Dawn and Twilight of Zoroastrianism* (1961).

ZOROASTRIANISM

The chief problems attendant upon the study of Iranian religion are laid out in G. Widengren, *Stand und Aufgaben der iranischen Religionsgeschichte* (1955). Both of Zaehner's cited works take up the difficult question of the evolution of Zoroastrianism into the Sasanian period, as does P. J. Menasce, "L'Église Mazdéenne dans l'empire Sassanide," *Journal of World History* II (1954–1955), pp. 554–565. On the important figure of Kartir there is M. Sprengling, "Kartir, Founder of Sasanian Zoroastrianism," *American Journal of Semitic Languages* LVII (1940), pp. 197–228; and, on Plutarch's *Isis and Osiris*, the analysis of J. Hani, "Plutarque en face du dualisme iranien," *Revue des Études Grecques* LXXVII (1964), pp. 489–525.

MANICHAEISM

There are a number of good introductions to both Mani and Manichaeism: H. H. Schaeder, "Urform und Fortbildungen des Manichäischen Systems," *Bibliothek Warburg, Vorträge IV* (1924–1925), pp. 65–127; H. Puech, *Le Manichéisme, son fondateur, sa doctrine* (1949); and G. Widengren, *Mani and Manichaeism* (1965). Some basic texts out of a great number and wide variety of finds from Egypt to Chinese Turkestan have been assembled in A. Adam, *Texte zum Manichäismus* (1954), with notices on their original publication. On the afterlife of the system see S. Runciman, *The Medieval Manichee* (1947; r-p. 1955).

GNOSTICISM

There are histories of Gnosticism, including H. Jonas' magisterial *Gnosis und spätantiker Zeit*,[2] 2 vols. (1954), abridged in his *The Gnostic Religion*[2] (1963), but scholars are still struggling to define the phenomenon. This was the main point of the symposium papers edited by U. Bianci, *The Origins of Gnosticism* (1967), and contributed by most of the international scholars working on the subject. In it M. Krause reports on the current status of the most important Gnostic texts, those discovered at Nag Hamadi in Egypt, and there is a more detailed description of the original find and its fate in J. Doresse, *The Secret Books of the Egyptian Gnostics*[2] (1960). Among the other contributors to the symposium was R. M. Grant, whose *Gnosticism and Early Christianity*[2] (1966) is important and informative, and the possible Jewish affiliations are traced by another contributor, R. McLean Wilson, in his *The Gnostic Problem* (1958). On Marcion's version of Gnosticism there is E. C. Blackman, *Marcion and His Influence* (1948).

THE SECOND CENTURY

Imperial Rome seemed almost oblivious to these new growths. Eastern commerce and imperialism were the order of the day, the first traced in M. P. Charlesworth, *The Trade Routes and Commerce of the Roman Empire* (1926; r-p. 1961), and J. I. Miller, *The Spice Trade of the Roman Empire* (1968); the latter in F. A. Lepper, *Trajan's Parthian War* (1948). The glories of the Second Sophistic are on display in the biographical collections of Philostratus and Eunapius, both available in English in the Loeb Classical Library, and more magnificently in Aelius Aristides, a new collection of whose *Discourses* is in preparation. There are two major studies on Aristides, a personal and a rhetorical one: C. A. Behr, *Aelius Aristides and the Sacred Tales* (1968), and A. Boulanger, *Aelius Aristide et la sophistique dans la province d'Asie au IIᵉ siècle de notre ère* (1923). Lucian is well served in English in both the Loeb Classical Library and elsewhere, and there is a full-scale bibliography by J. Schwartz, *Bibliographie de Lucien de Samosate* (1965). There is a general treatment of the movement in G. W. Bowersock, *Greek Sophists in the Roman Empire* (1969), and three other studies touch upon the diverse literary and artistic currents of the time: G. M. A. Grube, *The Greek and Roman Critics* (1965); B. E. Perry, *The Ancient Romances* (1967); and J. M. C. Toynbee, *The Hadrianic School: A Chapter in the History of Greek Art* (1934).

THE THIRD CENTURY

The gold turned to iron in the third century. The entire tale can be read from beginning to end in M. Rostovtzeff, *The Social and Economic History of the Roman Empire*,[2] 3 vols. (1957), and, with the emphasis on the end, in R. Remondon, *La Crise de l'empire romain de Marc Aurèle à Anastase* (1964), and R. Macmullen, *Enemies of the Roman Order. Treason, Unrest, and Alienation in the Empire* (1967). Among the latter enemies were chiefly the Christians and the Jews, with whom the Romans now dealt more severely. The Jews' history under the Empire was a complex but unhappy one, related in J. Juster, *Les Juifs dans l'empire romain*, 2 vols. (1914; r-p. 1964), and it was further complicated by their dealings with an increasingly hostile Christianity: M. Simon, *Verus Israel: Étude sur les relations entre Chrétiens et Juifs dans l'empire romain (135-452)* (1948; r-p. 1964).

CHRISTIAN PERSECUTIONS

The Christians had their own problems with the authorities. These have been studied by J. Moreau, *La Persécution du Christianisme dans l'empire romain* (1956), and W. Frend, *Martyrdom and Persecution in the Early Church* (1965), and the documents brought together in P. R. Coleman-Norton, *Roman State and Christian Church*, 3 vols. (1966). The chief issue was, of course, the cult of the emperor, and the question has been studied in great detail from its Hellenistic origins down to the late Empire: F. Taeger, *Charisma*, 2 vols. (1957); L. Cerfaux and L. Tondriau, *Le Culte des souverains dans la civilisation gréco-romain* (1957); and, with emphasis on the Romans, L. R. Taylor, *The Divinity of the Roman Emperor* (1931), and M. P. Charlesworth, "Some Observations on Ruler-Cult, Especially in Rome," *Harvard Theological Review* XXVIII (1935), pp. 5-44.

DIOCLETIAN

The tide, of economic decline if not of Christianity, was stemmed in the East by Diocletian, who began a new era in the ancient world; the "decline and fall" debate is, however, essentially a western question, and so may be passed over here. For Diocletian himself there are D. Van Berchem, *L'armée de Dioclétien et la reforme constantinienne* (1952), and W. Seston, *Dioclétien et la Tétrarchie* (1947), in addition to the work of Rostovtzeff cited above. Many of the basic reform texts are presented with comment in the second volume of N. Lewis and M. Reinhold, *Roman Civilization* (1955; r-p. 1966).

HELLENIC CHRISTIANITY

In the intervals between persecutions the eastern Christians were moving out among the intelligentsia of the *oikoumene* and producing the earliest literature of the Gentile Church. The ground is surveyed in J. Quasten, *Patrology*, 3 vols. (1950–1960), and E. J. Goodspeed and R. M. Grant, *A History of Early Christian Literature* (1966), with indications on the texts and studies devoted to individual Fathers. The consequent Hellenic influence was considerable and can be seen most clearly in the development of positions in the new Greek-style theology: J. Daniélou, *A History of Early Christian Doctrine before Nicaea* (1964); H. Chadwick, *Early Christian Thought and the Classical Tradition* (1966); and H. A. Wolfson, *The Philosophy of the Church Fathers* (1956). The more general contacts, and conflicts, between the two "cultures," the Christian and the Hellenic, are traced in C. N. Cochrane, *Christianity and Classical Culture*[2] (1957); M. Laistner, *Christianity and Pagan Culture;* W. Jaeger, *Early Christianity and Greek Paideia* (1962); and A. Momigliano, ed., *Paganism and Christianity in the Fourth Century* (1963).

MONASTICISM

Monasticism began as a turning in the other direction, away from the Hellenic *paideia*. Its origins are considered in R. Heussi, *Der Ursprung des Mönchtums* (1936). The subsequent history of eastern monasticism is preserved in both word and stone. For the literary evidence, most of it hagiographical, and the methods of dealing with it, the best introduction is R. Aigrain, *L'Hagiographie: Ses Sources, ses méthodes, son histoire* (1953), and the more particular *Le tréfonds orientale de l'hagiographie byzantine* (1950), by P. Peeters. The most thorough investigations of the monastic sites are those carried out in Egypt by the New York Metropolitan Museum of Art and described in the various *Publications of the Egyptian Expedition*. The Fathers of the Egyptian desert are accessible in their own words, as, for example, in H. Waddell, *The Desert Fathers* (1936; r-p. 1957), and major studies have been devoted to the founder, collected in B. Steidle, ed., *Antonius Magnus Eremita* (1956). The general context of monastic spirituality is described in I. Hausherr, "Les grands courants de la spiritualité orientale," *Orientalia Christiana Periodica* I (1935), pp. 114–138, and the Egyptian version is more specifically explored in L. Bouyer, *Saint Antoine et la spiritualité du monachisme primitif* (1950).

SYRIAN MONASTICISM

More recently Syrian monasticism, described in the ancient sources as an importation from Egypt, is receiving closer attention. A. Vööbus has devoted a number of studies to it, particularly his *A History of Asceticism in the Syrian Church* (1958), and the interesting *Celibacy, a Requirement of Admission to Baptism in the Early Christian Church* (1951), with its stress on the Manichaean connections. There is also S. Jargy, "Les origines du monachisme en Syrie et en Mesopotamie," *Proche-Orient Chrétien* II (1952), pp. 110–124, and G. Widengren, "Researches on Syrian Mysticism. Mystical Experiences and Spiritual Exercises," *Numen* VIII (1961), pp. 161–198. On the peculiar Syrian growth of the Stylites, see H. Delehaye, *Les Saints stylites* (1923).

CONSTANTINE

With the conversion of Constantine the fortunes of both Christianity and the Empire changed. The historical problems of Constantine's conversion are surveyed in N. H. Baynes, *Constantine the Great and the Christian Church* (1930), and its implications are traced in A. Alföldi, *The Conversion of Constantine and Pagan Rome* (1948), and A. H. M. Jones, *Constantine and the Conversion of Europe*[2] (1962).

THE FOURTH CENTURY

Life and society in the fourth century are the most thoroughly documented in antiquity. The richness can be seen in works as different in scale as A. H. M. Jones, *The Later Roman Empire*, 3 vols. (1964); P. Petit, *Libanius et la vie municipale à Antioche au IVᵉ siècle après J.C.* (1955); and G. Downey, *Antioch in the Age of Theodosius the Great* (1962). The standard account of the life of Julian is still J. Bidez, *La vie de l'empereur Julien* (1930; r-p. 1965), but some measure of the work done over the last four decades since Bidez can be gained from the supportive material cited in the appropriate chapters of G. Downey, *A History of Antioch* (1961).

THE IMPERIAL CHURCH

The evolution of the Imperial Church is traced in all the standard ecclesiastical histories, such as B. J. Kidd, *A History of the Church to*

A.D. 461, 3 vols. (1922), or Vols. III–V of A. Fliche and V. Martin, *Histoire de l'Église* (1947–1948), and, from a literary point of view, in the indispensable H. G. Beck, *Kirche und theologische Literatur im byzantinischen Reich* (1959), with rich bibliographies on the eastern Patriarchates and the eastern liturgies. The relations of Church and state during this early period are discussed in S. L. Greenslade, *Church and State from Constantine to Theodosius* (1954), and H. Dorries, *Constantine and Religious Liberty* (1961).

THEOLOGY

There are two excellent treatments of the early doctrinal disputes centering around the teaching of Arius and culminating in the Council of Nicaea: G. L. Prestige, *Fathers and Heretics* (1940; r-p. 1963) and *God in Patristic Thought*[2] (1952). There is a great deal more detail in J. N. D. Kelly, *Early Christian Creeds* (1950) and *Early Christian Doctrines* (1958), and A. Grillmeier, *Christ in the Christian Tradition* (1965). The political implications, important in Arianism, are traced in N. Q. King, *The Emperor Theodosius and the Establishment of Christianity* (1961).

Theology

Index